Rapid GUI Programming with Python and Qt

Rapid GUI Programming with Python and Qt

The Definitive Guide to PyQt Programming

Mark Summerfield

PRENTICE HALL

Upper Saddle River, NJ · Boston · Indianapolis · San Francisco
New York · Toronto · Montreal · London · Munich · Paris · Madrid
Capetown · Sydney · Tokyo · Singapore · Mexico City

The publisher offers excellent discounts on this book when ordered in quantity for bulk purchases or special sales, which may include electronic versions and/or custom covers and content particular to your business, training goals, marketing focus, and branding interests. For more information, please contact:

U.S. Corporate and Government Sales
(800) 382-3419
corpsales@pearsontechgroup.com

For sales outside the United States, please contact:

International Sales
international@pearsoned.com

Visit us on the Web: www.prenhallprofessional.com

Library of Congress Cataloging-in-Publication Data is on file

This product is printed digitally on demand. This book is the paperback version of an original hardcover book.

ISBN-10:   0-13-439333-3

Second printing, February 2009, with minor corrections

This book is dedicated to

Andrea Summerfield

Contents

Foreword xiii

Introduction 1

Part I: Python Programming

Chapter 1. Data Types and Data Structures 9
    Executing Python Code 10
    Variables and Objects 12
    Numbers and Strings 15
        Integers and Long Integers 16
        Floats and Decimals 17
        Bytestrings, Unicode Strings, and QStrings 20
    Collections 29
        Tuples 29
        Lists 31
        Dictionaries 35
        Sets 37
    Built-in Functions 37
    Summary 41
    Exercises 42

Chapter 2. Control Structures 45
    Conditional Branching 46
    Looping 49
        List Comprehensions and Generators 53
    Functions 55
        Generator Functions 58
        Using Keyword Arguments 59
        Lambda Functions 61
        Dynamic Function Creation 62
        Partial Function Application 63
    Exception Handling 66

Summary 72
Exercises 72

Chapter 3. Classes and Modules 75
Creating Instances 77
Methods and Special Methods 79
    Static Data, and Static Methods and Decorators 85
    Example: The Length Class 86
    Collection Classes 92
    Example: The OrderedDict Class 92
Inheritance and Polymorphism 99
Modules and Multifile Applications 104
    Using the doctest Module 105
Summary 107
Exercises 108

Part II: Basic GUI Programming

Chapter 4. Introduction to GUI Programming 111
A Pop-Up Alert in 25 Lines 112
An Expression Evaluator in 30 Lines 116
A Currency Converter in 70 Lines 121
Signals and Slots 127
Summary 136
Exercise 137

Chapter 5. Dialogs 139
Dumb Dialogs 141
Standard Dialogs 147
    Modal OK/Cancel-Style Dialogs 148
Smart Dialogs 154
    Modeless Apply/Close-Style Dialogs 155
    Modeless "Live" Dialogs 159
Summary 162
Exercise 163

Chapter 6. Main Windows 165
Creating a Main Window 166
    Actions and Key Sequences 171
    Resource Files 172

Creating and Using Actions 174
Restoring and Saving the Main Window's State 181
Handling User Actions 190
Handling File Actions 191
Handling Edit Actions 197
Handling Help Actions 200
Summary 201
Exercise 202

Chapter 7. Using Qt Designer 205
Designing User Interfaces 208
Implementing Dialogs 216
Testing Dialogs 221
Summary 223
Exercise 224

Chapter 8. Data Handling and Custom File Formats 227
Main Window Responsibilities 229
Data Container Responsibilities 235
Saving and Loading Binary Files 240
Writing and Reading Using QDataStream 240
Writing and Reading Using the pickle Module 246
Saving and Loading Text Files 249
Writing and Reading Using QTextStream 250
Writing and Reading Using the codecs Module 255
Saving and Loading XML Files 256
Writing XML 256
Reading and Parsing XML with PyQt's DOM Classes 259
Reading and Parsing XML with PyQt's SAX Classes 262
Summary 265
Exercise 266

Part III: Intermediate GUI Programming

Chapter 9. Layouts and Multiple Documents 269
Layout Policies 270
Tab Widgets and Stacked Widgets 272
Extension Dialogs 276
Splitters 280
Single Document Interface (SDI) 283

Multiple Document Interface (MDI) 290

Summary 300

Exercise 301

Chapter 10. Events, the Clipboard, and Drag and Drop 303

The Event-Handling Mechanism 303

Reimplementing Event Handlers 305

Using the Clipboard 310

Drag and Drop 312

     Handling Custom Data 313

Summary 317

Exercise 318

Chapter 11. Custom Widgets 321

Using Widget Style Sheets 322

Creating Composite Widgets 325

Subclassing Built-in Widgets 326

Subclassing QWidget 328

     Example: A Fraction Slider 331

     Example: A Flow-Mixing Widget 339

Summary 345

Exercise 346

Chapter 12. Item-Based Graphics 349

Custom and Interactive Graphics Items 351

Animation and Complex Shapes 368

Summary 378

Exercise 379

Chapter 13. Rich Text and Printing 381

Rich Text Editing 382

     Using QSyntaxHighlighter 382

     A Rich Text Line Edit 389

Printing Documents 398

     Printing Images 400

     Printing Documents Using HTML and QTextDocument 401

     Printing Documents Using QTextCursor and QTextDocument 403

     Printing Documents Using QPainter 407

Summary 411

Exercise 412

Chapter 14. Model/View Programming 413

    Using the Convenience Item Widgets 415

    Creating Custom Models 423

        Implementing the View Logic 424

        Implementing the Custom Model 427

    Creating Custom Delegates 436

    Summary 442

    Exercise 443

Chapter 15. Databases 445

    Connecting to the Database 446

    Executing SQL Queries 446

    Using Database Form Views 451

    Using Database Table Views 457

    Summary 470

    Exercise 471

Part IV: Advanced GUI Programming

Chapter 16. Advanced Model/View Programming 475

    Custom Views 476

    Generic Delegates 483

    Representing Tabular Data in Trees 492

    Summary 505

    Exercise 505

Chapter 17. Online Help and Internationalization 509

    Online Help 510

    Internationalization 512

    Summary 519

    Exercise 520

Chapter 18. Networking 521

    Creating a TCP Client 523

    Creating a TCP Server 529

    Summary 534

    Exercise 534

Chapter 19. Multithreading 537

    Creating a Threaded Server 539

    Creating and Managing Secondary Threads 544

    Implementing a Secondary Thread 552

    Summary 557

    Exercise 558

    This Is Not Quite the End 559

Appendix A. Installing 561

    Installing on Windows 561

    Installing on Mac OS X 566

    Installing on Linux and Unix 570

Appendix B. Selected PyQt Widgets 575

Appendix C. Selected PyQt Class Hierarchies 581

Index 585

Foreword

As PyQt's creator, I'm delighted to see that this book has been written. Although I served as one of the book's technical reviewers, I'm happy to confess that I learned a few things myself.

The PyQt documentation covers the APIs of all the PyQt classes. This book shows you how to use all those classes, how to combine them to create dialogs, main windows, and entire applications—all of which look good and work well, with no arbitrary limits, and using a programming language that is a joy to use.

What I particularly like about the book is that the examples aren't trivial ones designed to illustrate a simple point, but are potentially useful in their own right. The way that different approaches are considered will reward the reader who wants to develop a deeper understanding of how to apply PyQt to the development of large scale, production quality applications.

I began the PyQt story back in the late 1990s. I had been using Tcl/Tk for some time, but I felt that Tk applications looked ugly, especially when I saw what had been achieved with the first version of KDE. I had wanted to switch to Python, and so I thought I would combine the change of language with a change of GUI library.

Initially I used some wrappers that had been written using SWIG, but I concluded that I could produce a more suitable wrapper tool myself. I set to work creating SIP, and released PyQt 0.1 supporting Qt 1.41 in November 1998. Development has continued regularly ever since, both to keep up with new releases of Qt and to broaden the scope of PyQt with, for example, the addition of support tools and improved documentation. By 2000, PyQt 2.0 supported Qt 2.2 on both Linux and Windows. Qt 3 support appeared in 2001, and Mac OS X support in 2002. The PyQt4 series began with PyQt 4.0 in June 2006 with support for Qt 4.

My primary goal has always been to allow Python and Qt to work together in a way that feels natural to Python programmers, while allowing them to do anything they want in Python that can be done in C++. The key to achieving this was the development of SIP. This gave me a specialized code generator over which I had complete control and ensures that Python and Qt will always fit snugly together.

The essential process of developing and maintaining PyQt is now well established. Much of the work is now automated, which means that keeping up with new releases of Qt from Trolltech is no longer the problem it once was, and en-surs that PyQt will continue for years to come.

It's been very gratifying to watch the growth of the PyQt community over the years. If this book is part of your introduction to PyQt, then welcome!

— Phil Thompson
Wimborne, Dorset, U.K.
August 25, 2007

Introduction

This book teaches how to write GUI applications using the Python programming language and the Qt application development framework. The only essential prior knowledge is that you can program in *some* object-oriented programming language, such as C++, C#, Java, or of course, Python itself. For the rich text chapter, some familiarity with HTML and with regular expressions is assumed, and the databases and threading chapters assume some basic knowledge of those topics. A knowledge of GUI programming is not required, since all the key concepts are covered.

The book will be useful to people who program professionally as part of their job, whether as full-time software developers, or those from other disciplines, including scientists and engineers, who need to do some programming in support of their work. It is also suitable for undergraduate and post-graduate students, particularly those doing courses or research that includes a substantial computing element. The exercises (with solutions) are provided especially to help students.

Python is probably the easiest to learn and nicest scripting language in widespread use, and Qt is probably the best library for developing GUI applications. The combination of Python and Qt, "PyQt", makes it possible to develop applications on any supported platform and run them unchanged on all the supported platforms—for example, all modern versions of Windows, Linux, Mac OS X, and most Unix-based systems. No compilation is required thanks to Python being interpreted, and no source code changes to adapt to different operating systems are required thanks to Qt abstracting away the platform-specific details. We only have to copy the source file or files to a target machine that has both Python and PyQt installed and the application will run.

If you are new to Python: Welcome! You are about to discover a language that is clear to read and write, and that is concise without being cryptic. Python supports many programming paradigms, but because our focus is on GUI programming, we will take an object-oriented approach everywhere except in the very early chapters.

Python is a very expressive language, which means that we can usually write far fewer lines of Python code than would be required for an equivalent application written in, say, C++ or Java. This makes it possible to show some small but complete examples throughout the text, and makes PyQt an ideal tool for rapidly and easily developing GUI applications, whether for prototyping or for production use.

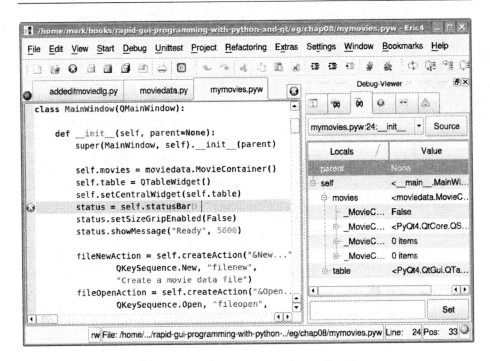

Figure 1 *The Eric4 IDE—a PyQt4 application*

Since the emphasis of the book is on GUI programming, Part I provides a fast-paced Python tutorial as well as some PyQt coverage. This material is clearly marked (just like this paragraph, with "Qt" in the margin) to make it easy for experienced Python programmers to skip the Python they already know. Parts II, III, and IV of the book are all PyQt-specific and assume that readers can already program in Python, whether from previous experience or from reading Part I.

Quite often in programming we reach decision points when there are several possible approaches we could take. Reference books and the online documentation identify what classes, methods, and functions are available, and in some cases provide examples, but such documents rarely provide a broader context. This book gives the necessary context, highlighting the key decision points for GUI programming and offering insights into the pros and cons so that you can decide for yourself what the right policy is for your particular circumstances. For example, when you create a dialog, should it be modal or modeless? (See Chapter 5 for an explanation and policy recommendations on this issue.)

PyQt is used to write all kinds of GUI applications, from accounting applications, to visualization tools used by scientists and engineers. Figure 1, for example, shows Eric4, a powerful integrated development environment that is written in PyQt. It is possible to write PyQt applications that are just tens of lines long, and medium-size projects of 1 000 to 10 000 lines are very common. Some commercial companies have built 100 000-line PyQt applications, with programming teams varying in size from just one person to more than a dozen people. Many in-house tools are written using PyQt, but because these are often used to gain competitive advantage, the companies involved generally do not permit their use of PyQt to be made public. PyQt is also widely used in the open source world, with games, utilities, visualization tools, and IDEs all written using it.

This book is specifically about PyQt4, the Python bindings for the Qt 4 C++ application development framework.* PyQt4 is provided in the form of ten Python modules which between them contain around 400 classes and about 6 000 methods and functions. All the example programs have been tested on Windows, Linux, and Mac OS X, using Python 2.5, Qt 4.2, and PyQt 4.2, and additionally on Windows and Linux using Qt 4.3 and PyQt 4.3, and also with Python 2.6 using Qt 4.4 and PyQt 4.4. Backporting to earlier versions is possible in some cases, but we recommend using the most up-to-date versions of Python, Qt, and PyQt.

Python, PyQt, and Qt can be used free of charge for noncommercial purposes, but the license used by Python is different from that used by PyQt and Qt. Python is available with a very liberal license that allows it to be used to develop both commercial and noncommercial applications. Both PyQt and Qt are dual-licensed: This essentially allows them to be used to develop noncommercial applications—which must in turn be licensed using an acceptable open source license such as the GNU General Public License (GPL); or to be used to develop commercial applications—in this case, a commercial PyQt license *and* a commercial Qt license must be purchased.

The Structure of the Book

The book is divided into four parts. Part I is primarily a rapid conversion course aimed at non-Python programmers who are familiar with an object-oriented language, although it also has some (clearly marked) PyQt content. Because the core Python language is mostly simple and is quite small, these chapters can teach the basics of Python to a sufficient extent that real Python applications can be written.

If you think that you can pick up the Python syntax simply through reading it, you might be tempted to skip Part I and dive straight into the GUI programming that begins in Part II. The early chapters in Part II include back-references to the relevant pages in Part I to support readers who choose this approach. However, even for readers familiar with Python, we recommend reading about QString in Chapter 1. If you are unfamiliar with partial function application (currying), it is important to read the subsection that covers this in Chapter 2, since this technique is sometimes used in GUI programming.

---

*There are also Python bindings for the older Qt 3 library, but there is no reason to use that library for new projects, especially since Qt 4 offers far more functionality and is easier to use.

Part II begins by showing three tiny PyQt GUI applications to give an initial impression of what PyQt programming is like. It also explains some of the fundamental concepts involved in GUI programming, including PyQt's high-level signals and slots communication mechanism. Chapter 5 shows how to create dialogs and how to create and lay out widgets ("controls" in Windows-speak—the graphical elements that make up a user interface such as buttons, listboxes, and such) in a dialog. Dialogs are central to GUI programming: Most GUI applications have a single main window, and dozens or scores of dialogs, so this topic is covered in depth.

After the dialogs chapter comes Chapter 6, which covers main windows, including menus, toolbars, dock windows, and keyboard shortcuts, as well as loading and saving application settings. Part II's final chapters show how to create dialogs using *Qt Designer*, Qt's visual design tool, and how to save data in binary, text, and XML formats.

Part III gives deeper coverage of some of the topics covered in Part II, and introduces many new topics. Chapter 9 shows how to lay out widgets in quite sophisticated ways, and how to handle multiple documents. Chapter 10 covers low-level event handlers, and how to use the clipboard as well as drag and drop, text, HTML, and binary data. Chapter 11 shows how to modify and subclass existing widgets, and how to create entirely new widgets from scratch, with complete control over their appearance and behavior. This chapter also shows how to do basic graphics. Chapter 12 shows how to use Qt 4.2's new graphics view architecture, which is particularly suited to handling large numbers of independent graphical objects. Qt's HTML-capable rich text engine is covered in Chapter 13. This chapter also covers printing both to paper and to PDF files.

Part III concludes with two chapters on model/view programming: Chapter 14 introduces the subject and shows how to use Qt's built-in views and how to create custom data models and custom delegates, and Chapter 15 shows how to use the model/view architecture to perform database programming.

Part IV continues the model/view theme, with coverage of three different advanced model/view topics in Chapter 16. The first section of Chapter 17 describes the techniques that can be used for providing online help, and the second section explains how to internationalize an application, including how to use Qt's translation tools to create translation files. The Python standard library provides its own classes for networking and for threading, but in the last two chapters of Part IV we show how to do networking and threading using PyQt's classes.

Appendix A explains where Python, PyQt, and Qt can be obtained, and how to install them on Windows, Mac OS X, and Linux. PyQt is much easier to learn if you install it and try out some of the exercises, and if you inspect some of the example code. Appendix B presents screenshots and brief descriptions of selected PyQt widgets; this is helpful for those new to GUI programming. Appendix C presents diagrams of some of PyQt's key class hierarchies; this is useful for getting to know what classes PyQt has to offer and how they are related.

If you have never used Python before, you should begin by reading Chapters 1–6 in order. If you already know Python, at least read the string policy (in bullet points on page 28), and skim the material in Chapter 2 (apart from the first section, which you'll know well). Make sure that you are comfortable with lambda and partial function application, both of which are covered in Chapter 2. It is probably also worth skimming Chapter 3 as well. Then read Chapters 4, 5, and 6 in order.

Once you have covered the first six chapters, you have covered the essentials of Python and the fundamentals of PyQt.

Chapter 7 is useful if you want to know how to create dialogs using a visual design tool rather than purely by hand coding, something that can save a lot of time. For file handling, at least read the first three sections of Chapter 8. If you plan to write and read text files, also read Chapter 8's fourth section, and similarly the fifth section if you are going to use XML files.

For Part III, at the least read Chapter 10's first section, on event handling, and all of Chapter 11. Chapter 12 and the first section of Chapter 13 assume that you have read about PyQt's event handling, and that you have read Chapter 11. Chapters 9 and 14 can be read stand-alone in this part, but Chapter 15 assumes that you have read Chapter 14.

In Part IV, Chapter 16 assumes that you have read Chapters 14 and 15, but the other chapters can be read independently.

If you find errors in the text or in the examples, or have other comments, please write to mark@qtrac.eu quoting "PyQt book" in the subject line. The book's home page, where any corrections will be published, and from where the examples and exercise solutions can be downloaded, is http://www.qtrac.eu/pyqtbook.html.

If you want to participate in the PyQt community, it is worthwhile joining the mailing list. Go to http://www.riverbankcomputing.com/mailman/listinfo/pyqt to find a link to the archive, so that you can see what the mailing list is like, and also for a form for joining. Python also has mailing lists and other community activities. For these, go to http://www.python.org/community.

Acknowledgments

I have many people to thank, and I will begin with those who have been intimately involved with the book.

Jasmin Blanchette is a senior software developer at Trolltech, a Qt expert, and a fine editor and writer in his own right. I have cowritten two C++/Qt books with him. Jasmin has made a huge number of suggestions and criticisms that have immensely improved the quality of this book.

David Boddie, Trolltech's documentation manager, is an active PyQt open source developer who has made many contributions to PyQt itself. His input has helped ensure that I have covered everything necessary, and done so in a sensible order.

Richard Chamberlain is cofounder and chief technology officer of Jadu Ltd., a content management company. His feedback and insights have helped ensure that the book is as broadly accessible as possible. He has also helped refine and improve the code used in the examples and exercises.

Trenton Schulz is a Trolltech developer who has been a valuable reviewer of my previous books. For this book, he has brought his Python and Qt knowledge to bear, giving considerable feedback on the manuscript. Along with Richard, he also ensured that Mac OS X users were never forgotten. In addition, he spotted many subtle errors that I had missed.

Phil Thompson is PyQt's creator and maintainer. He has been supportive of the book from the start, even adding features and improvements to PyQt as a direct result of discussions we have had regarding the book. He has made numerous suggestions for the book's improvement, and corrected many mistakes and misunderstandings.

Special thanks to Samuel Rolland, who let me loose on his Mac laptop, to install PyQt, test the examples, and take screenshots.

Thanks are also due to Guido van Rossum, creator of Python, as well as to the wider Python community who have contributed so much to make Python, and especially its libraries, so useful and enjoyable to use.

Thanks also to Trolltech, for developing and maintaining Qt, and in particular to the Trolltech developers both past and present, many of whom I have had the pleasure of working with, and who ensure that Qt is the best cross-platform GUI development framework in existence.

Particular thanks to Jeff Kingston, creator of the Lout typesetting language. I use Lout for all my books and for most of my other writing projects. Over the years, Jeff has made many improvements and added numerous features to Lout in response to feedback from users, including many that I have asked for myself. Thanks also to James Cloos who created the condensed version of the DejaVu Sans Mono font (itself derived from Jim Lyles' Vera font) from which this book's monospaced font is derived.

The publisher, in the person of Editor-in-Chief Karen Gettman, was supportive of this book from the very beginning. And special thanks to my editor, Debra Williams Cauley, for her support, and for making the entire process as smooth as possible. Thanks also to Lara Wysong who managed the production process so well, and to the proofreader, Audrey Doyle, who did such fine work.

Last but not least, I want to acknowledge my wife, Andrea. Her love, loyalty, and support always give me strength and hope.

Part I

Python Programming

1

- Executing Python Code
- Variables and Objects
- Numbers and Strings
- Collections
- Built-in Functions

Data Types and Data Structures

In this chapter, we begin a Python conversion course that shows non-Python programmers how to program with Python. We introduce some fundamental data types and data structures, as well as some of Python's procedural syntax. The approach taken throughout is to emphasize realistic code like that used in practice, rather than giving the formal definitions and explanations that are already available in the documentation that is supplied with Python and available online at http://www.python.org.

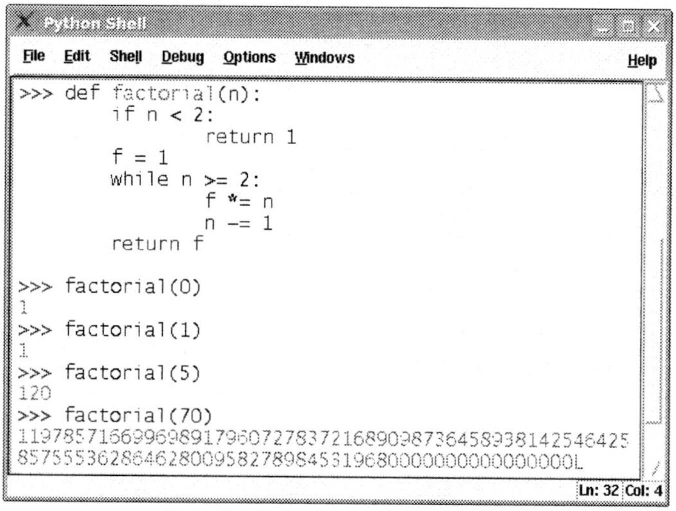

Figure 1.1 *The IDLE Python Shell window*

If you have not already installed Python and PyQt, it would be a good idea to do so: That way you will be able to try out the examples that accompany this book (downloadable from http://www.qtrac.eu/pyqtbook.html). See Appendix A for installation details. One advantage of installing the software is that the IDLE integrated development environment is installed along with Python.

9

The IDLE Development Environment

The full installation of Python includes IDLE, a basic but very useful integrated development environment. When IDLE is launched (click Start→All Programs→Python 2.x→IDLE on Windows, or click Finder→Applications→MacPython 2.x→IDLE on Mac OS X, or run `idle &` in a console on Linux), it presents its Python Shell window.

As the screenshot in Figure 1.1 shows, IDLE has a rather retro Windows 95 look. This is because it is written in Tkinter rather than in PyQt. We've chosen to use IDLE because IDLE comes as standard with Python and is very simple to learn and use. If you want to use a much more powerful and modern-looking IDE, you might prefer Eric4 which is written in PyQt, or one of the other Python IDEs that are available. However, if you are new to Python, we recommend that you start out with the simpler IDLE, and once you are more experienced with PyQt, then trying the other IDEs to see if you prefer one of them. And of course, you could simply use a plain text editor and debug using `print` statements and not use an IDE at all.

IDLE provides three key facilities: the ability to enter Python expressions and code and to see the results directly in the Python Shell; a code editor that provides Python-specific color syntax highlighting; and a debugger that can be used to step through code to help identify and kill bugs. The Python Shell is especially useful for trying out simple algorithms, snippets of code, and regular expressions, and can also be used as a very powerful and flexible calculator.

Executing Python Code

Before we can really explore the Python language we need to know how to execute Python code. We will show this by reviewing a tiny example program that is just one line long.

We must use a plain text editor for working with Python files.* On Windows it is possible to use Notepad, but IDLE includes a suitable Python editor designed specifically for editing Python code: Simply start IDLE and then click File→New Window.

We will type the following line into a file, called `hello.py`:

```
print "Hello World"
```

Note that no semicolon is necessary: In Python newline acts as a statement separator. Also, we do not need a newline, "\n", in the string, since `print` automatically adds a newline unless we suppress it with a trailing comma.

---

*The programs in this book are written using ASCII characters, with escape sequences where Unicode is required. It is possible to use Latin-1, UTF-8, or other encodings for strings and comments in Python programs, as explained in the documentation under "Encoding declarations".

Assuming that we have saved the code in the file `hello.py` (in the directory `C:\pyqt\chap01` if using Windows), we can start up a console (click Start→All Programs→Accessories→Console on Windows XP—sometimes Console is called Command Prompt; or run `Terminal.app` from `/Applications/Utilities` on Mac OS X), change to that directory, and execute the program like this:

```
C:\>cd c:\pyqt\chap01
C:\pyqt\chap01>hello.py
```

As·long as Python is correctly installed, Windows will recognize the `.py` file extension and give the file to `python.exe` to execute. The program will print "Hello World" on the console as we would expect.*

On Mac OS X and Linux we must explicitly run the interpreter by typing its name and the file's name at the console's prompt, like this:

```
% python hello.py
```

This will work providing that Python is installed and in your `PATH`. Alternatively, for Linux and Mac OS X, we can add an additional "shebang" (shell execute) comment line which tells the operating system to use a Python interpreter, making the `hello.py` file two lines long:

```
#!/usr/bin/env python
print "Hello World"
```

For this to work on Mac OS X and Linux, the file's permissions must be set correctly. For example, at the console prompt in the same directory as the file, enter `chmod +x hello.py` to make the file executable.

Python comments start with "#" and continue until the end of the line. This means that it is perfectly safe to add the "shebang" line to *all* Python programs, since the comment is ignored on Windows but on Linux it tells the operating system to execute the file using a Python interpreter. Appendix A shows how to associate the Python interpreter with `.py` and `.pyw` files on Mac OS X.

When we speak of executing a Python program, what happens behind the scenes is that Python reads the `.py` (or `.pyw`) file into memory, and parses it, to get a bytecode program that it then goes on to execute. For each module that is imported by the program, Python first checks to see whether there is a precompiled bytecode version (in a `.pyo` or `.pyc` file) that has a timestamp which corresponds to its `.py` file. If there is, Python uses the bytecode version; otherwise, it parses the module's `.py` file, saves it into a `.pyc` file, and uses the bytecode it just generated. So, unlike Java, we don't have to explicitly bytecode-compile any modules, whether they are supplied with Python or are ones we have written ourselves. And in most Python installations, the supplied modules are com-

---

*Mac OS X users note that whenever we refer to a console, this is the same as a Mac Terminal.

piled as part of the installation process so as to avoid having to compile them whenever a Python application that uses them is run.

Variables and Objects

In most programming languages, including C++ and Java, we must declare each variable, specifying its type, before it can be used. This is called *static typing*, because the compiler knows at compile time what type each variable is. Python, like most very high level languages, uses a different approach: Variables have no type restrictions (dynamic typing), and they don't need to be declared.

We could learn about Python's variables and identifiers by creating and executing a file, as we did with hello.py in the preceding section. But for trying out small code snippets we don't need to create a file at all. We can just enter the lines directly in the IDLE Python Shell window at the >>> prompt:

```
>>> x = 71
>>> y = "Dove"
```

The whitespace around the assignment operator = is optional but is included because it makes the code easier to read. As a matter of style we will always put one space before and after binary operators. On the other hand, it is important that each statement occupies its own line and has no extraneous leading whitespace. This is because Python uses indentation and line breaks to signify its block structure, rather than the braces and semicolons used by many other programming languages.

Now we are ready to review what the two lines actually do. The first line creates an object of type int and binds the name x to it.* The second line creates an object of type str (an 8-bit string type) and binds the name y to it.

Some Python programmers refer to names (such as the x and y used earlier), as *object references* since they refer to objects rather than being objects in their own right. For basic data types like int and str it makes no difference whether we see their variables as "objects" or as "object references"; they behave in the same way as they do in other programming languages:

```
>>> x = 82
>>> x += 7
>>> x
89
```

Later on we will see cases where the fact that Python variables are object references makes a difference.

Lists
☞ 31

---

*This is similar to the Java assignment, Integer x = new Integer(71); for C++ a near-equivalent would be int xd = 71; int &x = xd;.

Functions, Methods, and Operators Terminology

The term *function* is used to refer to a subroutine that can be executed independently, and the term *method* is used to refer to a function that can only be executed when bound to an object, that is, called on an instance of a particular class.

An *operator* may be independent or it may be bound to an object, but unlike functions and methods, operators do not use parentheses. Operators that are represented by symbols such as +, *, and < are rather obviously called operators, but operators that have names such as del and print are often called *statements*.

Python functions do not have to be pure in the mathematical sense: They do not have to return a value and they can modify their arguments. Python functions are like C and C++ functions, or like Pascal functions that take var parameters. Python methods are like C++ or Java member functions.

Python has two ways of comparing objects: by "identity" and by "value". An object's identity is effectively its address in memory, and this is what an object reference holds. If we use comparison operators, such as == and <, we get value comparison. For example, two strings are equal using == if they both contain the same text. If we use is we get identity comparison, which is fast because we are just comparing two addresses and don't have to look at the objects themselves. An object's identity can be obtained by calling id() on an object reference.

Python has a special object called None. This can be assigned to any variable and it means that the variable has no value. There is only ever one instance of the None object, so we can always use the fast is and is not comparisons when testing for it.

Notice that we wrote x on its own at the >>> prompt. If we write an expression or variable in IDLE, its value is automatically printed. In a program, we must use an explicit print statement to print an expression. For example:

```
print x
```

Python's print statement is an operator, not a function, and for this reason it is invoked without using parentheses (just as we use + and other operators without them).

Earlier we said that Python uses *dynamic* typing. There are two factors involved in this. First, we can assign any object to any variable; for example, we could write:

```
x = 47
x = "Heron"
```

After the first line x's type is int, and after the second line x's type is str, so clearly the type associated with the name x is determined by what the name is bound to, and not by any intrinsic property of its own. For this reason , we do not need to associate a particular type with a particular name.

The second aspect of Python's dynamic typing is that the typing is strong: Python does not permit operations between incompatible types, as the following example, typed into IDLE, shows:

```
>>> x = 41
>>> y = "Flamingo"
>>> x + y

Traceback (most recent call last):
  File <pyshell#2>, line 1, in <module>
    x + y
TypeError:  unsupported operand type(s) for +: 'int' and 'str'
```

When we attempted to apply the binary + operator, Python raised a TypeError exception and refused to perform the operation.★ (Exceptions are covered in Chapter 2.)

If we were to assign to y a type compatible with x's type, such as an int or float, the addition would work fine:

```
>>> x = 41
>>> y = 8.5
>>> x + y
49.5
```

Although x and y are of different types (int and float), Python provides the same kind of automatic type promotion that other languages use, so the x is converted to a float and the calculation performed is actually 41.0 + 8.5.

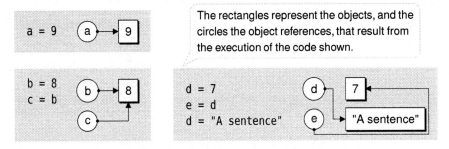

The rectangles represent the objects, and the circles the object references, that result from the execution of the code shown.

Figure 1.2 *Object references and objects*

Assigning a value to a variable is called *binding*, since we bind names to objects. If we assign a new object to an existing variable, we are said to be

---

★The line of the traceback, File "<pyshell#2>", and so on, varies every time, so your line may be different from the one shown here.

rebinding the name. This is illustrated in Figure 1.2. When we do this, what happens to the object the name was originally bound to? For example:

```
>>> x = "Sparrow"
>>> x = 9.8
```

What has happened to the str object that holds the text "Sparrow"? Once an object has no names bound to it, it is scheduled for garbage collection, and in due course it may be deleted from memory. This is very similar to how things work in Java.

Python variable names consist of ASCII letters, digits, and underscores (_). Variable names should begin with a letter, and they are case-sensitive (rowan, Rowan, and roWan are three different variables). No Python variable should be given the name of any of Python's keywords (see Table 1.1), nor of Python's built-in constants such as None, True, or False.

Numbers and Strings

Python provides several numeric types and two string types. What all these types have in common is that they are *immutable*. This means that in Python, numbers and strings cannot be changed. This sounds rather limiting, but thanks to Python's augmented assignment operators (+=, *=, etc.), it simply is not a problem.

Before looking at the specific data types we will look at one important consequence of the immutability. Let us type some simple expressions into IDLE:

```
>>> x = 5
>>> y = x
>>> x, y
(5, 5)
```

Here we have created an object of type int with the value 5 and bound the name x to it. We have then assigned x to y which has the effect of binding y to the same object that x is bound to. So, when we print them in IDLE (in a program we would have to write print x, y, but in IDLE we just write an expression and IDLE automatically prints it), IDLE outputs the values as a *tuple*—essentially a read-only list of values.

Tuples
☞ 29

Now let us increment y:

```
>>> y += 1
>>> x, y
(5, 6)
```

We might have expected both x and y to have the value 6 since both referred to the same integer object. But because Python numbers (and strings) are immutable, this does not happen. The augmented assignment operators when applied to immutable objects are mere syntactic sugar: They do not change

Table 1.1 *Python's Keywords*[*]

and	class	elif	finally	if	lambda	print	while
as[2.6]	continue	else	for	import	not	raise	with[2.6]
assert[1.5]	def	except	from	in	or	return	yield[2.3]
break	del	exec	global	is	pass	try	

the objects they are applied to. So what really happened is this: y = y + 1, so a *new* integer object was created (with value 6), and y was bound to this new object. As a result, when we asked IDLE to print x and y, they were referring to different objects, each with a different value.

We need to bear in mind the fact that the = operator performs a *binding* operation rather than an assignment. The name on the left-hand side is bound (or rebound if the name already exists) to the object on the right-hand side. For immutable objects, it makes no difference at all, as we will see in a moment. But for mutable objects, it means that using = will not give us a copy (it just binds another name to the original object), so when we really need a copy we must use a copy() method, or a function from Python's copy module, as discussed shortly.

Shallow and Deep Copying sidebar ☞ 34

In practice, the immutability of numbers and strings is very convenient. For example:

```
>>> s = "Bath"
>>> t = " Hat"
>>> u = s
>>> s += t
>>> s, t, u
('Bath Hat', ' Hat', 'Bath')
```

Notice that we assigned string s to u. Intuitively we would expect that u holds the value "Bath" that was, in effect, assigned to it, and we do not expect that applying += to s will have any side effects, even though both s and u refer to the same string. And our intuition is correct: u's value is not changed because when += is applied to s, a *new* string object is created and bound to s, and u is left as the only object now referring to the original "Bath" string.

Integers and Long Integers

Python provides three integral types: bool, int, and long. The bool type can only take the values True or False, and when used in a numeric context these are treated as 1 and 0. The long type can hold an integer whose size is limited only by the machine's available memory, so integers hundreds of digits long can be created and processed. The only downside is that the long type is slower to pro-

---

[*]The numbers beside some of the keywords indicate the version of Python that introduced them.

cess than the int type. The int type is the same signed integer type provided by most programming languages; however, if an operation is applied to an int that would make its value exceed its range (for example, a value greater than 2^{31} - 1 or less than -2^{31} on some machines), the int is automatically type promoted into a long.

Python uses the suffix L to signify a long, and we can do the same in code when necessary. For example:

```
>>> p = 5 ** 35
>>> q = 7L
>>> r = 2 + q
>>> p, q, r
(2910383045673370361328125L, 7L, 9L)
```

Integer literals are assumed to be base 10 (decimal) numbers, except those that start with a 0x, which are treated as hexadecimal (base 16), for example, 0x3F, which is decimal 63, and those that start with 0 which are treated as octal (base 8). Any kind of integer literal can have L appended to it to make it into a long.

Python supports the common operators that we would expect for numbers, including +, -, *, /, %, and their augmented cousins, +=, -=, *=, /=, and %=. Python also provides ** for raising a number to a power.

By default, Python's / division operator performs truncating division when both operands are of type int. For example, 5 / 3, produces 1. This is the norm in most programming languages, but it can be inconvenient in Python since dynamic typing means that a variable might be an int or a float at different times. The solution is to tell Python to *always* do "true division", which produces floating-point results whenever necessary, and to use the // operator when we really want truncation to occur. We will see how to do this in Chapter 3.

Floats and Decimals

Python provides three kinds of floating-point values: float, Decimal, and complex. Type float holds double-precision floating-point numbers whose range depends on the C (or Java) compiler Python was built with; they have limited precision and cannot be reliably compared for equality. Numbers of type float are written with a decimal point, or using scientific notation, for example, 0.0, 5.7, 8.9e-4. It is salutary to type these into IDLE:

```
>>> 0.0, 5.7, 8.9e-4
(0.0, 5.7000000000000002, 0.00088999999999999995)
```

The inaccuracy is *not* a Python-specific problem: Computers represent floating-point numbers using base 2, which can represent some decimals exactly (such as 0.5) but others only approximately (such as 0.1). Furthermore, the representation uses a fixed number of bits, so there is a limit to the number of digits that can be held.

In practice this is rarely a problem since most floating-point numbers use 64 bits which is more than sufficient in most cases. But if we need high precision, Python's Decimal numbers from the decimal module can be used. These perform calculations that are accurate to the level of precision we specify (by default, to 28 decimal places) and can represent periodic numbers like 0.1 exactly; but processing is a lot slower than with normal floats. Because of their accuracy, Decimal numbers are suitable for financial calculations.

Before Decimal numbers can be used, the decimal module must be imported. The syntax for doing this is the same whether we are writing code in a .py file, or typing in IDLE as we are here:

```
>>> import decimal
```

Here we have imported the decimal module into our IDLE Shell window. (The import semantics are explained in the Importing Objects sidebar.) Integer literals can be passed to the Decimal constructor, but because Decimals are high-precision and floats are not, we cannot pass floats; instead, we must provide floating-point values as strings. For example:

```
>>> decimal.Decimal(19), decimal.Decimal("5.1"),
decimal.Decimal("8.9e-4")
(Decimal("19"), Decimal("5.1"), Decimal("0.00089"))
```

The number decimal.Decimal("5.1") is held exactly; as a float it would probably be something like 5.0999999999999996. Similarly, decimal.Decimal("0.00089") would be something like 0.00088999999999999995. We can easily convert from Decimal to float, although we may lose precision by doing so:

```
>>> d = decimal.Decimal("1.1")
>>> f = float(d)
>>> f
1.1000000000000001
```

Python also provides complex numbers as a built-in data type. These numbers consist of a real and an imaginary component, the latter indicated by the suffix j.* For example:

```
>>> c = 5.4+0.8j
>>> type(c)
<type 'complex'>
```

Here we have entered a complex number (with the syntax *real_part+imaginary_part*j), and used Python's type() function to tell us what type the c is bound to.

---

*Mathematicians use *i* for imaginary numbers, whereas engineers, and Python, use *j*.

Importing Objects

Python has a large and comprehensive library of modules that provides a huge amount of predefined functionality. We can use this functionality by importing the constants, variables, functions, and classes that we want. The general syntax for importing is:

```
import moduleName
```

We can then access objects inside the module using the dot operator. For example, the `random` module provides the `randint()` function, which can be imported and used like this:

```
import random
x = random.randint(1, 10)
```

Note that it is common to put `import` statements at the beginning of `.py` files, but they can be put elsewhere—for example, inside a function definition.

One benefit of Python's module system is that each module acts as a name-space, so we avoid name collisions effortlessly. For example, we may have defined our own `randint()` function, but there is no name conflict because the imported one in the example is accessed using the fully qualified name `random.randint()`. And as we will see in Chapter 3, we can create our own modules and import our own objects.

Modules themselves can contain other modules, and for very large modules, it is more convenient to import objects directly into the current namespace. Python provides a syntax for this. For example:

```
from PyQt4.QtCore import *
x = QString()
y = QDate()
```

Here we have imported every object, that is, all the classes from the `PyQt4` module's `QtCore` module, and this allows us to use their unqualified names. Using this syntax is frowned on by some developers, but since we know that almost all of the PyQt objects begin with a capital "Q", providing we don't create any of our own objects with names beginning with "Q", we will not get any name collisions and can type far less. However, for those who prefer to use fully qualified names in all cases, the plain import syntax can be used:

```
import PyQt4
x = PyQt4.QtCore.QString()
y = PyQt4.QtCore.QDate()
```

For the sake of brevity we will use the `from ... import` syntax for the `PyQt4` modules, although we will use the plain import syntax for everything else.

Python's floating-point numbers provide the same basic operations as its integral numbers, with integers being promoted to floating-point when numeric types are mixed in the same expression.

Bytestrings, Unicode Strings, and QStrings

There are two built-in string types in Python: str which holds bytes, and unicode which holds Unicode characters. Both types support a common set of string-processing operations. Like numbers, Python strings are immutable. They are also sequences, so they can be passed to functions that accept sequences and can use Python's sequence operations, for example, the len() function which returns the length of a sequence. PyQt provides a third string type, QString.

QString ☞ 28

If we only deal with 7-bit ASCII characters, that is, characters in the range 0–127, and if we want to save some memory, we can use strs. However, if we use an 8-bit character set, we must be careful that we know which codec we are using. In Western Europe, for example, 8-bit strings are often encoded using the Latin-1 encoding. In general, it is not always possible simply by examining the bytes to determine which 8-bit encoding is used for a particular string (or file). Modern GUI libraries, including Qt, use Unicode strings, so the safest route is to use strs for 7-bit ASCII and for raw binary 8-bit bytes, and unicode or QString otherwise.

Python strings are created by using quotes:

```
>>> g = "Green"
>>> t = ' trees'
>>> g + t
'Green trees'
```

Python does not mind whether we use double or single quotes as long as we use the same kind at both ends.

To force a string literal to be of type unicode, we precede its initial quote with u:

```
>>> bird = "Sparrow"
>>> beast = u"Unicorn"
>>> type(bird), type(beast), type(bird + beast)
(<type 'str'>, <type 'unicode'>, <type 'unicode'>)
```

Notice that we can use binary + to concatenate strings, and that if we involve str and unicode objects in the same operation the str operands are promoted to unicode and the resultant object is of type unicode. (If the str contains characters outside the 7-bit ASCII range, Python raises a UnicodeEncodeError exception; exceptions are covered in Chapter 2.)

In Python there is no separate "character" type: A single character is a string of length 1. We can get a character from a byte value using chr(), which accepts an integer value in the range 0–255. The Python documentation does not specify which encoding is used for values outside the ASCII range, (i.e., above 127). For Unicode, we can use `unichr()`, which accepts an integer in the range 0–65 535.* To convert the other way, from a character to its integer value (ASCII value or Unicode code point), we can use `ord()`. For example:

```
>>> euro = unichr(8364)
>>> print euro
€
>>> ord(euro)
8364
```

Why did we use `print` instead of letting IDLE output the result? Because IDLE shows non-ASCII characters in strings using hexadecimal escapes, so without `print` IDLE will output `u'\u20ac'`.

It is also possible to access Unicode characters by name:

```
>>> euro = u"\N{euro sign}"
>>> print euro
€
```

If we need to include special characters in a string we can escape them using a backslash, ("\"). Table 1.2 shows the escapes available; the Unicode ones only make sense inside `unicode` strings.

Here are two examples that show how to escape quotes:

```
"He said \"No you don't!\" again."
'What\'s up with him?'
```

We don't need to escape single quotes inside strings delimited by double quotes, and we don't need to escape double quotes inside strings delimited by single quotes.

For multiline strings we can use "triple" quotes:

```
'''This string has three lines in it, with a 'quote',
another "quote", and with just one embedded newline \
since we have escaped one of them.'''
```

These kinds of strings can include escaped characters just like normal strings, and can be delimited by three single quotes as shown, or by three double quotes. Newlines in triple-quoted strings, and in Python code, can be escaped by preceding them with a backslash. (This works correctly on Windows too, even though Windows uses two characters at the end of lines rather than one.)

---

*The range extends to 1 114 111 if Python was configured to use the UCS-4 representation.

Table 1.2 *Python's String Escapes*

Escape	Meaning
newline	Escape (i.e., ignore) the newline
\\\\	Backslash (\\)
\\'	Single quote (')
\\"	Double quote (")
\\a	ASCII bell (BEL)
\\b	ASCII backspace (BS)
\\f	ASCII formfeed (FF)
\\n	ASCII linefeed (LF)
\\N{*name*}	Unicode character name
\\r	ASCII carriage return (CR)
\\t	ASCII tab (TAB)
\\u*hhhh*	Unicode character with the given 16-bit hexadecimal value
\\U*hhhhhhhh*	Unicode character with the given 32-bit hexadecimal value
\\v	ASCII vertical tab (VT)
ooo	Character with the given octal value
\\x*hh*	Character with the given hexadecimal value

Python strings are *sequences* where individual characters can be accessed by positional indexing, with the first character at index position 0. It is also possible to index from the end of the string, with the last character's index position being -1. For example:

```
>>> phrase = "The red balloon"
>>> phrase[0], phrase[5], phrase[-1]
('T', 'e', 'n')
```

Negative indexes are used to access characters from right to left, with the right most character position being -1, the one to the left of that at position -2, and so on.

Python sequences support *slicing*, which means that we can copy subsequences from a sequence. A slice has one, two, or three colon-separated components: the start (which defaults to index 0), the end (which defaults to the length of the sequence), and another one which we will ignore. Slices are taken from and including the start index up to but excluding the end index. Here are some examples:

```
>>> phrase = "The red balloon"
>>> phrase[:3]
```

```
'The'
>>> phrase[-3:]
'oon'
>>> phrase[4:7]
'red'
```

Since Python strings are immutable it is not possible to assign to a character or slice inside a string:

```
>>> p = "pad"
>>> p[1] = "o"     # WRONG
Traceback (most recent call last):
  File <pyshell#64>, line 1, in <module>
    p[1] = o
TypeError:  object does not support item assignment
```

The easiest way to insert a character into a string is by using the slicing syntax:

```
>>> p = "pad"
>>> p = p[:1] + "o" + p[2:]
>>> p
'pod'
```

It may appear annoying that we have to specify literal numbers, but in practical programming we normally get the indexes using method calls—for example, using the find() method.

Other approaches are possible. For example:

```
>>> p = "pad"
>>> p = "o".join((p[:1], p[2:]))
>>> p
'pod'
```

Programmers from a Pascal or C++ background who are used to mutable strings may find the immutability of strings awkward at first. Python does, of course, offer mutable strings; they are provided by the StringIO module and the (faster) cStringIO module. PyQt's QString class is also mutable. But with practice, the Python way of working with immutable strings, and in particular, the idiom shown above, concatenating using the join() method, will soon be second nature. We will look at another idiom, used for "composing" strings, shortly.

Python strings have many useful methods, but we will concentrate on the most commonly used ones. In Python, methods are invoked on object references by using the dot . operator to access the method, and parentheses () to signify that we are performing a method (member function) call.* For example:

---

*As noted earlier, parentheses are not used with operators such as + and print.

```
>>> line = "The quick brown fox."
>>> line.find("q")
4
```

The find() method returns the index position of the leftmost occurrence of the string it is given as an argument, inside the string it is applied to. It returns -1 on failure.

Python also provides an index() method that has identical usage, but which raises a ValueError exception on failure. Other sequence classes (such as lists) also have an index() method, so having one for strings gives consistency.

Since we can use either find() or index() on strings, is there any reason to prefer one over the other? For one-off searches, it is often convenient to use find() and just check the return value. But if we have a block of code where we are performing lots of searches, using find() forces us to check the return value of every search, whereas using index() allows us to assume the result is always valid, and if it isn't, to handle any errors in a single exception handler. Of course, if we don't catch the exception, it will be passed up the call stack, and if it isn't caught anywhere it will cause the application to terminate. We use both approaches throughout the book, using whichever one is most appropriate on a case-by-case basis.

Exceptions vs. testing for errors ☞ 68

String methods can be applied both to string objects and to string literals:

```
>>> "malthusian catastrophe".title()
'Malthusian Catastrophe'
```

The title() method returns a string that is a copy of the string it is applied to, but with the first letter of every word capitalized. Python provides string formatting of data types using a syntax that is very similar to the C library's printf() function.

To achieve formatting we use the binary % operator, which takes a format string left-hand argument and a right-hand object (often a tuple of objects), which are to be formatted. For example:

Tuples ☞ 29

```
>>> "There are %i items" % 5
'There are 5 items'
```

The %i in the string is replaced by the number 5. The letter following the % in a string format specifies the type of object that is expected, with %i signifying an integer.

Here is an example that shows three different types being replaced, with arrows showing which % item is replaced by which tuple element:

```
>>> "The %i %s cost %f dollars" % (3, "fish", 17.49)
'The 3 fish cost 17.490000 dollars'
```

Table 1.3 *Selected String Methods and Functions*

Syntax	Description
`x in s`	Returns `True` if string `x` is a substring of string `s`
`x not in s`	Returns `True` if `x` is not a substring of string `s`
`x + s`	Returns the concatenation of strings `x` and `s`
`s * i`	Returns a string consisting of `int i` concatenations of string `s`. For example, `"Abc" * 3` produces `"AbcAbcAbc"`.
`len(s)`	Returns the length of string `s`; this is a byte count if `s` is of type `str` and a character count if `s` is of type `unicode`
`s.count(x)`	Returns the number of times string `x` occurs in string `s`. This method, and several others, can take optional start and end arguments to restrict the search to a slice of the string they are called on.
`s.endswith(x)`	Returns `True` if string `s` ends with string `x`
`s.startswith(x)`	Returns `True` if string `s` starts with string `x`
`s.find(x)`	Returns the index position of the leftmost occurrence of `x` in `s`; returns -1 if `x` is not found
`s.rfind(x)`	Like `find()`, but searches from right to left
`s.index(x)`	Returns the index position of the leftmost occurrence of `x` in `s`; raises a `ValueError` exception if no `x` is found
`s.rindex(x)`	Like `index()`, but searches from right to left
`s.isdigit()`	Returns `True` if the string is not empty and the character or characters it contains are *all* digits
`s.isalpha()`	Like `isdigit()`, but checks for letters
`s.join((x,...))`	Returns a string which is the concatenation of the given sequence delimited by the string on which the method is called. For example, `":".join(("A", "BB", "CCC"))` returns `"A:BB:CCC"`. The delimiter can be empty.
`s.lower()`	Returns a lower-cased copy of string `s`
`s.upper()`	Returns an upper-cased copy of string `s`
`s.replace(x, y)`	Returns a copy of string `s` with any occurrences of string `x` replaced by copies of string `y`
`s.split()`	Returns a list of strings, splitting on whitespace. For example, `"ab\tc d   e".split()` returns `["ab", "c", "d", "e"]`. This method can be given a first argument which is a string to split on, and a second argument which is the maximum number of splits to make.
`s.strip()`	Returns a copy of the string with leading and trailing whitespace removed. Accepts an optional string argument specifying which characters should be removed.

The % items are called format specifiers, and format strings contain at least one. Format specifiers consist of a percent (%) symbol followed by a formatting character. The percent symbol itself is specified by using %%. In the example, we used %i which is the format specifier for an int, %s which is the specifier for a string, and %f which is the specifier for a float.

Earlier we looked at how to insert a substring into a string. We showed how to do this using slicing, and the more Pythonic way using the string join() method. Here is a third way, using format specifiers:

```
>>> p = "pad"
>>> p = "%so%s" % (p[:1], p[2:])
>>> p
'pod'
```

Here we create a new string which consists of a string (which comes from the first slice of p), "o", and another string (from the second slice of p). The join() approach shown earlier is used for concatenating strings; this approach is used for "composing" strings.

We can exercise some control over the formatting of % items by putting some information between the % and the letter. For example, to show only two digits after the decimal place for a float we can use the specifier %.2f:

```
>>> "The length is %.2f meters" % 72.8958
'The length is 72.90 meters'
```

Here are a few more examples, two of which show the use of the % operator in conjunction with the print statement:

```
>>> print "An integer", 5, "and a float", 65.3
An integer 5 and a float 65.3
>>> print "An integer %i and a float %f" % (5, 65.3)
An integer 5 and a float 65.300000
>>> print "An integer %i and a float %.1f" % (5, 65.3)
An integer 5 and a float 65.3
```

In many cases, %i (and its synonym, %d), %f, and %s suffice. The full details of what format specifiers are available and how they can be modified to give specific results are given in the Python documentation; in this case, look for "String Formatting Operations". Other approaches to string formatting are also possible with Python, for example, Perl-like interpolation is provided by the Template class in the string module. It is even possible to use a C++-like syntax; see the recipe "Using a C++-like iostream Syntax", in the *Python Cookbook*. (See the Python Documentation sidebar.)

Notice that the print statement automatically outputs a space between each argument it prints. It is possible to avoid this using sys.stdout.write() instead of print; more coverage of write() is given in Chapter 6.

Python Documentation

Python is supplied with a large amount of documentation. Most of the documentation is of good quality, but there are a few areas where the coverage is rather thin. Navigating the documentation using the HTML version takes practice because it is organized more like a physical book than an online document and has far too few cross-reference links between pages.

Windows users are fortunate here because for them the documentation is supplied in Windows help file format. Click Start→All Programs→Python 2.x→Python Manuals to launch the Windows help browser. This tool has both an Index and a Search function that makes finding documentation easy. For example, to find the information about string format specifiers, simply enter "formatting" in the Index line edit and the entry "formatting, string (%)" will appear.

It is well worth skimming through the documentation. We suggest that you look at the "Library Reference" page (lib.html) to see what Python's standard library offers, and clicking through to the documentation of whichever topics are of interest. This should provide an initial impression of what is available and should also help you to establish a mental picture of where you can find the documentation you are interested in.

Note that some topics are covered under more than one heading. For example, to read about strings, see "Sequence Types", "String Methods", "String Formatting Operations", and "String Services". Similarly, for files and directories, see "File and Directory Access", "Data Compression and Archiving", and "Files and Directories".

For those who prefer printed information, the following books are worth considering.

- *Core PYTHON Programming* by Wesley Chun. This is a Python tutorial that may be suitable if you are completely new to Python and want a slower pace than Part I of this book provides.

- *Python in a Nutshell* by Alex Martelli. This is an excellent reference book that gives detailed and accurate coverage of the Python language and Python's standard library.

- *Python Cookbook 2nd Edition*, edited by Alex Martelli, Anna Martelli Ravenscroft, and David Ascher. This book provides lots of small practical functions, classes, snippets, and ideas, and will help broaden any Python programmer's awareness of what can be done with Python. The recipes are also available online at http://aspn.activestate.com/ASPN/Python/Cookbook.

For online Python information, the starting point is http://www.python.org. This site is also home to the Python wiki. PyQt-specific information is provided at http://www.riverbankcomputing.co.uk. The PyQt wiki is at http://www.diotavelli.net/PyQtWiki.

When using PyQt we have access to an additional string type, QString. Unlike Python's str and unicode, QString is mutable; this means that we can change QStrings in place, inserting and removing substrings, and changing individual characters. QString has a rather different API from that provided by str and unicode. (Qt provides QString because Qt is written in C++, which does not yet have built-in Unicode support.)

QString holds Unicode characters, but depending on which version of Python we are using, the internal representation may be different from Python's Unicode representation; this doesn't really matter, since PyQt can easily convert between unicode and QString. For example:

```
>>> from PyQt4.QtCore import *
>>> a = QString("apple")
>>> b = unicode("baker")
>>> print a + b
applebaker
>>> type(a + b)
<class 'PyQt4.QtCore.QString'>
```

Here we import all the classes from the QtCore module, made available to us through the PyQt4 module. When we perform operations involving QStrings and Python strings, the resultant strings are always QStrings as the type() function reveals.

When using PyQt, Qt methods that take string arguments can be given str, unicode, or QString types, and PyQt will perform any necessary conversion automatically. Qt methods that return strings always return QStrings. In view of Python's dynamic typing, we can easily become confused and not be sure whether we have a QString or a Python string. For this reason, it is wise to decide on a policy for string usage so that we always know where we stand.

The policy we use with PyQt is as follows:

- Use type str only when working with strictly 7-bit ASCII strings or with raw 8-bit data, that is, with raw bytes.

- For strings that will be used only by PyQt functions, for example, strings that are returned by one PyQt function only to be passed at some point to another PyQt function—do not convert such strings. Simply keep them as QStrings.

- In all other cases, use unicode strings, converting QStrings to unicode as soon as possible. In other words, as soon as a QString has been returned from a Qt function, always immediately convert it to type unicode.

This policy means that we avoid making incorrect assumptions about 8-bit string encodings (because we use Unicode). It also ensures that the strings we pass to Python functions have the methods that Python expects: QStrings have different methods from str and unicode, so passing them to Python functions can lead to errors. PyQt uses `QString` rather than `unicode` because when PyQt was first created, Python's Unicode support was nowhere near as good as it is today.

Collections

Once we have variables, that is, individual named object references to objects of particular types, it is natural to want to have entire collections of object references. Python's standard collection types hold object references, so they can, in effect, hold collections of any type of object. Another consequence of collections using object references is that they can refer to objects of different types: They are not restricted to holding items that are all of a single type.

The built-in collection types are `tuple`, `list`, `dict` (dictionary), `set`, and `frozenset`. All except `tuple` and `frozenset` are mutable, so items can be added and deleted from lists, dictionaries, and sets. Some additional mutable collection types are provided in the `collections` module.★

Python has one collection type in its standard library that does not hold object references; instead, it holds numbers of a specified type. This is the `array` type and it is used in situations where large numbers of numbers need to be stored and processed as efficiently as possible.

In this section, we will look at Python's built-in collection types.

Tuples

String
slicing

22 ☜

A tuple is an ordered sequence of zero or more object references. Like strings (and as we will see shortly, like lists), tuples support sequence functions such as `len()` as well as the same slicing syntax that we saw earlier. This makes it really easy to extract items from a tuple. However, tuples are immutable so we cannot replace or delete any of their items. If we want to be able to modify an ordered sequence, we simply use a list instead of a tuple; or if we already have a tuple but want to modify it, we just convert it to a list and then apply our changes.

We have already had some informal exposure to tuples; for example, some of our interactions in IDLE produced results that were wrapped up as tuples, and we also used tuples to provide multiple arguments to the `%` operator.

Here are some examples that show how to construct tuples:

```
>>> empty = ()
>>> type(empty)
<type 'tuple'>
>>> one = ("Canary")
```

★The Qt library provides its own rich set of container classes for C++, but these are not available in PyQt, and in any case, Python's own collection classes are perfectly good to use.

```
>>> type(one)
<type 'str'>
>>> one = ("Canary",)
>>> type(one)
<type 'tuple'>
```

Creating an empty tuple is simple, but for a one item tuple, we must use a comma to distinguish it from a parenthesized expression:

```
>>> things = ("Parrot", 3.5, u"\u20AC")
>>> type(things)
<type 'tuple'>
```

Tuples can hold items of any type; here we have str, float, and unicode items. It is also possible to drop the parentheses for tuples that have at least two items and where the meaning is unambiguous:

```
>>> items = "Dog", 99, "Cow", 28
>>> type(items)
<type 'tuple'>
```

Tuples can be arbitrarily nested and can be sliced, as these examples show:

```
>>> names = "Albert", "Brenda", "Cecil", "Donna"
>>> names[:3]
('Albert', 'Brenda', 'Cecil')
>>> names[1]
'Brenda'
```

We create a tuple of names, then take a slice of the first three items, and then look at the item at index position 1. Like all Python sequences, the first item is at position 0:

```
>>>names = names[0], names[1], "Bernadette", names[2], names[3]
>>> names
('Albert', 'Brenda', 'Bernadette', 'Cecil', 'Donna')
```

Now we have changed the names tuple to refer to a new tuple with an extra item in the middle. It might be tempting to write names[:2] instead of names[0], names[1], and similarly names[2:] for the last two names, but if we did so we would end up with a three-item tuple:

```
(('Albert', 'Brenda'), 'Bernadette', ('Cecil', 'Donna'))
```

This is because when we use slicing on a tuple the slices are always tuples themselves.

```
>>> names
('Albert', 'Brenda', 'Bernadette', 'Cecil', 'Donna')
>>> names = names[:4]
```

```
>>> names
('Albert', 'Brenda', 'Bernadette', 'Cecil')
```

Here, we have, in effect, chopped off the last name by taking a tuple of the first 4 items, that is, those with index positions 0, 1, 2, and 3. In slicing, the first number is the first index and this item is *included* in the result, and the second number is the last index and this item is *excluded* from the result.

```
>>> names
('Albert', 'Brenda', 'Bernadette', 'Cecil')
>>> names = names[:-1]
>>> names
('Albert', 'Brenda', 'Bernadette')
```

Another way of chopping off the last item is to index from the end; this way we don't have to know what the length of the tuple is. But if we want to know the length we can use the len() function:

```
>>> pets = (("Dog", 2), ("Cat", 3), ("Hamster", 14))
>>> len(pets)
3
>>> pets
(('Dog', 2), ('Cat', 3), ('Hamster', 14))
>>> pets[2][1]
14
>>> pets[1][0:2]
('Cat', 3)
>>> pets[1]
('Cat', 3)
```

Tuples can be nested and items accessed using as many square brackets as necessary.

Any sequence can be given to the tuple constructor to create a tuple. For example:

```
>>> tuple("some text")
('s', 'o', 'm', 'e', ' ', 't', 'e', 'x', 't')
```

Tuples are useful when we need fixed ordered collections of objects. They are also used as arguments to some functions and methods. For example, starting with Python 2.5, the str.endswith() method accepts either a single string argument (e.g., ".png") or a tuple of strings (e.g., (".png", ".jpg", ".jpeg")).

Lists

The list type is an ordered sequence type similar to the tuple type. All the sequence functions and the slicing that we have seen working with strings and tuples work in exactly the same way for lists. What distinguishes tuples from lists is that lists are mutable and have methods that we can use to modify them.

And whereas tuples are created using parentheses, lists are created using square brackets (or by using the list() constructor).

Let us look at some slicing examples that extract parts of a list:

```
>>> fruit = ["Apple", "Hawthorn", "Loquat", "Medlar", "Pear", "Quince"]
>>> fruit[:2]
['Apple', 'Hawthorn']
>>> fruit[-1]
'Quince'
>>> fruit[2:5]
['Loquat', 'Medlar', 'Pear']
```

Here, we have used the familiar slicing syntax that we have already used for strings and tuples.

Because lists are mutable we can insert and delete list items. This is achieved by using method calls, or by using the slicing syntax where slices are used on both sides of the assignment operator. First we will look at the method calls:

```
>>> fruit.insert(4, "Rowan")
>>> fruit
['Apple', 'Hawthorn', 'Loquat', 'Medlar', 'Rowan', 'Pear',
'Quince']
>>> del fruit[4]
>>> fruit
['Apple', 'Hawthorn', 'Loquat', 'Medlar', 'Pear', 'Quince']
```

We have inserted a new item and then deleted it, using a method call and an operator. The del statement is used to remove an item at a particular index position, whereas the remove() method is used to remove an item that matches remove()'s parameter. So, in this example, we could also have less efficiently deleted using fruit.remove("Rowan").

Now we will do the same thing using slicing:

```
>>> fruit[4:4] = ["Rowan"]
>>> fruit
['Apple', 'Hawthorn', 'Loquat', 'Medlar', 'Rowan', 'Pear',
'Quince']
>>> fruit[4:5] = []
>>> fruit
['Apple', 'Hawthorn', 'Loquat', 'Medlar', 'Pear', 'Quince']
```

When we assigned "Rowan" we used square brackets because we were inserting a list slice (a one-item list) into a list slice. If we had omitted the brackets, Python would have treated the word "Rowan" as a list in its own right, and would have inserted "R", "o", and so on, as separate items.

Table 1.4 *Selected List Methods and Functions*

Syntax	Description
x in L	Returns True if item x is in list L
x not in L	Returns True if item x is not in list L
L + m	Returns a list containing all the items of list L and of list m; the extend() method does the same but more efficiently
len(L)	Returns the length of list L
L.count(x)	Returns the number of times item x occurs in list L
L.index(x)	Returns the index position of the leftmost occurrence of item x in list L, or raises a ValueError exception
L.append(x)	Appends item x to the end of list L
L.extend(m)	Appends all list m's items to the end of list L
L.insert(i, x)	Inserts item x into list L at index position int i
L.remove(x)	Removes the leftmost occurrence of item x from list L, or raises a ValueError exception if no x is found
L.pop()	Returns and removes the rightmost item of list L
L.pop(i)	Returns and removes the item at index position int i in L
L.reverse()	Reverses list L in-place
L.sort()	Sorts list L in-place; this method accepts optional arguments such as a comparison function or a "key" to facilitate DSU (decorate, sort, undecorate) sorting

When inserting using slices, the source and target slices can be of different lengths. If the target slice is of zero length, such as fruit[4:4], only insertion takes place; but if the target's length is greater than zero, the number of items in the target slice are replaced by the items in the slice that is inserted. In this example, we replaced a one-item slice with a zero-item slice, effectively deleting the one item.

Here are a few more examples:

```
>>> fruit[2:3] = ["Plum", "Peach"]
>>> fruit
['Apple', 'Hawthorn', 'Plum', 'Peach', 'Medlar', 'Pear', 'Quince']
>>> fruit[4:4] = ["Apricot", "Cherry", "Greengage"]
>>> fruit
['Apple', 'Hawthorn', 'Plum', 'Peach', 'Apricot', 'Cherry',
 'Greengage', 'Medlar', 'Pear', 'Quince']
>>> bag = fruit[:]
>>> bag
['Apple', 'Hawthorn', 'Plum', 'Peach', 'Apricot', 'Cherry',
 'Greengage', 'Medlar', 'Pear', 'Quince']
```

Shallow and Deep Copying

We saw earlier (on page 16) that if we have two variables referring to the same string and we change one of them, for example using += to append—Python creates a new string. This occurs because Python strings are immutable. For mutable types such as lists (and dictionaries, covered shortly), the situation is different.

For example, if we create a list with two variables referring to it, and we change the list through one of the variables, *both* variables now refer to the *same* changed list:

```
>>> seaweed = ["Aonori", "Carola", "Dulse"]
>>> macroalgae = seaweed
>>> seaweed, macroalgae
(['Aonori', 'Carola', 'Dulse'], ['Aonori', 'Carola', 'Dulse'])
>>> macroalgae[2] = "Hijiki"
>>> seaweed, macroalgae
(['Aonori', 'Carola', 'Hijiki'], ['Aonori', 'Carola', 'Hijiki'])
```

This is because by default, Python uses *shallow* copying when copying mutable data. We can force Python to do a *deep* copy by taking a slice that consists of the entire list:

```
>>> seaweed = ["Aonori", "Carola", "Dulse"]
>>> macroalgae = seaweed[:]
>>> seaweed, macroalgae
(['Aonori', 'Carola', 'Dulse'], ['Aonori', 'Carola', 'Dulse'])
>>> macroalgae[2] = "Hijiki"
>>> seaweed, macroalgae
(['Aonori', 'Carola', 'Dulse'], ['Aonori', 'Carola', 'Hijiki'])
```

Slices always copy the items sliced, whether we slice a part of a list, or the whole list as we have done here. However, this works only one level deep, so if we had a list of lists, the sublists would only be shallow-copied. Some other collection types—for example, dict—provide a copy() method which is their equivalent of [:].

For deep copying that works to any depth we must import the copy module and use the deepcopy() function. In practice though, this is very rarely a problem, and when it does trip us up, using deepcopy() sorts it out for us.

We have replaced a slice of length one, fruit[2:3] ("Loquat"), with a slice of length two. We have also inserted a slice of three items without removing any. In the last example we copied all of fruit's items to bag; this could have been done using bag = fruit, but with subtly different semantics; see the Shallow and Deep Copying sidebar for more about copying lists.

Multiple consecutive items can be deleted using del on a slice, or by assigning a zero-length slice to a slice. To insert multiple items we can use slicing, or we can slice with operator +, and to add at the end we can use extend(). See Table 1.4 for a summary of the methods and functions applicable to lists.

Dictionaries

The dict type is a data dictionary, also known as an associative array. A dictionary holds a set of unordered key–value pairs and provides very fast key lookup. Keys are unique and must be of an immutable type, such as a Python string, a number, or a tuple; the value can be of any type including collection types, so it is possible to create arbitrarily nested data structures. Although dictionaries are not sequences, we can get sequences of their keys and values, as we will see in the next chapter.

Similar data structures exist in other languages—for example, Perl's hash, Java's HashMap, and C++'s unordered_map.

Notice that a tuple can be a dictionary key, but a list cannot, since a dictionary's keys must be immutable. In languages that offer only simple keys like strings and numbers, programmers who want multi-item keys must resort to converting their items into a string, but thanks to tuples this kind of hack is not necessary in Python.

Here are some examples that show how to create a dictionary and access items in it:

```
>>> insects = {"Dragonfly": 5000, "Praying Mantis": 2000,
"Fly": 120000, "Beetle": 350000}
>>> insects
{'Fly': 120000, 'Dragonfly': 5000, 'Praying Mantis': 2000,
'Beetle': 350000}
>>> insects["Dragonfly"]
5000
>>> insects["Grasshopper"] = 20000
>>> insects
{'Fly': 120000, 'Dragonfly': 5000, 'Praying Mantis': 2000,
'Grasshopper': 20000, 'Beetle': 350000}
```

Items can be deleted from a dictionary in the same way they can be deleted from a list. For example:

```
>>> del insects["Fly"]
>>> insects
{'Dragonfly': 5000, 'Praying Mantis': 2000, 'Grasshopper': 20000,
'Beetle': 350000}
>>> insects.pop("Beetle")
350000
>>> insects
{'Dragonfly': 5000, 'Praying Mantis': 2000, 'Grasshopper': 20000}
```

Table 1.5 *Selected Dictionary Methods and Functions*

Syntax	Description
x in d	Returns True if item x is in dict d
x not in d	Returns True if x is not in dict d
len(d)	Returns the number of items in dict d
d.clear()	Removes all items from dict d
d.copy()	Returns a shallow copy of dict d
d.keys()	Returns a list of all the keys in dict d
d.values()	Returns a list of all the values in dict d
d.items()	Returns a list of tuples of all the (key, value) pairs in dict d
d.get(k)	Returns the value with key k, or None
d.get(k, x)	Returns the value with key k if k is in dict d; otherwise, returns x
d.setdefault(k, x)	The same as the get() method, except that if the key is not in dict d, a new item is inserted with the given key and a value of None or x if x is given
d.pop(k)	Returns and removes the item with key k; raises a KeyError exception if there is no such key in dict d
d.pop(k, x)	Returns and removes the item with key k if k is in dict d; otherwise, returns x

Dictionaries can be constructed using the dict() constructor, and if the keys happen to be valid identifiers (i.e., alphanumeric beginning with an alphabetic character and with no whitespace), we can use a more convenient syntax:

```
>>> vitamins = dict(B12=1000, B6=250, A=380, C=5000, D3=400)
>>> vitamins
{'A': 380, 'C': 5000, 'B12': 1000, 'D3': 400, 'B6': 250}
```

We mentioned earlier that dictionary keys can be tuples; here is one last example to show this in action:

```
>>> points3d = {(3, 7, -2): "Green", (4, -1, 11): "Blue",
(8, 15, 6): "Yellow"}
>>> points3d
{(4, -1, 11): 'Blue', (8, 15, 6): 'Yellow', (3, 7, -2): 'Green'}
>>> points3d[(8, 15, 6)]
'Yellow'
```

In Chapter 2 we will see how to iterate over dictionaries in their "natural" arbitrary order, and also in key order.

Sets

Python provides two set types: `set` and `frozenset`. Both are unordered, so neither is a sequence. Sets are mutable, so items can be added and removed. Frozensets are immutable and cannot be changed; however, this means that they are suitable for use as dictionary keys.

Every item in a set is unique; if we try to add an item that is already in a set the `add()` call does nothing. Two sets are equal if they contain the same items, no matter what order those items were inserted in. Sets are similar to dictionaries that have only keys and no values. Lists, on the other hand keep their items in insertion order (unless they are sorted), and allow duplicates.

A frozenset is constructed with a single sequence parameter—for example a tuple or a list. A set can be constructed in the same way. For example:

```
>>> unicorns = set(("Narwhal", "Oryx", "Eland"))
>>> "Mutant Goat" in unicorns
False
>>> "Oryx" in unicorns
True
```

Since we created a set rather than a frozenset we can add and remove items. For example:

```
>>> unicorns.add("Mutant Goat")
>>> unicorns
set(['Oryx', 'Mutant Goat', 'Eland', 'Narwhal'])
>>> unicorns.add("Eland")
>>> unicorns
set(['Oryx', 'Mutant Goat', 'Eland', 'Narwhal'])
>>> unicorns.remove("Narwhal")
>>> unicorns
set(['Oryx', 'Mutant Goat', 'Eland'])
```

The set classes also support the standard set operations—for example, union, intersection, and difference—and for some operations provide both methods and operators, as Table 1.6 shows.

Built-in Functions

As we have already seen, Python has a number of built-in functions and operators: for example, `del`, `print`, `len()`, and `type()`. Tables 1.7–1.9 show some others that are useful, some of which we will discuss here.

In IDLE, or when using the Python interpreter directly, we can use the `help()` function to get information about an object, or to enter Python's interactive help system. For example:

```
>>> help(str)
```

Table 1.6 *Selected Set Methods and Functions*

Syntax	Description
x in s	Returns True if item x is in set s
x not in s	Returns True if item x is not in set s
len(s)	Returns the number of items in set s
s.clear()	Removes all the items from set s
s.copy()	Returns a shallow copy of set s
s.add(x)	Adds item x to set s if it is not already in s
s.remove(x)	Removes item x from set s, or raises a KeyError exception if x is not in s
s.discard(x)	Removes item x from set s if it is in s
s.issubset(t) s <= t	Returns True if set s is a subset of set t
s.issuperset(t) s >= t	Returns True if set s is a superset of set t
s.union(t) s | t	Returns a new set that has all the items from set s and from set t
s.intersection(t) s & t	Returns a new set that has each item that is both in set s and in set t
s.difference(t) s – t	Returns a new set that has every item that is in set s that is not in set t

Table 1.7 *Selected Sequence-Related Built-ins*

Syntax	Description
all(q)	Returns True if all items in q are True; q is an *iterable*—for example, a sequence such as a string or a list
any(q)	Returns True if any item in q is True
x in q	Returns True if item x is in sequence q; also works for dictionaries
x not in q	Returns True if item x is not in sequence q; also works for dictionaries
len(q)	Returns the number of items in sequence q; also works for dictionaries
max(q)	Returns the maximum item of sequence q
min(q)	Returns the minimum item of sequence q
sum(q)	Returns the sum of the items in sequence q

Table 1.8 *Some Useful Built-ins*

Syntax	Description
chr(i)	Returns a one-character str whose ASCII value is given by int i
unichr(i)	Returns a one-character unicode string whose Unicode code point is given by int i
ord(c)	Returns the int that is the byte value (0–255) if c is a one-character str string, or the int for the Unicode code point if c is a one-character unicode string
dir(x)	Returns a list of most of object x's attributes, including all its method names
help(x)	In IDLE, prints a brief description of object x's type and a list of its attributes including all its methods
hasattr(x, a)	Returns True if the object x has the attribute called a
id(x)	Returns the unique ID of the object that object reference x refers to
isinstance(x, C)	Returns True if x is an instance of class C or a subclass of class C
type(x)	Returns the type of x; isinstance() is preferred since it accounts for inheritance; type() is most often used for debugging
eval(s)	Returns the result of evaluating the string s which can contain an arbitrary Python expression
open(f, m)	Opens the file named in string f using mode m, and returns the file handle; covered in Chapter 6
range(i)	Returns a list of int i ints numbered from 0 to i – 1; additional arguments specify start, end, and step values

range() ex-amples ☞ 50

This will display all the str class's methods with a brief explanation of each. Quite a lot of information is provided, so we often have to scroll up using the PageUp key or using the scrollbar.

```
>>> help()
```

With no arguments the help() function takes us into the interactive help system. Type quit to return to normal IDLE interaction.

Once we are familiar with Python's classes and we need just a quick reminder, we can use dir() to get a bare list of a class's methods, for example:

```
>>> dir(str)
```

Table 1.9 *Selected Math-Related Built-ins*

Syntax	Description
`abs(n)`	Returns the absolute value of number n
`divmod(i, j)`	Returns a tuple containing the quotient and remainder that result from dividing i by j
`hex(i)`	Returns a hexadecimal string representing number i
`oct(i)`	Returns an octal string representing number i
`float(x)`	Returns x converted to a `float`; x may be a string or a number
`int(x)`	Returns x converted to an `int`; x may be a string or a number
`long(x)`	Returns x converted to a `long`; x may be a string or a number
`pow(x, y)`	Returns x raised to the power y; can accept a third modulo argument—the two-argument form is the same as using operator `**`
`round(x, n)`	Returns `float` value x rounded to n digits after the decimal place

The `range()` function is covered in Chapter 2 when we look at looping, and the `open()` function is covered in Chapter 6 when we look at reading and writing files. The `hasattr()` and `isinstance()` functions are covered in Chapter 3.

For the sequence-related functions, `max()` and `min()` work on sequences that contain strings as well as those that contain numbers, but may give suprising results:

```
>>> x = "Zebras don't sail"
>>> max(x), min(x)
('t', ' ')
```

The ordering is based on the byte values for `str` strings and on code points for unicode strings. For example, `ord("Z")` is 90, whereas `ord("t")` is 116.

Some of Python's built-in mathematical functions are shown in Table 1.9. Python is also supplied with a mathematics library that has all the standard functions we would expect. We can discover what they are by importing the `math` module, and using `dir()`:

```
>>> import math
>>> dir(math)
['__doc__', '__file__', '__name__', 'acos', 'asin', 'atan', 'atan2',
'ceil', 'cos', 'cosh', 'degrees', 'e', 'exp', 'fabs', 'floor', 'fmod',
'frexp', 'hypot', 'ldexp', 'log', 'log10', 'modf', 'pi', 'pow',
'radians', 'sin', 'sinh', 'sqrt', 'tan', 'tanh']
```

The first three items are special methods (indicated by leading and trailing double underscores); we will learn more about special methods in Chapter 3. All the rest are functions, except for `math.e` and `math.pi`, which are constants. We can find out what type an item is interactively. For example:

```
>>> import math
>>> type(math.pi), type(math.sin)
(<type 'float'>, <type 'builtin_function_or_method'>)
>>> math.pi, math.sin
(3.1415926535897931, <built-in function sin>)
>>> math.sin(math.pi)
1.2246063538223773e-16★
```

At first it is quite useful to explore what Python offers in this interactive way, but reading the documentation, particularly skimming the "Library Reference", will provide a broad overview of what Python's standard libraries have to offer.

Summary

In this chapter, we saw the use of the assignment using operator =, numeric addition using + (with type-promotion of an `int` to a `float`), and augmented assignment with +=. We also saw the `print` operator and learned that since IDLE automatically prints expressions, we use `print` much less often when using IDLE. We also saw that comments are introduced by a # and continue until the end of the line. In fact Python can separate statements with semicolons but it is very unusual to do this: In Python, a statement occupies a single line; newline is the statement separator.

We have learned how Python strings are created by using quotes, and how strings can be sliced and concatenated using the [] and + operators. We also summarized some of the key methods that Python strings provide: We will see numerous examples of their use in working code throughout the book. We saw that `QString` is a distinct Unicode string type and that we need to have a policy governing our use of `QStrings` and Python strings (normally `unicode` strings) when programming using PyQt.

The chapter introduced Python's major collection types. Tuples provide a nice way of grouping items together and can be used as dictionary keys. Lists are ordered and can hold duplicates. They provide fast insertions and deletions, and fast index-based lookup. Dictionaries are unordered and have unique keys. Like lists, they provide fast insertions and deletions. They also provide fast key-based lookup. Sets can be thought of as dictionaries that don't hold values. We will make great use of all these types in the rest of the book.

★The value 0.00000000000000012246063538223773 is close to 0 as expected.

Finally, we had a quick glimpse at some of Python's built-in functionality and at one of its mathematics modules. In Chapter 3, we will see how to create our own modules. But before that, we need to learn about Python's control structures so that we can branch, loop, call our own functions, and handle exceptions—all of which are the subject of the next chapter.

Exercises

The purpose of the exercises here, and throughout the book, is to encourage you to try out Python, and from Part II onward, PyQt, to get some hands-on experience. The exercises are designed to require as little typing as possible, and they are graded from least to most challenging.

The exercises for this chapter can all be tried out directly in IDLE; from Chapter 2 onward, they are slightly longer and will need to be typed into files, as we will explain.

1. Run IDLE, and type in the following:

   ```
   one = [9, 36, 16, 25, 4, 1]
   two = dict(india=9, golf=17, juliet=5, foxtrot=61, hotel=8)
   three = {11: "lima", 13: "kilo", 12: "mike"}
   ```

   Try to predict what the len(), max(), min(), and sum() functions will produce for each of the three collections, and then apply the functions and see the results. Do they do what you expected?

2. Continuing in IDLE, assign a dictionary's keys to two variables, and then change one of them like this:

   ```
   d = dict(november=11, oscar=12, papa=13, quebec=14)
   v1 = v2 = d.keys()
   v1, v2 # This will show the contents of the lists
   v1[3] = "X"
   ```

   After this, do you expect v1 and v2 to be the same or different? Why? Print out v1 and v2 to see. Now try assigning to v1 and v2 separately, and again change one:

   ```
   v1 = d.keys()
   v2 = d.keys()
   v1[3] = "X"
   ```

   Will v1 and v2 be the same as before? Print them out to see. If any of this is mysterious, try rereading the sidebar on page 34.

3. In the documentation, string-related methods and functions are covered in several places—find and read or skim these pages: "Sequence types", "String methods", "String formatting operations", and "String constants".

If you are comfortable with regular expressions, also look at the "Regular expression operations" pages.

Still in IDLE, create two floating-point values:

```
f = -34.814
g = 723.126
```

Based on your reading of the string-formatting documentation, create a single format string that when used with the % operator will produce the string < -34.81> when applied to f and <+723.13> when applied to g.

Solutions to the exercises, and all the source code for the examples, is available online from the author's Web site at http://www.qtrac.eu/pyqtbook.html. In the pyqtbook.zip file (and in the pyqtbook.tar.gz file) there are subdirectories, chap01, chap02, and so on, and in these are the relevant examples and answers. This chapter's answers are in chap01/answers.txt.

2

- Conditional Branching
- Looping
- Functions
- Exception Handling

Control Structures

To write programs we need data types, with variables and data structures in which to store them, and we need control structures such as branches and loops to provide control of program flow and iteration. In this chapter, we will learn how to use Python's if statement and how to loop using for and while loops. Exceptions can affect the flow of control, so we also cover both handling and creating exceptions.

One fundamental way of encapsulating functionality is to put it into functions and methods. This chapter shows how to define functions, and the next chapter shows how to define classes and methods. Programmers coming from a C++ or similar background are used to functions being defined just once. The same is true in Python, but with an additional possibility: In Python, we can create functions at runtime in a way that reflects the current circumstances, as we will see later in this chapter.

In the preceding chapter, we used IDLE to experiment with snippets of Python code. In this chapter, we will almost always simply show the code as it would be written in a file as part of a program. However, it is perfectly possible to type the snippets used in this chapter into IDLE to see the results "live", and this is certainly worth doing for anything covered that you are not sure about.

Some of Python's functions and operators work on Boolean values. For example, the binary operator in returns True if its left-hand operand is in its right-hand operand. Similarly, the if and while statements evaluate the expressions they are given, as we will see shortly.

In Python, a value evaluates to False if it is the predefined constant False, the number 0, the special object None, an empty sequence (e.g., an empty string or list), or an empty collection; otherwise, the value is True.

In PyQt an empty QString and any "null" object, that is, any object of a PyQt data type that has an isNull() method (and where isNull() returns True), evaluates to False. For example, an empty QStringList, a null QDate, a null QDateTime, and a null `QTime` are all `False`. Correspondingly, nonempty and non-null PyQt objects are `True`.

We can test any object to see its Boolean value by converting it to a `bool` type. For example:

```
from PyQt4.QtCore import *
now = QDate.currentDate()
never = QDate()
print bool(now), bool(never)    # Prints "True False"
```

The `QDate()` constructor with no arguments creates a null date; the `QDate.currentDate()` static method returns today's date which, of course, is not null.

Conditional Branching

Python provides an `if` statement with the same semantics as languages like C++ and Java, although with its own sparse syntax:

```
if expression1:
    suite1
elif expression2:
    suite2
else:
    suite3
```

The first thing that stands out to programmers used to C++ or Java is that there are no parentheses and no braces. The other thing to notice is the colon: This is part of the syntax and is easy to forget when starting out. Colons are used with `else`, `elif`, and in many other places to indicate that a block of code (a *suite* in Python-speak) is to follow. As we would expect, there can be any number of `elif`s (including none), and optionally, there can be a single `else` at the end.

Unlike most other programming languages, Python uses indentation to signify its block structure. Some programmers don't like this, at least at first, and some get quite emotional about the issue. But it takes just a few days to get used to, and after a few months, brace-free code seems much nicer and less cluttered to read than code that uses braces.

Since suites are indicated using indentation, the question that naturally arises is, "What kind of indentation?". The Python style guidelines recommend four spaces per level of indentation, and only spaces (no tabs). Most modern text editors can be set up to handle this automatically (IDLE's editor does, of course). Python will work fine with any number of spaces or with tabs, providing that the indentation used is consistent. In this book, we will follow the official Python guidelines.

Let's begin with a very simple example:

Table 2.1 *Logical Operations*

Group	Operators	Description
Comparison	<, <=, ==, !=, >=, >	The <> operator is also permitted as a synonym for != but is deprecated
Identity	is, is not	These are used to determine if two object references refer to the same underlying object
Membership	in, not in	These are used on lists, dictionaries, and strings, as we saw in Chapter 1
Logical	not, and, or	Both and and or short-circuit; the bit-wise equivalents are: ~ (not), & (and), | (or), and ^ (xor)

```
if x > 0:
    print x
```

In this case, the suite is just one statement (print x). In general, a suite is a single statement, or an indented block of statements (which themselves may contain nested suites), or the keyword pass which does absolutely nothing. The reason we need pass is because Python's syntax *requires* a suite, so if we want to put in a stub, or indicate that we are handling a "do nothing" case, we must use something, so Python provides pass; for example:

```
if x == 5:
    pass    # do nothing in this case
```

In general, whenever Python's syntax has a colon followed by a suite, the suite can be on the same line if it is just a single statement. For example:

```
if x == 5: pass
```

If the suite is more than a single statement, it must begin on the following line at the next level of indentation.

Python supports the standard comparison operators, and for logical operations it uses names (not, and, and or) rather than symbols. It is also possible to combine comparison expressions in a way that is familiar to mathematicians:

```
if 1 <= x <= 10:
    print x
```

Here, we print x if it is between 1 and 10. If x is an expression with no side effects, the above statement is equivalent to:

```
if 1 <= x and x <= 10:
    print x
```

No Dangling Else Trap

One additional benefit of using indentation is that the "dangling else ambiguity" is impossible in Python. For example, here is some C++ code:

```
if (x > 0)
    if (y > 0)
        z = 1;
else
    z = 5;
```

The code sets z to 1 if both x and y are greater than 0, and it looks like it will set z to 5 if x is less than or equal to 0. But in fact, it sets z to 5 only if x is greater than 0 *and* if y is less than or equal to 0. Here is what it means in Python:

```
if x > 0:
    if y > 0:
        z = 1
    else:
        z = 5
```

And if we really want z set to 5 if x is less than or equal to 0, we would write this:

```
if x > 0:
    if y > 0:
        z = 1
else:
    z = 5
```

Thanks to Python's indentation-based block structure, we avoid the "dangling else" trap.

The first form is preferred: It is clearer and simpler, it is more efficient (since x may be a complex expression involving some overhead to evaluate), and it is easier to maintain (again because the x is used only once rather than twice).

Python provides multiway branching using elif and else; there is no case (or switch) statement.

```
if x < 10:
    print "small"
elif x < 100:
    print "medium"
elif x < 1000:
    print "large"
else:
    print "huge"
```

Python 2.5 introduced a conditional expression. It is a kind of `if` statement that can be used in expressions, and it is equivalent to the ternary operators used by some other languages. The Python syntax is quite different from C++'s and Java's, which use ? : for their ternary operators, and it has the form *trueResult* if *expression* else *falseResult*; so the expression is in the middle:

```
print "x is zero or positive" if x >= 0 else "x is negative"
```

This will print "x is zero or positive" if x >= 0 evaluates to True; otherwise, it will print "x is negative".*

Looping

Python provides two loop constructs. One is the `while` loop, whose basic syntax is:

```
while expression:
    suite
```

Here is an example:

```
count = 10
while count != 0:
    print count,
    count -= 1
```

This will print "10 9 8 7 6 5 4 3 2 1"—all on one line, due to the `print` statement's trailing comma. Notice that we must have a colon before the indented suite.

Loops can be broken out of prematurely, using the `break` statement. This is particularly helpful in loops which will not otherwise terminate, that is, because their conditional expression is always true:

```
while True:
    item = getNextItem()
    if not item:
        break
    processItem(item)
```

Python's `while` loop can also have an associated `else` statement using the following syntax:

```
while expression:
    suite1
else:
    suite2
```

---

*Andrew Kuchling, author of the "What's New in Python" documents, recommends always using parentheses with conditional expressions. In this book, we use them only when necessary.

The else clause (with its associated suite) is optional. It is executed if the loop
terminates at the condition, rather than due to a break statement. It is not
often used, but can be useful in some situations:

```
i = 0
while i < len(mylist):
    if mylist[i] == item:
        print "Found the item"
        break
    i += 1
else:
    print "Didn't find the item"
```

The while loop is very versatile, but since it is so common to want to loop over
all the items in a list, or to loop a specific number of times, Python provides an
additional loop construct that is more convenient in such cases. This is the for
loop, whose syntax is:

```
for variable in iterable:
    suite1
else:
    suite2
```

The else works the same as in the while loop, that is, its suite is executed if
the for loop completes, but not if it was terminated by a break statement. An
iterable is an object that can be iterated over, such as a string, a tuple, a list, a
dictionary, or an iterator (such as a generator, covered later). In the case of a
dictionary, it is the keys that are iterated over.

Here, we iterate over a string, that is, over each character in the string:

```
for char in "aeiou":
    print "%s=%d" % (char, ord(char)),
```

This prints "a=97 e=101 i=105 o=111 u=117". The variable char takes each
value from the iterable in turn (in this case "a", then "e", and so on up to "u"),
and for each iteration executes the associated suite.

The range() built-in function returns a list of integers that can conveniently be
used in for loops. For example:

```
for i in range(10):
    print i,
```

This prints "0 1 2 3 4 5 6 7 8 9". By default, the range() function returns a list
of integers starting at 0, increasing by 1, up to but excluding the given value.
It also has two- and three-argument forms:

```
range(3, 7)         # Returns [3, 4, 5, 6]
range(-4, 12, 3)    # Returns [-4, -1, 2, 5, 8, 11]
```

Python also provides an xrange() function with the same semantics, but which is more memory-efficient in a for loop, because it evaluates lazily rather than generating the entire list of integers in one go. We will normally use range() and substitute it with xrange() only if it makes a significant difference to performance.

If the for loop's iterable is mutable (e.g., a list or a dictionary), it must not be changed inside the loop. If we want to change a list or dictionary as we iterate over it, we must iterate over a list of the list's indexes or a list of the dictionary's keys, or use a shallow copy, rather than working directly on the collections themselves. For example:

```
presidents = dict(Washington=(1789, 1797), Adams=(1797, 1801),
                  Jefferson=(1801, 1809), Madison=(1809, 1817))
for key in presidents.keys():
    if key == "Adams":
        del presidents[key]
    else:
        print key, presidents[key]
```

This removes the "Adams" key (and its associated value) from the presidents dictionary, and prints:

```
Madison (1809, 1817)
Jefferson (1801, 1809)
Washington (1789, 1797)
```

Notice that although Python normally uses newline as a statement separator, this does *not* occur inside parentheses. The same is true when we create lists in square brackets or dictionaries in braces. This is why we can spread the construction of the presidents dictionary over a couple of lines without having to escape the intervening newline with a backslash (\).

Since dictionaries hold pairs of keys and values, Python provides methods for iterating over the keys, the values, and the pairs. And as a convenience, if we simply iterate over a dictionary, we don't even have to call the keys() method to get the keys:

```
presidents = dict(Washington=(1789, 1797), Adams=(1797, 1801),
                  Jefferson=(1801, 1809), Madison=(1809, 1817))
for key in presidents:
    print "%s: %d-%d" % (key, presidents[key][0], presidents[key][1])
```

This prints (not necessarily in this order):

```
Madison: 1809-1817
Jefferson: 1801-1809
Washington: 1789-1797
Adams: 1797-1801
```

When we iterate over a dictionary in a for loop the variable is set to each dictionary key in turn.* Dictionaries are unordered, so their keys are returned in an undefined order.

To get the values rather than the keys we can use the values() method—for example, for dates in presidents.values(): and to get pairs we can use the items() method. For example:

```
for item in presidents.items():
    print "%s: %d-%d" % (item[0], item[1][0], item[1][1])
```

This produces the same output as the previous example, as does the following:

```
for president, dates in presidents.items():
    print "%s: %d-%d" % (president, dates[0], dates[1])
```

Here we have unpacked each pair returned by the items() method, the dates being the two-element tuple of dates.

If we want to iterate in order, we must explicitly sort the list before we iterate on it. For example, to iterate in name order we can do this:

```
for key in sorted(presidents):
    print "%s: %d-%d" % (key, presidents[key][0], presidents[key][1])
```

Both for loops and the sorted() function can work on sequences or on iterators. Iterators are objects that support Python's iterator protocol, which means that they provide a next() method, and raise a StopIteration exception when they have no more items. Not surprisingly, lists and strings implement the protocol: A list iterator returns each item in the list in turn, and a string iterator returns each character of the string in turn. Dictionaries also support the protocol: They return each of their keys in turn (in an arbitrary order). So, when we use a for loop or call sorted() on a dictionary, we actually operate on the dictionary's keys. For example:

```
names = list(presidents)
# names == ['Madison', 'Jefferson', 'Washington', 'Adams']
```

So in the for loop, we effectively called sorted(list(presidents)) which is the same as sorted(presidents.keys()). If we want to be more explicit, we could break things down into steps:

```
keys = presidents.keys()     # Or: keys = list(presidents)
keys.sort()
for key in keys:
    print "%s: %d-%d" % (key, presidents[key][0], presidents[key][1])
```

---

*Note for C++/Qt programmers: Python's for loop iterates over a dictionary's keys, whereas Qt's foreach loop iterates over a QMap's values.

Python's sort() method and sorted() function can take additional arguments. So, for example, we could sort the presidents dictionary by dates.

In addition to the keys(), values(), and items() methods, dictionaries also provide iterkeys(), itervalues(), and iteritems() methods. These additional methods can be used just like the plain versions, and they provide better performance. However, they cannot be used to iterate over a dictionary whose keys will change during the iteration.

Just like while loops, we can use break to leave a for loop before the iterations are complete. We can also use continue in both kinds of loop to immediately jump to the next iteration. For example:

```
for x in range(-5, 6):
    if x == 0:
        continue # goes directly to the next iteration
    print 1.0 / x,
```

This will produce output like this: "-0.2 -0.25 -0.333333333333 -0.5 -1.0 1.0 0.5 0.333333333333 0.25 0.2". Without the continue, we would eventually attempt division by zero and get an exception.

As mentioned earlier, Python's loops can have an optional else clause that is executed *only* if the loop completed, that is, the else clause will not be executed if break was called inside the loop. An example will make this clearer; here is an inefficient way of generating a list of primes:

```
primes = [2]
for x in range(2, 50):
    if x % 2:
        for p in primes:
            if x % p == 0:
                break # exits the loop and skips the else
        else:
            primes.append(x)
```

%
operator
24 ☞

When we saw the % operator earlier, it was used with string operands and produced a formatted string as its result. Here, we use the % operator with integer operands, and in this context it performs the modulus (remainder) operation, and produces an integer as its result.

At the end, the primes list is [2, 3, 5, 7, 11, 13, 17, 19, 23, 29, 31, 37, 41, 43, 47]. The append() method is called only if the iteration over the primes list completes, that is, if x is not divisible by any previous prime.

List Comprehensions and Generators

Producing lists using a for loop in conjunction with range() is easy. In addition, Python provides an alternative approach called *list comprehensions*—these are expressions that generate lists. (Note that this and other advanced sections in

Parts I, II, and III, are indicated by a rocket in the margin. You can skip these on first reading since back-references are given where appropriate.)

Let us generate a list of numbers divisible by 5:

```
fives = []
for x in range(50):
    if x % 5 == 0:
        fives.append(x)
# fives = [0, 5, 10, 15, 20, 25, 30, 35, 40, 45]
```

This involves the familiar combination of `for` and `range()`.

Now we will see how to generate a simple list of consecutive numbers using a list comprehension:

```
[x for x in range(10)]
```

This produces the list [0, 1, 2, 3, 4, 5, 6, 7, 8, 9]. List comprehensions can have conditions attached:

```
fives = [x for x in range(50) if x % 5 == 0]
```

This generates the same `fives` list as our original `for` loop. More complex list comprehensions with nested `for` loops are perfectly possible, although the more conventional syntax may be easier to read in such cases.

One drawback of list comprehensions is that they generate the entire list in one go, which can consume a lot of memory if the list is very large. This problem also applies to the conventional syntax, but you can get around it by using `xrange()` instead of `range()`. Python *generators* provide another solution. These are expressions that work like list comprehensions, except that they generate their lists lazily.

```
fives = (x for x in range(50) if x % 5 == 0)
```

This is almost identical to the list comprehension (the only obvious difference being the use of parentheses rather than square brackets), but the object returned is not a list! Instead, a *generator* is returned. A generator is an iterator, so we can do things like this:

```
for x in (x for x in range(50) if x % 5 == 0):
    print x,
```

which will print "0 5 10 15 20 25 30 35 40 45".

List comprehensions are not strictly necessary in Python programming; the coverage here is mostly to ensure that they are recognizable when reading other people's code, and to provide a taste of some of Python's more advanced features. When we use them later on, we will generally show equivalent code that uses `for` loops, for example. On the other hand, generators, although an advanced and relatively new feature of Python, cannot easily be mimicked. We will create a simple generator function in the next section, and some very short generator methods in an example class in Chapter 3.

Functions

In general, functions allow us to package up and parameterize commonly used functionality. Python provides three types of functions: ordinary functions, lambda functions, and methods. In this section, we will concentrate on ordinary functions, with a very brief mention of lambda functions; we will cover methods in Chapter 3.

In Python, every function has either "global" or "local" scope. Broadly speaking, global scope means that the function is visible within the file in which it is defined and is accessible from any file which imports that file. Local scope means that the function was defined inside another scope (e.g., inside another function) and is visible only within the enclosing local scope. We will not concern ourselves further with this issue here, but will return to it in Chapter 3.

Functions are defined using the def statement, using the syntax:

```
def functionName(optional_parameters):
    suite
```

For example:

```
def greeting():
    print "Welcome to Python"
```

The function name must be a valid identifier. Functions are called using parentheses, so to execute the greeting() function we do this:

```
greeting()    # Prints "Welcome to Python"
```

A function's name is an object reference to the function, and like any other object reference it can be assigned to another variable or stored in a data structure:

```
g = greeting
g()              # Prints "Welcome to Python"
```

This makes keeping lists or dictionaries of functions trivial in Python.

Functions that accept parameters can be given the parameter values by position ("positional arguments"), by name ("keyword arguments"; but nothing to do with the language's keywords), or by a combination of both. Let us look at a concrete example: Python does not provide a range() function that operates on floats, so we will create one ourselves.

```
def frange(start, stop, inc):
    result = []
    while start < stop:
        result.append(start)
        start += inc
    return result
```

If we call this function as frange(0, 5, 0.5) the list we get back is [0, 0.5, 1.0, 1.5, 2.0, 2.5, 3.0, 3.5, 4.0, 4.5], as we expect.

Like normal Python variables, we do not specify types for our parameters. And since we have not given any default arguments, every parameter *must* be specified, otherwise we will get a TypeError exception. For those unfamiliar with default arguments, Python allows us to give values to parameters in a function's signature. Each such value is a "default argument", and it is used if the corresponding argument is not given when the function is called.

In many cases we create functions where one or more arguments will almost always have the same values. Python allows us to provide default arguments for such situations, and we have taken advantage of this to provide a default argument for the third parameter, as this revised def line shows:

```
def frange(start, stop, inc=1.0):
```

This works fine; for example, we can now call frange(0, 5) to get [0, 1.0, 2.0, 3.0, 4.0] since the increment defaults to 1.0. In common with other languages that allow default arguments, Python does not permit a parameter without a default argument to follow one that has a default argument; so we could *not* have frange(start=0, 5). Nor does Python allow overloaded functions. Neither of these restrictions is ever a problem in practice, as we will see shortly when we discuss keyword arguments.

Unfortunately, our frange() function does not provide the same argument logic as range() provides. For range(), if one argument is given it is the upper bound, if two are given they are the lower and upper bounds, and if three are given they are the bounds and the step size. So we will create a final frange() function, which more carefully mimics range()'s behavior:[*]

```
def frange(arg0, arg1=None, arg2=None):
    """Returns a list of floats using range-like syntax

    frange(start, stop, inc)    # start = arg0  stop = arg1  inc = arg2
    frange(start, stop)         # start = arg0  stop = arg1  inc = 1.0
    frange(stop)                # start = 0.0   stop = arg0  inc = 1.0
    """
    start = 0.0
```

---

[*]For a more sophisticated frange(), see "Writing a range-like Function with Float Increments" in the *Python Cookbook*.

```
            inc = 1.0
            if arg2 is not None:     # 3 arguments given
                start = arg0
                stop = arg1
                inc = arg2
            elif arg1 is not None:  # 2 arguments given
                start = arg0
                stop = arg1
            else:                     # 1 argument given
                stop = arg0
            # Build and return a list
            result = []
            while start < (stop - (inc / 2.0)):
                result.append(start)
                start += inc
            return result
```

For example, frange(5) returns [0.0, 1.0, 2.0, 3.0, 4.0], frange(5, 10) returns [5, 6.0, 7.0, 8.0, 9.0], and frange(2, 5, 0.5) returns [2, 2.5, 3.0, 3.5, 4.0, 4.5].

The loop condition is different from the one we used earlier. It is designed to prevent you from accidentally reaching the stop value due to floating-point rounding errors.

After the def line, we have a triple-quoted string—and the string is not assigned to anything. An unassigned string that follows a def statement—or that is the first thing in a .py or .pyw file or that follows a class statement, as we will see later on in Part I—is called a "docstring". It is the natural place to document functions. By convention, the first line is a brief summary, separated from the rest by a blank line.

In most of the examples shown in the rest of the book, we will omit the doc-strings to save space. They are included in the source code that accompanies the book where appropriate.

The use of None is a more convenient default than, say, 0 since 0 might be a legitimate upper bound. We could have compared to None using the syntax arg2 != None, but using is not is more efficient and better Python style. This is because if we use is we get identity comparison rather than value comparison, which is fast because we are just comparing two addresses and don't have to look at the objects themselves. Python has one global None object, so comparing with it using is or is not is very fast.

The parameters passed to Python functions are always object references. In the case of references to immutable objects like strings and numbers, we can treat the parameters as though they were passed by value. This is because if an immutable parameter is "changed" inside a function, the parameter is simply bound to a new object, and the original object it referred to is left intact.

Conversely, mutable objects, that is, parameters that are object references to mutable types like lists and dictionaries, can be changed inside functions. These parameter-passing behaviors are the same as in Java.*

All Python functions return a value. This is done either explicitly by using a return or yield statement (covered next), or implicitly, in which case Python will return None for us. Unlike C++ or Java, we are not tied down to specifying one particular return type: We can return any type we want since what we return is an object reference that is bound to a variable of any type. Python functions always return a single value, but because that value can be a tuple or a list or any other collection, for all practical purposes, Python functions can return any number of values.

Generator Functions

If we replace the code at the end of the frange() function as shown in the following code snippet, we will turn the function into a generator. Generators do not have return statements; instead, they have yield statements. If a generator runs out of values, that is, if control reaches the end of the function, instead of returning, Python automatically raises a StopIteration exception:

```
# Build and return a list          # Return each value on demand
result = []                        while start < (stop - (inc / 2.0)):
while start < (stop - (inc / 2.0)):    yield start
    result.append(start)               start += inc
    start += inc
return result
```

Now, if we call frange(5), we will get back a generator object, not a list. We can force the generator to give us a list by doing this: list(frange(5)). But a more common use of generators is in loops:

```
for x in frange(10):
    print x,
```

This will output "0.0 1.0 2.0 3.0 4.0 5.0 6.0 7.0 8.0 9.0" whichever version we use. But for long lists the generator version will be much more efficient, because rather than creating the whole list in memory like the list version, it creates only one item at a time.

The yield statement behaves like a return statement, but for one crucial difference: After yield has returned a value, when the generator is next called it will continue from the statement following the yield with all its previous state intact. So the first time the frange() generator is called, assuming, say frange(5), it returns 0.0; the second time it returns 1.0, and so on. After returning 9.0 the while expression evaluates to False and the function terminates.

---

*Mutable parameters in Python are similar to Pascal's var parameters and to C++'s non-const references.

Because the function is a generator (and this is the case purely because we have used yield), when it finishes it does not return a value, but instead raises a StopIteration exception. In the context of a for loop, the for gracefully handles this particular exception, taking it not as an error, but as an indication that the iteration has completed, so the for loop ends and the flow of control moves to the for loop's else suite, or to the statement following the for loop's suite, if there is no else. Similarly, if we coerce a generator into a list, the list constructor will automatically handle the StopIteration exception.

A generator is an object that has a next() function, so we can explore the behavior of our frange() generator interactively if we wish:

```
>>> list(frange(1, 3, 0.75))
[1, 1.75, 2.5]
>>> gen = frange(1, 3, 0.75)
>>> gen.next()
1
>>> gen.next()
1.75
>>> gen.next()
2.5
>>> gen.next()
Traceback (most recent call last):
  File <pyshell#126>, line 1, in -toplevel-
    gen.next()
StopIteration
```

We generated the whole three-item list using list(), and then we used the generator returned by frange() to produce each successive value in the same way that a for loop does.

Using Keyword Arguments

Python's argument-handling abilities are very versatile. So far we have provided parameters using positional syntax. For example, the first parameter we gave to our frange() function always went to arg0, the second to arg1, and the third to arg2. We have also used default arguments so that some arguments could be omitted. But what happens if we want to pass, say, the first and third arguments, but accept the default second argument? In the next example, we will see how we can achieve this.

Python provides a strip() method for stripping whitespace (or other unwanted characters) from the ends of a string, but it does not provide a function for cleaning up the whitespace inside a string; something that we often need to do when we get strings from users. Here is a function that strips whitespace from both ends of a string and replaces each sequence of internal whitespace with a single space:

Experimenting with Functions in Files

Both `frange()` and a generator version, `gfrange()`, are in the file `chap02/frange.py`. If we want to try these or any other functions interactively, we can start up IDLE, and append the path where the file we want to use is located to the paths it searches; for example:

```
>>> import sys
>>> sys.path.append("C:/pyqt/chap02")
```

Now the relevant module can be loaded into IDLE:

```
>>> import frange
```

The file we wish to import from must have a .py extension, and we must not include the extension in the `import` statement. Now we can use `frange()` and `gfrange()` inside IDLE:

```
>>> frange.frange(3, 5, 0.25)
[3, 3.25, 3.5, 3.75, 4.0, 4.25, 4.5, 4.75]
```

Importing Objects sidebar 19 ☞

The first name `frange` is the module name, and within that module we wish to access the `frange` function, which is why we write `frange.frange()`. We did the same thing a moment ago, when we imported the `sys` module and accessed its `path` list using `sys.path`.

Although we prefer to use IDLE, it is also possible to directly use the Python interpreter when experimenting interactively. If we simply run the Python executable itself (`python.exe`, for example) in a console, we will get the familiar `>>>` prompt and be able to use the interpreter interactively.

```
def simplify(text, space=" \t\r\n\f", delete=""):
    result = []
    word = ""
    for char in text:
        if char in delete:
            continue
        elif char in space:
            if word:
                result.append(word)
                word = ""
        else:
            word += char
    if word:
        result.append(word)
    return " ".join(result)
```

The function iterates over every character in the text string. If the character is in the delete string (which, by default, is empty), we ignore it. If it is a "space" (i.e., it is in the space string), we append the word we have been building up to our list of words, and set the next word to be empty. Otherwise, we append the character to the word we are building up. At the end, we tack on the last word to our list of words. Finally, we return the list of words as a single string with each word separated by a single space, using the string join() method.*

Now let us look at how we can use the function:

```
simplify(" this    and\n that\t too")    # Returns "this and that too"
simplify("  Washington    D.C.\n",
        delete=",;:.")                      # Returns "Washington DC"
simplify(delete="aeiou", text=" disemvoweled ")    # Returns "dsmvwld"
```

In the first case, we use the default arguments for the space and delete parameters. In the second case, we use Python's keyword argument syntax to specify the third parameter while accepting the default for the second parameter. In the last case, we use keyword syntax for both of the arguments we want to use. Notice that if we use keyword syntax, the order of the keyword arguments is up to us—providing that if we also use positional arguments, these precede the keyword arguments, as the second call shows.

The code we have used for simplify() is not as Pythonic as it could be. For example, we should really store word as a list of characters rather than as a string, and we don't need the space parameter since we could use the string object's isspace() method instead. The file chap02/simplified.py contains the simplify() shown here and a similar function, simplified(), which uses the more Pythonic approach. And as noted earlier, although we usually don't show the docstrings in the book, they are in the files.

Python's argument passing is even more sophisticated than we have shown so far. In addition to named arguments, Python functions can be given signatures that accept a variable number of positional arguments and a variable number of keyword arguments. This is a much more versatile and powerful version of C++'s and Java's variable argument lists, but it is rarely needed, so we will not cover it.

Lambda Functions

So far, we've always defined functions using def, but Python provides a second way of creating functions:

```
cube = lambda x: pow(x, 3)
```

The lambda keyword is used to create simple anonymous functions. Lambda functions cannot contain control structures (no branches or loops), nor do they have a return statement: The value returned is simply whatever the expression

---

*The QString.simplified() method is like our simplify() function called with just one argument.

evaluates to. Lambda functions can be closures, a topic covered later. In this example, we have assigned the lambda function to the variable cube, which we can now use, for example: cube(3) which will return 27.

Clo-
sures
☞ 64

Some Python programmers dislike lambda; certainly it is not needed since def can be used to create any function we want. However, when we start on GUI programming we will see one context where lambda can be useful, although we will also show alternatives that don't use it.

Dynamic Function Creation

The Python interpreter starts reading from the top of the .py or .pyw file. When the interpreter encounters a def statement it executes the statement, thereby creating the function and binding the name following the def to it. Any code that is not inside a def statement (or inside a class statement, as we will see in the next chapter) is executed directly.

Python cannot call functions or use objects that have not been defined. So Python programs that occupy a single file tend to have a Pascal-like structure with lots of function definitions from the top down, and at the end a call to one of them to start the processing off.

Unlike C++ and Java, Python programs do not have a fixed entry point, and the name "main" is not special. The Python interpreter simply executes the code it encounters from the first line down. For example, here is a complete Python program:

```
#!/usr/bin/env python

def hello():
    print "Hello"

def world():
    print "World"

def main():
    hello()
    world()

main()
```

The interpreter executes def hello(), that is, it creates the hello() function, then creates the world() function, and then creates the main() function. Finally the interpreter reaches a function call, to main() in this case, so the interpreter executes the function call, at which point what we normally think of as program execution commences.

Python programmers usually put only one statement at the top level, a call to the first function they want to execute. They usually call this function main(), and call their other functions from it, resulting in a structure similar to that used by C++ and Java.

Since `def` statements are executed at runtime, it is possible to use different definitions depending on the situation. This is especially useful when we want to use functionality in one version of Python that is not available in an earlier one, without forcing our users to upgrade.

For example, Python 2.4 introduced the `sorted()` function. What if we had some code that needed `sorted()`, but some of our users were using Python 2.3 and some were using 2.4 or later? We could simply rely on the `sorted()` method for 2.4 or later, and provide our own equivalent function for older Pythons:

```
import sys

if sys.version_info[:2] < (2, 4):
    def sorted(items):
        items = list(items)
        items.sort()
        return items
```

We begin by importing the `sys` module, which provides the `version_info` tuple. Then we use this tuple to get the major and minor version numbers. Only if the version is lower than 2.4 do we define our own `sorted()` function. Notice also that we can compare tuples: Python can compare data structures, including nested ones, providing all the types they contain can be compared.

Partial Function Application

As we will see when we begin GUI programming, we sometimes have situations where we need to call a particular function, but we actually know what one of the parameters will be when we are writing the code. For example, we might have several buttons that all need to invoke the same function, but parameterized in some way by which particular button is the cause of the invocation.

In the simplest case we want to store a function (i.e., an object reference to a function) that we can then call later. A function stored like this is known as a *callback*. Here is a trivial example:

```
def hello(who):
    print "Hello", who

def goodbye(who):
    print "Goodbye", who

funclist = [hello, goodbye]
# Some time later
for func in funclist:
    func("Me")
```

This prints "Hello Me", and then "Goodbye Me". Here, we have stored two functions and then called them later on. Notice that we passed the same argument, `"Me"`, each time we called `func()`. Since we know what the argument is in advance, it would be nice to be able to somehow package up both the function to be called and the parameter we want to use into a single callable object.

A solution to this is *partial function application* (also known as "currying"), which simply means that we take a function and zero, one, or more parameters for it, and wrap them up into a new function which, when invoked, will call the original function with the parameters we wrapped, and with any others that are passed at call time. Such wrapped functions are called *closures* because they encapsulate some of their calling context when they are created.

To get a flavor for how this works, let us imagine a very simple GUI program where we have two buttons that, when pressed, will call the same `action()` function. (We won't worry about how we transform button presses into function calls right now; it is very easy, and fully explained in Chapter 4.)

```
def action(button):
    print "You pressed button", button
```

Now when we create our buttons, naturally we know which ones they are, so we want to tell the first button to make the call `action("One")` and the second to call `action("Two")`. But this presents us with a problem. We know what we want called, but we don't want the call to take place until a button is pressed. So, for example, we want to give the first button a function which wraps `action()` and the parameter `"One"`, so that when the first button is pressed it can call `action()` with the right parameter.

So, what we need is a function that will take a function and an argument and return a function, that when, called will call the original function with the original argument. In Python 2.5, this is easy assuming our previous definition of `action()`:

```
import functools

buttonOneFunc = functools.partial(action, "One")
buttonTwoFunc = functools.partial(action, "Two")
```

The `functools.partial()` function takes a function as the first argument, and then any number of other arguments, and returns a function that, when called, will call the passed function with the passed arguments, and with any additional arguments that are given at call time.

So, when `buttonOneFunc()` is called, it will simply call `action("One")` just as we want. As we mentioned earlier, a function's name is simply an object reference that happens to refer to a function, so it can be passed as a parameter like any other object reference.

But where does this leave users of earlier versions of Python? We could provide our own very simple and less powerful version of `partial()`. For example:

```
def partial(func, arg):
    def callme():
        return func(arg)
    return callme
```

Inside the partial() function we create an inner function, callme(), that, when called, will call the function and argument that were passed to the partial() function. After creating the callme() function, we then return an object reference to it so that it can be called later.

This means that we can now write:

```
buttonOneFunc = partial(action, "One")
buttonTwoFunc = partial(action, "Two")
```

Ideally, it would be nice to use functools.partial() when it is available, and fall back on our own simple partial() function otherwise. Well, since we can define functions at runtime, this is perfectly possible:

```
import sys

if sys.version_info[:2] < (2, 5):
    def partial(func, arg):
        def callme():
            return func(arg)
        return callme
else:
    from functools import partial
```

The if statement ensures that if we are using a version of Python older than 2.5 we create a partial() function that takes a function and a single argument and returns a function that, when called, will call the function passed in with the argument. But if we are using a later version of Python, we use the functools.partial() function, so in our code we can always call partial(), and whichever version was created will be the one used.

Now, just as before, we can write:

```
buttonOneFunc = partial(action, "One")
buttonTwoFunc = partial(action, "Two")
```

Only this time the code will work with both old and new versions of Python.

The partial() function we have defined is just about the simplest possible. It is also possible to create much more sophisticated wrappers that can take positional and keyword arguments at the time they are wrapped, and additional positional and keyword arguments at the time they are called; functionality that functools.partial() already provides. We use partial() in several places from Part II onward, but in each case the simple partial() function shown in this section could be used if Python 2.5 or later was not available.

In the next section, we will continue to take a fairly high-level view of functions, and look at the possibilities that are available to us for the notification and handling of error conditions.

Exception Handling

Many primers push exception handling quite far back, often after covering object-oriented programming. We put them here in the control structures chapter because exception handling is relevant in both procedural and object-oriented programming, and because exception handling can cause the flow of execution to change dramatically, which certainly qualifies exception handlers as a kind of control structure.

An *exception* is an object that is "raised" (or "thrown") under some specific circumstances. When an exception is raised, the normal flow of execution ceases and the interpreter looks for a suitable exception handler to pass the exception to. It begins by looking at the enclosing block and works its way out. If no suitable exception handler is found in the current function, the interpreter will go up the call stack, looking for a handler in the function's caller, and if that fails in the caller's caller, and so on.

As the interpreter searches for a suitable exception handler, it may encounter finally blocks; any such blocks are executed, after which the search for an exception handler is resumed. (We use finally blocks for cleaning up—for example, to ensure that a file is closed, as we will see shortly.)

If a handler is found, the interpreter passes control to the handler, and execution continues from there. If, having gone all the way up the call stack to the top level, no handler is found, the application will terminate and report the exception that was the cause.

In Python, exceptions can be raised by built-in or library functions and methods, or by us in our code. The exceptions that are raised can be of any of the built-in exception types or our own custom exception types.

Exception handlers are blocks with the general syntax:

```
try:
    suite1
except exceptions:
    suite2
else:
    suite3
```

Here, the code in *suite1* is executed, and if an exception occurs, control will pass to the except statement. If the except statement is suitable, *suite2* will be executed; we will discuss what happens otherwise shortly. If no exception occurs, *suite3* is executed after *suite1* is finished.

The except statement has more than one syntax; here are some examples:

```
    except IndexError: pass
    except ValueError, e: pass
    except (IOError, OSError), e: pass
    except: pass
```

In the first case we are asking to handle IndexError exceptions but do not require any information about the exception if it is raised. In the second case we handle ValueError exceptions, and we want the exception object (which is put in variable e). In the third case we handle both IOError and OSError exceptions, and if either occurs, we also want the exception object, and again this is put in variable e. The last case should not be used, since it will catch any exception: Using such a broad exception handler is usually unwise because it will catch all kinds of exception, including those we don't expect, thereby masking logical errors in our code. Because we have used pass for the suites, if an exception is caught, no further action is taken, and execution will continue from the finally block if there is one, and then from the statement following the try block.

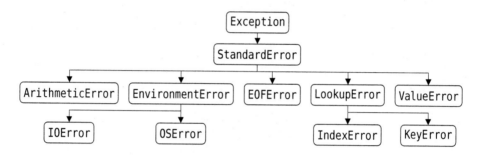

Figure 2.1 *Some of Python's exception hierarchy*

It is also possible for a single try block to have more than one exception handler:

```
try:
    process()
except IndexError, e:
    print "Error: %s" % e
except LookupError, e:
    print "Error: %s" % e
```

The order of the handlers is important. In this case, IndexError is a subclass of LookupError, so if we had LookupError first, control would never pass to the IndexError handler. This is because LookupError matches both itself and all its subclasses. Just like C++ and Java, when we have multiple exception handlers for the same try block they are examined in the order that they appear. This means that we must order them from most specific to least specific. Some of Python's exception hierarchy is shown in Figure 2.1; the least specific exception is at the top, going down to the most specific at the bottom.

Now that we have a broad overview of exceptions, let's see how their use compares with a more conventional error handling approach; this will also give us a feel for their use and syntax. We will look at two code snippets that have the same number of lines and that do exactly the same thing: They extract the first angle-bracketed item from a string. In both cases we assume that the variable text holds the string we are going to search.

```
# Testing for errors                    # Exception handling
result = ""                             try:
i = text.find("<")                          i = text.index("<")
if i > -1:                                   j = text.index(">", i + 1)
    j = text.find(">", i + 1)                result = text[i:j + 1]
    if j > -1:                          except ValueError:
        result = text[i:j + 1]              result = ""
print result                            print result
```

Both approaches ensure that result is an empty string if no angle-bracketed substring is found. However, the right-hand snippet focuses on the positive with each line in the try block able to assume that the previous lines executed correctly—because if they hadn't, they would have raised an exception and execution would have jumped to the except block.

If we were searching for a single substring, using find() would be more convenient than using the exception handling machinery; but as soon as we need to do two or more things that could fail, exception handling, as here, usually results in cleaner code with a clear demarcation between the code we are expecting to execute and the code we've written to cope with errors and out-cases.

When we write our own functions, we can have them raise exceptions in failure cases if we wish; for example, we could put a couple of lines at the beginning of the simplify() function we developed in a previous section:

```
def simplify(text, space=" \t\r\n\f", delete=""):
    if not space and not delete:
        raise Exception, "Nothing to skip or delete"
```

This will work, but unfortunately, the Exception class (which is the conventional base class for Python exceptions) isn't specific to our circumstances. This is easily solved by creating our own custom exception and raising that instead:

```
class SimplifyError(Exception): pass

def simplify(text, space=" \t\r\n\f", delete=""):
    if not space and not delete:
        raise SimplifyError, "Nothing to skip or delete"
```

Exceptions are class instances, and although we don't cover classes until Chapter 3, the syntax for creating an exception class is so simple that there seems to be no reason not to show it here. The class statement has a similar structure to a def statement, with the class keyword, followed by the name, except that in the parentheses we put the base classes rather than parameter names. We've used pass to indicate an empty suite, and we have chosen to inherit Exception. We could have inherited from one of Exception's subclasses instead; for example, ValueError.

In practice, though, raising an exception in this particular case may be overkill. We could take the view that the function will always be called with space or delete or both nonempty, and we can assert this belief rather than use an exception:

```
def simplify(text, space=" \t\r\n\f", delete=""):
    assert space or delete
```

This will raise an AssertionError exception if both space and delete are empty, and probably expresses the logic of the function's preconditions better than the previous two attempts. If the exception is not caught (and an assertion should not be), the program will terminate and issue an error message saying that an AssertionError was the cause and providing a traceback that identifies the file and line where the assertion failed.

Another context where exception handling can be useful is breaking out of deeply nested loops. For example, imagine that we have a three-dimensional grid of values and we want to find the first occurrence of a particular target item. Here is the conventional approach:

```
found = False
for x in range(len(grid)):
    for y in range(len(grid[x])):
        for z in range(len(grid[x][y])):
            if grid[x][y][z] == target:
                found = True
                break
        if found:
            break
    if found:
        break
if found:
    print "Found at (%d, %d, %d)" % (x, y, z)
else:
    print "Not found"
```

This is 15 lines long. It is easy to understand, but tedious to type and rather inefficient. Now we will use an approach that uses exception handling:

```
class FoundException(Exception): pass

try:
```

```
    for x in range(len(grid)):
        for y in range(len(grid[x])):
            for z in range(len(grid[x][y])):
                if grid[x][y][z] == target:
                    raise FoundException
except FoundException:
    print "Found at (%d, %d, %d)" % (x, y, z)
else:
    print "Not found"
```

This version is only 11 lines long. If the target is found, we raise the exception and handle that situation. If no exception is raised, the try block's else suite is executed.

In some situations, we want some cleanup code to be called no matter what. For example, we may want to guarantee that we close a file or a network or database connection even if our code has a bug. This is achieved using a try ... finally block, as the next example shows:

```
filehandle = open(filename)
try:
    for line in filehandle:
        process(line)
finally:
    filehandle.close()
```

Here we open a file with the given filename and get a file handle. We then iterate over the file handle—which is a generator and gives us one line at a time in the context of a for loop. If any exception occurs, the interpreter looks for the except or finally that is nearest in scope. In this case, it does not find an except, but it does find a finally, so the interpreter switches control to the finally suite and executes it. If no exception occurs, the finally block will be executed after the try suite has finished. So either way, the file will be closed.

Python versions prior to 2.5 do not support try ... except ... finally blocks. So if we need both except and finally we must use two blocks, a try ... except and a try ... finally, with one nested inside the other. For example, in Python versions up to 2.4, the most robust way to open and process a file is like this:

```
fh = None
try:
    try:
        fh = open(fname)
        process(fh)
    except IOError, e:
        print "I/O error: %s" % e
finally:
    if fh:
        fh.close()
```

This code makes use of things we have already discussed, but to make sure we have a firm grip on exception handling, we will consider the code in detail.

If the file can't be opened in the first place, the except block is executed and then the finally block—which will do nothing since the file handle will still be None because the file could not be opened. On the other hand, if the file is opened and processing commences, there might be an I/O error. If this happens, the except block is executed, and again control will then pass to the finally block, and the file will be closed.

If an exception occurs that is not an IOError, or an IOError subclass, for example, perhaps a ValueError occurs in our process() function—the interpreter will consider the except block to be unsuitable and will look for the nearest enclosing exception handler that is suitable. As it looks, the interpreter will first encounter the finally block which it will then execute, after which, (i.e., after closing the file), it will then look for a suitable exception handler.

If the file is opened and processing completes with no exception being raised, the except block is skipped, but the finally block is still executed since finally blocks are executed no matter what happens. So, in all cases, apart from the interpreter being killed by the user (or, in very rare cases, crashing), if the file was opened, it will be closed.

In Python 2.5 and later, we can use a simpler approach that has the same semantics because we can have try ... except ... finally blocks:

```
fh = None
try:
    fh = open(fname)
    process(fh)
except IOError, e:
    print "I/O error: %s" % e
finally:
    if fh:
        fh.close()
```

Using this syntax, it is still possible to have an else block for when no exception occurred; it is placed after the last except block and before the one and only finally block. We will revisit this topic in the context of files in Chapter 6.

No matter what version of Python we use, finally blocks are always executed whether an exception occurs or not, exactly once, either when the try suite is finished, or when an exception is raised that shifts the flow of control outside the try block.

Python 2.6 (and Python 2.5 with a from __future__ import with_statement statement) offers another approach entirely: "context managers". For file handling, we prefer the try ... finally approach, but in other cases, we prefer context managers. For example, we show how to use context managers for locking and unlocking read/write locks used by threads in Chapter 19.

Summary

In this chapter we saw how to branch using if, and how to create multiway branches using if with elifs and, optionally, with else. We also saw how to loop using while and for, and how to generate lists of integers using range(). We learned about the dictionary methods that provide a dictionary's keys, values, and key–value pairs (items), and we took a brief look at sorting. We also had a glimpse at how to use Python's list comprehensions and generators.

We saw how to create functions using def (and with lambda). We used positional and keyword arguments, and we developed two useful functions, frange() and simplify(). We saw how Python creates functions dynamically as it reads a .py file, and how we can use this dynamism to provide similar functionality in older Python versions to that which is available in newer versions. And we saw how to use partial function application to create wrapper functions that encapsulate a function with its arguments (closures).

We also learned how to raise exceptions, how to create custom exceptions, and how to handle exceptions. We saw how to use finally to guarantee cleanup, and we discussed some of the more complex exception-handling possibilities that Python offers. We also saw that exception handling can lead to cleaner code when we have suites where multiple exceptions could occur, and how they can be used to cleanly exit a set of deeply nested loops.

Creating custom exceptions led us on to creating simple classes; classes that have no attributes (no member data) and no methods. In the next chapter we will look more formally at classes, and learn how to create them and instantiate instances of them, with any attributes and methods we wish.

Exercises

In Chapter 1, the exercises were short enough to be typed into IDLE. From now on we recommend that you type your solutions into a file with a .py extension, and add some test calls at the end. For example, you might write a file with this structure:

```
#!/usr/bin/env python

def mysolution(arg0, arg1):
    pass     # Whatever code is needed

mysolution(1, 2)          # Call with one set of parameters
mysolution("a", "b")      # Call with another set of parameters
# Additional calls to make sure all boundary cases are tested
```

If you are using Windows, make sure that you run your test programs inside a console window; similarly, Mac OS X users should use a Terminal. You may also need to include print statements so that you can see the results. (Exercises involving GUI applications begin in Part II.)

If you look at the book's source code, including this chapter's answers.py file, you will find that the code often has long docstrings, in many cases occupying far more lines than the code itself. This is because the docstrings usually include usage examples which do double duty as unit tests, as we will see in Chapter 3's "Using the doctest Module" subsection.

1. Write a function with signature:

   ```
   valid(text, chars="ABCDEFGHIJKLMNOPQRSTUVWXYZ0123456789")
   ```

   The function should return a (possibly empty) string which is a copy of text that only contains characters in chars. For example:

   ```
   valid("Barking!")                          # Returns "B"
   valid("KL754", "0123456789")               # Returns "754"
   valid("BEAN", "abcdefghijklmnopqrstuvwxyz")  # Returns ""
   ```

   It can be done in half a dozen lines, using a for loop and an if statement, not counting the docstring, which should also be written.

2. Write a function with signature:

   ```
   charcount(text)
   ```

   This should return a dictionary with 28 keys, "a", "b", ..., "z", plus "whitespace" and "others". For every character in a lowercased copy of text, if the character is alphabetic, increment the corresponding key; if the character is whitespace, increment the "whitespace" key; otherwise, increment the "others" key. For example, the call:

   ```
   stats = charcount("Exceedingly Edible")
   ```

   will mean that stats is a dictionary with the following contents:

   ```
   {'whitespace': 1, 'others': 0, 'a': 0, 'c': 1, 'b': 1, 'e': 5,
   'd': 2, 'g': 1, 'f': 0, 'i': 2, 'h': 0, 'k': 0, 'j': 0, 'm': 0,
   'l': 2, 'o': 0, 'n': 1, 'q': 0, 'p': 0, 's': 0, 'r': 0, 'u': 0,
   't': 0, 'w': 0, 'v': 0, 'y': 1, 'x': 1, 'z': 0}
   ```

   Using a dictionary and a for loop, it can be done in slightly more than a dozen lines of code.

3. Create a function with signature:

   ```
   integer(number)
   ```

   The number parameter is either a number or a string that can be converted to a number. The function should return the number as type int, rounding it if the number passed in is a float. If the conversion fails, catch the ValueError exception, and return 0. Make sure it works for both strings and literal numbers, such as 4.5, 32, "23", and "-15.1", and that it correctly

returns zero for invalid numbers like "tonsils". This can be done in half a
dozen lines. (Hint: To work with all the cases you'll always need to convert
to type `float` first, that is, by calling `float()` on the input.)

4. Now write a function with signature:

```
incrementString(text="AAAA")
```

The function must "increment" the given string. Here are some examples:

```
incrementString("A")        # Returns "B"
incrementString("Z")        # Returns "AA"
incrementString("AM")       # Returns "AN"
incrementString("AZ")       # Returns "BA"
incrementString("BA")       # Returns "BB"
incrementString("BZ")       # Returns "CA"
incrementString("ZZA")      # Returns "ZZB"
incrementString("ZZZ")      # Returns "AAAA"
incrementString("AAAA")     # Returns "AAAB"
incrementString("AAAZ")     # Returns "AABA"
incrementString("ABC2")     # Raises a ValueError
```

The characters in `text` must be A–Z (or a–z, in which case the function
must upper-case them); otherwise the function should raise a `ValueError`
exception.

This is a bit more challenging than the previous exercises. The code can
be written in less than 20 lines if you use a couple of list comprehensions,
although it can also be written without them. It is a bit tricky to get right.
(Hint: The `reversed()` function returns a sequence in reverse order.)

5. If you read the section on function generators, try writing a generator
with signature:

```
leapyears(yearlist)
```

The `yearlist` parameter is a sequence of year numbers—for example,
[1600, 1604, 1700, 1704, 1800, 1900, 1996, 2000, 2004]. Given this input,
the output would be the years 1600, 1604, 1704, 1996, 2000, and 2004, one
at a time. This can be done in about half a dozen lines. (Hint: Leap years
are divisible by 4, but if they are divisible by 100, must also be divisible
by 400.)

Model answers for this chapter's exercises are in the file `chap02/answers.py`.

3

● Creating Instances

● Methods and Special Methods

● Inheritance and Polymorphism

● Modules and Multifile Applications

Classes and Modules

Python fully supports procedural and object-oriented programming, and leaves us free to use either approach, or to combine the two. So far we have done procedural programming, although we have already used some Python classes—for example, the `str` string class. What we have not yet done is defined our own classes. In this chapter we will learn how to create classes and methods, and how to do object-oriented programming with Python. And in all subsequent chapters, we will almost always use an object-oriented approach in the programs we write.

We assume that you are familiar with object-oriented programming—for example using C++ or Java—but will take the opportunity to clarify our terminology. We use the term "object", and occasionally the term "instance", to refer to an instance of a particular class. We use the terms "class", "type", and "data type", interchangeably. Variables that belong to a specific instance are called "attributes" or "instance variables". Variables that are used inside methods that are not instance variables are called "local variables", or simply "variables". We use the term "base class" to refer to a class that is inherited from; a base class may be the immediate ancestor, or may be further up the inheritance tree. Some people use the term "super class" for this concept. We use the terms "subclass" and "derived class" for a class that inherits from another class.

In Python, any method can be overridden (reimplemented) in a subclass; this is the same as Java (apart from Java's "final" methods).[*] Overloading, that is, having methods with the same name but with different parameter lists in the same class, is not supported, although this is not a limitation in practice because of Python's versatile argument-handling capabilities. In fact, the underlying Qt C++ API makes extensive use of overloading, but PyQt handles this seamlessly behind the scenes, so in practice, we can call any "overloaded" Qt method and rely on PyQt to do the right thing.

Qt

---

[*]In C++ terminology, all Python methods are virtual.

This chapter begins with the basic syntax for creating classes. We then look at how to construct and initialize objects, and how to implement methods. One of the nicest features of Python's object-oriented support is that it allows us to reimplement "special methods". This means we can make our classes seamlessly blend in so that they behave just like built-in classes. For example, it is easy to make our classes work with the comparison operators such as == and <. We then look at the numeric special methods: these allow us to overload operators such as + and += which can be useful when creating complete custom data types, especially numeric ones. If our class is a collection, there are some additional special methods we can reimplement so that, for example, our collection will support the in operator and the len() function. The chapter concludes with a section on Python's support for inheritance and polymorphism.

For historical reasons, there are two kinds of user-defined types (classes) that Python provides: "old-style" and "new-style". The only obvious difference is that old-style classes either have no base class, or have only old-style base classes. New-style classes always derive from a new-style class, for example, object, Python's ultimate base class. Since there is no reason to use old-style classes, and because they will be dropped from the language from Python 3.0, we will always use new-style classes.

The syntax for creating a class is simple:

```
class className(base_classes):
    suite
```

In the class's suite we can have def statements; and in such a context they create methods for their enclosing class rather than functions.

It is also possible to have "empty" classes, with no methods or attributes (data members) of their own, as we saw at the end of the preceding chapter when we derived our own custom exception class.

New-style classes *always* have at least one base class—for example, object. Unlike Java, Python supports multiple inheritance, that is, Python classes can inherit from one, two, or more base classes. We will mostly avoid this feature because it can lead to unnecessary and confusing complexity. Python does not support abstract classes (classes that cannot be instantiated, and that can only be derived from—useful for defining interfaces), but the effect of having an abstract class can be achieved all the same. We will look at a small example of multiple inheritance where one of the base classes is "abstract" and is used purely to provide an API (rather like a Java interface).

In Python, all methods and attributes are accessible from both inside and outside the class; there are no access specifiers such as "public" and "private". Python does have a concept of "private"—objects with names that begin with a single leading underscore are considered to be private. As far as methods and instance variables are concerned, their privacy is merely a convention that we are invited to respect. And as for modules, private classes and functions, that is, those whose name begins with a leading underscore, are not imported when using the `from moduleName import *` syntax. Python also has a concept of "very private"—methods and attributes with names that begin with two leading underscores. Very private objects are still accessible, but the Python interpreter mangles their names to make it difficult to access them by mistake.

Now that we know the basic syntax for creating a class and have a broad overview of Python's object-oriented features, we are ready to see how to create a class and some instances.

Creating Instances

In most object-oriented languages, objects are created in two steps: First, the object is constructed, and second, the object is initialized. Some languages merge these two steps into one, but Python keeps them separate. Python has the `__new__()` special method which is called to construct an object, and the `__init__()` special method which is called to initialize a newly constructed object. It is very rare to actually need to implement `__new__()` ourselves; not one of the custom classes in this book needs it—and older versions of Python did not even have the `__new__()` special method. Python is perfectly capable of constructing our objects for us, so in almost every case the only method we need to implement is `__init__()`.

In view of Python's two-step object creation, we will normally talk of object creation rather than construction. Also, we will generally refer to a class's initializer (its `__init__()` method), since that is the method that is normally reimplemented in custom classes and the one that is closer to the idea of a constructor that is used in languages like C++ and Java.

Let's see how to create a class in practice. We will create one that stores a string (the name of a kind of chair) and a number (how many legs the chair has):

```
class Chair(object):
    """This class represents chairs."""

    def __init__(self, name, legs=4):
        self.name = name
        self.legs = legs
```

It is conventional to follow a `class` statement with a docstring as shown in the preceding code. We will not normally show docstrings in the book, but they are included where appropriate in the accompanying example code. The blank line is purely for aesthetics and clarity.

Methods with names beginning *and* ending with two underscores are "special" methods. Python uses such methods to integrate custom classes so that they can have the same usage patterns as built-in classes, as we will soon see.

The `__init__()` method, and indeed every method, has a first parameter that is the Python equivalent to the C++ or Java "this" variable, that is, a variable that refers to the object itself. This variable is conventionally called `self`. We must put `self` as the first item of every (nonstatic*) method's parameter list, although we never need to pass it since Python will do that for us.

Although the name "self" is merely conventional, we will always use it. Inside the object, we must use `self` explicitly when we want to refer to instance methods or attributes. For example, in the `Chair` class's initializer, we have created two data attributes using `self`. Thanks to Python's dynamic nature, it is possible to create additional attributes in other methods, and even to add additional attributes to particular instances if we wish; but we will take a more conservative line that is sufficient for the GUI programming we are working toward.

To create an instance of a class, we use the following syntax:

```
instance = className(arguments)
```

The parentheses are mandatory, even if we don't pass any arguments. Behind the scenes, Python constructs the object by calling the class's static `__new__()` method (which is inherited from `object`, or in rare cases is implemented by us), and then calls `__init__()` on the newly constructed object. The resulting initialized object is returned.

In the case of our `Chair` class, we must pass either one or two arguments (Python passes the first `self` argument automatically for us); for example:

```
chair1 = Chair("Barcelona")
chair2 = Chair("Bar Stool", 1)
```

Since the attributes are public, they can be read or assigned to using the dot (.) operator; for example: `print chair2.name` will print "Bar Stool", and `chair1.legs = 2` will change `chair1`'s `legs` attribute's value from 4 to 2.

Object-oriented purists will no doubt be uncomfortable with this kind of direct access to attributes from outside the instance, whereas those with a taste for extreme programming may be perfectly happy with it since we can always add accessor methods later.

Now that we have seen how construction and initialization are handled, we need to consider object destruction. C++ programmers are used to using destructors and relying on the fact that they can delete objects at a time of their own choosing. Java and Python programmers do not have that particular luxury. Instead, they have automatic garbage collection, which makes programming much easier in general but with the one drawback of not giving fine control over exactly when objects are deleted. If resources need to be protected, the solution is normally to use a `try ... finally` block to guarantee cleanup. When an object is about to be garbage-collected its `__del__()` special method is called, with `self` as its only argument. As is common practice in Python (and in Java regarding the finalize() method), we very rarely use this particular special

---

*A static method is one that can be called on a class or an instance and has no `self` parameter. Normal methods are non-static, that is, they have a `self` parameter and must be called on instances.

method. To put this in perspective, out of more than 170 classes in this book's examples and exercise solutions, not one reimplements __del__().

We have now learned how to create and initialize an object of a custom class. Next, we will see how to provide additional methods to give our class distinctive behavior. We will also learn how to ensure that our classes smoothly integrate with the rest of Python, and act just like built-in classes where that is appropriate.

Methods and Special Methods

We will begin by looking at a class that uses accessor methods to get and set the value of attributes, rather than using direct attribute access.

```
class Rectangle(object):

    def __init__(self, width, height):
        self.width = width
        self.height = height

    def getWidth(self):
        return self.width

    def setWidth(self, width):
        self.width = width

    def getHeight(self):
        return self.height

    def setHeight(self, height):
        self.height = height

    def area(self):
        return self.getWidth() * self.getHeight()
```

We have chosen to use a Java-style naming convention for both getters and setters. Now we can write code like this:

```
rect = Rectangle(50, 10)
print rect.area()    # Prints "500"
rect.setWidth(20)
```

We could just as easily have implemented the area() method like this:

```
def area(self):
    return self.width * self.height
```

Writing trivial accessor methods as we have done here is the right approach for languages like C++ because it provides maximum flexibility, and no overhead in the compiled code. And if at a later stage we needed to perform some computation in an accessor, we can simply add in the functionality without requir-

ing users of our class to change their code. But in Python, it is not necessary
to write such accessors. Instead, we can directly read and write attributes, and
if at a later stage we need to perform some computation, we can use Python's
property() function. This function allows us to create named properties that
can replace attributes. Properties are accessed just like attributes, but behind
the scenes they call the methods that we specify to get and set the value.

Here is a second version of the Rectangle class, this time using direct attribute
access for the width and height, and a property for the area:

```
class Rectangle(object):

    def __init__(self, width, height):
        self.width = width
        self.height = height

    def _area(self):
        return self.width * self.height
    area = property(fget=_area)
```

This allows us to write code like this:

```
rect = Rectangle(5, 4)
print rect.width, rect.height, rect.area    # Prints (5, 4, 20)
rect.width = 6
```

Python's property() function can be used to specify a getter, a setter, a deletion
method, and a docstring. Since we specified only a getter, the area property is
read-only. If later on we needed to perform some computation when the width
was accessed, we could simply turn it into a property, like this:

```
def _width(self):
    return self.__width

def _setWidth(self, width):
    # Perform some computation
    self.__width = width

width = property(fget=_width, fset=_setWidth)
```

Notice that we have changed the name of the instance variable from width to
__width to avoid a name collision with the width property. In general, properties
whose values are held in instance variables use private names (names with
two leading underscores) for the instance variables, to avoid name collisions
with the property name that the class's user uses. For example, users of the
Rectangle class with the width property, can get and set the width attribute
exactly the same as before, only now, the _width() and _setWidth() methods are
used behind the scenes to perform these operations, and the attribute's data is
held in the __width instance variable.

Discussion of private names ☞ 88

Table 3.1 *Basic Special Methods*

Method	Syntax	Description
__init__(self, args)	x = X()	Initializes a newly created instance
__call__(self, args)	x()	Makes instances callable, that is, turns them into functors. The args are optional. (Advanced)
__cmp__(self, other)	x == y x < y # etc	Returns -1 if self < other, 0 if they are equal, and 1 otherwise. If __cmp__() is implemented, it will be used for any comparison operators that are not explicitly implemented.
__eq__(self, other)	x == y	Returns True if x is equal to y
__ne__(self, other)	x != y	Returns True if x is not equal to y
__le__(self, other)	x <= y	Returns True if x is less than or equal to y
__lt__(self, other)	x < y	Returns True if x is less than y
__ge__(self, other)	x >= y	Returns True if x is greater than or equal to y
__gt__(self, other)	x > y	Returns True if x is greater than y
__nonzero__(self)	if x: pass	Returns True if x is nonzero
__repr__(self)	y = eval(`x`)	Returns an eval()-able representation of x. Using backticks is the same as calling repr().★
__str__(self)	print x	Returns a human-readable representation of x
__unicode__(self)	print x	Returns a human-readable Unicode representation of x

Python offers even more control over attribute access than we have shown here, but since this is not necessary to our goal of GUI programming, we will leave this as a topic to look up if it ever becomes of interest. The starting point is the documentation for the __getattr__(), __getattribute__(), and __setattr__() special methods.

The mechanics of Python methods, including special methods, are exactly the same as for functions, but with the addition of the self first argument, and the ability to access self's attributes and call self's methods. We just have to remember that when we call methods or access instance variables, we must specify the instance using self. For example, in the Rectangle class's setHeight()

★It is best to use repr() rather than backticks since backticks will be dropped in Python 3.0.

method, we used `self.height` to refer to the instance variable and plain `height` to refer to the parameter, that is, to a local variable. Similarly, in the `area()` method, we call two `Rectangle` methods, again using `self`. This is quite different from C++ and Java, where the instance is assumed.

In C++ it is possible to implement operators, that is, to provide our own implementations of operators for our data types. The C++ syntax uses the keyword `operator` followed by the operator itself—for example, `operator+()`—but in Python every operator has a name, so to implement a class's + operator in Python we would implement an `__add__()` method. All the Python methods for implementing operators are special methods, and this is signified by them having names that begin and end with two underscores.

To better integrate our custom classes into Python, there are some additional general special methods which may be worth implementing. For example, we might want to provide support for the comparison operators, and a Boolean value for instances of our class. We will add a few more methods to the `Rectangle` class to show the possibilities in action, but for brevity we won't repeat the `class` statement and the methods we have already implemented. We will start with comparisons:

```
def __cmp__(self, other):
    return cmp(self.area, other.area)
```

If we want we can implement a special method for every one of the comparison operators. For example, if we implement `__lt__()` "less than", we will be able to compare instances of our class with the < operator. However, if we don't want to implement the comparison operators individually, we can simply implement `__cmp__()` as we have done here. Python will use the specific special method for comparisons if it has been implemented, but will fall back on `__cmp__()` otherwise. So just by implementing this one special method, *all* the comparison operators (<, <=, ==, !=, >=, >) will work with `Rectangle` objects:

```
rectA = Rectangle(4, 4)
rectB = Rectangle(8, 2)
rectA == rectB    # True because both have the same area
rectA < rectB     # False
```

We used the built-in `cmp()` function to implement `__cmp__()`. The `cmp()` function takes two objects and returns -1 if the first is less than the second, 0 if they are equal, and 1 otherwise. We used the rectangles' areas as the basis for comparison, which is why we got the rather surprising `True` result in our example. A stricter, and perhaps better implementation might be:

```
def __cmp__(self, other):
    if (self.width != other.width):
        return cmp(self.width, other.width)
    return cmp(self.height, other.height)
```

Here we return the result of comparing the heights if the widths are the same; otherwise, we return the result of comparing the widths.

If we do not reimplement any comparison special methods, in most cases Python will happily perform comparisons for us, although not necessarily in the way we would want. If we are creating a class where comparisons make sense, we ought to implement __cmp__(). For other classes, the safest thing to do is to implement __cmp__() with a body of return NotImplementedError.

```
def __nonzero__(self):
    return self.width or self.height
```

This special method is used when the object is in a Boolean context; for example, bool(rectA), or if rectB: and returns True if the object is "nonzero".

```
def __repr__(self):
    return "Rectangle(%d, %d)" % (self.width, self.height)
```

The "representation" special method must return a string which, if evaluated (e.g., using eval()), will result in the construction of an object with the same properties as the object it is called on. Some objects are too complex to support this, and for some objects, such as a window or a button in a GUI, it doesn't make sense; so such classes don't provide a __repr__() implementation. In a string % operator's format string we use %r to get the result of this special method; we can also use the repr() function or the backticks `` operator. Backticks are just a syntactic alternative to using repr(). For example, repr(x) and `x` both return identical results: the representation of object x as returned by x's __repr__() method.

There is also a __str__() special method that must return a string representation of the object it is called on (like Java's toString() method), but unlike __repr__(), the representation is meant to be human-readable and does not have to be eval()-able. If, as in this case, the __str__() method is not implemented, Python will use the __repr__() method instead. For example:

```
rect = Rectangle(8, 9)
print rect    # Prints "Rectangle(8, 9)" using __repr__()
```

If we want a human-readable Unicode string representation of our class, we can implement __unicode__().

There are a few more general special methods that we could implement, but which are not appropriate for the Rectangle class. All the commonly implemented general special methods are listed in Table 3.1.

At this point, C++ programmers might be wondering where the copy constructor and assignment operators are, and Java programmers might be wondering about the clone() method. Python does not use a copy constructor and reimplementing the assignment operator is not necessary. If we want to do an assignment we just use = and Python will bind a new name to our existing

Table 3.2 *Selected Numeric Special Methods*

Method	Syntax	Method	Syntax
__float__(self)	float(x)	__int__(self)	int(x)
__abs__(self)	abs(x)	__neg__(self)	-x
__add__(self, other)	x + y	__sub__(self, other)	x - y
__iadd__(self, other)	x += y	__isub__(self, other)	x -= y
__radd__(self, other)	y + x	__rsub__(self, other)	y - x
__mul__(self, other)	x * y	__mod__(self, other)	x % y
__imul__(self, other)	x *= y	__imod__(self, other)	x %= y
__rmul__(self, other)	y * x	__rmod__(self, other)	y % x
__floordiv__(self, other)	x // y	__truediv__(self, other)	x / y
__ifloordiv__(self, other)	x //= y	__itruediv__(self, other)	x /= y
__rfloordiv__(self, other)	y // x	__rtruediv__(self, other)	y / x

object. If we really do need a copy of our object, we can use the copy() or deep-copy() function from the copy module, the first for objects that don't have nested attributes or when a shallow copy suffices, and the second for objects that must be copied in full. Alternatively, we can provide our own copy method, which we usually call copy() since this is conventional Python practice.

For numerical classes, it is often convenient to provide functionality to support the standard numeric operators, such as + and +=. This is achieved in Python's usual way, by implementing various special methods. If we implement only +, Python will use it to provide +=, but it is often best to implement both since that gives us finer control and makes it easier to optimize the operations.

The most commonly implemented numeric special methods are listed in Table 3.2. Those not listed include bit-shifting operators and hexadecimal and octal conversion operators.

The reason for two different division operators is that Python can perform either integer or floating-point division, as explained on page 17.

Some special methods have two or three versions; for example, __add__(), __radd__(), and __iadd__(). The "r" versions (e.g., __radd__()), are for situations where the left-hand operand does not have a suitable method, but the right-hand operand does. For example, if we have the expression x + y, with x and y of types X and Y, Python will first try to evaluate the expression by calling X.__add__(x, y). But if type X does not have this method, Python will then try Y.__radd__(x, y). If Y has no such method, an exception will be raised.

In the "i" versions, the "i" stands for "in-place". They are used for augmented assignment operators such as +=. We will shortly see an example that shows many of these methods in practice, but first we must learn how to create static data and static methods.

Static Data, and Static Methods and Decorators

In some situations it is useful to have data that is associated with a class as a whole rather than with its instances. For example, if we have a Balloon class, we might want to know how many unique colors have been used:

```
class Balloon(object):

    unique_colors = set()

    def __init__(self, color):
        self.color = color
        Balloon.unique_colors.add(color)

    @staticmethod
    def uniqueColorCount():
        return len(Balloon.unique_colors)

    @staticmethod
    def uniqueColors():
        return Balloon.unique_colors.copy()
```

Static data is created inside a class block, but outside of any def statements. To access static data, we must qualify the name, and the easiest way to do so is by using the class name, as we do in the Balloon class's static methods. We will see static data and methods in more realistic contexts in the next subsection.

The @staticmethod is a *decorator*. A decorator is a function that takes a function as an argument, wraps it in some way, and assigns the wrapped function back to the original function's name, so it has the same effect as writing this:

```
    def uniqueColors():
        return Balloon.unique_colors.copy()
    uniqueColors = staticmethod(uniqueColors)
```

The @ symbol is used to signify a decorator. The staticmethod() function is one of Python's built-in functions.

We can use more than one decorator. For example, a suitable decorator could be written to instrument functions and methods, or to log each time a method is called. For example:

```
    @logger
    @recalculate
    def changeWidth(self, width):
        self.width = width
```

Here, whenever the object's width is changed two decorators are applied: logger(), which might record the change in a log file or database, and recalculate(), which might update the object's area.

In addition to static methods, Python also supports "class methods". These are
similar to static methods in that they do not have a `self` first argument, and so
can be called using a class or an instance. What distinguishes them from static
methods is that they have a Python-supplied first argument, the class they are
called on. This is conventionally called `cls`.

Example: The Length Class

Now that we have seen a lot of Python's general and numerical special methods, we are in a position to create a complete custom data type. We will create
the `Length` class to hold physical lengths. We want to be able to create lengths
using syntax like this: `distance = Length("22 miles")`. And we want to be able to
retrieve lengths in the units we prefer—for example, `km = distance.to("km")`.
The class must not support the multiplication of lengths by lengths (since that
would produce an area), but should support multiplication by amounts; for example `distance * 2`.

As usual, although the source code, in `chap03/length.py`, has docstrings, we
will not show them in the following snippets, both to save space and to avoid
distracting us from the code itself.

```
from __future__ import division
```

Trun-
cating
division

17 ☜

The first statement in the file is rather intriguing. The `from __future__ import`
syntax is used to switch on Python features that will be on by default in a later
version. Such statements must always come first. In this case, we are saying
that we want to switch on Python's future division behavior, which is for / to
do "true", or floating-point division, rather than what it does normally, that is,
truncating division. (The // operator does truncating division, if that is what
we really need.)

```
class Length(object):

    convert = dict(mi=621.371e-6, miles=621.371e-6, mile=621.371e-6,
                   yd=1.094, yards=1.094, yard=1.094,
                   ft=3.281, feet=3.281, foot=3.281,
                   inches=39.37, inch=39.37,
                   mm=1000, millimeter=1000, millimeters=1000,
                   millimetre=1000, millimetres=1000,
                   cm=100, centimeter=100, centimeters=100,
                   centimetre=100, centimetres=100,
                   m=1.0, meter=1.0, meters=1.0, metre=1.0, metres=1.0,
                   km=0.001, kilometer=0.001, kilometers=0.001,
                   kilometre=0.001, kilometres=0.001)
    convert["in"] = 39.37
    numbers = frozenset("0123456789.eE")
```

We begin with a `class` statement to give our class a name, and to provide a
context in which we can create static data and methods. We have inherited

from `object`, so our class is new-style. Then we create some static data. First we create a dictionary that maps names to conversion factors. We can't use "in" as an argument name because it is a Python keyword, so we insert it into the dictionary separately using the [] operator. We also create a set of the characters that are valid in floating-point numbers.

```
def __init__(self, length=None):
    if length is None:
        self.__amount = 0.0
    else:
        digits = ""
        for i, char in enumerate(length):
            if char in Length.numbers:
                digits += char
            else:
                self.__amount = float(digits)
                unit = length[i:].strip().lower()
                break
        else:
            raise ValueError, "need an amount and a unit"
        self.__amount /= Length.convert[unit]
```

Inside the initializer, the local variables `length`, `digits`, `i`, `char`, and `unit` all go out of scope at the end of the method. We refer only to one instance variable, `self.__amount`. This variable always holds the given length in meters, no matter what units were used in the initializer, and is accessible from any method. We also refer to two static variables, `Length.numbers` and `Length.convert`.

When a `Length` object is created, Python will call the `__init__`() method. We give the user two options: Pass no arguments, in which case the length will be 0 meters, or pass a string that specifies an amount and a unit with optional whitespace separating the two.

If a string is given, we want to iterate over the characters that are valid in numbers, and then take the remainder to be the units. Python's `enumerate()` function returns an iterator that returns a tuple of two values on each iteration, an index number starting from 0, and the corresponding item from the sequence. So if the string in `length` was `"7 mi"`, the tuples returned would be (0, "7"), (1, " "), (2, "m"), and (3, "i"). We can unpack a tuple in a `for` loop simply by providing enough variables.

As long as we retrieve characters that are in the `numbers` set we add them to our `digits` string. Once we reach a character that isn't in the set, we attempt to convert the `digits` string to a `float`, and take the rest of the `length` string to be the units. We strip off any leading and trailing whitespace from the units string, and lowercase the string. Finally, we calculate how many meters the given length is by using the conversion factor from the static `convert` dictionary.

We called our data attribute __amount, rather than, say, amount, because we want this data to be private. Python will name-mangle any name in a class that begins with two underscores (and which does not end in two underscores) to be preceded by an underscore and the class name to make the attribute's name unique. In this case, __amount will be mangled to be _Length__amount. When we look at some of the special methods, we will see a practical reason why this is beneficial.

Clearly many things could go wrong. The floating-point conversion could fail, there may be no units given (in which case we raise an exception, along with a "reason" string), or the units may not match any in the convert dictionary. In this method, we have chosen to let the possible exceptions be raised, documenting them in the method's docstring so that users of the class know what to expect.

```
def set(self, length):
    self.__init__(length)
```

We want our lengths to be mutable, so we have provided a set() method. It takes the same argument as __init__(), and because __init__() is an initializer rather than a constructor, we can safely pass the work on to it.

```
def to(self, unit):
    return self.__amount * Length.convert[unit]
```

We store lengths inside the class as meters. This means that we need to maintain only a single floating-point value, rather than, say, a value and a unit. But just as we can specify our preferred units when we create a length, we also want to be able to retrieve a length as a value in the units of our choice. This is what the to() method achieves. It uses the convert dictionary to convert the meters value to the units specified.

```
def copy(self):
    other = Length()
    other.__amount = self.__amount
    return other
```

As we know, if we use the = operator, we will simply bind (or rebind) a name, so if we want a genuine copy of a length we need some means of doing it. Here we have chosen to provide a copy() method. But we did not have to: Instead, we could have simply relied on the copy module. For example:

```
import copy
import length

x = length.Length("3 km")
y = copy.copy(x)
```

We have imported both the standard copy module and our own length module, (assuming that chap03 is in sys.path, and that the module is called length.py).

Then we created two independent lengths. If, instead, we had done y = x and then changed x using the set() method, y would have changed too. Of course, since we have implemented our own copy() method, we could also have copied by writing y = x.copy().

We could have implemented the copy() method differently. For example:

```
def copy(self):     # Alternative #1
    import copy
    return copy.copy(self)

def copy(self):     # Alternative #2
    return eval(repr(self))
```

The first of these uses Python's standard copy module to implement the copy() function. The second uses the repr() method to provide an eval()-able string version of the length—for example, Length('3000.000000m')—and then uses eval() to evaluate this code; in this case, it constructs a new length of the same size as the original.

```
@staticmethod
def units():
    return Length.convert.keys()
```

We have provided this static method to give users of our class access to the names of the units we support. By using keys(), we ensure that a list of unit names is returned, rather than an object reference to our static dictionary.

With the exception of the __init__() initialization method, none of the methods we have looked at so far has been a special method. But we want our Length class to work like a standard Python class, so that it can be used with operators like * and *=, compared, and converted to suitable compatible types. All these things are achievable by implementing special methods. We will begin with comparisons.

```
def __cmp__(self, other):
    return cmp(self.__amount, other.__amount)
```

This method is easy to implement since we can just compare how long each length is.

The other object could be an object of any type. Thanks to Python's name mangling, the actual comparison is made between self._Length__amount and other._Length__amount. If the other object does not have a _Length__amount attribute, that is, if it is not a length, Python will raise an AttributeError which is what we want. This is true of all the other methods that take a length argument in addition to self.

Without the name mangling, there is a small risk of the other object not being a length, yet happening to have an __amount attribute. To prevent this risk we might have used type testing, even though this is often poor practice in object-oriented programming.

```
def __repr__(self):
    return "Length('%.6fm')" % self.__amount

def __str__(self):
    return "%.3fm" % self.__amount
```

Python's floating-point accuracy depends on the compiler it was built with, but it is very likely to be accurate to much more than the six decimal places we have chosen to use for our "representation" method.

For the string representation, we don't need to be as accurate, nor do we need to return a string that can be eval()'d, so we just return the raw length and the meters unit. If users of our Length class want a string representation with a different unit, they can use to()—for example, "%s miles" % length.Length("200 ft").to("miles").

```
def __add__(self, other):
    return Length("%fm" % (self.__amount + other.__amount))

def __iadd__(self, other):
    self.__amount += other.__amount
    return self
```

We have used two special methods to support addition. The first supports binary + with a length operand on either side. It constructs and returns a new Length object. The second supports += for incrementing a length by another length.

They allow us to write code like this:

```
x = length.Length("30ft")
y = length.Length("250cm")
z = x + y     # z == Length('11.643554m')
x += y        # x == Length('11.643554m')
```

It is also possible to implement __radd__() for mixed-type arithmetic, but we have not done so because it does not make sense for the Length class.

We will omit the code that provides support for subtraction since it is almost identical to the code for addition (and is in the source file).

```
def __mul__(self, other):
    if isinstance(other, Length):
        raise ValueError, \
                "Length * Length produces an area not a Length"
    return Length("%fm" % (self.__amount * other))
```

```
def __rmul__(self, other):
    return Length("%fm" % (other * self.__amount))

def __imul__(self, other):
    self.__amount *= other
    return self
```

For the multiplication methods, we provide support for multiplying a length by a number. If we assume that x is a length, __mul__() supports uses like x * 5, and __rmul__() supports uses like 5 * x. We must explicitly disallow multiplying lengths together in __mul__() since the result would be an area and not a length. We do not need to do this in __rmul__() because __mul__() is always tried first, and if it raises an exception, Python does not try __rmul__(). The __imul__() method supports in-place (augmented) multiplication—for example, x *= 5.

```
def __truediv__(self, other):
    return Length("%fm" % (self.__amount / other))

def __itruediv__(self, other):
    self.__amount /= other
    return self
```

The implementation of the division special methods has a similar structure to the other arithmetic methods. One reason for showing them is to remind ourselves that the reason the / and /= operators perform floating-point division is because of the from __future__ import division directive at the beginning of the length.py file. It is also possible to reimplement truncating division, but that isn't appropriate for the Length class.

Another reason for showing them is that they are subtly different from the addition methods we have just seen. Although addition and subtraction operate only on lengths, multiplication and division operate on a length and a number.

```
def __float__(self):
    return self.__amount

def __int__(self):
    return int(round(self.__amount))
```

We have chosen to support two type conversions, both of which are easy to write and understand. The __str__() method implemented earlier is also a type conversion (to type str).

Now that we have seen how to implement a custom data type, we will turn our attention to implementing a custom collection class.

Collection Classes

In Python, collections are sequences such as lists and strings, mappings such as dictionaries, or sets. If we implement our own collection classes we can use special methods to make our collections usable with the same syntax and semantics as the built-in collection types. Table 3.3 lists the special methods common to collections, and in this section we discuss some of the specifics of each kind of collection.

In the case of sequences, it is common to implement `__add__()` and `__radd__()` to support concatenation with +, and in the case of a mutable collection, to implement `__iadd__()`, for +=, too. Similarly, the `__mul__()` methods should be implemented to support * for repeating the collection. If an invalid index is given, we should raise an `IndexError` exception. In addition to special methods, a custom sequence collection ought to implement `append()`, `count()`, `index()`, `insert()`, `extend()`, `pop()`, `remove()`, `reverse()`, and `sort()`.

For mappings, we should raise `KeyError` if an invalid key is given, and in addition to the special methods, we should at least implement `copy()` and `get()`, along with `items()`, `keys()`, and `values()`, and their iterator versions, such as `iteritems()`. A Python iterator is a function or method that returns successive values—for example, each character in a string, or each item in a list or dictionary. They are often implemented by generators.

Generator functions

58 ☜

For sets, we should also raise `KeyError` if an invalid key is used; for example, when calling `remove()`. Set collections should implement `issubset()`, `issuperset()`, `union()`, `intersection()`, `difference()`, `symmetric_difference()`, and `copy()`. For mutable sets, additional methods should be provided, including `add()`, `remove()`, and `discard()`.

Example: The OrderedDict Class

A rare omission from Python's standard library is an ordered dictionary. Plain dictionaries provide very fast lookup, but do not provide ordering. For example, if we wanted to iterate over a dictionary's values in key order, we would copy the keys to a list, sort the list, and iterate over the list, using the list's elements to access the dictionary's values. For small dictionaries, or where we do this rarely, sorting may be fine, but when the dictionary is large or sorted frequently, sorting every time may be computationally expensive.

An obvious solution is to create an ordered dictionary, and that is what we will do here.

Understanding the `OrderedDict` example is not necessary for learning GUI programming, but we do use the techniques and methods explained here in some of the programs that we will cover later on. For now, though, you could safely skip to the next section, starting on page 99, and then return here to understand the techniques when you encounter them in later chapters.

Table 3.3 *Selected Collection Special Methods*

Method	Syntax	Description
`__contains__(self, x)`	`x in y`	Returns `True` if x is in sequence y or if x is a key in `dict` y. This method is also used for `not in`.
`__len__(self)`	`len(y)`	Returns the number of items in y
`__getitem__(self, k)`	`y[k]`	Returns the k-th item of sequence y or the value for key k in `dict` y
`__setitem__(self, k, v)`	`y[k] = v`	Sets the k-th item of sequence y or the value for key k in `dict` y, to v
`__delitem__(self, k)`	`del y[k]`	Deletes the k-th item of sequence y or the item with key k in `dict` y
`__iter__(self)`	`for x in y: pass`	Returns an iterator into collection y

One approach would be to inherit `dict`, but we will instead use aggregation (also called composition), and defer consideration of inheritance until the next section.

To get an ordered dictionary, we will create a class that stores a normal dictionary, and alongside it, an ordered list of the dictionary's keys. We will implement all of the `dict` API, but we will not show `update()` or `fromkeys()` because they both go beyond what we have covered and what we need for GUI programming. (Of course, both of these methods are in the source code, `chap03/ordereddict.py`.)

The first executable statement in the file is an `import` statement:

```
import bisect
```

The `bisect` module provides methods for searching ordered sequences such as lists using the binary chop algorithm. We will discuss it shortly when we see it in use.

For this class we don't need any static data, so we will begin by looking at both the `class` statement and the definition of `__init__()`:

```
class OrderedDict(object):

    def __init__(self, dictionary=None):
        self.__keys = []
        self.__dict = {}
        if dictionary is not None:
            if isinstance(dictionary, OrderedDict):
                self.__dict = dictionary.__dict.copy()
                self.__keys = dictionary.__keys[:]
            else:
```

```
        self.__dict = dict(dictionary).copy()
        self.__keys = sorted(self.__dict.keys())
```

We create a list called __keys and a dictionary called __dict. If the OrderedDict is initialized with another dictionary, we need to get that dictionary's data. The simplest and most direct way of doing this is how we do it in the else suite. We convert the object to a dictionary (which costs nothing if it is already a dictionary), and take a shallow copy of it. Then we take a sorted list of the dictionary's keys.

The approach used in the else suite works in all cases, but purely for efficiency, we have introduced a type test using isinstance(). This function returns True if its first argument is an instance of the class or classes (passed as a tuple) given as its second argument, or any of their base classes. So if we are initializing from another OrderedDict (or from an OrderedDict subclass) we can simply shallow-copy its dictionary, which costs the same as before, and shallow-copy its keys, which is cheaper because they are already sorted.

Since our dictionary is ordered, in addition to the normal dictionary methods we should also be able to access the value of a dictionary item at a particular index position in the dictionary. That is what the first two methods we are going to implement provide:

```
    def getAt(self, index):
        return self.__dict[self.__keys[index]]

    def setAt(self, index, value):
        self.__dict[self.__keys[index]] = value
```

The getAt() method returns the index-th item in the dictionary. It does this by accessing the dictionary using the key the list holds in the index-th position. The setAt() method uses the same logic, except that it sets the value for the dictionary item that is at the index-th position.

```
    def __getitem__(self, key):
        return self.__dict[key]
```

Dictionary methods
36 ☞

If we have a dictionary, d, and use the syntax value = d[key], the __getitem__() special method is called. We simply pass the work on to the dictionary we are holding inside our OrderedDict class. If the key is not in __dict it will raise a KeyError, which is what we want, since we want OrderedDict to have the same behavior as a dict, except when key order is an issue.

```
    def __setitem__(self, key, value):
        if key not in self.__dict:
            bisect.insort_left(self.__keys, key)
        self.__dict[key] = value
```

If the user assigns to a dictionary using the syntax d[key] = value, we again rely on the __dict to do the work. But if the key is not already in the __dict, it can't be in the list of keys either, so we must add it.

The insort_left() function takes a sorted sequence, such as a sorted list, and an item to insert. It locates the position in the sequence where the item should go to preserve the sequence's order, and inserts the item there. The insort_left() function, like all the bisect module's functions, uses a binary chop, so performance is excellent even on very long sequences.

Another approach would have been to simply append the new key and then call sort() on the list. Python's sorting functionality is highly optimized for partially sorted data, so performance might not be too bad, but we prefer the more efficient solution.

```
def __delitem__(self, key):
    i = bisect.bisect_left(self.__keys, key)
    del self.__keys[i]
    del self.__dict[key]
```

Deleting an item is quite simple. The bisect_left() function takes a sorted sequence, such as a sorted list, and an item. It returns the index position where the item is in the sequence (or where the item would have been if it was in the sequence). We assume the key is in the list, relying on an exception being raised if it isn't. We delete the key by index position from the keys list, and delete the (key, value) by key from the dictionary.

We could instead have deleted the key from the keys list with a single statement, self.__keys.remove(key), but that would have used a slow linear search.

```
def get(self, key, value=None):
    return self.__dict.get(key, value)
```

This method returns the value for the given key, unless the key is not present in the dictionary, in which case it returns the specified value (which defaults to None). Since key order is not involved, we can simply pass on the work.

```
def setdefault(self, key, value):
    if key not in self.__dict:
        bisect.insort_left(self.__keys, key)
    return self.__dict.setdefault(key, value)
```

This method is similar to get(), but with one important difference: If the key is not in the dictionary, it is inserted with the given value. And in the case of a key that isn't in the dictionary, we must, of course, insert it into our key list.

```
def pop(self, key, value=None):
    if key not in self.__dict:
        return value
    i = bisect.bisect_left(self.__keys, key)
```

```
        del self.__keys[i]
        return self.__dict.pop(key, value)
```

This method is also similar to get(), except that it removes the item with the given key if it is in the dictionary. Naturally, if a key is removed from the dictionary, we must also remove it from the list of keys.

```
def popitem(self):
    item = self.__dict.popitem()
    i = bisect.bisect_left(self.__keys, item[0])
    del self.__keys[i]
    return item
```

This method removes and returns an arbitrary item, that is, a (key, value) tuple. We first remove the arbitrary item from the dictionary (since we don't know what it will be in advance), then remove its key from our list of keys, and finally return the item that was removed.

```
def has_key(self, key):
    return key in self.__dict


def __contains__(self, key):
    return key in self.__dict
```

The has_key() method is supported for backward compatibility; nowadays programmers use in, which is implemented by the __contains__() special method.

```
def __len__(self):
    return len(self.__dict)
```

This returns how many items are in the dictionary. We could just as easily have returned len(self.__keys).

```
def keys(self):
    return self.__keys[:]
```

We return our dictionary's keys as a shallow copy of our key list, so they are in key order. A standard dict returns its keys in an arbitrary order.

```
def values(self):
    return [self.__dict[key] for key in self.__keys]
```

List
compre-
hen-
sions

53 ☜

We return the dictionary's values in key order. To do this we create a list of the values by iterating over the key list in a list comprehension. This could also be done using a for loop:

```
result = []
for key in self.__keys:
    result.append(self.__dict[key])
return result
```

Writing one line of code rather than four obviously makes the list comprehension more appealing, although the syntax can take some getting used to.

```
def items(self):
    return [(key, self.__dict[key]) for key in self.__keys]
```

We use a similar approach for returning items, as (key, value) tuples, and again we could use a conventional loop instead:

```
result = []
for key in self.__keys:
    result.append((key, self.__dict[key]))
return result
```

By now, though, list comprehensions should start to become more familiar.

```
def __iter__(self):
    return iter(self.__keys)

def iterkeys(self):
    return iter(self.__keys)
```

An iterator is a "callable object" (typically a function or method) that returns the "next" item each time it is called. (Such objects have a next() function which is what Python calls.)

An iterator for a sequence such as a string, list, or tuple, can be obtained by using the iter() function, which is what we do here. For dictionaries, when an iterator is requested, an iterator to the dictionary's keys is returned, although for consistency, the dict API also provides an iterkeys() method, since it also provides itervalues() and iteritems() methods. If iter() is called on a dictionary, such as an OrderedDict instance, Python uses the __iter__() special method.

```
def itervalues(self):
    for key in self.__keys:
        yield self.__dict[key]
```

If itervalues() is called, we must return a generator that returns the dictionary's values. For a plain dict, the generator returns each value in an arbitrary order, but for the OrderedDict we want to return the values in key order.

Generator functions

58 ☞

Any function or method that contains a yield statement is a generator. The yield statement behaves like a return statement, except that after the yield has returned a value, when the generator is next called it will continue from the statement following the yield with all its previous state intact. So in this method, after each dictionary value is returned, the next iteration of the for loop takes place, until all the values have been returned.

```
def iteritems(self):
    for key in self.__keys:
```

```
        yield key, self.__dict[key]
```

This is almost identical to `itervalues()`, except that we return a (key, value) tuple. (We don't need to use parentheses to signify a tuple here, because there is no ambiguity.)

```
    def copy(self):
        dictionary = OrderedDict()
        dictionary.__keys = self.__keys[:]
        dictionary.__dict = self.__dict.copy()
        return dictionary
```

For copying, we perform a shallow copy of the keys list and of the internal dictionary, so the cost is proportional to the dictionary's size.

```
    def clear(self):
        self.__keys = []
        self.__dict = {}
```

This is the easiest function. We could have used `list()` and `dict()` rather than `[]` and `{}`.

```
    def __repr__(self):
        pieces = []
        for key in self.__keys:
            pieces.append("%r: %r" % (key, self.__dict[key]))
        return "OrderedDict({%s})" % ", ".join(pieces)
```

We have chosen to provide an `eval()`-able form of our dictionary. (And since we have not implemented `__str__()`, this will also be used when the dictionary is required as a string—for example, in a `print` statement.) For each (key, value) pair, we use the `%r` "representation" format so, for example, strings will be quoted, but numbers will not be. Here are two examples that show `repr()` in action:

```
    d = OrderedDict(dict(s=1, a=2, n=3, i=4, t=5))
    print repr(d)
    # Prints "OrderedDict({'a': 2, 'i': 4, 'n': 3, 's': 1, 't': 5})"
    d = OrderedDict({2: 'a', 3: 'm', 1: 'x'})
    print `d`      # Same as print repr(d)
    # Prints "OrderedDict({1: 'x', 2: 'a', 3: 'm'})"
```

Naturally, this method could have been implemented using a list comprehension, but in this case a `for` loop seems to be easier to understand.

We have now completed our review of the `OrderedDict` class. One piece of functionality that may appear to be missing from this and the other Python collections is the ability to load and save to a file. In fact, Python has the ability to load and save collections, including nested collections, to bytestrings and to files, providing they contain objects that can be represented, such as Booleans, numbers, strings, and collections of such objects. (Actually, Python can even load and save functions, classes, and in some cases, instances.) We will learn about this functionality in Chapter 8.

Inheritance and Polymorphism

Just as we would expect from a language that supports object-oriented programming, Python supports inheritance and polymorphism. We have already used inheritance because the classes we have created so far have inherited object, but in this section we will go into more depth. All Python methods are virtual, so if we reimplement a method in a base class the reimplemented method will be the one that is called. We will see shortly how we can access base class methods, for example, when we want to use them as part of a reimplemented method.

Let us begin with a simple class that holds some basic information about a work of art:

```
class Item(object):

    def __init__(self, artist, title, year=None):
        self.__artist = artist
        self.__title = title
        self.__year = year
```

We have inherited the object base class and given our class three private data attributes. Since we have made the attributes private, we must either provide accessors for them, or create properties through which we can access them. In this example, we have chosen to use accessors:

```
    def artist(self):
        return self.__artist

    def setArtist(self, artist):
        self.__artist = artist
```

The accessors for the __title and __year attributes are structurally the same as those for the __artist attribute, so we have not shown them.

```
    def __str__(self):
        year = ""
        if self.__year is not None:
            year = " in %d" % self.__year
        return "%s by %s%s" % (self.__title, self.__artist, year)
```

If a string representation is required, we return a string in the form *"title* by *artist"* if __year is None, and *"title* by *artist* in *year"* otherwise.

Now that we can encapsulate some basic information about a work of art, we can create a `Painting` subclass to hold information on paintings:

```
class Painting(Item):

    def __init__(self, artist, title, year=None):
        super(Painting, self).__init__(artist, title, year)
```

The preceding code is the entire subclass. We have not added any data attributes or new methods, so we just use the super() built-in function to initialize the Item base class. The super() function takes a class and returns the class's base class. If the function is also passed an instance (as we do here), the returned base class object is bound to the instance we passed in, which means we can call (base class) methods on the instance.

It is also possible to call the base class by naming it explicitly—for example, Item.__init__(self, artist, title, year); notice that we must pass the self parameter ourselves if we use this approach.

We don't have to call the base class __init__() at all—for example, if the base class has no data attributes. And if we do call it, the super() call does not have to be the first call we make, although it usually is in __init__() implementations.

Now we will look at a slightly more elaborate subclass:

```
class Sculpture(Item):

    def __init__(self, artist, title, year=None, material=None):
        super(Sculpture, self).__init__(artist, title, year)
        self.__material = material
```

The Sculpture class has an additional attribute, so after initializing through the base class we also initialize the extra attribute.

We won't show the accessors since they are structurally the same as those used for the artist's name.

```
    def __str__(self):
        materialString = ""
        if self.__material is not None:
            materialString = " (%s)" % self.__material
        return "%s%s" % (super(Sculpture, self).__str__(),
                         materialString)
```

The __str__() method uses the base class's __str__() method, and if the material is known, it tacks it on to the end of the resultant string. We cannot call str(self) because that would lead to an infinite recursion (calling __str__() again and again), but there is no problem calling a special method explicitly when necessary, as we do here.

Because of Python's polymorphism, the right __str__() method will always be called. For example:

```
a = Painting("Cecil Collins", "The Sleeping Fool", 1943)
print a    # Prints "The Sleeping Fool by Cecil Collins in 1943"
b = Sculpture("Auguste Rodin", "The Secret", 1925, "bronze")
print b    # Prints "The Secret by Auguste Rodin in 1925 (bronze)"
```

Although we have shown polymorphism using a special method, it works exactly the same for ordinary methods.

Python uses dynamic typing, also called duck typing ("If it walks like a duck and it quacks like a duck, it is a duck"). This is very flexible. For example, suppose we had a class like this:

```
class Title(object):

    def __init__(self, title)
        self.__title = title

    def title(self):
        return self.__title
```

Now we could do this:

```
items = []
items.append(Painting("Cecil Collins", "The Poet", 1941))
items.append(Sculpture("Auguste Rodin", "Naked Balzac", 1917,
                       "plaster"))
items.append(Title("Eternal Springtime"))
for item in items:
    print item.title()
```

This will print the title of each item, even though the items are of different types. All that matters to Python is that they all support the required method, in this case title().

But what if we had a collection of items, but we were not sure if all of them supported the title() method? With the code as it stands we would get an AttributeError as soon as we reached an item that didn't support title(). One solution is to use exception handling:

```
try:
    for item in items:
        print item.title()
except AttributeError:
    pass
```

That contains the problem, but stops the loop as soon as an unsuitable item is encountered. This might tempt us to use type checking, with type() or isinstance(), for example:

```
for item in items:
    if isinstance(item, Item):
        print item.title()
```

This will work perfectly for Paintings and Sculptures since they are both Item subclasses, but will fail on Title objects. Furthermore, this approach is not really good object-oriented style. What we really want to do is say "can it quack?", and we can do this using hasattr():

```
for item in items:
    if hasattr(item, "title"):
        print item.title()
```

Now our items can be Paintings, Sculptures, Titles, or even strings (since strings have a title() method).

One question remains, though: How do we know that the attribute is a method—that it is callable—rather than a data attribute? One approach is to use callable(). For example:

```
for item in items:
    if hasattr(item, "title") and callable(item.title):
        print item.title()
```

We still need to use hasattr() because we must call callable() only on something that exists (otherwise, we will get an exception), in this case an instance attribute that is a method.

Python's introspection is very powerful, and it has more features than those we have covered here. But whether it is wise to use it, apart from isinstance(), is debatable.

Sometimes it is useful to define an abstract base class (an interface) that simply defines a particular API. For example, works of art and other kinds of items have dimensions, so it might be useful to have a Dimension interface that had area() and volume() methods. Although Python provides no formal support for interfaces, we can achieve what we want by implementing a class that has no data attributes, and whose methods raise the NotImplementedError exception. For example:

```
class Dimension(object):

    def area(self):
        raise NotImplementedError, "Dimension.area()"

    def volume(self):
```

```
raise NotImplementedError, "Dimension.volume()"
```

This defines the `Dimension` interface as having the two methods we want. If we multiply-inherit `Dimension` and forget to reimplement the methods, we will get a `NotImplementedError` exception if we try to use them. Here is a new version of the `Painting` class that makes use of the interface:

```
class Painting(Item, Dimension):

    def __init__(self, artist, title, year=None, width=None,
                 height=None):
        super(Painting, self).__init__(artist, title, year)
        self.__width = width
        self.__height = height
```

To calculate a painting's area we need its width and height, so we add these to the constructor, and assign them to suitable attributes:

```
    def area(self):
        if self.__width is None or self.__height is None:
            return None
        return self.__width * self.__height

    def volume(self):
        return None
```

We must implement `area()` and `volume()`. Although the `volume()` method does not make sense for a painting, we must provide an implementation anyway (since the interface requires one), so we do so and return `None`. An alternative would have been to have raised an exception—for example, `ValueError`.

It would be natural to rework the `Sculpture` class to accept width, height, and depth arguments, and to provide a `volume()` implementation. But an `area()` implementation may or may not make sense for a sculpture. We might mean the overall area of the total volume, or the area of a face from a particular viewpoint. Since there is ambiguity, we could either pass an additional argument to disambiguate, or give up and either return `None` or raise an exception.

Multiply inheriting just involves listing two or more base classes in the `class` statement. The order in which the base classes appear does not matter in our example, but can matter in more complex hierarchies.

Python's object-oriented functionality goes beyond what we have covered in this chapter. For instances that need to store a fixed set of attributes as compactly as possible, it is possible to use the `__slots__` class attribute. We mention this only to highlight the fact that this is completely different from the PyQt slots (which are functions and more commonly methods) that we will encounter in the GUI chapters. It is also possible to create meta-classes, but again this is beyond the scope of what we need for GUI programming, so we do not need to cover the topic here.

Signals and slots ☞ 127

Modules and Multifile Applications

Import-
ing
Objects
sidebar
19 ☞

Object-oriented programming allows us to package up functionality (e.g., methods and data attributes), into classes. Python modules allow us to package up functionality at a higher level—for example, entire sets of classes, functions, and instance variables. A module is simply a file with a .py extension. Modules may have code that is executed when they are imported, but more commonly they simply provide functions and classes which are instantiated when they are imported. We have already seen examples of this: The Length class is in a file called length.py, and is therefore accessible as the length module. When importing a module, we specify the name of the module file without the extension. For example:

```
import length
a = length.Length("4.5 yd")
```

Only modules that are in the current directory, or in Python's sys.path list, can be imported. If we need access to modules that are elsewhere in the filesystem, we can add additional paths to sys.path. In addition to a file, a module can be an entire directory of files. In these cases, the directory must contain a file called __init__.py. This file can be (and often is) empty; it is simply used as a marker to tell Python that the directory contains .py files and that the directory name is the top-level module name. For example, we might create a directory called mylibrary and put length.py, ordereddict.py, and an empty __init__.py in it. As long as we add the directory that contains the mylibrary directory to Python's path, we could do this:

```
import mylibrary.length
a = mylibrary.length.Length("14.3 km")
```

In practice, we might prefer to alias mylibrary.length to something shorter. For example:

```
import mylibrary.length as length
a = length.Length("948mm")
```

Python's module handling is a lot more sophisticated than we have shown, but what we have covered is sufficient for the GUI programming which is our main concern.* Python and PyQt applications can be written in a single file or can be spread over multiple files. We will show both approaches in the coming chapters.

---

*The module import semantics are due to change in Python 2.7, with imports becoming absolute rather than relative. See http://www.python.org/dev/peps/pep-0328 for details.

Using the doctest Module

Python has considerable support for testing, with the doctest and unittest modules for unit testing and the test module for regression testing. PyQt also provides unit-testing functionality with the QtTest module.

When we create modules, such as the length and ordereddict modules we wrote earlier, they are designed to be imported and the objects they provide (e.g., the Length and OrderedDict classes), used by the importing application. But since .py files can also be executables, we can easily include unit-testing code: When the module is imported the unit-testing code is simply ignored; but when the module is run the unit tests are executed. This approach is supported by the doctest module.

The doctest module makes unit testing as simple and painless as possible. To use it all we need to do is add examples to our docstrings, showing what we would type into the interactive Python interpreter (or IDLE) and what response we expect back. For example, here is the OrderedDict class's get() method in full:

```
def get(self, key, value=None):
    """Returns the value associated with key or value if key isn't
    in the dictionary

    >>> d = OrderedDict(dict(s=1, a=2, n=3, i=4, t=5, y=6))
    >>> d.get("X", 21)
    21
    >>> d.get("i")
    4
    """
    return self.__dict.get(key, value)
```

The docstring contains a brief description of the method's purpose, and then some examples written as though they were typed into the interpreter. We begin by creating an OrderedDict object; we don't need to import or qualify since we are inside the ordereddict module. We then write a call to the method we are testing and what the interpreter (or IDLE) is expected to respond. And then we do another call and response.

The doctest module uses this syntax because it is so familiar to Python programmers through their use of the interactive Python interpreter or of IDLE, or of any other Python IDE, such as Eric4, that embeds a Python interpreter. When the tests are run, the doctest module will import the module itself, then read every docstring (using Python's introspection capabilities) and then execute each statement that begins with the >>> prompt. It then checks the result against the expected output (which may be nothing), and will report any failures.

To make a module able to use `doctest` like this we just need to add three lines at the end of the module:

```
if __name__ == "__main__":
    import doctest
    doctest.testmod()
```

Whether a module is imported by being the subject of an `import` statement, or is invoked on the command line, all the module's code is executed. This causes the module's functions and classes to be created ready for use.

We can tell whether a module was imported because in this case its __name__ attribute is set to the module's name. On the other hand, if a module is invoked its __name__ attribute is set to __main__.

As shown earlier, we can use an `if` statement to see whether the module was imported, in which case we do nothing else. But if the module was invoked on the command line, we import the `doctest` module and execute the `testmod()` function which performs all our tests.

We can perform a test run from inside a console window. For example:

```
C:\>cd c:\pyqt\chap03
C:\pyqt\chap03>ordereddict.py
```

If there are no test failures, the module will run silently. If there are any errors, these will be output to the console. We can force the `doctest` module to be more verbose by using the –v flag:

```
C:\pyqt\chap03>ordereddict.py –v
```

This shows every single test that is performed, and a summary at the end.

It is also possible to test for expected failures, for example, out-cases where we expect an exception to be raised. For these we just write the first and last lines of the expected output (because the traceback in the middle may vary) and use an ellipsis, ..., to indicate the traceback. For example, here is the OrderedDict class's setAt() method in full:

```
    def setAt(self, index, value):
        """Sets the index-th item's value to the given value

        >>> d = OrderedDict(dict(s=1, a=2, n=3, i=4, t=5, y=6))
        >>> d.getAt(5)
        6
        >>> d.setAt(5, 99)
        >>> d.getAt(5)
        99
        >>> d.setAt(19, 42)
        Traceback (most recent call last):
        ...
```

```
IndexError: list index out of range
"""
self.__dict[self.__keys[index]] = value
```

We created an OrderedDict of six items, but in the last test attempted to set the nonexistent twentieth item's value. This causes the dictionary to raise an IndexError, so we write what the interactive Python interpreter would output, and the doctest module understands this and will pass the test if the exception was correctly raised.

The doctest module is less sophisticated than the unittest module, but it is both easy to use and unobtrusive. We have used it in all the examples shown so far, as can be seen by looking at the book's source code.

Summary

This chapter took us from being users of classes to being creators of classes. We saw how to initialize newly created instances using the __init__() special method, and how to implement many of the other special methods so that our custom data types (classes) can behave just like Python's built-in classes. We also learned how to create both ordinary methods and static methods, and how to store and access both per-instance and static data.

We reviewed two complete examples. The Length class, a numeric data type, and the OrderedDict class, a collection class. We also made use of much of the knowledge gained from the previous chapters, including some of Python's advanced features, such as list comprehensions and generator methods.

This chapter also shownend how to do both single and multiple inheritance, and gave an example of how to create a simple interface class. We learned more about using isinstance() for type testing, and about hasattr() and duck typing.

We concluded the chapter with an overview of how Python modules and multifile applications work. We also looked at the doctest module and saw how easy it is to create unit tests that look like examples in our docstrings.

We now know the Python language fundamentals. We can create variables, use collections, and create our own data types and collection types. We can branch, loop, call functions and methods, and raise and handle exceptions. Clearly, there is a lot more to learn, but we can cover everything else we require as the need arises. We are now ready to start GUI application programming, a topic that begins in the next chapter and which occupies the rest of the book.

Exercises

1. Implement a Tribool data type. This is a data type that can have one of
three values: True, False, or unknown (for which you should use None). In
addition to __init__(), implement __str__(), __repr__(), and __cmp__();
also, implement __nonzero__() for conversion to bool(), __invert__() for
logical not (~), __and__() for logical and (&), and __or__() for logical or (|).
There are two possible logics that can be used: propagating, where any expression involving unknown (i.e., None) is unknown, and nonpropagating,
where any expression involving unknown that can be evaluated is evaluated. Use nonpropagating logic so that your Tribools match the truth table shown here, and where t is Tribool(True), f is Tribool(False), and n is
Tribool(None) (for unknown):

Expression	Result	Expression	Result	Expression	Result
~t	False	~f	True	~n	None
t & t	True	t & f	False	t & n	None
f & f	False	f & n	False	n & n	None
t | t	True	t | f	True	t | n	True
f | f	False	f | n	None	n | n	None

For example, with nonpropagating logic, True | None is True, because as long
as one operand to logical or is true, the expression is true. But False | None
is None (unknown), because we cannot determine the result.

Most of the methods can be implemented in just a few lines of code.
Make sure that you use the doctest module and write unit tests for all
the methods.

2. Implement a Stack class and an EmptyStackError exception class. The Stack
class should use a list to store its items, and should provide pop() to return
and remove the item at the top of the stack (the rightmost item), top() to
return the item at the top of the stack, and push() to push a new item onto
the stack. Also provide special methods so that len() and str() will work
sensibly. Make sure that pop() and top() raise EmptyStackError if the stack
is empty when they are called. The methods can be written using very few
lines of code. Make sure that you use the doctest module and write unit
tests for all the methods.

The model answers are provided in the files chap03/tribool.py and chap03/
stack.py.

Part II

Basic GUI Programming

4

- A Pop-Up Alert in 25 Lines
- An Expression Evaluator in 30 Lines
- A Currency Converter in 70 Lines
- Signals and Slots

Introduction to GUI Programming

In this chapter we begin with brief reviews of three tiny yet useful GUI applications written in PyQt. We will take the opportunity to highlight some of the issues involved in GUI programming, but we will defer most of the details to later chapters. Once we have a feel for PyQt GUI programming, we will discuss PyQt's "signals and slots" mechanism—this is a high-level communication mechanism for responding to user interaction that allows us to ignore irrelevant detail.

Although PyQt is used commercially to build applications that vary in size from hundreds of lines of code to more than 100 000 lines of code, the applications we will build in this chapter are all less than 100 lines, and they show just how much can be done with very little code.

In this chapter we will design our user interfaces purely by writing code, but in Chapter 7, we will learn how to create user interfaces using Qt's visual design tool, *Qt Designer*.

Python console applications and Python module files always have a .py extension, but for Python GUI applications we use a .pyw extension. Both .py and .pyw are fine on Linux, but on Windows, .pyw ensures that Windows uses the pythonw.exe interpreter instead of python.exe, and this in turn ensures that when we execute a Python GUI application, no unnecessary console window will appear.* On Mac OS X, it is essential to use the .pyw extension.

The PyQt documentation is provided as a set of HTML files, independent of the Python documentation. The most commonly referred to documents are those covering the PyQt API. These files have been converted from the original C++/Qt documentation files, and their index page is called classes.html; Win-

---

*If you use Windows and an error message box titled, "pythonw.exe - Unable To Locate Component" pops up, it almost certainly means that you have not set your path correctly. See Appendix A, page 564, for how to fix this.

dows users will find a link to this page in their Start button's PyQt menu. It is well worth looking at this page to get an overview of what classes are available, and of course to dip in and read about those classes that seem interesting.

The first application we will look at is an unusual hybrid: a GUI application that must be launched from a console because it requires command-line arguments. We have included it because it makes it easier to explain how the PyQt event loop works (and what that is), without having to go into any other GUI details. The second and third examples are both very short but standard GUI applications. They both show the basics of how we can create and lay out widgets ("controls" in Windows-speak)—labels, buttons, comboboxes, and other on-screen elements that users can view and, in most cases, interact with. They also show how we can respond to user interactions—for example, how to call a particular function or method when the user performs a particular action.

In the last section we will cover how to handle user interactions in more depth, and in the next chapter we will cover layouts and dialogs much more thoroughly. Use this chapter to get a feel for how things work, without worrying about the details: The chapters that follow will fill in the gaps and will familiarize you with standard PyQt programming practices.

A Pop-Up Alert in 25 Lines

Our first GUI application is a bit odd. First, it must be run from the console, and second it has no "decorations"—no title bar, no system menu, no X close button. Figure 4.1 shows the whole thing.

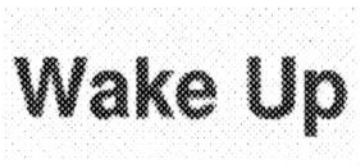

Wake Up

Figure 4.1 *The Alert program*

To get the output displayed, we could enter a command line like this:

```
C:\>cd c:\pyqt\chap04
C:\pyqt\chap04>alert.pyw 12:15 Wake Up
```

When run, the program executes invisibly in the background, simply marking time until the specified time is reached. At that point, it pops up a window with the message text. About a minute after showing the window, the application will automatically terminate.

The specified time must use the 24-hour clock. For testing purposes we can use a time that has just gone; for example, by using 12:15 when it is really 12:30, the window will pop up immediately (well, within less than a second).

Now that we know what it does and how to run it, we will review the implementation. The file is a few lines longer than 25 lines because we have not counted comment lines and blank lines in the total—but there are only 25 lines of executable code. We will begin with the imports.

```
import sys
import time
from PyQt4.QtCore import *
from PyQt4.QtGui import *
```

We import the `sys` module because we want to access the command-line arguments it holds in the `sys.argv` list. The `time` module is imported because we need its `sleep()` function, and we need the PyQt modules for the GUI and for the `QTime` class.

```
app = QApplication(sys.argv)
```

We begin by creating a `QApplication` object. Every PyQt GUI application must have a `QApplication` object. This object provides access to global-like information such as the application's directory, the screen size (and which screen the application is on, in a multihead system), and so on. This object also provides the *event loop*, discussed shortly.

When we create a `QApplication` object we pass it the command-line arguments; this is because PyQt recognizes some command-line arguments of its own, such as –geometry and –style, so we ought to give it the chance to read them. If `QApplication` recognizes any of the arguments, it acts on them, and removes them from the list it was given. The list of arguments that `QApplication` recognizes is given in the `QApplication`'s initializer's documentation.

```
try:
    due = QTime.currentTime()
    message = "Alert!"
    if len(sys.argv) < 2:
        raise ValueError
    hours, mins = sys.argv[1].split(":")
    due = QTime(int(hours), int(mins))
    if not due.isValid():
        raise ValueError
    if len(sys.argv) > 2:
        message = " ".join(sys.argv[2:])
except ValueError:
    message = "Usage: alert.pyw HH:MM [optional message]" # 24hr clock
```

At the very least, the application requires a time, so we set the `due` variable to the time right now. We also provide a default message. If the user has not given at least one command-line argument (a time), we raise a `ValueError` exception. This will result in the time being now and the message being the "usage" error message.

If the first argument does not contain a colon, a ValueError will be raised when
we attempt to unpack two items from the split() call. If the hours or minutes
are not a valid number, a ValueError will be raised by int(), and if the hours or
minutes are out of range, due will be an invalid QTime, and we raise a ValueError
ourselves. Although Python provides its own date and time classes, the PyQt
date and time classes are often more convenient (and in some respects more
powerful), so we tend to prefer them.

If the time is valid, we set the message to be the space-separated concatenation
of the other command-line arguments if there are any; otherwise, we leave it as
the default "Alert!" that we set at the beginning. (When a program is executed
on the command line, it is given a list of arguments, the first being the invoking
name, and the rest being each sequence of nonwhitespace characters, that is,
each "word", entered on the command line. The words may be changed by the
shell—for example, by applying wildcard expansion. Python puts the words it
is actually given in the sys.argv list.)

Now we know when the message must be shown and what the message is.

```
while QTime.currentTime() < due:
    time.sleep(20) # 20 seconds
```

We loop continuously, comparing the current time with the target time. The
loop will terminate if the current time is later than the target time. We could
have simply put a pass statement inside the loop, but if we did that Python
would loop as quickly as possible, gobbling up processor cycles for no good
reason. The time.sleep() command tells Python to suspend processing for
the specified number of seconds, 20 in this case. This gives other programs
more opportunity to run and makes sense since we don't want to actually do
anything while we wait for the due time to arrive.

Apart from creating the QApplication object, what we have done so far is
standard console programming.

```
label = QLabel("<font color=red size=72><b>" + message + "</b></font>")
label.setWindowFlags(Qt.SplashScreen)
label.show()
QTimer.singleShot(60000, app.quit) # 1 minute
app.exec_()
```

We have created a QApplication object, we have a message, and the due time
has arrived, so now we can begin to create our application. A GUI application
needs widgets, and in this case we need a label to show the message. A QLabel
can accept HTML text, so we give it an HTML string that tells it to display bold
red text of size 72 points.[*]

---

[*]The supported HTML tags are listed at http://doc.trolltech.com/richtext-html-subset.html.

In PyQt, any widget can be used as a top-level window, even a button or a label. When a widget is used like this, PyQt automatically gives it a title bar. We don't want a title bar for this application, so we set the label's window flags to those used for splash screens since they have no title bar. Once we have set up the label that will be our window, we call show() on it. At this point, the label window is not shown! The call to show() merely schedules a "paint event", that is, it adds a new event to the QApplication object's event queue that is a request to paint the specified widget.

Next, we set up a single-shot timer. Whereas the Python library's time.sleep() function takes a number of seconds, the QTimer.singleShot() function takes a number of milliseconds. We give the singleShot() method two arguments: how long until it should time out (one minute in this case), and a function or method for it to call when it times out.

In PyQt terminology, the function or method we have given is called a "slot", although in the PyQt documentation the terms "callable", "Python slot", and "Qt slot" are used to distinguish slots from Python's __slots__, a feature of new-style classes that is described in the Python Language Reference. In this book we will use the PyQt terminology, since we never use __slots__.

Signals and slots

☞ 127

So now we have two events scheduled: A paint event that wants to take place immediately, and a timer timeout event that wants to take place in a minute's time.

The call to app.exec_() starts off the QApplication object's event loop.* The first event it gets is the paint event, so the label window pops up on-screen with the given message. About one minute later the timer timeout event occurs and the QApplication.quit() method is called. This method performs a clean termination of the GUI application. It closes any open windows, frees up any resources it has acquired, and exits.

Event loops are used by all GUI applications. In pseudocode, an event loop looks like this:

```
while True:
    event = getNextEvent()
    if event:
        if event == Terminate:
            break
        processEvent(event)
```

When the user interacts with the application, or when certain other things occur, such as a timer timing out or the application's window being uncovered (maybe because another application was closed), an event is generated inside PyQt and added to the event queue. The application's event loop continuously

---

*PyQt uses exec_() rather than exec() to avoid conflicting with Python's built-in exec statement.

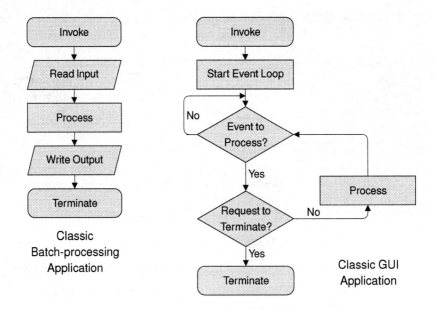

Figure 4.2 *Batch processing applications versus GUI applications*

checks to see whether there is an event to process, and if there is, it processes it (or passes it on to the event's associated function or method for processing).

Although complete, and quite useful if you use consoles, the application uses only a single widget. Also, we have not given it any ability to respond to user interaction. It also works rather like traditional batch-processing programs. It is invoked, performs some processing (waits, then shows a message), and terminates. Most GUI programs work differently. Once invoked, they run their event loop and respond to events. Some events come from the user—for example, key presses and mouse clicks—and some from the system, for example, timers timing out and windows being revealed. They process in response to requests that are the result of events such as button clicks and menu selections, and terminate only when told to do so.

The next application we will look at is much more conventional than the one we've just seen, and is typical of many very small GUI applications generally.

An Expression Evaluator in 30 Lines

This application is a complete dialog-style application written in 30 lines of code (excluding blank and comment lines). "Dialog-style" means an application that has no menu bar, and usually no toolbar or status bar, most commonly with some buttons (as we will see in the next section), and with no central widget. In contrast, "main window-style" applications normally have a menu bar, toolbars, a status bar, and in some cases buttons too; and they have a central widget (which may contain other widgets, of course). We will look at main window-style applications in Chapter 6.

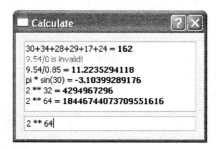

Figure 4.3 *The Calculate application*

This application uses two widgets: A QTextBrowser which is a read-only multi-line text box that can display both plain text and HTML; and a QLineEdit, which is a single-line text box that displays plain text. All text in PyQt widgets is Unicode, although it can be converted to other character sets when necessary.

The Calculate application (shown in Figure 4.3), can be invoked just like any normal GUI application by clicking (or double-clicking depending on platform and settings) its icon. (It can also be launched from a console, of course.) Once the application is running, the user can simply type mathematical expressions into the line edit and when they press Enter (or Return), the expression and its result are appended to the QTextBrowser. Any exceptions that are raised due to invalid expressions or invalid arithmetic (such as division by zero) are caught and turned into error messages that are simply appended to the QTextBrowser.

As usual, we will look at the code in sections. This example follows the pattern that we will use for all future GUI applications: A form is represented by a class, behavior in response to user interaction is handled by methods, and the "main" part of the program is tiny.

```
from __future__ import division
import sys
from math import *
from PyQt4.QtCore import *
from PyQt4.QtGui import *
```

Truncating division

17 ☜

Since we are doing mathematics and don't want any surprises like truncating division, we make sure we get floating-point division. Normally we import non-PyQt modules using the import *moduleName* syntax; but since we want all of the math module's functions and constants available to our program's users, we simply import them all into the current namespace. As usual, we import sys to get the sys.argv list, and we import everything from both the QtCore and the QtGui modules.

```
class Form(QDialog):
```

```
    def __init__(self, parent=None):
        super(Form, self).__init__(parent)
        self.browser = QTextBrowser()
        self.lineedit = QLineEdit("Type an expression and press Enter")
        self.lineedit.selectAll()
        layout = QVBoxLayout()
        layout.addWidget(self.browser)
        layout.addWidget(self.lineedit)
        self.setLayout(layout)
        self.lineedit.setFocus()
        self.connect(self.lineedit, SIGNAL("returnPressed()"),
                     self.updateUi)
        self.setWindowTitle("Calculate")
```

As we have seen, any widget can be used as a top-level window. But in most cases when we create a top-level window we subclass QDialog, or QMainWindow, or occasionally, QWidget. Both QDialog and QMainWindow, and indeed all of PyQt's widgets, are derived from QWidget, and all are new-style classes. By inheriting QDialog we get a blank form, that is, a gray rectangle, and some convenient behaviors and methods. For example, if the user clicks the close X button, the dialog will close. By default, when a widget is closed it is merely hidden; we can, of course, change this behavior, as we will see in the next chapter.

We give our Form class's __init__() method a default parent of None, and use super() to initialize it. A widget that has no parent becomes a top-level window, which is what we want for our form. We then create the two widgets we need and keep references to them so that we can access them later, outside of __init__(). Since we did not give these widgets parents, it would seem that they will become top-level windows—which would not make sense. We will see shortly that they get parents later on in the initializer. We give the QLineEdit some initial text to show, and select it all. This will ensure that as soon as the user starts typing, the text we gave will be overwritten.

We want the widgets to appear vertically, one above the other, in the window. This is achieved by creating a QVBoxLayout and adding our two widgets to it, and then setting the layout on the form. If you run the application and resize it, you will find that any extra vertical space is given to the QTextBrowser, and that both widgets will grow horizontally. This is all handled automatically by the layout manager, and can be fine-tuned by setting layout policies.

One important side effect of using layouts is that PyQt automatically reparents the widgets that are laid out. So although we did not give our widgets a parent of self (the Form instance), when we call setLayout() the layout manager gives ownership of the widgets and of itself to the form, and takes ownership of any nested layouts itself. This means that none of the widgets that are laid out is a top-level window, and all of them have parents, which is what we want. So when the form is deleted, all its child widgets and layouts will be deleted with it, in the correct order.

Object Ownership

All PyQt classes that derive from QObject—and this includes all the widgets, since QWidget is a QObject subclass—can have a "parent". The parent–child relationship is used for two complementary purposes. A widget that has no parent is a top-level window, and a widget that has a parent (always another widget) is contained (displayed) within its parent. The relationship also defines *ownership*, with parents owning their children.

PyQt uses the parent–child ownership model to ensure that if a parent—for example, a top-level window—is deleted, all its children, for example, all the widgets the window contains, are automatically deleted as well. To avoid memory leaks, we should always make sure that any QObject, including all QWidgets, has a parent, the sole exception being top-level windows.

Most PyQt QObject subclasses have constructors that take a parent object as their last (optional) argument. But for widgets we generally do not (and need not) pass this argument. This is because widgets used in dialogs are laid out with layout managers, and when this occurs they are automatically reparented to the widget in which they are laid out, so they end up with the correct parent without requiring us to take any special action.

There are some cases where we must explicitly pass a parent—for example, when constructing QObject subclass objects that are not widgets, or that are widgets but which will not be laid out (such as dock widgets); we will see several examples of such cases in later chapters.

One final point is that it is possible to get situations where a Python variable is referring to an underlying PyQt object that no longer exists. This issue is covered in Chapter 9, in the "aliveness" discussion starting on page 287.

The widgets on a form can be laid out using a variety of techniques. We can use the resize() and move() methods to give them absolute sizes and positions; we can reimplement the resizeEvent() method and calculate their sizes and positions dynamically, or we can use PyQt's layout managers. Using absolute sizes and positions is very inconvenient. For one thing, we have to perform lots of manual calculations, and for another, if we change the layout we have to redo the calculations. Calculating the sizes and positions dynamically is a better approach, but still requires us to write quite a lot of tedious calculating code.

Using layout managers makes things a lot easier. And layout managers are quite smart: They automatically adapt to resize events and to content changes. Anyone used to dialogs in many versions of Windows will appreciate the benefits of having dialogs that can be resized (and that do so sensibly), rather than being forced to use small, nonresizable dialogs which can be very inconvenient when their contents are too large to fit. Layout managers also make life easier for internationalized programs since they adapt to content, so translated labels will not be "chopped off" if the target language is more verbose than the original language.

PyQt provides three layout managers: one for vertical layouts, one for horizontal layouts, and one for grid layouts. Layouts can be nested, so quite sophisticated layouts are possible. And there are other ways of laying out widgets, such as using splitters or tab widgets. All of these approaches are considered in more depth in Chapter 9.

As a courtesy to our users, we want the focus to start in the QLineEdit; we call setFocus() to achieve this. We must do this after setting the layout.

The connect() call is something we will look at in depth later in this chapter. Suffice it to say that every widget (and some other QObjects) announce state changes by emitting "signals". These signals (which are nothing to do with Unix signals) are usually ignored. However, we can choose to take notice of any signals we are interested in, and we do this by identifying the QObject that we want to know about, the signal it emits that we are interested in, and the function or method we want called when the signal is emitted.

Signals and slots ☞ 127

So in this case, when the user presses Enter (or Return) in the QLineEdit, the returnPressed() signal will be emitted as usual, but because of our connect() call, when this occurs, our updateUi() method will be called. We will see what happens then in a moment.

The last thing we do in __init__() is set the window's title.

As we will see shortly, the form is created and show() is called on it. Once the event loop begins, the form is shown—and nothing more appears to happen. The application is simply running the event loop, waiting for the user to click the mouse or press a key. Once the user starts interacting, the results of their interaction are processed. So if the user types in an expression, the QLineEdit will take care of displaying what they type, and if they press Enter, our updateUi() method will be called.

```
def updateUi(self):
    try:
        text = unicode(self.lineedit.text())
        self.browser.append("%s = <b>%s</b>" % (text, eval(text)))
    except:
        self.browser.append(
                "<font color=red>%s is invalid!</font>" % text)
```

PyQt string policy 28 ☜

When updateUi() is called it retrieves the text from the QLineEdit, immediately converting it to a unicode object. We then use Python's eval() function to evaluate the string as an expression. If this is successful, we append a string to the QTextBrowser that has the expression text, an equals sign, and then the result in bold. Although we normally convert QStrings to unicode as soon as possible, we can pass QStrings, unicodes, and strs to PyQt methods that expect a QString, and PyQt will automatically perform any necessary conversion. If any exception occurs, we append an error message instead. Using a catch-all except block like this is not good general practice, but for a 30-line program it seems reasonable.

By using eval() we avoid all the work of parsing and error checking that we would have to do ourselves if we were using a compiled language.

```
app = QApplication(sys.argv)
form = Form()
form.show()
app.exec_()
```

Now that we have defined our Form class, at the end of the calculate.pyw file, we create the QApplication object, instantiate an instance of our form, schedule it to be painted, and start off the event loop.

And that is the complete application. But it isn't quite the end of the story. We have not said how the user can terminate the application. Because our form derives from QDialog, it inherits some behavior. For example, if the user clicks the close button X, or if they press the Esc key, the form will close. When a form closes, it is hidden. When the form is hidden PyQt will detect that the application has no visible windows and that no further interaction is possible. It will therefore delete the form and perform a clean termination of the application.

In some cases, we want an application to continue even if it is not visible—for example, a server. For these cases, we can call QApplication.setQuitOnLast-WindowClosed(False). It is also possible, although rarely necessary, to be notified when the last window is closed.

On Mac OS X, and some X Windows window managers, like twm, an application like this will *not* have a close button, and on the Mac, choosing Quit on the menu bar will not work. In such cases, pressing Esc will terminate the application, and in addition on the Mac, Command+. will also work. In view of this, for applications that are likely to be used on the Mac or with twm or similar, it is best to provide a Quit button. Adding buttons to dialogs is covered in this chapter's last section.

We are now ready to look at the last small, complete example that we will present in this chapter. It has more custom behavior, has a more complex layout, and does more sophisticated processing, but its fundamental structure is very similar to the Calculate application, and indeed to that of many other PyQt dialogs.

A Currency Converter in 70 Lines

One small utility that is often useful is a currency converter. But since exchange rates frequently change, we cannot simply create a static dictionary of conversion rates as we did for the units of length in the Length class we created in the previous chapter. Fortunately, the Bank of Canada provides exchange rates in a file that is accessible over the Internet, and which uses an easy-to-parse format. The rates are sometimes a few days old, but they are good enough for estimating the cash required for trips or how much a foreign contract is likely to pay. The application is shown in Figure 4.4.

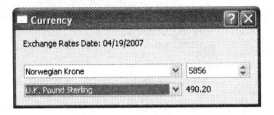

Figure 4.4 *The Currency application*

The application must first download and parse the exchange rates. Then it must create a user interface which the user can manipulate to specify the currencies and the amount that they are interested in.

As usual, we will begin with the imports:

```
import sys
import urllib2
from PyQt4.QtCore import *
from PyQt4.QtGui import *
```

Both Python and PyQt provide classes for networking. In Chapter 18, we will use PyQt's classes, but here we will use Python's urllib2 module because it provides a very useful convenience function that makes it easy to grab a file over the Internet.

```
class Form(QDialog):

    def __init__(self, parent=None):
        super(Form, self).__init__(parent)

        date = self.getdata()
        rates = sorted(self.rates.keys())

        dateLabel = QLabel(date)
        self.fromComboBox = QComboBox()
        self.fromComboBox.addItems(rates)
        self.fromSpinBox = QDoubleSpinBox()
        self.fromSpinBox.setRange(0.01, 10000000.00)
        self.fromSpinBox.setValue(1.00)
        self.toComboBox = QComboBox()
        self.toComboBox.addItems(rates)
        self.toLabel = QLabel("1.00")
```

After initializing our form using super(), we call our getdata() method. As we will soon see, this method gets the exchange rates, populates the self.rates dictionary, and returns a string holding the date the rates were in force. The dictionary's keys are currency names, and the values are the conversion factors.

We take a sorted copy of the dictionary's keys so that we can present the user with sorted lists of currencies in the comboboxes. The date and rates variables, and the dateLabel, are referred to only inside __init__(), so we do not keep references to them in the class instance. On the other hand, we do need to access the comboboxes and the toLabel (which displays the amount of the target currency), so we make these instance variables by using self.

Inst-
ance
vari-
ables
77 ☞

We add the same sorted list of currencies to both comboboxes, and we create a QDoubleSpinBox, a spinbox that handles floating-point values. We provide a minimum and maximum value for the spinbox, and also an initial value. It is good practice to always set a spinbox's range before setting its value, since if we set the value first and this happens to be outside the default range, the value will be reduced or increased to fit the default range.

Since both comboboxes will initially show the same currency and the initial value to convert is 1.00, the result shown in the toLabel must also be 1.00, so we set this explicitly.

```
grid = QGridLayout()
grid.addWidget(dateLabel, 0, 0)
grid.addWidget(self.fromComboBox, 1, 0)
grid.addWidget(self.fromSpinBox, 1, 1)
grid.addWidget(self.toComboBox, 2, 0)
grid.addWidget(self.toLabel, 2, 1)
self.setLayout(grid)
```

A grid layout seems to be the simplest solution to laying out the widgets. When we add a widget to a grid we give the row and column position it should occupy, both of which are 0-based. The layout is shown schematically in Figure 4.5. Much more can be done with grid layouts. For example, we can have spanning rows and columns; all of this is covered later, in Chapter 9.

dateLabel (0, 0)	
self.fromComboBox (1, 0)	self.fromSpinBox (1, 1)
self.toComboBox (2, 0)	self.toLabel (2, 1)

Figure 4.5 *The Currency application's grid layout*

If we look at the screenshot, or run the application, it is clear that column 0 of the grid layout is much wider than column 1. But there is nothing in the code that specifies this, so why does it happen? Layouts are smart enough to adapt to their environment, both to the space available and to the contents and size policies of the widgets they are managing. In this case, the comboboxes are stretched horizontally to be wide enough to show the widest currency text in full, and the spinbox is stretched horizontally to be wide enough to show its maximum value. Since comboboxes are the widest items in column 0, they effectively set that column's minimum width; and similarly for the spinbox in column 1. If we run the application and try to make the window narrower, nothing will happen because it is already at its minimum width. But we can make the window wider and both columns will stretch to occupy the extra space. It is, of course, possible to bias the layout so that it gives more horizontal space to, say, column 0, when extra space is available.

None of the widgets is initially stretched vertically because that is not necessary for any of them. But if we increase the window's height, all of the extra space will go to the dateLabel because that is the only widget on the form that likes to grow in every direction and has no other widgets to constrain it.

Now that we have created, populated, and laid out the widgets, it is time to set up the form's behavior.

```
self.connect(self.fromComboBox,
        SIGNAL("currentIndexChanged(int)"), self.updateUi)
self.connect(self.toComboBox,
        SIGNAL("currentIndexChanged(int)"), self.updateUi)
self.connect(self.fromSpinBox,
        SIGNAL("valueChanged(double)"), self.updateUi)
self.setWindowTitle("Currency")
```

If the user changes the current item in one of the comboboxes, the relevant combobox will emit a currentIndexChanged() signal with the index position of the new current item. Similarly, if the user changes the value held by the spinbox, a valueChanged() signal will be emitted with the new value. We have connected all these signals to just one Python slot: updateUi(). This does not have to be the case, as we will see in the next section, but it happens to be a sensible choice for this application.

And at the end of __init__() we set the window's title.

```
def updateUi(self):
    to = unicode(self.toComboBox.currentText())
    from_ = unicode(self.fromComboBox.currentText())
    amount = (self.rates[from_] / self.rates[to]) * \
            self.fromSpinBox.value()
    self.toLabel.setText("%0.2f" % amount)
```

This method is called in response to the currentIndexChanged() signal emitted by the comboboxes, and in response to the valueChanged() signal emitted by the spinbox. All the signals involved also pass a parameter. As we will see in the next section, we can ignore signal parameters, as we do here.

No matter which signal was involved, we go through the same process. We extract the "to" and "from" currencies, calculate the "to" amount, and set the toLabel's text accordingly. We have given the "from" text's variable the name from_ because from is a Python keyword and therefore not available to us. We had to escape a newline when calculating the amount to make the line narrow enough to fit on the page; and in any case, we prefer to limit line lengths to make it easier to read two files side by side on the screen.

```
def getdata(self): # Idea taken from the Python Cookbook
    self.rates = {}
    try:
        date = "Unknown"
        fh = urllib2.urlopen("http://www.bankofcanada.ca"
                             "/en/markets/csv/exchange_eng.csv")
        for line in fh:
            line = line.rstrip()
            if not line or line.startswith(("#", "Closing ")):
                continue
            fields = line.split(",")
            if line.startswith("Date "):
                date = fields[-1]
            else:
                try:
                    value = float(fields[-1])
                    self.rates[unicode(fields[0])] = value
                except ValueError:
                    pass
        return "Exchange Rates Date: " + date
    except Exception, e:
        return "Failed to download:\n%s" % e
```

This method is where we get the data that drives the application. We begin by creating a new instance attribute, self.rates. Unlike C++, Java, and similar languages, Python allows us to create instance attributes as and when we need them—for example, in the constructor, in the initializer, or in any other method. We can even add attributes to specific instances on the fly.

Since a lot can go wrong with network connections—for example, the network might be down, the host might be down, the URL may have changed, and so on, we need to make the application more robust than in the previous two examples. Another possible problem is that we may get an invalid floating-point value such as the "NA" (Not Available) that the currency data sometimes contains. We have an inner try ... except block that catches invalid numbers. So if we fail to convert a currency value to a floating-point number, we simply skip that particular currency and continue.

We handle every other possibility by wrapping almost the entire method in an outer try ... except block. (This is too general for most applications, but it seems acceptable for a tiny 70-line application.) If a problem occurs, we catch the exception raised and return it as a string to the caller, __init__(). The string that is returned by getdata() is shown in the dateLabel, so normally this label will show the date applicable to the exchange rates, but in an error situation it will show the error message instead.

Notice that we have split the URL string into two strings over two lines because it is so long—and we did not need to escape the newline. This works because the strings are within parentheses. If that wasn't the case, we would either have to escape the newline or concatenate them using + (and still escape the newline).

We initialize the date variable with a string indicating that we don't know what dates the rates were calculated. We then use the urllib2.urlopen() function to give us a file handle to the file we are interested in. The file handle can be used to read the entire file in one go using its read() method, but in this case we prefer to read line by line by using the file handle as an iterable.

Here is the data from the exchange_eng.csv file on one particular day. Some columns, and most rows, have been omitted; these are indicated by ellipses.

```
...
#
Date (<m>/<d>/<year>),01/05/2007,...,01/12/2007,01/15/2007
Closing Can/US Exchange Rate,1.1725,...,1.1688,1.1667
U.S. Dollar (Noon),1.1755,...,1.1702,1.1681
Argentina Peso (Floating Rate),0.3797,...,0.3773,0.3767
Australian Dollar,0.9164,...,0.9157,0.9153
...
Vietnamese Dong,0.000073,...,0.000073,0.000073
```

The exchange_eng.csv file's format uses several different kinds of lines. Comment lines begin with "#", and there may also be blank lines; we ignore all these. The exchange rates are listed by name, followed by rates, all comma-separated. The rates are those applying on particular dates, with the last one on each line being the most recent. We split each of these lines on commas and take the first item to be the currency name, and the last item to be the exchange rate. There is also a line that begins with "Date"; this lists the dates applying to each column. When we encounter this line we take the last date, since that is the one that corresponds with the exchange rates we are using. There is also a line that begins "Closing"; we ignore it.

For each exchange rate line we insert an item into the self.rates dictionary, using the currency's name for the key and the exchange rate as the value. We have assumed that the file's text is either 7-bit ASCII or Unicode; if it isn't one of these we may get an encoding error. If we knew the encoding, we could specify it as a second argument when we call unicode().

```
app = QApplication(sys.argv)
form = Form()
form.show()
app.exec_()
```

We have used exactly the same code as the previous example to create the QApplication object, instantiate the Currency application's form, and start off the event loop.

As for program termination, just like the previous example, because we have subclassed QDialog, if the user clicks the close X button or presses Esc, the window will close and then PyQt will terminate the application. In Chapter 6, we will see how to provide more explicit means of termination, and how to ensure that the user has the opportunity to save any unsaved changes and program settings.

By now it should be clear that using PyQt for GUI programming is straightforward. Although we will see more complex layouts later on, they are not intrinsically difficult, and because the layout managers are smart, in most cases they "just work". Naturally, there is a lot more to be covered—for example, creating main window-style applications, creating dialogs that the user can pop-up for interaction, and so on. But we will begin with something fundamental to PyQt, that so far we have glossed over: the signals and slots communication mechanism, which is the subject of the next section.

Signals and Slots

Every GUI library provides the details of events that take place, such as mouse clicks and key presses. For example, if we have a button with the text Click Me, and the user clicks it, all kinds of information becomes available. The GUI library can tell us the coordinates of the mouse click relative to the button, relative to the button's parent widget, and relative to the screen; it can tell us the state of the Shift, Ctrl, Alt, and NumLock keys at the time of the click; and the precise time of the click and of the release; and so on. Similar information can be provided if the user "clicked" the button without using the mouse. The user may have pressed the Tab key enough times to move the focus to the button and then pressed Spacebar, or maybe they pressed Alt+C. Although the outcome is the same in all these cases, each different means of clicking the button produces different events and different information.

The Qt library was the first to recognize that in almost every case, programmers don't need or even want all the low-level details: They don't care *how* the button was pressed, they just want to know *that* it was pressed so that they can respond appropriately. For this reason Qt, and therefore PyQt, provides two communication mechanisms: a low-level event-handling mechanism which is similar to those provided by all the other GUI libraries, and a high-level mechanism which Trolltech (makers of Qt) have called "signals and slots". We will look at the low-level mechanism in Chapter 10, and again in Chapter 11, but in this section we will focus on the high-level mechanism.

Every QObject—including all of PyQt's widgets since they derive from QWidget, a QObject subclass—supports the signals and slots mechanism. In particular, they are capable of announcing state changes, such as when a checkbox becomes checked or unchecked, and other important occurrences, for example when a button is clicked (by whatever means). All of PyQt's widgets have a set of predefined signals.

Whenever a signal is emitted, by default PyQt simply throws it away! To take notice of a signal we must connect it to a *slot*. In C++/Qt, slots are methods that must be declared with a special syntax; but in PyQt, they can be any callable we like (e.g., any function or method), and no special syntax is required when defining them.

Most widgets also have predefined slots, so in some cases we can connect a predefined signal to a predefined slot and not have to do anything else to get the behavior we want. PyQt is more versatile than C++/Qt in this regard, because we can connect not just to slots, but also to any callable, and from PyQt 4.2, it is possible to dynamically add "predefined" signals and slots to QObjects. Let's see how signals and slots works in practice with the Signals and Slots program shown in Figure 4.6.

Figure 4.6 *The Signals and Slots program*

Both the QDial and QSpinBox widgets have valueChanged() signals that, when emitted, carry the new value. And they both have setValue() slots that take an integer value. We can therefore connect these two widgets to each other so that whichever one the user changes, will cause the other to be changed correspondingly:

```
class Form(QDialog):

    def __init__(self, parent=None):
        super(Form, self).__init__(parent)

        dial = QDial()
        dial.setNotchesVisible(True)
        spinbox = QSpinBox()

        layout = QHBoxLayout()
        layout.addWidget(dial)
        layout.addWidget(spinbox)
        self.setLayout(layout)

        self.connect(dial, SIGNAL("valueChanged(int)"),
                     spinbox.setValue)
        self.connect(spinbox, SIGNAL("valueChanged(int)"),
                     dial.setValue)
```

```
self.setWindowTitle("Signals and Slots")
```

Since the two widgets are connected in this way, if the user moves the dial—say to value 20—the dial will emit a `valueChanged(20)` signal which will, in turn, cause a call to the spinbox's `setValue()` slot with 20 as the argument. But then, since its value has now been changed, the spinbox will emit a `valueChanged(20)` signal which will in turn cause a call to the dial's `setValue()` slot with 20 as the argument. So it looks like we will get an infinite loop. But what happens is that the `valueChanged()` signal is not emitted if the value is not actually changed. This is because the standard approach to writing value-changing slots is to begin by comparing the new value with the existing one. If the values are the same, we do nothing and return; otherwise, we apply the change and emit a signal to announce the change of state. The connections are depicted in Figure 4.7.

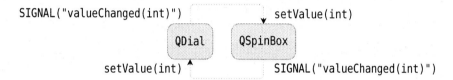

Figure 4.7 *The signals and slots connections*

Now let's look at the general syntax for connections. We assume that the PyQt modules have been imported using the `from ... import *` syntax, and that `s` and `w` are `QObjects`, normally widgets, with `s` usually being `self`.

```
s.connect(w, SIGNAL("signalSignature"), functionName)
s.connect(w, SIGNAL("signalSignature"), instance.methodName)
s.connect(w, SIGNAL("signalSignature"),
          instance, SLOT("slotSignature"))
```

The *signalSignature* is the name of the signal and a (possibly empty) comma-separated list of parameter type names in parentheses. If the signal is a Qt signal, the type names must be the C++ type names, such as `int` and `QString`. C++ type names can be rather complex, with each type name possibly including one or more of `const`, `*`, and `&`. When we write them as signal (or slot) signatures we can drop any `const`s and `&`s, but must keep any `*`s. For example, almost every Qt signal that passes a QString uses a parameter type of `const QString&`, but in PyQt, just using `QString` alone is sufficient. On the other hand, the `QListWidget` has a signal with the signature `itemActivated(QListWidgetItem*)`, and we must use this exactly as written.

PyQt signals are defined when they are actually emitted and can have any number of any type of parameters, as we will see shortly.

The *slotSignature* has the same form as a *signalSignature* except that the name is of a Qt slot. A slot may not have more arguments than the signal that is connected to it, but may have less; the additional parameters are then discarded. Corresponding signal and slot arguments must have the same types, so for example, we could not connect a QDial's valueChanged(int) signal to a QLineEdit's setText(QString) slot.

In our dial and spinbox example we used the *instance.methodName* syntax as we did with the example applications shown earlier in the chapter. But when the slot is actually a Qt slot rather than a Python method, it is more efficient to use the SLOT() syntax:

```
self.connect(dial, SIGNAL("valueChanged(int)"),
             spinbox, SLOT("setValue(int)"))
self.connect(spinbox, SIGNAL("valueChanged(int)"),
             dial, SLOT("setValue(int)"))
```

We have already seen that it is possible to connect multiple signals to the same slot. It is also possible to connect a single signal to multiple slots. Although rare, we can also connect a signal to another signal: In such cases, when the first signal is emitted, it will cause the signal it is connected to, to be emitted.

Connections are made using QObject.connect(); they can be broken using QObject.disconnect(). In practice, we rarely need to break connections ourselves since, for example, PyQt will automatically disconnect any connections involving an object that has been deleted.

So far we have seen how to connect to signals, and how to write slots—which are ordinary functions or methods. And we know that signals are emitted to signify state changes or other important occurrences. But what if we want to create a component that emits its own signals? This is easily achieved using QObject.emit(). For example, here is a complete QSpinBox subclass that emits its own custom atzero signal, and that also passes a number:

```
class ZeroSpinBox(QSpinBox):

    zeros = 0

    def __init__(self, parent=None):
        super(ZeroSpinBox, self).__init__(parent)
        self.connect(self, SIGNAL("valueChanged(int)"), self.checkzero)

    def checkzero(self):
        if self.value() == 0:
            self.zeros += 1
            self.emit(SIGNAL("atzero"), self.zeros)
```

We connect to the spinbox's own valueChanged() signal and have it call our checkzero() slot. If the value happens to be 0, the checkzero() slot emits the atzero signal, along with a count of how many times it has been zero; passing additional data like this is optional. The lack of parentheses for the signal is important: It tells PyQt that this is a "short-circuit" signal.

A signal with no arguments (and therefore no parentheses) is a short-circuit Python signal. When such a signal is emitted, any data can be passed as additional arguments to the `emit()` method, and they are passed as Python objects. This avoids the overhead of converting the arguments to and from C++ data types, and also means that arbitrary Python objects can be passed, even ones which cannot be converted to and from C++ data types. A signal with at least one argument is either a Qt signal or a non-short-circuit Python signal. In these cases, PyQt will check to see whether the signal is a Qt signal, and if it is not will assume that it is a Python signal. In either case, the arguments are converted to C++ data types.

Here is how we connect to the signal in the form's `__init__()` method:

```
zerospinbox = ZeroSpinBox()
...
self.connect(zerospinbox, SIGNAL("atzero"), self.announce)
```

Again, we must not use parentheses because it is a short-circuit signal. And for completeness, here is the slot it connects to in the form:

```
def announce(self, zeros):
    print "ZeroSpinBox has been at zero %d times" % zeros
```

If we use the `SIGNAL()` function with an identifier but no parentheses, we are specifying a short-circuit signal as described earlier. We can use this syntax both to emit short-circuit signals, and to connect to them. Both uses are shown in the example.

If we use the `SIGNAL()` function with a *signalSignature* (a possibly empty parenthesized list of comma-separated PyQt types), we are specifying either a Python or a Qt signal. (A Python signal is one that is emitted in Python code; a Qt signal is one emitted from an underlying C++ object.) We can use this syntax both to emit Python and Qt signals, and to connect to them. These signals can be connected to any callable, that is, to any function or method, including Qt slots; they can also be connected using the `SLOT()` syntax, with a *slotSignature*. PyQt checks to see whether the signal is a Qt signal, and if it is not it assumes it is a Python signal. If we use parentheses, even for Python signals, the arguments must be convertible to C++ data types.

We will now look at another example, a tiny custom non-GUI class that has a signal and a slot and which shows that the mechanism is not limited to GUI classes—any `QObject` subclass can use signals and slots.

```
class TaxRate(QObject):

    def __init__(self):
        super(TaxRate, self).__init__()
        self.__rate = 17.5
```

```
    def rate(self):
        return self.__rate

    def setRate(self, rate):
        if rate != self.__rate:
            self.__rate = rate
            self.emit(SIGNAL("rateChanged"), self.__rate)
```

Both the rate() and the setRate() methods can be connected to, since any Python callable can be used as a slot. If the rate is changed, we update the private __rate value and emit a custom rateChanged signal, giving the new rate as a parameter. We have also used the faster short-circuit syntax. If we wanted to use the standard syntax, the only difference would be that the signal would be written as SIGNAL("rateChanged(float)"). If we connect the rateChanged signal to the setRate() slot, because of the if statement, no infinite loop will occur. Let us look at the class in use. First we will declare a function to be called when the rate changes:

```
    def rateChanged(value):
        print "TaxRate changed to %.2f%%" % value
```

And now we will try it out:

```
    vat = TaxRate()
    vat.connect(vat, SIGNAL("rateChanged"), rateChanged)
    vat.setRate(17.5)    # No change will occur (new rate is the same)
    vat.setRate(8.5)     # A change will occur (new rate is different)
```

This will cause just one line to be output to the console: "TaxRate changed to 8.50%".

In earlier examples where we connected multiple signals to the same slot, we did not care who emitted the signal. But sometimes we want to connect two or more signals to the same slot, and have the slot behave differently depending on who called it. In this section's last example we will address this issue.

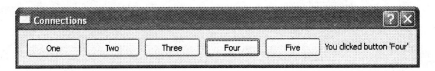

Figure 4.8 *The Connections program*

The Connections program shown in Figure 4.8, has five buttons and a label. When one of the buttons is clicked the signals and slots mechanism is used to update the label's text. Here is how the first button is created in the form's __init__() method:

```
        button1 = QPushButton("One")
```

All the other buttons are created in the same way, differing only in their variable name and the text that is passed to them.

We will start with the simplest connection, which is used by button1. Here is the __init__() method's connect() call:

```
self.connect(button1, SIGNAL("clicked()"), self.one)
```

We have used a dedicated method for this button:

```
def one(self):
    self.label.setText("You clicked button 'One'")
```

Connecting a button's clicked() signal to a single method that responds appropriately is probably the most common connection scenario.

But what if most of the processing was the same, with just some parameterization depending on which particular button was pressed? In such cases, it is usually best to connect each button to the same slot. There are two approaches to doing this. One is to use partial function application to wrap a slot with a parameter so that when the slot is invoked it is parameterized with the button that called it. The other is to ask PyQt to tell us which button called the slot. We will show both approaches, starting with partial function application.

Partial function application

63 ☜

Back on page 65 we created a wrapper function which used Python 2.5's functools.partial() function or our own simple partial() function:

```
import sys

if sys.version_info[:2] < (2, 5):
    def partial(func, arg):
        def callme():
            return func(arg)
        return callme
else:
    from functools import partial
```

Using partial() we can now wrap a slot and a button name together. So we might be tempted to do this:

```
self.connect(button2, SIGNAL("clicked()"),
                partial(self.anyButton, "Two")) # WRONG for PyQt 4.0-4.2
```

Unfortunately, this won't work for PyQt versions prior to 4.3. The wrapper function is created in the connect() call, but as soon as the connect() call completes, the wrapper goes out of scope and is garbage-collected. From PyQt 4.3, wrappers made with functools.partial() are treated specially when they are used for connections like this. This means that the function connected to will not be garbage-collected, so the code shown here will work correctly.

PyQt
4.3

For PyQt 4.0, 4.1, and 4.2, we can still use partial(): We just need to keep a reference to the wrapper—we will not use the reference except for the connect() call, but the fact that it is an attribute of the form instance will ensure that the wrapper function will not go out of scope while the form exists, and will therefore work. So the connection is actually made like this:

```
self.button2callback = partial(self.anyButton, "Two")
self.connect(button2, SIGNAL("clicked()"),
             self.button2callback)
```

When button2 is clicked, the anyButton() method will be called with a string parameter containing the text "Two". Here is what this method looks like:

```
def anyButton(self, who):
    self.label.setText("You clicked button '%s'" % who)
```

We could have used this slot for all the buttons using the partial() function that we have just shown. And in fact, we could avoid using partial() at all and get the same results:

```
self.button3callback = lambda who="Three": self.anyButton(who)
self.connect(button3, SIGNAL("clicked()"),
             self.button3callback)
```

Lambda functions

61 ☞

Here we've created a lambda function that is parameterized by the button's name. It works the same as the partial() technique, and calls the same anyButton() method, only with lambda being used to create the wrapper.

Both button2callback() and button3callback() call anyButton(); the only difference between them is that the first passes "Two" as its parameter and the second passes "Three".

PyQt 4.1.1

If we are using PyQt 4.1.1 or later, and we use lambda callbacks, we don't have to keep a reference to them ourselves. This is because PyQt treats lambda specially when used to create wrappers in a connection. (This is the same special treatment that is extended to functools.partial() in PyQt 4.3.) For this reason we can use lambda directly in connect() calls. For example:

```
self.connect(button3, SIGNAL("clicked()"),
             lambda who="Three": self.anyButton(who))
```

The wrapping technique works perfectly well, but there is an alternative approach that is slightly more involved, but which may be useful in some cases, particularly when we don't want to wrap our calls. This other technique is used to respond to button4 and to button5. Here are their connections:

```
self.connect(button4, SIGNAL("clicked()"), self.clicked)
self.connect(button5, SIGNAL("clicked()"), self.clicked)
```

Notice that we do not wrap the clicked() method that they are both connected to, so at first sight it looks like there is no way to tell which button called the clicked() method.* However, the implementation makes clear that we can distinguish if we want to:

```
def clicked(self):
    button = self.sender()
    if button is None or not isinstance(button, QPushButton):
        return
    self.label.setText("You clicked button '%s'" % button.text())
```

Inside a slot we can always call sender() to discover which QObject the invoking signal came from. (This could be None if the slot was called using a normal method call.) Although we know that we have connected only buttons to this slot, we still take care to check. We have used isinstance(), but we could have used hasattr(button, "text") instead. If we had connected all the buttons to this slot, it would have worked correctly for them all.

Some programmers don't like using sender() because they feel that it isn't good object-oriented style, so they tend to use partial function application when needs like this arise.

There is actually one other technique that can be used to get the effect of wrapping a function and a parameter. It makes use of the QSignalMapper class, and an example of its use is shown in Chapter 9.

QSig-
nal-
Mapper

☞ 297

It is possible in some situations for a slot to be called as the result of a signal, and the processing performed in the slot, directly or indirectly, causes the signal that originally called the slot to be called again, leading to an infinite cycle. Such cycles are rare in practice. Two factors help reduce the possibility of cycles. First, some signals are emitted only if a real change takes place. For example, if the value of a QSpinBox is changed by the user, or programmatically by a setValue() call, it emits its valueChanged() signal only if the new value is different from the current value. Second, some signals are emitted only as the result of user actions. For example, QLineEdit emits its textEdited() signal only when the text is changed by the user, and not when it is changed in code by a setText() call.

If a signal–slot cycle does seem to have occurred, naturally, the first thing to check is that the code's logic is correct: Are we actually doing the processing we thought we were? If the logic is right, and we still have a cycle, we might be able to break the cycle by changing the signals that we connect to—for example, replacing signals that are emitted as a result of programmatic changes, with those that are emitted only as a result of user interaction. If the problem persists, we could stop signals being emitted at certain places in our code using QObject.blockSignals(), which is inherited by all QWidget classes and is

---

* It is conventional PyQt programming style to give a slot the same name as the signal that connects to it.

passed a Boolean—True to stop the object emitting signals and False to resume signalling.

This completes our formal coverage of the signals and slots mechanism. We will see many more examples of signals and slots in practice in almost all the examples shown in the rest of the book. Most other GUI libraries have copied the mechanism in some form or other. This is because the signals and slots mechanism is very useful and powerful, and leaves programmers free to focus on the logic of their applications rather than having to concern themselves with the details of how the user invoked a particular operation.

Summary

In this chapter, we saw that it is possible to create hybrid console–GUI applications. This can actually be taken much further—for example, by including all the GUI code within the scope of an if block and executing it only if PyQt is installed. This would allow us to create a GUI application that could fall back to "console mode" if some of our users did not have PyQt.

We also saw that unlike conventional batch-processing programs, GUI applications have an event loop that runs continuously, checking for user events like mouse clicks and key presses, and system events like timers timing out or windows being revealed, and terminating only when requested to do so.

The Calculate application showed us a very simple but structurally typical dialog __init__() method. The widgets are created, laid out, and connected, and one or more other methods are used to respond to user interaction. The Currency application used the same approach, only with a more sophisticated interface, and more complex behavior and processing. The Currency application also showed that we can connect multiple signals to a single slot without formality.

PyQt's signals and slots mechanism allows us to handle user interaction at a much higher level of abstraction than the specific details of mouse clicks and key presses. It lets us focus on what users want to do rather than on how they asked to do it. All the PyQt widgets emit signals to announce state changes and other important occurrences; and most of the time we can ignore the signals. But for those signals that we are interested in, it is easy to use QObject.connect() to ensure that the function or method of our choice is called when the signal is emitted so that we can respond to it. Unlike C++/Qt, which must designate certain methods specially as slots, in PyQt we are free to use any callable, that is, any function or method, as a slot.

We also saw how to connect multiple signals to a single slot, and how to use partial function application or the sender() method so that the slot can respond appropriately depending on which widget signalled it.

We also learned that we do not have to formally declare our own custom signals: We can simply emit them using QObject.emit(), along with any additional parameters we want to pass.

Exercise

Write a dialog-style application that calculates compound interest. The application should be very similar in style and structure to the Currency application, and should look like this:

The amount should be automatically recalculated every time the user changes one of the variable factors, that is, the principle, rate, or years. The years combobox should have the texts "1 year", "2 years", "3 years", and so on, so the number of years will be the combobox's current index + 1. The compound interest formula in Python is amount = principal * ((1 + (rate / 100.0)) ** years). The QDoubleSpinBox class has setPrefix() and setSuffix() methods which can be used for the "$" and "%" symbols. The whole application can be written in around 60 lines.

Hint: The updating can be done by connecting suitable spinbox and combobox signals to an updateUi() slot where the calculations are performed and the amount label is updated.

A model answer is provided in the file chap04/interest.pyw.

5

● Dumb Dialogs
● Standard Dialogs
● Smart Dialogs

Dialogs

Almost every GUI application has at least one dialog, and the majority of GUI applications have one main window with dozens or scores of dialogs. Dialogs can be used to make announcements that are too important to put in the status bar or into a log file. In such cases, they typically just have a label for the text and an OK button for the user to press when they've read the message. Mostly, dialogs are used to ask users questions. Some are simple and need just a yes or no answer. Others ask users to make another kind of choice—for example, what file, folder, color, or font do they want to use. For all these, PyQt provides built-in dialogs.

Our focus in this chapter is on creating custom dialogs so that we can ask users for their requirements and preferences when none of the built-in dialogs is suitable.

One question that we do not address, concerns which widget is suitable for a particular purpose. For example, if we want a user to make a choice between three options, we might provide three radio buttons, or a three-item list widget or combobox. Or we might use a tri-state checkbox. And these are not the only possibilities. For those new to GUI programming, Appendix B provides screenshots and brief descriptions of selected PyQt widgets which may be helpful when making these decisions.

Qt is supplied with *Qt Designer*, a visual design tool that makes it easy to "draw" dialogs without having to write any code for creating and laying out their widgets. It can also be used to set up some of a dialog's behavior. We cover *Qt Designer* later, in Chapter 7. In this chapter we will create all the dialogs in code. Some developers make all their dialogs this way, and others prefer to use *Qt Designer*. This book shows both approaches so that you can decide which is best to use on a case-by-case basis.

One way to classify dialogs is by their "intelligence", where they may be "dumb", "standard", or "smart", depending on how much knowledge about the application's data is built into them. These classifications affect how we implement and instantiate (create instances of) dialogs, and for each one we have devoted a section of this chapter. Each of these sections begins with an explanation of what the classification means, and explains the pros and cons through a worked example.

In addition to an intelligence classification, dialogs can also be categorized by their *modality*. An *application modal* dialog is a dialog that, once invoked, is the only part of an application that the user can interact with. Until the user closes the dialog, they cannot use the rest of the application. The user is, of course, free to interact with other applications, for example, by clicking one to give it the focus.

A *window modal* dialog is one that works in a similar way to an application modal dialog, except that it only prevents interaction with its parent window, parent's parent window, and so on up to the top-level parent, as well as the parent windows' sibling windows. For applications that have a single top-level window there is no practical difference between application modality and window modality. When referring to a "modal" window without specifying which kind, window modality is assumed.

The opposite of a modal dialog is a *modeless* dialog. When a modeless dialog is invoked, the user can interact with the dialog, and with the rest of the application. This has implications for how we design our code, since it may be that the user can affect program state both in the main window and in the modeless dialog, which then has an effect on the other.

Another important aspect of writing dialogs is how we handle validation. Wherever possible we try to choose suitable widgets and set their properties to avoid having to write any validation code ourselves. For example, if we need an integer we could use a QSpinBox and use its setRange() method to constrain the range to the values that are acceptable to us. We call validation that applies to individual widgets "widget-level" validation; database programmers often call this "field-level" validation. Sometimes we need to go further than widget-level validation, particularly when there are interdependencies. For example, a theater booking system might have two comboboxes, one to select a floor and the other to select a seat row. If the ground floor had seat rows A–R, and the first floor had seat rows M–T, then clearly only some floor and seat row combinations are valid. For these cases, we must perform "form-level" validation; database programmers often call this "record-level" validation.

Another validation issue concerns when the validation takes place. Ideally we don't want users to be able to enter invalid data at all, but sometimes this can be quite tricky to prevent. We break validation into two broad categories: "post-mortem", which is validation that takes place at the point when the user wants to have their settings accepted, and "preventative", which takes place as the user manipulates editing widgets.

Since dialogs can have different levels of intelligence, three kinds of modality, and a variety of validation strategies, it would appear that there are many possible combinations to choose from. In practice, the combinations we use tend to be the same ones each time. For example, in most situations we might make dumb and standard dialogs modal and smart dialogs modeless. As for validation, the right strategy is very dependent on circumstances. We will see examples of the most common use cases in this chapter, and we will see further dialog examples throughout the rest of the book.

Dumb Dialogs

We define a "dumb" dialog to be a dialog whose widgets are set to their initial values by the dialog's caller, and whose final values are obtained directly from the widgets, again by the dialog's caller. A dumb dialog has no knowledge of what data its widgets are used to present and edit. We can apply some basic validation to a dumb dialog's widgets, but it is not common (or always possible) to set up validation that incorporates interdependencies between widgets; in other words, form-level validation is not usually done in dumb dialogs. Dumb dialogs are normally modal dialogs with an "accept" button (e.g., OK) and a "reject" button (e.g., Cancel).

The main advantages of using dumb dialogs are that we do not have to write any code to provide them with an API, nor any code for additional logic. Both of these benefits are a consequence of all their widgets being publically accessible. The main disadvantages are that the code that uses them is tied to their user interface (because we access the widgets directly), so we cannot easily implement complex validation—and they are much less convenient than a standard or smart dialog if needed in more than one place.

We will begin with a concrete example. Suppose we have a graphics application and we want to let the user set some pen properties—for example, the pen's width, style, and whether lines drawn with it should have beveled edges. Figure 5.1 shows what we want to achieve.

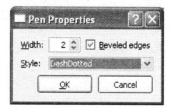

Figure 5.1 *The Pen Properties dialog*

In this case, we don't need "live" or interactive updating of the pen's properties, so a modal dialog is sufficient. And since the validation required is quite simple, we can use a dumb dialog in this situation.

We would use the dialog by popping it up modally in a slot that is connected to a menu option, toolbar button, or dialog button. If the user clicked OK, we would then update our pen properties; if they clicked Cancel, we would do nothing. Here is what the calling slot might look like:

```
def setPenProperties(self):
    dialog = PenPropertiesDlg(self)
    dialog.widthSpinBox.setValue(self.width)
    dialog.beveledCheckBox.setChecked(self.beveled)
    dialog.styleComboBox.setCurrentIndex(
            dialog.styleComboBox.findText(self.style))
    if dialog.exec_():
        self.width = dialog.widthSpinBox.value()
        self.beveled = dialog.beveledCheckBox.isChecked()
        self.style = unicode(dialog.styleComboBox.currentText())
        self.updateData()
```

We begin by creating a `PenPropertiesDlg` dialog—we will see the details of this shortly; all we need to know now is that it has a width spinbox, a beveled checkbox, and a style combobox. We pass a parent, `self` (the calling form) to the dialog, to take advantage of the fact that by default, PyQt centers a dialog over its parent, and also because dialogs that have a parent do not get a separate entry in the taskbar. We then access the widgets directly, setting their values to those held by the calling form. The `QComboBox.findText()` method returns the index position of the item with the matching text.

When we call `exec_()` on a dialog, the dialog is shown modally. This means that the dialog's parent windows and their sibling windows are blocked until the dialog is closed. Only when the user closes the dialog (either by "accepting" or by "rejecting" it) does the `exec_()` call return. The return value evaluates to `True` if the user accepted the dialog; otherwise, it evaluates to `False`. If the user accepted the dialog we know that they want their settings to take effect, so we read them out of the dialog's widgets and update our application's data. The `updateData()` call at the end is just one of our own custom methods that makes the application show the pen properties in the main window.

At the end of the `setPenProperties()` method the `PenPropertiesDlg` will go out of scope and will become a candidate for garbage collection. For this reason, we must always create a new dialog and populate its widgets whenever `setPenProperties()` is called. This approach saves memory, at the price of some speed overhead. For tiny dialogs like this, the overhead is too small for the user to notice, but later on we will show an alternative approach that avoids creating and destroying dialogs every time.

Using a dumb dialog means that the dialog is quite loosely coupled to the application. We could completely decouple it by making the labels accessible as instance variables. Then we could use the `PenPropertiesDlg` to edit any kind of data that required a spinbox, a checkbox, and a combobox, simply by changing the labels. For example, we could use it to record a weather reading with a "Temperature" spinbox, an "Is raining" checkbox, and a "Cloud cover" combobox.

Now that we have seen how we can use the dialog, let's look at the code that implements it. The PenPropertiesDlg has a single method, __init__(), which we will look at in parts.

```
class PenPropertiesDlg(QDialog):

    def __init__(self, parent=None):
        super(PenPropertiesDlg, self).__init__(parent)
```

Not surprisingly, our dialog is a QDialog subclass, and we initialize it in the way we have seen a few times already.

```
widthLabel = QLabel("&Width:")
self.widthSpinBox = QSpinBox()
widthLabel.setBuddy(self.widthSpinBox)
self.widthSpinBox.setAlignment(Qt.AlignRight|Qt.AlignVCenter)
self.widthSpinBox.setRange(0, 24)
self.beveledCheckBox = QCheckBox("&Beveled edges")
styleLabel = QLabel("&Style:")
self.styleComboBox = QComboBox()
styleLabel.setBuddy(self.styleComboBox)
self.styleComboBox.addItems(["Solid", "Dashed", "Dotted",
                             "DashDotted", "DashDotDotted"])
okButton = QPushButton("&OK")
cancelButton = QPushButton("Cancel")
```

For each editing widget, we also create a corresponding label so that the user can tell what they are editing. When we put an ampersand (&) in a label's text it can have two possible meanings. It can simply be a literal ampersand. Or it can signify that the ampersand should not be shown, but instead the letter following it should be underlined to show that it represents a keyboard accelerator. For example, in the case of the widthLabel, its text of "&Width:" will appear as <u>W</u>idth: and its accelerator will be Alt+W. On Mac OS X the default behavior is to ignore accelerators; for this reason, PyQt does not display the underlines on this platform.

What distinguishes between a literal ampersand and an accelerator ampersand is if the label has a "buddy": If it does, the ampersand signifies an accelerator. A buddy is a widget that PyQt will pass the keyboard focus to when the corresponding label's accelerator is pressed. So, when the user presses Alt+W, the keyboard focus will be switched to the widthSpinBox. This in turn means that if the user presses the up or down arrow keys or PageUp or PageDown, these will affect the widthSpinBox since it has the keyboard focus.

In the case of buttons, an underlined letter in the button's text is used to signify an accelerator. So in this case, the okButton's text, "&OK", appears as <u>O</u>K, and the user can press the button by clicking it with the mouse, by tabbing to it and pressing the spacebar, or by pressing Alt+O. It is not common to provide an accelerator for Cancel (or Close) buttons since these are normally connected to the dialog's reject() slot, and QDialog provides a keyboard shortcut for that, the Esc key.* Checkboxes and radio buttons are somewhat similar to buttons in that they have text that can have an accelerator. For example, the beveled checkbox has an underlined "B", so the user can toggle the checkbox's checked state by pressing Alt+B.

One disadvantage of creating buttons like this is that when we come to lay them out we will do so in one particular order. For example, we might put OK to the left of Cancel. But on some windowing systems this order is wrong. PyQt has a solution for this, covered in the Dialog Button Layout sidebar.

We have aligned the spinbox's number to the right, vertically centered, and set its valid range to be 0–24. In PyQt, a pen width (i.e., a line width) of 0 is allowed and signifies a 1-pixel-wide width regardless of any transformations. Pen widths of 1 and above are drawn at the given width, and respect any transformations, such as scaling, that are in force.

By using a spinbox and setting a range for it, we avoid the possibility of invalid pen widths that might have been entered had we used, for example, a line edit. Very often, simply choosing the right widget and setting its properties appropriately provides all the widget-level validation that is needed. This is also shown by our use of the beveled checkbox: Either the pen draws lines with beveled edges or it doesn't. And the same is true again with our use of a combobox of line styles—the user can choose only a valid style, that is, a style from a list that we have provided.

```
buttonLayout = QHBoxLayout()
buttonLayout.addStretch()
buttonLayout.addWidget(okButton)
buttonLayout.addWidget(cancelButton)
layout = QGridLayout()
layout.addWidget(widthLabel, 0, 0)
layout.addWidget(self.widthSpinBox, 0, 1)
layout.addWidget(self.beveledCheckBox, 0, 2)
layout.addWidget(styleLabel, 1, 0)
layout.addWidget(self.styleComboBox, 1, 1, 1, 2)
layout.addLayout(buttonLayout, 2, 0, 1, 3)
self.setLayout(layout)
```

We have used two layouts, one nested inside the other, to get the layout we want. We begin by laying out the buttons horizontally, beginning with a "stretch". The stretch will consume as much space as possible, which has the effect of pushing the two buttons as far to the right as they can go, and still fit.

---

*We use the terms "keyboard accelerator" and "accelerator" for the Alt+*Letter* key sequences that can be used to click buttons and switch focus in dialogs, and to pop up menus. We use the term "keyboard shortcut" for any other kind of key sequence—for example, the key sequence Ctrl+S, which is often used to save files. We will see how to create keyboard shortcuts in Chapter 6.

Dialog Button Layout

In some of our early examples, we have put the buttons on the right of the dialogs, with the OK button first and then the Cancel button next. This is the most common layout on Windows, but it is not always correct. For example, for Mac OS X or for the GNOME desktop environment, they should be swapped.

If we want our applications to have the most native look and feel possible and expect to deploy them on different platforms, issues like button ordering and positioning will matter to us. Qt 4.2 (PyQt 4.1) provides a solution for this particular problem: the QDialogButtonBox class.

Instead of creating OK and Cancel buttons directly, we create a QDialogButtonBox. For example:

```
buttonBox = QDialogButtonBox(QDialogButtonBox.Ok|
                             QDialogButtonBox.Cancel)
```

To make a button the "default" button, that is, the one that is pressed when the user presses Enter (assuming that the widget with keyboard focus does not handle Enter key presses itself), we can do this:

```
buttonBox.button(QDialogButtonBox.Ok).setDefault(True)
```

Since a button box is a single widget (although it contains other widgets), we can add it directly to the dialog's existing layout, rather than putting it in its own layout and nesting that inside the dialog's layout. Here is what we would do in the PenPropertiesDlg example's grid layout:

```
layout.addWidget(buttonBox, 3, 0, 1, 3)
```

And instead of connecting from the buttons' clicked() signals, we can make connections from the button box, which has its own signals that correspond to user actions:

```
self.connect(buttonBox, SIGNAL("accepted()"),
             self, SLOT("accept()"))
self.connect(buttonBox, SIGNAL("rejected()"),
             self, SLOT("reject()"))
```

We are still free to connect to individual buttons' clicked() signals, though, and often do so for dialogs that have many buttons.

The QDialogButtonBox defaults to using a horizontal layout, but can be set to use a vertical layout by passing Qt.Vertical to its constructor, or by calling setOrientation().

We use QDialogButtonBox for most of the examples, but it could always be replaced by individual QPushButtons if backward compatibility was an issue.

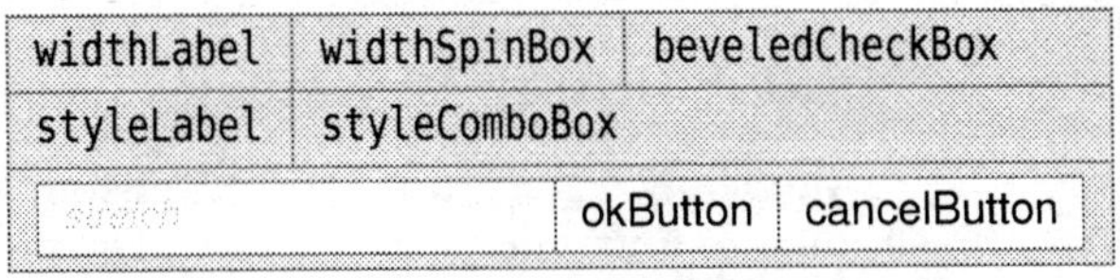

widthLabel	widthSpinBox	beveledCheckBox	
styleLabel	styleComboBox		
stretch		okButton	cancelButton

Figure 5.2 *The Pen Properties dialog's layout*

The width label, width spinbox, and bevel checkbox are laid out side by side in three columns using a grid layout. The style label and style combobox are put on the next row, with the style combobox set to span two columns. The arguments to the QGridLayout.addWidget() method are the widget, the row, the column, and then optionally, the number of rows to span, followed by the number of columns to span. We add the button layout as a third row to the grid layout, having it span all three columns. Finally, we set the layout on the dialog. The layout is shown schematically in Figure 5.2; the grid layout is shown shaded.

```
self.connect(okButton, SIGNAL("clicked()"),
             self, SLOT("accept()"))
self.connect(cancelButton, SIGNAL("clicked()"),
             self, SLOT("reject()"))
self.setWindowTitle("Pen Properties")
```

At the end of __init__() we make the necessary connections. We connect the OK button's clicked() signal to the dialog's accept() slot: This slot will

Table 5.1 *Selected Layout Methods*

Syntax	Description
b.addLayout(l)	Adds QLayout l to QBoxLayout b, which is normally a QHBoxLayout or a QVBoxLayout
b.addSpacing(i)	Adds a QSpacerItem of fixed size int i to layout b
b.addStretch(i)	Adds a QSpacerItem with minimum size 0 and a stretch factor of int i to layout b
b.addWidget(w)	Adds QWidget w to layout b
b.setStretchFactor(x, i)	Sets the stretch factor of layout b's layout or widget x to int i
g.addLayout(l, r, c)	Adds QLayout l to QGridLayout g at row int r and column int c; additional row span and column span arguments can be given
g.addWidget(w, r, c)	Adds QWidget w to QGridLayout g at row int r and column int c; additional row span and column span arguments can be given
g.setRowStretch(r, i)	Sets QGridLayout g's row r's stretch to int i
g.setColumnStretch(c, i)	Sets QGridLayout g's column c's stretch to int i

close the dialog and return a `True` value. The `Cancel` button is connected in a corresponding way. Finally, we set the window's title.

For small dumb dialogs that are only ever called from one place, it is possible to avoid creating a dialog class at all. Instead, we can simply create all the widgets in the invoking method, lay them out, connect them, and call `exec_()`. If `exec_()` returns `True`, we can then extract the values from the widgets and we are done. The file `chap05/pen.pyw` contains the Pen Properties dialog and a dummy program with two buttons, one to invoke the `PenPropertiesDlg` we have just reviewed and another that does everything inline. Creating dialogs inline is not an approach that we would recommend, so we will not review the code for doing it, but it is mentioned and provided in the example's `setPenInline()` method for completeness.

Dumb dialogs are easy to understand and use, but setting and getting values using a dialog's widgets is not recommended except for the very simplest dialogs, where only one, two, or at most, a few values are involved. We have shown them primarily as a gentle introduction to dialogs, since creating, laying out, and connecting the widgets is the same in any kind of dialog. In the next section, we will look at standard dialogs, both modal and modeless ones.

Standard Dialogs

We consider a dialog to be a "standard" dialog if it initializes its widgets in accordance with the values set through its initializer or through its methods, and whose final values are obtained by method calls or from instance variables—not directly from the dialog's widgets. A standard dialog can have both widget-level and form-level validation. Standard dialogs are either modal, with "accept" and "reject" buttons, or (less commonly) modeless, in which case they have "apply" and "close" buttons and notify state changes through signal and slot connections.

One key advantage of standard dialogs is that the caller does not need to know about their implementation, only how to set the initial values, and how to get the resultant values if the user clicked OK. Another advantage, at least for modal standard dialogs, is that the user cannot interact with the dialog's parent windows and their sibling windows, so the relevant parts of the application's state will probably not change behind the dialog's back. The main drawback of using a standard dialog is most apparent when it must handle lots of different data items, since all the items must be fed into the dialog and the results retrieved on each invocation, and this may involve many lines of code.

As with the previous section, we will explain by means of an example. In this case, the example will be used both in this section and in the next section so that we can see the different approaches and trade-offs between standard and smart dialogs more clearly.

Let us imagine that we have an application that needs to display a table of floating-point numbers, and that we want to give users some control over the format of the numbers. One way to achieve this is to provide a menu option, toolbar button, or keyboard shortcut that will invoke a modal dialog which the user can interact with to set their formatting preferences. Figure 5.3 shows a number format dialog that has been popped up over a table of numbers.

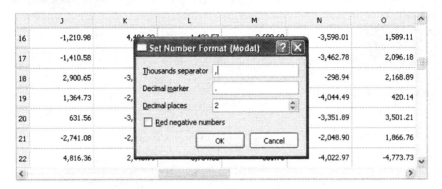

Figure 5.3 *The modal Set Number Format dialog in context*

The data that we want the dialog to make available to the user is held in a dictionary in the main form. Here is how the dictionary is initialized:

```
self.format = dict(thousandsseparator=",",
                   decimalmarker=".", decimalplaces=2,
                   rednegatives=False)
```

Using a dictionary like this is very convenient, and makes it easy to add additional items.

We have put the dialog in its own file, numberformatdlg1.py, which the application, numbers.pyw, imports. The number "1" in the filename distinguishes it from the other two versions of the dialog covered in the next section.

Modal OK/Cancel-Style Dialogs

Let us begin by seeing how the dialog is used; we assume that the setNumber-Format1() method is called in response to some user action.

```
def setNumberFormat1(self):
    dialog = numberformatdlg1.NumberFormatDlg(self.format, self)
    if dialog.exec_():
        self.format = dialog.numberFormat()
        self.refreshTable()
```

We start by creating the dialog and passing it the format dictionary from which the dialog will initialize itself, and `self` so that the dialog is tied to the calling form—centered over it and not having its own taskbar entry.

As we mentioned earlier, calling `exec_()` pops up the dialog it is called on as a modal dialog, so the user must either accept or reject the dialog before they can interact with the dialog's parents and their siblings. In the next section, we will use modeless versions of the dialog that don't impose this restriction.

If the user clicks OK, we set the format dictionary to have the values set in the dialog, and update the table so that the numbers are displayed with the new format. If the user cancels, we do nothing. At the end of the method, the dialog goes out of scope and is therefore scheduled for garbage collection.

To save space, and to avoid needless repetition, from now on we will not show any `import` statements, unless their presence is not obvious. So, for example, we will no longer show `from PyQt4.QtCore import *` or the `PyQt4.QtGui` import.

We are now ready to see the implementation of the dialog itself.

```
class NumberFormatDlg(QDialog):

    def __init__(self, format, parent=None):
        super(NumberFormatDlg, self).__init__(parent)
```

The `__init__()` method begins in the same way as all the other dialogs we have seen so far.

```
        thousandsLabel = QLabel("&Thousands separator")
        self.thousandsEdit = QLineEdit(format["thousandsseparator"])
        thousandsLabel.setBuddy(self.thousandsEdit)
        decimalMarkerLabel = QLabel("Decimal &marker")
        self.decimalMarkerEdit = QLineEdit(format["decimalmarker"])
        decimalMarkerLabel.setBuddy(self.decimalMarkerEdit)
        decimalPlacesLabel = QLabel("&Decimal places")
        self.decimalPlacesSpinBox = QSpinBox()
        decimalPlacesLabel.setBuddy(self.decimalPlacesSpinBox)
        self.decimalPlacesSpinBox.setRange(0, 6)
        self.decimalPlacesSpinBox.setValue(format["decimalplaces"])
        self.redNegativesCheckBox = QCheckBox("&Red negative numbers")
        self.redNegativesCheckBox.setChecked(format["rednegatives"])

        buttonBox = QDialogButtonBox(QDialogButtonBox.Ok|
                                     QDialogButtonBox.Cancel)
```

For each aspect of the format that we want the user to be able to change we create a label so that they know what they are editing, and a suitable editing widget. Since the `format` argument is mandatory, we assume that it has all the values we need, so we use it to initialize the editing widgets. We also use `setBuddy()` calls to support keyboard users since not all users are able to use the mouse.

Buddies
143 ☜

Table 5.2 *Selected QDialogButtonBox Methods and Signals*

Syntax	Description
d.addButton(b, r)	Adds QPushButton b, with QDialogButtonBox.ButtonRole r, to QDialogButtonBox d
d.addButton(t, r)	Adds a QPushButton with text t and with button role r to QDialogButtonBox d, and returns the added button
d.addButton(s)	Adds a QPushButton, specified as QDialogButtonBox.StandardButton s, to QDialogButtonBox d and returns the added button
d.setOrientation(o)	Sets the QDialogButtonBox's orientation to Qt.Orientation o (vertical or horizontal)
d.button(s)	Returns the QDialogButtonBox's QPushButton specified as StandardButton s, or None if there isn't one
d.accepted()	This signal is emitted if a button with the QDialogButtonBox.Accept role is clicked
d.rejected()	This signal is emitted if a button with the QDialogButtonBox.Reject role is clicked

The only validation we have put in place is to limit the range of the decimal places spinbox. We have chosen to do "post-mortem" validation, that is, to validate *after* the user has entered values, at the point where they click OK to accept their edits. In the next section, we will see "preventative" validation, which prevents invalid edits in the first place.

```
self.format = format.copy()
```

We need to take a *copy* of the format dictionary that was passed in, since we want to be able to change the dictionary inside the dialog without affecting the original dictionary.

```
grid = QGridLayout()
grid.addWidget(thousandsLabel, 0, 0)
grid.addWidget(self.thousandsEdit, 0, 1)
grid.addWidget(decimalMarkerLabel, 1, 0)
grid.addWidget(self.decimalMarkerEdit, 1, 1)
grid.addWidget(decimalPlacesLabel, 2, 0)
grid.addWidget(self.decimalPlacesSpinBox, 2, 1)
grid.addWidget(self.redNegativesCheckBox, 3, 0, 1, 2)
grid.addWidget(buttonBox, 4, 0, 1, 2)
self.setLayout(grid)
```

The layout is very similar in appearance to the one we used for the Pen Properties dialog, except that this time we have a QDialogButtonBox widget rather than a layout for the buttons. This makes it possible to create the entire layout using a single QGridLayout.

thousandsLabel	self.thousandsEdit	
decimalMarkerLabel	self.decimalMarkerEdit	
decimalPlacesLabel	self.decimalPlacesSpinBox	
self.redNegativesCheckBox		
	okButton	cancelButton

Figure 5.4 *The Set Number Format dialog's layout*

Both the "red negatives" checkbox and the button box are laid out so that they each span one row and two columns. Row and column spans are specified by the last two arguments to the QGridLayout's addWidget() and addLayout() methods. The layout is shown in Figure 5.4, with the grid shown shaded.

```
self.connect(buttonBox, SIGNAL("accepted()"),
             self, SLOT("accept()"))
self.connect(buttonBox, SIGNAL("rejected()"),
             self, SLOT("reject()"))
self.setWindowTitle("Set Number Format (Modal)")
```

The code for making the connections and setting the window's title is similar to what we used for the Pen Properties dialog, only this time we use the button box's signals rather than connecting directly to the buttons themselves.

```
def numberFormat(self):
    return self.format
```

If the user clicks OK, the dialog is accepted and returns a True value. In this case, the calling form's method overwrites its format dictionary with the dialog's dictionary, by calling the numberFormat() method. Since we have not made the dialog's self.format attribute very private (i.e., by calling it __format), we could have accessed it from outside the form directly; we will take that approach in a later example.

When the user clicks OK, because we are using post-mortem validation, it is possible that some of the editing widgets contain invalid data. To handle this, we reimplement QDialog.accept() and do our validation there. Because the method is quite long, we will look at it in parts.

```
def accept(self):
    class ThousandsError(Exception): pass
    class DecimalError(Exception): pass
    Punctuation = frozenset(" ,;:.")
```

We begin by creating two exception classes that we will use inside the accept() method. These will help to keep our code cleaner and shorter than would otherwise be possible. We also create a set of the characters that we will allow to be used as thousands separators and decimal place markers.

The only editing widgets we are concerned with validating are the two line edits. This is because the decimal places spinbox is already limited to a valid range, and because the "red negatives" checkbox can only be checked or unchecked, both of which are valid.

```python
thousands = unicode(self.thousandsEdit.text())
decimal = unicode(self.decimalMarkerEdit.text())
try:
    if len(decimal) == 0:
        raise DecimalError, ("The decimal marker may not be "
                             "empty.")
    if len(thousands) > 1:
        raise ThousandsError, ("The thousands separator may "
                               "only be empty or one character.")
    if len(decimal) > 1:
        raise DecimalError, ("The decimal marker must be "
                             "one character.")
    if thousands == decimal:
        raise ThousandsError, ("The thousands separator and "
                               "the decimal marker must be different.")
    if thousands and thousands not in Punctuation:
        raise ThousandsError, ("The thousands separator must "
                               "be a punctuation symbol.")
    if decimal not in Punctuation:
        raise DecimalError, ("The decimal marker must be a "
                             "punctuation symbol.")
except ThousandsError, e:
    QMessageBox.warning(self, "Thousands Separator Error",
                        unicode(e))
    self.thousandsEdit.selectAll()
    self.thousandsEdit.setFocus()
    return
except DecimalError, e:
    QMessageBox.warning(self, "Decimal Marker Error",
                        unicode(e))
    self.decimalMarkerEdit.selectAll()
    self.decimalMarkerEdit.setFocus()
    return
```

We begin by getting the text from the two line edits. Although it is acceptable to have no thousands separator, a decimal marker must be present, so we begin by checking that the decimalMarkerEdit has at least one character. If it doesn't, we raise our custom DecimalError with suitable error text. We also raise exceptions if either of the texts is longer than one character, or if they are the same character, or if either contains a character that is not in our Punctuation set. The if statements differ regarding punctuation because the thousands separator is allowed to be empty, but the decimal place marker is not.

Figure 5.5 *A QMessageBox warning*

We have used parentheses around the error strings that are in two parts to turn them into single expressions; an alternative syntax would have been to drop the parentheses, and instead concatenate the two parts and escape the newline.

Depending on whether we get a ThousandsError or a DecimalError, we display a "warning" message box with appropriate error text, as illustrated in Figure 5.5. We must convert the exception object e to be a string (we have used unicode() to do this) so that it is suitable as an argument to the QMessageBox's static warning() method. We will make more use of the QMessageBox static methods, including the use of additional arguments, both in this chapter and throughout the book.

QMess-
ageBox
sidebar

☞ 188

Once the user has acknowledged the error message by closing the message box, we select the text in the invalid line edit and give the focus to the line edit, ready for the user to make their correction. Then we return—so the dialog is not accepted and the user must either fix the problem or click Cancel to close the dialog and abandon their changes.

```
self.format["thousandsseparator"] = thousands
self.format["decimalmarker"] = decimal
self.format["decimalplaces"] = \
        self.decimalPlacesSpinBox.value()
self.format["rednegatives"] = \
        self.redNegativesCheckBox.isChecked()
QDialog.accept(self)
```

If no exception is raised, neither of the return statements is executed and execution falls through to this final part of the accept() method. Here we update the dialog's format dictionary with the values from the editing widgets, and call the base class's accept() method. The form will be closed (i.e., hidden) and a True value returned from the exec_() statement. As we saw earlier, the caller, on receiving a True value from exec_(), goes on to retrieve the dialog's format using the numberFormat() method.

Why didn't we use super() to call the base class's accept() at the end instead of naming QDialog explicitly? The short answer is that using super() in this context won't work. PyQt tries to be as efficient as possible by using lazy attribute lookup, but the result is that super() does not work as we would expect in PyQt subclasses. (For an explanation, see the PyQt `pyqt4ref.html` documentation, under "super and PyQt classes".)

Although the dialog is hidden only when it is accepted (or rejected), once it goes out of scope, that is, at the end of the caller's `setNumberFormat1()` method, the dialog is scheduled for garbage collection.

Creating modal dialogs like this one is usually straightforward. The only complications involved concern whether we have layouts and validation that require some care to get right, as we do here.

In some cases the user will want to be able to see the results of their choices, perhaps changing their choices a few times until they are satisfied. For these situations modal dialogs can be inconvenient since the user must invoke the dialog, perform their edits, accept, see the results, and then repeat the cycle until they are happy. If the dialog was modeless and was able to update the application's state without being closed, the user could simply invoke the dialog once, perform their edits, see the effects, and then do more edits, and so on: a much faster cycle. We will see how to achieve this in the next section; we will also look at a much simpler and more active validation strategy—preventative validation.

Smart Dialogs

We define a "smart" dialog to be one that initializes its widgets in accordance with data references or data structures that are passed to its initializer, and which is capable of updating the data directly in response to user interaction. Smart dialogs can have both widget-level and form-level validation. Smart dialogs are usually modeless, with "apply" and "close" buttons, although they can also be "live", in which case they may have no buttons, with changes to widgets reflected directly into the data they have access to. Smart modeless

Table 5.3 *Selected QDialog Methods*

Syntax	Description
`d.accept()`	Closes (hides) QDialog d, stops its event loop, and causes `exec_()` to return with a `True` value. The dialog is deleted if `Qt.WA_DeleteOnClose` is set
`d.reject()`	Closes (hides) QDialog d, stops its event loop, and causes `exec_()` to return with a `False` value
`d.done(i)`	Closes (hides) QDialog d, stops its event loop, and causes `exec_()` to return int i
`d.exec_()`	Shows QDialog d modally, blocking until it is closed
`d.show()`	Shows QDialog d modelessly; inherited from QWidget
`d.setSizeGrip-Enabled(b)`	Shows or hides QDialog d's size grip depending on `bool b`

dialogs that have "apply" buttons notify state changes through signal and slot connections.

The main benefit of using a smart modeless dialog is seen at the point of use. When the dialog is created, it is given references to the calling form's data structures so that the dialog can update the data structures directly with no further code required at the call point. The downsides are that the dialog must have knowledge of the calling form's data structures so that it correctly reflects the data values into its widgets and only applies changes that are valid, and that, being modeless, there is a risk of the data the dialog depends on being changed from under it if the user interacts with some other part of the application.

In this section we are going to continue with the theme of number format dialogs so that we can compare the various approaches.

Modeless Apply/Close-Style Dialogs

If we want our users to be able to repeatedly change the number format and see the results, it will be much more convenient for them if they could do so without having to keep invoking and accepting the number format dialog. The solution is to use a modeless dialog which allows them to interact with the number format widgets and to apply their changes and to see the effect, as often as they like. Dialogs like this usually have an Apply button and a Close button. Unlike a modal OK/Cancel-style dialog, which can be canceled, leaving everything as it was before, once Apply has been clicked the user cannot revert their changes. Of course we could provide a Revert button or a Defaults button, but this would require more work.

Superficially, the only difference between the modeless and the modal versions of the dialog is the button text. However, there are two other important differences: The calling form's method creates and invokes the dialog differently, and the dialog must make sure it is deleted, not just hidden, when it is closed. Let us begin by looking at how the dialog is invoked.

```
def setNumberFormat2(self):
    dialog = numberformatdlg2.NumberFormatDlg(self.format, self)
    self.connect(dialog, SIGNAL("changed"), self.refreshTable)
    dialog.show()
```

We create the dialog in the same way we created the modal version earlier; it is shown in Figure 5.6. We then connect the dialog's changed Python signal to the calling form's refreshTable() method, and then we just call show() on the dialog. When we call show(), the dialog is popped up as a modeless dialog. Application execution continues concurrently with the dialog, and the user can interact with both the dialog and other windows in the application.

Whenever the dialog emits its changed signal, the main form's refreshTable() method is called, and this will reformat all the numbers in the table using

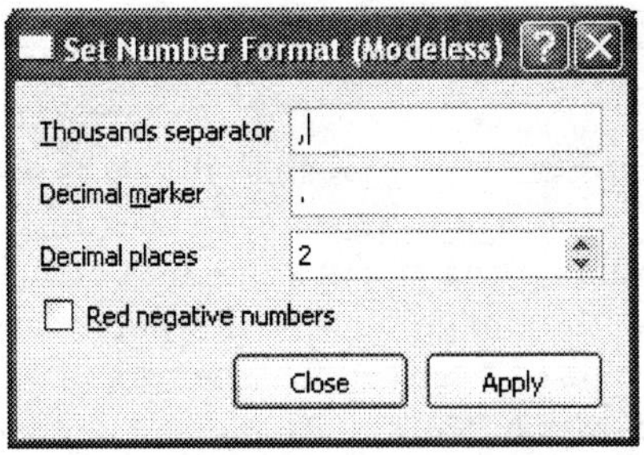

Figure 5.6 *The modeless Set Number Format dialog*

the format dictionary's settings. We can imagine that this means that when the user clicks the Apply button the format dictionary will be updated and the changed signal emitted. We will see shortly that this is indeed what happens.

Although the dialog variable goes out of scope, PyQt is smart enough to keep a reference to modeless dialogs, so the dialog continues to exist. But when the user clicks Close, the dialog would normally only be hidden, so if the user invoked the dialog again and again, more and more memory would be needlessly consumed, as more dialogs would be created but none deleted. One solution to this is to make sure that the dialog is deleted, rather than hidden, when it is closed. (We will see another solution when we look at a "live" dialog, shortly.)

We shall start with the dialog's __init__() method.

```
def __init__(self, format, parent=None):
    super(NumberFormatDlg, self).__init__(parent)
    self.setAttribute(Qt.WA_DeleteOnClose)
```

After calling super(), we call setAttribute() to make sure that when the dialog is closed it will be deleted rather than merely hidden.

```
punctuationRe = QRegExp(r"[ ,;:.]")

thousandsLabel = QLabel("&Thousands separator")
self.thousandsEdit = QLineEdit(format["thousandsseparator"])
thousandsLabel.setBuddy(self.thousandsEdit)
self.thousandsEdit.setMaxLength(1)
self.thousandsEdit.setValidator(
        QRegExpValidator(punctuationRe, self))

decimalMarkerLabel = QLabel("Decimal &marker")
self.decimalMarkerEdit = QLineEdit(format["decimalmarker"])
decimalMarkerLabel.setBuddy(self.decimalMarkerEdit)
self.decimalMarkerEdit.setMaxLength(1)
self.decimalMarkerEdit.setValidator(
        QRegExpValidator(punctuationRe, self))
self.decimalMarkerEdit.setInputMask("X")
```

```
decimalPlacesLabel = QLabel("&Decimal places")
self.decimalPlacesSpinBox = QSpinBox()
decimalPlacesLabel.setBuddy(self.decimalPlacesSpinBox)
self.decimalPlacesSpinBox.setRange(0, 6)
self.decimalPlacesSpinBox.setValue(format["decimalplaces"])

self.redNegativesCheckBox = QCheckBox("&Red negative numbers")
self.redNegativesCheckBox.setChecked(format["rednegatives"])

buttonBox = QDialogButtonBox(QDialogButtonBox.Apply|
                             QDialogButtonBox.Close)
```

The creation of the form's widgets is very similar to what we did before, but this time we are using preventative validation almost exclusively. We set a one-character maximum length on the thousands separator and decimal marker line edits, and in both cases we also set a QRegExpValidator. A validator will only allow the user to enter valid characters, and in the case of a regular expression validator, only characters that match the regular expression.[*] PyQt uses a regular expression syntax that is essentially a subset of the syntax offered by Python's re module.

The QRegExpValidator's initializer requires both a regular expression and a parent, which is why we have passed self in addition to the regular expression.

In this case, we have set the validation regular expression to be "[,;:.]". This is a *character class* and means that the only characters that are valid are those contained in the square brackets, that is, space, comma, semicolon, colon, and period. Notice that the regular expression string is preceded by "r". This signifies a "raw" string and means that (almost) all of the characters inside the string are to be taken as literals. This considerably reduces the need to escape regular expression special characters such as "\", although here it does not matter. Nonetheless, we always use "r" with regular expression strings as a matter of good practice.

Although we are happy to accept an empty thousands separator, we require a decimal marker. For this reason we have used an input mask. A mask of "X" says that one character of any kind is *required*—we don't have to concern ourselves with what the character will be because the regular expression validator will ensure that it is valid. Format masks are explained in the QLineEdit.inputMask property's documentation.[o]

The only other difference to the way we created the widgets in the modal version of the dialog is that we create Apply and Close buttons rather than OK and Cancel buttons.

---

[*] The QRegExp documentation provides a brief introduction to regular expressions. For in-depth coverage, see *Mastering Regular Expressions* by Jeffrey E. Friedl.

[o] Every PyQt QObject and QWidget has "properties". These are similar in principle to Python properties, except that they can be accessed using the property() and setProperty() methods.

```
self.format = format
```

In the modal dialog we took a copy of the caller's format dictionary; here we take a reference to it, so that we can change it directly from within the dialog.

We will not show the dialog's layout since it is identical to the layout used in the modal dialog shown earlier.

```
self.connect(buttonBox.button(QDialogButtonBox.Apply),
             SIGNAL("clicked()"), self.apply)
self.connect(buttonBox, SIGNAL("rejected()"),
             self, SLOT("reject()"))
self.setWindowTitle("Set Number Format (Modeless)")
```

We create two signal–slot connections. The first one is between the Apply button's clicked() signal and the apply() method. To make this connection, we must retrieve a reference to the button from the button box using its button() method, passing the same argument, QDialogButtonBox.Apply, that we used to create the button in the first place.

The connection to reject() will cause the dialog to close, and because of the Qt.WA_DeleteOnClose attribute, the dialog will be deleted rather than hidden. There is no connection to the dialog's accept() slot, so the only way to get rid of the dialog is to close it. If the user clicks the Apply button, the apply() slot, shown next, will be called. Naturally, we also set a window title.

The final method in this class is apply(), which we will review in two parts.

```
def apply(self):
    thousands = unicode(self.thousandsEdit.text())
    decimal = unicode(self.decimalMarkerEdit.text())
    if thousands == decimal:
        QMessageBox.warning(self, "Format Error",
                "The thousands separator and the decimal marker "
                "must be different.")
        self.thousandsEdit.selectAll()
        self.thousandsEdit.setFocus()
        return
    if len(decimal) == 0:
        QMessageBox.warning(self, "Format Error",
                            "The decimal marker may not be empty.")
        self.decimalMarkerEdit.selectAll()
        self.decimalMarkerEdit.setFocus()
        return
```

Form-level validation is normally necessary when two or more widgets' values are interdependent. In this example, we do not want to allow the thousands separator to be the same as the decimal place marker, so we check for this situation in the apply() method, and if it has occurred we notify the user, put the focus in the thousands separator line edit, and return without applying the user's edits.

We could have avoided this by connecting both line edits' textEdited() signals to a "check and fix" slot—we will do this in the next example.

We must also check that the decimal marker isn't empty. Although the decimal place marker's line edit regular expression validator wants a single character, it allows the line edit to be empty. This is because an empty string is a valid prefix for a string that has a valid character. After all, the line edit may have been empty when the user switched the focus into it.

```
self.format["thousandsseparator"] = thousands
self.format["decimalmarker"] = decimal
self.format["decimalplaces"] = \
        self.decimalPlacesSpinBox.value()
self.format["rednegatives"] = \
        self.redNegativesCheckBox.isChecked()
self.emit(SIGNAL("changed"))
```

If there are no validation problems, neither of the return statements is executed and we fall through to the end of the accept() slot. Here we update the format dictionary. The self.format variable is a reference to the caller's format dictionary, so the changes are applied directly to the caller's data structure. Finally, we emit a changed signal, and as we have seen, this causes the caller's refreshTable() method to be called, which in turn formats all the numbers in the table using the caller's format dictionary.

This dialog is smarter than the standard one we created in the preceding section. It works directly on the caller's data structure (the format dictionary), and notifies the caller when the data structure has changed so that the changes can be applied. We could have made it smarter still and given it a reference to the caller's refreshTable() method and had the dialog execute it directly: We will use this approach in the next example.

In situations where the user wants to repeatedly apply changes, it may be inconvenient for them to keep having to click an Apply button. They may just want to manipulate a dialog's widgets and see the effects immediately. We will see how to do this next.

Modeless "Live" Dialogs

For our last number format example, we will review a smart modeless "live" dialog—a dialog that works very similarly to the one we have just seen, but which has no buttons, and where changes are applied automatically and immediately. The dialog is shown in Figure 5.7.

In the modal version of the dialog we used post-mortem validation, and in the smart modeless version we used a mixture of post-mortem and preventative validation. In this example, we will use preventative validation exclusively. Also, instead of creating a signal–slot connection so that the dialog can notify

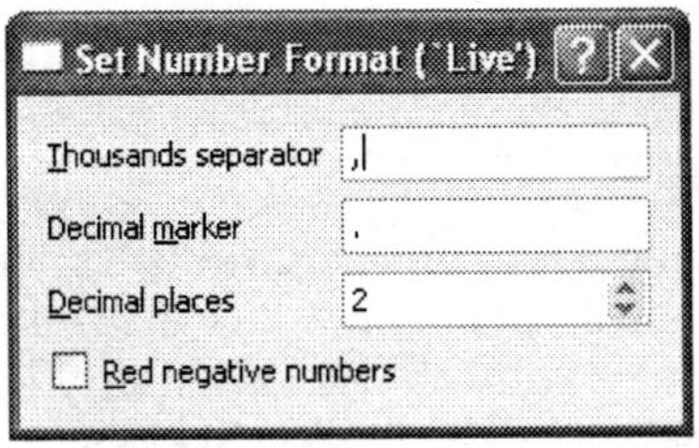

Figure 5.7 *The "live" Set Number Format dialog*

the caller of changes, we give the dialog the method to call when there are changes to be applied so that it can call this method whenever necessary.

We could create this dialog in exactly the same way as the previous dialog, but we will instead demonstrate a different approach. Rather than creating the dialog when it is needed and then destroying it, creating and destroying on every use, we will create it just once, the first time it is needed, and then hide it when the user is finished with it, showing and hiding on every use.

```
def setNumberFormat3(self):
    if self.numberFormatDlg is None:
        self.numberFormatDlg = numberformatdlg3.NumberFormatDlg(
                self.format, self.refreshTable, self)
    self.numberFormatDlg.show()
    self.numberFormatDlg.raise_()
    self.numberFormatDlg.activateWindow()
```

In the calling form's initializer, we have the statement `self.numberFormatDlg = None`. This ensures that the first time this method is called the dialog is created. Then, we show the dialog as before. But in this case, when the dialog is closed it is merely hidden (because we do *not* set the `Qt.WA_DeleteOnClose` widget attribute). So when this method is called, we may be creating and showing the dialog for the first time, or we may be showing a dialog that was created earlier and subsequently hidden. To account for the second possibility, we must both raise (put the dialog on top of all the other windows in the application) and activate (give the focus to the dialog); doing these the first time is harmless.[*]

Also, we have made the dialog even smarter than the previous one, and instead of setting up a signal–slot connection, we pass the bound `refreshTable()` method to the dialog as an additional parameter.

The `__init__()` method is almost the same as before, with just three differences. First, it does not set the `Qt.WA_DeleteOnClose` attribute so that when the dialog is closed, it will be hidden, not deleted. Second, it keeps a copy of the method it is passed (i.e., it keeps a reference to `self.refreshTable()` in `self.callback`), and

---

[*]PyQt uses raise_() rather than raise() to avoid conflict with the built-in raise statement.

third, its signal and slot connections are slightly different than before. Here are the connection calls:

```
self.connect(self.thousandsEdit,
        SIGNAL("textEdited(QString)"), self.checkAndFix)
self.connect(self.decimalMarkerEdit,
        SIGNAL("textEdited(QString)"), self.checkAndFix)
self.connect(self.decimalPlacesSpinBox,
        SIGNAL("valueChanged(int)"), self.apply)
self.connect(self.redNegativesCheckBox,
        SIGNAL("toggled(bool)"), self.apply)
```

As before, we can rely on the decimal places spinbox to ensure that only a valid number of decimal places is set, and similarly the "red negatives" checkbox can only be in a valid state, so changes to either of these can be applied immediately.

But for the line edits, we now connect their textEdited() signals. These signals are emitted whenever the user types in a character or deletes a character from them. The checkAndFix() slot will both ensure that the line edits hold valid text and apply the change immediately. There are no buttons in this dialog: The user can close it by pressing Esc, which will then hide it. The dialog will be deleted only when its calling form is deleted, because at that point the caller's self.numberFormatDlg instance variable will go out of scope, and with no other reference to the dialog, it will be scheduled for garbage collection.

```
def apply(self):
    self.format["thousandsseparator"] = \
            unicode(self.thousandsEdit.text())
    self.format["decimalmarker"] = \
            unicode(self.decimalMarkerEdit.text())
    self.format["decimalplaces"] = \
            self.decimalPlacesSpinBox.value()
    self.format["rednegatives"] = \
            self.redNegativesCheckBox.isChecked()
    self.callback()
```

The apply() method is the simplest we have seen so far. This is because it is called only when all the editing widgets hold valid data, so no post-mortem validation is required. It no longer emits a signal to announce a state change—instead, it calls the method it was given and this applies the changes directly to the caller's form.

```
def checkAndFix(self):
    thousands = unicode(self.thousandsEdit.text())
    decimal = unicode(self.decimalMarkerEdit.text())
    if thousands == decimal:
        self.thousandsEdit.clear()
        self.thousandsEdit.setFocus()
```

```
        if len(decimal) == 0:
            self.decimalMarkerEdit.setText(".")
            self.decimalMarkerEdit.selectAll()
            self.decimalMarkerEdit.setFocus()
    self.apply()
```

This method applies preventative validation as the user types in either of the line edits. We still rely on the line edit validators, maximum length properties, and in the case of the decimal place marker line edit, an input mask, with all of these combining to provide almost all the validation that we need. But it is still possible for the user to set the same text in both—in which case we delete the thousands separator and move the focus to its line edit, or (if the user tries hard) for the decimal place marker to be empty—in which case we set a valid alternative, select it, and give it the keyboard focus. At the end we know that both line edits are valid, so we call apply() and apply the changes.

One benefit of using the show/hide approach is that the dialog's state is maintained automatically. If we have to create the dialog each time it is used we must populate it with data, but for this dialog, whenever it is shown (after the first time), it already has the correct data. Of course, in this particular example we have three dialogs that are all used to edit the same data, which means that this dialog could become out of sync; we ignore this issue because having multiple dialogs editing the same data is not something we would do in a real application.

By passing in both the data structure (the format dictionary) and the caller's update method (refreshTable(), passed as self.callback), we have made this dialog very smart—and very tightly coupled to its caller. For this reason, many programmers prefer the "middle way" of using standard dialogs—dumb dialogs are too limited and can be inconvenient to use, and smart dialogs can be more work to maintain because of the tight coupling their knowledge of their callers' data structures implies.

Summary

We categorized dialogs into three "intelligences", dumb, standard, and smart, and showed that they can be used modally or modelessly. Dumb dialogs are easy to create, and are perfectly adequate for doing widget-level validation. Dumb dialogs are normally used modally, and if we are careful they can be generalized since they can be very loosely coupled to the application's logic. Nonetheless, using dumb dialogs usually ends up leading to programmer frustration and the need to rewrite in the form of a standard or smart dialog, so it is often best to avoid them except for those very simple cases where just one or two values are required and the built-in QInputDialog static dialogs are not suitable.

The most common choice is between a standard modal dialog and a smart modeless dialog, and in the latter case between the "apply" and "live" styles of updating. Modal dialogs are the easiest to program because they block any other interaction with the dialog's parent windows and their sibling windows, thereby reducing the risk that the data they are working on is changed from under them. But modeless dialogs are preferred by some users, and are particularly convenient when users want to try out various options before deciding which ones they want. Modal dialogs can also be used for this purpose if they provide some kind of preview; for example, font dialogs are often modal, and show sample text that reflects the user's font settings as they change them.

The two validation strategies that we have looked at, post-mortem and preventative, can be used on their own or in combination. From a usability point of view, preventative is often considered to be superior, although it can lead to user frustration. For example, a user might complain ("I want to set this to five but it won't let me") when the setting is invalid because of another setting elsewhere on the form.

It is possible to design a dialog so that it can be used both for adding and for editing items. These add/edit dialogs are no different from other kinds of dialogs when it comes to the creation, layout, and connection of their widgets. The key difference is that they may need to behave in different ways depending on whether they are adding or editing. When editing, the widgets are populated from the item passed in, and when adding, the widgets are populated with default values. If the dialog is accepted, it may simply provide accessors through which the values set can be retrieved, leaving the work to the caller, or it may be smart, able to update edited items directly, and to create new items if the user is adding. See the `AddEditMovieDlg` class in `chap08/additemmoviedlg.py` (its user interface design is in `chap08/additemmoviedlg.ui`), and the `TextItemDlg` class in `chap12/pagedesigner.pyw`, for examples of add/edit item dialogs.

Another possibility is to avoid using a dialog at all and to allow the user to edit data in-place—for example, in a list or table. This approach is covered in the chapters on model/view programming.

Exercise

Write a stand-alone string list editing dialog. The dialog should use `if __name__ == "__main__":` so that it can be run and tested independently. It should look like the dialog shown in Figure 5.8.

The strings should be held in a `QListWidget`. The Sort button is easy to implement since we can connect its `clicked()` signal directly to the `QListWidget.sortItems()` method.

The dialog should work on its own string list, either a copy of one passed in, or one it creates itself, and when accepted should emit a signal containing the list (as a `QStringList`), and also have a publically accessible data attribute, `stringlist`.

The `reject()` slot should be implemented like this:

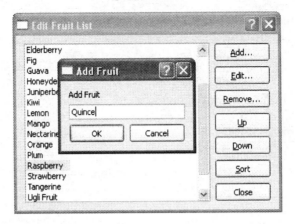

Figure 5.8 *The String List dialog with an item being added*

```
def reject(self):
    self.accept()
```

For testing purposes put the following code at the end of the file:

```
if __name__ == "__main__":
    fruit = ["Banana", "Apple", "Elderberry", "Clementine", "Fig",
             "Guava", "Mango", "Honeydew Melon", "Date", "Watermelon",
             "Tangerine", "Ugli Fruit", "Juniperberry", "Kiwi",
             "Lemon", "Nectarine", "Plum", "Raspberry", "Strawberry",
             "Orange"]
    app = QApplication(sys.argv)
    form = StringListDlg("Fruit", fruit)
    form.exec_()
    print "\n".join([unicode(x) for x in form.stringlist])
```

This creates a StringListDlg instance, with a string that names the kind of things in the list, and a list of strings, and then calls it modally. When the user closes the dialog we print the list of strings on the console so that we can see the effects of our edits.

You will need to read the documentation for QListWidget, and for QInputDialog.getText() which can be used for getting a string to be added and for editing an existing string. This exercise can be done in about 120 lines of code.

A model answer is provided by the file chap05/stringlistdlg.py. The program can be tested by running it. (On Windows, it should be run from a console; on Mac OS X, from a Terminal.)

6

Main Windows

Most applications are main-window-style applications, that is, they have a menu bar, toolbars, a status bar, a central area, and possibly dock windows, to provide the user with a rich yet navigable and comprehensible user interface. In this chapter, we will see how to create a main-window-style application which demonstrates how to create and use all of these features.

Figure 6.1 *The Image Changer application*

We will use the Image Changer application shown in Figure 6.1 to demonstrate how to create a main-window-style application. Like most such applications it has menus, toolbars, and a status bar; it also has a dock window. In addition to seeing how to create all these user interface elements, we will cover how to relate user interactions with them, to methods that perform the relevant actions.

This chapter also explains how to handle the creation of new files and the opening of existing files, including keeping the user interface synchronized with the application's state. Also covered is how to give the user the opportunity to save unsaved changes, and how to manage a recently used files list. We will also show how to save and restore user preferences, including the sizes and positions of the main window and of the toolbars and dock windows.

Most applications have a data structure for holding their data, and use one or more widgets through which users can view and edit the data. The Image Changer application holds its data in a single QImage object, and uses a QLabel widget as its data viewer. In Chapter 8, we will see a main-window-style application that is used to present and edit lots of data items, and in Chapter 9, we will see how to create main window applications that can handle multiple documents.

Before looking at how to create the application, we will discuss some of the state that a user interface must maintain. Quite often, some menu options and toolbar buttons are "checkable", that is, they can be in one of two states. For example, in a word processor, a toolbar button for toggling italic text could be "on" (pushed down) or "off". If there is also an italic menu option, we must make sure that the menu option and the toolbar button are kept in sync. Fortunately, PyQt makes it easy to automate such synchronization.

Some options may be interdependent. For example, we can have text left-aligned, centered, or right-aligned, but only one of these can be "on" at any one time. So if the user switched on centered alignment, the left and right alignment toolbar buttons and menu options must be switched off. Again, PyQt makes it straightforward to synchronize such interdependent options. In this chapter, we will cover options that are noncheckable, such as "file open", and both independent and interdependent checkable options.

Although some menu and toolbar options can have an immediate effect on the application's data, others are used to invoke dialogs through which users can specify precisely what they want done. Since we have given so much coverage to dialogs in the preceding two chapters, here we will concentrate on how they are used rather than on how they are created. In this chapter we will see how to invoke custom dialogs, and also how to use many of PyQt's built-in dialogs, including dialogs for choosing a filename, the print dialog, and dialogs for asking the user for an item of data, such as a string or a number.

Creating a Main Window

For most main-window-style applications, the creation of the main window follows a similar pattern. We begin by creating and initializing some data structures, then we create a "central widget" which will occupy the main window's central area, and then we create and set up any dock windows. Next, we create "actions" and insert them into menus and toolbars. It is quite common to also read in the application's settings, and for applications that restore the

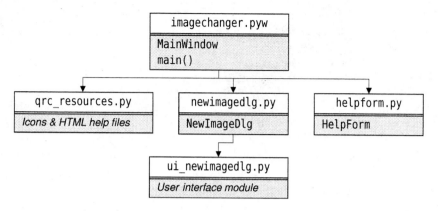

Figure 6.2 *The Image Changer's modules, classes, and functions*

user's workspace, to load the files that the application had open when it was last terminated.

The files that make up the Image Changer application are shown in Figure 6.2. The application's main window class is in the file chap06/imagechanger.pyw. The initializer is quite long, so we will look at it in pieces. But first we will look at the imports that precede the class definition.

```
import os
import platform
import sys
from PyQt4.QtCore import *
from PyQt4.QtGui import *
import helpform
import newimagedlg
import qrc_resources

__version__ = "1.0.0"
```

In this book, our policy is to import Python's standard modules, then third-party modules (such as PyQt), and then our own modules. We will discuss the items we use from the os and platform modules when we use them in the code. The sys module is used to provide sys.argv as usual. The helpform and newimagedlg modules provide the HelpForm and NewImageDlg classes. We will discuss the qrc_resources module later on.

It is common for applications to have a version string, and conventional to call it __version__; we will use it in the application's about box.

Now we can look at the beginning of the MainWindow class.

```
class MainWindow(QMainWindow):

    def __init__(self, parent=None):
        super(MainWindow, self).__init__(parent)
```

```
self.image = QImage()
self.dirty = False
self.filename = None
self.mirroredvertically = False
self.mirroredhorizontally = False
```

The initializer begins conventionally with the super() call. Next, we create a null QImage that we will use to hold the image the user loads or creates. A QImage is not a QObject subclass, so it does not need a parent; instead, we can leave its deletion to Python's normal garbage collection when the application terminates. We also create some instance variables. We use dirty as a Boolean flag to indicate whether the image has unsaved changes. The filename is initially set to None, which we use to signify that either there is no image, or there is a newly created image that has never been saved.

PyQt provides various mirroring capabilities, but for this example application we have limited ourselves to just three possibilities: having the image mirrored vertically, horizontally, or not at all. We need to keep track of the mirrored state so that we can keep the user interface in sync, as we will see when we discuss the mirroring actions.

```
self.imageLabel = QLabel()
self.imageLabel.setMinimumSize(200, 200)
self.imageLabel.setAlignment(Qt.AlignCenter)
self.imageLabel.setContextMenuPolicy(Qt.ActionsContextMenu)
self.setCentralWidget(self.imageLabel)
```

In some applications the central widget is a composite widget (a widget that is composed of other widgets, laid out just like those in a dialog), or an item-based widget (such as a list or table), but here a single QLabel is sufficient. A QLabel can display plain text, or HTML, or an image in any of the image formats that PyQt supports; later on we will see how to discover what these formats are, since they can vary. We have set a minimum size because initially the label has nothing to show, and would therefore take up no space, which would look peculiar. We have chosen to align our images vertically and horizontally centered.

PyQt offers many ways of creating context menus, but we are going to use the easiest and most common approach. First, we must set the context menu policy for the widget which we want to have a context menu. Then, we must add some actions to the widget—something we will do further on. When the user invokes the context menu, the menu will pop up, displaying the actions that were added.

Object Owner- ship sidebar

119 ☞

Unlike dialogs, where we use layouts, in a main-window-style application we only ever have one central widget—although this widget could be composite, so there is no limitation in practice. We only need to call setCentralWidget() and we are done. This method both lays out the widget in the main window's central area, and reparents the widget so that the main window takes ownership of it.

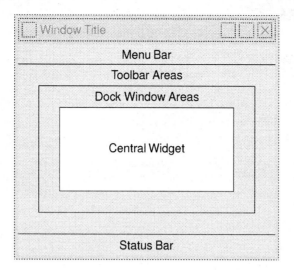

Figure 6.3 *QMainWindow's areas*

Toolbars are suitable for holding toolbar buttons, and some other kinds of widgets such as comboboxes and spinboxes. For larger widgets, for tool palettes, or for any widget that we want the user to be able to drag out of the window to float freely as an independent window in its own right, using a dock window is often the right choice.

Dock windows are windows that can appear in the dock areas shown in Figure 6.3. They have a small caption, and restore and close buttons, and they can be dragged from one dock area to another, or float freely as independent top-level windows in their own right. When they are docked they automatically provide a splitter between themselves and the central area, and this makes them easy to resize.

In PyQt, dock windows are instances of the QDockWidget class. We can add a single widget to a dock widget, just as we can have a single widget in a main window's central area, and in the same way this is no limitation, since the widget added can be a composite.

```
logDockWidget = QDockWidget("Log", self)
logDockWidget.setObjectName("LogDockWidget")
logDockWidget.setAllowedAreas(Qt.LeftDockWidgetArea|
                              Qt.RightDockWidgetArea)
self.listWidget = QListWidget()
logDockWidget.setWidget(self.listWidget)
self.addDockWidget(Qt.RightDockWidgetArea, logDockWidget)
```

Dock widgets are not put into a layout, so when we create them, in addition to providing their window caption, we must give them a parent. By setting a parent, we ensure that the dock widget does not go out of scope and get garbage-collected by Python at the wrong time. Instead, the dock widget will be deleted when its parent, the top-level window (the main window), is deleted.

Every PyQt object can be given an object name, although up to now we have never done so. Object names can sometimes be useful in debugging, but we have set one here because we want PyQt to save and restore the dock widget's size and position, and since there could be any number of dock widgets, PyQt uses the object name to distinguish between them.

By default, dock widgets can be dragged into any dock area and are movable, floatable, and closable. Since our dock widget is going to be used to store a list—a widget that is usually tall and narrow—it only makes sense for it to be in the left or right dock areas (or to float), so we use setAllowedAreas() to restrict the areas. Dock widgets also have a setFeatures() method which is used to control whether the dock widget can be moved, floated, or closed, but we do not need to use it here because the defaults are fine.

Once the dock widget has been set up, we create the widget it will hold, in this case a list widget. Then we add the widget to the dock widget, and the dock widget to the main window. We did not have to give the list widget a parent because when it is added to the dock widget the dock widget takes ownership of it.

```
self.printer = None
```

We want users to be able to print out their images. To do this we need to create a QPrinter object. We could create the printer whenever we need it and leave it to be garbage-collected afterward. But we prefer to keep an instance variable, initially set to None. The first time the user asks to print we will create a QPrinter and assign it to our printer variable. This has two benefits. First, we create the printer object only when it is needed, and second, because we keep a reference to it, it stays around—and keeps all its previous state such as the user's choice of printer, paper size, and so on.

```
self.sizeLabel = QLabel()
self.sizeLabel.setFrameStyle(QFrame.StyledPanel|QFrame.Sunken)
status = self.statusBar()
status.setSizeGripEnabled(False)
status.addPermanentWidget(self.sizeLabel)
status.showMessage("Ready", 5000)
```

For the application's status bar, we want the usual message area on the left, and a status indicator showing the width and height of the current image. We do this by creating a QLabel widget and adding it to the status bar. We also switch off the status bar's size grip since that seems inappropriate when we have an indicator label that shows the image's dimensions. The status bar itself is created for us the first time we call the QMainWindow's statusBar() method. If we call the status bar's showMessage() method with a string, the string will be displayed in the status bar, and will remain on display until either another showMessage()

call supplants it or until `clearMessage()` is called. We have used the two-argument form, where the second argument is the number of milliseconds (5000, i.e., 5 seconds), that the message should be shown for; after this time the status bar will clear itself.

So far we have seen how to create the main window's central widget, create a dock widget, and set up the status bar. Now we are almost ready to create the menus and toolbars, but first we must understand what PyQt actions are, and then take a brief detour to learn about resources.

Actions and Key Sequences

Qt's designers recognized that user interfaces often provide several different ways for the user to achieve the same thing. For example, creating a new file in many applications can be done via the File→New menu option, or by clicking the New File toolbar button, 🗎, or by using the Ctrl+N keyboard shortcut. In general, we do not care how the user asked to perform the action, we only care what action they asked to be done. PyQt encapsulates user actions using the `QAction` class. So, for example, to create a "file new" action we could write code like this:

```
fileNewAction = QAction(QIcon("images/filenew.png"), "&New", self)
fileNewAction.setShortcut(QKeySequence.New)
helpText = "Create a new image"
fileNewAction.setToolTip(helpText)
fileNewAction.setStatusTip(helpText)
self.connect(fileNewAction, SIGNAL("triggered()"), self.fileNew)
```

This assumes that we have a suitable icon and a `fileNew()` method. The ampersand in the menu item's text means that the menu item will appear as <u>N</u>ew (except on Mac OS X or unless the windowing system is set to suppress underlines), and that keyboard users will be able to invoke it by pressing Alt+F,N, assuming that the File menu's text is `"&File"` so that it appears as <u>F</u>ile. Alternatively, the user could use the shortcut that was created by `setShortcut()`, and simply press Ctrl+N instead.

Many key sequences are standardized, some even across different windowing systems. For example, Windows, KDE, and GNOME all use Ctrl+N for "new" and Ctrl+S for "save". Mac OS X is similar, with Command+N and Command+S for these actions. The `QKeySequence` class in PyQt 4.2 provides constants for the standardized key sequences, such as `QKeySequence.New`. This is especially useful when the standardized key sequences differ across windowing systems, or where more than one key sequence is associated with an action. For example, if we set a shortcut to `QKeySequence.Paste`, PyQt will trigger a "paste" action in response to Ctrl+V or Shift+Ins on Windows; Ctrl+V, Shift+Ins, or F18 on KDE and GNOME; and Command+V on Mac OS X.

Qt 4.2

For key sequences that are not standardized (or if we want backward compatibility with earlier PyQt releases), we can provide the shortcut as a string;

Table 6.1 *Selected QAction Methods*

Syntax	Description
a.data()	Returns QAction a's user data as a QVariant
a.setData(v)	Sets QAction a's user data to QVariant v
a.isChecked()	Returns True if QAction a is checked
a.setChecked(b)	Checks or unchecks QAction a depending on bool b
a.isEnabled()	Returns True if QAction a is enabled
a.setEnabled(b)	Enables or disables QAction a depending on bool b
a.setSeparator(b)	Sets QAction a to be a normal action or a separator depending on bool b
a.setShortcut(k)	Sets QAction a's keyboard shortcut to QKeySequence k
a.setStatusTip(s)	Sets QAction a's status tip text to string s
a.setText(s)	Sets QAction a's text to string s
a.setToolTip(s)	Sets QAction a's tooltip text to string s
a.setWhatsThis(s)	Sets QAction a's What's This? text to string s
a.toggled(b)	This signal is emitted when QAction a's checked status changes; bool b is True if the action is checked
a.triggered(b)	This signal is emitted when QAction a is invoked; the optional bool b is True if QAction a is checked

for example, setShortcut("Ctrl+Q"). This book uses the standardized key sequences that are available, and otherwise falls back to using strings.

Object Ownership sidebar 119 ☜

Notice that we give the QAction a parent of self (the form in which the action is applicable). It is important that every QObject subclass (except top-level windows) has a parent; for widgets this is usually achieved by laying them out, but for a pure data object like a QAction, we must provide the parent explicitly.

Once we have created the action, we can add it to a menu and to a toolbar like this:

```
fileMenu.addAction(fileNewAction)
fileToolbar.addAction(fileNewAction)
```

Now whenever the user invokes the "file new" action (by whatever means), the fileNew() method will be called.

Resource Files

Unfortunately, there is a small problem with the code we have written. It assumes that the application's working directory is the directory where it is located. This is the normal case under Windows where the .pyw (or a shortcut to it) is clicked (or double-clicked). But if the program is executed from the command line from a different directory—for example, ./chap06/imagechanger.pyw—none of the icons will appear. This is because we gave the icon's path as images, that is, a path relative to the application's working directory, so when invoked from elsewhere, the icons were looked for in the ./images directory (which might not even exist), when in fact they are in the ./chap06/images directory.

We might be tempted to try to solve the problem using Python's os.getcwd() function; but this returns the directory where we invoked the application, which as we have noted, may not be the directory where the application actually resides. Nor does PyQt's QApplication.applicationDirPath() method help, since this returns the path to the Python executable, not to our application itself. One solution is to use os.path.dirname(__file__) to provide a prefix for the icon filenames, since the __file__ variable holds the full name and path of the current .py or .pyw file.

Another solution is to put all our icons (and help files, and any other small resources) into a single .py module and access them all from there. This not only solves the path problem (because Python knows how to look for a module to be imported), but also means that instead of having dozens of icons, help files, and similar, some of which could easily become lost, we have a single module containing them all.

To produce a resource module we must do two things. First, we must create a .qrc file that contains details of the resources we want included, and then we must run pyrcc4 which reads a .qrc file and produces a resource module. The .qrc file is in a simple XML format that is easy to write by hand. Here is an extract from the resources.qrc file used by the Image Changer application:

```
<!DOCTYPE RCC><RCC version="1.0">
<qresource>
<file alias="filenew.png">images/filenew.png</file>
<file alias="fileopen.png">images/fileopen.png</file>
...
<file alias="icon.png">images/icon.png</file>

<file>help/editmenu.html</file>
<file>help/filemenu.html</file>
<file>help/index.html</file>
</qresource>
</RCC>
```

The ellipsis represents many lines that have been omitted to save space because they are all very similar. Each <file> entry must contain a filename, with its relative path if it is in a subdirectory. Now, if we want to use the "file new" action's image, we could write QIcon(":/images/filenew.png"). But thanks to the alias, we can shorten this to QIcon(":/filenew.png"). The leading :/ tells PyQt that the file is a resource. Resource files can be treated just like normal (read-only) files in the filesystem, the only difference being that they have the special path prefix. But before we can use resources, we must make sure we generate the resource module and import it into our application.

Earlier we showed the imports for the Image Changer application, and the last one was import qrc_resources. The qrc_resources.py module was generated by pyrcc4 using the following command line:

```
C:\pyqt\chap06>pyrcc4 -o qrc_resources.py resources.qrc
```

We must run this command whenever we change the resources.qrc file.

As a convenience for readers, two small Python programs are provided with the examples to make using pyrcc4, and some other PyQt command-line programs, much easier. One is mkpyqt.py, itself a command-line program, and the other is Make PyQt, a GUI application written in PyQt4. This means, for example, that instead of running pyrcc4 ourselves, we can simply type this:

```
C:\pyqt\chap06>mkpyqt.py
```

Both mkpyqt.py and Make PyQt do the same thing: They run pyuic4 and other PyQt tools, and for each one they automatically use the correct command-line arguments; they are described in the next chapter.

mk-pyqt.py and Make PyQt sidebar
☞ 207

Creating and Using Actions

The code we saw earlier for creating a "file new" action required six lines to create and set up the action. Most main-window-style applications have scores of actions, so typing six lines for each one would soon become very tedious. For this reason, we have created a helper method which allows us to reduce the code for creating actions to just two or three lines. We will look at the helper, and then see how it is used in the main window's initializer.

```python
def createAction(self, text, slot=None, shortcut=None, icon=None,
                 tip=None, checkable=False, signal="triggered()"):
    action = QAction(text, self)
    if icon is not None:
        action.setIcon(QIcon(":/%s.png" % icon))
    if shortcut is not None:
        action.setShortcut(shortcut)
    if tip is not None:
        action.setToolTip(tip)
        action.setStatusTip(tip)
    if slot is not None:
        self.connect(action, SIGNAL(signal), slot)
    if checkable:
        action.setCheckable(True)
    return action
```

This method does everything that we did by hand for the "file new" action. In addition, it handles cases where there is no icon, as well as "checkable" actions. Icons are optional, although for actions that will be added to a toolbar it is conventional to provide one. An action is checkable if it can have "on" and "off" states like the Bold or Italic actions that word processors normally provide.

Notice that the last argument to the QAction constructor is self; this is the action's parent (the main window) and it ensures that the action will not be garbage-collected when it goes out of the initializer's scope. In some cases, we make actions instance variables so that we can access them outside the form's initializer, something we don't need to do in this particular example.

Here is how we can create the "file new" action using the createAction() helper method:

```
fileNewAction = self.createAction("&New...", self.fileNew,
        QKeySequence.New, "filenew", "Create an image file")
```

With the exception of the "file quit" action (and "file save as", for which we don't provide a shortcut), the other file actions are created in the same way, so we won't waste space by showing them.

```
fileQuitAction = self.createAction("&Quit", self.close,
        "Ctrl+Q", "filequit", "Close the application")
```

The QKeySequence class does not have a standardized shortcut for application termination, so we have chosen one ourselves and specified it as a string. We could have just as easily used a different shortcut—for example, Alt+X or Alt+F4.

The close() slot is inherited from QMainWindow. If the main window is closed by invoking the "file quit" action (which we have just connected to the close() slot), for example, by clicking File→Quit or by pressing Ctrl+Q, the base class's close() method will be called. But if the user clicks the application's close button, X, the close() method is *not* called.

The only way we can be sure we are intercepting attempts to close the window is to reimplement the close event handler. Whether the application is closed by the close() method or via the close button, the close event handler is always called. So, by reimplementing this event handler we can give the user the opportunity to save any unsaved changes, and we can save the application's settings.

In general, we can implement an application's behavior purely through the high-level signals and slots mechanism, but in this one important case we must use the lower-level event-handling mechanism. However, reimplementing the close event is no different from reimplementing any other method, and it is not difficult, as we will see when we cover it further on. (Event handling is covered in Chapter 10.)

The editing actions are created in a similar way, but we will look at a few of them because of subtle differences.

```
editZoomAction = self.createAction("&Zoom...", self.editZoom,
                "Alt+Z", "editzoom", "Zoom the image")
```

It is convenient for users to be able to zoom in and out to see an image in more or less detail. We have provided a spinbox in the toolbar to allow mouse users to change the zoom factor (and which we will come to shortly), but we must also support keyboard users, so for them we create an "edit zoom" action which will be added to the Edit menu. When triggered, the method connected to this action will pop up a dialog box where the user can enter a zoom percentage.

There are standardized key sequences for zoom in and for zoom out, but there is not one for zooming generally, so we have chosen to use Alt+Z in this case. (We did not use Ctrl+Z, since that is the standardized key sequence for undo on most platforms.)

```
editInvertAction = self.createAction("&Invert",
                self.editInvert, "Ctrl+I", "editinvert",
                "Invert the image's colors", True, "toggled(bool)")
```

The "edit invert" action is a toggle action. We could still use the `triggered()` signal, but then we would need to call `isChecked()` on the action to find out its state. It is more convenient for us to use the `toggled(bool)` signal since that not only tells us that the action has been invoked, but also whether it is checked. Actions also have a `triggered(bool)` signal that is emitted only for user changes, but that is not suitable here because whether the checked status of the invert action is changed by the user or programmatically, we want to act on it.

The "edit swap red and blue" action is similar to the "edit invert" action, so we won't show it.

Like the "edit invert" action and the "edit swap red and blue" action, the mirror actions are also checkable, but unlike the "invert" and "swap red and blue" actions which are independent, we have chosen to make the mirror actions mutually exclusive, allowing only one to be "on" at any one time. To get this behavior we create the mirror actions in the normal way, but add each of them to an "action group". An action group is a class which manages a set of checkable actions and ensures that if one of the actions it manages is set to "on", the others are all set to "off".

```
mirrorGroup = QActionGroup(self)
```

Object Owner-ship sidebar

119 ☞

An action group is a QObject subclass that is neither a top-level window nor a widget that is laid out, so we must give it an explicit parent to ensure that it is deleted by PyQt at the right time.

Once we have created the action group, we create the actions in the same way as before, only now we add each one to the action group.

```
editUnMirrorAction = self.createAction("&Unmirror",
        self.editUnMirror, "Ctrl+U", "editunmirror",
        "Unmirror the image", True, "toggled(bool)")
mirrorGroup.addAction(editUnMirrorAction)
```

We have not shown the code for the "edit mirror vertically" or "edit mirror horizontally" actions since it is almost identical to the code shown earlier.

```
editUnMirrorAction.setChecked(True)
```

Checkable actions default to being "off", but when we have a group like this where exactly one must be "on" at a time, we must choose one to be on in the first place. In this case, the "edit unmirror" action is the most sensible to switch on initially. Checking the action will cause it to emit its toggled() signal, but at this stage the QImage is null, and as we will see, no change is applied to a null image.

We create two more actions, "help about", and "help help", with code very similar to what we have already seen.

Although the actions are all in existence, none of them actually works! This is because they become operational only when they have been added to a menu, a toolbar, or both.

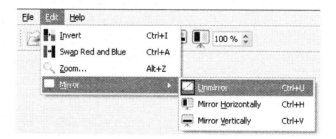

Figure 6.4 *The Edit menu and the Mirror submenu*

Menus in the menu bar are created by accessing the main window's menu bar (which is created the first time menuBar() is called, just like the status bar). Here is the code for creating the Edit menu:

```
editMenu = self.menuBar().addMenu("&Edit")
self.addActions(editMenu, (editInvertAction,
        editSwapRedAndBlueAction, editZoomAction))
```

We have created the Edit menu, and then used addActions() to add some actions to it. This is sufficient to produce the Edit menu shown in Figure 6.4, apart from the Mirror option, which we will look at in a moment.

Actions are added to menus and toolbars using addAction(). To reduce typing
we have created a tiny helper method which can be used to add actions to a
menu or to a toolbar, and which can also add separators. Here is its code:

```
def addActions(self, target, actions):
    for action in actions:
        if action is None:
            target.addSeparator()
        else:
            target.addAction(action)
```

The target is a menu or toolbar, and actions is a list or tuple of actions or
Nones. We could have used the built-in QWidget.addActions() method, but in that
case we would have to create separator actions (shown later) rather than use
Nones.

The last option on the Edit menu, Mirror, has a small triangle on its right. This
signifies that it has a submenu.

```
mirrorMenu = editMenu.addMenu(QIcon(":/editmirror.png"),
                              "&Mirror")
self.addActions(mirrorMenu, (editUnMirrorAction,
        editMirrorHorizontalAction, editMirrorVerticalAction))
```

Submenus are populated in exactly the same way as any other menu, but they
are added to their parent menu using QMenu.addMenu() rather than to the main
window's menu bar using QMainWindow.menuBar().addMenu(). Having created the
mirror menu, we add actions to it using our addActions() helper method, just
as we did before.

Most menus are created and then populated with actions in the same way as
the Edit menu, but the File menu is different.

```
self.fileMenu = self.menuBar().addMenu("&File")
self.fileMenuActions = (fileNewAction, fileOpenAction,
        fileSaveAction, fileSaveAsAction, None,
        filePrintAction, fileQuitAction)
self.connect(self.fileMenu, SIGNAL("aboutToShow()"),
             self.updateFileMenu)
```

We want the File menu to show recently used files. For this reason, we do not
populate the File menu here, but instead generate it dynamically whenever the
user invokes it. This is why we made the File menu an instance variable, and
also why we have an instance variable holding the File menu's actions. The connection ensures that whenever the File menu is invoked our updateFileMenu()
slot will be called. We will review this slot later on.

The Help menu is created conventionally, in the same way as the Edit menu, so
we won't show it.

Figure 6.5 *The File toolbar*

With the menus in place, we can now turn to the toolbars.

```
fileToolbar = self.addToolBar("File")
fileToolbar.setObjectName("FileToolBar")
self.addActions(fileToolbar, (fileNewAction, fileOpenAction,
                              fileSaveAsAction))
```

Creating a toolbar is similar to creating a menu: We call `addToolBar()` to create a `QToolBar` object and populate it using `addActions()`. We can use our `addActions()` method for both menus and toolbars because their APIs are very similar, with both providing `addAction()` and `addSeparator()` methods. We set an object name so that PyQt can save and restore the toolbar's position—there can be any number of toolbars and PyQt uses the object name to distinguish between them, just as it does for dock widgets. The resulting toolbar is shown in Figure 6.5.

The edit toolbar and the checkable actions ("edit invert", "edit swap red and blue", and the mirror actions) are all created in the same way. But as Figure 6.6 shows, the edit toolbar has a spinbox in addition to its toolbar buttons. In view of this, we will show the code for this toolbar in full, showing it in two parts for ease of explanation.

```
editToolbar = self.addToolBar("Edit")
editToolbar.setObjectName("EditToolBar")
self.addActions(editToolbar, (editInvertAction,
        editSwapRedAndBlueAction, editUnMirrorAction,
        editMirrorVerticalAction,
        editMirrorHorizontalAction))
```

Creating a toolbar and adding actions to it is the same for all toolbars.

We want to provide the user with a quick means of changing the zoom factor, so we provide a spinbox in the edit toolbar to make this possible. Earlier, we put a separate "edit zoom" action in the Edit menu, to cater to keyboard users.

```
self.zoomSpinBox = QSpinBox()
self.zoomSpinBox.setRange(1, 400)
self.zoomSpinBox.setSuffix(" %")
self.zoomSpinBox.setValue(100)
self.zoomSpinBox.setToolTip("Zoom the image")
self.zoomSpinBox.setStatusTip(self.zoomSpinBox.toolTip())
self.zoomSpinBox.setFocusPolicy(Qt.NoFocus)
self.connect(self.zoomSpinBox,
             SIGNAL("valueChanged(int)"), self.showImage)
editToolbar.addWidget(self.zoomSpinBox)
```

Figure 6.6 *The Edit toolbar*

The pattern for adding widgets to a toolbar is always the same: We create the widget, set it up, connect it to something to handle user interaction, and add it to the toolbar. We have made the spinbox an instance variable because we will need to access it outside the main window's initializer. The addWidget() call passes ownership of the spinbox to the toolbar.

We have now fully populated the menus and toolbars with actions. Although every action was added to the menus, some were not added to the toolbars. This is quite conventional; usually only the most frequently used actions are added to toolbars.

Earlier we saw the following line of code:

```
self.imageLabel.setContextMenuPolicy(Qt.ActionsContextMenu)
```

This tells PyQt that if actions are added to the imageLabel widget, they are to be used for a context menu, such as the one shown in Figure 6.7.

```
self.addActions(self.imageLabel, (editInvertAction,
        editSwapRedAndBlueAction, editUnMirrorAction,
        editMirrorVerticalAction, editMirrorHorizontalAction))
```

We can reuse our addActions() method to add actions to the label widget, providing we don't pass Nones since QWidget does not have an addSeparator() method. Setting the policy and adding actions to a widget are all that is necessary to get a context menu for that widget.

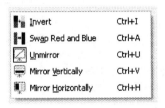

Figure 6.7 *The Image Label's context menu*

The QWidget class has an addAction() method that is inherited by the QMenu, QMenuBar, and QToolBar classes. This is why we can add actions to any of these classes. Although the QWidget class does not have an addSeparator() method, one is provided for convenience in the QMenu, QMenuBar, and QToolBar classes. If we want to add a separator to a context menu, we must do so by adding a separator action. For example:

```
separator = QAction(self)
separator.setSeparator(True)
self.addActions(editToolbar, (editInvertAction,
        editSwapRedAndBlueAction, separator, editUnMirrorAction,
        editMirrorVerticalAction, editMirrorHorizontalAction))
```

If we need more sophisticated context menu handling—for example, where the menu's actions vary depending on the application's state, we can reimplement the relevant widget's contextMenuEvent() event-handling method. Event handling is covered in Chapter 10.

context-Menu-Event()
☞ 307

When we create a new image or load an existing image, we want the user interface to revert to its original state. In particular, we want the "edit invert" and "edit swap red and green" actions to be "off", and the mirror action to be "edit unmirrored".

```
self.resetableActions = ((editInvertAction, False),
                (editSwapRedAndBlueAction, False),
                (editUnMirrorAction, True))
```

We have created an instance variable holding a tuple of pairs, with each pair holding an action and the checked state it should have when a new image is created or loaded. We will see resetableActions in use when we review the fileNew() and loadFile() slots.

In the Image Changer application, all of the actions are enabled all of the time. This is fine, since we always check for a null image before performing any action, but it has the disadvantage that, for example, "file save" will be enabled if there is no image or if there is an unchanged image, and similarly, the edit actions will be enabled even if there is no image. The solution is to enable or disable actions depending on the application's state, as the sidebar in Chapter 13 shows.

Enabling and Disabling Actions sidebar
☞ 385

Restoring and Saving the Main Window's State

Now that the main window's user interface has been fully set up, we are almost ready to finish the initializer method, but before we do we will restore the application's settings from the previous run (or use default settings if this is the very first time the application has been run).

Before we can look at application settings, though, we must make a quick detour and look at the creation of the application object and how the main window itself is created. The very last executable statement in the imagechanger.pyw file is the bare function call:

```
main()
```

As usual, we have chosen to use a conventional name for the first function we execute. Here is its code:

```
def main():
    app = QApplication(sys.argv)
    app.setOrganizationName("Qtrac Ltd.")
    app.setOrganizationDomain("qtrac.eu")
    app.setApplicationName("Image Changer")
    app.setWindowIcon(QIcon(":/icon.png"))
    form = MainWindow()
    form.show()
    app.exec_()
```

The function's first line is one we have seen many times before. The next three lines are new. Our primary use of them is for loading and saving application settings. If we create a QSettings object without passing any arguments, it will use the organization name or domain (depending on platform), and the application name that we have set here. So, by setting these once on the application object, we don't have to remember to pass them whenever we need a QSettings instance.

But what do these names mean? They are used by PyQt to save the application's settings in the most appropriate place—for example, in the Windows registry, or in a directory under $HOME/.config on Linux, or in $HOME/Library/ Preferences on Mac OS X. The registry keys or file and directory names are derived from the names we give to the application object.

We can tell that the icon file is loaded from the qrc_resources module because its path begins with :/.

After we have set up the application object, we create the main window, show it, and start off the event loop, in the same way as we have done in examples in previous chapters.

Now we can return to where we got up to in the MainWindow.__init__() method, and see how it restores system settings.

```
settings = QSettings()
self.recentFiles = settings.value("RecentFiles").toStringList()
size = settings.value("MainWindow/Size",
                      QVariant(QSize(600, 500))).toSize()
self.resize(size)
position = settings.value("MainWindow/Position",
                          QVariant(QPoint(0, 0))).toPoint()
self.move(position)
self.restoreState(
        settings.value("MainWindow/State").toByteArray())

self.setWindowTitle("Image Changer")
self.updateFileMenu()
QTimer.singleShot(0, self.loadInitialFile)
```

We begin by creating a QSettings object. Since we passed no arguments, the names held by the application object are used to locate the settings information. We begin by retrieving the recently used files list. The QSettings.value() method always returns a QVariant, so we must convert it to the data type we are expecting.

Next, we use the two-argument form of value(), where the second argument is a default value. This means that the very first time the application is run, it has no settings at all, so we will get a QSize() object with a width of 600 pixels and a height of 500 pixels.* On subsequent runs, the size returned will be whatever the size of the main window was when the application was terminated—so long as we remember to save the size when the application terminates. Once we have a size, we resize the main window to the given size. After getting the previous (or default) size, we retrieve and set the position in exactly the same way.

There is no flickering, because the resizing and positioning are done in the main window's initializer, before the window is actually shown to the user.

Qt 4.2 introduced two new QWidget methods for saving and restoring a top-level window's geometry. Unfortunately, a bug meant that they were not reliable in all situations on X11-based systems, and for this reason we have restored the window's size and position as separate items. Qt 4.3 has fixed the bug, so with Qt 4.3 (e.g., with PyQt 4.3), instead of retrieving the size and position and calling resize() and move(), everything can be done using a single line:

Qt
4.3

```
self.restoreGeometry(settings.value("Geometry").toByteArray())
```

This assumes that the geometry was saved when the application was terminated, as we will see when we look at the closeEvent().

close-
Event()

☞ 185

The QMainWindow class provides a restoreState() method and a saveState() method; these methods restore from and save to a QByteArray. The data they save and restore are the dock window sizes and positions, and the toolbar positions—but they work only for dock widgets and toolbars that have unique object names.

After setting the window's title, we call updateFileMenu() to create the File menu. Unlike the other menus, the File menu is generated dynamically; this is so that it can show any recently used files. The connection from the File menu's aboutToShow() signal to the updateFileMenu() method means that the File menu is created afresh whenever the user clicks File in the menu bar, or presses Alt+F. But until this method has been called for the first time, the File menu does not exist—which means that the keyboard shortcuts for actions that have not been added to a toolbar, such as Ctrl+Q for "file quit", will not work. In view of this, we explicitly call updateFileMenu() to create an initial File menu and to activate the keyboard shortcuts.

---

*PyQt's documentation rarely gives units of measurement because it is assumed that the units are pixels, except for QPrinter, which uses points.

Doing Lots of Processing at Start-Up

If we need to do lots of processing at start-up—for example, if we need to load in lots of large files, we always do so in a separate loading method. At the end of the main form's constructor, the loading method is called through a zero-timeout single-shot timer.

What would happen if we didn't use a single-shot timer? Imagine, for example, that the method was `loadInitialFiles()` and that it loaded lots of multimegabyte files. The file loading would be done when the main window was being created, that is, before the `show()` call, and before the event loop (`exec_()`) had been started. This means that the user might experience a long delay between launching the application and actually seeing the application's window appear on-screen. Also, if the file loading might result in message boxes being popped up—for example, to report errors—it makes more sense to have these appear after the main window is shown, and when the event loop is running.

We want the main window to appear as quickly as possible so that the user knows that the launch was successful, and so that they can see any long-running processes, like loading large files, through the main window's user interface. This is achieved by using a single-shot timer as we did in the Image Changer example.

This works because a single-shot timer with a timeout of zero does not execute the slot it is given immediately. Instead, it puts the slot to be called in the event queue and then simply returns. At this point, the end of the main window's initializer is reached and the initialization is complete. The very next statement (in `main()`) is a `show()` call on the main window, and this does nothing except add a show event to the event queue. So, now the event queue has a timer event and a show event. A timer event with a timeout of zero is taken to mean "do this when the event queue has nothing else to do", so when the next statement, `exec_()`, is reached and starts off the event loop, it always chooses to handle the show event first, so the form appears, and then, with no other events left, the single-shot timer's event is processed, and the `loadInitialFiles()` call is made.

The initializer's last line looks rather peculiar. A single-shot timer takes a timeout argument (in milliseconds), and a method to call when the timeout occurs. So, it looks as though the line could have been written like this instead:

```
self.loadInitialFile()
```

In this application, where we load at most only one initial file, and where that file is very unlikely to be as big even as 1 MB, we could use either approach without noticing any difference. Nonetheless, calling the method directly is not the same as using a single-shot timer with a zero timeout, as the Doing Lots of Processing at Start-Up sidebar explains.

We have finished reviewing the code for initializing the main window, so now we can begin looking at the other methods that must be implemented to provide the application's functionality. Although the Image Changer application is just one specific example, to the greatest extent possible we have made the code either generic or easily adaptable so that it could be used as the basis for other main-window-style applications, even ones that are completely different.

In view of the discussions we have just had, it seems appropriate to begin our coverage with the loadInitialFile() method.

```
def loadInitialFile(self):
    settings = QSettings()
    fname = unicode(settings.value("LastFile").toString())
    if fname and QFile.exists(fname):
        self.loadFile(fname)
```

This method uses a QSettings object to get the last image that the application used. If there was such an image, and it still exists, the program attempts to load it. We will review loadFile() when we cover the file actions.

We could just as easily have written if fname and os.access(fname, os.F_OK): It makes no noticable difference here, but for multiperson projects, it may be wise to have a policy of preferring PyQt over the standard Python libraries or vice versa in cases like this, just to keep things as simple and clear as possible.

We discussed restoring the application's state a little earlier, so it seems appropriate to cover the close event, since that is where we save the application's state.

```
def closeEvent(self, event):
    if self.okToContinue():
        settings = QSettings()
        filename = QVariant(QString(self.filename)) \
                if self.filename is not None else QVariant()
        settings.setValue("LastFile", filename)
        recentFiles = QVariant(self.recentFiles) \
                if self.recentFiles else QVariant()
        settings.setValue("RecentFiles", recentFiles)
        settings.setValue("MainWindow/Size", QVariant(self.size()))
        settings.setValue("MainWindow/Position",
                QVariant(self.pos()))
        settings.setValue("MainWindow/State",
                QVariant(self.saveState()))
    else:
        event.ignore()
```

If the user attempts to close the application, by whatever means (apart from killing or crashing it), the closeEvent() method is called. We begin by calling our own custom okToContinue() method; this returns True if the user really

Table 6.2 *Selected QMainWindow Methods*

Syntax	Description
`m.addDockWidget(a, d)`	Adds `QDockWidget` d into `Qt.QDockWidgetArea` a in `QMainWindow` m
`m.addToolBar(s)`	Adds and returns a new `QToolBar` called string s
`m.menuBar()`	Returns `QMainWindow` m's `QMenuBar` (which is created the first time this method is called)
`m.restoreGeometry(ba)`	Restores `QMainWindow` m's position and size to those encapsulated in `QByteArray` ba
`m.restoreState(ba)`	Restores `QMainWindow` m's dock widgets and toolbars to the state encapsulated in `QByteArray` ba
`m.saveGeometry()`	Returns `QMainWindow` m's position and size encapsulated in a `QByteArray`
`m.saveState()`	Returns the state of `QMainWindow` m's dock widgets and toolbars, that is, their sizes and positions, encapsulated in a `QByteArray`
`m.setCentralWidget(w)`	Sets `QMainWindow` m's central widget to be `QWidget` w
`m.statusBar()`	Returns `QMainWindow` m's `QStatusBar` (which is created the first time this method is called)
`m.setWindowIcon(i)`	Sets `QMainWindow` m's icon to `QIcon` i; this method is inherited from `QWidget`
`m.setWindowTitle(s)`	Sets `QMainWindow` m's title to string s; this method is inherited from `QWidget`

wants to close, and `False` otherwise. It is inside `okToContinue()` that we give the user the chance to save unsaved changes. If the user does want to close, we create a fresh `QSettings` object, and store the "last file" (i.e., the file the user has open), the recently used files, and the main window's state. The `QSettings` class only reads and writes `QVariant` objects, so we must be careful to provide either null `QVariant`s (created with `QVariant()`), or `QVariant`s with the correct information in them.

If the user chose not to close, we call `ignore()` on the close event. This will tell PyQt to simply discard the close event and to leave the application running.

 If we are using Qt 4.3 (e.g., with PyQt 4.3) and have restored the main window's geometry using `QWidget.restoreGeometry()`, we can save the geometry like this:

```
settings.setValue("Geometry", QVariant(self.saveGeometry()))
```

If we take this approach, we do not need to save the main window's size or position separately.

```
def okToContinue(self):
    if self.dirty:
```

```
                    reply = QMessageBox.question(self,
                                "Image Changer - Unsaved Changes",
                                "Save unsaved changes?",
                                QMessageBox.Yes|QMessageBox.No|
                                QMessageBox.Cancel)
                if reply == QMessageBox.Cancel:
                    return False
                elif reply == QMessageBox.Yes:
                    self.fileSave()
            return True
```

This method is used by the closeEvent(), and by the "file new" and "file open" actions. If the image is "dirty", that is, if it has unsaved changes, we pop up a message box and ask the user what they want to do. If they click Yes, we save the image to disk and return True. If they click No, we simply return True, so the unsaved changes will be lost. If they click Cancel, we return False, which means that the unsaved changes are not saved, but the current image will remain current, so it could be saved later.

All the examples in the book use yes/no or yes/no/cancel message boxes to give the user the opportunity to save unsaved changes. An alternative favored by some developers is to use Save and Discard buttons (using the QMessageBox.Save and QMessageBox.Discard button specifiers), instead.

The recently used files list is part of the application's state that must not only be saved and restored when the application is terminated and executed, but also kept current at runtime. Earlier we connected the fileMenu's aboutToShow() signal to a custom updateFileMenu() slot. So, when the user presses Alt+F or clicks the File menu, this slot is called *before* the File menu is shown.

```
        def updateFileMenu(self):
            self.fileMenu.clear()
            self.addActions(self.fileMenu, self.fileMenuActions[:-1])
            current = QString(self.filename) \
                    if self.filename is not None else None
            recentFiles = []
            for fname in self.recentFiles:
                if fname != current and QFile.exists(fname):
                    recentFiles.append(fname)
            if recentFiles:
                self.fileMenu.addSeparator()
                for i, fname in enumerate(recentFiles):
                    action = QAction(QIcon(":/icon.png"), "&%d %s" % (
                            i + 1, QFileInfo(fname).fileName()), self)
                    action.setData(QVariant(fname))
                    self.connect(action, SIGNAL("triggered()"),
                                 self.loadFile)
                    self.fileMenu.addAction(action)
```

The Static QMessageBox Methods

The QMessageBox class offers several static convenience methods that pop up a modal dialog with a suitable icon and buttons. They are useful for offering users dialogs that have a single OK button, or Yes and No buttons, and similar.

The most commonly used QMessageBox static methods are critical(), information(), question(), and warning(). The methods take a parent widget (over which they center themselves), window title text, message text (which can be plain text or HTML), and zero or more button specifications. If no buttons are specified, a single OK button is provided.

The buttons can be specified using constants, or we can provide our own text. In Qt 4.0 and Qt 4.1, it was very common to bitwise OR QMessageBox.Default with OK or Yes buttons—this means the button will be pressed if the user presses Enter, and to bitwise OR QMessageBox.Escape with the Cancel or No buttons, which will then be pressed if the user presses Esc. For example:

```
reply = QMessageBox.question(self,
        "Image Changer - Unsaved Changes", "Save unsaved changes?",
        QMessageBox.Yes|QMessageBox.Default,
        QMessageBox.No|QMessageBox.Escape)
```

The methods return the constant of the button that was pressed.

From Qt 4.2, the QMessageBox API has been simplified so that instead of specifying buttons and using bitwise ORs, we can just use buttons. For example, for a yes/no/cancel dialog we could write:

```
reply = QMessageBox.question(self,
        "Image Changer - Unsaved Changes", "Save unsaved changes?",
        QMessageBox.Yes|QMessageBox.No|QMessageBox.Cancel)
```

In this case, PyQt will automatically make the Yes (accept) button the default button, activated by the user pressing Enter, and the Cancel (reject) button the escape button, activated by the user pressing Esc. The QMessageBox methods also make sure that the buttons are shown in the correct order for the platform. We use the Qt 4.2 syntax for the examples in this book.

The message box is closed by the user clicking the "accept" button (often Yes or OK) or the "reject" button (often No or Cancel). The user can also, in effect, press the "reject" button by clicking the window's close button, X, or by pressing Esc.

If we want to create a customized message box—for example, using custom button texts and a custom icon—we can create a QMessageBox instance. We can then use methods such as QMessageBox.addButton() and QMessageBox.setIcon(), and pop up the message box by calling QMessageBox.exec_().

```
self.fileMenu.addSeparator()
self.fileMenu.addAction(self.fileMenuActions[-1])
```

We begin by clearing all the File menu's actions. Then we add back the original list of file menu actions, such as "file new" and "file open", but excluding the last one, "file quit". Then we iterate over the recently used files list, creating a local list which only contains files that still exist in the filesystem, and excluding the current file. Although it does not seem to make much sense, many applications include the current file, often showing it first in the list.

Now, if there are any recently used files in our local list we add a separator to the menu and then create an action for each one with text that just contains the filename (without the path), preceded by a numbered accelerator: 1, 2, ..., 9. PyQt's QFileInfo class provides information on files similar to some of the functions offered by Python's os module. The QFileInfo.fileName() method is equivalent to os.path.basename(). For each action, we also store an item of "user data"—in this case, the file's full name, including its path. Finally, we connect each recently used filename's action's triggered() signal to the loadFile() slot, and add the action to the menu. (We cover loadFile() in the next section.) At the end, we add another separator, and the File menu's last action, "file quit".

But how is the recently used files list created and maintained? We saw in the form's initializer that we initially populate the recentFiles string list from the application's settings. We have also seen that the list is correspondingly saved in the closeEvent(). New files are added to the list using addRecentFile().

```
def addRecentFile(self, fname):
    if fname is None:
        return
    if not self.recentFiles.contains(fname):
        self.recentFiles.prepend(QString(fname))
        while self.recentFiles.count() > 9:
            self.recentFiles.takeLast()
```

This method prepends the given filename, and then pops off any excess files from the end (the ones added longest ago) so that we never have more than nine filenames in our list. We keep the recentFiles variable as a QStringList, which is why we have used QStringList methods rather than Python list methods on it.

The addRecentFile() method itself is called inside the fileNew(), fileSaveAs(), and loadFile() methods; and indirectly from loadInitialFile(), fileOpen(), and updateFileMenu(), all of which either call or connect to loadFile(). So, when we save an image for the first time, or under a new name, or create a new image, or open an existing image, the filename is added to the recently used files list. However, the newly added filename will not appear in the File menu, unless we subsequently create or open another image, since our updateFileMenu() method does not display the current image's filename in the recently used files list.

Figure 6.8 *The File menu with some recently used files*

The approach to handling recently used files that we have taken here is just one of many possibilities. An alternative is to create the File menu just once, with a set of actions at the end for recently used files. When the menu is updated, instead of being cleared and re-created, the actions set aside for recently used files are simply hidden or shown, in the latter case having had their filenames updated to reflect the current set of recently used files. From the user's point of view, there is no discernable difference whichever approach we take under the hood, so in either case the File menu will look similar to the one shown in Figure 6.8.

Both approaches can be used to implement recently used files in a File menu, adding the list at the end as we have done in the Image Changer application, just before the Quit option. They can also both be used to implement the Open Recent File menu option that has all the recent files as a submenu, as used by OpenOffice.org and some other applications. The benefits of using a separate Open Recent File option is that the File menu is always the same, and full paths can be shown in the submenu—something we avoid when putting recently used files directly in the File menu so that it doesn't become extremely wide (and therefore, ugly).

Handling User Actions

In the preceding section, we created the appearance of our main-window-style application and provided its behavioral infrastructure by creating a set of actions. We also saw how to save and restore application settings, and how to manage a recently used files list.

Some of an application's behavior is automatically handled by PyQt—for example, window minimizing, maximizing, and resizing—so we do not have to do this ourselves. Some other behaviors can be implemented purely through signals and slots connections. In this section we are concerned with the actions that are directly under the control of the user and which can be used to view, edit, and output, their data.

Handling File Actions

The File menu is probably the most widely implemented menu in main-window-style applications, and in most cases it offers, at the least, "new", "save", and "quit" (or "exit") options.

```
def fileNew(self):
    if not self.okToContinue():
        return
    dialog = newimagedlg.NewImageDlg(self)
    if dialog.exec_():
        self.addRecentFile(self.filename)
        self.image = QImage()
        for action, check in self.resetableActions:
            action.setChecked(check)
        self.image = dialog.image()
        self.filename = None
        self.dirty = True
        self.showImage()
        self.sizeLabel.setText("%d x %d" % (self.image.width(),
                                            self.image.height()))
        self.updateStatus("Created new image")
```

okToCon-
tinue()

186 ☞

When the user asks to work on a new file we begin by seeing whether it is "okay to continue". This gives the user the chance to save or discard any unsaved changes, or to change their mind entirely and cancel the action.

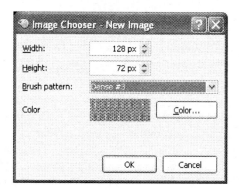

Figure 6.9 *The New Image dialog*

If the user continues, we pop up a modal NewImageDlg in which they can specify the size, color, and brush pattern of the image they want to create. This dialog, shown in Figure 6.9, is created and used just like the dialogs we created in the preceding chapter. However, the New Image dialog's user interface was created using *Qt Designer*, and the user interface file must be converted into a module file, using pyuic4, for the dialog to be usable. This can be done directly by running pyuic4, or by running either mkpyqt.py or Make PyQt, both of which are easier since they work out the correct command-line arguments automatically. We will cover all of these matters in the next chapter.

mk-
pyqt.py
and
Make
PyQt
sidebar
☞ 207

If the user accepts the dialog, we add the current filename (if any) to the recently used files list. Then we set the current image to be a null image, to ensure that any changes to checkable actions have no effect on the image. Next we go through the actions that we want to be reset when a new image is created or loaded, setting each one to our preferred default value. Now we can safely set the image to the one created by the dialog.

We set the filename to be None and the dirty flag to be True to ensure that the user will be prompted to save the image and asked for a filename, if they terminate the application or attempt to create or load another image.

We then call showImage() which displays the image in the imageLabel, scaled according to the zoom factor. Finally, we update the size label in the status bar, and call updateStatus().

```
def updateStatus(self, message):
    self.statusBar().showMessage(message, 5000)
    self.listWidget.addItem(message)
    if self.filename is not None:
        self.setWindowTitle("Image Changer - %s[*]" % \
                            os.path.basename(self.filename))
    elif not self.image.isNull():
        self.setWindowTitle("Image Changer - Unnamed[*]")
    else:
        self.setWindowTitle("Image Changer[*]")
    self.setWindowModified(self.dirty)
```

We begin by showing the message that has been passed, with a timeout of five seconds. We also add the message to the log widget to keep a log of every action that has taken place.

If the user has opened an existing file, or has saved the current file, we will have a filename. We put the filename in the window's title using Python's os.path.basename() function to get the filename without the path. We could just as easily have written QFileInfo(fname).fileName() instead, as we did earlier. If there is no filename and the image variable is not a null image, it means that the user has created a new image, but has not yet saved it; so we use a fake filename of "Unnamed". The last case is where no file has been opened or created.

Regardless of what we set the window title to be, we include the string "[*]" somewhere inside it. This string is never displayed as it is: Instead it is used to indicate whether the file is dirty. On Linux and Windows this means that the filename will be shown unadorned if it has no unsaved changes, and with an asterisk (*) replacing the "[*]" string otherwise. On Mac OS X, the close button will be shown with a dot in it if there are unsaved changes. The mechanism depends on the window modified status, so we make sure we set that to the state of the dirty flag.

```
def fileOpen(self):
    if not self.okToContinue():
        return
    dir = os.path.dirname(self.filename) \
            if self.filename is not None else "."
    formats = ["*.%s" % unicode(format).lower() \
                for format in QImageReader.supportedImageFormats()]
    fname = unicode(QFileDialog.getOpenFileName(self,
                        "Image Changer - Choose Image", dir,
                        "Image files (%s)" % " ".join(formats)))
    if fname:
        self.loadFile(fname)
```

If the user asks to open an existing image, we first make sure that they have had the chance to save or discard any unsaved changes, or to cancel the action entirely.

If the user has decided to continue, as a courtesy, we want to pop up a file open dialog set to a sensible directory. If we already have an image filename, we use its path; otherwise, we use ".", the current directory. We have also chosen to pass in a file filter string that limits the image file types the file open dialog can show. Such file types are defined by their extensions, and are passed as a string. The string may specify multiple extensions for a single type, and multiple types. For example, a text editor might pass a string of:

```
"Text files (*.txt)\nHTML files (*.htm *.html)"
```

If there is more than one type, we must separate them with newlines. If a type can handle more than one extension, we must separate the extensions with spaces. The string shown will produce a file type combobox with two items, "Text files" and "HTML files", and will ensure that the only file types shown in the dialog are those that have an extension of .txt, .htm, or .html.

In the case of the Image Changer application, we use the list of image type extensions for the image types that can be read by the version of PyQt that the application is using. At the very least, this is likely to include .bmp, .jpg (and .jpeg, the same as .jpg), and .png. The list comprehension iterates over the readable image extensions and creates a list of strings of the form "*.bmp", "*.jpg", and so on; these are joined, space-separated, into a single string by the string join() method.

List comprehensions

53 ☜

The `QFileDialog.getOpenFileName()` method returns a `QString` which either holds a filename (with the full path), or is empty (if the user canceled). If the user chose a filename, we call `loadFile()` to load it.

Here, and throughout the program, when we have needed the application's name we have simply written it. But since we set the name in the application object in `main()` to simplify our `QSettings` usage, we could instead retrieve the name whenever it was required. In this case, the relevant code would then become:

```
fname = unicode(QFileDialog.getOpenFileName(self,
              "%s - Choose Image" % QApplication.applicationName(),
              dir, "Image files (%s)" % " ".join(formats)))
```

It is surprising how frequently the name of the application is used. The file `imagechanger.pyw` is less than 500 lines, but it uses the application's name a dozen times. Some developers prefer to use the method call to guarantee consistency. We will discuss string handling further in Chapter 17, when we cover internationalization.

If the user opens a file, the `loadFile()` method is called to actually perform the loading. We will look at this method in two parts.

```
def loadFile(self, fname=None):
    if fname is None:
        action = self.sender()
        if isinstance(action, QAction):
            fname = unicode(action.data().toString())
            if not self.okToContinue():
                return
        else:
            return
```

If the method is called from the `fileOpen()` method or from the `loadInitial-File()` method, it is passed the filename to open. But if it is called from a recently used file action, no filename is passed. We can use this difference to distinguish the two cases. If a recently used file action was invoked, we retrieve the sending object. This should be a `QAction`, but we check to be safe, and then extract the action's user data, in which we stored the recently used file's full name including its path. User data is held as a `QVariant`, so we must convert it to a suitable type. At this point, we check to see whether it is okay to continue. We do not have to make this test in the "file open" case, because there, the check is made before the user is even asked for the name of a file to open. So now, if the method has not returned, we know that we have a filename in `fname` that we must try to load.

```
if fname:
    self.filename = None
    image = QImage(fname)
```

```
            if image.isNull():
                message = "Failed to read %s" % fname
            else:
                self.addRecentFile(fname)
                self.image = QImage()
                for action, check in self.resetableActions:
                    action.setChecked(check)
                self.image = image
                self.filename = fname
                self.showImage()
                self.dirty = False
                self.sizeLabel.setText("%d x %d" % (
                            image.width(), image.height()))
                message = "Loaded %s" % os.path.basename(fname)
            self.updateStatus(message)
```

We begin by making the current filename None and then we attempt to read the image into a local variable. PyQt does not use exception handling, so errors must always be discovered indirectly. In this case, a null image means that for some reason we failed to load the image. If the load was successful we add the new filename to the recently used files list, where it will appear only if another file is subsequently opened, or if this one is saved under another name. Next, we set the instance image variable to be a null image: This means that we are free to reset the checkable actions to our preferred defaults without any side effects. This works because when the checkable actions are changed, although the relevant methods will be called due to the signal–slot connections, the methods do nothing if the image is null.

add-
Recent-
File()

189 🖙

After the preliminaries, we assign the local image to the image instance variable and the local filename to the filename instance variable. Next, we call showImage() to show the image at the current zoom factor, clear the dirty flag, and update the size label. Finally, we call updateStatus() to show the message in the status bar, and to update the log widget.

```
        def fileSave(self):
            if self.image.isNull():
                return
            if self.filename is None:
                self.fileSaveAs()
            else:
                if self.image.save(self.filename, None):
                    self.updateStatus("Saved as %s" % self.filename)
                    self.dirty = False
                else:
                    self.updateStatus("Failed to save %s" % self.filename)
```

The fileSave() method, and many others, act on the application's data (a QImage instance), but make no sense if there is no image data. For this reason, many

of the methods do nothing and return immediately if there is no image data
for them to work on.

If there is image data, and the filename is None, the user must have invoked the
"file new" action, and is now saving their image for the first time. For this case,
we pass on the work to the fileSaveAs() method.

If we have a filename, we attempt to save the image using QImage.save(). This
method returns a Boolean success/failure flag, in response to which we update
the status accordingly. (We have deferred coverage of loading and saving
custom file formats to Chapter 8, since we are concentrating purely on main
window functionality in this chapter.)

```
def fileSaveAs(self):
    if self.image.isNull():
        return
    fname = self.filename if self.filename is not None else "."
    formats = ["*.%s" % unicode(format).lower() \
                for format in QImageWriter.supportedImageFormats()]
    fname = unicode(QFileDialog.getSaveFileName(self,
                    "Image Changer - Save Image", fname,
                    "Image files (%s)" % " ".join(formats)))
    if fname:
        if "." not in fname:
            fname += ".png"
        self.addRecentFile(fname)
        self.filename = fname
        self.fileSave()
```

When the "file save as" action is triggered we begin by retrieving the current
filename. If the filename is None, we set it to be ".", the current directory. We
then use the QFileDialog.getSaveFileName() dialog to prompt the user to give
us a filename to save under. If the current filename is not None, we use that as
the default name—the file save dialog takes care of giving a warning yes/no
dialog if the user chooses the name of a file that already exists. We use the
same technique for setting the file filters string as we used for the "file open"
action, but this time using the list of image formats that this version of PyQt
can write (which may be different from the list of formats it can read).

If the user entered a filename that does not include a dot, that is, it has no
extension, we set the extension to be .png. Next, we add the filename to the
recently used files list (so that it will appear if a different file is subsequently
opened, or if this one is saved under a new name), set the filename instance
variable to the name, and pass the work of saving to the fileSave() method
that we have just reviewed.

The last file action we must consider is "file print". When this action is invoked
the filePrint() method is called. This method paints the image on a printer.
Since the method uses techniques that we have not covered yet, we will defer

discussion of it until later. The technique it uses is shown in the Printing Images sidebar, and coverage of the `filePrint()` method itself is in Chapter 13 (from page 400), where we also discuss approaches to printing documents in general.

Print-
ing
Images
sidebar

☞ 363

The only file action we have not reviewed is the "file quit" action. This action is connected to the main window's `close()` method, which in turn causes a close event to be put on the event queue. We provided a reimplementation of the `closeEvent()` handler in which we made sure the user had the chance to save unsaved changes, using a call to `okToContinue()`, and where we saved the application's settings.

close-
Event()

185 ☜

Handling Edit Actions

Most of the functionality of the file actions was provided by the `MainWindow` subclass itself. The only work passed on was the image loading and saving, which the `QImage` instance variable was required to do. This particular division of responsibilities between a main window and the data structure that holds the data is very common. The main window handles the high-level file new, open, save, and recently used files functionality, and the data structure handles loading and saving.

It is also common for most, or even all, of the editing functionality to be provided either by the view widget or by the data structure. In the Image Changer application, all the data manipulation is handled by the data structure (the image `QImage`), and the presentation of the data is handled by the data viewer (the `imageLabel QLabel`). Again, this is a very common separation of responsibilities.

In this section, we will review most of the edit actions, omitting a couple that are almost identical to ones that are shown. We will be quite brief here, since the functionality is specific to the Image Changer application.

```
def editInvert(self, on):
    if self.image.isNull():
        return
    self.image.invertPixels()
    self.showImage()
    self.dirty = True
    self.updateStatus("Inverted" if on else "Uninverted")
```

If the user invokes the "edit invert" action, it will be checked (or unchecked). In either case, we simply invert the image's pixels using the functionality provided by `QImage`, show the changed image, set the dirty flag, and call `updateStatus()` so that the status bar briefly shows the action that was performed, and an additional item is added to the log.

The `editSwapRedAndBlue()` method (not shown) is the same except that it uses the `QImage.rgbSwapped()` method, and it has different status text.

```
def editMirrorHorizontal(self, on):
    if self.image.isNull():
        return
    self.image = self.image.mirrored(True, False)
    self.showImage()
    self.mirroredhorizontally = not self.mirroredhorizontally
    self.dirty = True
    self.updateStatus("Mirrored Horizontally" \
            if on else "Unmirrored Horizontally")
```

This method is structurally the same as editInvert() and editSwapRedAndBlue().
The QImage.mirrored() method takes two Boolean flags, the first for horizontal
mirroring and the second for vertical mirroring. In the Image Changer
application, we have deliberately restricted what mirroring is allowed, so users
can only have no mirroring, vertical mirroring, or horizontal mirroring, but not
a combination of vertical and horizontal. We also keep an instance variable
that keeps track of whether the image is horizontally mirrored.

The editMirrorVertical() method, not shown, is virtually identical.

```
def editUnMirror(self, on):
    if self.image.isNull():
        return
    if self.mirroredhorizontally:
        self.editMirrorHorizontal(False)
    if self.mirroredvertically:
        self.editMirrorVertical(False)
```

This method switches off whichever mirroring is in force, or does nothing if
the image is not mirrored. It does not set the dirty flag or update the status: It
leaves that for editMirrorHorizontal() or editMirrorVertical(), if it calls either
of them.

The application provides two means by which the user can change the zoom factor. They can interact with the zoom spinbox in the toolbar—its valueChanged()
signal is connected to the showImage() slot that we will review shortly—or they
can invoke the "edit zoom" action in the Edit menu. If they use the "edit zoom"
action, the editZoom() method is called.

```
def editZoom(self):
    if self.image.isNull():
        return
    percent, ok = QInputDialog.getInteger(self,
            "Image Changer - Zoom", "Percent:",
            self.zoomSpinBox.value(), 1, 400)
    if ok:
        self.zoomSpinBox.setValue(percent)
```

We begin by using one of the QInputDialog class's static methods to obtain a zoom factor. The getInteger() method takes a parent (over which the dialog will center itself), a caption, text describing what data is wanted, an initial value, and, optionally, minimum and maximum values.

The QInputDialog provides some other static convenience methods, including getDouble() to get a floating-point value, getItem() to choose a string from a list, and getText() to get a string. For all of them, the return value is a two-tuple, containing the value and a Boolean flag indicating whether the user entered and accepted a valid value.

If the user clicked OK, we set the zoom spinbox's value to the given integer. If this value is different from the current value, the spinbox will emit a valueChanged() signal. This signal is connected to the showImage() slot, so the slot will be called if the user chose a new zoom percentage value.

```
def showImage(self, percent=None):
    if self.image.isNull():
        return
    if percent is None:
        percent = self.zoomSpinBox.value()
    factor = percent / 100.0
    width = self.image.width() * factor
    height = self.image.height() * factor
    image = self.image.scaled(width, height, Qt.KeepAspectRatio)
    self.imageLabel.setPixmap(QPixmap.fromImage(image))
```

This slot is called when a new image is created or loaded, whenever a transformation is applied, and in response to the zoom spinbox's valueChanged() signal. This signal is emitted whenever the user changes the toolbar zoom spinbox's value, either directly using the mouse, or indirectly through the "edit zoom" action described earlier.

We retrieve the percentage and turn it into a zoom factor that we can use to produce the image's new width and height. We then create a *copy* of the image scaled to the new size and preserving the aspect ratio, and set the imageLabel to display this image. The label requires an image as a QPixmap, so we use the static QPixmap.fromImage() method to convert the QImage to a QPixmap.

Notice that zooming the image in this way has no effect on the original image; it is purely a change in view, not an edit. This is why the dirty flag does not need to be set.

According to PyQt's documentation, QPixmaps are optimized for on-screen display (so they are fast to draw), and QImages are optimized for editing (which is why we have used them to hold the image data).

Handling Help Actions

When we created the main window's actions, we provided each with help text, and set it as their status text and as their tooltip text. This means that when the user navigates the application's menu system, the status text of the currently highlighted menu option will automatically appear in the status bar. Similarly, if the user hovers the mouse over a toolbar button, the corresponding tooltip text will be displayed in a tooltip.

For an application as small and simple as the Image Changer, status tips and tooltips might be entirely adequate. Nonetheless, we have provided an online help system to show how it can be done, although we defer coverage until Chapter 17 (from page 510).

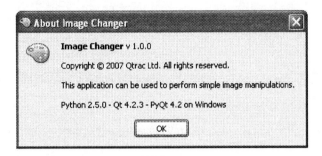

Figure 6.10 *The about Image Changer box*

Whether or not we provide online help, it is always a good idea to provide an "about" box. This should at least show the application's version and copyright notice, as Figure 6.10 illustrates.

```
def helpAbout(self):
    QMessageBox.about(self, "About Image Changer",
            """<b>Image Changer</b> v %s
            <p>Copyright &copy; 2007 Qtrac Ltd.
            All rights reserved.
            <p>This application can be used to perform
            simple image manipulations.
            <p>Python %s - Qt %s - PyQt %s on %s""" % (
            __version__, platform.python_version(),
            QT_VERSION_STR, PYQT_VERSION_STR, platform.system())))
```

The QMessageBox.about() static convenience method pops up a modal OK-style message box with the given caption and text. The text can be HTML, as it is here. The message box will use the application's window icon if there is one.

We display the application's version, and version information about the Python, Qt, and PyQt libraries, as well as the platform the application is running on. The library version information is probably of no direct use to the user, but it may be very helpful to support staff who are being asked for help by the user.

Summary

Main-window-style applications are created by subclassing QMainWindow. The window has a single widget (which may be composite and so contain other widgets) as its central widget.

Actions are used to represent the functionality the application provides to its users. These actions are held as QAction objects which have text (used in menus), icons (used in both menus and toolbars), tooltips and status tips, and that are connected to slots, which, when invoked, will perform the appropriate action. Usually, all the actions are added to the main window's menus, and the most commonly used ones are added to toolbars. To support keyboard users, we provide keyboard shortcuts for frequently used actions, and menu accelerators to make menu navigation as quick and convenient as possible.

Some actions are checkable, and some groups of checkable actions may be mutually exclusive, that is, one and only one may be checked at any one time. PyQt supports checkable actions by the setting of a single property, and supports mutually exclusive groups of actions through QActionGroup objects.

Dock windows are represented by dock widgets and are easy to create and set up. Arbitrary widgets can be added to dock widgets and to toolbars, although in practice we only usually add small or letterbox-shaped widgets to toolbars.

Actions, action groups, and dock windows must all be given a parent explicitly—the main window, for example—to ensure that they are deleted at the right time. This is not necessary for the application's other widgets and QObjects because they are all owned either by the main window or by one of the main window's children. The application's non-QObject objects can be left to be deleted by Python's garbage collector.

Applications often use resources (small files, such as icons, and data files), and PyQt's resource mechanism makes accessing and using them quite easy. They do require an extra build step, though, either using PyQt's pyrcc4 console application, or the mkpyqt.py or Make PyQt programs supplied with the book's examples.

Dialogs can be created entirely in code as we did in the preceding chapter, or using *Qt Designer*, as we will see in the next chapter. If we need to incorporate *Qt Designer* user interface files in our application, like resources they require an extra build step, either using PyQt's pyuic4 console application, or again, using mkpyqt.py or Make PyQt.

Once the main window's visual appearance has been created by setting its central widget and by creating menus, toolbars, and perhaps dock windows, we can concern ourselves with loading and saving application settings. Many settings are commonly loaded in the main window's initializer, and settings are normally saved (and the user given the chance to save unsaved changes) in a reimplementation of the closeEvent() method.

If we want to restore the user's workspace, loading in the files they had open the last time they ran the application, it is best to use a single-shot timer at the end of the main window's initializer to load the files.

Most applications usually have a dataset and one or more widgets that are used to present and edit the data. Since the focus of the chapter has been on the main window's user interface infrastructure, we opted for the simplest possible data and visualization widget, but in later chapters the emphasis will be the other way around.

It is very common to have the main window take care of high-level file handling and the list of recently used files, and for the object holding the data to be responsible for loading, saving, and editing the data.

At this point in the book, you now know enough Python and PyQt to create both dialog-style and main-window-style GUI applications. In the next chapter, we will show *Qt Designer* in action, an application that can considerably speed up the development and maintenance of dialogs. And in the last chapter of Part II, we will explore some of the key approaches to saving and loading custom file formats, using both the PyQt and the Python libraries. In Parts III and IV, we will explore PyQt both more deeply, looking at event handling and creating custom widgets, for example, and more broadly, learning about PyQt's model/view architecture and other advanced features, including threading.

Exercise

Create the dialog shown in Figure 6.11. It should have the class name ResizeDlg, and its initializer should accept an initial width and height. The dialog should provide a method called result(), which must return a two-tuple of the width and height the user has chosen. The spinboxes should have a minimum of 4 and a maximum of four times the width (or height) passed in. Both should show their contents right-aligned.

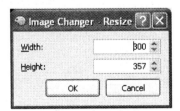

Figure 6.11 *The Image Changer resize dialog*

Modify the Image Changer application so that it has a new "edit resize" action. The action should appear on the Edit menu (after the "edit zoom" action). An icon called editresize.png is in the images subdirectory, but will need to be added to the resources.qrc file. You will also need to import the resize dialog you have just created.

The resize dialog should be used in an editResize() slot that the "edit resize" action should be connected to. The dialog is used like this:

```
form = resizedlg.ResizeDlg(self.image.width(),
                           self.image.height(), self)
if form.exec_():
    width, height = form.result()
```

Unlike the editZoom() slot, the image itself should be changed, so the size label, status bar, and dirty status must all be changed if the size is changed. On the other hand, if the "new" size is the same as the original size, no resizing should take place.

The resize dialog can be written in less than 50 lines, and the resize slot in less than 20 lines, with the new action just requiring an extra one or two lines in a couple of places in the main window's initializer.

A model solution is in the files chap06/imagechanger_ans.pyw and chap06/resize-dlg.py.

- Designing User Interfaces
- Implementing Dialogs
- Testing Dialogs

Using Qt Designer

In Chapter 5 we created dialogs purely by writing code. In our initializers we created the widgets we needed and set their initial properties. Then we created one or more layout managers to which we added the widgets to get the appearance we wanted. In some cases, when working with vertical or horizontal layouts we added a "stretch" which would expand to fill unwanted space. And after laying out the widgets we connected the signals we were interested in to the methods we wanted to handle them.

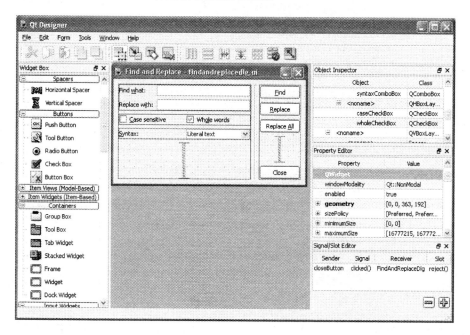

Figure 7.1 *Qt Designer*

Some programmers prefer to do everything in code, whereas others prefer to use a visual design tool to create their dialogs. With PyQt, we can do either, or even both. The Image Changer application from the preceding chapter had two custom dialogs: the ResizeDlg, which was created purely in code (in the exercise), and the NewImageDlg, which was created using *Qt Designer*. We showed how to do things in code first so that you would get a strong sense of how the layout managers work. But in this chapter we are going to create dialogs using *Qt Designer*, which is shown in Figure 7.1.

Qt Designer can be used to create user interfaces for dialogs, custom widgets, and main windows. We will only cover dialogs; custom widgets are almost the same, only they are based on the "Widget" template rather than one of the "Dialog" templates. Using *Qt Designer* for main windows offers fewer advantages, apart from the convenience of a visual QAction editor. *Qt Designer* can also be used to create and edit resource files.

The user interfaces are stored in .ui files, and include details of a form's widgets and layouts. In addition, *Qt Designer* can be used to associate labels with their "buddies", and to set the tab-order, that is, the order in which widgets get the keyboard focus when the user presses the Tab key. This can also be done in code with QWidget.setTabOrder(), but it is rarely necessary for hand-coded forms, since the default is the order of widget creation, which is usually what we want. *Qt Designer* can also be used to make signal–slot connections, but only between built-in signals and slots.

Buddies
143 ☞

Once a user interface has been designed and saved in a .ui file, it must be converted into code before it can be used. This is done using the pyuic4 command-line program. For example:

```
C:\pyqt\chap07>pyuic4 -o ui_findandreplacedlg.py findandreplacedlg.ui
```

mk-
pyqt.py
and
Make
PyQt
sidebar

☞ 207

As mentioned in the previous chapter, we can use either mkpyqt.py or Make PyQt to run pyuic4 for us. However, generating a Python module (a .py file) from a .ui file is not enough to make the user interface usable.* Note that the generated code (in the ui_*.py files) should never be hand-edited because any changes will be overwritten the next time pyuic4 is run.

From the end-user's perspective, it makes no difference whether a dialog's user interface is hand-coded or created with *Qt Designer*. However, there is a significant difference in the implementation of a dialog's initializer, since we must create, lay out, and connect the dialog's widgets if hand coding, but only need to call a particular method to achieve the same thing with a dialog that uses a *Qt Designer* user interface.

One great benefit of using *Qt Designer*, in addition to the convenience of designing dialogs visually, is that if we change the design, we only have to regenerate the user interface module (using pyuic4 directly, or via mkpyqt.py or Make PyQt), and we do not need to change our code. The only time that we must change our code is if we add, delete, or rename widgets that we refer to in our code. This

---

*It is possible, though uncommon, to load and use the .ui file directly using PyQt4.uic.loadUi().

`mkpyqt.py` and Make PyQt

The `mkpyqt.py` console application and the Make PyQt (`makepyqt.pyw`) GUI application, are build programs that run PyQt's `pyuic4`, `pyrcc4`, `pylupdate4`, and `lrelease` programs for us. They both do exactly the same job, automatically using the correct command-line arguments to run PyQt's helper programs, and they both check timestamps to avoid doing unnecessary work.

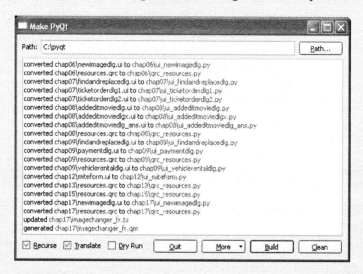

The build programs look for `.ui` files and run `pyuic4` on them to produce files with the same name but prefixed with `ui_` and with their extension changed to `.py`. Similarly, they look for `.qrc` files and run `pyrcc4` on them to produce files with the same name but prefixed with `qrc_`, and again with their extension changed to `.py`.

For example, if we run `mkpyqt.py` in the `chap06` directory, we get:

```
C:\pyqt\chap06>..\mkpyqt.py
./newimagedlg.ui -> ./ui_newimagedlg.py
./resources.qrc -> ./qrc_resources.py
```

The same thing can be achieved by running Make PyQt: click the Path button to set the path to `C:\pyqt\chap06`, and then click the Build button. If we make any changes we can simply run `mkpyqt.py` again, or click Build if using Make PyQt, and any necessary updates will be made.

Both build programs can delete the generated files ready for a fresh build, and both can work recursively on entire directory trees using the `-r` option for `mkpyqt.py` or by checking the Recurse checkbox for Make PyQt. Run `mkpyqt.py -h` in a console for a summary of its options. The Make PyQt program has tooltips for its checkboxes and buttons. In some cases, it may be necessary to set the tool paths; click More→Tool paths, on the first use.

means that using *Qt Designer* is much quicker and easier for experimenting with designs than editing hand-coded layouts, and helps maintain a separation between the visual design created using *Qt Designer*, and the behavior implemented in code.

In this chapter we will create an example dialog, using it to learn how to use *Qt Designer* to create and lay out widgets, to set buddies and tab order, and to make signal–slot connections. We will also see how to use the user interface modules generated by pyuic4, and how to create connections to our custom slots automatically without having to use connect() calls in the initializer.

For the examples, we have used the *Qt Designer* that comes with Qt 4.2. Earlier versions of *Qt Designer* do not have the QFontComboBox or QCalendarWidget widgets, and their "Dialog" templates use QPushButtons rather than a QDialogButtonBox.

Designing User Interfaces

Before we can begin we must start *Qt Designer*. On Linux, run designer & in a console (assuming it is in your path), or invoke it from your menu system. On Windows XP, click Start→Qt by Trolltech→Designer, and on Mac OS X launch it using Finder. *Qt Designer* starts with a New Form dialog; click Dialog with Buttons Bottom and then click Create. This will create a new form with a caption of "untitled", and with the QDialogButtonBox as shown in Figure 7.2.

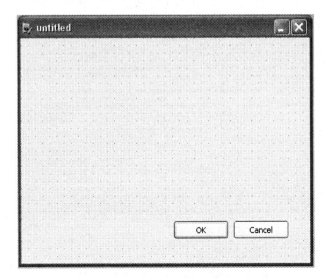

Figure 7.2 *A dialog with buttons bottom dialog*

When *Qt Designer* is run for the first time it defaults to "Multiple Top-Level Windows" mode—this can be confusing, except for Mac OS X users for whom this approach is the norm. To get everything in one window as shown in Figure 7.1, click Edit→User Interface Mode→Docked Window.* *Qt Designer* will remember this setting, so it needs to be done only once.

Qt Designer is not difficult to use, but it does take some initial practice. One thing that helps is to do things in a particular order, as shown in the following list of steps. For steps 1 and 2, always work from "back" to "front", that is, always start with containers (group boxes, tab widgets, frames), and then go on to the normal widgets that belong inside, that is, on top of them. We will go through an example step-by-step in a moment, but first here is a general description of how to create a dialog using *Qt Designer*.

1. Drag a widget onto the form and place it in approximately the right position; there is no need to place it exactly, and normally only container widgets need to be resized.

2. Set the widget's properties if necessary; if the widget will be referred to in code, at least give it a sensible name.

3. Repeat steps 1 and 2 until all the required widgets are on the form.

4. If there are large gaps, drag in horizontal or vertical spacers (these appear as blue springs) to fill them; sometimes, when gaps are obvious, spacers are added during steps 1 and 2.

5. Select two or more widgets (or spacers or layouts) to be laid out (Shift+Click each one), and then lay them out using a layout manager or a splitter.

6. Repeat step 5 until all the widgets and spacers are in layouts.

7. Click the form (to deselect everything) and lay out the form by using one of the layout managers.

8. Create buddies for the form's labels.

9. Set the form's tab order if the order is wrong.

10. Create signal–slot connections between built-in signals and slots where appropriate.

11. Preview the form and check that everything works as intended.

12. Set the form's object name (this is used in its class name), and the form's title, and save it so that it has a filename. For example, if the object name is "PaymentDlg", we would probably give it a title of "Payment" and a filename of paymentdlg.ui.

If the layout is wrong, use undo to go back to where you think you could start laying things out again, and have another go. If that is not possible or does not work, or if the layout is being changed some time after it was originally created, simply break the layouts that need changing and then redo them. Usually, it is necessary to break the form's layout (click the form, then the Break

---

*From Qt 4.3 this option is available by clicking Edit→Preferences.

Layout toolbar button) before changing the layouts within the form; so at the
end the form itself must be laid out again.

Although it is possible to drag layouts onto the form and then drag widgets
into the layouts, the best practice is to drag all the widgets and spacers onto the
form, and then repeatedly select some widgets and spacers and apply layouts
to them. The one situation where it makes sense to add widgets to an existing
layout is if we want to drag widgets into gaps—for example, into empty cells in
a grid layout.

Now that we have the overall principles in mind, we will go step by step
through the design of the Find and Replace dialog shown in Figure 7.3.

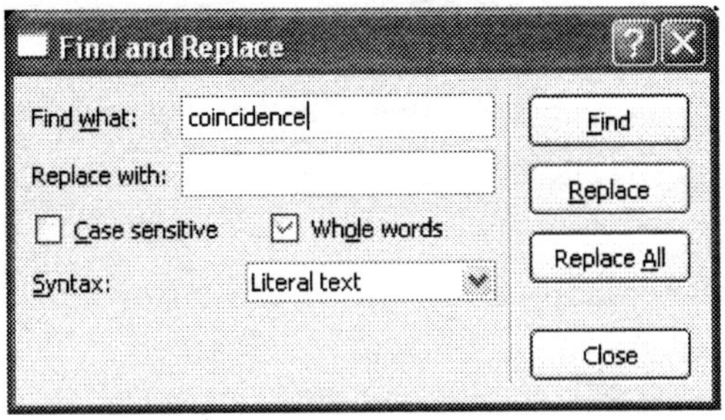

Figure 7.3 *A Find and Replace dialog*

Create a new form based on one of the "Dialog" templates. This will give us a
form with a button box. The button box has two buttons, OK and Cancel, with
signal–slot connections already set up.

Click the button box and then click Edit→Delete. This will leave us with a
completely blank form. For this example we will use QPushButtons instead
of a QDialogButtonBox. This will allow us to exercise finer control than can be
achieved using a QDialogButtonBox inside *Qt Designer*, and gives us the chance
to do signal–slot button connections in *Qt Designer*. In most of the other examples, and in the exercise, we use a QDialogButtonBox.

By default, *Qt Designer* has a dock window on the left called Widget Box.
This contains all the widgets that *Qt Designer* can handle. The widgets are
grouped into sections, and toward the end is a group called Display Widgets;
this contains the Label widget. (*Qt Designer* does not use class names for its
widgets, at least not in the user interface it presents to us, but in almost every
case it is obvious which class a particular name refers to.)

Click and drag a Label onto the form, toward the top left. We don't care what
this label is called because we will not refer to it in code, but the default text of
"TextLabel" is not what we want. When a widget is first dragged and dropped
it is automatically selected, and the selected widget is always the one whose
properties are shown in the property editor. Go to the Property Editor dock
window (normally on the right), and scroll down to the "text" property. Change
this to "Find &what:". It does not matter that the text now appears to be

truncated on the form; once the label is laid out the layout manager will make sure that the text is displayed in full.

Now drag a Line Edit (from the Input Widgets group), and put this to the right of the Label. Go to the property editor and change the Line Edit's "objectName" (the very first property of all widgets) to "findLineEdit". We are giving it a sensible name because we want to refer to this line edit in our code.

Now drag another Label and another Line Edit below the first two. The second Label should have the text "Replace w&ith" and the second Line Edit should be called "replaceLineEdit". The form should now look very similar to Figure 7.4.

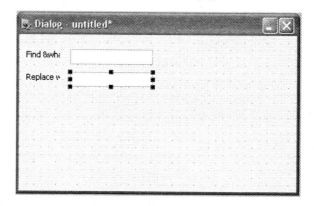

Figure 7.4 *Two Labels and two Line Edits*

At any time we can save the form by pressing Ctrl+S or File→Save. When we save we will use the filename, findandreplacedlg.ui.

Every editable property (and some read-only properties) are shown in the property editor. But in addition, *Qt Designer* provides a context menu. The first option in the context menu is normally one that allows us to change the widget's most "important" property (e.g., a Label's or a Line Edit's "text" property), and a second option that allows us to change the widget's object name. If we change a checkbox, radio button, or push button's text using the context menu, the editing is done in-place, in which case we must press Enter to finish. We will always talk of changing properties in the property editor, but you can, of course, use the context menu if you prefer.

We will now add the two checkboxes. Drag a Check Box from the Buttons group (near the top of the Widget Box) and put it underneath the second Label. Change its object name to "caseCheckBox" and its text to "&Case sensitive", by using the property editor or the context menu. Drag a second Check Box to the right of the first: Change its object name to "wholeCheckBox" and its text to "Wh&ole words", and set its "checked" state to "true". The form should now be similar to the one shown in Figure 7.5.

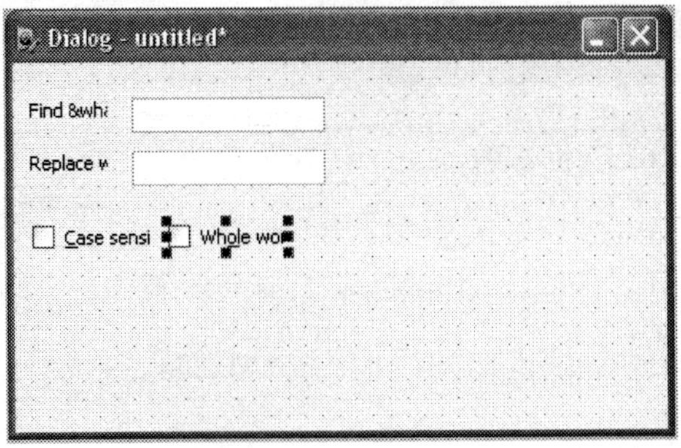

Figure 7.5 *Two Labels, two Line Edits, and two Checkboxes*

Now we will add the Syntax label and combobox. Drag a Label below the case-sensitive checkbox and set its text to "&Syntax:". Now drag a Combo Box (from the Input Widgets group) to the right of the Syntax Label. Change the Combo Box's object name to "syntaxComboBox". Right-click the Combo Box and choose the first menu option, Edit Items. Click the "+" icon, and type in "Literal text". Repeat this to add "Regular expression". Click the OK button to finish.

If the user resizes the form we want the widgets to stay neatly together rather than spreading out, so drag a Vertical Spacer (from the Spacers group near the top of the Widget Box) and put it below the Combo Box. When we design forms using code we use stretches, but when we design them visually we use spacers: They both expand to fill empty space. Adding a stretch to a layout is essentially the same as inserting a QSpacerItem into a layout, but is less to type.

To make the buttons visually separate from the widgets we have just created, we will put a vertical line between them and the other widgets. Drag a Vertical Line (actually a QFrame with shape QFrame.VLine) from the Display Widgets group (near the bottom of the Widget Box) and put it to the right of all the widgets in the form, but leaving space to the right of it for the buttons. Now the form should look like Figure 7.6.

We are now ready to create the buttons. Drag a Push Button (from the Buttons group near the top of the Widget Box) to the top right of the form. Change its object name to "findButton" and its text to "&Find". Drag another button beneath the Find button, and give it the object name "replaceButton" and set its text to be "&Replace". Create a third button, below the Replace button. Give it an object name of "replaceAllButton" and change its text to "Replace &All". Now drag a Vertical Spacer under the Replace All button. Finally, drag a fourth button below the spacer. Give this button the object name "closeButton" and change its text to "Close".

Now we have all the widgets and spacers we need and we have set all their properties appropriately. The form should look like that shown in Figure 7.7.

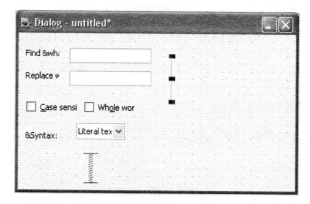

Figure 7.6 *A Find and Replace dialog without buttons*

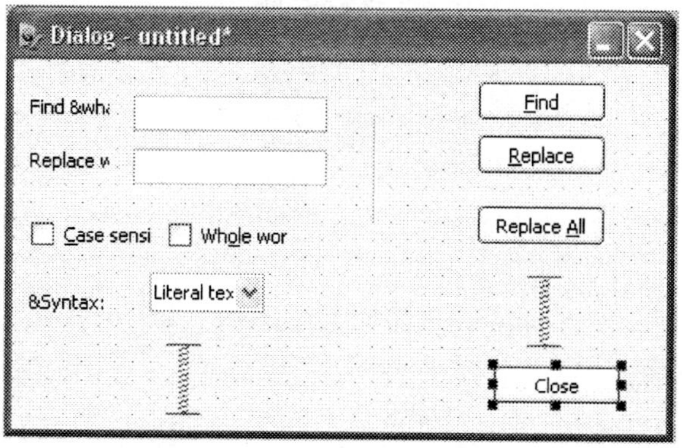

Figure 7.7 *A Find and Replace dialog that is not laid out*

What is the best way to lay out this form? What is the best design for this form? The answers to these questions are matters of taste and practice. Here, we simply show the mechanics, and leave the aesthetics to you.

We will begin by laying out the first two Labels and their Line Edits. Click the form to deselect everything, then Shift+Click the Find what Label and its Line Edit, and the Replace with Label and its Line Edit. Once these four widgets are selected, click Form→Lay Out in a Grid (or click the corresponding toolbar button). The layout is indicated by a red line—layout lines are not visible at runtime.

Now deselect everything (by clicking the form), and select the two Check Boxes. Click Form→Lay Out Horizontally. Again, deselect everything, and this time lay out the Syntax Label and Combo Box using a horizontal layout. There should now be three layouts—a grid and two horizontal layouts, like those shown in Figure 7.8.

We can now lay out the layouts on the left-hand side of the form. Click the form to deselect everything. It can be tricky to select layouts (rather than widgets), so instead of selecting by using Shift+Click, we will use a selection rectangle. Click near the bottom left of the form, and drag the selection rectangle: This

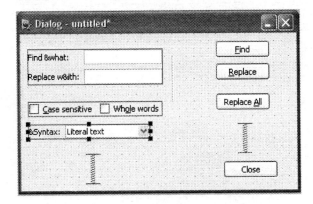

Figure 7.8 *A Find and Replace dialog with some layouts*

rectangle only needs to touch an object to select it, so drag up and right so that it touches the left-hand Vertical Spacer and the three layouts—and nothing else (not the Vertical Line, for example). Now, release and click Form→Lay Out Vertically.

We can use the same selection technique to lay out the buttons. Click the form to deselect everything. Now click near the bottom right of the form and drag so that the selection rectangle touches the Close button, the right-hand Vertical Spacer, and the other three buttons—and nothing else. Now, release and click Form→Lay Out Vertically. We should now have a form with every widget in the left- or right-hand layout and a Vertical Line in the middle, as shown in Figure 7.9.

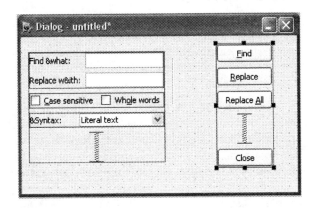

Figure 7.9 *A Find and Replace dialog almost laid out*

We are now ready to lay out the form itself. Deselect everything by clicking the form. Now click Form→Lay Out Horizontally. The form will now look a bit too tall, so just drag the bottom of the form up until the form looks better. If you drag a lot, the spacers may "disappear"; they are still there, but just too small to be seen.

We can now preview the form to see what the layout really looks like, and during the preview we can drag the form's corner to make it smaller and larger to check that its resizing behavior is sensible. To preview, click Form→Preview (or press Ctrl+R). It is also possible to preview in different styles using the Form→Preview in menu option. The form should now look like the one in Figure 7.10. If this is not the case, use Edit→Undo to unwind your changes, and then lay things out again. If you have to redo a layout, it sometimes helps to resize and reposition some of the widgets to give *Qt Designer* more of a clue about how you want the layout to go, especially when using grid layouts.

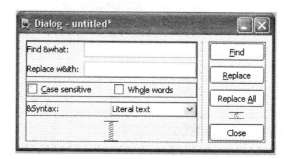

Figure 7.10 *A laid out Find and Replace dialog*

We are now ready to set the labels' buddies, set the form's tab order, do any connections we need, and name and save the form.

We will start with buddies. Click Edit→Edit Buddies to switch on buddy mode. To set up buddy relationships we click a Label and drag to the widget we want to be its buddy. So in this example, we must click the Find what Label and drag to its Line Edit, and then do the same for the Replace with Label and its Line Edit, and then for the Syntax Label and the Combo Box. To leave buddy mode, press F3. Now, no ampersands (&) should be visible in the Labels.

Next we will set the form's tab order. Click Edit→Edit Tab Order, and then click each numbered box in turn, in the tab order that you want. To leave tab order mode, press F3.

The Find, Replace, and Replace All buttons will need to be connected to our own custom methods; we will do this outside of *Qt Designer*. But the Close button can be connected to the dialog's reject() slot. To do this, click Edit→Edit Signals/Slots, and then drag from the Close button to the form. When you release, the Configure Connection dialog will pop up. Click the (no-argument) clicked() signal from the list of signals on the left, and the reject() slot from the list of slots on the right, and then click OK. To leave signal–slot mode, press F3.

Click the form to deselect everything. This also has the effect of making the property editor show the form's properties. Set the dialog's object name (which will be used in its class name) to "FindAndReplaceDlg", and set the "windowTitle" property to "Find and Replace". Now click File→Save to save the user interface, giving it a filename of findandreplacedlg.ui.

In this section, we have confined ourselves to using *Qt Designer* to create a custom dialog using one of the "Dialog" templates, since this is sufficient to learn the basics of how to use *Qt Designer*. However, *Qt Designer* can be used to create much more complex dialogs than the one we have created here, including dialogs with tab widgets and widget stacks that are often used for configuration dialogs that have dozens or even scores of options. It is also possible to extend *Qt Designer* with plug-ins that contain custom widgets. These widgets are normally written in C++, but from PyQt 4.2, it is also possible to incorporate custom widgets written in Python.

The Qt documentation includes a comprehensive *Qt Designer* manual that goes into more depth and covers more of the facilities available. The material covered in this section is sufficient to get started, but the only way to learn *Qt Designer* properly is to use it.

Having designed a user interface, the next step is to make it usable in our code.

Implementing Dialogs

When we create a user interface with *Qt Designer*, we create a subclass using multiple inheritance in which we put the code we need to give the user interface the behavior we need.* The first class we inherit is QDialog. If we were using the "Widget" template our first inherited class would be QWidget, and if we were using the "Main Window" template our first inherited class would be QMainWindow. The second class we inherit is the class that represents the user interface we designed using *Qt Designer*.

In the preceding section, we created a user interface with a form object name of "FindAndReplaceDlg", stored in the file findandreplacedlg.ui. We must run pyuic4 (directly, or via mkpyqt.py or Make PyQt) to generate the ui_findandreplacedlg.py module file. The module has a class in it whose name is the form's object name with a Ui_ prefix, so in this case the class name is Ui_FindAndReplaceDlg.

We will call our subclass FindAndReplaceDlg, and put it in the file findandreplacedlg.py.

Before we look at the class declaration and initializer, we will look at the imports.

```
import re
from PyQt4.QtCore import *
from PyQt4.QtGui import *
import ui_findandreplacedlg
```

---

*Other approaches are possible, and they are covered in the online documentation. None of them is quite as convenient as the approach we use here, though.

The first import is the regular expression module that we will use in the code. The second and third imports are the usual ones for PyQt programming. The last import is of the generated user interface module. Now we can look at our subclass.

```
class FindAndReplaceDlg(QDialog,
        ui_findandreplacedlg.Ui_FindAndReplaceDlg):

    def __init__(self, text, parent=None):
        super(FindAndReplaceDlg, self).__init__(parent)
        self.__text = unicode(text)
        self.__index = 0
        self.setupUi(self)
        if not MAC:
            self.findButton.setFocusPolicy(Qt.NoFocus)
            self.replaceButton.setFocusPolicy(Qt.NoFocus)
            self.replaceAllButton.setFocusPolicy(Qt.NoFocus)
            self.closeButton.setFocusPolicy(Qt.NoFocus)
        self.updateUi()
```

We inherit from both QDialog and from Ui_FindAndReplaceDlg. We rarely need to use multiple inheritance in Python programming, but for this situation it makes things much easier than would otherwise be the case. Our FindAndReplaceDlg subclass is, in effect, the union of the two classes it inherits from, and can access their attributes directly, prefixed with self, of course.

We have set our initializer to accept text that is the data the dialog will work on, and a parent widget. The super() call is made on the first inherited class, QDialog. We keep a copy of the text, and also an index position, in case the user clicks Find more than once to find subsequent occurrences of the same text.

The call to the setupUi() method is something we have not seen before. This method is provided by the generated module. When called it creates all the widgets specified in the user interface file, lays them out according to our design, sets their buddies and tab order, and makes the connections we set. In other words, it re-creates the form we designed in *Qt Designer*.

In addition, the setupUi() method calls QtCore.QMetaObject.connectSlotsBy-Name(), a static method that creates signal–slot connections between form widget signals and methods in our subclass that follow a particular naming convention. Any method whose name is of the form on_*widgetName*_*signalName* will have the named widget's named signal connected to it.

For example, our form has a widget called findLineEdit of type QLineEdit. One of the signals emitted by a QLineEdit is textEdited(QString). So, if we want to connect this signal, without calling the connect() method in the initializer, we can leave the job to setupUi(). This will work as long as we call the slot we want the signal to connect to, on_findLineEdit_textEdited. This is the approach we have used for all the connections in the form, apart from the Close button's clicked() signal that we connected visually in *Qt Designer*.

For Windows and Linux users, it is convenient to set the buttons' focus policies to "No Focus". This makes no difference to mouse users, but is often helpful to keyboard users. It means that pressing Tab moves the keyboard focus only among the editing widgets—in this example, the find line edit, the replace line edit, the checkboxes, and the combobox—which is usually more convenient than having to Tab over the buttons too. Keyboard users can still press any button using its keyboard accelerator (Esc in the case of the close button). Unfortunately, buddies and buttons don't provide Mac OS X keyboard users with accelerators (unless they switch on support for assistive devices), so these users need to be able to Tab to all controls, including the buttons. To cater to all platforms, instead of setting the buttons' focus policies in *Qt Designer*, we set them manually, after the user interface has been created by setupUi().

The MAC Boolean variable is True if the underlying window system is Mac OS X. It was set at the beginning of the file, after the imports, using the following rather enigmatic statement:

```
MAC = "qt_mac_set_native_menubar" in dir()
```

A clearer way of writing this is:

```
import PyQt4.QtGui
MAC = hasattr(PyQt4.QtGui, "qt_mac_set_native_menubar")
```

These work because the PyQt4.QtGui.qt_mac_set_native_menubar() function exists only on Mac OS X systems. We will use a similar technique for X Window System detection in Chapter 11.

The updateUi() method called at the end is our own custom method; we use it to enable or disable the buttons depending on whether the user has entered any text to find.

```
@pyqtSignature("QString")
def on_findLineEdit_textEdited(self, text):
    self.__index = 0
    self.updateUi()
```

Decora-
tors

85 ☜

Thanks to setupUi(), this method is automatically connected to by the findLine-Edit's textEdited() signal. Whenever we want an automatic connection we use the @pyqtSignature decorator to specify the signal's arguments. The purpose of the decorator is to distinguish between signals that have the same name but different parameters. In this particular case, there is only one textEdited() signal, so the decorator is not strictly necessary; but we always use the decorator as a matter of good practice. For example, if a later version of PyQt introduced another signal with the same name but with different arguments, code that used the decorator would continue to work, but code without it would not.

Since this slot is called when the user changes the find text, we reset the index position from which to start the search to 0 (the beginning). Here, and in the initializer, we end with a call to updateUi().

```
def updateUi(self):
    enable = not self.findLineEdit.text().isEmpty()
    self.findButton.setEnabled(enable)
    self.replaceButton.setEnabled(enable)
    self.replaceAllButton.setEnabled(enable)
```

We have already seen many examples of a method of this kind. Here, we enable the Find, Replace, and Replace All buttons, if the user has entered a find text. It does not matter whether there is any replace text, since it is perfectly valid to replace something with nothing, that is, to delete the text that is found. This method is the reason why the form starts with every button except the Close button disabled.

When the user closes the form, the text it holds (which may be different from the original text if the user has used replace or replace all) is accessible using the text() method.

```
def text(self):
    return self.__text
```

Some Python programmers would not provide a method for this; instead, they would have a self.text variable (rather than self.__text), and access the variable directly.

The rest of the dialog's functionality is implemented in methods that are invoked as a result of the user pressing one of the buttons (other than the Close button), plus a helper method. Their implementation is not specifically relevant to using *Qt Designer*, but we will briefly review them for completeness.

```
@pyqtSignature("")
def on_findButton_clicked(self):
    regex = self.makeRegex()
    match = regex.search(self.__text, self.__index)
    if match is not None:
        self.__index = match.end()
        self.emit(SIGNAL("found"), match.start())
    else:
        self.emit(SIGNAL("notfound"))
```

A button's clicked() signal has an optional Boolean argument that we are not interested in, so we specify an empty parameter list for the @pyqtSignature decorator. In contrast, we could not have used an empty parameter list for the on_findLineEdit_textEdited() slot's decorator, because the textEdited() signal's argument is not optional, so it must be included.

To perform the search, we create a regular expression to specify the find text and some of the search's characteristics. Then we search the text using the regular expression, from the current index position. If a match was found we update the index position to be at the match's end, ready for a subsequent

search, and emit a signal with the position in the text where the find text
was found.

```python
def makeRegex(self):
    findText = unicode(self.findLineEdit.text())
    if unicode(self.syntaxComboBox.currentText()) == "Literal":
        findText = re.escape(findText)
    flags = re.MULTILINE|re.DOTALL|re.UNICODE
    if not self.caseCheckBox.isChecked():
        flags |= re.IGNORECASE
    if self.wholeCheckBox.isChecked():
        findText = r"\b%s\b" % findText
    return re.compile(findText, flags)
```

We begin by getting the find text that the user has entered. We know that it
cannot be empty because the buttons (apart from the Close button) are enabled
only if there is some find text. If the user has chosen a literal text search, we
use the re.escape() function to escape any regular expression meta-characters
(like "\") that may be in the user's find text. Then we initialize our search
flags. We supplement the flags with the re.IGNORECASE flag if the caseCheckBox is
unchecked. If the user has asked to search for whole words, we put a \b before
and after the find text: This is a token in Python's (and QRegExp's) regular expression language that specifies a word boundary. The r in front of the string
literal indicates a "raw" string in which we can write characters like "\" un-
escaped. Finally we return the regular expression in compiled (ready-to-use)
form.★

Raw
strings

157 ✏

If we knew that the text to be searched was normally going to be a QString
rather than a unicode, it might be preferable to use the PyQt QRegExp class
rather than the Python standard library's re class.

```python
@pyqtSignature("")
def on_replaceButton_clicked(self):
    regex = self.makeRegex()
    self.__text = regex.sub(unicode(self.replaceLineEdit.text()),
                            self.__text, 1)
```

This method is quite simple because it passes on its preparation work to the
makeRegex() method. We use the sub method ("substitute") to replace the first
occurrence of the find text with the replacement text. The replacement text
could be empty. The 1 is the maximum number of replacements to make.

```python
@pyqtSignature("")
def on_replaceAllButton_clicked(self):
    regex = self.makeRegex()
```

★The QRegExp documentation provides a brief introduction to regular expressions. Python's regular
expression engine is covered in the re module documentation. For in-depth coverage see *Mastering
Regular Expressions* by Jeffrey E. Friedl.

```
        self.__text = regex.sub(unicode(self.replaceLineEdit.text()),
                            self.__text)
```

This method is almost identical to the one earlier. The only difference is that we do not specify a maximum number of replacements, so `sub()` will replace as many (nonoverlapping) occurrences of the find text as it finds.

We have now implemented the `FindAndReplaceDlg`. The implementation of the dialog's methods is not really any different from what we have done before, except for our use of the decorator and `setupUi()` to provide automatic connections.

To use the dialog in an application we must make sure that the `ui_findandreplacedlg.py` module file is generated, and we must import the `findandreplacedlg` module we have just written. We will see how the form is created and used in the next section.

Testing Dialogs

Since any PyQt widget, including any dialog, can be used as a top-level window in its own right, it is easy to test a dialog by instantiating it and starting the event loop.★ Often, though, we need to do a bit more. For example, we may need to set up some initial data, or provide methods to receive the dialog's signals so that we can see that they are working correctly.

In the case of the Find and Replace dialog, we need some initial text, and we need to check that the connections work and that the find and replace methods work.

So, at the end of the `findandreplacedlg.py` file, we have added some extra code. This code is executed only if the file is run stand-alone, so it does not affect performance or interfere with the use of the dialog when it is used in an application.

```
if __name__ == "__main__":
    import sys

    text = """US experience shows that, unlike traditional patents,
software patents do not encourage innovation and R&D, quite the
contrary. In particular they hurt small and medium-sized enterprises
and generally newcomers in the market. They will just weaken the market
and increase spending on patents and litigation, at the expense of
technological innovation and research. Especially dangerous are
attempts to abuse the patent system by preventing interoperability as a
means of avoiding competition with technological ability.
--- Extract quoted from Linus Torvalds and Alan Cox's letter
```

★When using `pyuic4` we can specify a command-line option of -x to get the dialog generated with a bit of extra code so that it can be tested stand-alone.

```
        to the President of the European Parliament
http://www.effi.org/patentit/patents_torvalds_cox.html"""

    def found(where):
        print "Found at %d" % where

    def nomore():
        print "No more found"

    app = QApplication(sys.argv)
    form = FindAndReplaceDlg(text)
    form.connect(form, SIGNAL("found"), found)
    form.connect(form, SIGNAL("notfound"), nomore)
    form.show()
    app.exec_()
    print form.text()
```

We begin by importing the sys module, and then we create a piece of text to work on. Next, we create a couple of simple functions for the dialog's signals to be connected to.

We create the QApplication object in the normal way, and then we create an instance of our dialog, passing it our test text. We connect the dialog's two signals to our slots, and call show(). Then we start off the event loop. When the event loop terminates we print the dialog's text: This will be different from the original text if the user replaced some text.

The dialog can now be run from a console and tested.

```
    C:\pyqt\chap07>python findandreplacedlg.py
```

Unless using automated testing tools, it is often helpful to add testing functionality to dialogs. It does not take too much time or effort to write them, and running them whenever a change is made to the dialog's logic will help minimize the introduction of bugs.

Sometimes we pass complex objects to dialogs that may appear to make testing impossible. But thanks to Python's duck typing we can always create a fake class that simulates enough behavior to be usable for testing. For example, in Chapter 12, we use a property editor dialog. This dialog operates on "Node" objects, so in the testing code we create a FakeNode class that provides the methods for setting and getting a node's properties that the dialog makes use of. (The relevant files are chap12/propertiesdlg.ui, from which ui_propertiesdlg.py is generated, and chap12/propertiesdlg.py where the PropertiesDlg is implemented.)

Summary

Qt Designer provides a quick and easy way to create user interfaces. Using a visual design tool makes it much easier to see whether a design "works". Another benefit of *Qt Designer* is that if we change a design, providing we have not added, removed, or renamed any widgets we refer to in code, our code will not need to be changed at all. And even if we do add, rename, or remove widgets, the changes to our code may be quite small, since *Qt Designer* handles all the widget creation and laying out for us.

The fundamental principles of using *Qt Designer* are always the same: We drag widgets onto a form, containers (such as frames, group boxes, and tab widgets) first, then ordinary widgets, and we set their properties. Then we add spacers to occupy gaps. Next we select particular widgets, spacers, and layouts, and apply layouts to them, repeating this process until everything is laid out. Then we lay out the form itself. At the end we set buddies, the tab order, and the signal–slot connections.

Implementing dialogs with user interfaces that have been created by *Qt Designer* is similar to implementing them by hand. The biggest difference is in the initializer, where we simply call `setupUi()` to create and lay out the widgets, and to create the signal–slot connections. The methods we implement can be done just as we have done them before (and their code will be no different), but usually we use the `on_widgetName_signalName` naming convention, along with the `@pyqtSignature` decorator to take advantage of `setupUi()`'s ability to automatically create connections.

A use case that we have not covered is to use the "Widget" template to create composite widgets (widgets made up of two or more other widgets laid out together). In some cases these widget designs can be used for entire forms, and in other cases they can be used as components of forms—for example, to provide the page of a tab widget or of a widget stack. Or two or more composite widgets could be laid out together in a form to create a more complex form. This use is possible by using *Qt Designer* and generating the Python modules in the normal way. Then we can import the generated modules, and in our form class, we call each custom widget's `setupUi()` method to create the user interface.

The questions about how smart a dialog is, what modality it should have, and how it validates are no different for dialogs created with *Qt Designer* than for those created by hand. The only exception that we can set widget properties in *Qt Designer*—for example, we could set a spinbox's range and initial value. We can, of course, do the same thing in code, but for widgets that need only simple validation, doing it all in *Qt Designer* is usually more convenient.

We must use `pyuic4` to generate Python modules from *Qt Designer* `.ui` files, either by running `pyuic4` directly or by using `mkpyqt.py` or Make PyQt, both of which also generate Python modules for resource files if `.qrc` files are present.

If we are not using testing tools, adding testing code that is executed only if the form is run stand-alone does not affect the performance of our dialogs, and can be very convenient both during development and when maintaining a dialog. If complex objects that the dialog depends on are not available, we can often create a "fake" class that provides the same methods as the complex object, and pass an instance of the fake class for testing purposes.

All PyQt programs can be written entirely by hand; there is never any need to use *Qt Designer*. However, designing dialogs with a visual design tool can be very helpful, since the results can be seen immediately, and changes to designs can be made quickly and easily. Another benefit of using *Qt Designer* is that a lot of fairly repetitive code for creating, laying out, and connecting widgets can be automatically generated rather than written by hand. *Qt Designer* was used to create a dialog in both this chapter, and the preceding one. We will see many more examples of dialogs created with *Qt Designer* in the following chapters.

Exercise

Use *Qt Designer* to create a user interface with one of the designs shown in Figure 7.11, or with a design of your own. You will probably need to use a Grid Layout, as well as Vertical and Horizontal Layouts. For grid layouts, you may have to try a few times, perhaps resizing and positioning widgets to help *Qt Designer* create the grid you want. Use QDialogButtonBoxes for the buttons.

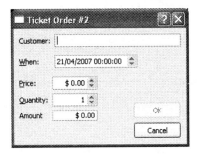

Figure 7.11 *A dialog with two different designs*

The price spinbox should have a range of 0.00–5 000.00, be right-aligned, and have a prefix of "$ ", as shown in Figure 7.11. The quantity spinbox should have a range of 1–50 and also be right-aligned. Set the date format to be whatever you prefer if you don't like the default.

The widgets you will refer to in code should have sensible names—for example, customerLineEdit and priceSpinBox.

Make the appropriate buddies, that is, from the "customer" Label to its Line Edit, from the "when" Label to the Date Time Edit, and so on. Also make sure that the Tab order is customer, when date, price, quantity, button box.

Create a subclass to use the user interface. The code should ensure that the OK button is enabled only if the customer Line Edit is not empty and the amount is greater than zero. To access a button in a `QDialogButtonBox`, use the `button()` method with the button's constant as the argument—for example, `buttonBox.button(QDialogButtonBox.Ok)`.

The amount should be recalculated and shown in the amount label every time the user changes one of the spinbox values. Set the when date's range to be from tomorrow, until next year. Provide a `result()` method that returns a four-tuple (`unicode, datetime.datetime, float, int`) for the customer, when date, price, and quantity. (If you are using a PyQt version prior to 4.1, return the date as a `QDateTime`; otherwise, use the `QDateTime.toPyDateTime()` method to get a `datetime.datetime`.)

Include enough test code at the end to create and show a `TicketOrderDlg` so that you can interact with it. After the event loop has finished print the tuple returned by the `result()` method on the console.

The subclass, including the test code, can be written in about 60 lines. If this is the first time you have used *Qt Designer* it may take 15–20 minutes to get the design right, but with practice a dialog like this should take just a few minutes.

Model solutions are provided in `chap07/ticketorderdlg1.ui` and `chap07/ticket-orderdlg2.ui`, with a test program in `chap07/ticketorderdlg.py`.

8

● Main Window Responsibilities

● Data Container Responsibilities

● Saving and Loading Binary Files

● Saving and Loading Text Files

● Saving and Loading XML Files

Data Handling and Custom File Formats

Most applications need to load and save data. Often the data format is predetermined because the application is reading data produced by some other application over which it has no control. But for applications where we create our own file formats, a lot of options are available.

In Chapter 6 we created a main-window-style application from which we learned how to create menus and toolbars, and how to handle file loading and saving. In this chapter we will work on another main-window-style application, but this time our focus will be on the application's data.

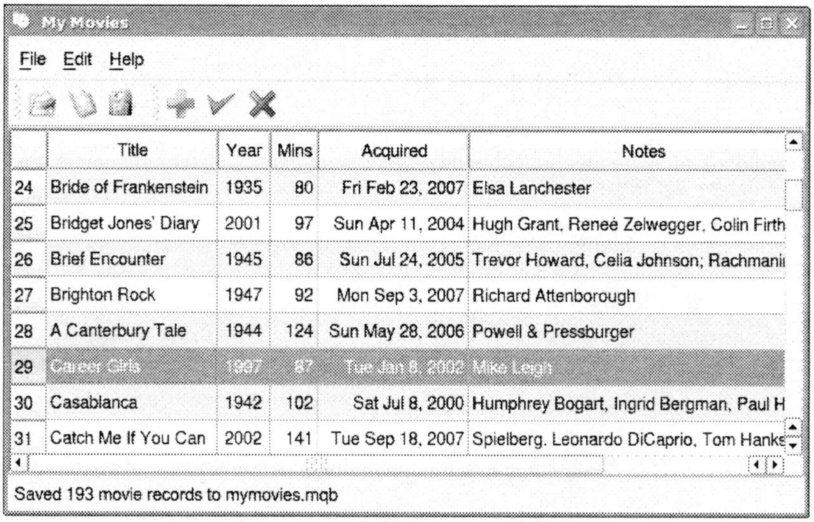

Figure 8.1 *The My Movies application*

The application we will take as our example is called My Movies; it is shown in Figure 8.1. It is used to store some basic information about the movies we

227

might have in our collection. The application will allow us to view and edit a collection of custom Movie objects (or movie *records* as we will call them), and to load and save these records from and to disk in a variety of formats.

If you just want to dive straight into file handling, you can jump ahead to the relevant sections. Coverage of saving and loading binary files begins on page 240, of text files on page 249, and of XML files on page 256. You can always come back to the first two sections to cover the relationship between the GUI and file handling.

String
policy
28 ☜

In all the previous examples we usually kept as much data as possible in Python data types and converted to and from PyQt types only when necessary. And for strings in particular, we proposed a policy that meant that we always converted QStrings to unicodes as soon as possible and always operated on unicode strings. But in this chapter we are going to take the opposite approach, and keep all our data in PyQt types, converting to Python types only when necessary. One reason for doing this is that PyQt provides excellent support for binary data, and uses the same binary formats as C++/Qt, which is useful when working with files that must be accessed by both C++ and Python programs. Another reason is that this will also provide a contrast that will help us understand the pros and cons of each approach so that we can make the right decisions in applications we work on later.

One immediate benefit of holding data in PyQt types is that we do not have to keep converting data that we give to or get from the widgets we use for viewing and editing. When dealing with a large collection of data, this could be a significant saving of processing overhead.

When we have custom data to load and save five options are available to us. We can use binary, plain text, or XML files, or we can use QSettings objects with an explicit filename, or we can use a database. In this chapter we will cover the first three options, and briefly mention the fourth, QSettings, here. We will defer coverage of databases until Chapter 15.

All the options apart from QSettings can be implemented using either Python's standard library or PyQt. In this chapter, we will discuss loading and saving both binary and text formats using both libraries so that we can compare and contrast them. For XML, we will use PyQt for loading and parsing, and we will do the saving ourselves. Python's standard library also provides considerable XML support, but covering it would not show anything that cannot be done with PyQt's XML classes.

In Chapter 6, we saw how to use a QSettings object to save and load user settings, such as the main window's size and position, and a list of recently used files. The class stores all data as QVariants, but this is perfectly acceptable for small amounts of data. We can use this class to store custom data by creating a QSettings instance with a filename—for example, iniFile = QSettings("curvedata.ini", QSettings.IniFormat). Now we can use the iniFile object to write data using setValue() and to read data using value(), in both cases converting between QVariant and the relevant type.

In the following section we will look at the high-level file handling and data presentation that are performed by the application's main window subclass. In the second section, we will look at the application's data module, including the implementation of individual data items, and of the data item container in which the application's data is held.

Then, in the subsequent sections, we will look at saving and loading data in various formats. In the section on binary files, we will look at how to use PyQt's QDataStream class and also the standard Python library's cPickle module to load and save our collection of movie records. In the section on text files, we will see how to load and save our movie records in plain text using PyQt's QTextStream and the Python standard library's codecs module. And in the last section we will write the code to save the records as XML by hand, and see how to use both DOM and SAX parsers to read back the XML data.

Main Window Responsibilities

The main window is usually given responsibility for offering the user the high-level file-handling actions, and for presenting the application's data. In this section, we will focus particularly on the file actions, since they differ from what we did in Chapter 6's Image Changer application and they are more representative of what happens in larger applications. We will also look at how the data is presented to the user. In the My Movies application, the data is held in a "container" (a MovieContainer), and all the work of saving and loading (and exporting and importing) is passed on to the container by the main window. We will look at the container in the next section, and at the container's saving and loading code in the sections that follow that.

The source code is in the chap08 directory, and it includes a *Qt Designer*-designed user interface for adding and editing movie records. Figure 8.2 shows the application's Python modules.

We have chosen to make a distinction between saving and exporting, and between loading and importing. When we load a file, the filename we used becomes the application's current filename for when we save. If we save a file, we use the application's current filename, so subsequent saves will be to the same file. We can change the current filename by using the "save as" action. When we import a file, we clear the current filename; this means that the data must be given a new filename if the user wants to save it. If the user exports the data, they are asked for a new filename, and the current filename is not affected.

Now we are ready to look at the main window's file-handling functionality. We will begin by looking at the start of the main window's initializer, to see

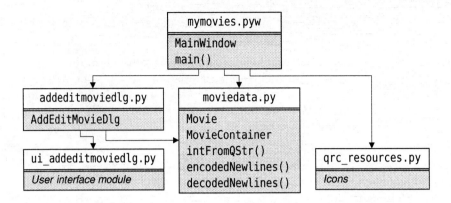

Figure 8.2 *The My Movie application's modules, classes, and functions*

the creation of the data-holding movie container and the data-presenting QTableWidget.

```
class MainWindow(QMainWindow):

    def __init__(self, parent=None):
        super(MainWindow, self).__init__(parent)

        self.movies = moviedata.MovieContainer()
        self.table = QTableWidget()
        self.setCentralWidget(self.table)
```

After calling super(), we create a new empty movies container. (We will look at the Movie and MovieContainer classes shortly.) Then we create a QTableWidget. This widget is used to present and optionally to edit tabular data. The table is set up and populated in updateTable(). We have omitted the rest of the initializer, since we already know from Chapter 6 how to set up the status bar, create the file, edit, and help actions, populate the menus and toolbars, and restore the application's state from the previous session's settings.

For completeness, we will now take a brief detour to review updateTable() to see how the table widget is set up and populated. (You could skip ahead to the fileNew() method on page 232 if you prefer to focus purely on the file handling.) The approach we are using is very simple and direct. PyQt also offers a more sophisticated approach to populating and editing item-based widgets such as lists, tables, and trees, using PyQt's model/view architecture—we will learn about this in Chapter 14.

```
    def updateTable(self, current=None):
        self.table.clear()
        self.table.setRowCount(len(self.movies))
        self.table.setColumnCount(5)
        self.table.setHorizontalHeaderLabels(["Title", "Year", "Mins",
                "Acquired", "Notes"])
```

```
        self.table.setAlternatingRowColors(True)
        self.table.setEditTriggers(QTableWidget.NoEditTriggers)
        self.table.setSelectionBehavior(QTableWidget.SelectRows)
        self.table.setSelectionMode(QTableWidget.SingleSelection)
        selected = None
```

This method is quite long, so we will review it in three parts. It can be called with no argument, in which case it simply populates the table; or it can be called with the id() of the current Movie, in which case it makes the specified movie's row selected and visible (scrolling if necessary), after populating the table. A current movie is passed if a movie has just been added or edited.

We begin by clearing the table; this gets rid of both the data and the headings. Next, we set the row and column counts, and the column headers. We set the table's properties so that the user cannot edit anything in-place, since we prefer to use a separate add/edit dialog in this particular application. We also ensure that users can select only a single row at a time. The selected variable holds the QTableWidgetItem that holds the title and id() of the current movie, if there is one.

```
        for row, movie in enumerate(self.movies):
            item = QTableWidgetItem(movie.title)
            if current is not None and current == id(movie):
                selected = item
            item.setData(Qt.UserRole, QVariant(long(id(movie))))
            self.table.setItem(row, 0, item)
            year = movie.year
            if year != movie.UNKNOWNYEAR:
                item = QTableWidgetItem("%d" % year)
                item.setTextAlignment(Qt.AlignCenter)
                self.table.setItem(row, 1, item)
            minutes = movie.minutes
            if minutes != movie.UNKNOWNMINUTES:
                item = QTableWidgetItem("%d" % minutes)
                item.setTextAlignment(Qt.AlignRight|Qt.AlignVCenter)
                self.table.setItem(row, 2, item)
            item = QTableWidgetItem(movie.acquired.toString(
                                    moviedata.DATEFORMAT))
            item.setTextAlignment(Qt.AlignRight|Qt.AlignVCenter)
            self.table.setItem(row, 3, item)
            notes = movie.notes
            if notes.length() > 40:
                notes = notes.left(39) + "..."
            self.table.setItem(row, 4, QTableWidgetItem(notes))
```

Each cell in a QTableWidget is represented by a QTableWidgetItem. These items can hold displayable text as well as "user" data. We iterate over every movie in the movie container, creating one row of items for each one. We store the movie's title in the first cell (item) of each row, and set this item's user data to hold the movie's id(). We must convert the ID to be a long, to ensure that it is held correctly inside the QVariant. Once the item has been created and set up, we put it in the table at the appropriate row and column.

We only populate the year and minutes cells if we have data for them. For the notes, we truncate and add an ellipsis if the data is long, since notes could be many paragraphs in size.

```
        self.table.resizeColumnsToContents()
        if selected is not None:
            selected.setSelected(True)
            self.table.setCurrentItem(selected)
            self.table.scrollToItem(selected)
```

Once all the table items have been added, we resize the table's columns to match their contents.

When we iterate over the movies in the movie container, the movies are returned in alphabetical order (but ignoring leading "A", "An", and "The", words). If the user adds a new movie or edits an existing movie, we want to ensure that the movie they have just added or edited is both selected and visible. This is achieved by calling updateTable() after the add or edit, with the ID of the movie they added or edited. At the end of updateTable(), if a movie ID was passed in, the selected variable will hold the item corresponding to the movie's title cell, and this item (and therefore the item's row) will be made both current and selected, and if necessary the table widget will scroll to make sure that the row is visible to the user.

```
    def fileNew(self):
        if not self.okToContinue():
            return
        self.movies.clear()
        self.statusBar().clearMessage()
        self.updateTable()
```

This method is similar to the method of the same name used for the Image Changer application. The key difference is that instead of the main window being responsible for the data, the work is delegated to the movie container held in self.movies. When updateTable() is called, there will be no movie records, so the widget will just show the column headers and nothing else.

The okToContinue() method is almost the same as the one we used in the Image Changer application. The only difference is that instead of the condition checking self.dirty (since the Image Changer's main window held the application's data) it calls self.movies.isDirty() because in this application, the movies container holds the data.

```
    def fileOpen(self):
        if not self.okToContinue():
```

```
                return
        path = QFileInfo(self.movies.filename()).path() \
                if not self.movies.filename().isEmpty() else "."
        fname = QFileDialog.getOpenFileName(self,
                    "My Movies - Load Movie Data", path,
                    "My Movies data files (%s)" % \
                    self.movies.formats())
        if not fname.isEmpty():
            ok, msg = self.movies.load(fname)
            self.statusBar().showMessage(msg, 5000)
            self.updateTable()
```

The file open method is structurally the same as we have seen before. The movie container holds the current filename as a QString. Normally, an application has just one custom file format, but for the sake of illustration the My Movies application supports several, so we have provided a formats() method to return the extensions that can be used.

The main window subclass passes on the work of loading to the movies container. We have designed our movie container's load and save methods to return a Boolean success/failure flag and a message. The message is either an error message, or a report of how many movie records were loaded or saved. In the My Movies application, we use only the message.

If the load is successful, the movie container will contain the new movie records and updateTable() will display them. If the load failed, the movie container will be empty, and updateTable() will show only the column headers.

```
        def fileSave(self):
            if self.movies.filename().isEmpty():
                self.fileSaveAs()
            else:
                ok, msg = self.movies.save()
                self.statusBar().showMessage(msg, 5000)
```

Again, the logic for this method is the same as we have seen before. The code used for saving and loading depends on the filename extension, as we will see later.

We will skip the code for fileSaveAs(); it is the same as for the Image Changer application, except that we use QString rather than unicode methods with the filename, and we use a default extension of .mqb (My Movies in Qt binary format).

```
        def fileImportDOM(self):
            self.fileImport("dom")


        def fileImportSAX(self):
            self.fileImport("sax")
```

```
def fileImport(self, format):
    if not self.okToContinue():
        return
    path = QFileInfo(self.movies.filename()).path() \
            if not self.movies.filename().isEmpty() else "."
    fname = QFileDialog.getOpenFileName(self,
                "My Movies - Import Movie Data", path,
                "My Movies XML files (*.xml)")
    if not fname.isEmpty():
        if format == "dom":
            ok, msg = self.movies.importDOM(fname)
        else:
            ok, msg = self.movies.importSAX(fname)
        self.statusBar().showMessage(msg, 5000)
        self.updateTable()
```

Normally we would provide a single import method and use either a SAX or a DOM parser. Here we have chosen to show both parsers in use, so we provide two separate import actions. Both produce the same results.

The file action code for importing is very similar to the "file open" action, only we use the import parser specified by the user. And as with all the file-handling code, we pass on the work to the movie container.

```
def fileExportXml(self):
    fname = self.movies.filename()
    if fname.isEmpty():
        fname = "."
    else:
        i = fname.lastIndexOf(".")
        if i > 0:
            fname = fname.left(i)
        fname += ".xml"
    fname = QFileDialog.getSaveFileName(self,
                "My Movies - Export Movie Data", fname,
                "My Movies XML files (*.xml)")
    if not fname.isEmpty():
        if not fname.contains("."):
            fname += ".xml"
        ok, msg = self.movies.exportXml(fname)
        self.statusBar().showMessage(msg, 5000)
```

We provide only one XML export method. The code is similar to the "file save as" action. Notice that we must use QString methods to ensure that the filename has the .xml extension, rather than the unicode methods we used in the Image Changer application, because the filename is held as a QString.

Data Container Responsibilities

The application's data container is responsible for holding all the data items, that is, the movie records, and for saving and loading them to and from disk. We saw in the preceding section when we looked at the `MainWindow.updateTable()` method how the container could be iterated over using a `for` loop to get all the movies so that they could be displayed in the application's `QTableWidget`. In this section, we will look at the functionality provided by the `moviedata` module, including the data structures used to hold the movie data, how we provide support for ordered iteration, and other aspects, but excluding the actual saving and loading code since that is covered in the sections that follow.

Why use a custom data container at all? After all, we could simply use one of Python's built-in data structures, such as a list or a dictionary. We prefer to take an approach where we wrap a standard data structure in a custom container class. This ensures that accesses to the data are controlled by our class, which helps to maintain data integrity. It also makes it easier to extend the container's functionality, and to replace the underlying data structure in the future, without affecting existing code. In other words, this is an object-oriented approach that avoids the disadvantages of simply using, say, a list, with some global functions.

We will begin with the `moviedata` module's imports and constants.

```
import bisect
import codecs
import copy_reg
import cPickle
import gzip
from PyQt4.QtCore import *
from PyQt4.QtXml import *
```

We store the movies in canonicalized title order, ignoring case, and ignoring leading "A", "An", and "The" words. To minimize insertion and lookup times we maintain the order using the `bisect` module, using the same techniques we used for the `OrderedDict` we implemented in Chapter 3.

Ordered-
Dict

92 ☜

The `codecs` module is necessary for reading and writing Python text files using a specific text codec. The `copy_reg` and `cPickle` modules are used for saving and loading Python "pickles"—these are files that contain arbitrary Python data structures. The `gzip` module is used to compress data; we will use it to compress and decompress our pickled data. The `PyQt4.QtCore` import is familiar, but we must also import the `PyQt4.QtXml` module to give us access to PyQt's SAX and DOM parsers. We will see all of these modules in use in the following sections. Note that we do not need the `PyQt4.QtGui` module, since the `moviedata` module is a pure data-handling module with no GUI functionality.

```
CODEC = "UTF-8"
```

```
NEWPARA = unichr(0x2029)
NEWLINE = unichr(0x2028)
```

We want to use the UTF-8 codec for text files. This is an 8-bit Unicode encoding that uses one byte for each ASCII character, and two or more bytes for any other character. It is probably the most widely used Unicode text encoding used in files. By using Unicode we can store text written in just about any human language in use today.

Although \n is a valid Unicode character, we will need to use the Unicode-specific paragraph break and line break characters when we use XML. This is because XML parsers do not normally distinguish between one ASCII whitespace character, such as newline, and another, such as space, which is not convenient if we want to preserve the user's line and paragraphs breaks.

```
class Movie(object):
    UNKNOWNYEAR = 1890
    UNKNOWNMINUTES = 0

    def __init__(self, title=None, year=UNKNOWNYEAR,
                 minutes=UNKNOWNMINUTES, acquired=None, notes=None):
        self.title = title
        self.year = year
        self.minutes = minutes
        self.acquired = acquired \
                if acquired is not None else QDate.currentDate()
        self.notes = notes
```

The Movie class is used to hold the data about one movie. We use instance variables directly rather than providing simple getters and setters. The title and notes are stored as QStrings, and the date acquired as a QDate. The year the movie was released and its duration in minutes are held as ints. We provide two static constants to indicate that we do not know when the movie was released or how long it is.

We are now ready to look at the movie container class. This class holds an ordered list of movies, and provides functionality for saving and loading (and exporting and importing) movies in a variety of formats.

```
class MovieContainer(object):
    MAGIC_NUMBER = 0x3051E
    FILE_VERSION = 100

    def __init__(self):
        self.__fname = QString()
        self.__movies = []
        self.__movieFromId = {}
        self.__dirty = False
```

The MAGIC_NUMBER and FILE_VERSION are used for saving and loading files using PyQt's QDataStream class.

id()
function

13 ☞

Object
refer-
ences

12 ☞

The filename is held as a QString. Each element of the __movies list is itself a two-element list, the first element being a sort key and the second a Movie. This is the class's main data structure, and it is used to hold the movies in order. The __movieFromId dictionary's keys are the id()s of Movie objects, and the values are Movies. As we saw in Chapter 1, every Python object very conveniently has a unique ID, available by calling id() on it. This dictionary is used to provide fast movie lookup when a movie's ID is known. For example, the main window stores movie IDs as "user" data in its first column of QTableWidgetItems. There is no duplication of data, of course, since the two data structures really hold references to Movie objects rather than Movie objects themselves.

```
def __iter__(self):
    for pair in iter(self.__movies):
        yield pair[1]
```

When the MainWindow.updateTable() method iterated over the movie container using a for loop, Python used the container's __iter__() method. Here we can see that we iterate over the ordered list of [key, movie] lists, returning just the movie item each time.

```
def __len__(self):
    return len(self.__movies)
```

This method allows us to use the len() function on movie containers.

In the following sections we will see the code for loading and saving the movies held in a movie container in various formats. But first we will look at how the container is cleared, and how movies are added, deleted, and updated, so that we can get a feel for how the container works, particularly regarding ordering.

```
def clear(self, clearFilename=True):
    self.__movies = []
    self.__movieFromId = {}
    if clearFilename:
        self.__fname = QString()
    self.__dirty = False
```

This method is used to clear all the data, possibly including the filename. It is called from MainWindow.fileNew(), which does clear the filename, and from the various save and load methods, which leave the filename untouched. The movie container maintains a dirty flag so that it always knows whether there are unsaved changes.

```
def add(self, movie):
    if id(movie) in self.__movieFromId:
```

```
        return False
    key = self.key(movie.title, movie.year)
    bisect.insert_left(self.__movies, [key, movie])
    self.__movieFromId[id(movie)] = movie
    self.__dirty = True
    return True
```

The first `if` statement ensures that we don't add the same movie twice. We use the `key()` method to generate a suitable order key, and then use the `bisect` module's `insert_left()` function to insert the two-element `[key, movie]` list into the `__movies` list. This is very fast because the `bisect` module uses the binary chop algorithm. We also make sure that the `__movieFromId` dictionary is up-to-date, and set the container to be dirty.

```
def key(self, title, year):
    text = unicode(title).lower()
    if text.startswith("a "):
        text = text[2:]
    elif text.startswith("an "):
        text = text[3:]
    elif text.startswith("the "):
        text = text[4:]
    parts = text.split(" ", 1)
    if parts[0].isdigit():
        text = "%08d " % int(parts[0])
        if len(parts) > 1:
            text += parts[1]
    return u"%s\t%d" % (text.replace(" ", ""), year)
```

This method generates a key string suitable for ordering our movie data. We do not guarantee key uniqueness (although it would not be difficult to do), because the ordered data structure is a list in which duplicate keys are not a problem. The code is English-specific, eliminating the definite and indefinite articles from movie titles. If the movie's title begins with a number, we pad the number with leading zeros so that, for example, "20" will come before "100". We do not need to pad the year, because years are always exactly four digits. All the other data is stored using PyQt data types, but we have chosen to use `unicode` for the key strings.

```
def delete(self, movie):
    if id(movie) not in self.__movieFromId:
        return False
    key = self.key(movie.title, movie.year)
    i = bisect.bisect_left(self.__movies, [key, movie])
    del self.__movies[i]
    del self.__movieFromId[id(movie)]
    self.__dirty = True
    return True
```

To delete a movie we must remove it from both data structures, and in the case of the __movies list, we must first find the movie's index position.

```python
def updateMovie(self, movie, title, year, minutes=None,
                notes=None):
    if minutes is not None:
        movie.minutes = minutes
    if notes is not None:
        movie.notes = notes
    if title != movie.title or year != movie.year:
        key = self.key(movie.title, movie.year)
        i = bisect.bisect_left(self.__movies, [key, movie])
        self.__movies[i][0] = self.key(title, year)
        movie.title = title
        movie.year = year
        self.__movies.sort()
    self.__dirty = True
```

If the user edits a movie, the application always calls this method with the user's changes. If the minutes or notes are passed as None, we take that to mean that they have not been changed. If the movie's title or year has changed, the movie may now be in the wrong position in the __movies list. In these cases, we find the movie using its original title and year, set the new title and year, and then re-sort the list. This is not as expensive in practice as it may at first appear. The list will contain, at most, one incorrectly sorted item, and Python's sort algorithm is highly optimized for partially sorted data.

If we ever found that we had a performance problem here, we could always reimplement updateMovie() using delete() and add() instead.

```python
@staticmethod
def formats():
    return "*.mqb *.mpb *.mqt *.mpt"
```

Normally, we would provide one, or at most two, custom data formats for an application, but for the purposes of illustration we provide three formats using four extensions. Extension .mqb is Qt binary format, and it uses the QDataStream class, and extension .mpb is Python pickle format (using gzip compression). Extension .mqt is Qt text format, and it uses the QTextStream class, and extension .mpt is Python text format. Both text formats are identical, but by using different extensions we can use different save and load code for the purposes of comparison.

```python
def save(self, fname=QString()):
    if not fname.isEmpty():
        self.__fname = fname
    if self.__fname.endsWith(".mqb"):
        return self.saveQDataStream()
```

```
        elif self.__fname.endsWith(".mpb"):
            return self.savePickle()
        elif self.__fname.endsWith(".mqt"):
            return self.saveQTextStream()
        elif self.__fname.endsWith(".mpt"):
            return self.saveText()
        return False, "Failed to save: invalid file extension"
```

When the user invokes the "file save" action we would expect the data container's save() method to be invoked. This is indeed what happens in My Movies and is the normal practice. However, here, instead of performing the save itself, the save() method hands the work to a method that is specific to the filename's extension. This is purely so that we can show how to save in the different formats; in a real application we would normally use only one format.

There is a corresponding load() method, that has the same logic as the save() method and passes its work to load methods that are extension-specific. All the load and save methods return a two-element tuple, the first element a Boolean success/failure flag and the second a message, either an error message or a report of what successfully occurred.

Approaches to File Error Handling sidebar ☞ 244

We have now seen the application's infrastructure for file handling, and the container's data structures that hold the data in memory. In the following sections, we will look at the code that performs the saving and loading of the container's data to and from disk.

Saving and Loading Binary Files

Both PyQt and the Python standard library provide facilities for writing and reading binary files. PyQt uses the QDataStream class, and the Python standard library uses the file class, either directly or in conjunction with the pickle module.

Binary formats are not human-readable, but they are the easiest to code and the fastest to write and read to and from disk. No parsing is necessary: Numbers, dates, and many PyQt types, including images, can be read and written without formality. PyQt's support for binary files is very strong: PyQt ensures that binary files are platform-independent, and it isn't difficult to version our binary file types so that we can extend our file format when required. The Python standard library's pickle module (and its faster cPickle counterpart) also provide fast platform-independent loading and saving, but may not be as efficient as PyQt's QDataStream for handling complex PyQt types, such as images.

Writing and Reading Using QDataStream

The QDataStream class can read and write Python Boolean and numeric types, and PyQt types, including images, in binary format. Files written by QData-

Stream are platform-independent; the class automatically takes care of endianness and word size.

Almost every new version of PyQt has a QDataStream that uses a new binary format for data storage—this is done so that QDataStream can accommodate new data types, and to support enhancements to existing data types. This is not a problem, because every version of QDataStream can read data stored in the formats used by all its previous versions. In addition, QDataStream always stores integers the same way, no matter which version of QDataStream is being used.

```
def saveQDataStream(self):
    error = None
    fh = None
    try:
        fh = QFile(self.__fname)
        if not fh.open(QIODevice.WriteOnly):
            raise IOError, unicode(fh.errorString())
        stream = QDataStream(fh)
        stream.writeInt32(MovieContainer.MAGIC_NUMBER)
        stream.writeInt32(MovieContainer.FILE_VERSION)
        stream.setVersion(QDataStream.Qt_4_2)
```

Since PyQt uses return values rather than exceptions, if the file cannot be opened we raise an exception ourselves since we prefer the exception-based approach to error handling. Having opened the file, we create a QDataStream object to write to it.

PyQt cannot guess what size integer we want to use to store int and long integers, so we must write integer values using the writeInt*n*() and writeUInt*n*() methods, where *n* is 8, 16, 32, or 64, that is, the number of bits to use to store the integer. For floating-point numbers, QDataStream provides the writeDouble() and readDouble() methods. These operate on Python floats (equivalent to C and C++ doubles), and are stored as 64-bit values in IEEE-754 format.

The first integer we write is the "magic number". This is an arbitrary number that we use to identify My Movies data files. This number will never change. We should give any custom binary data file a unique magic number, since filename extensions cannot always be relied upon to correctly identify a file's type. Next we write a "file version". This is the version of our file format (we have set it to be 100). If we decide to change the file format later, the magic number will remain the same—after all, the file will still hold movie data—but the file format will change (e.g., to 101) so that we can execute different code to load it to account for the difference in format.

Since integers are always saved in the same format, we can safely write them before setting the QDataStream version. But once we have written the magic number and file version, we should set the QDataStream version to the one that PyQt should use for writing and reading the rest of the data. If we want to take advantage of a later version we could use our original file format for version Qt_4_2, and another file format for the later version. Then, when we come to load the data, we could set the QDataStream version depending on our file format number.

Setting the QDataStream version is very important, since it will ensure that any PyQt data type is saved and loaded correctly. The only situation where it does not matter is if we are only saving and loading integers, since their representation never changes.

```
for key, movie in self.__movies:
    stream << movie.title
    stream.writeInt16(movie.year)
    stream.writeInt16(movie.minutes)
    stream << movie.acquired << movie.notes
```

Now we iterate over the movie data, writing each movie's data to the data stream. The data's format is illustrated in Figure 8.3. The QDataStream class overloads the << operator for many PyQt classes, including, for example, QString, QDate, and QImage, so we must use a C++-like streaming syntax to write our data. The << operator writes its right operand to the data stream that is its left operand. It can be applied repeatedly to the same stream, since it returns the stream it is applied to, but for integers, we must use the writeInt$n$() and writeUInt$n$() methods.

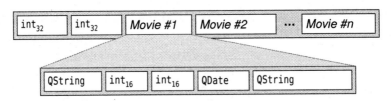

Figure 8.3 *The QDataStream My Movies file format*

Since we are writing binary data, we do not have to do any formatting. We just have to ensure that when we load the data back, we use the same QDataStream version, and that we load in the same data types in the same order as we saved. So, in this case, we will load back two integers (the magic and file version numbers), and then any number of movie records, each comprising a string, two integers, a date, and a string.

```
    except (IOError, OSError), e:
        error = "Failed to save: %s" % e
    finally:
        if fh is not None:
            fh.close()
        if error is not None:
            return False, error
    self.__dirty = False
```

```
        return True, "Saved %d movie records to %s" % (
                len(self.__movies),
                QFileInfo(self.__fname).fileName())
```

If there are any errors, we simply give up and return a failure flag and an error message. Otherwise, we clear the dirty flag and return a success flag and a message indicating how many records were saved.

The corresponding load method is just as straightforward, although it does have to do more error handling.

```
    def loadQDataStream(self):
        error = None
        fh = None
        try:
            fh = QFile(self.__fname)
            if not fh.open(QIODevice.ReadOnly):
                raise IOError, unicode(fh.errorString())
            stream = QDataStream(fh)
            magic = stream.readInt32()
            if magic != MovieContainer.MAGIC_NUMBER:
                raise IOError, "unrecognized file type"
            version = stream.readInt32()
            if version < MovieContainer.FILE_VERSION:
                raise IOError, "old and unreadable file format"
            elif version > MovieContainer.FILE_VERSION:
                raise IOError, "new and unreadable file format"
            stream.setVersion(QDataStream.Qt_4_2)
            self.clear(False)
```

We create the QFile object and QDataStream object the same as before, except this time using ReadOnly rather than WriteOnly mode. Then we read in the magic number. If this is not the unique My Movies data file number, we raise an exception. Next we read the file version, and make sure it is one that we can handle. At this point, we would branch depending on the file version, if we had more than one version of this file format in use. Then we set the QDataStream version.

The next step is to clear the movies data structures. We do this as late as possible so that if an exception was raised earlier, the original data will be left intact. The False argument tells the clear() method to clear __movies and __movieFromId, but not the filename.

```
            while not stream.atEnd():
                title = QString()
                acquired = QDate()
                notes = QString()
                stream >> title
                year = stream.readInt16()
```

Approaches to File Error Handling

The approach used for handling file errors in this chapter has the structure shown here on the left. Another equally valid approach, used, for example, in chap09/textedit.py and chap14/ships.py, is shown here on the right.

```
error = None                         exception = None
fh = None                            fh = None
try:                                 try:
    # open file and read data            # open file and read data
except (IOError, OSError), e:        except (IOError, OSError), e:
    error = unicode(e)                   exception = e
finally:                             finally:
    if fh is not None:                   if fh is not None:
        fh.close()                           fh.close()
    if error is not None:                if exception is not None:
        return False, error                  raise exception
    return True, "Success"
```

At the call point, and assuming we are dealing with a load() method, we might use code like this for the left-hand approach:

```
ok, msg = load(args)
if not ok:
    QMessageBox.warning(self, "File Error", msg)
```

And for the right-hand approach we could use code like this:

```
try:
    load(args)
except (IOError, OSError), e:
    QMessageBox.warning(self, "File Error", unicode(e))
```

Another approach, used in chap09/sditexteditor.pyw and chap12/pagedesign-er.pyw, is to do all the error handling inside the file-handling method itself:

```
fh = None
try:
    # open file and read data
except (IOError, OSError), e:
    QMessageBox.warning(self, "File Error", unicode(e))
finally:
    if fh is not None:
        fh.close()
```

At the call point we simply call load(args), leaving the load() method itself to report any problems to the user.

Table 8.1 *Selected QDataStream Methods*

Syntax	Description
s.atEnd()	Returns True if the end of QDataStream s has been reached
s.setVersion(v)	Sets QDataStream s's version to v, where v is one of Qt_1_0, Qt_2_0, ..., Qt_4_2, or Qt_4_3
s << x	Writes object x to QDataStream s; x can be of type QBrush, QColor, QDate, QDateTime, QFont, QIcon, QImage, QMatrix, QPainterPath, QPen, QPixmap, QSize, QString, QVariant, etc.
s.readBool()	Reads a bool from QDataStream s
s.readDouble()	Reads a float from QDataStream s
s.readInt16()	Reads a 16-bit int from QDataStream s. There is also a readUInt16() method.
s.readInt32()	Reads a 32-bit int from QDataStream s. There is also a readUInt32() method.
s.readInt64()	Reads a 64-bit long from QDataStream s. There is also a readUInt64() method.
x = QString() s >> x	Reads object x from QDataStream s; x must already exist (so that the data stream knows what data type to read), and can be any of the types writable by <<
s.writeBool(b)	Writes bool b to QDataStream s
s.write- Double(f)	Writes float f to QDataStream s
s.writeInt16(i)	Writes int i as a 16-bit int to QDataStream s. There is also a writeUInt16() method.
s.writeInt32(i)	Writes int i as a 32-bit int to QDataStream s. There is also a writeUInt32() method.
s.writeInt64(l)	Writes long l as a 64-bit int to QDataStream s. There is also a writeUInt64() method.

```
minutes = stream.readInt16()
stream >> acquired >> notes
self.add(Movie(title, year, minutes, acquired, notes))
```

We could have stored the number of movies at the beginning of the file, after the file version. But instead we simply iterate over the data stream until we reach the end. For non-numeric data types we must create variables that hold empty values of the correct type. Then we use the >> operator, which takes a data stream as its left operand and a variable as its right operand; it reads a value of the right operand's type from the stream and puts it into the right operand. The operator returns the file stream, so it can be applied repeatedly.

For integers we must always read using the readInt*n*() and readUInt*n*() methods with the same number of bits as we specified when writing.

Once we have read in a single movie's data, we create a new Movie object and immediately add it to the container's data structures using the add() method we reviewed in the preceding section.

```
except (IOError, OSError), e:
    error = "Failed to load: %s" % e
finally:
    if fh is not None:
        fh.close()
    if error is not None:
        return False, error
self.__dirty = False
return True, "Loaded %d movie records from %s" % (
        len(self.__movies),
        QFileInfo(self.__fname).fileName())
```

The error handling and the final return statement are structurally the same as we used for the save method.

Using the PyQt QDataStream class to write binary data is not very different in principle from using Python's file class. We must be careful to use the correct QDataStream version, and we ought to use a magic number and file version, or some equivalent approach. The use of the << and >> operators is not very Pythonic, but it is easy to understand.

We could have put code for writing a movie in the Movie class itself, perhaps with a method that took a QDataStream argument and wrote the movie's data to it. In practice it is usually more convenient, and almost always more flexible, to have the data container do the file handling rather than the individual data items.

Writing and Reading Using the pickle Module

Python's standard pickle module, and its faster cPickle counterpart, can save arbitrary Python data structures to disk and load them back again. These modules provide exactly the same functions and functionality. The only difference between them is that the pickle module is implemented purely in Python, and the cPickle module is implemented in C. These modules only understand the data types in the Python standard library, and classes that are built from them. If we want to pickle PyQt-specific data types with PyQt versions prior to PyQt 4.3, we must tell the pickle (or cPickle) module how to handle them.

```
def _pickleQDate(date):
    return QDate, (date.year(), date.month(), date.day())

def _pickleQString(qstr):
    return QString, (unicode(qstr),)
```

```
copy_reg.pickle(QDate, _pickleQDate)
copy_reg.pickle(QString, _pickleQString)
```

The copy_reg module is used to specify how to read and write nonstandard data types. The information is provided by calling copy_reg.pickle() with two arguments. The first argument is the new-style class that we want to be able to pickle, and the second is a function. The function must take a single argument, an instance of the class we want to pickle, and should return a two-tuple, whose first element is the class and whose second element is a tuple of standard Python types that can be fed into the class's constructor to create an instance that has the same value as the instance passed in.

With this information the pickle module can store instances of our class by storing the class name as text and the arguments as a tuple of standard Python types. Then, when we want to unpickle (load) the data back, Python can use eval() to re-create our instances.

PyQt 4.3 includes support for pickling basic Qt data types, including QByte-Array, QChar, QColor, QDate, QDateTime, QKeySequence, QLine, QLineF, QMatrix, QPoint, QPointF, QPolygon, QRect, QRectF, QSize, QSizeF, QString, QTime, and all PyQt enums. This means that we can "pickle" any of these types without having to write and register our own pickling functions.

```
def savePickle(self):
    error = None
    fh = None
    try:
        fh = gzip.open(unicode(self.__fname), "wb")
        cPickle.dump(self.__movies, fh, 2)
    except (IOError, OSError), e:
        error = "Failed to save: %s" % e
    finally:
        if fh is not None:
            fh.close()
        if error is not None:
            return False, error
        self.__dirty = False
        return True, "Saved %d movie records to %s" % (
                len(self.__movies),
                QFileInfo(self.__fname).fileName())
```

We can easily save any Python data structure, including recursive data structures, as a pickle. We do this by opening a file in binary mode and using the dump() function. In this example, we have chosen to save our pickle compressed (which may reduce file size by around 50 percent), but we could have avoided using compression like this:

```
fh = open(unicode(self.__fname), "wb")
```

We must convert the filename to unicode because it is held as a QString. The wb argument to open() means "write binary". The dump() function takes a Python data structure, in this case our list of [key, movie] lists, a file handle, and a format code. We always use format code 2, which means pickle binary format.

Since the keys are generated by the key() method, we really need to save only the Movie instances, rather than the [key, movie] lists. If disk space was at a premium we might do this, but it would require us to regenerate the keys when the data was loaded, so it represents a trade-off between disk space and speed of saving and loading. We have opted to sacrifice disk space for the sake of faster and easier saving and loading.

```
def loadPickle(self):
    error = None
    fh = None
    try:
        fh = gzip.open(unicode(self.__fname), "rb")
        self.clear(False)
        self.__movies = cPickle.load(fh)
        for key, movie in self.__movies:
            self.__movieFromId[id(movie)] = movie
    except (IOError, OSError), e:
        error = "Failed to load: %s" % e
    finally:
        if fh is not None:
            fh.close()
        if error is not None:
            return False, error
        self.__dirty = False
        return True, "Loaded %d movie records from %s" % (
                len(self.__movies),
                QFileInfo(self.__fname).fileName())
```

Unpickling is almost as easy as pickling. We must remember to open the file using gzip so that it gets uncompressed. The rb argument to open() means "read binary". We use the pickle load() function to retrieve the data; it takes a file handle and returns the entire data structure. We assign the data structure directly to our __movies list. Then we iterate over the movies to populate the __movieFromId dictionary: This cannot be saved because it depends on Movie id()s which will vary every time the application is run.

Pickling and unpickling is the easiest approach to saving and loading binary data, and is ideal for situations when our data is held in standard Python data types. If we hold our data as PyQt data types, it is usually best to use QData-Stream. This class is more efficient than the pickle module at storing complex PyQt data types like images (because there is none of the conversion overhead that is required when pickling), and it produces more compact files than the pickle module produces (unless the pickled data is compressed). It also makes it easy to provide seamless data format interoperability with C++/Qt applications.

Saving and Loading Text Files

PyQt and the Python standard library provide facilities for writing and reading text files. PyQt uses the QTextStream class, and the Python standard library uses the codecs module.

Plain text formats are usually human-readable, in a text editor, for example, and are usually easy to write. Any kind of data can be written as plain text one way or another. Numbers and dates can be written quite easily and compactly by using their string representations, and other types, such as images, can be written in more verbose forms—for example, using .xpm format.

Reading plain text that includes nontextual data or that has structure (for example, a record structure) means that we must write a parser, and this can be quite difficult, especially for complex data or complex data structures. Plain text formats can also be quite tricky to extend in a way that remains compatible with earlier formats, and they are vulnerable to being misread due to differences between the encoding read and the encoding written, since a user might edit them using a text editor that assumes a different encoding from the one that was actually used. These formats are most useful for simple file structures that store simple data types.*

Format	Example
{{MOVIE}} ␣ *title* ↵	{{MOVIE}} 12 Monkeys
year ␣ *minutes* ␣ *acquired* ↵	1995 129 2001-06-21
{NOTES} ↵	{NOTES}
notes ↵	Based on La Jetée
{{ENDMOVIE}} ↵	{{ENDMOVIE}}

Figure 8.4 *The My Movies text format*

The data we need to write contains only simple types: strings, integers, and a date. But we still need to structure the text file so that each movie record can be distinguished, and we must account for the fact that the notes text may extend over multiple lines.

The structure we have chosen is shown in Figure 8.4. In the Format column on the left, spaces are indicated by ␣ and newlines by ↵.

The notes may span multiple lines, but we have assumed that no line of notes begins with the text {{ENDMOVIE}}. A more robust solution would in-

---

*If the format is very simple, it may be easiest to use a QSettings object and have it read and write to a specified file rather than to hand-code.

volve escaping. For example, we could assume that for any line that begins with, say, \, we ignore the \ and take the rest of the line as literal text. This would allow us to include a line with the text {{ENDMOVIE}}", by writing it as \{{ENDMOVIE}}.

Writing and Reading Using QTextStream

The code for writing in text format using QTextStream is very similar to the code we used for writing using QDataStream.

```
def saveQTextStream(self):
    error = None
    fh = None
    try:
        fh = QFile(self.__fname)
        if not fh.open(QIODevice.WriteOnly):
            raise IOError, unicode(fh.errorString())
        stream = QTextStream(fh)
        stream.setCodec(CODEC)
        for key, movie in self.__movies:
            stream << "{{MOVIE}} " << movie.title << "\n" \
                   << movie.year << " " << movie.minutes << " " \
                   << movie.acquired.toString(Qt.ISODate) \
                   << "\n{NOTES}"
            if not movie.notes.isEmpty():
                stream << "\n" << movie.notes
            stream << "\n{{ENDMOVIE}}\n"
```

There are two crucial points to note. First we must specify the encoding we want to use. We are using UTF-8 in all cases; (CODEC holds the text UTF-8). If we do not do this, PyQt will use the local 8-bit encoding, which could be any of ASCII, Latin-1, or UTF-8 in the United States, Latin-1 or UTF-8 in Western Europe, and EUC-JP, JIS, Shift-JIS, or UTF-8 in Japan. By specifying the encoding, we ensure that we always write and read using the encoding we have specified so that characters are not misinterpreted. Unfortunately, we cannot guarantee that users will edit our text file using the correct encoding. If the files are likely to be edited, we could write the encoding on the first line in ASCII—for example, as encoding="UTF-8" in a similar way to XML—to at least provide a hint to the editor. This problem should diminish in the coming years since UTF-8 is becoming the de facto global standard for encoding text files.

The second point should be obvious: All data must be written as text. QTextStream overloads operator << to handle Booleans, numbers, and QStrings automatically, but other data types must be converted to their string representations. For dates we have chosen to use ISO (YYYY-MM-DD) format. We have also chosen to avoid having a blank line after the {NOTES} marker if the notes are empty.

We have omitted the code for the except and finally blocks since it is the same as we have seen a few times before—for example, in the saveQDataStream() method.

Although writing in text format is straightforward, reading it back is not so easy. For one thing, we will have to read each integer (year, minutes, and components of the acquired date) as text and convert it to the integer the text represents. But the main issue is that we must correctly parse the file to pick out each movie's record attributes.

Handling integers is not too difficult since QString provides a toInt() method; but the method returns a success/failure flag rather than raising an exception, and checking for this every time we handle a number will mean that we need three lines of code per number instead of one. For this reason, we have created a more Pythonic wrapper function for reading integers.

```
def intFromQStr(qstr):
    i, ok = qstr.toInt()
    if not ok:
        raise ValueError, unicode(qstr)
    return i
```

This function simply calls QString.toInt() and raises an exception on failure, or returns the integer on success.

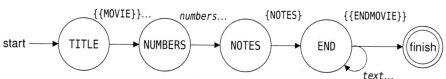

Figure 8.5 *The My Movies text format's finite state automaton for each movie*

To parse our movies text file we will use a finite state automaton to gather each movie's data. The automaton for parsing a single movie is illustrated in Figure 8.5. This just means that before we read each line, we have an expectation of what the line will contain. If the expectation is not met, we have an error; otherwise, we read the expected data and set the expectation for what the next line should contain.

```
def loadQTextStream(self):
    error = None
    fh = None
    try:
        fh = QFile(self.__fname)
        if not fh.open(QIODevice.ReadOnly):
            raise IOError, unicode(fh.errorString())
        stream = QTextStream(fh)
        stream.setCodec(CODEC)
        self.clear(False)
        lino = 0
```

The method begins familiarly enough. Once we have opened the file, created the QTextStream, and set the codec, we clear the existing movie data, and are ready to read in the data from disk.

For each movie we first expect a "title" line containing {{MOVIE}} followed by a space and the movie's title, then a "numbers" line that will have the year, minutes, and acquired date, then a "notes" line that just contains {NOTES}, then zero or more lines of notes text, and finally an "end" line containing just {{ENDMOVIE}}. We begin by expecting a "title" line.

To help the user find format errors we keep track of the current line number in the lino variable, which we will use in error messages.

The body of the while loop that we use to read through the file is quite long, so we will look at it in parts.

```
while not stream.atEnd():
    title = year = minutes = acquired = notes = None
    line = stream.readLine()
    lino += 1
    if not line.startsWith("{{MOVIE}}"):
        raise ValueError, "no movie record found"
    else:
        title = line.mid(len("{{MOVIE}}")).trimmed()
```

We begin by initializing the variables that will hold one movie's attributes to None so that it is easy to tell whether we have read them all.

We iterate over each line in the file. Unlike the Python standard library's file.readline() method, PyQt's QTextStream.readLine() strips off the line's trailing newline. Each time we read a line we increment lino.

The first line we expect for any movie is one beginning with the {{MOVIE}} marker. If the line is wrong we raise an exception with an error message; the exception handler will add the line number in the message passed up to the user. If we have a correct line, we extract the movie's title by reading the text that follows the {{MOVIE}} marker at the beginning of the line, stripping off any leading and trailing whitespace.

The QString.mid(*n*) method is the equivalent of unicode[*n*:], and QString. trimmed() is the same as unicode.strip().

Now we are ready to read the "numbers" line.

```
if stream.atEnd():
    raise ValueError, "premature end of file"
line = stream.readLine()
lino += 1
parts = line.split(" ")
if parts.count() != 3:
    raise ValueError, "invalid numeric data"
```

```
year = intFromQStr(parts[0])
minutes = intFromQStr(parts[1])
ymd = parts[2].split("-")
if ymd.count() != 3:
    raise ValueError, "invalid acquired date"
acquired = QDate(intFromQStr(ymd[0]),
                 intFromQStr(ymd[1]),
                 intFromQStr(ymd[2]))
```

We begin by checking that we haven't prematurely reached the end of the file, and if we have, we raise an exception. Otherwise, we read in the "numbers" line. This line should have an integer (the year), a space, an integer (the minutes), a space, and the acquired date in YYYY-MM-DD format. We initially split the line on the space character and this should give us three strings, year, minutes, and acquired date. We use our intFromQStr() function to convert the text to the integer it represents; if any conversion fails an exception is raised and handled in this method's exception handler. We convert the year and minutes directly, but for the acquired date we must split the string again, this time on the hyphen character, and then construct a QDate using the integer values extracted from each part.

Now we are ready to read the {NOTES} marker, optionally followed by lines of notes, and finally the {{ENDMOVIE}} marker.

```
if stream.atEnd():
    raise ValueError, "premature end of file"
line = stream.readLine()
lino += 1
if line != "{NOTES}":
    raise ValueError, "notes expected"
notes = QString()
while not stream.atEnd():
    line = stream.readLine()
    lino += 1
    if line == "{{ENDMOVIE}}":
        if title is None or year is None or \
            minutes is None or acquired is None or \
            notes is None:
            raise ValueError, "incomplete record"
        self.add(Movie(title, year, minutes,
                       acquired, notes.trimmed()))
        break
    else:
        notes += line + "\n"
else:
    raise ValueError, "missing endmovie marker"
```

Table 8.2 *Selected QTextStream Methods*

Syntax	Description
s.atEnd()	Returns True if the end of QTextStream s has been reached
s.setCodec(c)	Sets QTextStream s's text codec to the one specified in c—this can be a string (e.g., "UTF-8"), or a QTextCodec object
s << x	Writes object x to QTextStream s; x can be of type bool, float, int, long, QString, str, unicode, and a few others
s.readLine()	Reads one line, returning it as a QString stripped of any end-of-line characters
s.readAll()	Reads the entire file, returning it as a QString

We expect to get a single line containing the {NOTES} marker. At this point, we set the notes variable to be an empty QString. Even if no notes text is added, the fact that we have a QString rather than a None is enough to tell us that we read the notes, even if they were empty.

Now there are two possibilities. Either we have the {{ENDMOVIE}} marker, or we are reading a line of notes. In the latter case we simply append the line to the notes we have accumulated so far, adding back the newline that PyQt's readLine() method stripped off. Then we loop, and have either the {{ENDMOVIE}} marker or another line of notes.

If we get the marker, we check that none of our variables is None to ensure that we have read all the data for a movie record, and then we create and add a new movie with the data we have gathered. Now we break out of the inner while loop ready to read another movie, or to finish if the one just read was the last one in the file.

If we never get the {{ENDMOVIE}} marker, at some point the end of the file will be reached and the inner while loop will terminate. If this occurs, the while loop's else suite will execute and raise a suitable exception. A while or for loop's else suite is executed only if the loop completes, not if it is terminated by a break statement.

while
loop's
else
clause
50 ☞

```
        except (IOError, OSError, ValueError), e:
            error = "Failed to load: %s on line %d" % (e, lino)
        finally:
            if fh is not None:
                fh.close()
            if error is not None:
                return False, error
        self.__dirty = False
        return True, "Loaded %d movie records from %s" % (
                len(self.__movies),
                QFileInfo(self.__fname).fileName())
```

The error handling is almost identical to what we have seen before, only this time we include the line number where the error occurred.

Writing and Reading Using the codecs Module

An alternative to using the PyQt classes is to use Python's built-in and standard library classes for writing and reading text files. Files can be written and read directly using the file class, but if we want to specify the encoding, we must use the codecs module instead.

```
def saveText(self):
    error = None
    fh = None
    try:
        fh = codecs.open(unicode(self.__fname), "w", CODEC)
        for key, movie in self.__movies:
            fh.write(u"{{MOVIE}} %s\n" % unicode(movie.title))
            fh.write(u"%d %d %s\n" % (movie.year, movie.minutes,
                    movie.acquired.toString(Qt.ISODate)))
            fh.write(u"{NOTES}")
            if not movie.notes.isEmpty():
                fh.write(u"\n%s" % unicode(movie.notes))
            fh.write(u"\n{{ENDMOVIE}}\n")
```

We have used exactly the same text format as we used when writing with a QTextStream, so the code is very similar to saveQTextStream(). We open the file using the codecs.open() function rather than the open() function; we do not have to specify a "binary" flag. We have omitted the code from the except block to the end since it is the same as we have seen before.

```
def loadText(self):
    error = None
    fh = None
    try:
        fh = codecs.open(unicode(self.__fname), "rU", CODEC)
        self.clear(False)
        lino = 0
        while True:
            title = year = minutes = acquired = notes = None
            line = fh.readline()
            if not line:
                break
            lino += 1
            if not line.startswith("{{MOVIE}}"):
                raise ValueError, "no movie record found"
            else:
                title = QString(line[len("{{MOVIE}}"):].strip())
```

We have shown only the first few lines of the loadText() method that corresponds to saveText(). This is because the method uses the same algorithm and almost the same code as the loadQTextStream() method. The only significant differences are due to the fact that we read in the lines as Python unicodes, so we must convert the title and notes to QStrings. Also, Python keeps the newlines rather than discarding them, and returns an empty string to signify that the end of the file has been reached, so we must slightly modify the code to account for this. For the integers we can use Python's int() function rather than the intFromQStr() function we needed for QStrings.

We have chosen to read back in rU mode, which stands for "read universal newlines", rather than plain r mode, which stands for "read". This just means that the lines will be read correctly even if written on, say, Linux, and read back on say, Windows, even though the two operating systems use different line-ending conventions.

Saving and Loading XML Files

Both PyQt and the Python standard library can read and write XML files. PyQt provides two parsers for reading, and can write XML using its QDomDocument class. PyQt 4.3 adds two new XML classes. The QXmlStreamReader class is lightweight like SAX, but easier to use, and the QXmlStreamWriter class is much easier and more efficient for writing than writing by hand or using DOM. The Python standard library also provides extensive XML support, but in this section we will confine ourselves to the functionality offered by the PyQt library, since Python's XML classes are well covered by Python's documentation and in such books as *Python and XML* and *XML Processing in Python*.

XML formats tend to be a lot more verbose than plain text formats, and not so easy for humans to read. On the other hand, encoding issues are taken care of, so hand editing can be more reliable than with plain text, and the parsing of the overall file structure is usually a lot easier using a suitable XML library than for plain text files. XML formats are generally simpler to extend than either binary or plain text formats, although care must be taken when writing XML to ensure that data does not contain XML meta-characters. Writing XML is straightforward, but reading it requires the use of a parser. There are two very different and widely used XML parser APIs: DOM (Document Object Model), which loads entire XML documents into memory and is well suited to editing a document's structure, and SAX (Simple API for XML), which works incrementally, so is less resource-hungry and is suitable for searching and processing XML documents. We will show both parsers in action.

Writing XML

If we have read an XML document into a QDomDocument, or if we have created and populated a QDomDocument in code, the easiest way to save the document to disk is to use QDomDocument.toString() to get a QString of the entire document in XML format, and to save the string to disk. In practice, though, we often use XML only as a data-interchange format, and hold our data in custom data structures. In these cases, we need to write the XML ourselves, and that is what we will look at in a moment.

In XML, sequences of "whitespace" characters, such as newlines, tabs, and spaces, are usually treated as a single space. This is often convenient, but not in the case of our movie notes, since for the notes we want to preserve the newlines and paragraph breaks that the user has inserted.

```
def encodedNewlines(text):
    return text.replace("\n\n", NEWPARA).replace("\n", NEWLINE)

def decodedNewlines(text):
    return text.replace(NEWPARA, "\n\n").replace(NEWLINE, "\n")
```

The preceding two functions can be used to preserve the users' paragraph breaks and newlines. The first function encodes paragraph breaks and newlines into the Unicode character that represents them, and the second one decodes Unicode paragraph breaks and newlines back to the familiar \n character.

With these two functions available, we are ready to see how to export our movie data in XML format. Let us begin by looking at the format we are aiming to produce:

```
<?xml version='1.0' encoding='UTF-8'?>
<!DOCTYPE MOVIES>
<MOVIES VERSION='1.0'>
...
<MOVIE YEAR='1951' MINUTES='100' ACQUIRED='2002-02-07'>
<TITLE>The African Queen</TITLE>
<NOTES>
Katherine Hepburn, Humphrey Bogart
</NOTES>
</MOVIE>
...
</MOVIES>
```

The ellipses represent movie records that have been omitted to save space and are not part of the format. Although we will always write the <MOVIE> tag's attributes in the same order, as far as the XML parsers are concerned the order is arbitrary. Attribute values should not contain single or double quotes, or the XML meta-characters, <, >, or &.* This means that for attribute values, we should either escape them, or ensure that we only use values that we know do not contain these characters—for example, numbers, dates and times in ISO

---

*To escape XML text we must convert < to <, > to >, and & to &. In attribute values, in addition to these conversions, we must convert ' to ' and " to ".

format, and Booleans. For character data such as the title and notes, we can
include quotes, since only the meta-characters are not permitted.

```
def exportXml(self, fname):
    error = None
    fh = None
    try:
        fh = QFile(fname)
        if not fh.open(QIODevice.WriteOnly):
            raise IOError, unicode(fh.errorString())
        stream = QTextStream(fh)
        stream.setCodec(CODEC)
        stream << ("<?xml version='1.0' encoding='%s'?>\n"
                   "<!DOCTYPE MOVIES>\n"
                   "<MOVIES VERSION='1.0'>\n" % CODEC)
```

We have chosen to use PyQt's QTextStream to write our XML file; we could just
as easily have used the codecs module, although in that case we would need to
convert the QStrings to unicodes.*

The method starts off in the now familiar way. Once the QTextStream has been
created, we set its codec to UTF-8 as usual, and then we output the first three
lines—these are always the same.

```
    for key, movie in self.__movies:
        stream << ("<MOVIE YEAR='%d' MINUTES='%d' "
                   "ACQUIRED='%s'>\n" % (
                   movie.year, movie.minutes,
                   movie.acquired.toString(Qt.ISODate))) \
                << "<TITLE>" << Qt.escape(movie.title) \
                << "</TITLE>\n<NOTES>"
        if not movie.notes.isEmpty():
            stream << "\n" << Qt.escape(
                        encodedNewlines(movie.notes))
        stream << "\n</NOTES>\n</MOVIE>\n"
    stream << "</MOVIES>\n"
```

We iterate over our movie data in the same way as we have done previously.
The Qt.escape() function takes a QString and returns it with any XML meta-
characters properly escaped. And we use our encodedNewlines() function to convert any paragraph and line breaks in the notes to their Unicode equivalents.
We do not perform any escaping on the attributes because we know that they
cannot contain any unacceptable characters. We have omitted the end of the
method since the exception handling and return are structurally the same as
those we have seen before.

---

*PyQt 4.0 has a bug that prevents QTextStream from writing correctly, so for PyQt 4.0 we must use
the codecs module. The problem does not exist in PyQt 4.1 and later versions.

Reading and Parsing XML with PyQt's DOM Classes

PyQt's QDomDocument class can be used to read in an entire (well-formed) XML document in one go. But once we have a QDomDocument, we must be able to use it. Some applications reflect the document into a widget, often a QTreeWidget, whereas others, like My Movies, which use XML purely as a data-interchange format, traverse the document, populating their data structures as they go.

```
def importDOM(self, fname):
    dom = QDomDocument()
    error = None
    fh = None
    try:
        fh = QFile(fname)
        if not fh.open(QIODevice.ReadOnly):
            raise IOError, unicode(fh.errorString())
        if not dom.setContent(fh):
            raise ValueError, "could not parse XML"
    except (IOError, OSError, ValueError), e:
        error = "Failed to import: %s" % e
    finally:
        if fh is not None:
            fh.close()
        if error is not None:
            return False, error
    try:
        self.populateFromDOM(dom)
    except ValueError, e:
        return False, "Failed to import: %s" % e
    self.__fname = QString()
    self.__dirty = True
    return True, "Imported %d movie records from %s" % (
                len(self.__movies), QFileInfo(fname).fileName())
```

The first part of the load method should appear familiar, but notice that the entire file is read when we call QDomDocument.setContent(). If this method succeeds (returns True), we know that the XML was successfully parsed.

Once we have a QDomDocument, we need to extract our data from it, and that is what the populateFromDOM() method does.

The end of the method is different from what we have seen before. We clear the filename and set the dirty flag to True. This will ensure that if the user tries to save the XML movie data they have just imported, or if they try to quit the application, they will be given a "save as" dialog so that they get the chance to save the data in one of the application's binary or text formats.

Earlier we mentioned that a QDomDocument could easily be written to a file. Here is how we could do it, assuming that dom is a QDomDocument and filename is a valid filename, but with no error checking:

```
codecs.open(filename, "w", "utf-8").write(unicode(dom.toString()))
```

This will produce a file that is slightly different from the one produced by the exportXml() method. For example, the QDomDocument.toString() method indents nested tags, uses double quotes rather than single quotes for attributes, and may order the attributes differently. Nonetheless, the XML document produced is canonically identical to the one produced by exportXml().

Once the QDomDocument has read in the XML file we need to traverse its contents to populate the application's data structures, and to do this we begin by calling populateFromDOM() on the document.

```
def populateFromDOM(self, dom):
    root = dom.documentElement()
    if root.tagName() != "MOVIES":
        raise ValueError, "not a Movies XML file"
    self.clear(False)
    node = root.firstChild()
    while not node.isNull():
        if node.toElement().tagName() == "MOVIE":
            self.readMovieNode(node.toElement())
        node = node.nextSibling()
```

We start by checking that the XML file we read is indeed a movies XML file. If it is not we raise an exception, and if it is, we clear our data structures so that they are ready to be populated by the data extracted from the DOM document.

DOM documents are composed of "nodes", each of which represents an XML tag or the text between tags. A node may have children and it may have siblings. In the case of the movies XML format, we have sibling <MOVIE> nodes that have <TITLE> and <NOTES> child nodes, and these child nodes in turn have child text nodes. So to extract our data we iterate over the <MOVIE> nodes, and for each one we encounter, we extract its attributes and the data from its child nodes.

```
def readMovieNode(self, element):
    def getText(node):
        child = node.firstChild()
        text = QString()
        while not child.isNull():
            if child.nodeType() == QDomNode.TextNode:
                text += child.toText().data()
            child = child.nextSibling()
        return text.trimmed()
```

The readMovieNode() begins with a nested function definition. The getText() function takes a node as an argument—for example, a <TITLE> or <NOTES> opening tag—and iterates over its child text nodes, accumulating their text. Finally, it returns the text, with whitespace stripped from either end. As noted earlier, the QString.trimmed() method does the same job as unicode.strip().

```
year = intFromQStr(element.attribute("YEAR"))
minutes = intFromQStr(element.attribute("MINUTES"))
ymd = element.attribute("ACQUIRED").split("-")
if ymd.count() != 3:
    raise ValueError, "invalid acquired date %s" % \
            unicode(element.attribute("ACQUIRED"))
acquired = QDate(intFromQStr(ymd[0]), intFromQStr(ymd[1]),
                intFromQStr(ymd[2]))
```

The readMovieNode() method itself begins by extracting the <MOVIE> tag's attribute data and converting it from text into ints for the year and minutes, and into a QDate for the date acquired.

We could have avoided having to handle the details of the acquired date ourselves, and pushed the work onto the parser. For example, instead of having a single ACQUIRED attribute, we could have had ACQUIREDYEAR, ACQUIREDMONTH, and ACQUIREDDAY, each with an integer value. With these three attributes we would not need to do the split on hyphens, but the format would have been more verbose.

```
title = notes = None
node = element.firstChild()
while title is None or notes is None:
    if node.isNull():
        raise ValueError, "missing title or notes"
    if node.toElement().tagName() == "TITLE":
        title = getText(node)
    elif node.toElement().tagName() == "NOTES":
        notes = getText(node)
    node = node.nextSibling()
if title.isEmpty():
    raise ValueError, "missing title"
self.add(Movie(title, year, minutes, acquired,
                decodedNewlines(notes)))
```

Each <MOVIE> node has two child nodes, <TITLE> and <NOTES>. Although we always write them in the same order in the exportXml() method, we don't want to force the child nodes to have a particular order. For this reason, we iterate over the child nodes and use the nested getText() method to gather the text for whichever child node we encounter.

At the end, providing the movie has a title, we create a new Movie object and immediately add it to our data structures using add().

Using a DOM parser for importing XML into custom data structures works fine, although we often need to write small helper functions like getText(). DOM is best used in situations where we want to hold and manipulate the XML data inside a QDomDocument itself, rather than converting it into other data structures.

Reading and Parsing XML with PyQt's SAX Classes

Importing XML using a SAX parser works quite differently than using a DOM parser. With SAX, we define a handler class that implements just the methods that we are interested in, and then give an instance of the handler to the SAX parser to use as it parses the XML. Parsing is not done in one go as it is with DOM, but rather piece by piece, with our handler's methods being called when the data they handle is encountered. Any methods that we do not implement are provided by the base class, and in all cases they safely do nothing.

```
def importSAX(self, fname):
    error = None
    fh = None
    try:
        handler = SaxMovieHandler(self)
        parser = QXmlSimpleReader()
        parser.setContentHandler(handler)
        parser.setErrorHandler(handler)
        fh = QFile(fname)
        input = QXmlInputSource(fh)
        self.clear(False)
        if not parser.parse(input):
            raise ValueError, handler.error
    except (IOError, OSError, ValueError), e:
        error = "Failed to import: %s" % e
    finally:
        if fh is not None:
            fh.close()
        if error is not None:
            return False, error
        self.__fname = QString()
        self.__dirty = True
        return True, "Imported %d movie records from %s" % (
                len(self.__movies), QFileInfo(fname).fileName())
```

We begin by creating an instance of a custom SaxMovieHandler and of a SAX XML parser. The parser can be given a content handler, an error handler, and some other handlers; we have chosen to create just one handler, one that can handle both content and errors, so we set this same handler for these two purposes.

We get a QFile file handle and turn this into an XML "input source". At this point we clear our data structures, again as late as possible, and then we tell the parser to parse the XML file. The parser returns True on success and False on failure.

There is no separate phase for populating our data structures since we handle all of this inside our SaxMovieHandler class as parsing progresses. At the end we clear the filename and set the dirty flag to True, just as we did at the end of the importDOM() method.

The SaxMovieHandler class is a QXmlDefaultHandler subclass. For content handling it would normally implement at least startElement(), endElement(), and characters() to handle start tags with their attributes, end tags, and the text between tags. If we use the same handler for handling errors as we do here, we must also at least implement the fatalError() method.

```
class SaxMovieHandler(QXmlDefaultHandler):

    def __init__(self, movies):
        super(SaxMovieHandler, self).__init__()
        self.movies = movies
        self.text = QString()
        self.error = None
```

The super() call ensures that the base class is properly initialized. The movies parameter is the movie container itself. The text instance variable is used to hold between tags text—for example, the title or notes text—and the error variable will be given an error message if something goes wrong.

```
    def clear(self):
        self.year = None
        self.minutes = None
        self.acquired = None
        self.title = None
        self.notes = None
```

The first time this method is called it creates an instance variable for each of a movie's attributes. Every time it is called it sets the variables to None; this will make it easy to test whether we have read all of a movie's attributes.

```
    def startElement(self, namespaceURI, localName, qName, attributes):
        if qName == "MOVIE":
            self.clear()
            self.year = intFromQStr(attributes.value("YEAR"))
            self.minutes = intFromQStr(attributes.value("MINUTES"))
            ymd = attributes.value("ACQUIRED").split("-")
            if ymd.count() != 3:
                raise ValueError, "invalid acquired date %s" % \
                        unicode(attributes.value("ACQUIRED"))
            self.acquired = QDate(intFromQStr(ymd[0]),
```

```
                              intFromQStr(ymd[1]),
                              intFromQStr(ymd[2])))
        elif qName in ("TITLE", "NOTES"):
            self.text = QString()
        return True
```

This method is reimplemented from the base class, and for this reason we must use the same signature. We are interested in only the last two parameters: the qName (qualified name) that holds the tag's name, and attributes that hold's the tag's attribute data. This method is called whenever a new start tag is encountered.

If a new <MOVIE> tag is encountered we clear the corresponding instance variables, then populate the year, minutes, and acquired date from the tag's attribute data. This leaves the title and notes variables set to None.

If the tag is a <TITLE> or <NOTES> tag, we can expect to get its corresponding text (if there is any), so we set the text variable to be an empty string, ready to be appended to.

Every reimplemented method must return True on success or False on failure; so we return True at the end.

```
        def characters(self, text):
            self.text += text
            return True
```

Whenever text is encountered between tags, the characters() method is called. We simply append the text to the text variable. The end tag will tell us whether we are accumulating title or note text.

```
        def endElement(self, namespaceURI, localName, qName):
            if qName == "MOVIE":
                if self.year is None or self.minutes is None or \
                   self.acquired is None or self.title is None or \
                   self.notes is None or self.title.isEmpty():
                    raise ValueError, "incomplete movie record"
                self.movies.add(Movie(self.title, self.year,
                        self.minutes, self.acquired,
                        decodedNewlines(self.notes)))
                self.clear()
            elif qName == "TITLE":
                self.title = self.text.trimmed()
            elif qName == "NOTES":
                self.notes = self.text.trimmed()
            return True
```

This method is called whenever an end tag is reached. The tag's name is in the qName parameter. If the end tag is </MOVIE>, none of the movie data instance variables should be None (although the title or notes could be empty QStrings).

If none of the variables is None, and providing the movie has a title, we create a new Movie object and immediately add it to the movies container.

If we have reached a title or notes end tag, we know that the text that has been accumulated in the text QString has the text between the corresponding start and end tags, so we assign this text accordingly. If there was no text, the assignment will be of an empty QString.

```
def fatalError(self, exception):
    self.error = "parse error at line %d column %d: %s" % (
            exception.lineNumber(), exception.columnNumber(),
            exception.message())
    return False
```

If a parsing error occurs, the fatalError() method is called. We reimplement it to populate the handler's error text, and return False to indicate failure. This will cause the parser to finish parsing and to return False to its caller.

Using PyQt's SAX parser requires us to create at least one separate handler subclass. This is not difficult, especially since we need to reimplement only the methods we want to use. Parsing with SAX is also less memory-hungry than using DOM, since SAX works incrementally, and is noticeably faster, especially for larger documents.

Summary

With all the choices available, which is the best format to use, and should we use the Python or the PyQt classes?

Using a binary format is best for performance and platform independence, and it is also the simplest to implement. Using a plain text format is appropriate for small files that typically hold only simple values like strings, numbers, and dates, and that are intended to be hand-edited. Even so, there is a risk that the user's text editor will assume a different encoding from the one we have used. We recommend using UTF-8 for all plain text formats, since it is becoming the de facto standard encoding. Reading and writing XML is a lot slower than reading and writing binary files (except for small files, that is, less than ~1MB), but it is worth offering, at least as export and import formats. After all, if our users can export and import their data in XML format, it gives them the ability to export their data, process it with some other tool, and then import back the processed data, without having to know or care about the details of the binary format our application normally uses.

As for whether we use the Python or PyQt classes, it probably does not matter at all for small files holding simple data types. If we want to minimize our programming effort, using the cPickle module is probably the easiest route. But if we have large files (multimegabytes) or if we use complex PyQt types like QBrush, QCursor, QFont, QIcon, QImage, and so on, it is easiest and most efficient to use QDataStream since it can read and write all these types directly. The one drawback of using a binary format is that if we want to change our format, we must at least change our load method so that it can load both our new and our old formats. This is not a problem in practice, as long as we include a file version at the start of our data after the magic number, since we can use this to determine which loading code to use.

At this stage we have covered the fundamentals of GUI programming. We can create main window applications, with menus, toolbars, and dock windows, and we can create and pop up any kind of dialog we like. We have also learned how to use *Qt Designer* to simplify and speed up dialog design, and we saw how to load and save application data in various formats. In Part III we will both deepen and broaden our GUI programming knowledge, learning how to handle multiple documents and how to create complex dialogs that are manageable for the user. We will also explore some of PyQt's major architectural features, from its low-level event-handling mechanism to the creation of custom widgets, including coverage of 2D graphics, as well as higher-level features including item-based graphics, rich text (HTML) handling, and model/view programming.

Exercise

Modify the My Movies application so that each Movie object can store an extra piece of information: a QString called "location", which is where the movie is located—for example, the room and shelf. Provide only saving and loading of binary Qt format .mqb files and export and import of XML files, so remove the code for saving and loading pickles and text files. Make sure that your new My Movies application can still read the original application's .mqb and .xml files, that is, files that do not have location data.

The moviedata module's Movie class will need an extra QString attribute, called "location". The MovieContainer class will need several small changes. You will need to have both an old and a current file version number so you know which kind you are dealing with. The formats() method should now return only the string *.mqb, or could be eliminated entirely. The save() and load() methods need to handle only .mqb files, and must account for the location and the different file versions. Similarly the exportXml() method and the two import XML methods must also account for the possible presence of <LOCATION> tags. The changes to the user interface should be obvious, so we won't list them.

None of these changes involves many lines of code, but some are subtle and will take a bit of care to get right. Make sure that you test your changes. For example, load in an old file in .mqb format, and import a file in the old .xml format. Add some locations and save the data in a new .mqb file and export as XML. Read both of these back in to check that everything works properly.

A model solution is provided in the files, chap08/mymovies_ans.pyw, chap08/ moviedata_ans.pyw, chap08/addeditmoviedlg_ans.ui, and chap08/addeditmoviedlg-_ans.py.

Part III

Intermediate GUI Programming

9

● Layout Policies

● Tab Widgets and Stacked Widgets

● Splitters

● Single Document Interface (SDI)

● Multiple Document Interface (MDI)

Layouts and Multiple Documents

In every dialog we have created so far, all the widgets have been visible at the same time. But in some cases, such as, complex configuration dialogs or property editors, so many widgets are required that showing them all at once could confuse the user. For such situations we can use tab widgets or stacked widgets that allow us to group related widgets together, and show only the relevant group, or we can use extension dialogs that can show extra options on demand. These techniques can help make dialogs smaller and easier for users to navigate and use; we will cover them in this chapter's second section.

In the main-window-style applications we have created, we had one central widget. But in some situations, we need to show two or more widgets in the central area, and often want to give the user some control over their relative sizes. One way to achieve this is to use a single central widget with dock windows; we saw this approach in Chapter 6. Another approach is to use splitters, the subject of this chapter's third section.

Another issue that arises with main-window-style applications is how we deal with multiple documents. There are four main approaches to this. One is to use multiple instances of the application. In this approach, the user launches one instance of the application for each document they wish to work on. In theory this requires no programming effort at all, but in practice, we might want to implement some kind of file-locking scheme or use interprocess communication to ensure that the user does not start the application two or more times on the same document. All the applications we have created so far are of this kind, although none of them has used file locking.*

A second approach is to use SDI (Single Document Interface). This means that the user is expected to run only one instance of the application, but can use that application instance to create as many main windows as they need to handle all the documents they wish to work on. (It is possible to ensure that the user can only have one instance of an application running at the same

---

*For file-locking code, see "File Locking Using a Cross-Platform API" in the *Python Cookbook*.

time, but the technique varies from platform to platform and is beyond the scope of this book.) This approach is quite fashionable, and is recommended by the Apple Human Interface Guidelines for "document-style" applications. It is covered in the fourth section.

A third approach is to use MDI (Multiple Document Interface). Again, the user is expected to run only one instance of the application, but here, all the documents are kept within a single "workspace", that is, in child windows inside the main window's central area. MDI is less fashionable than SDI, and is also less resource hungry. For MDI applications, there is just one main window, no matter how many documents are being worked on, whereas SDI has a main window with its menu bar, toolbars, and so on for every document. The final section of this chapter will show how to implement an MDI application.

A fourth alternative is to use a tab widget with each document occupying its own tab page. This approach is used by many modern Web browsers. We will only cover tab widgets in the context of dialogs, although in the exercise you will get the chance to create a tab-widget-based main window application, and perhaps surprisingly, the code required is very similar to that used for an MDI application.

But before looking at tab widgets and stacked widgets in dialogs, and handling multiple documents, we will take a brief diversion to discuss layouts in a bit more depth than when we first encountered them.

Layout Policies

In earlier chapters, we saw many examples of PyQt's layout managers in action. It is possible in PyQt to set specific fixed sizes and positions for widgets, or to handle layouts manually by reimplementing each widget's resizeEvent() handler. But using layout managers is by far the easiest approach, and it offers additional benefits compared with manual approaches.

Layout managers allow widgets to grow and shrink to make the best use of the space available to them, dynamically responding to the user changing the containing form's size. Layout managers provide a minimum size for a form based on all the widgets' minimum sizes. This ensures that the form cannot be made too small to be usable, and is not fixed, but dependent on the widgets' contents—for example, a label might need more or less width depending on whether the text it is displaying is in English or German.

The QVBoxLayout, QHBoxLayout, and QGridLayout layout managers are very versatile. The box layouts can include "stretches" that consume space between widgets to prevent widgets from growing too tall or too wide. And grid layouts can have widgets that span multiple rows and columns. All the layout managers can be nested inside each other, so very sophisticated layouts can be created.

Nonetheless, sometimes the layout managers alone are not sufficient to achieve the layout we want. One simple way to help the layout managers is to

Table 9.1 *PyQt's Size Policies*

Policy		Effect
Fixed		The widget has the size specified by its size hint and never changes size
Minimum		The widget's size hint is its minimum size; it cannot be shrunk smaller than this, but it can grow bigger
Maximum		The widget's size hint is its maximum size; it cannot grow bigger than this, but it can shrink down to its minimum size hint
Preferred		The widget's size hint is its preferred size; it can be shrunk down to its minimum size hint, or it can grow bigger than its size hint
Expanding		The widget can be shrunk down to its minimum size hint, or it can grow bigger than its size hint, but it prefers to grow bigger

set the size policies of those widgets that are not being laid out satisfactorily. Every widget has vertical and horizontal size policies that can be set independently. (Every widget can also have a fixed minimum and maximum size, but using size policies usually provides better resizing behavior.) In addition, two sizes are associated with every widget: a size hint and a minimum size hint. The former is the widget's preferred size, and the latter is the smallest size the widget can be shrunk to. The sizes are used by the size policies as shown in Table 9.1.

For example, a QLineEdit might have a default horizontal policy of Expanding and a vertical policy of Fixed. This would mean that the line edit will take up as much horizontal space as it can get, but will always have the same vertical size. Every built-in PyQt widget has sensible size hints and size policies already set, so normally we need to change them for only one or two widgets when tweaking a layout.

Size policies also store a "stretch factor" in addition to a policy. This is used to indicate how layout managers should share space between widgets. For example, if we had a QVBoxLayout that contained two QListWidgets, both would want to grow in both directions. But if we wanted the bottom one to grow faster than the top one, we could give the top one a stretch factor of 1 and the bottom one a stretch factor of 3. This will ensure that if the user resizes, the extra space will be distributed between the two widgets in a proportion of 1:3.

If setting size policies and stretch factors is still not enough, we can always create a subclass and reimplement the sizeHint() and minimumSizeHint() methods to return the size we want. We will see examples of this in Chapter 11.

Tab Widgets and Stacked Widgets

Some dialogs require so many widgets to present all the options that they make available that they become difficult for the user to understand. The most obvious way to deal with this is to create two or more dialogs and to divide the options between them. This is a good approach when it is possible since it minimizes the demands made on the user, and may also be easier from a maintenance point of view than a single complex dialog. But often we need to use a single dialog because the options we are presenting to the user are related and need to be presented together.

When we must use a single dialog, there are two kinds of groups of options that we must consider. One kind is simply a group of related options. This is most easily handled by using a `QTabWidget`. A tab widget can have as many "pages" (child widgets and tab captions) as necessary, each one laid out with the widgets that are needed to present the relevant options. Figure 9.1 shows a `PaymentDlg`, an example of a three-page tab widget that was created using *Qt Designer*.

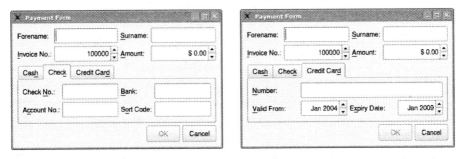

Figure 9.1 *A dialog that uses a tab widget for choosing a payment method*

In *Qt Designer*'s Widget Box's Containers section there is a Tab Widget. This can be dragged onto a form like any other widget. Like most container widgets, and unlike most other widgets, we normally have to manually resize the tab widget after dropping it on the form, to roughly the size we want. In *Qt Designer*, the tab widget has context menu options for deleting and adding pages. The current page can be set by clicking the relevant tab or by setting the "currentIndex" property. The current page's tab text can be set by setting the "currentTabText" property.

Once a tab widget has been dragged onto a form and resized, we can drag other widgets onto its pages. These widgets can be laid out in the normal way, and each tab page can be laid out in a similar way to the form itself: by deselecting all the widgets, then clicking the tab page, and then applying a layout manager.

Thanks to their labelled tabs, tab widgets make it obvious to the user that there are more options on other tab pages, and provide an easy means by which the user can navigate between pages. Tab widgets can have rounded or angled tab corners, and can have the tabs at the top, bottom, left, or right.

Although using *Qt Designer* is quicker and easier than creating the dialog by hand, it is interesting and useful to know how to achieve the same thing purely in code. We won't show the creation of the ordinary widgets, since we have seen that enough times by now; instead, we will focus on the tab widget and the form's overall layout. The following extracts are all from the `PaymentDlg` class's initializer in `chap09/paymentdlg.pyw`. (The *Qt Designer* version is in the files `paymentdlg.ui` and `paymentdlg.py`.)

```
tabWidget = QTabWidget()
cashWidget = QWidget()
cashLayout = QHBoxLayout()
cashLayout.addWidget(self.paidCheckBox)
cashWidget.setLayout(cashLayout)
tabWidget.addTab(cashWidget, "Cas&h")
```

We create the tab widget just like any other widget. Each page in a tab widget must contain a widget, so we create a new widget, `cashWidget`, and create a layout for it. Then we add the relevant widgets—in this case, just one, `paidCheckBox`—to the layout, and then set the layout on the containing widget. Finally, we add the containing widget as a new tab to the tab widget, along with the tab's label text.★

```
checkWidget = QWidget()
checkLayout = QGridLayout()
checkLayout.addWidget(checkNumLabel, 0, 0)
checkLayout.addWidget(self.checkNumLineEdit, 0, 1)
checkLayout.addWidget(bankLabel, 0, 2)
checkLayout.addWidget(self.bankLineEdit, 0, 3)
checkLayout.addWidget(accountNumLabel, 1, 0)
checkLayout.addWidget(self.accountNumLineEdit, 1, 1)
checkLayout.addWidget(sortCodeLabel, 1, 2)
checkLayout.addWidget(self.sortCodeLineEdit, 1, 3)
checkWidget.setLayout(checkLayout)
tabWidget.addTab(checkWidget, "Chec&k")
```

This tab is created in exactly the same way as the first one. The only differences are that we have used a grid layout, and we have more widgets to put in the layout.

We won't show the code for the third tab, because it is structurally the same as the ones we have already seen.

★In the PyQt documentation, and to some extent, the `QTabWidget`'s API, the term "tab" is used to refer to a tab's label alone, and to a tab's label and page together.

```
layout = QVBoxLayout()
layout.addLayout(gridLayout)
layout.addWidget(tabWidget)
layout.addWidget(self.buttonBox)
self.setLayout(layout)
```

For completeness, we have shown the heart of the dialog's layout, omitting only the creation of the grid layout that holds the labels, line edits, and spinboxes at the top of the form. The buttons are provided by a QDialogButtonBox, a widget that can be laid out like any other. Finally, we lay out the whole form in a vertical box layout: first the grid at the top, then the tab widget in the middle, and then the button box at the bottom.

Another kind of options group is one that is applicable only in certain circumstances. In the simple case where a group of options is applicable or not, we can use a checkable QGroupBox. If the user unchecks the group box, all the widgets it contains are disabled. This means that the user can see what options the group contains, even when they are unavailable, which is often helpful. In other cases, we might have two or more groups of options, only one of which is applicable at any one time. For this situation, a QStackedWidget provides a solution. Conceptually, a stacked widget is a tab widget that has no tabs. So the user has no visual clue that a stacked widget is present, and has no means of navigating between the stacked widget's pages.

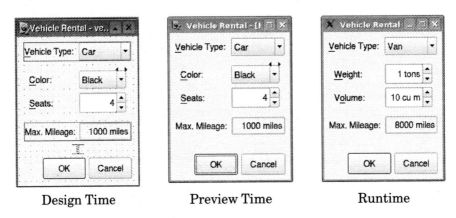

Design Time   Preview Time   Runtime

Figure 9.2 *A dialog that uses a stacked widget*

To use a stacked widget, we can drag a Stacked Widget onto a form in *Qt Designer*, and resize it in the same way as for a tab widget. Inside *Qt Designer* a stacked widget is indicated by two tiny arrowheads in its top right-hand corner. These arrowheads are also present when the form is previewed, but they do not appear at runtime—they are shown at the top right of the color combobox in the first two screenshots in Figure 9.2. Widgets can be dragged onto stacked widget pages and laid out in exactly the same way as for tab widgets. Stacked widgets have a context menu that has options for adding and deleting pages, just like a tab widget, and additional options for navigating between pages and for changing the page order.

Since stacked widgets have no tabs, we must provide the user with a means of navigating between pages. In the VehicleRentalDlg shown in Figure 9.2, the vehicle type combobox is used as a page selector. To make this work, in *Qt Designer* we have connected the combobox's currentIndexChanged(int) signal to the stacked widget's setCurrentIndex(int) slot. Another commonly used approach that lets users see all the pages available is to use a QListWidget containing the name of each page, and connecting its currentRowChanged(int) signal in the same way we connected the combobox's signal.

We will now see how to create a stacked widget in code. The following extracts are from the VehicleRentalDlg class's initializer in chap09/vehiclerentaldlg.pyw. (The *Qt Designer* version is in the files vehiclerentaldlg.ui and vehicle-rentaldlg.py.)

```
self.stackedWidget = QStackedWidget()
carWidget = QWidget()
carLayout = QGridLayout()
carLayout.addWidget(colorLabel, 0, 0)
carLayout.addWidget(self.colorComboBox, 0, 1)
carLayout.addWidget(seatsLabel, 1, 0)
carLayout.addWidget(self.seatsSpinBox, 1, 1)
carWidget.setLayout(carLayout)
self.stackedWidget.addWidget(carWidget)
```

Adding a "page" to a stacked widget is very similar to adding a tab to a tab widget. We begin by creating a plain widget, and then create a layout for it and lay out the widgets we want. Then we set the layout on the plain widget and add this widget to the widget stack. We have not shown the code for the vanWidget, because it is structurally identical.

```
topLayout = QHBoxLayout()
topLayout.addWidget(vehicleLabel)
topLayout.addWidget(self.vehicleComboBox)
bottomLayout = QHBoxLayout()
bottomLayout.addWidget(mileageLabel)
bottomLayout.addWidget(self.mileageLabel)
layout = QVBoxLayout()
layout.addLayout(topLayout)
layout.addWidget(self.stackedWidget)
layout.addLayout(bottomLayout)
layout.addWidget(self.buttonBox)
self.setLayout(layout)
```

Once again, for completeness we have shown the whole dialog's layout. We begin with a top layout that has the combobox that is used to set the stacked widget's current widget. Then we create a bottom layout of the mileage labels, and then a button layout for the buttons. Next, we add all of these layouts, and the stacked widget itself, to a vertical box layout.

```
self.connect(self.buttonBox, SIGNAL("accepted()"), self.accept)
self.connect(self.buttonBox, SIGNAL("rejected()"), self.reject)
self.connect(self.vehicleComboBox,
             SIGNAL("currentIndexChanged(QString)"),
             self.setWidgetStack)
self.connect(self.weightSpinBox, SIGNAL("valueChanged(int)"),
             self.weightChanged)
```

We must provide the user with a navigation mechanism, and we do this by connecting the vehicle combobox's `currentIndexChanged()` signal to a custom `setWidgetStack()` slot. The last slot is simply part of the form's validation; it is there to set the maximum mileage, which is fixed for cars but for vans is dependent on their weight.

```
def setWidgetStack(self, text):
    if text == "Car":
        self.stackedWidget.setCurrentIndex(0)
        self.mileageLabel.setText("1000 miles")
    else:
        self.stackedWidget.setCurrentIndex(1)
        self.weightChanged(self.weightSpinBox.value())

def weightChanged(self, amount):
    self.mileageLabel.setText("%d miles" % (8000 / amount))
```

The `setWidgetStack()` slot makes the appropriate widget visible, and handles part of the mileage setting since this varies depending on whether the vehicle is a car or a van.

We have used the combobox's current text to determine which widget to make visible. A possibly more robust approach would be to associate a data item with each combobox item (using the two-argument `QComboBox.addItem()` method), and use the current item's data item to choose which widget to show.

Extension Dialogs

There is another approach that we can take for complex dialogs: extension dialogs. These are typically used for cases where the dialog has "simple" and "advanced" options. Initially the dialog is shown with the simple options, but a toggle button is provided to show or hide the advanced options.

The extension dialog shown in Figure 9.3 shows the extra checkboxes when the More toggle button is depressed. Any `QPushButton` can be made into a toggle button by calling `setCheckable(True)` on it, or by setting its "checkable" property to `True` in *Qt Designer*.

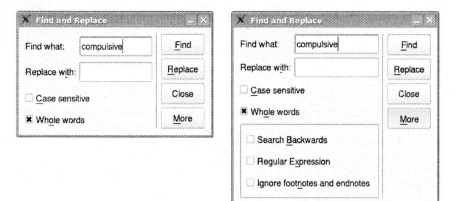

Figure 9.3 *An extension dialog*

To make the extension dialog work we have used two "tricks". The first trick is to put all the advanced options' widgets inside a QFrame. This means that we need to hide and show only the frame, since PyQt will automatically hide and show all the widgets inside the frame to reflect the frame's state of visibility. If we don't want the user to see the frame's outline when it is visible, we can simply set its "frameShape" property to QFrame.NoFrame.

The second trick is to make the dialog a fixed size. This will ensure that the dialog shrinks as small as possible (while keeping its margins), and takes account of the dialog's *visible* contents. The effect of this is to make the dialog short when the advanced options are hidden, and tall enough to show the advanced options when they are visible. We must also hide the frame when the dialog is created. Here is the code for the dialog's initializer (from chap09/findandreplacedlg.py):

```
class FindAndReplaceDlg(QDialog,
        ui_findandreplacedlg.Ui_FindAndReplaceDlg):

    def __init__(self, parent=None):
        super(FindAndReplaceDlg, self).__init__(parent)
        self.setupUi(self)
        self.moreFrame.hide()
        self.layout().setSizeConstraint(QLayout.SetFixedSize)
```

But how do we relate the More button to the shown/hidden state of the frame? Simply by connecting the moreButton's toggled(bool) signal to the moreFrame's setVisible(bool) slot. Note that if this connection is made in *Qt Designer*, we must check the Configure Connection dialog's "Show all signals and slots" checkbox; otherwise, the setVisible() slot will not appear.

For this section's final example, we will again look at how to achieve the layout in code. Unlike the previous two layouts which showed the use of new widgets (QTabWidget and QStackedWidget), this dialog's layout uses only widgets we have seen before—but does so in new ways. The following extracts are from the Find-

AndReplaceDlg class's initializer in chap09/findandreplacedlg.pyw. (The *Qt De-signer* version is in the files findandreplacedlg.ui and findandreplacedlg.py.)

We will only show the creation of the form's widgets that are specifically relevant to extension dialogs. The form's layout is shown in Figure 9.4.

```
moreFrame = QFrame()
moreFrame.setFrameStyle(QFrame.StyledPanel|QFrame.Sunken)
```

We create a frame in which we will put the extra checkboxes. If we didn't do the setFrameStyle() call, the frame would have no outline.

```
line = QFrame()
line.setFrameStyle(QFrame.VLine|QFrame.Sunken)
```

The line that we "draw" to visually separate the dialog's main widgets on the left from the buttons on the right is also a frame. Horizontal lines can be created by using a frame style of QFrame.HLine.

```
moreButton = QPushButton("&More")
moreButton.setCheckable(True)
```

The More button is different from other buttons in one respect: It is checkable. This means that it acts like a toggle button, staying down when clicked the first time, then coming up when clicked the next time, and so on.

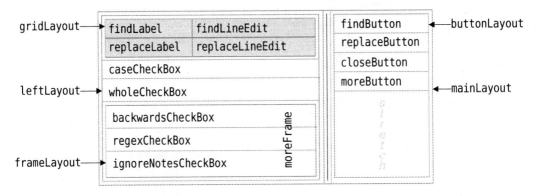

Figure 9.4 *The Find and Replace dialog's layout*

The labels and line edits are laid out in a grid; we will not show the code since we have seen this kind of layout many times before.

```
frameLayout = QVBoxLayout()
frameLayout.addWidget(self.backwardsCheckBox)
frameLayout.addWidget(self.regexCheckBox)
frameLayout.addWidget(self.ignoreNotesCheckBox)
moreFrame.setLayout(frameLayout)
```

We want the extra checkboxes to be laid out inside the more frame. To do this we create a layout, in this case a vertical box layout, and add the checkboxes to it. Then we set the layout on the frame. In previous examples, we have added layouts to layouts to achieve nesting, but here we nest by adding a layout to a frame. So in addition to being able to nest layouts inside one another, we can also nest frames and group boxes inside layouts, which gives us a great deal of flexibility.

```
leftLayout = QVBoxLayout()
leftLayout.addLayout(gridLayout)
leftLayout.addWidget(self.caseCheckBox)
leftLayout.addWidget(self.wholeCheckBox)
leftLayout.addWidget(moreFrame)
```

The left layout is a vertical box layout to which we add the grid layout (with the labels and line edits), the case sensitivity and whole words checkboxes, and then the more frame (that contains the extra checkboxes in a vertical box layout).

```
buttonLayout = QVBoxLayout()
buttonLayout.addWidget(self.findButton)
buttonLayout.addWidget(self.replaceButton)
buttonLayout.addWidget(closeButton)
buttonLayout.addWidget(moreButton)
buttonLayout.addStretch()
```

The button layout is very similar to ones we have seen before, only this time it is using a vertical box layout rather than a horizontal box layout.

```
mainLayout = QHBoxLayout()
mainLayout.addLayout(leftLayout)
mainLayout.addWidget(line)
mainLayout.addLayout(buttonLayout)
self.setLayout(mainLayout)
```

The dialog's main layout is a horizontal box layout, with the left layout on the left, then the dividing line, and then the button layout. The line will grow and shrink vertically according to whether the more frame is visible (and therefore whether the dialog is tall or short).

```
moreFrame.hide()
mainLayout.setSizeConstraint(QLayout.SetFixedSize)
```

We initially hide the more frame (and therefore the widgets it contains), and we use the set fixed size trick to ensure that the dialog resizes itself according to whether the more frame is visible.

```
self.connect(moreButton, SIGNAL("toggled(bool)"),
             moreFrame, SLOT("setVisible(bool)"))
```

The last thing we must do is connect the More button's `toggled()` signal to the more frame's `setVisible()` slot. When the frame is hidden (or shown), it will in turn hide (or show) all the widgets laid out inside it, because when `show()` or `hide()` is called on a widget, PyQt automatically propagates these calls to all the widget's children.

We have noted that there are two versions of each dialog shown in this section. One version is written entirely in code, for example, `paymentdlg.pyw`—and the other version has a *Qt Designer* user interface, with code in a module file—for example, `paymentdlg.ui` and `paymentdlg.py`. By comparing the "all in code" (`.pyw`) versions with the *Qt Designer* and module versions (`.py`), we can see clearly how much code writing we can avoid by using *Qt Designer*. An additional benefit of using *Qt Designer*, especially for complex widgets, is that it makes changing the design much easier than is the case when we do things manually.

Splitters

Some main-window-style applications need to use more than one widget in their central area. Two common types of applications that need to do this are email clients and network news readers. There are three approaches we can take to handle this. One is to create a composite widget, that is, a widget that is composed of other widgets (created and laid out like a dialog, but inheriting from `QWidget` instead of `QDialog`), and use this widget as the main window's central widget. Another approach is to have just one central widget and put the other widgets inside dock windows—we have already seen this in Chapter 6. The third approach is to use splitters, the topic of this section.

Composite widgets
☞ 325

Figure 9.5 shows a mock-up of a news reader application, and Figure 9.6 illustrates the relationship between the form's splitters and widgets. Splitters are fully supported by *Qt Designer*, and are used in much the same way as vertical and horizontal box layouts: We select two or more widgets, and click Form→Lay Out Horizontally in Splitter or Form→Lay Out Vertically in Splitter.

In this section we will show how to create splitters in code, including how to save and restore their relative positions. We will begin by looking at the relevant parts of the News Reader mock-up's initializer.

```
class MainWindow(QMainWindow):

    def __init__(self, parent=None):
        super(MainWindow, self).__init__(parent)
        self.groupsList = QListWidget()
        self.messagesList = QListWidget()
        self.messageView = QTextBrowser()
```

The initializer begins conventionally with the call to `super()`. The next three lines are slightly unusual, since although this is a main window, we have created three widgets instead of just one.

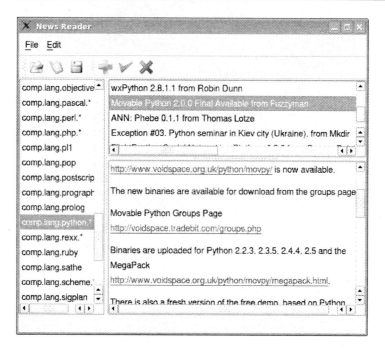

Figure 9.5 *The News Reader application mock-up*

```
self.messageSplitter = QSplitter(Qt.Vertical)
self.messageSplitter.addWidget(self.messagesList)
self.messageSplitter.addWidget(self.messageView)
self.mainSplitter = QSplitter(Qt.Horizontal)
self.mainSplitter.addWidget(self.groupsList)
self.mainSplitter.addWidget(self.messageSplitter)
self.setCentralWidget(self.mainSplitter)
```

We now create two splitters. The first is the messageSplitter; this holds the message list and message view widgets vertically, one above the other. The second splitter, mainSplitter, splits horizontally, with the group list widget on its left and the message splitter on its right. Like box layouts, splitters can hold more than two widgets, in which case they place a splitter in between each pair of widgets. The main splitter holds one widget and the other splitter, which in turn holds the other two widgets. So the main splitter ultimately holds everything else, and since splitters are widgets (unlike box layouts, which are layouts), a splitter can be added as a main window's central widget, as we have done here.

Some users find splitters annoying because they can resize them only by using the mouse. We will minimize this annoyance by saving and restoring the user's splitter sizes. This is helpful since the user can simply set the sizes once, and from then on the sizes they set will be honored.

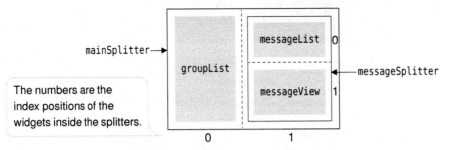

Figure 9.6 *The News Reader's splitters and widgets*

```
settings = QSettings()
size = settings.value("MainWindow/Size",
                      QVariant(QSize(600, 500))).toSize()
self.resize(size)
position = settings.value("MainWindow/Position",
                          QVariant(QPoint(0, 0))).toPoint()
self.move(position)
self.restoreState(
        settings.value("MainWindow/State").toByteArray())
self.messageSplitter.restoreState(
        settings.value("MessageSplitter").toByteArray())
self.mainSplitter.restoreState(
        settings.value("MainSplitter").toByteArray())
```

Saving the user's main window settings begins with some familiar code for restoring the window's size and position and the state of any toolbars and dock windows it may have. Splitters too have a state, and this is restored and saved in the same way as the main window's state.

```
def closeEvent(self, event):
    if self.okToContinue():
        settings = QSettings()
        settings.setValue("MainWindow/Size", QVariant(self.size()))
        settings.setValue("MainWindow/Position",
                QVariant(self.pos()))
        settings.setValue("MainWindow/State",
                QVariant(self.saveState()))
        settings.setValue("MessageSplitter",
            QVariant(self.messageSplitter.saveState()))
        settings.setValue("MainSplitter",
            QVariant(self.mainSplitter.saveState()))
    else:
        event.ignore()
```

In the main window's close event, again the code begins in a familiar way, only we now save the state of the splitters in addition to the main window's size, position, and state.

When the News Reader application is run for the very first time, by default the main splitter gives exactly half its width to the group list widget, and half to the message splitter. Similarly, the message splitter gives half its height to the message list widget and half to the message view widget. We want to change these proportions, making the group list narrower and the message viewer taller, and we can do so by applying stretch factors. For example:

```
self.mainSplitter.setStretchFactor(0, 1)
self.mainSplitter.setStretchFactor(1, 3)
self.messageSplitter.setStretchFactor(0, 1)
self.messageSplitter.setStretchFactor(1, 2)
```

The first argument to setStretchFactor() is the 0-based index position of the widget (from left to right, or from top to bottom), and the second argument is the stretch factor to be applied. In this case, we have said that the zero-th widget (the group list widget) should have a stretch factor of 1 and the first widget (the message splitter) should have a stretch factor of 3, thus dividing the horizontal space in a proportion of 1:3. Similarly, for the message splitter we split the vertical space in a proportion of 1:2 in favor of the message view widget. Since we save and restore the splitters' sizes, the stretch factors have an effect only the first time the application is run.

Single Document Interface (SDI)

For some applications, users want to be able to handle multiple documents. This can usually be achieved simply by running more than one instance of an application, but this can consume a lot of resources. Another disadvantage of using multiple instances is that it is not easy to provide a common Window menu that the user can use to navigate between their various documents.

There are three commonly used solutions to this. One is to use a single main window with a tab widget, and with each tab holding one document. This approach is fashionable for Web browsers, but it can be inconvenient when editing documents since it isn't possible to see two or more documents at once. We will not show this approach since the coverage of tab widgets in this chapter's second section is sufficient, and because you'll have the chance to try it for yourself in the exercise. The other two approaches are SDI, which we will cover in this section, and MDI, which we will cover in the next section.

The key to creating an SDI application is to create a window subclass that handles everything itself, including loading, saving, and cleanup, reducing the application to be essentially a collection of one or more such windows.

We will begin by looking at some extracts from the SDI Text Editor's initializer; the application itself is shown in Figure 9.7.

```
class MainWindow(QMainWindow):

    NextId = 1
```

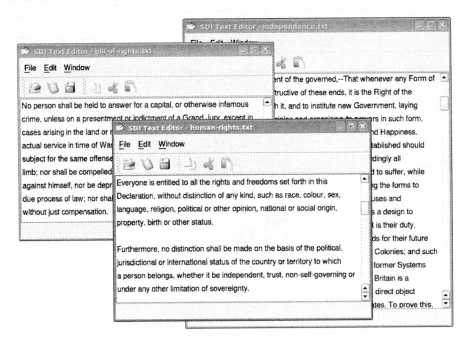

Figure 9.7 *SDI Text Editor with three documents*

```
Instances = set()

def __init__(self, filename=QString(), parent=None):
    super(MainWindow, self).__init__(parent)
    self.setAttribute(Qt.WA_DeleteOnClose)
    MainWindow.Instances.add(self)
```

The NextId static variable is used to provide numbers for new empty windows: "Unnamed-1.txt", "Unnamed-2.txt", and so on.

The application consists of one or more MainWindow instances, each of which must be able to act independently. However, there are three common situations where we need to access all of the instances from inside any one of them. One is to provide a "save all" option, another is to provide a Window menu through which the user can switch between the window instances, and another is to provide a "quit" option that the user can use to terminate the application, and which must implicitly close every window. The Instances static variable is what we use to keep track of all the instances.

When a new window instance is created, we set it to delete itself when closed. This means that windows can be closed directly by the user or indirectly by other instances (when the application is terminated, for example). One implication of using Qt.WA_DeleteOnClose is that the window should take care of saving unsaved changes and cleaning up itself. We also add the window to the static set of window instances so that any window instance can gain access to all the other windows. We will look into all of these matters further on.

```
        self.editor = QTextEdit()
        self.setCentralWidget(self.editor)
```

The QTextEdit is the ideal widget for our central widget, with some actions
being able to be passed directly to it, as we will see in a moment. We will now
look at just a few of the actions, skipping the createAction() method that we
have seen before.

create-
Action()
175 ☜

```
        fileSaveAllAction = self.createAction("Save A&ll",
                self.fileSaveAll, icon="filesave",
                tip="Save all the files")
```

This action is similar to almost all the other file actions, with a connection to
one of the MainWindow subclass's methods.

```
        fileCloseAction = self.createAction("&Close", self.close,
                QKeySequence.Close, "fileclose",
                "Close this text editor")
```

The "close" action is similar to those we have seen before. As usual, we do not
reimplement the close() method, but instead reimplement the closeEvent()
handler so that we can intercept any clean closure of the window. What is
different is that this action closes only the current window, not the application
(unless this is the application's only window).

```
        fileQuitAction = self.createAction("&Quit", self.fileQuit,
                "Ctrl+Q", "filequit", "Close the application")
```

The "quit" action terminates the application, and does so by closing each
of the SDI Text Editor's windows, as we will see when we review the file-
Quit() method.

```
        editCopyAction = self.createAction("&Copy", self.editor.copy,
                QKeySequence.Copy, "editcopy",
                "Copy text to the clipboard")
```

This action connects to the QTextEdit's relevant slot. The same is true of the
"cut" and "paste" actions.

The menus, toolbars, and status bar are all created in ways that we have seen
previously, except for the Window menu, which we will look at now.

```
        self.windowMenu = self.menuBar().addMenu("&Window")
        self.connect(self.windowMenu, SIGNAL("aboutToShow()"),
                self.updateWindowMenu)
```

We do not add any actions to the Window menu at all. Instead, we simply
connect the menu's aboutToShow() method to our custom updateWindowMenu()
method which, as we will see, populates the menu with all the SDI Text Editor
windows.

```
self.connect(self, SIGNAL("destroyed(QObject*)"),
                    MainWindow.updateInstances)
```

When the user closes a window, thanks to the Qt.WA_DeleteOnClose flag, the window will be deleted. But because we have a reference to the window in the static Instances set, the window cannot be garbage-collected. For this reason we connect the window's destroyed() signal to a slot that updates the Instances by removing any windows that have been closed. We will discuss this in more detail when we look at the updateInstances() method.

Since each window is responsible for a single file, we can have a single filename associated with each window. The filename can be passed to the window's initializer, and it defaults to an empty QString. The last lines of the initializer handle the filename.

```
self.filename = filename
if self.filename.isEmpty():
    self.filename = QString("Unnamed-%d.txt" % \
                            MainWindow.NextId)
    MainWindow.NextId += 1
    self.editor.document().setModified(False)
    self.setWindowTitle("SDI Text Editor - %s" % self.filename)
else:
    self.loadFile()
```

If the window has no filename, either because the application has just been started or because the user has invoked the "file new" action, we create a suitable window title; otherwise, we load the given file.

The closeEvent(), loadFile(), fileSave(), and fileSaveAs() methods are very similar to ones we have seen before, so we will not describe them here. (They are in the source code in chap09/sditexteditor.pyw, of course.) Instead, we will focus on those things that are special for an SDI application.

```
def fileNew(self):
    MainWindow().show()
```

When the user invokes the "file new" action, this method is called. Another instance of this class is created, and show() is called on it (so it is shown modelessly). At the end of the method, we would expect the window to go out of scope and be destroyed since it does not have a PyQt parent and it is not an instance variable. But inside the main window's initializer, the window adds itself to the static Instances set, so an object reference to the window still exists, and therefore, the window is not destroyed.

```
def fileOpen(self):
    filename = QFileDialog.getOpenFileName(self,
                        "SDI Text Editor -- Open File")
    if not filename.isEmpty():
```

```
        if not self.editor.document().isModified() and \
           self.filename.startsWith("Unnamed"):
            self.filename = filename
            self.loadFile()
        else:
            MainWindow(filename).show()
```

This method is slightly different from similar ones we have seen before. If the user gives a filename, and the current document is both unmodified and unnamed (i.e., a new empty document), we load the file into the existing window; otherwise, we create a new window, passing it the filename to load.

```
        def fileSaveAll(self):
            count = 0
            for window in MainWindow.Instances:
                if isAlive(window) and \
                   window.editor.document().isModified():
                    if window.fileSave():
                        count += 1
            self.statusBar().showMessage("Saved %d of %d files" % (
                    count, len(MainWindow.Instances)), 5000)
```

As a courtesy to users, we provide a Save All menu option. When it is invoked we iterate over every window in the Instances set, and for each window that is "alive" and modified, we save it.

A window is alive if it has not been deleted. Unfortunately, this is not quite as simple as it seems. There are two lifetimes associated with a QWidget: the lifetime of the Python variable that refers to the widget (in this case, the Main-Window instances in the Instances set), and the lifetime of the underlying PyQt object that is the widget as far as the computer's window system is concerned.

Normally, the lifetimes of a PyQt object and its Python variable are exactly the same. But here they may not be. For example, suppose we started the application and clicked File→New a couple of times so that we had three windows, and then we navigated to one of them and closed it. At this point the window that is closed (thanks to the Qt.WA_DeleteOnClose attribute) will be deleted.

Under the hood, PyQt actually calls the deleteLater() method on the deleted window. This gives the window the chance to finish anything it is in the middle of doing, so that it can be cleanly deleted. This will normally be all over in less than a millisecond, at which point the underlying PyQt object is deleted from memory and no longer exists. But the Python reference in the Instances set will still be in place, only now referring to a PyQt object that has gone. For this reason, we must always check any window in the Instances set for aliveness before accessing it.

```
    def isAlive(qobj):
        import sip
```

```
try:
    sip.unwrapinstance(qobj)
except RuntimeError:
    return False
return True
```

The sip module is one of PyQt's supporting modules that we do not normally need to access directly. But in cases where we need to dig a bit deeper, it can be useful. Here, the method tries to access a variable's underlying PyQt object. If the object has been deleted, a RuntimeError exception is raised, in which case we return False; otherwise, the object still exists and we return True.* By performing this check, we ensure that a window that has been closed and deleted is not inadvertently accessed, even if we have not yet deleted the variable that refers to the window.

```
@staticmethod
def updateInstances(qobj):
    MainWindow.Instances = set([window for window \
            in MainWindow.Instances if isAlive(window)])
```

Whenever a window is closed (and therefore deleted), it emits a destroyed() signal, which we connected to the updateInstances() method in the initializer. This method overwrites the Instances set with a set that contains only those window instances that are still alive.

So why do we need to check for aliveness when we iterate over the instances—for example, in the fileSaveAll() method—since this method ensures that the Instances set is kept up-to-date and is holding only live windows? The reason is that it is theoretically possible that between the time when a window is closed and the Instances set is updated, the window is iterated over in some other method.

Whenever the user clicks the Window menu in any SDI Text Editor window, a menu listing all the current windows appears. This occurs because the windowMenu's aboutToShow() signal is connected to the updateWindowMenu() slot that populates the menu.

```
def updateWindowMenu(self):
    self.windowMenu.clear()
    for window in MainWindow.Instances:
        if isAlive(window):
            self.windowMenu.addAction(window.windowTitle(),
                    self.raiseWindow)
```

First any existing menu entries are cleared; there will always be at least one, the current window. Next we iterate over all the window instances and add an

---

*The isAlive() function is based on Giovanni Bajo's PyQt (then PyKDE) mailing list posting, "How to detect if an object has been deleted". The list is used for both PyQt and PyKDE.

action for any that are alive. The action has text that is simply the window's title (the filename) and a slot—raiseWindow()—to be called when the menu option is invoked by the user.

```
def raiseWindow(self):
    action = self.sender()
    if not isinstance(action, QAction):
        return
    for window in MainWindow.Instances:
        if isAlive(window) and \
            window.windowTitle() == action.text():
            window.activateWindow()
            window.raise_()
            break
```

This method could be called by any of the Window menu's entries. We begin with a sanity check, and then we iterate over the window instances to see which one has a title whose text matches the action's text. If we find a match, we make the window concerned the "active" window (the application's top-level window that has the keyboard focus), and raise it to be on top of all other windows so that the user can see it.

In the MDI section that follows we will see how to create a more sophisticated Window menu, with accelerators and some additional menu options.

```
def fileQuit(self):
    QApplication.closeAllWindows()
```

PyQt provides a convenient method for closing all of an application's top-level windows. This method calls close() on all the windows, which in turn causes each window to get a closeEvent(). In this event (not shown), we check to see whether the QTextEdit's text has unsaved changes, and if it has we pop up a message box asking the user if they want to save.

```
app = QApplication(sys.argv)
app.setWindowIcon(QIcon(":/icon.png"))
MainWindow().show()
app.exec_()
```

At the end of the sditexteditor.pyw file, we create a QApplication instance and a single MainWindow instance and then start off the event loop.

Using the SDI approach is very fashionable, but it has some drawbacks. Since each main window has its own menu bar,[*] toolbar, and possibly dock windows, there is more resource overhead than for a single main window. Also, although it is easy to switch between windows using the Window menu, if we wanted

---

[*]On Mac OS X there is only one menu bar, at the top of the screen. It changes to reflect whichever window currently has the focus.

more control over window sizing and positioning, we would have to write the code ourselves. These problems can be solved by using the less fashionable MDI approach that we cover in the next section.

Multiple Document Interface (MDI)

MDI offers many benefits compared with SDI or with running multiple application instances. MDI applications are less resource-hungry, and they make it much easier to offer the user the ability to lay out their document windows in relation to each other. One drawback, however, is that you cannot switch between MDI windows using Alt+Tab (Command+Tab on Mac OS X), although this is rarely a problem in practice since for MDI applications, programmers invariably implement a Window menu for navigating between windows.

The key to creating MDI applications is to create a widget subclass that handles everything itself, including loading, saving, and cleanup, with the application holding these widgets in an MDI "workspace", and passing on to them any widget-specific actions.

In this section, we will create a text editor that offers the same kind of functionality as the SDI Text Editor from the preceding section, except that this time we will make it an MDI application. The application is shown in Figure 9.8.

Each document is presented and edited using an instance of a custom TextEdit widget, a QTextEdit subclass. The widget has the Qt.WA_DeleteOnClose attribute set, has a filename instance variable, and loads and saves the filename it is given. If the widget is closed (and therefore deleted), its close event handler gives the user the opportunity to save any unsaved changes. The TextEdit implementation is straightforward, and it is quite similar to code we have seen before, so we will not review it here; its source code is in the module chap09/textedit.py.

The code for the application proper is in the file chap09/texteditor.pyw. We will review the code for this, starting with some extracts from the MainWindow subclass's initializer.

```
class MainWindow(QMainWindow):

    def __init__(self, parent=None):
        super(MainWindow, self).__init__(parent)

        self.mdi = QWorkspace()
        self.setCentralWidget(self.mdi)
```

PyQt's MDI widget is called QWorkspace.* Like a tab widget or a stacked widget, a QWorkspace can have widgets added to it. These widgets are laid out by the workspace, rather like a miniature desktop, with the widgets tiled, cascaded, iconized, or dragged and resized by the user within the workspace's area.

---

*From Qt 4.3, MDI is provided by the QMdiArea class with an API similar to QWorkspace.

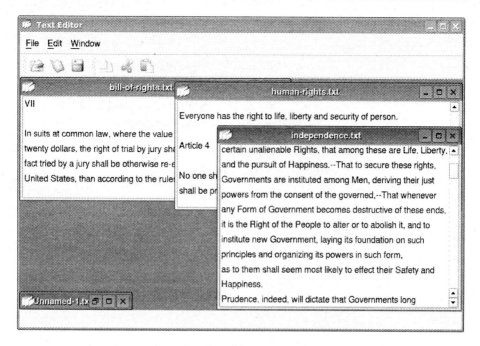

Figure 9.8 *MDI Text Editor with four documents*

It is possible to have a workspace that is larger than its window by calling QWorkspace.setScrollBarsEnabled(True). The workspace's background can be set by specifying a background brush.

```
fileNewAction = self.createAction("&New", self.fileNew,
        QKeySequence.New, "filenew", "Create a text file")
```

Most of the file actions are created as we have seen before. But as we will see, the MDI editor, like the SDI editor, does not have an okToContinue() method because each document window takes care of itself.

```
fileQuitAction = self.createAction("&Quit", self.close,
        "Ctrl+Q", "filequit", "Close the application")
```

If we close the application's window, the application will terminate. All the document windows will be closed, and any with unsaved changes are responsible for prompting the user and saving if asked to do so.

```
editCopyAction = self.createAction("&Copy", self.editCopy,
        QKeySequence.Copy, "editcopy",
        "Copy text to the clipboard")
```

In the SDI editor we passed on the "copy", "cut", and "paste" actions to each window's QTextEdit to handle. This is not possible in the MDI application because when the user triggers one of these actions, it must be applied to whichever

`TextEdit` window is active. For this reason the main window must do some work itself, as we will see when we review the implementation of these actions.

We have not shown the code for the other file and edit actions, because they all follow the same pattern as those shown earlier.

```
self.windowNextAction = self.createAction("&Next",
        self.mdi.activateNextWindow, QKeySequence.NextChild)
self.windowPrevAction = self.createAction("&Previous",
        self.mdi.activatePreviousWindow,
        QKeySequence.PreviousChild)
self.windowCascadeAction = self.createAction("Casca&de",
        self.mdi.cascade)
self.windowTileAction = self.createAction("&Tile",
        self.mdi.tile)
self.windowRestoreAction = self.createAction("&Restore All",
        self.windowRestoreAll)
self.windowMinimizeAction = self.createAction("&Iconize All",
        self.windowMinimizeAll)
self.windowArrangeIconsAction = self.createAction(
        "&Arrange Icons", self.mdi.arrangeIcons)
self.windowCloseAction = self.createAction("&Close",
        self.mdi.closeActiveWindow, QKeySequence.Close)
```

All the window actions are created as instance variables because we will be accessing them in another method. For some of the actions we can pass the work directly onto the `mdi` workspace instance, but minimizing and restoring all the MDI windows we must handle ourselves.

```
self.windowMapper = QSignalMapper(self)
self.connect(self.windowMapper, SIGNAL("mapped(QWidget*)"),
        self.mdi, SLOT("setActiveWindow(QWidget*)"))
```

In the Window menu that we will create, we need some way of making the window that the user chooses the active window. We saw a very simple solution to this problem in the preceding section. Another approach is to use partial function application, connecting each window action to `QWorkspace.setActiveWindow()` with the relevant `TextEdit` as argument. Here we have taken a pure PyQt approach, and we have used the `QSignalMapper` class. We will explain its use when we review the `updateWindowMenu()` method.

```
self.windowMenu = self.menuBar().addMenu("&Window")
self.connect(self.windowMenu, SIGNAL("aboutToShow()"),
        self.updateWindowMenu)
```

The connection to `aboutToShow()` ensures that our `updateWindowMenu()` method is called before the menu is shown.

```
        self.updateWindowMenu()
        self.setWindowTitle("Text Editor")
        QTimer.singleShot(0, self.loadFiles)
```

At the end of the constructor we call `updateWindowMenu()` to force the Window menu to be created. This may seem strange; after all, it will be created anyway when the user tries to use it, so why do so now? The reason is that if we automatically load in some documents at startup, the user might want to navigate between them using our keyboard shortcuts (F6 and Shift+F6), but the shortcuts will become active only after the menu has been created.

```
    def closeEvent(self, event):
        failures = []
        for textEdit in self.mdi.windowList():
            if textEdit.isModified():
                try:
                    textEdit.save()
                except IOError, e:
                    failures.append(str(e))
        if failures and \
           QMessageBox.warning(self, "Text Editor -- Save Error",
                    "Failed to save%s\nQuit anyway?" % \
                    "\n\t".join(failures),
                    QMessageBox.Yes|QMessageBox.No) == QMessageBox.No:
            event.ignore()
            return
        settings = QSettings()
        settings.setValue("MainWindow/Size", QVariant(self.size()))
        settings.setValue("MainWindow/Position",
                QVariant(self.pos()))
        settings.setValue("MainWindow/State",
                QVariant(self.saveState()))
        files = QStringList()
        for textEdit in self.mdi.windowList():
            if not textEdit.filename.startsWith("Unnamed"):
                files.append(textEdit.filename)
        settings.setValue("CurrentFiles", QVariant(files))
        self.mdi.closeAllWindows()
```

When the application is terminated we give the user the opportunity to save any unsaved changes. Then we save the main window's size, position, and state. We also save a list of all the filenames from all the MDI windows. At the end we call `QWorkspace.closeAllWindows()`, which will result in each window receiving a close event.

If any save fails, we take note, and after all the files have been processed, if there were errors we pop up a message box informing the user and give them the chance to cancel terminating the application.

In the TextEdit's close event there is code to give the user the chance to save any unsaved changes, but at this point there can't be any because we have already handled this by saving unsaved changes at the beginning of this method. We have the code in the TextEdit's close event because the user can close any window at any time, so each window must be able to cope with being closed. But we do not use this when the application is terminated, and instead call save() for modified files, because we want to keep a current files list, and to do that every file must have a proper filename before we reach the code for saving the current files list, and calling save() earlier achieves this.

```
def loadFiles(self):
    if len(sys.argv) > 1:
        for filename in sys.argv[1:31]: # Load at most 30 files
            filename = QString(filename)
            if QFileInfo(filename).isFile():
                self.loadFile(filename)
                QApplication.processEvents()
    else:
        settings = QSettings()
        files = settings.value("CurrentFiles").toStringList()
        for filename in files:
            filename = QString(filename)
            if QFile.exists(filename):
                self.loadFile(filename)
                QApplication.processEvents()
```

We have designed this application so that it will load back all the files that were open the last time the application was run. However, if the user specifies one or more files on the command line, we ignore the previously opened files, and open just those the user has specified. In this case, we have chosen to arbitrarily limit the number of files to 30, to protect the user from inadvertently giving a file specification of *.* in a directory with hundreds or thousands of files.

The QApplication.processEvents() calls temporarily yield control to the event loop so that any events that have accumulated—such as paint events—can be handled. Then processing resumes from the next statement. The effect in this application is that an editor window will pop up immediately after each file has been loaded, rather than the windows appearing only after all the files have been loaded. This makes it clear to the user that the application is doing something, whereas a long delay at the beginning might make the user think that the application has crashed. Another benefit of using processEvents() is that the user's mouse and keyboard events will get some processor time, keeping the application responsive even if a lot of other processing is taking place.

Doing Lots of Processing at Start-Up sidebar 184 ☞

Using processEvents() to keep an application responsive during long-running operations is much easier than using threading. Nonetheless, this method must be used with care because it could lead to events being handled that cause problems for the long-running operations themselves. One way to help reduce the risk is to pass extra parameters—for example, a flag that limits the kinds of events that should be processed, and a maximum time to be spent processing events. We will see another example of the use of processEvents() in Chapter 12; threading is the subject of Chapter 19.

```
def loadFile(self, filename):
    textEdit = textedit.TextEdit(filename)
    try:
        textEdit.load()
    except (IOError, OSError), e:
        QMessageBox.warning(self, "Text Editor -- Load Error",
                "Failed to load %s: %s" % (filename, e))
        textEdit.close()
        del textEdit
    else:
        self.mdi.addWindow(textEdit)
        textEdit.show()
```

When a file is loaded, as a result of either loadFiles() or fileOpen(), it creates a new TextEdit, with the given filename, and tells the editor to load the file. If loading fails, the user is informed in a message box, and the editor is closed and deleted. If loading succeeds, the editor is added to the workspace and shown. We do not need a static instances variable to keep the TextEdit instances alive, since QWorkspace takes care of this automatically for us.

```
def fileNew(self):
    textEdit = textedit.TextEdit()
    self.mdi.addWindow(textEdit)
    textEdit.show()
```

This method simply creates a new editor, adds it to the workspace, and shows it. The editor's window title will be "Unnamed-n.txt", where n is an incrementing integer starting from one. If the user types in any text and attempts to close or save the editor, they will be prompted to choose a proper filename.

```
def fileOpen(self):
    filename = QFileDialog.getOpenFileName(self,
                    "Text Editor -- Open File")
    if not filename.isEmpty():
        for textEdit in self.mdi.windowList():
            if textEdit.filename == filename:
                self.mdi.setActiveWindow(textEdit)
                break
        else:
            self.loadFile(filename)
```

If the user chooses to open a file, we check to see whether it is already in one of the workspace's editors. If it is we simply make that editor's window the active window. Otherwise we load the file into a new editor window. If our users wanted to be able to load the same file more than once—for example, to look at different parts of a long file—we could simply call loadFile() every time and not bother to see whether the file is in an existing editor.

```python
def fileSave(self):
    textEdit = self.mdi.activeWindow()
    if textEdit is None or not isinstance(textEdit, QTextEdit):
        return
    try:
        textEdit.save()
    except (IOError, OSError), e:
        QMessageBox.warning(self, "Text Editor -- Save Error",
                "Failed to save %s: %s" % (textEdit.filename, e))
```

When the user triggers the "file save" action, we determine which file they want to save by calling QWorkspace.activeWindow(). If this returns a TextEdit, we call save() on it.

```python
def fileSaveAll(self):
    errors = []
    for textEdit in self.mdi.windowList():
        if textEdit.isModified():
            try:
                textEdit.save()
            except (IOError, OSError), e:
                errors.append("%s: %s" % (textEdit.filename, e))
    if errors:
        QMessageBox.warning(self, "Text Editor -- Save All Error",
                "Failed to save\n%s" % "\n".join(errors))
```

As a convenience, we have provided a "save all" action. Since there might be a lot of windows, and if there is a problem saving one (for example, lack of disk space), the problem might affect many windows. So instead of giving error messages when each save() fails, we accumulate the errors in a list and show them all at the end, if there are any to show.

```python
def editCopy(self):
    textEdit = self.mdi.activeWindow()
    if textEdit is None or not isinstance(textEdit, QTextEdit):
        return
    cursor = textEdit.textCursor()
    text = cursor.selectedText()
    if not text.isEmpty():
        clipboard = QApplication.clipboard()
        clipboard.setText(text)
```

This method starts in the same way the previous one did—and the same way all the methods that apply to one particular window start—by retrieving the editor that the user is working on. The QTextCursor returned by QTextEdit.text-Cursor() is a programmatic equivalent to the cursor the user uses, but it is independent of the user's cursor; this class is discussed more fully in Chapter 13. If there is selected text, we copy it to the system's global clipboard.*

```
def editCut(self):
    textEdit = self.mdi.activeWindow()
    if textEdit is None or not isinstance(textEdit, QTextEdit):
        return
    cursor = textEdit.textCursor()
    text = cursor.selectedText()
    if not text.isEmpty():
        cursor.removeSelectedText()
        clipboard = QApplication.clipboard()
        clipboard.setText(text)
```

This method is almost the same as the copy method. The only difference is that if there is selected text, we remove it from the editor.

```
def editPaste(self):
    textEdit = self.mdi.activeWindow()
    if textEdit is None or not isinstance(textEdit, QTextEdit):
        return
    clipboard = QApplication.clipboard()
    textEdit.insertPlainText(clipboard.text())
```

If the clipboard has text, whether from a copy or cut operation in this application, or from another application, we insert it into the editor at the editor's current cursor position.

All the basic MDI window operations are provided by QWorkspace slots, so we do not need to provide tiling, cascading, or window navigation ourselves. But we do have to provide the code for minimizing and restoring all windows.

```
def windowRestoreAll(self):
    for textEdit in self.mdi.windowList():
        textEdit.showNormal()
```

The windowMinimizeAll() method (not shown) is the same, except that we call showMinimized() instead of showNormal().

A QSignalMapper object is one that emits a mapped() signal whenever its map() slot is called. The parameter it passes in its mapped() signal is the one that

---

* X Window System users have two clipboards: the default one and the mouse selection one. Mac OS X also has a "Find" clipboard. PyQt provides access to all the available clipboards using an optional "mode" second argument to setText() and text().

was set to correspond with whichever QObject called the map() slot. We use a signal mapper to relate actions in the Window menu with TextEdit widgets so that when the user chooses a particular window, the appropriate TextEdit will become the active window. This is set up in two places: the form's initializer, and in the updateWindowMenu() method, and is illustrated in Figure 9.9.

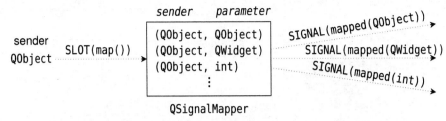

Figure 9.9 *The general operation of a QSignalMapper*

In the form's initializer we made a signal–slot connection from the signal mapper's mapped(QWidget*) signal to the MDI workspace's setActiveWindow(QWidget*) slot. To use this, the signal mapper must emit a signal that corresponds to the MDI window the user has chosen from the Window menu, and this is set up in the updateWindowMenu() method. The MDI Text Editor's signal mapper is illustrated in Figure 9.10.

```
def updateWindowMenu(self):
    self.windowMenu.clear()
    self.addActions(self.windowMenu, (self.windowNextAction,
            self.windowPrevAction, self.windowCascadeAction,
            self.windowTileAction, self.windowRestoreAction,
            self.windowMinimizeAction,
            self.windowArrangeIconsAction, None,
            self.windowCloseAction))
    textEdits = self.mdi.windowList()
    if not textEdits:
        return
```

We begin by clearing all the actions from the Window menu, and then we add back all the standard actions. Next, we get the list of TextEdit windows; if there are none we are finished and simply return; otherwise, we must add an entry for each window.

```
self.windowMenu.addSeparator()
i = 1
menu = self.windowMenu
for textEdit in textEdits:
    title = textEdit.windowTitle()
    if i == 10:
        self.windowMenu.addSeparator()
        menu = menu.addMenu("&More")
```

```
accel = ""
if i < 10:
    accel = "&%d " % i
elif i < 36:
    accel = "&%c " % chr(i + ord("@") - 9)
```

We iterate over all the windows. For the first nine, we create an "accel" string of &1, &2, and so on, to produce 1, 2, …, 9. If there are ten or more windows, we create a submenu with the text "More", and add the tenth and subsequent windows to this submenu. For the tenth to thirty-sixth windows, we create accel strings of &A, &B, …, &Z; for any other windows we do not provide an accel string. (The %c format string is used to specify a single character.) The More submenu's accelerators are English-specific; other languages may need different treatment.

```
action = menu.addAction("%s%s" % (accel, title))
self.connect(action, SIGNAL("triggered()"),
            self.windowMapper, SLOT("map()"))
self.windowMapper.setMapping(action, textEdit)
i += 1
```

We create a new action with the (possibly empty) accel text and the title text—the window's title, which is the filename without the path. Then we connect the action's triggered() signal to the signal mapper's map() slot. This means that whenever the user chooses a window from the Window menu, the signal mapper's map() slot will be called. Notice that neither the signal nor the slot has parameters; it is up to the signal mapper to figure out which action triggered it—it could use sender(), for example. After the signal–slot connection, we set up a mapping inside the signal mapper from the action to the corresponding TextEdit.

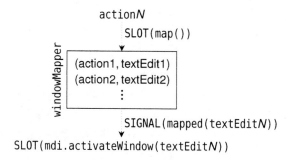

Figure 9.10 *The MDI Editor's signal mapper*

When the signal mapper's map() slot is called, the signal mapper will find out which action called it, and use the mapping to determine which TextEdit to pass as a parameter. Then the signal mapper will emit its own mapped(QWidget*) signal, with the parameter. We connected the mapped() signal to the MDI workspace's `setActiveWindow()` slot, so this slot is in turn called, and the Text-Edit passed as a parameter will become the active window.

That completes our review of the MDI Text Editor. We have skipped the code for creating the application object and the main window since it is the same as many code examples we have seen in previous examples.

Summary

When we have dialogs with lots of options, we can often make things more manageable for the user by using tab widgets and stacked widgets. Tab widgets are especially useful for when we want the user to be able to view and edit all the available options. Stacked widgets are suitable for when we want the user to see only the currently relevant page of options. For stacked widgets we must provide a means by which the user can select the current page—for example, a combobox or a list widget of page names. When some of a dialog's options are "advanced" or infrequently needed, we can use an extension dialog, hiding the extra options unless the user asks to see them. Checked group boxes can be used to enable or disable the widgets they contain; this is useful if we want the user to be able to see the options available, even when they are disabled. For some dialogs, all of these approaches can be used in combination, although in such complex cases, the validation logic might become rather convoluted.

Splitters are very useful for creating multiple-widget main windows and give the user control over the relative sizes of the widgets. An alternative approach is to have a single central widget, and to put the other widgets in dock windows. Dock windows automatically put a splitter between themselves and the central widget when docked, and can be dragged from one dock area to another or floated free.

SDI makes it easy for users to open multiple documents inside the same application. SDI also makes possible some interaction across the windows, such as having "save all" and "quit" actions and a Window menu, that are not very easily achieved using a separate application instance for each document. The SDI approach is very fashionable, and although it is more resource-hungry than MDI, it is probably easier for very inexperienced users to understand than MDI.

MDI provides the same benefits as SDI, except that the document windows are constrained to appear within a single main window's central area. This avoids duplicating menus and toolbars, and it makes it easier to arrange windows in relation to one another. One drawback of MDI is that some users find it more difficult to understand than SDI, at least at first. MDI is not limited to having windows of just one widget type, although most modern MDI applications that use more than one widget type in the main window have one type for document windows, and the other types are put in dock windows.

In both the SDI and MDI example applications, all of the actions are enabled all of the time. This is not a problem since any actions that don't make sense harmlessly do nothing. However, to avoid confusing some users, it might be better to enable or disable actions depending on the application's state; the sidebar in Chapter 13 shows how this can be done.

En-
abling
and
Dis-
abling
Actions
sidebar

☞ 385

Layouts, splitters, tab widgets, stacked widgets, dock windows, SDI, and MDI together provide a wide range of user interface design options. In addition, it is possible to create our own layouts in code, or to create our own layout managers, so the possibilities really are limitless.

Exercise

Modify the MDI Text Editor application (texteditor.pyw) so that instead of using MDI it uses a QTabWidget and becomes a tabbed editor.

The Window menu will not be required, so all the code associated with it can be removed. A new "file close tab" action will be needed, as will a corresponding method to handle it. Instead of using QWorkspace.windowList(), use a for loop to iterate from 0 to QTabWidget.count(), and use QTabWidget.widget() to access each window in turn.

The closeEvent() will need changing, and it is probably the trickiest to get right. Change loadFiles() to limit the number of files loaded on the command line to 10. fileNew() will need to create a TextEdit as before, and then add it to the tab widget using QTabWidget.addTab(), giving the widget and its window title as parameters. Instead of calling show() on the widget, use QTabWidget.setCurrentWidget(). The fileOpen(), loadFile(), fileSave(), fileSaveAs(), and fileSaveAll() methods will need small changes. The edit methods need to change only their first line of code to use QTabWidget.currentWidget() instead of QWorkspace.activeWindow().

Once everything is working, add two keyboard shortcuts, one for QKey-Sequence.PreviousChild and the other for QKeySequence.NextChild, along with suitable methods, prevTab() and nextTab(), to make them work.

The changes amount to about a dozen lines, plus an extra twenty lines or so for the shortcuts and their methods; as always the emphasis is on thought and understanding rather than on typing.

A model solution is provided in the file chap09/tabbededitor.pyw.

10

- The Event-Handling Mechanism
- Reimplementing Event Handlers
- Using the Clipboard
- Drag and Drop

Events, the Clipboard, and Drag and Drop

In this short chapter we begin by describing the key concepts involved in event handling. In the second section we build on this knowledge to show how to control a widget's behavior and appearance by reimplementing low-level event handlers. Later chapters build on the material covered in the first two sections, particularly Chapter 11, which shows how to create custom widgets.

The chapter's third section shows how to use the clipboard, and in particular how to pass and retrieve plain text, HTML, and images to and from the system's global clipboard. The last section shows how to implement drag and drop, both by using PyQt's easy-to-use built-in functionality, and by handling it ourselves to drag and drop custom data. The exercise builds on the coverage of dragging and dropping custom data to allow the user to choose whether to move or copy when dropping.

The Event-Handling Mechanism

PyQt provides two mechanisms for dealing with events: the high-level signals and slots mechanism, and low-level event handlers. The signals and slots approach is ideal when we are concerned with what actions the user wants to perform, without getting bogged down in the details of how specifically they asked. Signals and slots can also be used to customize some aspects of how widgets behave. But when we need to go deeper, particularly when creating custom widgets, we need to use low-level event handlers.

Signals
and
slots

127 ☜

PyQt provides a rich variety of event handlers, some concerned with widget behavior, such as those that handle key presses and mouse events, and others concerned with widget appearance, such as those that handle paint events and resize events.

PyQt's event-handling mechanism works in the logical way we would expect. For example, if the user clicks the mouse or presses a key on a widget with key-

303

board focus, the widget is given the event. If the widget handles the event, that is the end of the story. But if the widget does not handle the event, the event is propagated to the widget's parent—another benefit of PyQt's parent–child hierarchy. This passing of unhandled events from child to parent continues right up to the top-level widget, and if that doesn't handle the event, the event is simply thrown away.

PyQt provides five different ways of intercepting and handling events. The first two approaches are the most heavily used, with the others needed rarely, if ever.

The simplest approach is to reimplement a specific event handler. So far, we have seen just one example of this: the reimplementation of a widget's closeEvent(). As we will see in this chapter and in subsequent chapters, we can control a widget's behavior by reimplementing other event handlers—for example, keyPressEvent(), mousePressEvent(), and mouseReleaseEvent(). We can also control a widget's appearance by reimplementing resizeEvent() and paintEvent(). When we reimplement these events we often don't call the base class implementation since we want our own code executed only as a result of the event handler being called.

Before any specific event handler is called, the event() event handler is called. Reimplementing this method allows us to handle events that cannot be handled properly in the specific event handlers (in particular, overriding the Tab key's keyboard focus changing behavior), or to implement events for which no specific handler exists, such as QEvent.ToolBarChange. When we reimplement this handler, we call the base class implementation for any events we don't handle ourselves.

The third and fourth approaches use event filters. We can call installEvent-Filter() on any QObject. This will mean that all events for the QObject are passed to our event filter first: We can discard or modify any of the events before they reach the target object. An even more powerful version of this approach is to install an event filter on the QApplication object, although its only practical uses are for debugging and for handling mouse events sent to disabled widgets. It is possible to install multiple event filters on an object or on QApplication, in which case they are executed in order from most to least recently installed.

Event filters provide a very powerful means of handling events, and newcomers to PyQt programming are often tempted to use them. But we recommend avoiding the use of event filters, at least until you have a lot of PyQt programming experience. If very large numbers of event filters are installed, application performance can suffer; also, they can considerably increase code complexity compared with simply reimplementing specific event handlers, or the event() handler. We will not look at any event filter examples, since they should be avoided in general PyQt programming—they are really relevant only when creating custom widgets—and even then they are rarely necessary.

The fifth approach is to subclass `QApplication` and reimplement its `notify()` method. This method is called before any event filter or event handler, so it provides the ultimate in control. In practice, this would be done only for debugging, and even then, using event filters is probably more flexible.

Reimplementing Event Handlers

The screenshot in Figure 10.1 shows a `QWidget` subclass that has some reimplemented event handlers. The Events application in `chap10/events.pyw` reports certain events and conditions, and we will use it to see how event handling is done in PyQt. Later chapters use the same techniques that we describe here to do much more sophisticated and realistic event handling. We will begin by looking at an extract from the application's initializer to see its instance data.

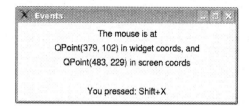

Figure 10.1 *Testing custom event handlers*

```
class Widget(QWidget):

    def __init__(self, parent=None):
        super(Widget, self).__init__(parent)
        self.justDoubleClicked = False
        self.key = QString()
        self.text = QString()
        self.message = QString()
```

We hold the text of the most recent key press in key, the text to be painted—for example, "The mouse is at..."—in text, and a message text in message. We also keep track of whether the user has just done a double-click.

The first event handler we will consider is the paint event. We will defer a proper discussion of painting to Chapter 11.

```
    def paintEvent(self, event):
        text = self.text
        i = text.indexOf("\n\n")
        if i >= 0:
            text = text.left(i)
        if not self.key.isEmpty():
            text += "\n\nYou pressed: %s" % self.key
        painter = QPainter(self)
        painter.setRenderHint(QPainter.TextAntialiasing)
```

```
        painter.drawText(self.rect(), Qt.AlignCenter, text)
        if self.message:
            painter.drawText(self.rect(),
                    Qt.AlignBottom|Qt.AlignHCenter, self.message)
            QTimer.singleShot(5000, self.message.clear)
            QTimer.singleShot(5000, self.update)
```

The text to be displayed consists of two parts. The first part usually contains the mouse coordinates, and the second part (which may be empty) contains the last key that the user pressed. In addition, message text may be painted at the bottom of the widget, in which case the single-shot timers clear the message text after 5 seconds and schedule a paint event to repaint the widget without the message text.

In paint events it is quite common to ignore the event as we have done here. (The event can tell us the exact region that needs repainting so it can be used to optimize painting by just painting the region that needs updating, a technique we will use in Chapter 16.) The rect() method returns a QRect with the widget's dimensions, so we simply draw the text centered in the given rectangle. We do not call the base class's paint event; this is standard practice in PyQt paint event handlers, and in any case, the QWidget paint event does nothing.

```
        def resizeEvent(self, event):
            self.text = QString("Resized to QSize(%d, %d)" % (
                            event.size().width(),
                            event.size().height()))
            self.update()
```

Whenever the widget is resized—for example, by the user dragging a corner or side—a resize event is generated. We set our instance text to show the new size, and call update() to schedule a paint event. A resize event also has the previous size, available from the QResizeEvent.oldSize() method. We do not call the base class's resize event, since it does nothing.

```
        def keyPressEvent(self, event):
            self.key = QString()
            if event.key() == Qt.Key_Home:
                self.key = "Home"
            elif event.key() == Qt.Key_End:
                self.key = "End"
            elif event.key() == Qt.Key_PageUp:
                if event.modifiers() & Qt.ControlModifier:
                    self.key = "Ctrl+PageUp"
                else:
                    self.key = "PageUp"
            elif event.key() == Qt.Key_PageDown:
                if event.modifiers() & Qt.ControlModifier:
                    self.key = "Ctrl+PageDown"
```

```
            else:
                self.key = "PageDown"
        elif Qt.Key_A <= event.key() <= Qt.Key_Z:
            if event.modifiers() & Qt.ShiftModifier:
                self.key = "Shift+"
            self.key += event.text()
        if self.key:
            self.key = QString(self.key)
            self.update()
        else:
            QWidget.keyPressEvent(self, event)
```

If the user presses a key, we are informed through the keyPressEvent(). There is also a corresponding keyReleaseEvent(), but that is rarely reimplemented. The QKeyEvent parameter provides several useful methods, including key(), which returns the key code for the key that was pressed, and modifiers(), which returns a bit flag indicating the state of the Shift, Ctrl, and Alt keys.

We have chosen to handle the Home, End, PageUp, Ctrl+PageUp, PageDown, and Ctrl+PageDown key sequences, and the alphabetic keys A..Z as well as Shift+A...Shift+Z. We store a textual representation of what was pressed in the key variable and call update() to schedule a paint event. If the user pressed a key that we do not handle, we pass on the key press to the base class implementation, a practice that is common when handling key events.

```
    def contextMenuEvent(self, event):
        menu = QMenu(self)
        oneAction = menu.addAction("&One")
        twoAction = menu.addAction("&Two")
        self.connect(oneAction, SIGNAL("triggered()"), self.one)
        self.connect(twoAction, SIGNAL("triggered()"), self.two)
        if not self.message:
            menu.addSeparator()
            threeAction = menu.addAction("Thre&e")
            self.connect(threeAction, SIGNAL("triggered()"),
                         self.three)
        menu.exec_(event.globalPos())
```

The easiest way to create a context menu is to add actions to a widget using QWidget.addAction(), and to set the widget's context menu policy to Qt.Actions-ContextMenu; we saw how this was done in Chapter 6 on page 180. But if we want fine control over what happens as a result of a context menu event—for example, offering different options depending on the application's state—we can reimplement the context menu event handler as we have done here.

The globalPos() method returns the mouse position at the time the context menu was invoked; we pass the position to QMenu.exec_() to ensure that the menu is popped up where the user expects it.

```
def mouseDoubleClickEvent(self, event):
    self.justDoubleClicked = True
    self.text = QString("Double-clicked.")
    self.update()
```

If the user double-clicks, this event handler is called. In this example, we need to keep track of whether the user has just double-clicked because we are also reimplementing the mouse release and mouse move events. A mouse release event will occur as the result of a double-click, and a mouse move event is almost certain to occur on a double-click because the user's hand is unlikely to be perfectly steady.

We take the same approach as we have done in the other event handlers: We set the text and schedule a repaint to show it. It is quite common not to call the base class for mouse events that we handle ourselves.

```
def mouseReleaseEvent(self, event):
    if self.justDoubleClicked:
        self.justDoubleClicked = False
    else:
        self.setMouseTracking(not self.hasMouseTracking())
        if self.hasMouseTracking():
            self.text = QString("Mouse tracking is on.\n"
                                "Try moving the mouse!\n"
                                "Single click to switch it off")
        else:
            self.text = QString("Mouse tracking is off.\n"
                                "Single click to switch it on")
        self.update()
```

If the user has just released the mouse, except just after a double-click, we toggle mouse tracking. When tracking is on, mouse move events are produced for all mouse movements; when tracking is off, mouse move events are produced only when the mouse is dragged. By default, mouse tracking is off. Here we use a mouse click (i.e., the release after a click) to toggle mouse tracking on or off. As before, we set the text, and schedule a paint event to show it.

```
def mouseMoveEvent(self, event):
    if not self.justDoubleClicked:
        globalPos = self.mapToGlobal(event.pos())
        self.text = QString("The mouse is at\nQPoint(%d, %d) "
                            "in widget coords, and\n"
                            "QPoint(%d, %d) in screen coords" % (
                            event.pos().x(), event.pos().y(),
                            globalPos.x(), globalPos.y()))
        self.update()
```

Table 10.1 *Selected QWidget Event-Handling Methods*

Syntax	Description
`w.closeEvent(e)`	Reimplement to give the user the opportunity to save unsaved changes and to save user settings; `w` is a custom `QWidget` subclass, and `e` is a handler-specific `QEvent` subclass
`w.contextMenu-Event(e)`	Reimplement to provide custom context menus. An easier alternative is to call `setContextMenu-Policy(Qt.ActionsContextMenu)` and add actions to the widget using `QWidget.addAction()`.
`w.dragEnterEvent(e)`	Reimplement to indicate whether the widget will accept or reject the drop in `QDragEnterEvent e`
`w.dragMoveEvent(e)`	Reimplement to set the acceptable drop actions—for example, not accepted, or one or more of, move, copy, and link, for `QDragMoveEvent e`
`w.dropEvent(e)`	Reimplement to handle the drop in `QDropEvent e`
`w.event(e)`	Reimplement for events that don't have specific event handlers—for example, for Tab key handling. This is inherited from `QObject`.
`w.keyPressEvent(e)`	Reimplement to respond to key presses
`w.mouseDoubleClick-Event(e)`	Reimplement to respond to double-clicks specified in `QMouseEvent e`
`w.mouseMoveEvent(e)`	Reimplement to respond to mouse moves specified in `QMouseEvent e`. This event handler is affected by `QWidget.setMouseTracking()`.
`w.mousePressEvent(e)`	Reimplement to respond to mouse presses
`w.mouseReleaseEvent(e)`	Reimplement to respond to mouse releases
`w.paintEvent(e)`	Reimplement to draw the widget
`w.resizeEvent(e)`	Reimplement to resize the widget

If the user has toggled mouse tracking on (by clicking the mouse), mouse move events will be produced and this method will be called for each of them. We retrieve the mouse's position in screen coordinates, that is, coordinates relative to the top left of the screen, and in widget coordinates, that is, coordinates relative to the top left of the widget. Both coordinate systems have a top left of $(0, 0)$, with y coordinates increasing downward and x coordinates increasing rightward.

```
def event(self, event):
    if event.type() == QEvent.KeyPress and \
       event.key() == Qt.Key_Tab:
        self.key = QString("Tab captured in event()")
```

```
                self.update()
                return True
        return QWidget.event(self, event)
```

When an event is passed to a widget the widget's event() method is called first. This method returns True if it handled the event, and False otherwise. In the case of returning False, PyQt will send the event to the widget's parent, and then to the parent's parent, until one of the handlers returns True, or until it reaches the top level (no parent), in which case the event is thrown away. The event() method may handle the event itself, or may delegate the work to a specific event handler like paintEvent() or mousePressEvent().

When the user presses Tab, in almost every case, the widget with the keyboard focus's event() method will call setFocus() on the next widget in the tab order and will return True without passing the event to any of the key handlers. (The QTextEdit class reimplements the event handler to insert literal tabs into the text, but can be told to revert to the normal focus-switching behavior.)

We cannot stop Tab from changing keyboard focus by reimplementing a key event handler, because the key press is never passed onto them. So we must instead reimplement the event() method and handle Tab presses there.

In this example, if the user presses Tab, we simply update the text that is displayed. We also return True indicating that we have handled the event. This prevents the event from being propagated any further. For all other events, we call the base class implementation.

Realistic event handlers are often more sophisticated than the ones shown here, but our purpose at the moment is just to see how the event-handling mechanism works. In the next chapter and in subsequent chapters, we will often reimplement event handlers including paintEvent() and resizeEvent(), as well as contextMenuEvent(), wheelEvent(), keyPressEvent(), and mousePressEvent(), all in realistic contexts. And in the last section of this chapter we will reimplement some of the drag-and-drop-related events.

Using the Clipboard

PyQt provides clipboard support for text in QTextEdit, QLineEdit, QTableWidget, and the other widgets where textual data can be edited. PyQt's clipboard and drag-and-drop systems use data in MIME (Multipurpose Internet Mail Extensions) format, a format that can be used to store any arbitrary data.

Occasionally, it is convenient to pass data to the clipboard or retrieve data from the clipboard directly in code. PyQt makes this easy. The QApplication class provides a static method that returns a QClipboard object, and we can set or get text, images, or other data to or from the clipboard through this object.

The clipboard holds only one object at a time, so if we set, say, a string, and then we set an image, only the image will be available because the string will be deleted when we set the image.

Here is how we set text on the clipboard:

```
clipboard = QApplication.clipboard()
clipboard.setText("I've been clipped!")
```

The text is set as plain text; we will see how to handle HTML shortly.

```
clipboard = QApplication.clipboard()
clipboard.setPixmap(QPixmap(os.path.join(
        os.path.dirname(__file__), "images/gvim.png")))
```

Image data can be set on the clipboard using setImage() for QImages, or set-Pixmap() for pixmaps, as we have done here. Both QImage and QPixmap can handle a wide variety of standard image formats.

Retrieving data from the clipboard is just as easy:

```
clipboard = QApplication.clipboard()
self.textLabel.setText(clipboard.text())
```

If the clipboard has no text—for example, if it has an image, or some custom data type—QClipboard.text() will return an empty string.

```
clipboard = QApplication.clipboard()
self.imageLabel.setPixmap(clipboard.pixmap())
```

If the clipboard has no image—for example, if it has text, or some custom data type—QClipboard.pixmap() will return a null image.

In addition to handling plain text and images we can handle some other kinds of data. For example, here is how we would copy HTML text to the clipboard:

```
mimeData = QMimeData()
mimeData.setHtml(
        "<b>Bold and <font color=red>Red</font></b>")
clipboard = QApplication.clipboard()
clipboard.setMimeData(mimeData)
```

If we want to retrieve HTML text, including HTML wrapped in a QMimeData object, we can use QClipboard.text("html"). This will return an empty string if there is no text, or if the text is not in HTML format—for example, if it is plain text. Here is the generic way to retrieve data that has been wrapped in a QMimeData object:

```
clipboard = QApplication.clipboard()
mimeData = clipboard.mimeData()
```

```
    if mimeData.hasHtml():
        self.textLabel.setText(mimeData.html())
```

In some situations we want to set and get our own custom data formats to and from the clipboard. We can do this using the QMimeData class, as we will see in the next section.

Data set on or retrieved from the clipboard usually works on the operating system's global clipboard. In addition, by specifying the clipboard mode, it is possible to use the selection clipboard (an additional clipboard that exists on Linux and other systems that use the X Window System), or the find pasteboard used on Mac OS X.

Drag and Drop

Many PyQt widgets support drag and drop out of the box, only requiring us to switch on the support to make it work. For example, the application shown in Figure 10.2 starts out with items in the left hand QListWidget, and with nothing in the QListWidget in the middle or in the QTableWidget on the right. The screenshot shows the application after some items have been dragged and dropped.

The application's source code is in the file chap10/draganddrop.pyw.

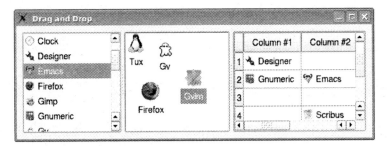

Figure 10.2 *PyQt's built-in drag-and-drop facilities*

The drag-and-drop functionality is achieved purely by setting properties on the widgets involved. Here is the code that created the left-hand list widget:

```
    listWidget = QListWidget()
    listWidget.setAcceptDrops(True)
    listWidget.setDragEnabled(True)
```

The middle list widget is similar, except that we have set it to icon view mode instead of list view mode:

```
    iconListWidget = QListWidget()
    iconListWidget.setAcceptDrops(True)
    iconListWidget.setDragEnabled(True)
```

```
iconListWidget.setViewMode(QListWidget.IconMode)
```

Making the QTableWidget support drag and drop is achieved in exactly the same way, with a call of setAcceptDrops(True) and a call of setDragEnabled(True).

No other code is necessary; what is shown is sufficient to allow users to drag icon and text items from one list widget to another, and to and from cells in the table.

The built-in drag-and-drop facilities are very convenient, and are often sufficient. But if we need to be able to handle our own custom data, we must reimplement some event handlers, as we will see in the following subsection.

Handling Custom Data

The application shown in Figure 10.3 supports drag and drop for custom data; in particular, icons and text. (The source code is in chap10/customdragand-drop.pyw.) Although this is the same functionality as the built-in drag-and-drop facilities offer, the techniques used are generic and can be applied to any arbitrary data we like.

The icons and text can be dragged from the list widget on the left to the list widget on the right (which is in icon mode), or to the custom widget at the bottom left, or to the custom line edit at the bottom right—although in this last case only the text is used.

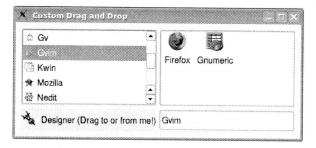

Figure 10.3 *Dragging and dropping custom data*

For custom data that is put on the clipboard or used by PyQt's drag-and-drop system, we use QMimeData objects, with our own custom MIME types. MIME is a standardized format for handling multipart custom data. MIME data has a type and a subtype—for example, text/plain, text/html, or image/png. To handle custom MIME data we must choose a custom type and subtype, and wrap the data in a QMimeData object.

For this example we have created a MIME type of application/x-icon-and-text. It is good practice for custom MIME subtypes to begin with x-. We have stored the data in a QByteArray, a resizable array of bytes, and which for this example holds a QString and a QIcon, although it could hold any arbitrary data.

We will begin by seeing how to make a `QLineEdit` subclass that can accept drops of MIME type application/x-icon-and-text, making use of the text and ignoring the icon.

```
class DropLineEdit(QLineEdit):

    def __init__(self, parent=None):
        super(DropLineEdit, self).__init__(parent)
        self.setAcceptDrops(True)
```

The initializer simply sets the line edit to accept drops.

```
    def dragEnterEvent(self, event):
        if event.mimeData().hasFormat("application/x-icon-and-text"):
            event.accept()
        else:
            event.ignore()
```

When the user drags over the line edit we want to display an icon if the MIME data being dragged is a type that we can handle; otherwise the line edit will display the "no drop" icon (which often appears as ⃠). By accepting the drag enter event we signify that we can accept drops of the type of MIME data on offer; by ignoring we say that we cannot accept such data. The icon used for acceptable data is set when the drag is initiated as we will see later on.

The drag-related event handlers are called automatically by PyQt when necessary because we set accept drops in the initializer.

```
    def dragMoveEvent(self, event):
        if event.mimeData().hasFormat("application/x-icon-and-text"):
            event.setDropAction(Qt.CopyAction)
            event.accept()
        else:
            event.ignore()
```

As the user drags over the widget `dragMoveEvent()`s occur; we want the data to be copied (rather than moved), so we set the drop action accordingly.

```
    def dropEvent(self, event):
        if event.mimeData().hasFormat("application/x-icon-and-text"):
            data = event.mimeData().data("application/x-icon-and-text")
            stream = QDataStream(data, QIODevice.ReadOnly)
            text = QString()
            stream >> text
            self.setText(text)
            event.setDropAction(Qt.CopyAction)
            event.accept()
        else:
            event.ignore()
```

Stream-
ing to
QData-
Stream

242 ☜

If the user drops the data on the widget we must handle it. We do this by extracting the data (a QByteArray), and then creating a QDataStream to read the data. The QDataStream class can read and write from and to any QIODevice including files, network sockets, external processes, and byte arrays. Since we are only interested in the string, that is all that we extract from the byte array. Note that to be able to stream QIcons to or from a QDataStream we must use PyQt 4.1 or later.

The DropLineEdit only supports dropping, so for our next example, we will create a QListWidget subclass which supports both dragging and dropping.

```
class DnDListWidget(QListWidget):

    def __init__(self, parent=None):
        super(DnDListWidget, self).__init__(parent)
        self.setAcceptDrops(True)
        self.setDragEnabled(True)
```

The initializer is similar to what we used before, except that we enable both dragging and dropping.

```
    def dragMoveEvent(self, event):
        if event.mimeData().hasFormat("application/x-icon-and-text"):
            event.setDropAction(Qt.MoveAction)
            event.accept()
        else:
            event.ignore()
```

This is almost identical to the DropLineEdit's dragMoveEvent(); the difference is that here we set the drop action to be Qt.MoveAction rather than Qt.CopyAction. The code for the dragEnterEvent() is not shown: It is the same as for the DropLineEdit.

```
    def dropEvent(self, event):
        if event.mimeData().hasFormat("application/x-icon-and-text"):
            data = event.mimeData().data("application/x-icon-and-text")
            stream = QDataStream(data, QIODevice.ReadOnly)
            text = QString()
            icon = QIcon()
            stream >> text >> icon
            item = QListWidgetItem(text, self)
            item.setIcon(icon)
            event.setDropAction(Qt.MoveAction)
            event.accept()
        else:
            event.ignore()
```

Stream-
ing from
QData-
Stream

245 📖

This code is again similar to the DropLineEdit, only now we want the icon as well as the text. To add an item to a QListWidget we must create a new QListWidgetItem and pass the list widget (self) as the item's parent.

```python
def startDrag(self, dropActions):
    item = self.currentItem()
    icon = item.icon()
    data = QByteArray()
    stream = QDataStream(data, QIODevice.WriteOnly)
    stream << item.text() << icon
    mimeData = QMimeData()
    mimeData.setData("application/x-icon-and-text", data)
    drag = QDrag(self)
    drag.setMimeData(mimeData)
    pixmap = icon.pixmap(24, 24)
    drag.setHotSpot(QPoint(12, 12))
    drag.setPixmap(pixmap)
    if drag.start(Qt.MoveAction) == Qt.MoveAction:
        self.takeItem(self.row(item))
```

This is the only method that is not in the DropLineEdit, and it is the one that makes it possible to drag from DnDListWidgets. We don't have to check the return value of currentItem() because only items can be dragged, so we know that if startDrag() is called there will be an item to drag. The startDrag() method is called automatically by PyQt when needed because we set drag enabled in the initializer.

We create a new empty byte array, and use QDataStream to populate it with the QListWidgetItem's icon and text. There is no need to call setVersion() on QDataStream when we use it purely for handling in-memory data that exists only during the runtime of the application and that is not exchanged with any other application. Once we have populated the byte array, we wrap it in a QMimeData object. Then we create a QDrag object, and give it the MIME data. We have chosen to use the data's icon as the icon to be used for the drag: If we had not done so, PyQt would provide a default icon. We have also set the drag's "hotspot" to be the center of the icon. The mouse's hotspot will always coincide with the icon's hotspot.

The call to QDrag.start() initiates the drag; we give as a parameter the action or actions that we will accept. If the drag succeeds, that is, if the data is successfully dropped, the start() method returns the action that occurred—for example, copy or move. If the action was move, we remove the dragged QListWidgetItem from this list widget. From Qt 4.3, QDrag.exec_() should be used instead of QDrag.start().

Qt 4.3

The setAcceptDrops() method is inherited from QWidget, but setDragEnabled() is not, so by default it is available in only certain widgets. If we want to create a custom widget that supports drops, we can simply call setAcceptDrops(True) and reimplement dragEnterEvent(), dragMoveEvent(), and dropEvent(), as we have done in the preceding examples. If we also want the custom widget to support drags, and the widget inherits QWidget or some QWidget subclass that does not have setDragEnabled(), we must do two things to make the widget support dragging. One is to provide a startDrag() method so that a QDrag object can be created, and another is to make sure the startDrag() method is called at an appropriate time. The easiest way to ensure that startDrag() is called is to reimplement the mouseMoveEvent():

```
def mouseMoveEvent(self, event):
    self.startDrag()
    QWidget.mouseMoveEvent(self, event)
```

The widget at the bottom left of the example application is a direct QWidget subclass and uses this technique. Its startDrag() method is very similar to the one we have just seen, and only a tiny bit simpler because it initiates copy drags rather than move drags, so we don't have to do anything regardless of whether the drag is dropped successfully.

Summary

When we use existing widgets, PyQt's signals and slots mechanism is often all we need to get the behaviors we want. But when we create custom widgets—for example, to exercise fine control over the appearance and behavior of a widget—we must reimplement low-level event handlers.

For appearance, reimplementing paintEvent() is often sufficient, although in some cases we may also need to reimplement resizeEvent(). We normally don't call the base class implementation for these events. For behavior it is common to reimplement keyPressEvent() and some of the mouse events such as mouse-PressEvent() or mouseMoveEvent(). We often don't call the base class implementation for mouse events, although it is usually harmless to do so. If we exercise lower-level control by reimplementing QWidget.event(), we must return True for those events that we handle ourselves, and we must return the result of calling the base class implementation for those events that we don't handle.

We don't often need to handle the clipboard in our own code, since most of PyQt's text editing widgets automatically interact with the clipboard in the way we would expect. But if we do want to work with the clipboard in code, setting and getting text and image data is straightforward, using the QClipboard object returned by QApplication.clipboard(). Setting HTML data is slightly more involved since we must wrap the HTML in a QMimeData object, although retrieving HTML is easy. When we use MIME data with the clipboard we are not limited to HTML; we can store and retrieve any kind of data by using the same techniques we used to handle drag-and-drop data.

The built-in drag-and-drop support provided by the standard PyQt widgets is very easy to set up and use. In some cases though, we need to drag and drop our own custom data types. The code required to do so is not difficult to write, and using QByteArray ensures that we can drag and drop any amount of data of any C++ or PyQt data type. However, if the amount of data is very large, it may be faster and less memory demanding to pass a token to stand for the data (say, an index position in a data structure), rather than the data itself, and actually copy data only when necessary.

It is also possible to bypass PyQt's drag-and-drop facilities entirely, and implement our own drag-and-drop system by reimplementing the mouse event handlers. This is not as difficult as it sounds, but it is clearly less convenient than using what PyQt already provides.

PyQt's event-handling system is very powerful, and yet quite easy to use. In most cases using the higher-level signals and slots mechanism is much easier and is more appropriate. But when we need fine control and customization, reimplementing event handlers will let us get the precise appearance and behavior we want—and we will see this in action in the next chapter, when we implement some custom widgets.

Exercise

Modify the DnDListWidget class so that when the user drops they get a pop-up menu at the mouse position with two options, Copy and Move. Modify the dragMoveEvent() to have a drop action of move rather than copy. The menu will need to go in the dropEvent(), *before* creating the new list item.

The QMenu.exec_() method takes a QPoint argument which tells it where to pop up; the QCursor.pos() method provides the current mouse position. The drop event's drop action must be set to copy or move depending on what the user chose.

The startDrag() method will need to be modified slightly: The start() call must be given both move and copy actions as acceptable actions, and should remove the item only if the user chose to move.

The trickiest part is deciding how to respond to the menu actions. You could use functools.partial() or lambda functions for example. In the model solution, we simply use an instance variable that holds the drop action and have two methods, one that sets the drop action to be move and the other to be copy, and simply connect the menu actions to these methods.

A subtler approach is also possible. Instead of using a pop-up menu, in the drag move event examine the keyboard modifiers and set the drop action to move by default, or to copy if the Ctrl key is pressed. Similarly, in the drop event set the drop action depending on the state of the Ctrl key. This is less intrusive than a pop-up menu, but also less obvious for casual or naive users.

In the solution, we have created two QListWidget subclasses, DnDMenuListWidget and DndCtrlListWidget, to show both of these approaches. Only about 25 lines need to be added or changed (once you have copied/pasted DndListWidget and renamed each of the two versions) to implement both of the approaches described here.

A model solution is provided in the file `chap10/customdraganddrop_ans.pyw`.

11

- Using Widget Style Sheets
- Creating Composite Widgets
- Subclassing Built-in Widgets
- Subclassing QWidget

Custom Widgets

One of PyQt's greatest and longest-standing strengths is the ease with which it is possible to create custom widgets. The custom widgets we create with PyQt are made the same way as the standard built-in widgets, so they integrate seamlessly and have no arbitrary restrictions on their appearance or behavior. Creating custom widgets in PyQt is not a matter of "one size fits all". Rather, we can choose from a number of approaches that give us increasing levels of control over our widgets' behavior and appearance.

The most basic level of customization is to simply set some of the properties of an existing widget. We have already done this a number of times in earlier chapters. For example, in the preceding chapter we enabled PyQt's default drag-and-drop behavior simply by calling setAcceptDrops(True) and setDragEnabled(True) on our widgets. For spinboxes, we can constrain their behavior—for example, by calling setRange() to set a minimum and maximum value—and can affect their appearance by using setPrefix() and setSuffix(). We will not show examples of this approach in this chapter because we have already seen it in action many times before.

If setting the properties of an existing widget is insufficient, we can use a style sheet to customize the widget's appearance and some aspects of its behavior. The ability to set style sheets on widgets was introduced with Qt 4.2, and we will see a simple example to give a taste of what is possible in this chapter.

Sometimes we need not so much to customize a particular widget, but to create a composite widget that combines two or more other widgets. We will look at a simple example of how this can be done.

If we need to change the behavior of an existing widget beyond what can be achieved by setting properties, we can subclass the widget and reimplement whichever event handlers are necessary to achieve the control we want.

But in some cases, we need a widget that is different from any of the standard built-in widgets. For these situations we can subclass QWidget directly and can completely define the behavior and appearance of the widget ourselves. We will show two examples of this, the first a "generic" widget that might be used in many places and many applications and the second an application-specific widget of the kind that might be created for just one program.

Using Widget Style Sheets

We have already seen many examples of customizing widgets by changing their properties. Some of these have affected widget behavior, such as setting a QSpinBox's range, and others have affected widget appearance, such as setting a QLabel's frame. Qt 4.2 introduced a new widget property, the style sheet property. This property holds a QString and uses a syntax borrowed from HTML's CSS (Cascading Style Sheets).*

The screenshot in Figure 11.1 shows a dialog that has a style sheet set. Style sheets apply to the widget they are set on, and all the widget's child widgets. In this case, we have set the combobox to use dark blue text and the line edits to used dark green text. We have also set line edits that are "mandatory" to have a yellow background.

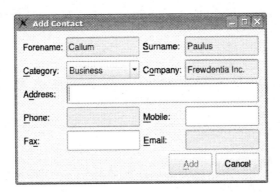

Figure 11.1 *A dialog customized using a style sheet*

No PyQt widget has a "mandatory" property, but from Qt 4.2 it is possible to add properties dynamically to QObjects. Note that Qt properties are different from Python properties—for example, they are accessed using property() and setProperty(). From PyQt 4.2, the QtCore.pyqtProperty() function can be used to create properties that are both Python and Qt properties at the same time.

```
self.lineedits = (self.forenameEdit, self.surnameEdit,
                  self.companyEdit, self.phoneEdit,
                  self.emailEdit)
for lineEdit in self.lineedits:
    lineEdit.setProperty("mandatory", QVariant(True))
```

---

*Style sheets are not officially supported on Mac OS X, so they may not behave predictably. They are expected to be supported from Qt 4.4 onward.

```
self.connect(lineEdit, SIGNAL("textEdited(QString)"),
             self.updateUi)
```

The preceding code is from the form's initializer. It adds a "mandatory" property to those line edits that we do not want the user to be able to leave blank. All Qt properties are held as QVariants. The signal–slot connections are discussed shortly.

We have created a style sheet for the widget as a class static variable, and set it on the form toward the end of the constructor. We could just as easily have read the style sheet from a file (since it is simply plain text), or from a PyQt resource.

```
StyleSheet = """
QComboBox { color: darkblue; }
QLineEdit { color: darkgreen; }
QLineEdit[mandatory="true"] {
    background-color: rgb(255, 255, 127);
    color: darkblue;
}
"""

...

self.setStyleSheet(ContactDlg.StyleSheet)
```

The style sheet syntax essentially consists of "selectors" and property name: value pairs. In the preceding snippet, the first line has a selector of QComboBox, which means that its property values will apply to any QComboBox or QComboBox subclass that is a child of the widget on which the style sheet is set. In this case, the effect is to set the text color to dark blue. The second selector is a QLineEdit, and this works similarly.

The third selector is more specific: It specifies both a class, and a property of that class whose state must be matched. In other words, this third selector will apply only to QLineEdit and QLineEdit subclasses that have a "mandatory" property, and where that property's value is True. For such cases, the background color is set to yellow (specified as an RGB triple), and the text color is set to dark blue.

The dialog is slightly subtler than it may at first appear. This is because the company line edit is mandatory only if the category combobox is set to "Business". To achieve this we need the signal–slot connections shown earlier, and one other connection:

```
self.connect(self.categoryComboBox, SIGNAL("activated(int)"),
             self.updateUi)
```

All the connections are to the updateUi() method:

```
def updateUi(self):
    mandatory = self.companyEdit.property("mandatory").toBool()
    if self.categoryComboBox.currentText() == "Business":
        if not mandatory:
            self.companyEdit.setProperty("mandatory",
                                         QVariant(True))
    elif mandatory:
        self.companyEdit.setProperty("mandatory", QVariant(False))
    if mandatory != \
        self.companyEdit.property("mandatory").toBool():
        self.setStyleSheet(ContactDlg.StyleSheet)
    enable = True
    for lineEdit in self.lineedits:
        if lineEdit.property("mandatory").toBool() and \
            lineEdit.text().isEmpty():
            enable = False
            break
    self.buttonBox.button(QDialogButtonBox.Ok).setEnabled(enable)
```

If the user has changed the category, we must reapply the style sheet to force the widgets to be restyled. This ensures that the background of the company line edit is correctly set to white or yellow depending on whether it is mandatory. Unfortunately, on slower machines, there is a slight flicker when the style sheet is reset—for this reason we have slightly long-winded code to ensure that the style sheet is reapplied only if necessary. Reapplying a style sheet is not necessary for changes to "pseudostates" such as enabled, checked, and hover.

Style sheets have a much richer syntax, and are much more powerful, than this simple example might suggest. For example, if we precede a selector with a dot, as in .QLineEdit, the selector will apply only to the class specified and not to its subclasses. If we want to a selector to apply to one specific widget we can call setObjectName() on the widget and then use that name as part of the selector. For example, if we had a button with an object name of "findButton", the selector that would apply only to that button would be QPushButton#findButton.

Some widgets have "subcontrols". For example, a QComboBox has an arrow that the user can click to make its list drop down. Subcontrols can be specified as part of the selector—for example, QComboBox::drop-down. Pseudostates can be specified using a single colon—for example, QCheckBox:checked.

In addition to setting colors, style sheets can also be used to set fonts, borders, margins, paddings, and backgrounds. One quick and easy way to experiment with simple style sheets is to run *Qt Designer*, create a new form, drag some widgets onto the form, and then enter and edit a style sheet for the form.

A style sheet can be set on a particular widget in a form, or on the form (QDialog or QMainWindow) itself. In either case, the style sheet will automatically be applied to any child widgets. It is also possible (and quite common) to set a single style sheet for the entire application, in which case we set it on the QApplication object.

Creating Composite Widgets

A composite widget is a widget that is composed of two or more other widgets. We are already experienced composite widget creators: For example, every dialog we have created is a composite widget. We are dedicating some space to a topic we have already covered because unlike the dialogs we created earlier (which were QDialog subclasses), we want to create composite widgets that are not dialogs, and that instead can be used inside dialogs (or as a main window's central widget).

The kind of composite widget we want is very similar to a dialog: We create the child widgets, lay them out, and do any signal–slot connections we need. The main difference is that we inherit from QWidget rather than from QDialog.

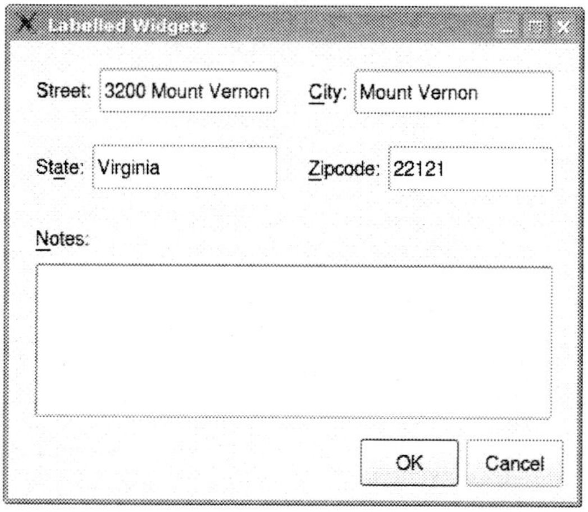

Figure 11.2 *A dialog using labelled widgets*

The screenshot in Figure 11.2 shows what looks like a conventional dialog, but in fact we have explicitly created only six widgets rather than twelve. This is because we have used four custom LabelledLineEdits, and one custom LabelledTextEdit, along with a QDialogButtonBox.

Our labelled editors are special in two ways. First, they automatically set up buddy relationships, and second, they can lay out the label either to the left or above their editing widget.

```
self.zipcode = LabelledLineEdit("&Zipcode:")
self.notes = LabelledTextEdit("&Notes:", ABOVE)
```

Creating labelled editors is easy, as this snippet from the form's initializer shows. The LabelledLineEdit exposes its widgets as instance variables, so we

can access its QLabel as LabelledLineEdit.label and its QLineEdit as Labelled-
LineEdit.lineEdit. The LabelledTextEdit has the same label, and has a textEdit
for its QTextEdit. The ABOVE is just a module constant; there is also a corresponding LEFT.

```
class LabelledLineEdit(QWidget):

    def __init__(self, labelText=QString(), position=LEFT,
                 parent=None):
        super(LabelledLineEdit, self).__init__(parent)
        self.label = QLabel(labelText)
        self.lineEdit = QLineEdit()
        self.label.setBuddy(self.lineEdit)
        layout = QBoxLayout(QBoxLayout.LeftToRight \
                 if position == LEFT else QBoxLayout.TopToBottom)
        layout.addWidget(self.label)
        layout.addWidget(self.lineEdit)
        self.setLayout(layout)
```

The preceding code is the complete LabelledLineEdit class. If we want to
connect signals and slots to its label or line edit, we can do so by accessing them
directly since they are held as public instance variables. Instead of using a
QVBoxLayout or a QHBoxLayout, we have used their base class so that we can set
the layout direction when the labelled line edit is created. We won't show the
code for the LabelledTextEdit since it differs only in that we create a QTextEdit
instead of a QLineEdit and call it textEdit instead of lineEdit.

Although we have created the composite labelled editing widgets purely in
code, it is possible to create composite widgets using *Qt Designer*, basing them
on the "Widget" template.

Creating composite widgets that are used repeatedly can save time in large
projects. They are also useful when we want to create a main-window-style application whose central widget must consist of two or more widgets, and where
using an MDI workspace, splitters, or dock windows is not a suitable solution.

Subclassing Built-in Widgets

Sometimes we need a widget that is similar in appearance and behavior to an
existing widget, but with more customization required than can be achieved
by using a style sheet or by setting other widget properties. In these cases, we
can subclass the similar widget and customize it to our needs.[*]

To show how to subclass an existing widget, let us imagine that we need a
spinbox that works on Roman numerals rather than on decimals, like the one
shown in Figure 11.3. Providing we know how to convert integers to Roman

---

[*]Appendix B provides screenshots and brief descriptions of selected PyQt widgets, and Appendix C
shows selected PyQt class hierarchies.

numeral strings and back again, it is straightforward to subclass QSpinBox for this purpose.

Figure 11.3 *A Roman spinbox*

When subclassing a spinbox we will need to reimplement three methods: validate(), which is used by the spinbox to prevent invalid data from being entered; valueFromText(), which is used to convert text entered by the user into an integer; and textFromValue(), which is used to convert an integer into its textual representation. We will also need to do some setting up in the initializer, so it is with that method that we will begin.

```
class RomanSpinBox(QSpinBox):

    def __init__(self, parent=None):
        super(RomanSpinBox, self).__init__(parent)
        regex = QRegExp(r"^M?M?M?(?:CM|CD|D?C?C?C?)"
                        r"(?:XC|XL|L?X?X?X?)(?:IX|IV|V?I?I?I?)$")
        regex.setCaseSensitivity(Qt.CaseInsensitive)
        self.validator = QRegExpValidator(regex, self)
        self.setRange(1, 3999)
        self.connect(self.lineEdit(), SIGNAL("textEdited(QString)"),
                     self.fixCase)
```

PyQt provides its own regular expression class, with a syntax very similar to that used by Python's re module. The main difference is that QRegExp does not support nongreedy quantifiers, although it will allow the entire regular expression to be nongreedy. The regular expression sets out which combinations of letters constitute valid Roman numbers in the range 1–3 999.★

We make the regular expression case-insensitive because we don't mind whether the user enters lower or uppercase letters—and anyway, we will force the input to be uppercase ourselves. Validators can either be one of PyQt's predefined validators (for integers and for floating-point numbers), or be based on a regular expression such as the one we have used here. The signal–slot connection is set up so that whenever the user enters any text we can force it to be uppercase.

```
    def fixCase(self, text):
        self.lineEdit().setText(text.toUpper())
```

A QSpinBox has a QLineEdit component, and it provides an accessor method to retrieve it. We use this to uppercase whatever the user has typed in. (The user

---

★The regular expression is adapted from one given in *Dive into Python* by Mark Pilgrim.

cannot type invalid letters like "A", "B", "1", or "2", because the validator will
not accept them.)

```
def validate(self, text, pos):
    return self.validator.validate(text, pos)
```

We must provide a validate() method. This will automatically be called
whenever the user changes the text, since this behavior is part of the QSpinBox's
API. We can simply pass on the work to the validator object we created in the
initializer.

```
def valueFromText(self, text):
    return intFromRoman(unicode(text))
```

If the user enters text, the spinbox needs to know the integer value it represents. We simply pass this on to an intFromRoman() function adapted from the
"Roman Numerals" recipe in the *Python Cookbook*.

```
def textFromValue(self, value):
    return romanFromInt(value)
```

The spinbox must be able to convert integers to their textual
representation—for example, when setValue() is called or when the user increments or decrements the value using the spinbox buttons. Again we pass on the
work, this time to a romanFromInt() function, adapted from the feedback given
on the "Decimal to Roman Numerals" recipe in the *Python Cookbook*.

The RomanSpinBox can be used anywhere a conventional QSpinBox is used, the
only limitation being the range of numbers it can cope with. A much more
complex example of subclassing an existing widget is presented in Chapter 13,
where a QTextEdit is used to create a RichTextLineEdit.

Subclassing QWidget

When we cannot get the custom widget we need by setting properties, using
a style sheet, or subclassing an existing widget, we can create the widget we
need from scratch. In practice, we always create custom widgets by subclassing
QWidget, since this provides a lot of behind-the-scenes convenience that we
don't need or want to worry about, leaving us free to focus on what matters: the
appearance and behavior of our custom widget.

In this section, we will look at two different custom widgets. The first, FractionSlider, is a generic "range control"-type widget that might be used many
times. The second, YPipeWidget, is an application-specific widget that may be
needed in only one particular program.

Before we go into the details of these two widgets, we will first discuss painting
in PyQt, and in particular the coordinate systems that are used by QPainter. A
QPainter has two separate coordinate systems: a device (physical) coordinate

system that matches the pixels in the widget's area, and a logical coordinate system. By default, the logical coordinate system is set to exactly match the physical coordinate system.

In fact, the physical coordinates are not necessarily pixels since they depend on the underlying paint device. This can be a `QGLPixelBuffer` (for 2D and 3D painting), a `QImage`, a `QPicture`, a `QPixmap`, a `QPrinter` (in which case the coordinates are points, $\frac{1}{72}$"), a `QSvgGenerator` (introduced with Qt 4.3), or a `QWidget`.

In PyQt terminology the physical coordinate system is called the "viewport", and confusingly, the logical coordinate system is called the "window".

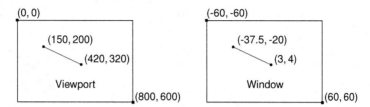

Figure 11.4 *The viewport and window coordinate systems*

In Figure 11.4, we have a physical widget size of 800×600. By calling `setWindow(-60, -60, 120, 120)` we can create a "window" with a top-left coordinate of (-60, -60), a width of 120, a height of 120, and centered at point (0, 0). The window's coordinate system is a logical coordinate system that `QPainter` automatically maps to the underlying physical device. After the `setWindow()` call, all our painting takes place using the logical (window) coordinate system.

In this case, the widget is rectangular, but our window has the same width and height. This means that the items we paint will be stretched out horizontally, since coordinates in the y-axis will be scaled by `QPainter` in the ratio 120:600 (1:5), whereas those in the x-axis will be scaled in the ratio 120:800 (1:$6\frac{2}{3}$).

For most widgets, a rectangular region works perfectly well, but in some cases—for example, if we really want our logical window to be square—we can change the viewport so that we operate on only a proportion of the widget's area.

```
side = min(self.width(), self.height())
painter.setViewport((self.width() - side) / 2,
                    (self.height() - side) / 2, side, side)
```

This code, executed inside a widget's `paintEvent()`, changes the widget's viewport to be the largest centered square region that will fit. In the example earlier, this will produce a viewport of 600×600 pixels with no top or bottom margins, but with a 100-pixel margin on the left and on the right. The window will now be an exact square, and the aspect ratio of anything we paint in it will be preserved.

Table 11.1 *Selected QWidget Methods*

Syntax	Description
w.addAction(a)	Adds QAction a to QWidget w; useful for context menus
w.close()	Hides QWidget w; or deletes it if Qt.WA_DeleteOnClose is set
w.hasFocus()	Returns True if QWidget w has the keyboard focus
w.height()	Returns QWidget w's height
w.hide()	Hides QWidget w
w.move(x, y)	Moves the top-level QWidget w to position (x, y)
w.raise_()	Raises QWidget w to the top of the parent widget's stack
w.rect()	Returns QWidget w's dimensions as a QRect
w.restore-Geometry(ba)	Restores top-level QWidget w's geometry to that encoded in QByteArray ba
w.save-Geometry()	Returns a QByteArray that encodes QWidget w's geometry
w.setAccept-Drops(b)	Sets whether QWidget w will accept drops depending on bool b
w.setAttrib-ute(wa, b)	Sets Qt.WidgetAttribute wa on or off depending on bool b. The most common attribute used is Qt.WA_DeleteOnClose.
w.setContext-MenuPolicy(p)	Sets QWidget w's context menu policy to policy p. Policies include Qt.NoContextMenu and Qt.ActionsContextMenu.
w.setCursor(c)	Sets QWidget w's cursor to c, a QCursor or a Qt.CursorShape
w.setEnabled(b)	Sets QWidget w to be enabled or disabled depending on b
w.setFocus()	Gives the keyboard focus to QWidget w
w.setFont(f)	Sets QWidget w's font to QFont f
w.setLayout(l)	Sets QWidget w's layout to QLayout l
w.setSize-Policy(hp, vp)	Sets QWidget w's horizontal and vertical QSizePolicys to hp and vp
w.setStyle-Sheet(s)	Sets QWidget w's style sheet to the CSS text in string s
w.setWindow-Icon(i)	Sets top-level QWidget w's icon to QIcon i
w.setWindow-Title(s)	Sets top-level QWidget w's title to string s
w.show()	Shows top-level QWidget w modelessly. It can be shown modally by using setWindowModality().
w.update()	Schedules a paint event for QWidget w
w.update-Geometry()	For non-top-level widgets, notifies any containing layouts that QWidget w's geometry may have changed
w.width()	Returns QWidget w's width

The main benefit of using a window is that it allows us to paint using logical coordinates. This is very convenient because it means that all the scaling that is needed—for example, when the user resizes the widget—is taken care of automatically by PyQt. This benefit also turns out to have a drawback: If we want to paint text, the text will be scaled along with everything else. For this reason, it is often easiest to work in physical (viewport) coordinates for custom widgets that paint text, and logical (window) coordinates otherwise. We show both approaches, with the FractionSlider using viewport coordinates and the YPipeWidget using window coordinates.

Example: A Fraction Slider

The FractionSlider is a widget that allows the user to choose a fraction between 0 and 1 inclusive; it is shown in Figure 11.5. We will allow programmers who use our slider to set a denominator in the range 3–60, and will emit value-Changed(int, int) signals (with the numerator and denominator) whenever the user changes the fraction. We provide both mouse and keyboard control, and we paint the entire widget ourselves. We also ensure that the widget's minimum size hint is always proportional to the size of the denominator, so that the widget cannot be resized to be too small to show the fraction texts.

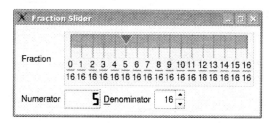

Figure 11.5 *A dialog using a Fraction Slider*

We will begin by looking at the static data and the initializer.

```
class FractionSlider(QWidget):

    XMARGIN = 12.0
    YMARGIN = 5.0
    WSTRING = "999"

    def __init__(self, numerator=0, denominator=10, parent=None):
        super(FractionSlider, self).__init__(parent)
        self._numerator = numerator
        self._denominator = denominator
        self.setFocusPolicy(Qt.WheelFocus)
        self.setSizePolicy(QSizePolicy(QSizePolicy.MinimumExpanding,
                                       QSizePolicy.Fixed))
```

The XMARGIN and YMARGIN are used to give some horizontal and vertical spacing around the edges of the widget. The WSTRING is a string containing text that is the longest we could possibly need: two digits to display, and an extra digit to provide some margin.

Size
policies
271 ⬆
We provide default values that start the widget off as showing zero tenths. We chose a focus policy of Qt.WheelFocus because that is the "strongest" one, which means that the widget will accept focus if tabbed to or clicked on, or if the user uses the mouse wheel on it. We set the size policies for the horizontal and vertical directions. By doing this we help ensure that our widget will cooperate properly with the layout managers. Here we have said that in the horizontal direction, the widget can be shrunk to its minimum size but prefers to grow, and in the vertical direction the widget has a fixed size of whatever height its sizeHint() method returns.

```
def decimal(self):
    return self.__numerator / float(self.__denominator)


def fraction(self):
    return self.__numerator, self.__denominator
```

We provide two convenience methods for returning the value, the first returning a floating-point value and the second a pair of integers.

```
def setFraction(self, numerator, denominator=None):
    if denominator is not None:
        if 3 <= denominator <= 60:
            self.__denominator = denominator
        else:
            raise ValueError, "denominator out of range"
    if 0 <= numerator <= self.__denominator:
        self.__numerator = numerator
    else:
        raise ValueError, "numerator out of range"
    self.update()
    self.updateGeometry()
```

This method can be used just to set the numerator, or to set both numerator and denominator. Once the fraction has been changed we call update() to schedule a paint event so that the gold triangle that marks the current fraction is repainted in the right place.

We also call updateGeometry(). This is to tell any layout manager that is responsible for this widget that the widget's geometry might have changed. This may appear strange—after all, we have changed only the fraction. But if we changed the denominator, the widget's size hint will have changed to allow for more (or less) fractions to be displayed. As a result, if there is a layout manager for the widget, it will recalculate its layout, asking the widget for its size hints and adjusting the layout if necessary.

We have chosen to deal with invalid values by raising exceptions. This is because setFraction() is normally called programmatically, and so should never be given out-of-range values in the normal run of things. An alternative approach would be to force the numerator and denominator to be within range: This approach is taken in the keyboard and mouse event handlers that give the widget its behavior, and it is to these that we now turn.

```
def mousePressEvent(self, event):
    if event.button() == Qt.LeftButton:
        self.moveSlider(event.x())
        event.accept()
    else:
        QWidget.mousePressEvent(self, event)
```

If the user clicks the widget, we want to set the numerator to the nearest fraction. We could do the calculations in the mouse press event, but since we want to support dragging the gold triangle as well as clicking to move it, we have factored out this code into a separate moveSlider() method that takes the mouse's *x* coordinate as an argument. After changing the fraction, we accept the event, since we have handled it. If we did not handle the click (for example, if it was a right-click), we call the base class implementation, although this is not strictly necessary.

```
def moveSlider(self, x):
    span = self.width() - (FractionSlider.XMARGIN * 2)
    offset = span - x + FractionSlider.XMARGIN
    numerator = int(round(self.__denominator * \
                    (1.0 - (offset / span))))
    numerator = max(0, min(numerator, self.__denominator))
    if numerator != self.__numerator:
        self.__numerator = numerator
        self.emit(SIGNAL("valueChanged(int,int)"),
                    self.__numerator, self.__denominator)
        self.update()
```

We begin by calculating the "span" of the widget, excluding the horizontal margins. Then we find how far along the *x*-axis the mouse was clicked (or dragged) and calculate the numerator as a proportion of the widget's width. If the user clicked or dragged in the left margin area, we set the numerator to 0, and if they clicked or dragged in the right margin area, we set it to equal the denominator (so the fraction will be 1). If the numerator has changed from before, we set the instance variable accordingly and emit a signal announcing that the value has changed. We then call update() to schedule a paint event (to move the gold triangle).

Short-circuit signals 131 ☜ We have chosen to emit a Python non-short-circuit signal; we could just as easily have made it a short-circuit signal by dropping the (int,int). It is also possible to define signals using the __pyqtSignals__ class attribute, although this is really useful only for custom widgets written in PyQt that are to be integrated with *Qt Designer.*★

```
def mouseMoveEvent(self, event):
    self.moveSlider(event.x())
```

This tiny method is all that we need to support dragging the gold triangle to change the fraction. This method is called only if the mouse is being dragged, that is, if the left mouse button is pressed at the same time the mouse is being moved. This is QWidget's standard behavior—we can have mouse move events generated for all mouse moves, regardless of the mouse buttons, by calling QWidget.setMouseTracking(True), if we wish.

```
def keyPressEvent(self, event):
    change = 0
    if event.key() == Qt.Key_Home:
        change = -self.__denominator
    elif event.key() in (Qt.Key_Up, Qt.Key_Right):
        change = 1
    elif event.key() == Qt.Key_PageUp:
        change = (self.__denominator // 10) + 1
    elif event.key() in (Qt.Key_Down, Qt.Key_Left):
        change = -1
    elif event.key() == Qt.Key_PageDown:
        change = -((self.__denominator // 10) + 1)
    elif event.key() == Qt.Key_End:
        change = self.__denominator
    if change:
        numerator = self.__numerator
        numerator += change
        numerator = max(0, min(numerator, self.__denominator))
        if numerator != self.__numerator:
            self.__numerator = numerator
            self.emit(SIGNAL("valueChanged(int,int)"),
                      self.__numerator, self.__denominator)
            self.update()
        event.accept()
    else:
        QWidget.keyPressEvent(self, event)
```

For keyboard support, we want Home to set the fraction to 0, End to set it to 1, up or right arrow keys to move to the next fraction up, and down or left arrow keys to move to the next fraction down. We have also set PageUp to move one-tenth of the way up and PageDown to move one-tenth of the way down.

★See the PyQt pyqt4ref.html documentation, under "Writing *Qt Designer* Plugins".

The code for ensuring that the numerator is in range, and for setting the instance variable, and so on, is identical to what we did in the mouse press event handler. And again we pass on unhandled key presses to the base class implementation—which does nothing, just as the base class mouse click handler does nothing.

```
def sizeHint(self):
    return self.minimumSizeHint()
```

We have decided that the widget's preferred size is its minimum size. Strictly speaking we did not have to reimplement this method, but by doing so we make our intention clear. Thanks to the size policies we set in the initializer, the widget can grow horizontally to occupy as much horizontal space as is available.

```
def minimumSizeHint(self):
    font = QFont(self.font())
    font.setPointSize(font.pointSize() - 1)
    fm = QFontMetricsF(font)
    return QSize(fm.width(FractionSlider.WSTRING) * \
            self.__denominator,
            (fm.height() * 4) + FractionSlider.YMARGIN)
```

A QFontMetricsF object is initialized by a QFont object, in this case the widget's default font.* This font is inherited from the widget's parent, which in turn inherits from its parent, and so on, with top-level widgets inheriting their fonts (and color schemes and other user settings) from the QApplication object, which itself takes them from the user preferences reported by the underlying windowing system. We can of course ignore the users' preferences and set an explicit font in any widget.

The QFontMetricsF object provides the real metrics, i.e., those of the font actually used—and this may be different from the font that was specified. For example, if the Helvetica font is used, it will almost certainly be found and used on Linux or Mac OS X, but on Windows, Ariel is likely to be used in its place. We have chosen to use a font size one less than the user's preferred font size to show the fractions, which is why we call setPointSize().

We set the widget's minimum width to be the width necessary to display all the fractions, assuming that each one is three digits wide, i.e., two digits plus some empty margin either side. The overall width is actually slightly less than this because we don't include the horizontal margins. We set the widget's minimum height to be four times the height of one character, i.e., enough vertical space for the fraction "segments" (the rectangles that signify each fraction), the vertical lines, the numerator, and the denominator. And just as for the width, the actual height is slightly less than this, because we only account for half of the vertical margin.

---

*PyQt also has a QFontMetrics class which gives integer rather than floating-point values. Similarly PyQt has QLine, QLineF, QPoint, QPointF, QPolygon, QPolygonF, QRect, QRectF, and some others.

Having implemented the key and mouse event handlers, set the size policies, and implemented the size hint methods, we have made the widget have appropriate behavior for user interaction and in relation to any layout manager that might be asked to lay out the widget. There is only one thing left to do: We must paint the widget when required to do so. The paintEvent() is rather long, so we will look at it in pieces.

```
def paintEvent(self, event=None):
    font = QFont(self.font())
    font.setPointSize(font.pointSize() - 1)
    fm = QFontMetricsF(font)
    fracWidth = fm.width(FractionSlider.WSTRING)
    indent = fm.boundingRect("9").width() / 2.0
    if not X11:
        fracWidth *= 1.5
    span = self.width() - (FractionSlider.XMARGIN * 2)
    value = self.__numerator / float(self.__denominator)
```

We begin by getting the font we want to use, as well as its font metrics. Then we calculate fracWidth, the width of one fraction, as well as an indent for each fraction's dividing line. The if statement is used to compensate for differences between the font metrics on the X Window System and other window systems such as Windows and Mac OS X. The span is the width of the widget excluding the horizontal margins, and the value is the floating-point value of the fraction.

The X11 Boolean variable is True if the underlying window system is the X Window System, as it normally is on Linux, BSD, Solaris, and similar, and False otherwise—for example, on Windows and Mac OS X. It was set at the beginning of the file, after the imports, using the following statement:

```
X11 = "qt_x11_wait_for_window_manager" in dir()
```

We could write it more clearly as:

```
import PyQt4.QtGui
X11 = hasattr(PyQt4.QtGui, "qt_x11_wait_for_window_manager")
```

These work because the PyQt4.QtGui.qt_x11_wait_for_window_manager() function exists only on systems that are using the X Window System. We used a similar technique for Mac OS X detection in Chapter 7.

```
painter = QPainter(self)
painter.setRenderHint(QPainter.Antialiasing)
painter.setRenderHint(QPainter.TextAntialiasing)
painter.setPen(self.palette().color(QPalette.Mid))
painter.setBrush(self.palette().brush(QPalette.AlternateBase))
painter.drawRect(self.rect())
```

We create a QPainter and set its render hints to give us antialiased drawing. Then we set the pen (which is used for shape outlines and for drawing text) and the brush (which is used for fills), and draw a rectangle over the entire widget. Because we used different shades for the pen and brush, this has the effect of giving the widget a border and a slightly indented look.

The QApplication object has a QPalette that contains colors for various purposes, such as text foreground and background colors, button colors, and so on. The colors are identified by their roles, such as QPalette.Text or QPalette.Highlight, although we have used rather more obscure roles in this example. There are, in fact, three sets of these colors, one for each of the widget states: "active", "disabled", and "inactive". Every QWidget also has a QPalette, with colors inherited from the QApplication palette—which in turn is initialized with colors from the underlying window system and therefore reflects the user's preferences. PyQt tries very hard to ensure that the colors in a palette work well together, providing good contrast, for example. As programmers, we are free to use whatever colors we like, but especially for standard requirements such as text colors and backgrounds, it is best to use the palette.

```
segColor = QColor(Qt.green).dark(120)
segLineColor = segColor.dark()
painter.setPen(segLineColor)
painter.setBrush(segColor)
painter.drawRect(FractionSlider.XMARGIN,
                 FractionSlider.YMARGIN, span, fm.height())
```

We create a dark green color for the segments, and an even darker green for the vertical lines that mark them out. Then we draw a rectangle that encompasses all the segments.

```
textColor = self.palette().color(QPalette.Text)
segWidth = span / self.__denominator
segHeight = fm.height() * 2
nRect = fm.boundingRect(FractionSlider.WSTRING)
x = FractionSlider.XMARGIN
yOffset = segHeight + fm.height()
```

Here, we set the text color to use based on the user's palette. Then we work out the width and height of each segment, and set an initial x position and a yOffset. The nRect is a rectangle large enough to contain a number with some left and right margin space.

```
for i in range(self.__denominator + 1):
    painter.setPen(segLineColor)
    painter.drawLine(x, FractionSlider.YMARGIN, x, segHeight)
    painter.setPen(textColor)
    y = segHeight
    rect = QRectF(nRect)
```

```
            rect.moveCenter(QPointF(x, y + fm.height() / 2.0))
            painter.drawText(rect, Qt.AlignCenter, QString.number(i))
            y = yOffset
            rect.moveCenter(QPointF(x, y + fm.height() / 2.0))
            painter.drawText(rect, Qt.AlignCenter,
                             QString.number(self.__denominator))
            painter.drawLine(QPointF(rect.left() + indent, y),
                             QPointF(rect.right() - indent, y))
            x += segWidth
```

In this loop we draw the vertical lines that mark out each segment, the numerator below each segment, and the denominator below each numerator, along with the dividing line between them. For the drawText() calls we provide a rectangle in which the text should be drawn, and by using Qt.AlignCenter, we ensure that the text is vertically and horizontally centered inside the specified rectangle. We use the same rectangle, but indented at the left and right, to calculate the end points of the dividing line, which we then draw. The y offsets are fixed for every line, numerator, and denominator, but the x offsets increase by one segment width after drawing each fraction.

```
        span = int(span)
        y = FractionSlider.YMARGIN - 0.5
        triangle = [QPointF(value * span, y),
                    QPointF((value * span) + \
                            (2 * FractionSlider.XMARGIN), y),
                    QPointF((value * span) + \
                            FractionSlider.XMARGIN, fm.height())]
        painter.setPen(Qt.yellow)
        painter.setBrush(Qt.darkYellow)
        painter.drawPolygon(QPolygonF(triangle))
```

At the end we draw the gold triangle that shows the user which fraction is selected. We specify polygons by providing a list of points. We don't have to duplicate the first point at the end, since if we use drawPolygon(), PyQt will automatically join the first and last points and fill the enclosed area. In the next chapter we will see more advanced drawing techniques, including the use of the very versatile QPainterPath class.

We have now completed the generic FractionSlider widget. It has both keyboard and mouse support, looks reasonable on all platforms, and interacts properly with the layout managers.

The QPainter class offers many more possibilities than we have needed for this widget, but in the next subsection we will see more of what can be done, including drawing unfilled polygons and polygons that use gradient fills. We will also see how to include other widgets inside a custom widget.

Example: A Flow-Mixing Widget

It is sometimes appropriate to create custom widgets for particular applications. For this example, we will assume that we have an application in which we are modeling the flow of fluid through a "Y"-shaped pipe, as depicted in Figure 11.6.

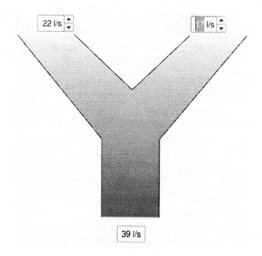

Figure 11.6 *A YPipe widget*

The widget must draw three gradient-filled polygons and three black outlines (to give a clear border to the pipe shapes), and must allow the user to set the left and right flows, as well as show the combined flow. We have chosen to provide spinboxes for the user to set the flows and to use a label to show the resultant flow. The advantages of using these built-in widgets include that we need concern ourselves only with their positioning and connections; we can leave PyQt to provide mouse and keyboard interaction and to display them properly. Another benefit is that we can paint our custom widget using a "window", that is, using logical rather than device (viewport) coordinates, and do not have to worry about scaled text because the text appears only in widgets that are overlaid on top of the custom widget, and are not affected by the window settings.

We will start by looking at the initializer, taking it in two parts.

```
class YPipeWidget(QWidget):

    def __init__(self, leftFlow=0, rightFlow=0, maxFlow=100,
                 parent=None):
        super(YPipeWidget, self).__init__(parent)

        self.leftSpinBox = QSpinBox(self)
        self.leftSpinBox.setRange(0, maxFlow)
        self.leftSpinBox.setValue(leftFlow)
        self.leftSpinBox.setSuffix(" l/s")
```

```
self.leftSpinBox.setAlignment(Qt.AlignRight|Qt.AlignVCenter)
self.connect(self.leftSpinBox, SIGNAL("valueChanged(int)"),
             self.valueChanged)
```

After the `super()` call, we create the left spinbox, set some of its parameters, and connect it to a `valueChanged()` method that we will look at in a moment. Notice that we give the spinbox a parent of `self` (the YPipeWidget instance); this is because the spinbox will not be laid out, so no layout manager will reparent the spinbox to the parent widget for us. We have omitted the creation and setup of the right spinbox because the code is almost identical.

```
self.label = QLabel(self)
self.label.setFrameStyle(QFrame.StyledPanel|QFrame.Sunken)
self.label.setAlignment(Qt.AlignCenter)
fm = QFontMetricsF(self.font())
self.label.setMinimumWidth(fm.width(" 999 l/s "))

self.setSizePolicy(QSizePolicy(QSizePolicy.Expanding,
                               QSizePolicy.Expanding))
self.setMinimumSize(self.minimumSizeHint())
self.valueChanged()
```

We create the label that we will use to show the combined flow, and set some of its properties. We give it a minimum width so that it will not resize disconcertingly—for example, if the flow rate changes between 9 and 10, or 99 and 100. We set the size policies of the YPipeWidget to expanding, which means that the widget wants to grow in both directions as much as possible. We also set the widget's minimum size to its minimum size hint, and call `valueChanged()` to give the label an initial value.

```
def valueChanged(self):
    a = self.leftSpinBox.value()
    b = self.rightSpinBox.value()
    self.label.setText("%d l/s" % (a + b))
    self.emit(SIGNAL("valueChanged"), a, b)
    self.update()
```

Whenever the user changes one of the flow spinboxes, this method is called. It updates the label, emits its own `valueChanged` Python signal, which any external widget could connect to, and schedules a repaint. The reason for the repaint is that the gradient fills are colored in proportion to the spinbox values.

```
def values(self):
    return self.leftSpinBox.value(), self.rightSpinBox.value()
```

This method provides the flow spinbox values as a two-tuple.

```
def minimumSizeHint(self):
    return QSize(self.leftSpinBox.width() * 3,
```

```
                    self.leftSpinBox.height() * 5)
```

We have made the widget's minimum width and height proportional to the spinboxes. This ensures that the "Y" shape never becomes too small to be understandable.

```
def resizeEvent(self, event=None):
    fm = QFontMetricsF(self.font())
    x = (self.width() - self.label.width()) / 2
    y = self.height() - (fm.height() * 1.5)
    self.label.move(x, y)
    y = self.height() / 60.0
    x = (self.width() / 4.0) - self.leftSpinBox.width()
    self.leftSpinBox.move(x, y)
    x = self.width() - (self.width() / 4.0)
    self.rightSpinBox.move(x, y)
```

The resize event is particularly important for widgets that contain other widgets and that do not have a layout. This is because we use this event to position the child widgets. A resize event is always called before a widget is first shown, so we automatically get the chance to position the child widgets before the widget is seen by the user for the first time.

The label is horizontally centered, and drawn near the bottom of the widget. (The y coordinates increase downward, so self.height() returns the greatest—bottommost—y value.) The two spinboxes are drawn near the top, $\frac{1}{60}$ of the height below the least—topmost—y value, and $\frac{1}{4}$ of the widget's width in from the left or right edge.

Because we have used QSpinBoxes and a QLabel, along with a couple of signal–slot connections, all the user interaction is taken care of, so we need to concern ourselves only with resizing and painting. Although the painting is simplified by having the spinboxes and label drawn by PyQt, it is still a little involved, so we will look at the paint event in pieces.

```
def paintEvent(self, event=None):
    LogicalSize = 100.0

    def logicalFromPhysical(length, side):
        return (length / side) * LogicalSize

    fm = QFontMetricsF(self.font())
    ymargin = (LogicalSize / 30.0) + \
            logicalFromPhysical(self.leftSpinBox.height(),
                                    self.height())
    ymax = LogicalSize - \
        logicalFromPhysical(fm.height() * 2, self.height())
    width = LogicalSize / 4.0
    cx, cy = LogicalSize / 2.0, LogicalSize / 3.0
```

```
ax, ay = cx - (2 * width), ymargin
bx, by = cx - width, ay
dx, dy = cx + width, ay
ex, ey = cx + (2 * width), ymargin
fx, fy = cx + (width / 2), cx + (LogicalSize / 24.0)
gx, gy = fx, ymax
hx, hy = cx - (width / 2), ymax
ix, iy = hx, fy
```

Rather than work in device (physical) coordinates and have to scale all the coordinates ourselves, we have created a logical coordinate system, with a top left of (0, 0) and a width and height of 100 (LogicalSize). We have defined a tiny helper function used to calculate a *y* margin above which the spinboxes are drawn, and a maximum *y* below which the label is drawn.

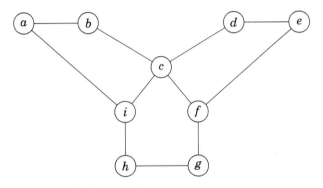

Figure 11.7 *The YPipe's coordinate points*

As Figure 11.7 indicates, we do all our painting in terms of the points needed to draw the "Y" shape. For each point in the figure, we calculate an *x* coordinate and a *y* coordinate. For example, the top-left point is *a*, so its coordinates in the code are ax and ay. Most of the calculations are done in terms of point *c*, (cx, cy).

```
painter = QPainter(self)
painter.setRenderHint(QPainter.Antialiasing)
side = min(self.width(), self.height())
painter.setViewport((self.width() - side) / 2,
                    (self.height() - side) / 2, side, side)
painter.setWindow(0, 0, LogicalSize, LogicalSize)
```

We create the painter and set its viewport to be the largest centered square area that will fit inside its rectangle. We then set a window, that is, impose our own logical coordinate system, leaving PyQt to take care of transforming logical to physical coordinates.

```
painter.setPen(Qt.NoPen)
```

Table 11.2 *Selected QPainter Methods (Excluding Drawing-Related Methods)*

Syntax	Description
`p.restore()`	Restores QPainter p's state to the last saved state
`p.rotate(a)`	Rotates QPainter p by int a°
`p.save()`	Saves QPainter p's state, including its transformation matrix, pen, and brush
`p.scale(x, y)`	Scales QPainter p horizontally by float x and vertically by float y; 1.0 is unscaled, 0.5 is half size, 3.0 is three times the size
`p.setMatrix(m)`	Sets QPainter p's transformation matrix to QMatrix m
`p.setRenderHint(h)`	Turns on the QPainter.RenderHint h. Hints include QPainter.Antialiasing, QPainter.TextAntialiasing, and QPainter.SmoothPixmapTransform.
`p.setView-port(x, y, w, h)`	Constrains QPainter p's viewport (physical coordinates) to the rectangle with top-left corner at point (x, y), and with width w and height h; all the arguments are ints
`p.setWin-dow(x, y, w, h)`	Sets QPainter p's logical coordinate system to the rectangle with top-left corner at point (x, y), and with width w and height h; all the arguments are ints
`p.shear(x, y)`	Shears QPainter p's coordinate system horizontally by float x and vertically by float y
`p.translate(dx, dy)`	Moves QPainter p's coordinate system horizontally by int dx and vertically by int dy

We turn off the pen because we do not want an outline around the polygons we will draw for each part of the pipe. Instead, we will draw in the lines we want at the end of the paint event.

```
gradient = QLinearGradient(QPointF(0, 0), QPointF(0, 100))
gradient.setColorAt(0, Qt.white)
a = self.leftSpinBox.value()
gradient.setColorAt(1, Qt.red if a != 0 else Qt.white)
painter.setBrush(QBrush(gradient))
painter.drawPolygon(
        QPolygon([ax, ay, bx, by, cx, cy, ix, iy]))
```

For the left part of the "Y" shape representing the left spinbox—the shape (*a, b, c, i*)—we use a linear color gradient going from white to red.

```
gradient = QLinearGradient(QPointF(0, 0), QPointF(0, 100))
gradient.setColorAt(0, Qt.white)
b = self.rightSpinBox.value()
gradient.setColorAt(1, Qt.blue if b != 0 else Qt.white)
```

Table 11.3 *Selected QPainter Drawing-Related Methods*

Syntax	Description
p.drawArc(r, a, s)	Draws an arc on QPainter p in the circle bounded by QRect r, starting at angle int a°, and spanning $\frac{s}{16}$°
p.drawChord(r, a, s)	Draws a chord on QPainter p in the circle bounded by QRect r, starting at angle int a°, and spanning $\frac{s}{16}$°
p.drawConvex-Polygon(pl)	Draws a convex polygon on QPainter p connecting the list of QPoints in pl, and connects the last point back to the first
p.drawEllipse(r)	Draws an ellipse on QPainter p bounded by QRect r; draws a circle if r is square
p.drawImage(pt, i)	Draws QImage i at QPoint pt on QPainter p; different arguments allow drawing just part of the image
p.drawLine(p1, p2)	Draws a line between QPoints p1 and p2 on QPainter p. Many argument variations are possible; there are also drawLines() methods.
p.drawPath(pp)	Draws the QPainterPath pp on QPainter p
p.drawPie(r, a, s)	Draws a pie segment in the circle bounded by QRect r, starting at angle int a°, and spanning $\frac{s}{16}$°
p.drawPixmap(pt, px)	Draws QPixmap px at QPoint pt on QPainter p; different arguments allow drawing just part of the pixmap
p.drawPoint(pt)	Draws QPoint pt on QPainter p; there are also draw-Points() methods
p.drawPolygon(pl)	Draws a polygon on QPainter p connecting the list of QPoints in pl, and connects the last point back to the first
p.drawPolyline(pl)	Draws a polyline on QPainter p connecting the list of QPoints in pl; does not connect the last point to the first
p.drawRect(r)	Draws a QRect r on QPainter p
p.drawRound-Rect(r, x, y)	Draws a rounded rectangle on QPainter p bounded by QRect r, and using rounding factors ints x and y
p.drawText(r, s, o)	Draws string s on QPainter p bounded by QRect r, and using the optional QTextOption o
p.drawText(x, y, s)	Draws string s on QPainter p at point (x, y)
p.fillPath(pp, b)	Fills QPainterPath pp with QBrush b on QPainter p
p.fillRect(r, b)	Fills QRect r with QBrush b on QPainter p
p.setBrush(b)	Sets the brush for filled shapes to QBrush b
p.setPen(pn)	Sets the pen for lines and outlines to QPen pn
p.setFont(f)	Sets QPainter p's text font to QFont f

```
painter.setBrush(QBrush(gradient))
painter.drawPolygon(
        QPolygon([cx, cy, dx, dy, ex, ey, fx, fy]))
```

The right part—shape (d, e, f, c)—is very similar to the left part, only it uses a gradient going from white to blue.

```
if (a + b) == 0:
    color = QColor(Qt.white)
else:
    ashare = (a / (a + b)) * 255.0
    bshare = 255.0 - ashare
    color = QColor(ashare, 0, bshare)
gradient = QLinearGradient(QPointF(0, 0), QPointF(0, 100))
gradient.setColorAt(0, Qt.white)
gradient.setColorAt(1, color)
painter.setBrush(QBrush(gradient))
painter.drawPolygon(
        QPolygon([cx, cy, fx, fy, gx, gy, hx, hy, ix, iy]))
```

The stem of the "Y"—shape (c, f, g, h, i)—is drawn with a linear gradient that goes from white to a red/blue color that is proportional to the left/right flow rates.

```
painter.setPen(Qt.black)
painter.drawPolyline(QPolygon([ax, ay, ix, iy, hx, hy]))
painter.drawPolyline(QPolygon([gx, gy, fx, fy, ex, ey]))
painter.drawPolyline(QPolygon([bx, by, cx, cy, dx, dy]))
```

We finish by drawing the lines that represent the sides of the pipe. The first line goes from a to i to h, marking out the left of the pipe, the second from g to f to e, marking out the right of the pipe, and the third, from b to c to d, marks the "V"-shaped part at the top.

Just like the built-in PyQt widgets, both the YPipeWidget and the Fraction-Slider can be used as top-level widgets, and this is particularly useful when developing and testing custom widgets. Both chap11/fractionslider.py and chap11/ypipewidget.py can be run as stand-alone programs because both have an if __name__ == "__main__": statement after the QWidget subclass, with code that creates a QApplication, and that creates and shows the custom widget.

Summary

PyQt offers several different ways of customizing widget appearance and behavior. The simplest and most frequently used approach is to set existing widget properties to the values we want. From Qt 4.2, the style sheet property is available, and this allows us to have a dramatic effect on the appearance of our widgets simply by entering plain text using the CSS syntax. One common and very easy use of style sheets is to set the background color of mandatory widgets.

Composite widgets allow us to lay out two or more widgets together and to then treat the resultant widget as a single widget. This can save time if the composite widget is used a lot, and also provides a way of having more than one widget in a main window-style application's central area. Some programmers make the constituent widgets private and forward their signals and slots, but in many cases the simplest approach is to leave the constituent widgets as public instance variables and to access and connect to them directly.

Subclassing existing widgets to adapt their appearance and especially their behavior is a lot easier than creating a QWidget subclass and doing everything ourselves. This approach works well with almost every PyQt widget, since most of them are designed to be subclassed. The only limitation of this approach is that it can be applied only to widgets that are similar enough to the widget we want, to make the adaptation feasible.

If we need to create a widget unlike any other, or if we want complete control over the appearance and behavior of our custom widget, we can subclass QWidget. Our subclass must reimplement paintEvent(), sizeHint(), and minimumSizeHint(), and will almost always reimplement keyPressEvent() and some of the mouse event handlers. Most of the built-in widgets are created in this way, with the rest being subclasses of other built-in widgets.

All the widgets we have customized or created in this chapter, and indeed throughout the book, are quite conventional in their appearance and behavior. PyQt does not enforce such conservatism, and we are free to create widgets with any appearance and any behaviors we can imagine.

Exercise

Create the Counters custom widget shown in Figure 11.8. The widget should show a 3×3 grid, with each square either blank (showing just the background color) or with a red or yellow ellipse. The state of any grid square should change from blank to red to yellow and back to blank in an endless cycle. Changes of state should occur when the user clicks a square or presses the spacebar on a square. The keyboard focus should be shown by drawing the square with a thick blue pen instead of the normal thin black pen used for the other squares. The user should be able to change the focused square by clicking a square or by using the up, down, left, and right arrow keys to move the focus.

Make sure that you provide a size hint and minimum size hint so that the widget has good resizing behavior and cannot be shrunk too small. The paint event is quite short, but slightly subtle; you will probably need to save and restore the painter's state, using QPainter.save() and QPainter.restore(), so that pen and brush colors intended for one square don't propagate to others.

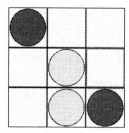

Figure 11.8 *The Counters custom widget*

Include an if __name__ == "__main__": statement at the end, and create a QApplication object and an instance of the Counters widget so that you can test it. The whole thing can be done in less than 130 lines.

A solution is given in chap11/counters.py.

## 12

- Custom and Interactive Graphics Items
- Animation and Complex Shapes

Item-Based Graphics

If we create a custom widget and reimplement its paint event, we can draw any graphics we like. This approach was shown in the preceding chapter, and it is ideal for drawing custom widgets, for drawing graphs, and for drawing small numbers of items. But if we need to draw lots of independent items, anything from dozens to tens of thousands of them, or if we need to draw items that the user can interact with individually—for example, clicking, dragging, and selecting them—or if we need to animate items, PyQt's graphics view classes are a much better choice than reimplementing a custom widget's paint event.

The graphics view classes—QGraphicsView, QGraphicsScene, and QGraphics-Item—along with the QGraphicsItem subclasses, were introduced with Qt 4.2, so the examples in this chapter will work only with a version of PyQt that has bindings to Qt 4.2 or later, such as PyQt 4.1. However, we strongly recommend that you use PyQt 4.2 or later for graphics-view-based applications.

To use the graphics view classes we must create a scene, represented by a QGraphicsScene object. Scenes are pure data, and they can be visualized only by associating them with one or more QGraphicsView objects. The items that are drawn in a scene are QGraphicsItem subclasses. PyQt provides several prede-fined subclasses, including QGraphicsLineItem, QGraphicsPixmapItem, QGraphics-SimpleTextItem (plain text), and QGraphicsTextItem (HTML). It is also possible to create custom graphics item subclasses, as we will see later in this chapter.

Once a scene has been created, and has had items added to it, it can be visual-ized using a QGraphicsView. One powerful feature of graphics views is that we can apply transformations to them, such as scaling and rotation, that change how the scene appears, but without changing any of the scene's items them-selves. It is also possible to associate more than one graphics view with a par-ticular scene, to allow different parts of the scene to be viewed, and with each view having its own independent transformations.

The graphics view classes are essentially two-dimensional; nonetheless, every item has a z value, with higher z-valued items being drawn on top of those with lower z values. Collision detection is based on item (x, y) positions. In addition to information about collisions, the scene can tell us which items contain a particular point or are in a particular region, and which are selected. Scenes have a foreground layer, useful, for example, to draw a grid that overlays all the items in the scene; they also have a background layer that is drawn underneath all the items, useful for providing a background image or color.

Items are either children of the scene (rather like PyQt's normal parent–child widget relationships), or a child of another item. When transformations are applied to an item, they are automatically applied to all the item's children, recursively to the greatest grandchild. This means that if an item is moved—for example, dragged by the user—all its children will be dragged with it. It is also possible to have groups of peer items, that is, transformations on one item in the group affect only that item's children, not the other members of the group.

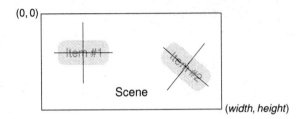

Figure 12.1 *Graphics items use local logical coordinates*

The graphics view classes use three different coordinate systems, although in practice we usually care about only two of them. Views use the physical coordinate system. Scenes use a logical coordinate system that we choose when we create them. PyQt automatically maps scene coordinates to view coordinates. In essence, scenes use "window" coordinates and views use "viewport" coordinates. So, when we are positioning items we place them in terms of scene coordinates. The third coordinate system is the one used by items. This is particularly convenient because it is a logical coordinate system centered on point (0, 0). Each item's (0, 0) is actually at the item's position in the scene. This means that in practice, we can always draw items in terms of their center point—and we do not have to care about any transformations that have been applied to them by parent items, since the scene will automatically take care of these for us. Figure 12.1 illustrates the relationship between scene and item coordinates.

Viewport and window coordinates

329 ☞

In this chapter we will look at two examples that between them show many different aspects of the graphics view classes. The first example is typical of the kind of application where the user creates items one by one, and manipulates items either individually or in selected groups. This application also shows user interaction, including selecting, moving, and resizing items. The second example shows animated composite items with complex shapes. It also shows how to minimize the work done to draw items depending on the scene's level of detail (how zoomed in or out it is).

Custom and Interactive Graphics Items

The predefined graphics items can be made movable, selectable, and focusable by calling setFlags() on them with suitable constants. Users can drag movable items with the mouse, and they can select selectable items by clicking them, and by using Ctrl+Click to select multiple items. Focusable items will receive key events, but will ignore them unless we create an item subclass with a key event handler. Similarly, we can make items responsive to mouse events by subclassing and implementing appropriate mouse event handlers.

In this section, we will use two of the predefined graphics items, and create two custom graphics item subclasses to show how to use graphics items, and how to control their behavior and appearance. We will also see how to load and save scenes, and how to print them. To do these things we will look at the Page Designer application shown in Figure 12.2. This program allows the user to create a page that can contain text, images, and boxes. Users can also create lines—these are just boxes that are 1 pixel wide or high. The images created by the user can be saved and loaded as .pgd files, a custom file format specific to this application, and they can be printed (or saved as PDF files) using a print dialog.

For the text items, a QGraphicsTextItem subclass is used, extended to allow the user to set the item's font and text by double-clicking. For the box (and line) items a QGraphicsItem subclass is used. This has a context menu, plus keyboard support for resizing, and it handles all its own drawing. The pixmap items simply use the built-in QGraphicsPixmapItem class, and the page and margin guidelines use the built-in QGraphicsRectItem class. The view that shows the scene is a QGraphicsView subclass that supports rubber-band selection and mouse-wheel scaling.

We will begin by looking at the QGraphicsView subclass. Then we will review the main form, and finally we will review the custom QGraphicsItem subclasses.

```
class GraphicsView(QGraphicsView):

    def __init__(self, parent=None):
        super(GraphicsView, self).__init__(parent)
        self.setDragMode(QGraphicsView.RubberBandDrag)
        self.setRenderHint(QPainter.Antialiasing)
        self.setRenderHint(QPainter.TextAntialiasing)

    def wheelEvent(self, event):
        factor = 1.41 ** (-event.delta() / 240.0)
        self.scale(factor, factor)
```

The preceding code is the complete GraphicsView subclass. In the initializer we set the drag mode: This means that dragging on the view will cause PyQt to give us a rubber band, and every item touched by the rubber band will be

Figure 12.2 *The Page Designer application*

selected. The render hints are propagated to any item that is painted inside the view, so we do not need to set the hints for each individual graphics item.

The wheel event is called whenever the user rolls the mouse wheel, and it will cause the view to scale smaller or larger depending on which way the wheel is rolled. The effect of this is to change the apparent size of the page—the underlying scene is not changed at all. The math used in this event handler is rather tricky, but this isn't a problem since the method can be copied and pasted "as is".

Near the top of `chap12/pagedesigner.pyw` we have some global declarations.

```
PageSize = (612, 792)
PointSize = 10

MagicNumber = 0x70616765
FileVersion = 1

Dirty = False
```

The page size is in points for U.S. Letter-size paper. (The source code also has the A4 page size, commented out.) The magic number and file version are used by QDataStream, as we have seen in Chapter 8 and elsewhere. We also have a global dirty flag.

Partial function application

63 ☞ We have not shown the imports, but they include functools. This is needed because in the context menu we use the functools.partial() function to wrap the methods to call with a suitable argument.

The main form's initializer is quite long, so we will look at it in parts but omit code that is similar to what we have seen elsewhere—for example, where we create and lay out the form's buttons.

```python
class MainForm(QDialog):

    def __init__(self, parent=None):
        super(MainForm, self).__init__(parent)

        self.filename = QString()
        self.copiedItem = QByteArray()
        self.pasteOffset = 5
        self.prevPoint = QPoint()
        self.addOffset = 5
        self.borders = []

        self.printer = QPrinter(QPrinter.HighResolution)
        self.printer.setPageSize(QPrinter.Letter)
```

The copied item is essentially a lump of binary data that describes the most recent item to be cut or copied. We store this data inside the application rather than on the clipboard because it is of no use to any other application. The paste offset is used when the user repeatedly pastes the same item, and the previous point and add offset are used when the user repeatedly adds the same item type. In both cases the newly added items are added at offset positions rather than exactly on top of the previous item. This makes it easier for the user to see where they are.

The borders list will contain two graphics items, both yellow rectangles: one giving the page outline and the other giving an outline inside the page allowing for some margin space. They are used as guidelines and are not saved or printed.

Although it is possible to create a QPrinter object when it is needed, by creating one and keeping it as an instance variable, we ensure that the user's settings, such as page size, are preserved between uses in the same session.

```python
        self.view = GraphicsView()
        self.scene = QGraphicsScene(self)
        self.scene.setSceneRect(0, 0, PageSize[0], PageSize[1])
        self.addBorders()
        self.view.setScene(self.scene)
```

Table 12.1 *Selected QGraphicsScene Methods*

Syntax	Description
s.addEllipse(r, pn, b)	Adds an ellipse bounded by QRectF r, outlined by QPen pn and filled with QBrush b, to QGraphicsScene s
s.addItem(g)	Adds QGraphicsItem g to QGraphicsScene s. The other add*() methods are conveniences for creating and adding some of the built-in graphics items.
s.addLine(l, pn)	Adds QLineF l, drawn with QPen pn, to s
s.addPath(pp, pn, b)	Adds QPainterPath pp, outlined by QPen pn and filled with QBrush b, to QGraphicsScene s
s.addPixmap(px)	Adds QPixmap px to QGraphicsScene s
s.addPolygon(pg, pn, b)	Adds QPolygon pg, outlined by QPen pn and filled with QBrush b, to QGraphicsScene s
s.addRect(r, pn, b)	Adds QRect r, outlined by QPen pn and filled with QBrush b, to QGraphicsScene s
s.addText(t, f)	Adds text t using QFont f, to QGraphicsScene s
s.collidingItems(g)	Returns a (possibly empty) list of the QGraphicsItems that QGraphicsItem g collides with
s.items()	Returns all the QGraphicsItems in QGraphicsScene s; using different arguments, those items that are at a particular point, or that are within or that intersect with a given rectangle, polygon, or painter path, can be returned
s.removeItem(g)	Removes QGraphicsItem g from QGraphicsScene s; ownership passes to the caller
s.render(p)	Renders QGraphicsScene s on QPainter p; additional arguments can be used to control the source and destination rectangle
s.setBackgroundBrush(b)	Sets QGraphicsScene s's background to QBrush b
s.setSceneRect(x, y, w, h)	Sets QGraphicsScene s's rectangle to position (x, y), with width w and height h; the arguments are floats
s.update()	Schedules a paint event for QGraphicsScene s
s.views()	Returns a (possibly empty) list of QGraphicsViews that are showing QGraphicsScene s

We create an instance of our custom GraphicsView class, as well as a standard QGraphicsScene. The rectangle we set on the scene is the "window", that is, the logical coordinate system that the scene will use—in this case, a rectangle with a top-left point of $(0, 0)$, and a width and height corresponding to the page's size in points.

The rest of the initializer creates and connects the buttons, and lays out the buttons and the view.

```
def addBorders(self):
    self.borders = []
    rect = QRectF(0, 0, PageSize[0], PageSize[1])
    self.borders.append(self.scene.addRect(rect, Qt.yellow))
    margin = 5.25 * PointSize
    self.borders.append(self.scene.addRect(
            rect.adjusted(margin, margin, -margin, -margin),
            Qt.yellow))
```

This method creates two QGraphicsRectItems, the first corresponding to the size of a page and the second (indicating the margins) inside the first. The QRect.adjusted() method returns a rectangle with its top-left and bottom-right points adjusted by the two sets of *dx* and *dy* pairs. In this case, the top left is moved right and down (by each being increased by margin amount) and the bottom right is moved left and up (by each being reduced by margin amount).

```
def removeBorders(self):
    while self.borders:
        item = self.borders.pop()
        self.scene.removeItem(item)
        del item
```

When we print or save we do not want to include the borders. This method destructively retrieves each item from the self.borders list (in a random order), and removes the items from the scene. When an item is removed from a scene the scene automatically notifies its views so that they can repaint the uncovered area. An alternative to deleting is to call setVisible(False) to hide the borders.

The call to QGraphicsScene.removeItem() removes the item (and its children) from the scene, but it does not delete the item, instead passing ownership to its caller. So after the removeItem() call, the item still exists. We could just leave the item to be deleted when each item reference goes out of scope, but we prefer to explicitly delete the items to make it clear that we have taken ownership and really are deleting them.

```
def addPixmap(self):
    path = QFileInfo(self.filename).path() \
        if not self.filename.isEmpty() else "."
    fname = QFileDialog.getOpenFileName(self,
                    "Page Designer - Add Pixmap", path,
                    "Pixmap Files (*.bmp *.jpg *.png *.xpm)")
    if fname.isEmpty():
```

```
        return
    self.createPixmapItem(QPixmap(fname), self.position())
```

When the user clicks the Add Pixmap button this method is called. We simply obtain the name of the image file the user wants to add to the page, and pass the work on to a createPixmapItem() method. We don't do everything in one method because splitting the functionality is more convenient—for example, for when we load pixmaps from a Page Designer .pgd file. The position() method is used to get the position where an item should be added; we will review it shortly.

```
    def createPixmapItem(self, pixmap, position, matrix=QMatrix()):
        item = QGraphicsPixmapItem(pixmap)
        item.setFlags(QGraphicsItem.ItemIsSelectable|
                        QGraphicsItem.ItemIsMovable)
        item.setPos(position)
        item.setMatrix(matrix)
        self.scene.clearSelection()
        self.scene.addItem(item)
        item.setSelected(True)
        global Dirty
        Dirty = True
```

The graphics view classes include QGraphicsPixmapItem which is perfect for showing images in scenes. QGraphicsItem's have three flags in Qt 4.2, ItemIsMovable, ItemIsSelectable and ItemIsFocusable. (Qt 4.3 adds ItemClipsToShape, ItemClipsChildrenToShape, and ItemIgnoresTransformations, this last particularly useful for showing text that we don't want the view to transform.)

Having created the item, we set its position in the scene. The setPos() method is the only item method that works in terms of scene coordinates; all the others work in item local logical coordinates. We do not have to set a transformation matrix (and the one returned by QMatrix() is the identity matrix), but we want an explicit matrix so that we can use it when we come to save and load (or copy and paste) the scene's items.*

The QMatrix class holds a 3×3 matrix and is specifically designed for graphical transformations, rather than being a general matrix class. As such, it is a rare example of a poorly named Qt class. From Qt 4.3, QMatrix has been superceded by the more sensibly named QTransform class, which is also capable of more powerful transformations since it uses a 4×4 matrix.

Once the item is set up, we clear any existing selections and add the item to the scene. Then we select it, ready for the user to interact with it.

```
    def position(self):
        point = self.mapFromGlobal(QCursor.pos())
        if not self.view.geometry().contains(point):
```

---

*An identity matrix in this context is one that, when set, causes no transformations to occur.

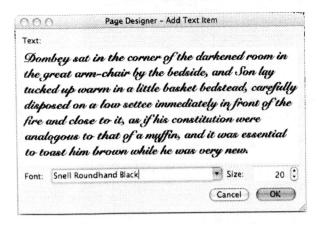

Figure 12.3 *Adding a new text item*

...t the user to be able to cut, copy, and paste items inside Page Designer,
...ce the items are not meaningful for other applications we will not use
...board.

```
def copy(self):
    item = self.selectedItem()
    if item is None:
        return
    self.copiedItem.clear()
    self.pasteOffset = 5
    stream = QDataStream(self.copiedItem, QIODevice.WriteOnly)
    self.writeItemToStream(stream, item)
```

...ser invokes the copy action we start by seeing whether there is exactly
...ected item. If there is, we clear the copied item byte array, and create a
...ream to write to the byte array. There is no need to use QDataStream.set-
...() because the data stream is used only for cutting, copying, and past-
...ring a single run of the application, so using whatever happens to be the
...t version is fine. We will look at the writeItemToStream() and the corre-
...ng readItemFromStream() methods later.

```
def selectedItem(self):
    items = self.scene.selectedItems()
    if len(items) == 1:
        return items[0]
    return None
```

...ethod returns the one selected item, or None if there are no selected items
...here are two or more selected items. The QGraphicsScene.selectedItems()
...d returns a list of the selected items. There are also items() methods
...eturn lists of the items that intersect a particular point or are inside
...icular rectangle or polygon, and there is a collidingItems() method to
...collisions.

```
        coord = random.randint(36, 144)
        point = QPoint(coord, coord)
    else:
        if point == self.prevPoint:
            point += QPoint(self.addOffset,
            self.addOffset += 5
        else:
            self.addOffset = 5
            self.prevPoint = point
    return self.view.mapToScene(point)
```

This method is used to provide a position in the sce
item should go. If the mouse is over the view, we
provided by QCursor.pos()—"cursor" in this context m
add an offset if an item has just been added at the sam
if the user repeatedly presses an Add button, each succ
from the one before, making it easier for the user to see
If the mouse is outside the view, we put the item at a se
the top left of the scene.

The mapFromGlobal() method converts a screen coordin
get coordinate as used by the view. But scenes use thei
system, so we must use QGraphicsView.mapToScene() to
ordinate into a scene coordinate.

```
    def addText(self):
        dialog = TextItemDlg(position=self.positi
                             scene=self.scene, pa
        dialog.exec_()
```

This method is called when the user clicks the Add Te;
smart add/edit item dialog, shown in Figure 12.3. If th
item is added with the text and font of their choice.
dialog, since it isn't relevant to graphics programming
chap12/pagedesigner.pyw.

We do not need to keep a reference to the added item be
ship of it to the scene inside the smart dialog.

```
    def addBox(self):
        BoxItem(self.position(), self.scene)
```

This method is called when the user clicks the Add Box
resize the box, even turning it into a line (by reducing th
pixel) by using the arrow keys, as we will see.

Again, we don't need to keep a reference to the adde
ownership is given to the scene.

We wa
but si
the cl

If the
one s
data
Versi
ing d
curr
spon

This
or if
met
tha
a pa
rep

```
def cut(self):
    item = self.selectedItem()
    if item is None:
        return
    self.copy()
    self.scene.removeItem(item)
    del item
```

This method copies the selected item using copy(), and then removes it from the scene. As mentioned when we discussed removing the border rectangles, removeItem() only removes an item from the scene; it does not delete the item. We could leave the item to be deleted when the item reference goes out of scope, but we prefer to explicitly delete it to make it clear that we have taken ownership and are really deleting the item.

```
def paste(self):
    if self.copiedItem.isEmpty():
        return
    stream = QDataStream(self.copiedItem, QIODevice.ReadOnly)
    self.readItemFromStream(stream, self.pasteOffset)
```

If an item has been cut or copied to the copied item, we simply create a data stream and read the item's data from the copied item byte array. The readItemFromStream() method takes care of creating the item and adding it to the scene.

```
def writeItemToStream(self, stream, item):
    if isinstance(item, QGraphicsTextItem):
        stream << QString("Text") << item.pos() << item.matrix() \
            << item.toPlainText() << item.font()
    elif isinstance(item, QGraphicsPixmapItem):
        stream << QString("Pixmap") << item.pos() \
            << item.matrix() << item.pixmap()
    elif isinstance(item, BoxItem):
        stream << QString("Box") << item.pos() << item.matrix() \
            << item.rect
        stream.writeInt16(item.style)
```

This method is used by copy(), cut() (indirectly), and save(). For each item it writes a string that describes the item's type, then the item's position and transformation matrix, and then any extra item-specific data. For text items, the extra data is the item's text and font; for pixmap items, the extra data is the pixmap itself—which means that the .pgd file could be quite large; and for boxes, the extra data is the box's rectangle and line style.

```
def readItemFromStream(self, stream, offset=0):
    type = QString()
    position = QPointF()
```

```
matrix = QMatrix()
stream >> type >> position >> matrix
if offset:
    position += QPointF(offset, offset)
if type == "Text":
    text = QString()
    font = QFont()
    stream >> text >> font
    TextItem(text, position, self.scene, font, matrix)
elif type == "Box":
    rect = QRectF()
    stream >> rect
    style = Qt.PenStyle(stream.readInt16())
    BoxItem(position, self.scene, style, rect, matrix)
elif type == "Pixmap":
    pixmap = QPixmap()
    stream >> pixmap
    self.createPixmapItem(pixmap, position, matrix)
```

This method is used both by paste() and by open() (which loads a .pgd file). It
begins by reading in the type, position, and matrix which are stored for every
type of item. Then, it adjusts the position by the offset—this is used only if the
item is being pasted. Next, the item-specific data is read and a suitable item
created using the data that has been gathered.

The TextItem and BoxItem initializers, and the createPixmapItem() method, all
create the appropriate graphics items and pass ownership to the scene.

```
def rotate(self):
    for item in self.scene.selectedItems():
        item.rotate(30)
```

If the user clicks Rotate, any selected items are rotated by 30°. There are no
child items used in this application, but if any of the rotated items had child
items, these too would be rotated.

```
def delete(self):
    items = self.scene.selectedItems()
    if len(items) and QMessageBox.question(self,
            "Page Designer - Delete",
            "Delete %d item%s?" % (len(items),
            "s" if len(items) != 1 else ""),
            QMessageBox.Yes|QMessageBox.No) == QMessageBox.Yes:
        while items:
            item = items.pop()
            self.scene.removeItem(item)
            del item
        global Dirty
```

```
                    Dirty = True
```

If the user clicks Delete and there is at least one selected item, they are asked whether they want to delete the selected items, and if they do, each selected item is deleted.

```
    def print_(self):
        dialog = QPrintDialog(self.printer)
        if dialog.exec_():
            painter = QPainter(self.printer)
            painter.setRenderHint(QPainter.Antialiasing)
            painter.setRenderHint(QPainter.TextAntialiasing)
            self.scene.clearSelection()
            self.removeBorders()
            self.scene.render(painter)
            self.addBorders()
```

A QPrinter is a paint device, just like a QWidget or a QImage, so we can easily paint onto a printer. Here we have taken advantage of the QGraphicsScene.render() convenience method, which paints the entire scene (or a selected portion of it) onto a paint device. Before painting, we remove the borders (the yellow rectangles), and after painting we restore the borders. We also clear the selection before painting, since some items may be rendered differently if they are selected. A similar QGraphicsView.render() method can be used to render the scene (or a selected portion of it) as seen.

We will omit the code for saving and loading .pgd files, since it is very similar to what we have seen before when working with binary files. For saving, we create a QDataStream, call setVersion() on it, and write a magic number and a file version. Then we iterate over all the items in the scene, calling writeItemToStream() parameterized by the data stream and by the item for each call. For loading, we also create a QDataStream. Then we read in the magic number and file version, and if they are correct, we delete all the existing items. As long as the file has data in it, we call readItemFromStream() parameterized by the stream. This method reads the item data and creates the items, adding them to the scene as it goes.

We have seen how the application works as a whole, and how to create and use items of two of the predefined graphics item classes, namely, QGraphicsRectItem and QGraphicsPixmapItem. Now we will turn our attention to custom graphics view items. We will begin by looking at the TextItem subclass; this extends the QGraphicsTextItem class with additional behavior, but leaves all the drawing to the base class. Then we will look at the BoxItem class; this class has code for both behavior and drawing.

```
    class TextItem(QGraphicsTextItem):

        def __init__(self, text, position, scene,
                    font=QFont("Times", PointSize), matrix=QMatrix()):
```

```
            super(TextItem, self).__init__(text)
            self.setFlags(QGraphicsItem.ItemIsSelectable|
                          QGraphicsItem.ItemIsMovable)
            self.setFont(font)
            self.setPos(position)
            self.setMatrix(matrix)
            scene.clearSelection()
            scene.addItem(self)
            self.setSelected(True)
            global Dirty
            Dirty = True
```

The TextItem's initializer is very similar to the createPixmapItem() method that creates and initializes QGraphicsPixmapItems. We provide a default font and a default matrix (the identity matrix) if none is supplied to the initializer.

```
        def parentWidget(self):
            return self.scene().views()[0]
```

An item's parent is either another item or a scene. But sometimes we need to know the visible widget in which the item appears, that is, the item's view. The scene is available to items and can return a list of the views that are showing the scene. For convenience, we have assumed that there is always at least one view showing our scene and that we consider the first view to be the "parent" view.

```
        def itemChange(self, change, variant):
            if change != QGraphicsItem.ItemSelectedChange:
                global Dirty
                Dirty = True
            return QGraphicsTextItem.itemChange(self, change, variant)
```

If the user interacts with an item—for example, moving or selecting it—this method is called. If the interaction is not merely a change in selection status, we set the global dirty flag.

Two caveats apply to itemChange() reimplementations. First, we must always return the result of calling the base class implementation, and second, we must never do anything inside this method that will lead to another (recursive) item-Change() call. In particular, we must never call setPos() inside itemChange().

```
        def mouseDoubleClickEvent(self, event):
            dialog = TextItemDlg(self, self.parentWidget())
            dialog.exec_()
```

If the user double-clicks the item, we pop up a smart dialog through which the user can change the item's text and font. This is the same dialog that we used for adding a text item.

Printing Images

Printing images in general is just as simple as printing scenes. Here is a printImage() method that will print any QImage or QPixmap (both of which can load .bmp, .png, .jpg, and various other graphics file types) on a single page, assuming that printer is a QPrinter:

```
def printImage(image, printer, scaleToFillPage=False):
    dialog = QPrintDialog(printer)
    if dialog.exec_():
        painter = QPainter(printer)
        painter.setRenderHint(QPainter.Antialiasing)
        rect = painter.viewport()
        size = image.size()
        size.scale(rect.size(), Qt.KeepAspectRatio)
        painter.setViewport(rect.x(), rect.y(),
                            size.width(), size.height())
        if scaleToFillPage:
            painter.setWindow(image.rect())
        if isinstance(image, QPixmap):
            painter.drawPixmap(0, 0, image)
        else:
            painter.drawImage(0, 0, image)
```

Printing a QPicture is very similar, except that we must calculate the size ourselves based on the picture's bounding rectangle, and call QPainter.draw-Picture() to do the drawing.

SVG images can also be printed. The approach is very similar to that used for drawing QGraphicsScenes. The QSvgRenderer class can load in an SVG image and has a render() method that can paint the image on any paint device, including a QPrinter. And with Qt 4.3, it is now possible to create SVG images by painting using the QSvgGenerator class, which is a paint device.[*]

This completes the text item class. It is quite small because we were concerned only with changing its behavior. For the BoxItem class that we will look at next, we provide code to govern both its behavior and its appearance.

```
class BoxItem(QGraphicsItem):

    def __init__(self, position, scene, style=Qt.SolidLine,
                 rect=None, matrix=QMatrix()):
        super(BoxItem, self).__init__()
        self.setFlags(QGraphicsItem.ItemIsSelectable|
                      QGraphicsItem.ItemIsMovable|
                      QGraphicsItem.ItemIsFocusable)
```

---

[*]Printing documents, including images, is covered in the next chapter.

```
        if rect is None:
            rect = QRectF(-10 * PointSize, -PointSize,
                          20 * PointSize, 2 * PointSize)
        self.rect = rect
        self.style = style
        self.setPos(position)
        self.setMatrix(matrix)
        scene.clearSelection()
        scene.addItem(self)
        self.setSelected(True)
        self.setFocus()
        global Dirty
        Dirty = True
```

Box items must be able to receive keyboard focus, because we want users to be able to resize boxes by using the arrow keys. If no explicit size is given—for example when the user clicks Add Box, rather than when a box is being re-created from file or being pasted from the copied item—we provide a default size which gives a letterbox shape. We also provide a default line style of a solid line, and a default identity matrix. The rest of the initializer is the same as we used before for text items.

We will omit the code for parentWidget() and itemChange() because their implementations are the same as the ones we used for the TextItem class.

```
    def setStyle(self, style):
        self.style = style
        self.update()
        global Dirty
        Dirty = True
```

This method is used to set the box's line style. It notifies the scene that the item needs repainting, and it sets the dirty flag since we record box line styles when we save into .pgd files.

```
    def contextMenuEvent(self, event):
        wrapped = []
        menu = QMenu(self.parentWidget())
        for text, param in (
                ("&Solid", Qt.SolidLine),
                ("&Dashed", Qt.DashLine),
                ("D&otted", Qt.DotLine),
                ("D&ashDotted", Qt.DashDotLine),
                ("DashDo&tDotted", Qt.DashDotDotLine)):
            wrapper = functools.partial(self.setStyle, param)
            wrapped.append(wrapper)
            menu.addAction(text, wrapper)
        menu.exec_(event.screenPos())
```

If the user invokes the context menu on the item (for example, by right-clicking on some platforms), this method will be called.* This context menu uses partial function application to wrap a method to be called, setStyle(), and a parameter to call it with, one of PyQt's built-in line styles. The wrappers must stay alive long enough for the menu to finish, since it is only at that point that one of them will be called. For this reason we keep a local list of the wrappers; the list will go out of scope only after the menu's exec_() call has finished, when the contextMenuEvent() itself completes.

```python
def keyPressEvent(self, event):
    factor = PointSize / 4
    changed = False
    if event.modifiers() & Qt.ShiftModifier:
        if event.key() == Qt.Key_Left:
            self.rect.setRight(self.rect.right() - factor)
            changed = True
        elif event.key() == Qt.Key_Right:
            self.rect.setRight(self.rect.right() + factor)
            changed = True
        elif event.key() == Qt.Key_Up:
            self.rect.setBottom(self.rect.bottom() - factor)
            changed = True
        elif event.key() == Qt.Key_Down:
            self.rect.setBottom(self.rect.bottom() + factor)
            changed = True
    if changed:
        self.update()
        global Dirty
        Dirty = True
    else:
        QGraphicsItem.keyPressEvent(self, event)
```

If the user presses the arrow keys and the view has scrollbars, the view will scroll appropriately. This method intercepts arrow key presses that occur with a Shift key press when the item has the keyboard focus, to give the user a means of resizing the box. The QRect.setRight() and QRect.setBottom() methods change the size of the rectangle because they change the width and height. If we handled the key press event, we call update() to schedule a paint event, and mark the page as dirty; otherwise, we call the base class implementation.

Now that we have seen how the box's behavior is implemented, we are ready to turn our attention to how the box is drawn. When subclassing QGraphicsItem we must at least provide implementations of the boundingRect() and paint() methods. It is also common to reimplement shape(), but we will defer that to the example in the next section.

---

* Note that this method will not be called if the view has been told to handle context menu events—for example, by having its context menu policy set to Qt.ActionsContextMenu.

Table 12.2 *Selected QGraphicsItem Methods #1*

Syntax	Description
`g.boundingRect()`	Returns `QGraphicsItem` g's bounding `QRectF`; subclasses should reimplement this
`g.collidesWith-Path(pp)`	Returns `True` if `QGraphicsItem` g collides with `QPainterPath` pp
`g.collidingItems()`	Returns a (possibly empty) list of the `QGraphicsItems` that `QGraphicsItem` g collides with
`g.contains(pt)`	Returns `True` if `QGraphicsItem` g contains `QPointF` pt
`g.isObscured()`	Returns `True` if `QGraphicsItem` g is obscured by its colliding items, providing their z values are larger
`g.isSelected()`	Returns `True` if `QGraphicsItem` g is selected
`g.itemChange(c, v)`	Does nothing; subclasses can reimplement this method to detect changes—for example, in selected status or position. Do not call `QGraphicsItem.setPos()` directly or indirectly in this method.
`g.moveBy(dx, dy)`	Moves `QGraphicsItem` g by `float` dx horizontally and by `float` dy vertically in scene coordinates
`g.paint(p, o)`	Does nothing; subclasses should reimplement this to draw themselves on `QPainter` p and with the option `QStyleOptionGraphicsItem` o; painting is done in local logical coordinates, by default centered at (0, 0)
`g.pos()`	Returns `QGraphicsItem` g's position as a `QPointF`. If g is a child of another `QGraphicsItem`, the point is in terms of the parent item's local logical coordinates; otherwise, it is in terms of scene coordinates.
`g.resetMatrix()`	Resets `QGraphicsItem` g's transformation matrix to the identity matrix; for PyQt 4.3, use `resetTransform()` instead
`g.rotate(a)`	Rotates `QGraphicsItem` g by `float` a°
`g.scale(x, y)`	Scales `QGraphicsItem` g horizontally by `float` x and vertically by `float` y; 1.0 is unscaled, 0.5 is half size, and 3.0 is three times the size
`g.scene()`	Returns `QGraphicsItem` g's `QGraphicsScene`, or `None` if it has not been added to a scene
`g.sceneBounding-Rect()`	Returns `QGraphicsItem` g's bounding `QRectF` in scene coordinates—this accounts for transformations
`g.setCursor(c)`	Sets g's cursor to c, a `QCursor` or a `Qt.CursorShape`
`g.setEnabled(b)`	Sets g to be enabled or disabled depending on b
`g.setFocus()`	Gives the keyboard focus to `QGraphicsItem` g
`g.setFlag(f)`	Sets the given `QGraphicsItem.ItemFlag` f on g

Table 12.3 *Selected QGraphicsItem Methods #2*

Syntax	Description
g.setMatrix(m)	Sets QGraphicsItem g's matrix to QMatrix m; for PyQt 4.3, use setTransform() with a QTransform argument
g.setPos(x, y)	Sets QGraphicsItem g's position. If g is a child of another QGraphicsItem, the position is in the parent item's local logical coordinates; otherwise, it is in scene coordinates.
g.setSelect-ed(b)	Sets QGraphicsItem g to be selected or unselected depending on bool b
g.setZValue(z)	Sets QGraphicsItem g's *z* value to float z. The default is 0; items with higher values appear in front of those with lower values.
g.shape()	Returns QGraphicsItem g's shape as a QPainterPath. The default implementation calls boundingRect() to determine the painter path to return; reimplementations normally create and return the exact shape. By default, collision detection is based on shape.
g.shear(x, y)	Shears QGraphicsItem g's coordinate system horizontally by float x and vertically by float y
g.trans-late(dx, dy)	Moves QGraphicsItem g's coordinate system horizontally by int dx and vertically by int dy
g.update()	Schedules a paint event for QGraphicsItem g where it is visible in the scene's views
g.zValue()	Returns QGraphicsItem g's *z* value

```
def boundingRect(self):
    return self.rect.adjusted(-2, -2, 2, 2)
```

This method should return the bounding rectangle of the item, plus half the pen width if the item has an outline. Here we have cheated and made the bounding rectangle a bit larger. This makes it much easier for the user to click the box, even if they have reduced it to being a line with a height or width of just 1 pixel.

We have not implemented the shape() method, so the base class's shape() method will be used, and will produce a shape that is based on the bounding rectangle. Since we have given a larger rectangle than is really the case, the shape will also be larger. The shape is used when determining collision detection, but it does not matter here because we don't use collision detection in this application; we will in the next one, though.

```
def paint(self, painter, option, widget):
    pen = QPen(self.style)
    pen.setColor(Qt.black)
    pen.setWidth(1)
```

```
        if option.state & QStyle.State_Selected:
            pen.setColor(Qt.blue)
        painter.setPen(pen)
        painter.drawRect(self.rect)
```

Painting the box is quite easy. We begin by creating a pen with the line style the user has set, and with a fixed width of 1 logical unit. We change the pen's color if the rectangle is selected, and then we set the pen and draw the rectangle.

Using the graphics view classes and painting graphics items is often easier than reimplementing paint events. This is because each item has its own paint() method, and because the items use a local logical coordinate system whose center is (0, 0), which is especially convenient for rotation.

In this section, we have seen the use of predefined graphics items, and custom items, both of which provide custom behavior and the second of which, BoxItem, also does custom drawing. In the example covered in the next section, we will see more sophisticated item painting, as well as collision detection and a simple form of animation.

Animation and Complex Shapes

In the preceding section, we looked at a graphics view application in which user interaction was central. In this section, we will look at a very different kind of application, one where we simulate a population of creatures, "multipedes", by visualizing each member of the population using a set of graphics items, as shown in Figure 12.4. Each multipede has internal timers. At each time interval the multipede moves, and if it has collisions, its coloring is changed slightly, and eventually it disappears.

We will begin by looking at an extract from the main form's initializer. Then we will review the form's populate() method, which is used to create and position the multipedes. Next we will look at the action of the Pause/Resume button and at the implementation of the zoom slider. Then we will look at the form's timer event, a kind of event handler we have not used before. Once we can see how the application works as a whole, we will look at the implementations of the graphics item subclasses that are used to visualize the multipedes.

```
    class MainForm(QDialog):

        def __init__(self, parent=None):
            super(MainForm, self).__init__(parent)

            self.scene = QGraphicsScene(self)
            self.scene.setSceneRect(0, 0, SCENESIZE, SCENESIZE)
            self.view = QGraphicsView()
            self.view.setRenderHint(QPainter.Antialiasing)
            self.view.setScene(self.scene)
```

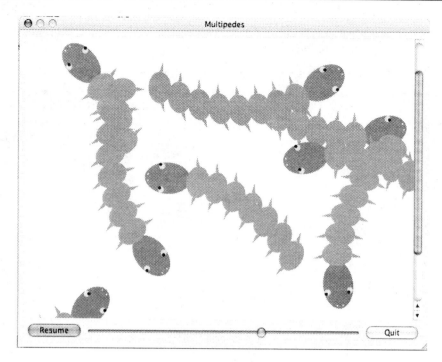

Figure 12.4 *The Multipedes application*

```
self.view.setFocusPolicy(Qt.NoFocus)
zoomSlider = QSlider(Qt.Horizontal)
zoomSlider.setRange(5, 200)
zoomSlider.setValue(100)
self.pauseButton = QPushButton("Pa&use")
quitButton = QPushButton("&Quit")
```

The form begins by creating a graphics scene. As usual for nonvisual QObject subclasses, we give the scene a parent. The SCENESIZE is a global integer of value 500. Setting up the view is similar to what we saw in the previous example. The zoom slider is used to zoom the scene in or out. We set its initial value to 100 (100%), and give it a range of 5% to 200%. The Pause button is used to pause and resume the animation.

```
self.connect(zoomSlider, SIGNAL("valueChanged(int)"),
            self.zoom)
self.connect(self.pauseButton, SIGNAL("clicked()"),
            self.pauseOrResume)
self.connect(quitButton, SIGNAL("clicked()"), self.accept)

self.populate()
self.startTimer(INTERVAL)
self.setWindowTitle("Multipedes")
```

We have omitted the layout since we have seen it so many before, and this one is not unusual. The connections contain no surprises, but they are shown so that we can see how the user interaction is handled.

Every QObject subclass (which includes all QWidgets since they are QObject subclasses) can set off a timer that causes a timer event to occur at every time interval. Here the INTERVAL is 200 milliseconds. The accuracy of timers depends on the underlying operating system, but it should be at least as good as 20 milliseconds, unless the machine is very heavily loaded. The startTimer() method returns a timer ID which is useful if we want to call the method more than once to set up multiple timers; we ignore it here because we want just one timer.

At the end of the initializer, we call populate() to create the multipedes, and set the application's window title as usual.

```
def pauseOrResume(self):
    global Running
    Running = not Running
    self.pauseButton.setText("Pa&use" if Running else "Res&ume")
```

If the user clicks the Pause button, we set the global Running Boolean to the opposite of what it was, and change the button's caption. The form's timer and the multipede timers refer to this variable, doing nothing if it is False.

```
def zoom(self, value):
    factor = value / 100.0
    matrix = self.view.matrix()
    matrix.reset()
    matrix.scale(factor, factor)
    self.view.setMatrix(matrix)
```

To zoom the scene, all that we need to do is change the scale of the view that shows the scene. This is achieved by getting the view's current transformation matrix, clearing any transformations (i.e., scaling) that may be in force, and then rescaling it to a factor that is proportional to the slider's setting.

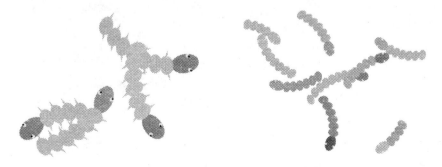

Figure 12.5 *Multipedes at two different zoom levels*

Zooming has a significant effect on how the multipedes are drawn. This is because in the QGraphicsItem.paint() method, we can find out how zoomed in or out a scene is and can use this information to determine how much detail to draw. This means, for example, that we can draw in a faster and more simplified way if the scene is zoomed out with users unable to discern the details anyway, and that we can draw in increasing detail as users zoom in. The effect of zooming is shown in Figure 12.5.

```
def populate(self):
    red, green, blue = 0, 150, 0
    for i in range(random.randint(6, 10)):
        angle = random.randint(0, 360)
        offset = random.randint(0, SCENESIZE // 2)
        half = SCENESIZE / 2
        x = half + (offset * math.sin(math.radians(angle)))
        y = half + (offset * math.cos(math.radians(angle)))
        color = QColor(red, green, blue)
        head = Head(color, angle, QPointF(x, y))
        color = QColor(red, green + random.randint(10, 60), blue)
        offset = 25
        segment = Segment(color, offset, head)
        for j in range(random.randint(3, 7)):
            offset += 25
            segment = Segment(color, offset, segment)
        head.rotate(random.randint(0, 360))
        self.scene.addItem(head)
    global Running
    Running = True
```

This method is used to generate a random population of 6–10 multipedes. Each multipede is made up of a head, and between four and eight body segments. For each multipede, the head is created first, with a semirandom color, with a random angle of direction, and at a random position inside a circle with its center in the middle of the scene. Then the multipede's first segment is created, with the head being its parent. This means that whatever transformation is applied to the head, for example, moving or rotating it, will also be applied to the first segment. Next, 3–7 additional segments are created. Each one is made a child of its preceding segment. The effect of this is that if the head is transformed, the first segment is transformed correspondingly, and so is the first segment's child segment, and so on, for all the multipede's segments.

Once the head and segments have been created, we rotate the head and add it to the scene. Adding a graphics item to a scene automatically adds all the item's children recursively, so by adding just the head, the entire multipede is added.

At the end, we set the global Running Boolean to True. In addition to the form's timer, each multipede part has a timer, and as long as Running is True, the part will move at each time interval.

The red color we have used is significant for head items. The red color component is set to 0 for all multipedes when they are first created. If the red color component of a multipede's head reaches the maximum (255)—which can occur as the result of collisions—the multipede will "die", that is, it will be removed. The culling is done in the timer event.

```
def timerEvent(self, event):
    if not Running:
        return
    dead = set()
    items = self.scene.items()
    if len(items) == 0:
        self.populate()
        return
    heads = set()
    for item in items:
        if isinstance(item, Head):
            heads.add(item)
            if item.color.red() == 255:
                dead.add(item)
    if len(heads) == 1:
        dead = heads
    del heads
    while dead:
        item = dead.pop()
        self.scene.removeItem(item)
        del item
```

At every time interval the form's timerEvent() method is called. If the Running Boolean is False, the method does nothing and returns immediately. If there are no items in the scene (they all died), we call populate() and begin a fresh run. Otherwise we iterate over all the items in the scene, populating two sets: one the set of head items that have a red color component with value 255, and the other with the set of all head items in the scene.

If there is just one head item, we overwrite the dead set with the heads set containing the one remaining head. This ensures that if there is just one multipede left, it will be killed off. We then delete the heads set so that there are no references that could keep items alive. Finally, we iterate over the dead items, removing each one from the scene at random and, since ownership passes to us, deleting each one that we remove. Thanks to the parent–child relationships, when we delete a multipede's head, the head's child (the first segment) is deleted, and in turn the first segment's child (the second segment) is deleted, and so on, to the greatest grandchild so that simply by deleting a multipede's head, we delete all the segments too.

We have now seen how the application works, so we can turn our attention to the implementation of the multipedes themselves. As the population() method shows, multipedes are made up of one Head and at least four Segments—both of these classes are QGraphicsItem subclasses, and both are smart enough to draw only the amount of detail that makes sense for the current zoom level. We will look at the Head first, and then at the Segment.

```
class Head(QGraphicsItem):

    Rect = QRectF(-30, -20, 60, 40)

    def __init__(self, color, angle, position):
        super(Head, self).__init__()
        self.color = color
        self.angle = angle
        self.setPos(position)
        self.timer = QTimer()
        QObject.connect(self.timer, SIGNAL("timeout()"), self.timeout)
        self.timer.start(INTERVAL)
```

All heads have the same shape: an ellipse that fits inside the static Rect rectangle. When the head is initialized we record its color and angle in instance variables and move it to the given position in the scene.

The QGraphicsItem class is not a QObject subclass and does not provide built-in timers. This is not a problem since we can simply use a QTimer as we have done here.* A QTimer's timeouts do not result in timer events, but instead are signified by timeout() signals being emitted. Here we create a timer which will time out every INTERVAL (200) milliseconds, that is, five times per second. We have connected the timer's timeout() signal to our own timeout() method; we will review this method shortly.

```
    def boundingRect(self):
        return Head.Rect
```

The bounding rectangle is easy—it is simply the static Rect rectangle that serves as the basic shape for all multipede heads.

```
    def shape(self):
        path = QPainterPath()
        path.addEllipse(Head.Rect)
        return path
```

---

*C++/Qt programmers might be tempted to multiply-inherit from QGraphicsItem and QObject, but PyQt permits inheritance only from a single Qt class.

This method is the default one used for collision detection, unless we specify a coarser-grained approach that uses just the bounding rectangle. A painter path is a series of rectangles, ellipses, arcs, and other shapes (including painter paths) that together completely describe an item's shape. In this case, the path is just one ellipse.

Using a painter path for a graphics item's shape ensures that collisions are detected accurately. For example, two multipede heads may cross at the corners of their rectangles without colliding, since their ellipses don't occupy the corners.

```
def paint(self, painter, option, widget=None):
    painter.setPen(Qt.NoPen)
    painter.setBrush(QBrush(self.color))
    painter.drawEllipse(Head.Rect)
    if option.levelOfDetail > 0.5:
        painter.setBrush(QBrush(Qt.yellow)) # Outer eyes
        painter.drawEllipse(-12, -19, 8, 8)
        painter.drawEllipse(-12, 11, 8, 8)
        if option.levelOfDetail > 0.9:
            painter.setBrush(QBrush(Qt.darkBlue)) # Inner eyes
            painter.drawEllipse(-12, -19, 4, 4)
            painter.drawEllipse(-12, 11, 4, 4)
            if option.levelOfDetail > 1.3:
                painter.setBrush(QBrush(Qt.white)) # Nostrils
                painter.drawEllipse(-27, -5, 2, 2)
                painter.drawEllipse(-27, 3, 2, 2)
```

The head in full detail is an ellipse, two eyes, each of which is two ellipses, one inside the other, and two tiny nostrils, again ellipses. The paint() method begins by getting rid of the pen and by setting a solid brush to the multipede's color. Then the basic head shape is drawn.

The option variable is of type QStyleOptionGraphicsItem, and it holds various useful information, including the item's transformation matrix, font metrics, palette, and state (selected, "on", "off", and many others). It also holds the "level of detail", a measure of how zoomed in or out the scene is. If the scene is not zoomed at all, the level of detail is 1.0; if it is zoomed in to be twice the size, the level of detail will be 2.0, and if it is zoomed out to half the size, the level of detail will be 0.5.

If the scene is being shown at 50% of its natural size or larger, we draw the multipede's yellow outer eyes. We can hard-code the coordinates because graphics items use their own local logical coordinate system and any externally applied transformations are taken care of automatically for us. If the scene is being show at 90% of its natural size or larger, we also draw the inner eyes, and if the scene is zoomed in enough to be viewed at 130% or larger, we also draw the multipedes' tiny nostrils.

The last method we must consider is the timeout() method that is called every INTERVAL milliseconds by the timer. We will look at the method in two parts, since there are two aspects to what it does.

```
def timeout(self):
    if not Running:
        return
    angle = self.angle
    while True:
        angle += random.randint(-9, 9)
        offset = random.randint(3, 15)
        x = self.x() + (offset * math.sin(math.radians(angle)))
        y = self.y() + (offset * math.cos(math.radians(angle)))
        if 0 <= x <= SCENESIZE and 0 <= y <= SCENESIZE:
            break
    self.angle = angle
    self.rotate(random.randint(-5, 5))
    self.setPos(QPointF(x, y))
```

If the global Running Boolean is False, we do nothing and return. Otherwise, we calculate a new position for the head based on a small random change to its angle of direction (±9°), and a small movement (3–15 logical units). To avoid the multipede wandering out of the scene, we keep moving and turning it until its new (x, y) position is within the scene's boundaries.

Once we have the new coordinates, we record the angle that was used, rotate the head slightly, and set the head's position. At this point, collisions may have occurred as a result of the movement.

```
for item in self.scene().collidingItems(self):
    if isinstance(item, Head):
        self.color.setRed(min(255, self.color.red() + 1))
    else:
        item.color.setBlue(min(255, item.color.blue() + 1))
```

We ask the scene for all the items that the head has collided with. If it has hit another head, we make this head a bit redder, and if it has hit a segment, we make the segment it has hit a bit bluer. If a head's red color component reaches 255, the head (and therefore the entire multipede, including all the segments) will be removed from the scene. The removals take place in the form's timer event, as we saw earlier (page 372).

Now we will look at the Segment implementation. Its initializer is a bit longer than the Head's initializer, but the boundingRect(), shape(), and paint() methods are much simpler as a result.

```
class Segment(QGraphicsItem):

    def __init__(self, color, offset, parent):
```

```
super(Segment, self).__init__(parent)
self.color = color
self.rect = QRectF(offset, -20, 30, 40)
self.path = QPainterPath()
self.path.addEllipse(self.rect)
x = offset + 15
y = -20
self.path.addPolygon(QPolygonF([QPointF(x, y),
        QPointF(x - 5, y - 12), QPointF(x - 5, y)]))
self.path.closeSubpath()
y = 20
self.path.addPolygon(QPolygonF([QPointF(x, y),
        QPointF(x - 5, y + 12), QPointF(x - 5, y)]))
self.path.closeSubpath()
self.change = 1
self.angle = 0
self.timer = QTimer()
QObject.connect(self.timer, SIGNAL("timeout()"), self.timeout)
self.timer.start(INTERVAL)
```

The first thing to notice is that we accept a parent parameter and pass it on to the base class. We did not do this for the Head because when an item is added to a scene, the scene automatically takes ownership of the item, so there was no need. But segments are not explicitly added to the scene since they are all children of other items. The first segment's parent is the multipede's head, the second segment's parent is the first segment, the third segment's parent is the second segment, and so on. When the head is added to the scene the segments are added too; but the scene takes ownership of only the head. Although we could have given the segments no parent and added them directly to the scene, it is much more convenient to make them child items. In particular, the parent–child relationship between graphics items is used to propagate transformations from parent to child.

The offset is an x offset relative to the head, no matter which segment we are initializing. The rectangle is used to draw the segment's ellipse, but unlike the head, it does not encompass the entire shape because segments have protruding legs. Because the segment's shape isn't simple, we create it using a painter path. We begin with the segment's "body", a simple ellipse. Then we draw one leg (a very flat triangle), and then the other leg. The addPolygon() method takes a QPolygonF(), which itself is constructed with a list of QPointF objects. After each leg is added, we call closeSubpath(); alternatively, we could simply have added an extra point at the end, a copy of the first point. The change and angle instance variables are used for movement; we will cover them in the timeout() event.

```
def boundingRect(self):
    return self.path.boundingRect()
```

The bounding rectangle must account for the entire shape, including the legs, but is it easy to obtain using QPainterPath.boundingRect().

```
def shape(self):
    return self.path
```

The shape isn't straightforward, but thanks to the path being calculated in the initializer, this method is simple.

```
def paint(self, painter, option, widget=None):
    painter.setPen(Qt.NoPen)
    painter.setBrush(QBrush(self.color))
    if option.levelOfDetail < 0.9:
        painter.drawEllipse(self.rect)
    else:
        painter.drawPath(self.path)
```

Thanks to precalculating the rectangle and painter path, the paint() method is much easier and faster than it would otherwise have been. If the scene is zoomed in to 90% or less, we just draw an ellipse; otherwise, we draw the shape in full detail using the painter path.

```
def timeout(self):
    if not Running:
        return
    matrix = self.matrix()
    matrix.reset()
    self.setMatrix(matrix)
    self.angle += self.change
    if self.angle > 5:
        self.change = -1
        self.angle -= 1
    elif self.angle < -5:
        self.change = 1
        self.angle += 1
    self.rotate(self.angle)
```

When a multipede's head moves, its first (child) segment moves with it, and that segment's child segment moves with it, and so on. This is fine, but it means that the multipede's shape is rigid. We want the segments to gently sway from side to side as the multipede moves, and for this reason we have given the segments their own timers.

We retrieve the segment's transformation matrix, clear any transformations (rotations) that have been applied, and then rotate the segment. The change variable starts out as 1 and the rotation angle starts out at 0°. At every time interval, the change is added to the angle. If the angle reaches 6 (or -6), we make it 5 (or -5) and negate the change value. This means that the angle has the sequence 1, 2, 3, 4, 5, 4, 3, 2, 1, 0, -1, -2, -3, -4, -5, -4, -3, -2, -1, 0, 1, 2, and so on, which produces a nice swaying effect.

This completes our review of animating complex shapes. Using painter paths, shapes of arbitrary complexity can be created, and by storing the paths as static or as instance variables, a lot of calculation can be done one-off rather than in every call to a paint method. The approach we have used to achieve animation is not the only one possible. For example, we could use QGraphics-ItemAnimation items in conjunction with a QTimeLine. Another approach would be to take the timers out of the items themselves and instead keep a set of references to them. Then, a timer in the form could be used, and at each interval each item in the set could be moved and collisions could be resolved from the form's timeout handler. There is no one and only right approach; rather, the best approach will depend on the needs of the application itself.

Summary

The graphics view classes are ideal for situations where we have lots of individual items to draw, from dozens to hundreds of thousands. They are also perfect for when we want to allow the user to interact with items—for example, clicking, dragging, and selecting them—as well as being ideal for doing animation.

Scenes use their own logical coordinate system and contain graphics items. Scenes are viewed using QGraphicsView, and more than one view can be associated with a scene if we want the user to be able to view the scene using two or more different transformations (for example, at different zoom levels or rotation angles).

The graphics view classes include a number of useful predefined items that can be used "as is". We can also subclass QGraphicsItem or one of its subclasses to provide custom behavior (for example context menus and key event handling) as well as custom painting so that we can draw any shapes we like.

If we want to save and load scenes to and from files, one simple approach is to make sure that every item has a transformation matrix, and to save an item description, the item's position in the scene, the item's matrix, and any additional item-specific data that may be necessary. Doing this using QDataStream is very easy.

Any scene can be drawn on any paint device, including a printer, a PDF file, or a QImage (for example, to save as a .png file), by using the render() methods provided by the scene and view classes. And from Qt 4.3, scenes can also be rendered in SVG format using the QSvgGenerator paint device class.

Painting graphics view items is made as easy as possible because of the convenient local coordinate system that allows us to ignore any externally applied transformations—for example, from parent items. The QPainter class offers many convenient drawing methods for drawing such things as arcs, chords, ellipses, polygons, lines, polylines, rectangles, images, and text. In addition, complex shapes can be created using `QPainterPath` objects, and these can be painted directly using `QPainter.drawPath()`.

Even more complex shapes can be created by composing two or more items together using parent–child relationships. Such relationships ensure that transformations applied to a parent item are automatically applied to the child items, down to the furthest grandchild. This, in conjunction with the use of local logical coordinates, makes animating complex shapes much easier than having to orchestrate all the transformations manually ourselves.

Simulations, games, and the visualization of time series data can be done using the graphics view classes. One simple approach to animation is to give each item its own timer and to move it whenever the timer times out, although several other approaches are possible. For painting, using pre-calculated shapes can save time in the paint methods, as can using the view's level of detail to decide how much detail to draw.

For graphing, creating a custom widget and reimplementing its paint event, as described in the preceding chapter, is probably the best approach. For general scientific and engineering applications, the PyQwt library (Qt Widgets for Technical Applications) provides a lot of functionality out of the box, including 2D plotting, whereas the PyQwt3D bindings extend PyQwt to include 3D plotting. To get the best out of these add-ons, and for fast numerical processing, installing the NumPy package is also recommended. See `http://pyqwt.sourceforge.net` and `http://numpy.scipy.org` for more information.

PyQt's graphics view classes have even more to offer than we have had the space to cover here. In addition to many more features offered by the graphics view classes, it is also possible to do both 2D and 3D graphics using the `QtOpenGL` module. In addition, this module can be used in conjunction with PyQt's other graphics classes. For example, we can use a `QGLWidget` instead of a `QWidget` for painting on by calling `QGraphicsView.setViewport(QGLWidget())`, and we can use `QPainter` to overlay a `QGLWidget` with annotations.

Exercise

Enhance the Page Designer application by adding a new button, Align, which has a pop-up menu of Align Left, Align Right, Align Top, and Align Bottom. Provide a single method, `setAlignment()`, that takes an alignment argument. Be sure to keep an instance variable with the wrappers so they don't get garbage-collected. To perform the alignment there must be at least two items selected (because items are aligned with respect to each other).

The algorithm in the solution has two phases: First it finds the item to align every other item in relation to; for example, if doing Align Left, it finds the leftmost item. Note that this must be done in terms of the `sceneBoundingRect()`, not the `boundingRect()` (which is different if the item is rotated). Second, it works out the x or y difference to be applied to the other items and then applies it. Adding the extra button and its menu will take less than 15 lines of code, and `setAlignment()` can be written in less than 45 lines, so the whole thing can be done in about 60 lines.

A solution is provided in `chap12/pagedesigner_ans.pyw`.

## 13

- Rich Text Editing
- Printing Documents

Rich Text and Printing

PyQt supports *rich text*, essentially a subset of HTML that also includes some support for CSS (cascading style sheets).[*] This means that in practice, we can pass strings that contain HTML markup to many of PyQt's text-handling classes and rely on PyQt to render the HTML properly in the user interface.

We have already seen examples of passing HTML to QLabels. The graphics item class QGraphicsTextItem can also accept HTML. The QTextBrowser class supports basic HTML display including hyperlinks, and although it is by no means a full-blown Web browser, many developers find it sufficient for displaying help text. For editing HTML, PyQt provides the QTextEdit class. Although this class can render all the PyQt-supported HTML tags, it does not provide users with the means to create or edit some of the tags—for example, it can show HTML tables, but it does not provide a means of inserting or editing them. These deficiencies can, of course, be remedied by subclassing and providing the functionality ourselves.

Another use case for QTextEdit is to provide source code editing, with syntax highlighting provided by custom QSyntaxHighlighter subclasses. A dedicated open source component, specifically designed for source code editing, is also available. This component is called Scintilla (http://www.scintilla.org), and the Qt port of it, QScintilla, can also be used with PyQt.

All of the widgets that can handle rich text store the text internally in a QTextDocument. This pure data class is also available for our use.

In this chapter, we will explore some of the features of QTextEdit, including its use as a source code editor using QSyntaxHighlighter. Although PyQt provides a set of widgets that covers most situations, from simple labels and frames all the way to tab widgets, tree views, and more, it does not include a one-line HTML text-editing widget. We will create our own widget for this purpose by subclassing QTextEdit; this will deepen our knowledge of QTextEdit and QText-

---

[*]The list of supported HTML tags and CSS properties is available at http://doc.trolltech.com/richtext-html-subset.html.

Document, and it will be a useful widget in later chapters when we want to provide the ability for users to edit single lines of HTML text in database-type applications.

Print-
ing
images
sidebar

363 ☜

This chapter's second section is devoted to printing. We have already seen how to print images and graphics scenes on a page, but in this section we will see how to print multiple page documents, including ones with embedded images. PyQt provides three different techniques for printing documents: one based on composing and printing HTML, another based on creating and printing QTextDocuments, and another based on using QPainter to paint directly onto the printer's pages. We will show and discuss all three approaches.

Rich Text Editing

In this section we will look at rich text editing from two different perspectives. In the first subsection we will create a plain text editor that uses QSyntaxHighlighter to provide syntax highlighting for Python source code. In the second subsection we will create a single-line rich text editor similar to QLineEdit, that has pop-up menus, and that supports various formatting shortcuts such as Ctrl+B and Ctrl+I to toggle bold and italic on and off. In both cases, we use QText-Edit as the foundation on which we build.

Using QSyntaxHighlighter

If we want a Python-savvy text editor with syntax highlighting, we need not create one ourselves. The Tkinter-based IDLE application provides both a "sandbox" in which we can experiment with Python code, and a perfectly good Python code editor. And for more power, we can use Eric4, itself written in PyQt and using QScintilla for its text editing. However, no off-the-shelf editor will necessarily work in just the way we want, and since creating our own is instructive and revealing of what is involved, we will create a simple Python Editor to learn how to use QTextEdit and QSyntaxHighlighter. As the screenshot in Figure 13.1 shows, the Python Editor is a simple main-window-style application with two menus and toolbars. Since we have covered the creation of such applications before, we will focus just on those parts that are relevant to rich text editing, starting with the beginning of the main window's initializer.

```
class MainWindow(QMainWindow):

    def __init__(self, filename=None, parent=None):
        super(MainWindow, self).__init__(parent)

        font = QFont("Courier", 11)
        font.setFixedPitch(True)
        self.editor = TextEdit()
        self.editor.setFont(font)
        self.highlighter = PythonHighlighter(self.editor.document())
        self.setCentralWidget(self.editor)
```

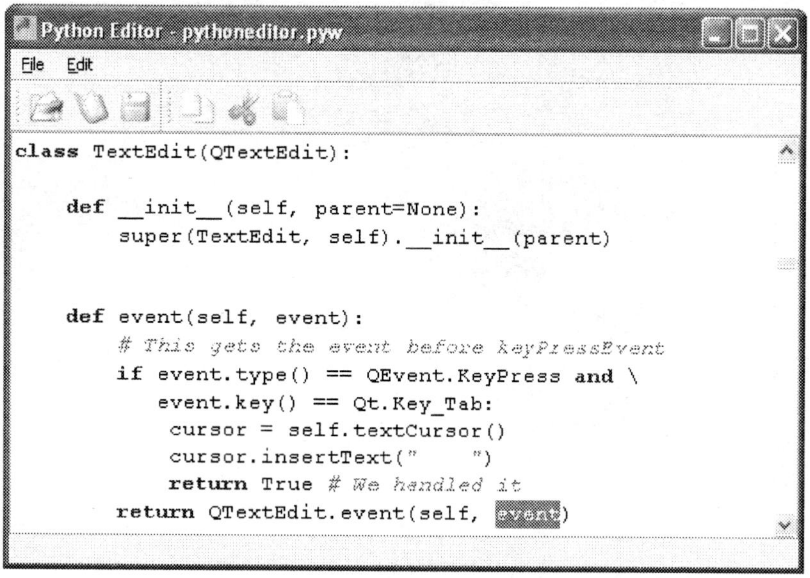

Figure 13.1 *The Python Editor editing itself*

We begin by creating a fixed-pitch font (a font where every character is the same width). Then we create a TextEdit, a custom QTextEdit class that differs from QTextEdit in that it converts Tab key presses into insertions of four spaces. Next we create a PythonHighlighter, a QSyntaxHighlighter subclass, passing it the text editor's QTextDocument—this is the object in which the editor's text and formatting are actually stored. We make the editor the main window's central widget.

The rest of the initializer is concerned with the creation of the actions, menus, and toolbars, things that we are very familiar with and can therefore skip. The only other methods we will look at are two of the three basic file-handling ones, since they involve the text editor.

```python
def fileNew(self):
    if not self.okToContinue():
        return
    document = self.editor.document()
    document.clear()
    document.setModified(False)
    self.filename = None
    self.setWindowTitle("Python Editor - Unnamed")
    self.updateUi()
```

This method simply retrieves and clears the QTextDocument that actually holds the text, and sets the modified flag to False. The result is a blank QTextEdit with no unsaved changes. The updateUi() method is used to enable and disable actions depending on the application's state; see the Enabling and Disabling Actions sidebar on page 385.

```
def loadFile(self):
    fh = None
    try:
        fh = QFile(self.filename)
        if not fh.open(QIODevice.ReadOnly):
            raise IOError, unicode(fh.errorString())
        stream = QTextStream(fh)
        stream.setCodec("UTF-8")
        self.editor.setPlainText(stream.readAll())
        self.editor.document().setModified(False)
        self.setWindowTitle("Python Editor - %s" % \
                QFileInfo(self.filename).fileName())
    except (IOError, OSError), e:
        QMessageBox.warning(self, "Python Editor -- Load Error",
                "Failed to load %s: %s" % (self.filename, e))
    finally:
        if fh is not None:
            fh.close()
```

If a file is loaded—for example, by the user invoking the File→Open action—this method is called. The file-handling code is similar to what we have seen before; the only real difference is that we set the QTextDocument's modified flag to False.

The code for saving (not shown) is very similar to that for loading. We get the file handle, create a QTextStream, set the encoding to UTF-8, and output the entire text using QTextEdit.toPlainText(). We also set the QTextDocument's modified flag to False.

```
class TextEdit(QTextEdit):

    def __init__(self, parent=None):
        super(TextEdit, self).__init__(parent)

    def event(self, event):
        if event.type() == QEvent.KeyPress and \
           event.key() == Qt.Key_Tab:
            cursor = self.textCursor()
            cursor.insertText("    ")
            return True
        return QTextEdit.event(self, event)
```

The preceding code shows the complete TextEdit subclass. Every QTextDocument can be manipulated through a QTextCursor object, which is the programmatic equivalent of a user interacting with the document using key presses and mouse actions.

Enabling and Disabling Actions

Sometimes particular actions are applicable only in certain circumstances. For example, it doesn't make much sense to allow "file save" on a document with no unsaved changes, or, arguably, to allow "file save as" on an empty document. Similarly, neither "edit copy" nor "edit cut" makes sense if there is no selected text. One way to deal with this is to leave all the actions enabled all the time, but to make sure that they do nothing in cases where they don't make sense; for example, if we call QTextEdit.cut(), it will safely do nothing if there is no selected text.

Another solution is to enable and disable actions depending on the application's state. This can be achieved by doing three things: First, making actions that will be enabled and disabled into instance variables so that they can be accessed outside of the initializer; second, creating a method (e.g., updateUi()) that enables and disables actions depending on the application's state; and third, making application-specific signal–slot connections to updateUi() so that it is called whenever the application's state changes.

Using the Python Editor as an example, we need these connections:

```
self.connect(self.editor,
        SIGNAL("selectionChanged()"), self.updateUi)
self.connect(self.editor.document(),
        SIGNAL("modificationChanged(bool)"), self.updateUi)
self.connect(QApplication.clipboard(),
        SIGNAL("dataChanged()"), self.updateUi)
```

These connections mean that if the editor's selection changes, or if the document is modified, or if the clipboard's data changes, we can enable or disable the relevant actions.

```
def updateUi(self, arg=None):
    self.fileSaveAction.setEnabled(
            self.editor.document().isModified())
    self.fileSaveAsAction.setEnabled(
            not self.editor.document().isEmpty())
    enable = self.editor.textCursor().hasSelection()
    self.editCopyAction.setEnabled(enable)
    self.editCutAction.setEnabled(enable)
    self.editPasteAction.setEnabled(self.editor.canPaste())
```

This method is called in response to the signal–slot connections earlier. It is also called explicitly at the end of the initializer to set the user interface's initial state, and at the end of the fileNew() method. The QTextEdit.canPaste() method was introduced with Qt 4.2; for earlier versions, use not QApplication.clipboard().text().isEmpty(). The text cursor and text document classes are covered later in this chapter.

Qt
4.2

QWidget.
event()

310 ☞
The event() handler is called before any of the specific key and mouse event handlers, and it is the only place where we can intercept and handle Tab key presses. If the user pressed Tab we get a QTextCursor from the QTextEdit; this allows us to programmatically interact with the underlying QTextDocument that holds the text. By default, the text cursor returned by a text edit is at the current insertion point (also called the cursor position), so we can simply insert four spaces. Then we return True to tell the event-handling system that we have handled the Tab key press and that no further action (such as changing focus) should take place.
Insert-
ing text
with
QText-
Cursor

☞ 404

To provide syntax highlighting we must create a QSyntaxHighlighter subclass, reimplement the highlightBlock() method, and create an instance of our highlighter with the QTextDocument we want it to apply to as an argument. We did the last part in the MainWindow's initializer, so now we will turn to our QSyntaxHighlighter subclass.

The QSyntaxHighlighter works on a line-by-line basis and provides a simple means of keeping track of state across multiple lines. For the Python Editor we will use regular expressions to identify the Python keywords, comments, and strings, including triple-quoted strings that span multiple lines, so that we can apply highlighting to them. We begin by setting up the regular expressions in the subclass's initializer, which we will look at in two parts.

```
class PythonHighlighter(QSyntaxHighlighter):

    Rules = []

    def __init__(self, parent=None):
        super(PythonHighlighter, self).__init__(parent)

        keywordFormat = QTextCharFormat()
        keywordFormat.setForeground(Qt.darkBlue)
        keywordFormat.setFontWeight(QFont.Bold)
        for pattern in ((r"\band\b", r"\bas\b", r"\bassert\b",
            ...
                r"\byield\b")):
            PythonHighlighter.Rules.append((QRegExp(pattern),
                                            keywordFormat))
```

The Rules static list holds a list of pairs. The first element of each pair is a regular expression (a QRegExp) that is used to match a syntactic construct that can occupy only a single line (such as a Python keyword). The second element is a QTextCharFormat, an object that can hold information regarding how a piece of text should be formatted, such as its font and the pen that should be used to paint it.

We have created a rule for each Python keyword, giving each one the same keywordFormat format. (Most of the keywords are not shown in the snippet as indicated by the ellipsis.) Each keyword has a \b before and after it; this is a regular expression symbol that does not match any text, but rather matches at a word boundary. This means, for example, that in the expression a and b, and will be recognized as a keyword, whereas in the expression a = sand, the and in sand will (correctly) not be recognized.

```python
commentFormat = QTextCharFormat()
commentFormat.setForeground(QColor(0, 127, 0))
commentFormat.setFontItalic(True)
PythonHighlighter.Rules.append((QRegExp(r"#.*"),
                                commentFormat))
self.stringFormat = QTextCharFormat()
self.stringFormat.setForeground(Qt.darkYellow)
stringRe = QRegExp(r"""(?:'[^']*'|"[^"]*")""")
stringRe.setMinimal(True)
PythonHighlighter.Rules.append((stringRe, self.stringFormat))
self.stringRe = QRegExp(r"""(:?"["]".*"["]"|'''.*''')""")
self.stringRe.setMinimal(True)
PythonHighlighter.Rules.append((self.stringRe,
                                self.stringFormat))
self.tripleSingleRe = QRegExp(r"""'''(?!")""")
self.tripleDoubleRe = QRegExp(r'''"""(?!')''')
```

After the keywords, we create a format and regular expression for handling Python comments. The regular expression is not perfect; it does not account for quoted # characters for example.

For strings, we keep the string format as an instance variable since we will need it in the highlightBlock() method when we handle multiline strings. Single-line strings are handled by naive (but fast) regular expressions set up in the initializer and added to the Rules list. At the end we create two more regular expressions. These both use negative lookahead; for example, (?!") means "not followed by "". They are for use in the highlightBlock() method, which we will review next in two parts.

```python
def highlightBlock(self, text):
    NORMAL, TRIPLESINGLE, TRIPLEDOUBLE = range(3)

    for regex, format in PythonHighlighter.Rules:
        i = text.indexOf(regex)
        while i >= 0:
            length = regex.matchedLength()
            self.setFormat(i, length, format)
            i = text.indexOf(regex, i + length)
```

The highlightBlock() method is called for every line that is displayed with the line in the QString text argument.

We begin by setting three possible states: normal, inside a triple-quoted string, and inside a triple double-quoted string. Then we iterate over every rule and wherever we find a match to the rule's regular expression, we set the text's format to the corresponding format for the length of the regular expression's match. The combination of a list of regular expression and format pairs and the for loop shown in the preceding code is sufficient for all syntax highlighting where each syntactic component only ever occupies a single line and where each is capable of being represented by a regular expression.

```
self.setCurrentBlockState(NORMAL)
if text.indexOf(self.stringRe) != -1:
    return
for i, state in ((text.indexOf(self.tripleSingleRe),
                  TRIPLESINGLE),
                 (text.indexOf(self.tripleDoubleRe),
                  TRIPLEDOUBLE)):
    if self.previousBlockState() == state:
        if i == -1:
            i = text.length()
            self.setCurrentBlockState(state)
        self.setFormat(0, i + 3, self.stringFormat)
    elif i > -1:
        self.setCurrentBlockState(state)
        self.setFormat(i, text.length(), self.stringFormat)
```

Next we set the current block's state to normal. The state is an integer of our choice that the QSyntaxHighlighter will associate with the current line. We then test to see whether we have a complete triple quoted string, that is, one that begins and ends in the line; if we do, we have already formatted it, so we are finished and can return.

In PyQt's text-handling classes such as QTextDocument, QTextEdit, and QSyntax-Highlighter, a block of text is essentially a sequence of characters delimited by a newline. For word processor-type documents this equates to a paragraph (since the text-handling class does the line wrapping), but for source code we insert newlines manually, so in this case each block is effectively a single line of code.

We now have three cases to deal with. We are either in a triple-quoted string that began on a previous line and that has not finished in this line; or we have the beginning or end of a triple-quoted string in this line.

If the previous line was in a triple-quoted string and there is no triple quote in this line, this entire line is still in a triple-quoted string, so we set the current block state to the same value as the previous line and format the entire line as triple-quoted. If the previous line's state is triple-quoted and we have a triple quote, it must be the closing triple quote, so we format triple-quoted up to and including the triple quote. In this case we leave the state as normal since that will apply from the end of the triple-quoted string onward. On the other hand, if the previous line's state was not triple-quoted and we find triple quotes, we set the state to triple-quoted and format from these quotes to the end of the line.

This completes our syntax highlighting example. Clearly we could use more sophisticated regular expressions, or even avoid them altogether and use a finite state automaton or a parser to identify which portions of each line require particular formatting. For large texts with complex syntax, syntax highlighting can be computationally expensive, but QSyntaxHighlighter helps to keep the overhead down by formatting only enough lines to correctly highlight the lines that are visible.

A Rich Text Line Edit

In some applications it is a requirement that users can enter single lines of rich text. For example, a database application may have a "description" field where we want the user to be able to use bold, italic, and colors for particular words if they want. We will see examples of this in Chapter 14 and Chapter 16. Unfortunately, PyQt does not provide such a widget. In this subsection we will create a RichTextLineEdit, a subclass of QTextEdit that provides the functionality we need; it is shown in Figure 13.2. In the process we will learn how to programmatically format pieces of text in a QTextEdit, and how to iterate over a QTextEdit's QTextDocument to extract the text and its formatting.

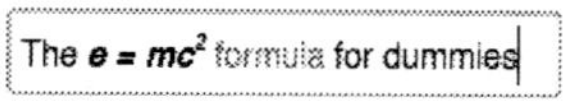

The $e = mc^2$ formula for dummies

Figure 13.2 *The Rich Text Line Edit*

The rich text line edit will support the most common kinds of text formatting that apply to single lines: bold, italic, underline, strikeout, superscript, and subscript. In addition, three font styles will be supported—monospaced, sans serif, and serif—and the ability to set the text's color to a limited range of colors. We will begin with some static constants and the initializer.

```
class RichTextLineEdit(QTextEdit):

    (Bold, Italic, Underline, StrikeOut, Monospaced, Sans, Serif,
     NoSuperOrSubscript, Subscript, Superscript) = range(10)

    def __init__(self, parent=None):
        super(RichTextLineEdit, self).__init__(parent)

        self.monofamily = QString("courier")
        self.sansfamily = QString("helvetica")
        self.seriffamily = QString("times")
        self.setLineWrapMode(QTextEdit.NoWrap)
        self.setTabChangesFocus(True)
        self.setVerticalScrollBarPolicy(Qt.ScrollBarAlwaysOff)
        self.setHorizontalScrollBarPolicy(Qt.ScrollBarAlwaysOff)
        fm = QFontMetrics(self.font())
        h = int(fm.height() * (1.4 if platform.system() == "Windows" \
                               else 1.2))
```

```
            self.setMinimumHeight(h)
            self.setMaximumHeight(int(h * 1.2))
            self.setToolTip("Press <b>Ctrl+M</b> for the text effects "
                    "menu and <b>Ctrl+K</b> for the color menu")
```

We begin by setting some default font families. Nowadays, every platform can be expected to provide Courier, Helvetica, and Times fonts (or fonts for which these names are aliases). Since the widget is a single line, we switch off line wrapping and scrollbars. We also ensure that Tab causes a change of focus rather than the insertion of a Tab character. Calculating a minimum and maximum height will help when we implement the size hint methods, but it is complicated slightly by differences in font metrics across platforms. The tooltip is there to give users a hint that the widget has some special key presses.

Notice that the conditional expression is enclosed in parentheses. They are essential in this case, since without them, on non-Windows platforms, h would always be set to 1 instead of the 20 or 30 or so that we would expect.

```
            def sizeHint(self):
                return QSize(self.document().idealWidth() + 5,
                            self.maximumHeight())
```

The preferred size is the "ideal" width of the text (taking into account font sizes and attributes like bold and italic), with a bit of padding to give a little margin, and the maximum height. The QTextDocument.idealWidth() method was introduced with Qt 4.2.

```
            def minimumSizeHint(self):
                fm = QFontMetrics(self.font())
                return QSize(fm.width("WWWW"), self.minimumHeight())
```

For the minimum size, we take the width of four "W" characters in the widget's default font. Alternatively, we could have simply used an arbitrary amount, say, 40 pixels.

One thing that distinguishes the RichTextLineEdit from a QLineEdit is the user's ability to change the format and color of words and characters. To support this we must provide some means by which the user can apply such changes. We have done this by providing a text effects menu and a color menu, and by supporting some key sequences for formatting. Both menus are invoked by particular key sequences, and the text effects menu is also popped up when a context menu event occurs.

```
            def contextMenuEvent(self, event):
                self.textEffectMenu()
```

A context menu event occurs when the user right-clicks on some platforms, or presses a particular key or key sequence on others. In this case, we simply call the custom textEffectMenu() method, which will pop up a suitable menu. By default, `QTextEdit` provides its own context menu, but by reimplementing the context menu event handler, our code takes precedence.

```
def keyPressEvent(self, event):
    if event.modifiers() & Qt.ControlModifier:
        handled = False
        if event.key() == Qt.Key_B:
            self.toggleBold()
            handled = True
        elif event.key() == Qt.Key_I:
            self.toggleItalic()
            handled = True
        elif event.key() == Qt.Key_K:
            self.colorMenu()
            handled = True
        elif event.key() == Qt.Key_M:
            self.textEffectMenu()
            handled = True
        elif event.key() == Qt.Key_U:
            self.toggleUnderline()
            handled = True
        if handled:
            event.accept()
            return
    if event.key() in (Qt.Key_Enter, Qt.Key_Return):
        self.emit(SIGNAL("returnPressed()"))
        event.accept()
    else:
        QTextEdit.keyPressEvent(self, event)
```

Since users are typing in text, it is natural to provide a keyboard interface for changing the text's format. We have set Ctrl+B to toggle bold, Ctrl+I to toggle italic, and Ctrl+U to toggle underlining. In addition, Ctrl+K invokes the color menu, and Ctrl+M invokes the text effects menu (in addition to being invoked by a context menu event). By calling `accept()` on the key presses we handle ourselves, we are indicating that no further event handling of these key presses is necessary.

If the user presses Return we emit a `returnPressed()` signal since this can be useful; no newline is inserted into the text. Any other key presses are passed on to the base class. The `QTextEdit` class supports its own key sequences—for example, Ctrl+Left Arrow for move left one word, Ctrl+Del for delete the word to the right, Ctrl+C to copy any selected text to the clipboard, and, of course, simple letters, such as a, b, Shift+A, and Shift+B, that are inserted literally.

```
def toggleBold(self):
    self.setFontWeight(QFont.Normal \
            if self.fontWeight() > QFont.Normal else QFont.Bold)
```

PyQt supports several levels of boldness, but we have chosen to take a simple bold on or off approach. The QTextEdit.fontWeight() method returns the font weight at the current insertion point, and similarly the setFontWeight() method is applied at the current insertion point or to the selected text. The QTextEdit is quite smart about formatting, at least on Linux. For example, if text is selected the formatting is applied only to the selection, whereas if there is no selection and the insertion point is at the end of the text, the formatting is applied from that point onward, and if there is no selection and the insertion point is in the middle of a word the formatting is applied to the whole word.

```
def toggleItalic(self):
    self.setFontItalic(not self.fontItalic())

def toggleUnderline(self):
    self.setFontUnderline(not self.fontUnderline())
```

Both italic and underline are simple on/off settings, and on Linux, toggling them works in the same smart way as applying bold or other formatting.

```
def colorMenu(self):
    pixmap = QPixmap(22, 22)
    menu = QMenu("Colour")
    for text, color in (("&Black", Qt.black), ("B&lue", Qt.blue),
            ("Dark Bl&ue", Qt.darkBlue), ("&Cyan", Qt.cyan),
            ("Dar&k Cyan", Qt.darkCyan), ("&Green", Qt.green),
            ("Dark Gr&een", Qt.darkGreen),
            ("M&agenta", Qt.magenta),
            ("Dark Mage&nta", Qt.darkMagenta),
            ("&Red", Qt.red), ("&Dark Red", Qt.darkRed)):
        color = QColor(color)
        pixmap.fill(color)
        action = menu.addAction(QIcon(pixmap), text, self.setColor)
        action.setData(QVariant(color))
    self.ensureCursorVisible()
    menu.exec_(self.viewport().mapToGlobal(
                            self.cursorRect().center()))
```

The color menu is invoked by Ctrl+K. To create the menu we iterate over a list of text and color constants, adding a new menu option for each one. We set the data for each action to be the relevant color; we use this in the setColor() implementation.

We want the menu to pop up at the insertion point, that is, at the text cursor position. This is not necessarily straightforward, because it is possible for the RichTextLineEdit to have more text than it is wide enough to show, and the insertion point could be outside the visible area.

We solve this problem by doing two things. First, we call the base class's QTextEdit.ensureCursorVisible() method; this has the effect of scrolling the editor so that the insertion point is in the visible area—and it does nothing if the insertion point is already visible. Second, we pop up the menu at the center of the insertion point's rectangle. The `cursorRect()` method returns a `QRect` that is in widget coordinates, so we must convert the coordinates of the `QPoint` we get from `QRect.center()` accordingly. We do this by calling `viewport()`, which effectively returns a widget that has the exact dimensions of the visible area, and that knows what region of the editor it represents. We then use the viewport widget's `mapToGlobal()` method to convert the point from the widget coordinate system to the global (screen) coordinate system that is used by `QMenu.exec_()` to position itself.

```python
def setColor(self):
    action = self.sender()
    if action is not None and isinstance(action, QAction):
        color = QColor(action.data())
        if color.isValid():
            self.setTextColor(color)
```

If the user chooses a color the `setColor()` method is called. We retrieve the color that was stored in the calling action's user data, and apply that color to the text. Again, the same logic used for bold, italic, and underlining is used to apply the color to the selected text, or to the current word, or from the end of the text onward.

```python
def textEffectMenu(self):
    format = self.currentCharFormat()
    menu = QMenu("Text Effect")
    for text, shortcut, data, checked in (
            ("&Bold", "Ctrl+B", RichTextLineEdit.Bold,
             self.fontWeight() > QFont.Normal),
            ("&Italic", "Ctrl+I", RichTextLineEdit.Italic,
             self.fontItalic()),
            ...
            ("Subs&cript", None, RichTextLineEdit.Subscript,
             format.verticalAlignment() == \
             QTextCharFormat.AlignSubScript)):
        action = menu.addAction(text, self.setTextEffect)
        if shortcut is not None:
            action.setShortcut(QKeySequence(shortcut))
        action.setData(QVariant(data))
        action.setCheckable(True)
        action.setChecked(checked)
    self.ensureCursorVisible()
    menu.exec_(self.viewport().mapToGlobal(
                        self.cursorRect().center()))
```

The text effects menu method, invoked by `Ctrl+M` or by a context menu event, is similar in structure to the color menu method, but slightly more involved.

We begin by retrieving the text formatting that is currently in force, since we need this information to determine whether to check the various menu options. Then we create a menu made from a list of quadruples (text, shortcut, constant, checked status). The menu is shown in Figure 13.3.

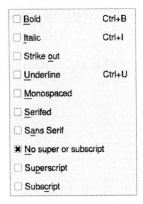

Figure 13.3 *The text effects menu*

We have set keyboard shortcuts for some of the actions—for example, Ctrl+B for bold. We have not used standardized key sequences because we have hard-coded the key presses in the key press event handler shown earlier and so we must be sure to match the key presses that the handler is expecting.

In fact, these shortcuts have no effect in practice because they exist only for the lifetime of the actions they are associated with and the actions exist only while the menu exists, that is, for the duration of the textEffectMenu() method. But this does not matter since we have reimplemented the key event handler to provide these shortcuts ourselves. Shortcuts in menus are useful only for permanent menus such as those added to a main window's menu bar. So, why do we bother with shortcuts in the menu at all? Because adding the shortcuts makes them appear in the menu, which helps the user to learn them. It doesn't solve the problem of how the user finds out about the Ctrl+M and Ctrl+K menus in the first place, but hopefully they will see the tooltip or read about them in the application's manual.

The menu itself is created and popped up in exactly the same way as the color menu. If the user clicks any of the text effects options, the setTextEffect() method is called. We will look at this method in two parts.

```
def setTextEffect(self):
    action = self.sender()
    if action is not None and isinstance(action, QAction):
        what = action.data().toInt()[0]
        if what == RichTextLineEdit.Bold:
            self.toggleBold()
            return
```

```
        if what == RichTextLineEdit.Italic:
            self.toggleItalic()
            return
        if what == RichTextLineEdit.Underline:
            self.toggleUnderline()
            return
```

Each text effect menu action had a constant stored in its user data; this constant is retrieved and held in the what variable. For the simple toggle actions, we only need to call the appropriate toggle method and we are finished.

```
        format = self.currentCharFormat()
        if what == RichTextLineEdit.Monospaced:
            format.setFontFamily(self.monofamily)
        elif what == RichTextLineEdit.Serif:
            format.setFontFamily(self.seriffamily)
        elif what == RichTextLineEdit.Sans:
            format.setFontFamily(self.sansfamily)
        if what == RichTextLineEdit.StrikeOut:
            format.setFontStrikeOut(not format.fontStrikeOut())
        if what == RichTextLineEdit.NoSuperOrSubscript:
            format.setVerticalAlignment(
                    QTextCharFormat.AlignNormal)
        elif what == RichTextLineEdit.Superscript:
            format.setVerticalAlignment(
                    QTextCharFormat.AlignSuperScript)
        elif what == RichTextLineEdit.Subscript:
            format.setVerticalAlignment(
                    QTextCharFormat.AlignSubScript)
        self.mergeCurrentCharFormat(format)
```

To change the font family, strikeout format, or vertical alignment, we must retrieve the current formatting, apply the change that the user has asked for, and then merge the updated format with the current format to make it take effect.

We have now covered all the formatting options that the rich text line edit supports. Once the user has entered their rich text we will no doubt want to retrieve it so that we can store it, search it, or manipulate it. We could use the QTextEdit.toPlainText() method—but that will strip out all the HTML, leaving us no better off than if we had used a QLineEdit. A more suitable alternative is to use QTextEdit.toHtml(), but the HTML returned by this method is quite verbose since it must be general enough to cater for all the PyQt-supported HTML tags.

To put this in perspective, if we have the text "The **bold** cat." (13 characters), where the word "bold" is in bold and the word "cat" is colored red, the toHtml() method returns 503 characters:

```
<html><head><meta name="qrichtext" content="1" />
<style type="text/css"> p, li { white-space: pre-wrap; } </style>
</head>
<body style=" font-family:'Nimbus Sans L'; font-size:11pt;
font-weight:400; font-style:normal; text-decoration:none;">
<p style=" margin-top:0px; margin-bottom:0px; margin-left:0px;
margin-right:0px; -qt-block-indent:0; text-indent:0px;">The
<span style=" font-weight:600;">bold</span>
<span style=" color:#ff0000;">cat</span>
<span style=" color:#000000;">.</span></p></body></html>
```

We have added some newlines to make the output fit neatly on the page. The text may vary slightly depending on the platform and Qt version, but it will still be around 500 characters long. Since the rich text line edit needs to support only a limited subset of tags, a simpler HTML could be used. For example:

```
The <b>bold </b><font color="#ff0000">cat</font>.
```

This is a mere 49 characters. To achieve this simpler HTML format we have provided a toSimpleHtml() method; it is a bit long, so we will review it in three parts.

```
def toSimpleHtml(self):
    html = QString()
    black = QColor(Qt.black)
    block = self.document().begin()
```

We begin by creating an empty target QString and assuming that the text color is black. The QTextDocument class, returned by QTextEdit.document(), provides a means of iterating over the text and the formatting that it contains. Essentially, each major text component, such as a paragraph or a table, is contained in a "block", and we can traverse the blocks using QTextDocument.begin() to retrieve the first block, and QTextBlock.next() to retrieve each subsequent block. An empty document will have an invalid first block.

Each text block contains one or more text "fragments", each of which has its own formatting characteristics. In fact, the structure of QTextDocuments is more complicated than this, but we can ignore the additional details, such as tables, lists, and images, since they are not used in the rich text line edit.

```
while block.isValid():
    iterator = block.begin()
    while iterator != block.end():
        fragment = iterator.fragment()
        if fragment.isValid():
            format = fragment.charFormat()
            family = format.fontFamily()
            color = format.foreground().color()
            text = Qt.escape(fragment.text())
```

```
            if format.verticalAlignment() == \
                QTextCharFormat.AlignSubScript:
                text = QString("<sub>%1</sub>").arg(text)
            elif format.verticalAlignment() == \
                QTextCharFormat.AlignSuperScript:
                text = QString("<sup>%1</sup>").arg(text)
            if format.fontUnderline():
                text = QString("<u>%1</u>").arg(text)
            if format.fontItalic():
                text = QString("<i>%1</i>").arg(text)
            if format.fontWeight() > QFont.Normal:
                text = QString("<b>%1</b>").arg(text)
            if format.fontStrikeOut():
                text = QString("<s>%1</s>").arg(text)
```

For each text fragment in the current block, we extract the character formatting, font family, and text color. Then we extract the text itself with any HTML characters ("&", "<", and ">") converted to the appropriate entities ("&", "<", and ">") by the Qt.escape() function. We then check to see whether the fragment is a subscript or superscript, surrounding the text with appropriate HTML tags if necessary. Then, similar tests are done for other formatting characteristics—specifically, underlining, italics, bold, and strikeout—and in each case the text has the appropriate HTML tags added to it.

```
            if color != black or not family.isEmpty():
                attribs = ""
                if color != black:
                    attribs += ' color="%s"' % color.name()
                if not family.isEmpty():
                    attribs += ' face="%s"' % family
                text = QString("<font%1>%2</font>")\
                                  .arg(attribs).arg(text)
            html += text
            iterator += 1
        block = block.next()
    return html
```

If the font family is not empty or if the color is not black, we must use a <font> tag with the face or color (or both) attributes. At the end of the fragment we append the text that represents the fragment to the html string that holds the entire line of rich text. Since each block may contain one or more fragments, we increment the iterator, dropping out of the inner while loop when it equals QTextBlock.end(), that is, after we have processed the last fragment in the block. Then we call QTextBlock.next() and process the next block's fragments, finally dropping out of the outer while loop when we reach an invalid block which signifies that all the blocks have been processed. And at the very end we return the `html` string that contains the valid (but minimal) HTML necessary to represent the rich text line edit's line of rich text.

This concludes the `RichTextLineEdit` class. We will use it in a couple of later chapters. Although this subclass provides only a single line HTML editor, the techniques we have seen can easily be applied to a `QTextEdit` subclass that is designed to edit entire HTML documents. In such cases, we would probably still provide some additional keyboard support, such as Ctrl+B and Ctrl+I for bold and italic, and perhaps even the text effects context menu. But the other text effects, colors, and formatting that are more appropriate to larger documents such as lists and tables, we would provide through menu options and toolbar buttons like any conventional HTML editor or word processor.

Printing Documents

Getting printed output from PyQt applications can be achieved in a number of ways. One approach is to produce output in a form that another program can print, such as producing HTML for a Web browser to print or SVG for an SVG-savvy drawing program to print.

From Qt 4.1, users can produce PDF documents through the Print dialog by checking the "print to file" option. It is also possible to produce PDF documents programmatically. For example, assuming that `document` is a `QTextDocument`:

```
printer = QPrinter()
printer.setPageSize(QPrinter.Letter)
printer.setOutputFormat(QPrinter.PdfFormat)
printer.setOutputFileName(filename)
document.print_(printer)
```

These approaches are not as convenient for users as having a printing facility within the application itself, and to do this PyQt offers three main choices.

1. We can generate HTML, give it to a `QTextDocument`, and use `QTextDocument.print_()` passing in a `QPrinter`, or `QTextDocument.drawContents()`, passing in a `QPainter` to render the document.

2. We can create a `QTextDocument` and retrieve a `QTextCursor` from it through which we can generate the document programmatically, and again using the `print_()` or `drawContents()` methods to render it.

3. We can create a `QPainter` to paint directly onto a `QPrinter`, that is, onto the printed pages. This is the most tedious approach, but it provides the greatest level of control.

The example application covered in this section shows all three techniques. It prints customer statements, with each `Statement` object holding a company name, contact name, address, and list of transactions, each of which is a (`QDate`, `float`) tuple. The `Statement` class also provides a `balance()` method that returns

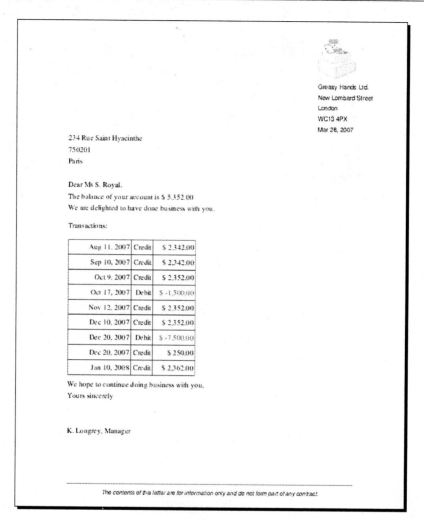

Figure 13.4 *A page printed using QPainter*

the sum of the transactions. We want to print the issuer's logo and address at the top right, below that the date, and on the left, the customer's address, then a form letter where the contents vary depending on whether the customer is in credit or debit, then a table of transactions, and a closing paragraph. Naturally, we also want each statement to begin on a fresh page. We will assume that all the statements are held in a list called `self.statements`, and that our printing is done using the methods of a form which holds these statements. The pages will look like the one shown in Figure 13.4.

But before looking at the three general printing techniques, we will look at how to print images, in particular showing the implementation of the `filePrint()` method used by the Image Changer application that we covered in Chapter 6.

Printing Images

Back in Chapter 6, we had a MainWindow.filePrint() method for printing an image, but we did not look at its implementation at that point because we had not covered QPainter. Now that we have seen QPainter in Chapter 11, and have seen a generic "print image" function, we can look at the implementation of the filePrint() method used by the Image Changer application. (The source code is in chap06/imagechanger.pyw.)

Print-
ing
Images
sidebar

363 ☜

```
def filePrint(self):
    if self.image.isNull():
        return
    if self.printer is None:
        self.printer = QPrinter(QPrinter.HighResolution)
        self.printer.setPageSize(QPrinter.Letter)
    form = QPrintDialog(self.printer, self)
    if form.exec_():
        painter = QPainter(self.printer)
        rect = painter.viewport()
        size = self.image.size()
        size.scale(rect.size(), Qt.KeepAspectRatio)
        painter.setViewport(rect.x(), rect.y(), size.width(),
                            size.height())
        painter.drawImage(0, 0, self.image)
```

If this is the first time the user has tried to print an image the printer instance variable will be None, so we instantiate it and provide a sensible default for the page size. (The default page size is QPrinter.A4.) Once we have a printer object, we create and pop up a modal QPrintDialog; the user can use this to choose the printer they want to print on and various other print-related options. This dialog varies from system to system since PyQt uses the system's native print dialog if one is available. If the user clicks Print, we are able to print the image.

PyQt has a notion of a "paint device", something on which lines, text, shapes, and images can be painted. As we have seen in earlier chapters, a widget is a paint device—its appearance is drawn, with the illusions of depth achieved by drawing shadows and highlights. A QImage is a paint device, and so is a QPrinter. All paint devices can be drawn on using a QPainter, so we create a new QPainter primed to paint on the QPrinter.

View-
port and
window
coordi-
nates

329 ☜

We get the rectangle that represents the painter's viewport. The viewport is the painter's drawing area, and in the case of a painter that is tied to a printer, this means the area of the page that can actually be drawn on. (Many printers cannot draw right up to the edges of the paper.) We then obtain the image's size as a QSize object, and then scale that object to fit inside the printer's viewport rectangle while preserving the size's aspect ratio. This has no effect if the image is already small enough to fit. Next, we change the printer's viewport rectangle to match our scaled rectangle, preserving its original origin, but with the scaled width and height. Finally we draw the image at the painter's origin and we are done.

If the user wants a PDF file, they can invoke the "print" action and choose the "print to file" option. On some platforms it is also possible to get PostScript output by changing the "print to file" filename's extension to .ps.

Printing Documents Using HTML and QTextDocument

The first approach we will show involves creating a string containing HTML, and using a QTextDocument to render the HTML to a QPrinter. The printVia-Html() method is quite long, so we will look at it in three parts.

```python
def printViaHtml(self):
    html = u""
    for statement in self.statements:
        date = QDate.currentDate().toString(DATE_FORMAT)
        address = Qt.escape(statement.address).replace(",", "<br>")
        contact = Qt.escape(statement.contact)
        balance = statement.balance()
        html += ("<p align=right><img src=':/logo.png'></p>"
                 "<p align=right>Greasy Hands Ltd."
                 "<br>New Lombard Street"
                 "<br>London<br>WC13 4PX<br>%s</p>"
                 "<p>%s</p><p>Dear %s,</p>"
                 "<p>The balance of your account is %s.") % (
                date, address, contact,
                QString("$ %L1").arg(float(balance), 0, "f", 2))
        if balance < 0:
            html += (" <p><font color=red><b>Please remit the "
                     "amount owing immediately.</b></font>")
        else:
            html += (" We are delighted to have done business "
                     "with you.")
        html += ("</p><p> </p><p>"
                 "<table border=1 cellpadding=2 "
                 "cellspacing=2><tr><td colspan=3>"
                 "Transactions</td></tr>")
```

We create an empty unicode variable called html. Then we iterate over all the statements. The contact and address contain text, so we take the precaution of escaping any HTML characters. The address is stored as a single line with commas separating each part; we replace commas with line breaks. The logo is in a resource file, as indicated by the :/ prefix; it could have been any file in the filesystem, and it could be in any of the image formats that PyQt supports.

Up to now we have formatted strings using Python's % operator. But in some cases, using PyQt's string formatting is advantageous. The QString class has an arg() method that can be given an object, usually a string or a number, with some optional parameters. Each arg() call replaces the leftmost %n item in the QString with suitable text. For example:

```
QString("Copied %1 bytes to %2").arg(5387).arg("log.txt")
```

results in the string:

```
Copied 5387 bytes to log.txt
```

The %n items have no formatting syntax like Python's % operator, but formatting can be achieved by passing additional arguments to the arg() method. It is also possible to localize the formatting by using %Ln. For example:

```
QString("Copied %L1 bytes to %2").arg(5387).arg("log.txt")
```

results in the string:

```
Copied 5,387 bytes to log.txt
```

in the United States and the United Kingdom, with the number coming out as 5.387 in some other countries.

In the case of our example, we want to print the amounts using two decimal digits, and with the whole number part having its digits grouped in threes. This can be achieved by using arg() with four arguments—the amount as a float, the minimum number of characters for the number to occupy, the output format ("f" for normal floating-point numbers and "e" or "E" for scientific notation) and the number of digits after the decimal place. It is also possible to give a fifth argument, a padding character, if a minimum number of characters is specified.

In the example we have used:

```
QString("$ %L1").arg(float(balance), 0, "f", 2))
```

A balance of 64 325.852 would be output as the string $ 64,325.85 in the United States.

Returning to the code, we add some text that varies depending on whether the customer is in debit or credit. Then we create the head of an HTML table with three columns, with the first row spanning all the columns and containing the title "Transactions". The   is an HTML entity that signifies a nonbreaking space.

```
for date, amount in statement.transactions:
    color, status = "black", "Credit"
    if amount < 0:
        color, status = "red", "Debit"
```

```
            html += ("<tr><td align=right>%s</td>"
                    "<td>%s</td><td align=right>"
                    "<font color=%s>%s</font></td></tr>" % (
                    date.toString(DATE_FORMAT), status, color,
                    QString("$ %L1").arg(
                            float(abs(amount)), 0, "f", 2)))
        html += ("</table></p><p style='page-break-after:always;'>"
                "We hope to continue doing "
                "business with you,<br>Yours sincerely,"
                "<br><br>K. Longrey, Manager</p>")
```

We iterate over each transaction, adding a new row to the table for each one. Then we add the closing table tag and add the final paragraph. We want a page break to follow the last paragraph, and this can be achieved by setting the page-break-after style option to always. This style option was added in Qt 4.2 and is ignored in earlier versions.

```
        dialog = QPrintDialog(self.printer, self)
        if dialog.exec_():
            document = QTextDocument()
            document.setHtml(html)
            document.print_(self.printer)
```

At the end we simply pop up a print dialog, and if the user clicks Print, we create a new QTextDocument, set its text to the HTML we have generated in the html string, and tell the document to print itself on the printer.

Creating an HTML string and printing it using a QTextDocument is probably the quickest and easiest way to produce printed output in PyQt. The only downside is that it can be tricky to exercise fine control, although we can use style attributes and set a style sheet.

Printing Documents Using QTextCursor and QTextDocument

We will now see how to achieve the same thing by creating a QTextDocument programmatically, rather than by creating an HTML string and using set-Html(). The code is more than twice as long (as is the code that uses QPainter that follows), but we should not infer from this particular example that these techniques will necessarily require more code in general.

```
    def printViaQCursor(self):
        dialog = QPrintDialog(self.printer, self)
        if not dialog.exec_():
            return
        logo = QPixmap(":/logo.png")
        headFormat = QTextBlockFormat()
        headFormat.setAlignment(Qt.AlignLeft)
```

```
headFormat.setTextIndent(
        self.printer.pageRect().width() - logo.width() - 216)
bodyFormat = QTextBlockFormat()
bodyFormat.setAlignment(Qt.AlignJustify)
lastParaBodyFormat = QTextBlockFormat(bodyFormat)
lastParaBodyFormat.setPageBreakPolicy(
        QTextFormat.PageBreak_AlwaysAfter)
rightBodyFormat = QTextBlockFormat()
rightBodyFormat.setAlignment(Qt.AlignRight)
headCharFormat = QTextCharFormat()
headCharFormat.setFont(QFont("Helvetica", 10))
bodyCharFormat = QTextCharFormat()
bodyCharFormat.setFont(QFont("Times", 11))
redBodyCharFormat = QTextCharFormat(bodyCharFormat)
redBodyCharFormat.setForeground(Qt.red)
tableFormat = QTextTableFormat()
tableFormat.setBorder(1)
tableFormat.setCellPadding(2)
```

We have chosen to create the document only if the user clicks Print in the Print dialog, rather than creating it and only asking them at the end, as we did before. We create a set of text formats—some are QTextBlockFormats that have attributes which are applicable to entire paragraphs, and others are QTextCharFormats with attributes that are applicable to fragments of paragraphs, such as phrases, words, and individual characters. We use the paragraph formats to set up text alignments, and the character formats to set up fonts and colors. The value, 216, is just an offset in points, $\frac{216''}{72}$, that is, 3 inches, by which the logo and address text will be indented.

The programmatic equivalent of setting the page-break-after style option in an HTML <p> tag is to use the QTextBlockFormat.setPageBreakPolicy() method on a paragraph format, but this is available only from Qt 4.2. In addition to the text and table formats used in this example, there are also formats for lists, frames, and images.

```
document = QTextDocument()
cursor = QTextCursor(document)
mainFrame = cursor.currentFrame()
page = 1
```

Once we have the formats ready, we create a QTextDocument. Then we create a QTextCursor for the document that gives us the programmatic equivalent of the user's insertion point in a QTextEdit.

Earlier we mentioned that QTextDocuments consist of a series of blocks; in fact, they consist of a root frame that itself contains a series of items which can be blocks (e.g., text blocks and table blocks), or frames, in a potentially recursive structure. In our case, we have a document with a single root frame that contains a series of text blocks and tables. Each cell in our tables holds a text block, and when we have finished inserting the cells in a table we need to go back up the document's hierarchy to the point that follows the table (but is not inside the table) so that we can insert the text that follows each table. For this reason we keep a reference to the currentFrame(), the one frame we are using, in the mainFrame variable.

```
for statement in self.statements:
    cursor.insertBlock(headFormat, headCharFormat)
    cursor.insertImage(":/logo.png")
    for text in ("Greasy Hands Ltd.", "New Lombard Street",
                 "London", "WC13 4PX",
                 QDate.currentDate().toString(DATE_FORMAT)):
        cursor.insertBlock(headFormat, headCharFormat)
        cursor.insertText(text)
    for line in statement.address.split(", "):
        cursor.insertBlock(bodyFormat, bodyCharFormat)
        cursor.insertText(line)
    cursor.insertBlock(bodyFormat)
    cursor.insertBlock(bodyFormat, bodyCharFormat)
    cursor.insertText("Dear %s," % statement.contact)
    cursor.insertBlock(bodyFormat)
    cursor.insertBlock(bodyFormat, bodyCharFormat)
    balance = statement.balance()
    cursor.insertText(QString(
            "The balance of your account is $ %L1.").arg(
            float(balance), 0, "f", 2))
    if balance < 0:
        cursor.insertBlock(bodyFormat, redBodyCharFormat)
        cursor.insertText("Please remit the amount owing "
                          "immediately.")
    else:
        cursor.insertBlock(bodyFormat, bodyCharFormat)
        cursor.insertText("We are delighted to have done "
                          "business with you.")
    cursor.insertBlock(bodyFormat, bodyCharFormat)
    cursor.insertText("Transactions:")
    table = cursor.insertTable(len(statement.transactions), 3,
                               tableFormat)
```

Once the document is set up and we have a QTextCursor through which we can insert items into the document, we are ready to iterate over each of the statements.

For each paragraph we want to insert, we insert a new block with a paragraph and a character format. We then insert the text or image we want the paragraph to contain. We can insert empty paragraphs (to consume vertical space) by inserting a block without inserting anything into it.

To insert a table we must specify how many rows and columns it should have, as well as its format.

```
row = 0
for date, amount in statement.transactions:
    cellCursor = table.cellAt(row, 0).firstCursorPosition()
    cellCursor.setBlockFormat(rightBodyFormat)
    cellCursor.insertText(date.toString(DATE_FORMAT),
                          bodyCharFormat)
    cellCursor = table.cellAt(row, 1).firstCursorPosition()
    if amount > 0:
        cellCursor.insertText("Credit", bodyCharFormat)
    else:
        cellCursor.insertText("Debit", bodyCharFormat)
    cellCursor = table.cellAt(row, 2).firstCursorPosition()
    cellCursor.setBlockFormat(rightBodyFormat)
    format = bodyCharFormat
    if amount < 0:
        format = redBodyCharFormat
    cellCursor.insertText(QString("$ %L1").arg(
            float(amount), 0, "f", 2), format)
    row += 1
```

Each row of the table represents a single transaction, with a date, some text ("Debit" or "Credit"), and the amount, colored red in the case of debits. To insert items into a table we must obtain a QTextCursor that gives access to a cell at a specified row and column. We do not have to insert a new block into a cell (unless we want more than one paragraph in a cell), so we simply set the cell's paragraph format and insert the text we want.

```
cursor.setPosition(mainFrame.lastPosition())
cursor.insertBlock(bodyFormat, bodyCharFormat)
cursor.insertText("We hope to continue doing business "
                  "with you,")
cursor.insertBlock(bodyFormat, bodyCharFormat)
cursor.insertText("Yours sincerely")
cursor.insertBlock(bodyFormat)
if page == len(self.statements):
    cursor.insertBlock(bodyFormat, bodyCharFormat)
else:
    cursor.insertBlock(lastParaBodyFormat, bodyCharFormat)
cursor.insertText("K. Longrey, Manager")
page += 1
```

Once we have finished populating a table and want to add items after it, we must reset the position of our text cursor to be just after the table. If we do not do this, the cursor will simply insert inside the table and we will end up with the rest of the first page inside the table, and the second page inside the first, and so on recursively! To avoid this problem we set the text cursor to be at the last position in the document, which is the position following the last thing we inserted, that is, just after the table.

Finishing the page is simply a matter of inserting additional blocks with the appropriate formats, followed by inserting the relevant texts. For all pages except the last, we set the last block's format to be lastParaBodyFormat, which (using Qt 4.2) will ensure that what follows will be on a fresh page.

```
document.print_(self.printer)
```

The very last statement is where we print the document on the printer. At this point the document is complete, so we could call toHtml() on it to get it in HTML format if that was preferred. It also means that we can use a QTextCursor in conjunction with a QTextDocument to create HTML pages programmatically if we wanted.

The advantage of using QTextDocument, whether we give it an HTML string or whether we populate it using a QTextCursor, is that we can avoid doing lots of calculations to see where text should be placed on the page. The disadvantage is that PyQt puts page numbers on our documents whether we like them or not, and it does not give us fine positional control. Neither of these problems occurs if we use a QPainter.

Printing Documents Using QPainter

We will conclude this section by looking at how to print using QPainter. Taking this approach means that we have the chore of doing all the position calculations ourselves, but also the benefit of being able to draw anything anywhere on the page, without being limited to what can be represented by HTML or by a QTextDocument. In addition, the painting itself uses the same methods and techniques that we have seen in the previous two chapters, since PyQt has a uniform approach to painting whether on widgets, on images, or on printed pages.

```
def printViaQPainter(self):
    dialog = QPrintDialog(self.printer, self)
    if not dialog.exec_():
        return
    LeftMargin = 72
    sansFont = QFont("Helvetica", 10)
    sansLineHeight = QFontMetrics(sansFont).height()
    serifFont = QFont("Times", 11)
    fm = QFontMetrics(serifFont)
    DateWidth = fm.width(" September 99, 2999 ")
    CreditWidth = fm.width(" Credit ")
    AmountWidth = fm.width(" W999999.99 ")
    serifLineHeight = fm.height()
```

```
logo = QPixmap(":/logo.png")
painter = QPainter(self.printer)
pageRect = self.printer.pageRect()
page = 1
```

We begin by presenting the user with the Print dialog, bailing out if they
click Cancel. If the print is to go ahead, we set up some fonts, widths, and line
heights, and create a QPainter to draw directly on the printer. If the specified
fonts are not available, PyQt will use the most closely matching fonts it can
find instead.

```
for statement in self.statements:
    painter.save()
    y = 0
    x = pageRect.width() - logo.width() - LeftMargin
    painter.drawPixmap(x, 0, logo)
    y += logo.height() + sansLineHeight
    painter.setFont(sansFont)
    painter.drawText(x, y, "Greasy Hands Ltd.")
    y += sansLineHeight
    painter.drawText(x, y, "New Lombard Street")
    y += sansLineHeight
    painter.drawText(x, y, "London")
    y += sansLineHeight
    painter.drawText(x, y, "WC13 4PX")
    y += sansLineHeight
    painter.drawText(x, y,
            QDate.currentDate().toString(DATE_FORMAT))
    y += sansLineHeight
    painter.setFont(serifFont)
    x = LeftMargin
    for line in statement.address.split(", "):
        painter.drawText(x, y, line)
        y += serifLineHeight
    y += serifLineHeight
```

For each statement we print the logo, address, date, and customer's address.
We save the painter's state, including its font, pen, brush, and transformation
matrix, at the beginning of each statement, and restore the state at the end
of each statement. This ensures that we always start each statement with a
clean slate.

```
    painter.drawText(x, y, "Dear %s," % statement.contact)
    y += serifLineHeight
    balance = statement.balance()
    painter.drawText(x, y, QString("The balance of your "
            "account is $ %L1").arg(float(balance), 0, "f", 2))
    y += serifLineHeight
```

```
            if balance < 0:
                painter.setPen(Qt.red)
                text = "Please remit the amount owing immediately."
            else:
                text = ("We are delighted to have done business "
                        "with you.")
            painter.drawText(x, y, text)
```

After the addresses we print the form letter with its text depending on the state of the account as usual.

```
            painter.setPen(Qt.black)
            y += int(serifLineHeight * 1.5)
            painter.drawText(x, y, "Transactions:")
            y += serifLineHeight
            option = QTextOption(Qt.AlignRight|Qt.AlignVCenter)
```

For the table of transactions we begin by writing the table's title and then we create a `QTextOption` object. These objects can be used to specify a variety of text-formatting options, including alignment and word wrapping.

```
            for date, amount in statement.transactions:
                x = LeftMargin
                h = int(fm.height() * 1.3)
                painter.drawRect(x, y, DateWidth, h)
                painter.drawText(
                        QRectF(x + 3, y + 3, DateWidth - 6, h - 6),
                        date.toString(DATE_FORMAT), option)
                x += DateWidth
                painter.drawRect(x, y, CreditWidth, h)
                text = "Credit"
                if amount < 0:
                    text = "Debit"
                painter.drawText(
                        QRectF(x + 3, y + 3, CreditWidth - 6, h - 6),
                        text, option)
                x += CreditWidth
                painter.drawRect(x, y, AmountWidth, h)
                if amount < 0:
                    painter.setPen(Qt.red)
                painter.drawText(
                        QRectF(x + 3, y + 3, AmountWidth - 6, h - 6),
                        QString("$ %L1").arg(float(amount), 0, "f", 2),
                        option)
                painter.setPen(Qt.black)
                y += h
```

To draw the transactions table we must draw both the text and the lines ourselves. We have cheated slightly by drawing a rectangle for each of the table's cells rather than just drawing the lines that separate the cells. This means that rectangles that share common lines—for example, the right edge of one rectangle and the left edge of the rectangle beside it—will overstrike one another—but visually this is not noticeable.

```
y += serifLineHeight
x = LeftMargin
painter.drawText(x, y, "We hope to continue doing "
                       "business with you,")
y += serifLineHeight
painter.drawText(x, y, "Yours sincerely")
y += serifLineHeight * 3
painter.drawText(x, y, "K. Longrey, Manager")
```

The final paragraph is the same as the one in the previous two methods, but this time we will add a disclaimer at the bottom of the page.

```
x = LeftMargin
y = pageRect.height() - 72
painter.drawLine(x, y, pageRect.width() - LeftMargin, y)
y += 2
font = QFont("Helvetica", 9)
font.setItalic(True)
painter.setFont(font)
option = QTextOption(Qt.AlignCenter)
option.setWrapMode(QTextOption.WordWrap)
painter.drawText(
        QRectF(x, y,
               pageRect.width() - 2 * LeftMargin, 31),
        "The contents of this letter are for information "
        "only and do not form part of any contract.",
        option)
```

It is much easier adding footers when using a QPainter because we know exactly what the page's dimensions are and can paint at any (x, y) position we like.

```
page += 1
if page <= len(self.statements):
    self.printer.newPage()
painter.restore()
```

Finally, we switch to a new page after every statement except the last one. This works with all Qt 4 versions, unlike the previous two approaches which can paginate properly only with Qt 4.2 or later.

Although printing using a QPainter requires more care and calculation than using a QTextDocument, it does give us complete control over the output.

Summary

Using QSyntaxHighlighter to provide syntax highlighting for plain text that has a regular syntax, such as source code, is quite straightforward. Handling multiline constructs can also be done quite easily. The hardest part is handling ambiguous and some special cases, such as quotes inside quoted strings or start-of-comment symbols that are inside quotes or other constructs that cancel their syntactic meaning. An alternative is to use the QScintilla editor.

The QTextEdit class is very powerful and versatile. Out of the box it can be used to edit both plain text and HTML. It is not difficult to create QTextEdit subclasses that provide key and context menu event handlers to give the user basic formatting options, and the techniques can easily be extended to provide menus and toolbars through which users could add, edit, and delete lists, tables, and images, and could apply formatting whether at the character level, such as underlining and strikeout, or at the paragraph level, such as aligning left, right, centered, or justified.

The HTML returned by QTextEdit.toHtml() is rather verbose because it must support a wide range of HTML tags. We can provide our own methods to traverse a QTextDocument's structure and output our own format. In the example we output a much simpler and shorter HTML, but the same approach could be used to output XML or other kinds of markup.

Applying most simple formatting to the underlying QTextDocument used by QTextEdit, QTextBrowser, QLabel, and QGraphicsTextItem is quite straightforward. Applying more advanced formatting, such as tables can be trickier because we must be careful not to keep nesting blocks inside each other.

Printed documents can be produced indirectly by outputting HTML or SVG, or directly by using a QPrinter to print on a physical printer, or from Qt 4.1 to output PDF files. Printed documents can be produced by creating an HTML string and giving it to a QTextDocument, or by programmatically inserting items into a blank QTextDocument. In both cases, the QTextDocument can be asked to print itself on a printer, or to draw itself on a QPainter.

Using HTML is the easiest approach for those familiar with HTML tags, and a fair amount of control can be achieved by using style attributes and a style sheet. Using a QTextCursor to insert into a QTextDocument makes finer control quite easy to achieve, especially for those unfamiliar with style sheets. The greatest control over page appearance is achieved by using a QPainter directly. This is also the easiest approach for those who are comfortable using the QPainter API, or who want to reuse the same code for painting and for printing. Such code reuse can also be achieved using a QTextDocument, since they can be rendered in QLabels and other widgets that use QTextDocuments. They can also be drawn onto arbitrary paint devices, such as widgets, using a QPainter, and they can be printed.

Exercise

Add two new actions, Indent and Unindent, with the shortcuts Ctrl+] and Ctrl+[. Suitable icons are provided in the images subdirectory, and are already in the resources.qrc file. Both actions should be added to the Edit menu and to the edit toolbar. Implement the methods editIndent() and editUnindent(). They should indent or unindent the current line by inserting or removing four spaces at the beginning of the line, no matter where the insertion point is in the line. At the end, the insertion point should be at the same relative position as it was before the indent or unindent. The actions should be instance variables and should be enabled only if the document is not empty.

Make sure that you use QTextCursor.beginEditBlock() and QTextCursor.endEditBlock() so that the indent or unindent can be undone as a single action—QTextEdit supports Ctrl+Z for undo. The two methods can be written in a total of about 20 lines.

If you want to achieve something more ambitious, try extending the two methods so that if there is a selection, the indent or unindent is applied to all the lines in the selection. This will add about another 40 lines, and it is slightly tricky. Make sure that at the end the original selection is in place.

You will need to read the documentation for QTextCursor and, especially, the anchor(), position(), setPosition(), and movePosition() methods.

A solution is provided in chap13/pythoneditor_ans.pyw.

14

● Using the Convenience Item Widgets
● Creating Custom Models
● Creating Custom Delegates

Model/View Programming

Model/view programming is a technique that involves separating data from its visual representation. It was first popularized as the MVC (model/view/controller) paradigm used in the Smalltalk programming language.

A *model* is a class that provides a uniform interface through which data items can be accessed. A *view* is a class that can present the data items from a model to the user on-screen. A *controller* is a class that mediates between the user interface (e.g., mouse events and key presses) to provide a means by which users can manipulate data items.

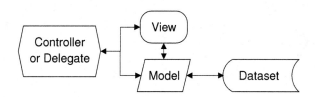

Figure 14.1 *Model / view / controller and model / view / delegate*

The MVC approach offers several benefits. For example, huge datasets can be handled, because only the data that is actually displayed or edited is read or written from or to the data source. Different views of the same dataset access the same underlying data with no data duplication: This is useful for viewing the same data in different ways using two or more views, or for viewing different parts of a large dataset. Also, if we change how the dataset is stored, for example, from a binary file to a database, only the model needs to be adapted—all the logic in the view and the controller will continue to work because the model fully insulates them from the data.

PyQt uses a slight variation on MVC, called model/view/delegate, that provides all the same benefits as MVC. Both are depicted schematically in Figure 14.1. The key difference is that some of the functionality that classic MVC reserves

413

for the controller can be implemented either in the delegate or in the model with the model/view/delegate approach.

Conceptually, the model/view/delegate approach works like this: The data is read and written from and to the data source by the model. The view asks the model for the data items that the view wants to display, that is, those items that are visible in the user interface. For each item that the view displays, it gives the item and a painter to the delegate, and asks the delegate to paint the item. Similarly, if the user initiates editing, the view asks the delegate to provide a suitable editor, and if the user accepts their edit (i.e., if the user does not press Esc to cancel), the updated data is passed back to the model. An editor can be any widget, and it is drawn in-place exactly on top of the item, giving the application's user the illusion that the item has become editable.

Every data item in the model (and therefore implicitly every item of data in the dataset), can be identified by a unique QModelIndex. Each model index has three important attributes: a row, a column, and a parent.

1. For one-dimensional models (e.g., lists) only the row is used.

2. For two-dimensional models (e.g., tables, including database tables) only the row and column are used.

3. For hierarchical models (e.g., trees) all three attributes are used.

Although QModelIndexes can refer to any data item in any model, we need to bear in mind that conceptually there are really two kinds of model. The first kind are tables, which include lists since these are just tables with a single column. When we work with tables we work in terms of rows and columns. The second kind are trees. For trees we work in terms of parents and children. (It is possible to take a rows-and-columns approach with trees, but this goes against the grain and will lead to code that is slow and difficult to maintain.)

No matter what the underlying dataset, whether the data is in memory, databases, or files, PyQt models provide the same uniform interface for data access—in particular, the QAbstractItemModel.data() and QAbstractItem-Model.setData() methods. It is also possible to create custom models that contain the dataset inside themselves, such as a model that is a wrapper around a dictionary or a list.

All data held in a model is stored as QVariants. This does not mean that all the dataset's data must be QVariants—the model is an interface to a dataset and in any given session may only ever access a small portion of the entire dataset, so only those data items that are actually used will be stored as QVariants, and then only in the model. The model is responsible for converting from the underlying dataset's data types to and from the QVariants the model uses internally.

Some PyQt widgets, including QListWidget, QTableWidget, and QTreeWidget, are views with models and delegates aggregated inside them. These are the convenience item view widgets and they are especially useful for small and ad hoc datasets. We will see them in use in this chapter's first section.

PyQt also provides some pure view widgets, including QListView, QTableView, and QTreeView. These must be used in conjunction with external models, either ones we create ourselves or one of the built-in models such as QStringListModel, QDirModel, or QSqlTableModel. In the second section, we will see how to create a custom model that can be used with a view widget.

All the convenience views and pure views use a default delegate that controls how data items are presented and edited. In this chapter's last section, we will see how to create a custom delegate to exercise complete control over the editing and presentation of data items. Custom delegates can be used with any view, whether it is a convenience view or a pure view.

This chapter provides a foundation in using PyQt's model/view classes. In Chapter 15, we will see how to use the model/view classes to work with databases, and in Chapter 16, we will cover more advanced uses, including the creation of custom views, improving code reuse in delegates, and presenting tabular data in trees.

We use the same dataset for all the examples in this chapter to make it easier to compare and contrast the techniques used. The dataset's items are described in the first section.

Using the Convenience Item Widgets

The convenience item widgets are view widgets that have built-in models. They use a default delegate for presenting and editing data, but this can be replaced by a custom delegate if we wish.

The screenshot in Figure 14.2 shows the same dataset in three different convenience view widgets. This means that the data is copied into each widget separately, so there is considerable data duplication. Another issue is that if we allow the user to edit the data, we must write code to ensure that all the views stay in sync. These problems would not exist if we used a custom model, as we will see in the next section.

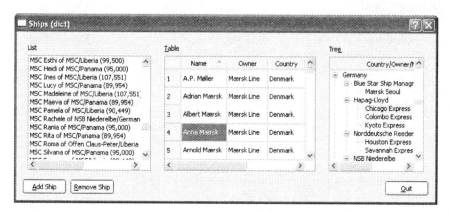

Figure 14.2 *QListWidget, QTableWidget, and QTreeWidget in action*

The dataset we are using is a set of information about container ships. Each ship is represented by a Ship object, defined in the chap14/ships.py module.

```
class Ship(object):

    def __init__(self, name, owner, country, teu=0, description=""):
        self.name = QString(name)
        self.owner = QString(owner)
        self.country = QString(country)
        self.teu = teu
        self.description = QString(description)

    def __cmp__(self, other):
        return QString.localeAwareCompare(self.name.toLower(),
                                          other.name.toLower())
```

The preceding code is the complete Ship class. The integer teu attribute stands for "twenty-foot equivalent units", that is, how many 20-foot containers the ship can hold. (Nowadays most containers are 40 feet, so each counts as 2 TEUs.) The name, owner, and country attributes are all plain text, but the description attribute holds one line of HTML.

The __cmp__() special method provides a means of comparison for the purpose of sorting. The QString.localeAwareCompare() method does string comparisons in a locale-sensitive way—for example, correctly handling accented characters.

Since we are using convenience views with no custom delegates, we have only limited control over the editing of the data items. For example, we cannot offer drop-down comboboxes for editing owners and countries, or use spinboxes for editing TEUs. Also, the description text is shown raw, rather than being interpreted as HTML. We will, of course, solve all of these problems as the chapter progresses, but for now we will just focus on using the convenience views.

For the list, table, and tree items that are used with the convenience view widgets, it is possible to set their font, text alignment, text color, and background color, and to give them an icon or make them checkable. For the pure view widgets, we can exercise similar control over the appearance of items through the custom model; or exercise complete control over both the appearance and the editing of items by using a custom delegate.

The code for this section's example is in chap14/ships-dict.pyw. The data is held in a Python dictionary that itself is wrapped in the ships.ShipContainer class. We will discuss only the code that is relevant to model/view programming here—the rest of the code uses ideas and idioms that we already saw earlier in the book—for example, in Chapter 8—and is not hard to follow.

```
class MainForm(QDialog):

    def __init__(self, parent=None):
```

```
super(MainForm, self).__init__(parent)

listLabel = QLabel("&List")
self.listWidget = QListWidget()
listLabel.setBuddy(self.listWidget)

tableLabel = QLabel("&Table")
self.tableWidget = QTableWidget()
tableLabel.setBuddy(self.tableWidget)

treeLabel = QLabel("Tre&e")
self.treeWidget = QTreeWidget()
treeLabel.setBuddy(self.treeWidget)
```

For each convenience view we create a label and set up a buddy to make keyboard navigation easier. The layout code is similar to what we have seen before, so we have omitted it and will concern ourselves only with the connections and with creating the data structure.

```
self.connect(self.tableWidget,
        SIGNAL("itemChanged(QTableWidgetItem*)"),
        self.tableItemChanged)
self.connect(addShipButton, SIGNAL("clicked()"), self.addShip)
self.connect(removeShipButton, SIGNAL("clicked()"),
            self.removeShip)
self.connect(quitButton, SIGNAL("clicked()"), self.accept)

self.ships = ships.ShipContainer(QString("ships.dat"))
self.setWindowTitle("Ships (dict)")
```

By default, list widgets are not editable, so all users can do is select an item. This is also true of tree widgets. But table widgets are editable by default, with users able to initiate editing by pressing F2 or by double-clicking a cell. We can exercise full control over whether a view widget is editable using QAbstract-ItemView.setEditTriggers(); so, for example, we can make tables read-only or lists editable.

This application allows users to edit ship data in the table, and to add and remove ships. It also keeps all three views up-to-date by repopulating them after the data is loaded, and whenever a change occurs.

```
def populateList(self, selectedShip=None):
    selected = None
    self.listWidget.clear()
    for ship in self.ships.inOrder():
        item = QListWidgetItem(QString("%1 of %2/%3 (%L4)") \
                .arg(ship.name).arg(ship.owner).arg(ship.country) \
                .arg(ship.teu))
        self.listWidget.addItem(item)
        if selectedShip is not None and selectedShip == id(ship):
```

```
            selected = item
        if selected is not None:
            selected.setSelected(True)
            self.listWidget.setCurrentItem(selected)
```

This method, like the other populating methods, is used both to populate the widget and to select the item that corresponds to the selectedShip—a Ship's id()—if one is passed in.

We begin by clearing the widget. Then we iterate over every ship in the ships container. The inOrder() method is provided by our custom ShipContainer class. For each ship we create a single list widget item that holds a single string. We use QString.arg() so that we can use %L to show the TEUs with the appropriate digit separators (e.g., commas).

QString
.arg()
402 ☞

If we reach a list widget item that is showing the selected ship, we keep a reference to the item in selected, and after the list widget has been populated, we make the selected item both current and selected.

```
        def populateTable(self, selectedShip=None):
            selected = None
            self.tableWidget.clear()
            self.tableWidget.setSortingEnabled(False)
            self.tableWidget.setRowCount(len(self.ships))
            headers = ["Name", "Owner", "Country", "Description", "TEU"]
            self.tableWidget.setColumnCount(len(headers))
            self.tableWidget.setHorizontalHeaderLabels(headers)
```

The populate table method is quite similar to the populate list method. We begin by clearing the table—this clears both the cells and the vertical and horizontal headers (the row numbers and column titles). We then set the number of rows and columns, as well as the column titles.

We want users to be able to click a column to have the table sort by that column's contents. This functionality is built into QTableWidget, but it *must* be switched off before populating the table.* We will switch sorting back on once the table is populated.

```
            for row, ship in enumerate(self.ships):
                item = QTableWidgetItem(ship.name)
                item.setData(Qt.UserRole, QVariant(long(id(ship))))
                if selectedShip is not None and selectedShip == id(ship):
                    selected = item
                self.tableWidget.setItem(row, ships.NAME, item)
                self.tableWidget.setItem(row, ships.OWNER,
                        QTableWidgetItem(ship.owner))
```

---

*In Qt 4.0 and 4.1, forgetting to switch off sorting before repopulating a table is harmless, but from Qt 4.2 it *must* be done.

```
                    self.tableWidget.setItem(row, ships.COUNTRY,
                            QTableWidgetItem(ship.country))
                    self.tableWidget.setItem(row, ships.DESCRIPTION,
                            QTableWidgetItem(ship.description))
                    item = QTableWidgetItem(QString("%L1") \
                            .arg(ship.teu, 8, 10, QChar(" ")))
                    item.setTextAlignment(Qt.AlignRight|Qt.AlignVCenter)
                    self.tableWidget.setItem(row, ships.TEU, item)
                self.tableWidget.setSortingEnabled(True)
                self.tableWidget.resizeColumnsToContents()
                if selected is not None:
                    selected.setSelected(True)
                    self.tableWidget.setCurrentItem(selected)
```

For each ship we must create a separate table item for each cell in the row that
is used to show its data. The column indexes, NAME, OWNER, and so on, are integers
from the ships module.

In the first item of each row we set the text (the ship's name) and, as user data,
the ship's ID. Storing the ID gives us a means of going from a table item to the
ship that the item's row represents. This works because the ShipContainer is a
dictionary whose keys are ship IDs and whose values are ships.

For simple text items we can usually create the item and insert it into the table
in a single statement: We have done this for the owner, country, and description
attributes. But if we want to format the item or store user data in it, we must
create the item separately, then call its methods, and finally put it in the table
with setItem(). We used this second approach to store the ships' IDs as user
data, and to right-align the TEU values.

The TEU values are integers, and the QString.arg() method used takes four
arguments: an integer, a minimum field width, a number base, and a character
to pad with, should padding be necessary to reach the minimum field width.

Once the table is populated we switch sorting back on, resize each column
to the width of its widest cell, and make the selected item (if any) current
and selected.

Populating lists and tables is very similar because they both use a rows-and-
columns approach. Populating trees is quite different because we must use
a parents-and-children approach. The tree view of the ships data has two
columns. The first column is the tree with the root items being countries, the
next level items being owners, and the bottom-level items being the ships themselves. The second column shows just the TEUs. We could have added a third
column to show the descriptions, but doing so does not make any difference in
terms of understanding how the tree widget works.

```
        def populateTree(self, selectedShip=None):
            selected = None
            self.treeWidget.clear()
```

```
self.treeWidget.setColumnCount(2)
self.treeWidget.setHeaderLabels(["Country/Owner/Name", "TEU"])
self.treeWidget.setItemsExpandable(True)
parentFromCountry = {}
parentFromCountryOwner = {}
```

We start off in a similar way to before, clearing the tree and setting up its columns and column titles. We also set the tree's items to be expandable. We will explain the two dictionaries in a moment.

```
for ship in self.ships.inCountryOwnerOrder():
    ancestor = parentFromCountry.get(ship.country)
    if ancestor is None:
        ancestor = QTreeWidgetItem(self.treeWidget,
                                   [ship.country])
        parentFromCountry[ship.country] = ancestor
    countryowner = ship.country + "/" + ship.owner
    parent = parentFromCountryOwner.get(countryowner)
    if parent is None:
        parent = QTreeWidgetItem(ancestor, [ship.owner])
        parentFromCountryOwner[countryowner] = parent
    item = QTreeWidgetItem(parent, [ship.name,
                           QString("%L1").arg(ship.teu)])
    item.setTextAlignment(1, Qt.AlignRight|Qt.AlignVCenter)
    if selectedShip is not None and selectedShip == id(ship):
        selected = item
    self.treeWidget.expandItem(parent)
    self.treeWidget.expandItem(ancestor)
```

Each ship must have an owner parent in the tree, and each owner must have a country parent in the tree.

For each ship we check to see whether there is an item in the tree for the ship's country. We do this by looking in the parentFromCountry dictionary. If there is not, we create a new country item with the tree widget as its parent, and keep a reference to the item in the dictionary. At this point, we have either retrieved or created the country (ancestor) item.

Then we check to see whether there is an item for the ship's owner in the tree. We look in the parentFromCountryOwner dictionary for this. Again, if there is not, we create a new owner item, with a parent of the country (ancestor) item we just found or created, and keep a reference to the owner item in the dictionary. At this point, we have either retrieved or created the owner (parent) item. Now we create a new item for the ship with the owner as its parent.

We have a parentFromCountryOwner rather than a parentFromOwner dictionary because a particular owner may operate in more than one country.

Tree widget items can have multiple columns, which is why we pass them a list in addition to their parent when we create them. We use the additional columns for ships, just one extra column in fact, to store the ships' TEUs. We right align the TEU number by calling QTreeWidgetItem.setTextAlignment() passing the column number as its first argument.

When adding items to convenience view widgets, we can either create the items with no parent and then add them, for example, using QTableWidget.setItem(), or we can create them with a parent, in which case PyQt will add them for us. We have chosen this second approach for populating the tree.

We have opted to expand every item so that the tree is fully expanded from the start. This is fine for relatively small trees, but not recommended for large ones.

```
self.treeWidget.resizeColumnToContents(0)
self.treeWidget.resizeColumnToContents(1)
if selected is not None:
    selected.setSelected(True)
    self.treeWidget.setCurrentItem(selected)
```

We finish by resizing the two columns and making the selected item (if any) current and selected.

We have left the list and tree views in their default read-only state. This means that the data can be changed only if the user edits items in the table, or if they add or remove ships; so in these cases, we must make sure that we keep the views in sync. In the case of editing, the tableItemChanged() method is called whenever an edit is completed. Users complete an edit by changing focus, for example, clicking outside the item or by pressing Tab, or by pressing Enter; they cancel an edit by pressing Esc.

```
def tableItemChanged(self, item):
    ship = self.currentTableShip()
    if ship is None:
        return
    column = self.tableWidget.currentColumn()
    if column == ships.NAME:
        ship.name = item.text().trimmed()
    elif column == ships.OWNER:
        ship.owner = item.text().trimmed()
    elif column == ships.COUNTRY:
        ship.country = item.text().trimmed()
    elif column == ships.DESCRIPTION:
        ship.description = item.text().trimmed()
    elif column == ships.TEU:
        ship.teu = item.text().toInt()[0]
    self.ships.dirty = True
    self.populateList()
```

```
self.populateTree()
```

If the user edits an item in the table, we retrieve the corresponding ship and update the appropriate attribute. We use `QString.trimmed()` to get rid of any leading and trailing whitespace.* We don't have to do anything to the table itself since the edit has already updated it, so we simply repopulate the list and the tree. Repopulating like this is fine for small datasets (up to hundreds of items), but for larger datasets it can be noticably slow. The solution is to update only those items that have been changed and that are visible in the widget. This is done automatically if we use a custom model with a view widget, as we will see in the next section.

```
def currentTableShip(self):
    item = self.tableWidget.item(self.tableWidget.currentRow(), 0)
    if item is None:
        return None
    return self.ships.ship(item.data(Qt.UserRole).toLongLong()[0])
```

The `QTableWidget.item()` method returns the table item for the given row and column. We always want the item for the current row and the first column since it is in these items that we store each row's corresponding ship ID.

We then use the `ShipContainer.ship()` method to retrieve the ship with the given ID. This is fast because the ships are held in a dictionary whose keys are their IDs.

```
def addShip(self):
    ship = ships.Ship(" Unknown", " Unknown", " Unknown")
    self.ships.addShip(ship)
    self.populateList()
    self.populateTree()
    self.populateTable(id(ship))
    self.tableWidget.setFocus()
    self.tableWidget.editItem(self.tableWidget.currentItem())
```

Adding a new ship is comparatively easy, in part because we don't do any validation. We simply create a new ship with "unknown" values (the leading spaces are to make the values stand out), and add the ship to the ships dictionary. Then we repopulate the list, tree, and table, all of which will retrieve all the ships, including the one we have just created. We pass the new ship's ID to the populate table method to make sure that its first column is the current and selected table item, and give it the keyboard focus. The `editItem()` call is the programmatic equivalent of the user pressing F2 or double-clicking to initiate editing, and it results in the first field, the ship's name, being editable. The user can edit the remaining fields just by pressing Tab, since the editing state will be preserved until they leave the row or press Enter (or cancel by pressing Esc).

---

*The `QString.simplified()` method is also very handy. It removes whitespace from the ends and reduces each internal sequence of one or more whitespace characters to a single space.

```
def removeShip(self):
    ship = self.currentTableShip()
    if ship is None:
        return
    if QMessageBox.question(self, "Ships - Remove",
            QString("Remove %1 of %2/%3?").arg(ship.name) \
                .arg(ship.owner).arg(ship.country),
            QMessageBox.Yes|QMessageBox.No) == QMessageBox.No:
        return
    self.ships.removeShip(ship)
    self.populateList()
    self.populateTree()
    self.populateTable()
```

Removing ships is even easier than adding them. We retrieve the current ship and then pop up a message box asking the user if they are sure they want to remove the ship. If they click Yes, we remove the ship from the ShipContainer and repopulate the view widgets.

Although using three different views as we have done here is unconventional, the techniques we have used, particularly with the QTableWidget are perfectly general.

The convenience widgets are very useful for small and ad hoc datasets, and can be used without necessarily having a separate dataset—showing, editing, and storing the data themselves. We chose to separate out the data in this example to prepare the ground for using the model/view techniques and in particular, custom models, the subject of the next section.

Creating Custom Models

In this section, we will create a custom model to hold the ship data, and display the same model in two different table views. An application that makes use of the model is shown in Figure 14.3. The user can scroll the tables independently, and can edit the data in either of them, safe in the knowledge that any changes will be automatically reflected in both views.

We will begin by showing extracts from the application's main form. This will show us some of the model/view API in use. Then we will look at the implementation of the model itself. One important benefit of PyQt's model/view architecture is that the same coding patterns are used again and again, so once we know how to create one table model, we know how to create any table (or list) model.

The model is provided by class ShipTableModel in chap14/ships.py and the application is in chap14/ships-model.pyw. We have improved the appearance of the data in the view by setting background and foreground colors, but these could have been done in the convenience views by calling the appropriate methods on

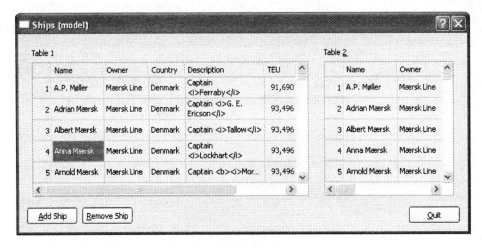

Figure 14.3 *A custom table model in two QTableViews*

the table items. The problems that existed in the previous example, in particular, no comboboxes for owners or countries, no spinbox for TEUs, and showing the HTML description text raw, remain. These can be solved only by using a delegate, something we will do in the next section.

Implementing the View Logic

Superficially, it would appear that there is no difference between what we can achieve using a convenience view with its built-in model, and a pure view with a separate model. In the preceding example, we had three views presenting the same underlying data, and it was our responsibility to keep them in sync. In this example, we will use two views on the same data, and can leave the work of synchronization to PyQt since both views use the same model. Another benefit is that the views only retrieve or store data that is actually seen or edited, and this can give considerable performance benefits when using large datasets.

We will begin with some extracts from the form's initializer.

```
class MainForm(QDialog):

    def __init__(self, parent=None):
        super(MainForm, self).__init__(parent)

        self.model = ships.ShipTableModel(QString("ships.dat"))
        tableLabel1 = QLabel("Table &1")
        self.tableView1 = QTableView()
        tableLabel1.setBuddy(self.tableView1)
        self.tableView1.setModel(self.model)
        tableLabel2 = QLabel("Table &2")
        self.tableView2 = QTableView()
        tableLabel2.setBuddy(self.tableView2)
        self.tableView2.setModel(self.model)
```

First we create a new model. Then we create two table views and accompanying labels to ease navigation. Each table view is given the same model to work on. We have omitted the layout code since it is not relevant.

```
for tableView in (self.tableView1, self.tableView2):
    header = tableView.horizontalHeader()
    self.connect(header, SIGNAL("sectionClicked(int)"),
                 self.sortTable)
self.connect(addShipButton, SIGNAL("clicked()"), self.addShip)
self.connect(removeShipButton, SIGNAL("clicked()"),
             self.removeShip)
self.connect(quitButton, SIGNAL("clicked()"), self.accept)

self.setWindowTitle("Ships (model)")
```

When we use a custom model we must handle sorting ourselves. We connect each table view's horizontal (columns) header to a sortTable() method. The other connections are similar to what we had before. But notice that we have no connection for when a table item is edited: There is no need, since the view will handle editing for us, automatically reflecting changes back into the model, which in turn will keep both views up-to-date.

```
def accept(self):
    if self.model.dirty and \
       QMessageBox.question(self, "Ships - Save?",
               "Save unsaved changes?",
               QMessageBox.Yes|QMessageBox.No) == QMessageBox.Yes:
        try:
            self.model.save()
        except IOError, e:
            QMessageBox.warning(self, "Ships - Error",
                    "Failed to save: %s" % e)
    QDialog.accept(self)
```

If the user terminates the application and there are unsaved changes, we give them the chance to save before exiting. The model's dirty attribute and its save() method are our own extensions to the QAbstractTableModel's API so that the model can load and save its data from and to files.

The base class for models is QAbstractItemModel, but row/column-based models normally inherit QAbstractTableModel, one of QAbstractItemModel's subclasses.

```
def sortTable(self, section):
    if section in (ships.OWNER, ships.COUNTRY):
        self.model.sortByCountryOwner()
    else:
        self.model.sortByName()
    self.resizeColumns()
```

We have provided only two sorts, but there is no reason why more could not be supported. Again, the sortBy*() methods are extensions that we have added to the standard API. When the user sorts we take the opportunity to resize the columns. We do this because editing may have changed the widths that the columns need, and since the sort will change the view anyway, it seems a sensible place to resize without disturbing the user.

```
def resizeColumns(self):
    for tableView in (self.tableView1, self.tableView2):
        for column in (ships.NAME, ships.OWNER, ships.COUNTRY,
                ships.TEU):
            tableView.resizeColumnToContents(column)
```

Here we have chosen to resize every column except the description column in both table views.

```
def addShip(self):
    row = self.model.rowCount()
    self.model.insertRows(row)
    index = self.model.index(row, 0)
    tableView = self.tableView1
    if self.tableView2.hasFocus():
        tableView = self.tableView2
    tableView.setFocus()
    tableView.setCurrentIndex(index)
    tableView.edit(index)
```

Adding a new ship is similar to what we did in the preceding section, but a little neater. We insert a new row as the last row in the model. Then we retrieve a model index that refers to the first column of the new row. We then find out which table view has (or last had) the keyboard focus, and we set the focus back to that view. We set the view's index to the model index we have retrieved and initiate editing on it.

The rowCount(), insertRows(), and index() methods are part of the standard QAbstractTableModel's API.

```
def removeShip(self):
    tableView = self.tableView1
    if self.tableView2.hasFocus():
        tableView = self.tableView2
    index = tableView.currentIndex()
    if not index.isValid():
        return
    row = index.row()
    name = self.model.data(
            self.model.index(row, ships.NAME)).toString()
    owner = self.model.data(
            self.model.index(row, ships.OWNER)).toString()
```

```
            country = self.model.data(
                    self.model.index(row, ships.COUNTRY)).toString()
            if QMessageBox.question(self, "Ships - Remove",
                    QString("Remove %1 of %2/%3?").arg(name).arg(owner) \
                        .arg(country),
                    QMessageBox.Yes|QMessageBox.No) == QMessageBox.No:
                return
            self.model.removeRows(row)
            self.resizeColumns()
```

If the user clicks the Remove button we retrieve the model index for the current table view's current item. We extract the row from this model index and use it with the QAbstractTableModel.data() method to retrieve the ship's name, owner, and country. The data() method takes a model index as a mandatory argument and returns a QVariant. We use QAbstractTableModel.index() to create model indexes for the row/column combinations we want, and use QVariant.toString() to convert the returned values to QStrings.

If the user confirms their deletion, we simply remove the relevant row from the model. The model will automatically notify the views, which in turn will update themselves. We have added a call to resizeColumns() since the maximum column widths may have changed after the deletion.

Implementing the Custom Model

We have now seen some of the QAbstractTableModel's API in use, along with some extensions of our own. The methods in a model subclass can be divided into three categories:

- Methods that are necessary for implementing read-only models

- Methods that are necessary for implementing editable models

- Methods that we need to extend the API for particular circumstances

The essential methods for read-only table models are data(), rowCount(), and columnCount(), although headerData() is almost always implemented too.

Editable models require reimplementations of the same methods as those needed for read-only models, and in addition, flags() and setData(). If the model is to support adding and removing rows as well as editing existing data, insertRows() and removeRows() must also be implemented.

Other methods can be implemented as well, but those listed in the two preceding paragraphs are the only essential ones.

For the ship model we store the ships in a list in memory and in a binary file on disk. To support this functionality we have extended the model API by adding sortByName(), sortByCountryOwner(), load(), and save().

The ShipTableModel is in chap14/ships.py.

```
class ShipTableModel(QAbstractTableModel):

    def __init__(self, filename=QString()):
        super(ShipTableModel, self).__init__()
        self.filename = filename
        self.dirty = False
        self.ships = []
        self.owners = set()
        self.countries = set()
```

We want to load and save the model's data from and to a binary file, so we keep an instance variable with the filename. The ships themselves are stored in a list which is initially unordered. We also keep two sets, one of owners and the other of countries: These will be used to populate comboboxes when we create a custom delegate in the next section.

```
    def rowCount(self, index=QModelIndex()):
        return len(self.ships)

    def columnCount(self, index=QModelIndex()):
        return 5
```

The row and column counts are easy to provide. It is very common for table models to have a fixed column count.

```
    def data(self, index, role=Qt.DisplayRole):
        if not index.isValid() or \
           not (0 <= index.row() < len(self.ships)):
            return QVariant()
        ship = self.ships[index.row()]
        column = index.column()
        if role == Qt.DisplayRole:
            if column == NAME:
                return QVariant(ship.name)
            elif column == OWNER:
                return QVariant(ship.owner)
            elif column == COUNTRY:
                return QVariant(ship.country)
            elif column == DESCRIPTION:
                return QVariant(ship.description)
            elif column == TEU:
                return QVariant(QString("%L1").arg(ship.teu))
```

The data() method has one mandatory argument—the model index of the item concerned—and one optional argument—the "role". The role is used to indicate what kind of information is required. The default role, Qt.DisplayRole, means that the data as displayed is wanted.

If the model index is invalid or if the row is out of range we return an invalid QVariant. PyQt's model/view architecture does not raise exceptions or give error messages; it simply uses invalid QVariants. If the index is valid we retrieve the ship at the row corresponding to the index's row. If the role is Qt.DisplayRole we return the data for the requested column as a QVariant. In the case of the TEU, instead of returning an integer, we return the number as a localized string.

```
        elif role == Qt.TextAlignmentRole:
            if column == TEU:
                return QVariant(int(Qt.AlignRight|Qt.AlignVCenter))
            return QVariant(int(Qt.AlignLeft|Qt.AlignVCenter))
        elif role == Qt.TextColorRole and column == TEU:
            if ship.teu < 80000:
                return QVariant(QColor(Qt.black))
            elif ship.teu < 100000:
                return QVariant(QColor(Qt.darkBlue))
            elif ship.teu < 120000:
                return QVariant(QColor(Qt.blue))
            else:
                return QVariant(QColor(Qt.red))
        elif role == Qt.BackgroundColorRole:
            if ship.country in (u"Bahamas", u"Cyprus", u"Denmark",
                    u"France", u"Germany", u"Greece"):
                return QVariant(QColor(250, 230, 250))
            elif ship.country in (u"Hong Kong", u"Japan", u"Taiwan"):
                return QVariant(QColor(250, 250, 230))
            elif ship.country in (u"Marshall Islands",):
                return QVariant(QColor(230, 250, 250))
            else:
                return QVariant(QColor(210, 230, 230))
        return QVariant()
```

If data() is being called with the Qt.TextAlignmentRole, we return a right-alignment for TEUs and a left-alignment for the other columns. QVariants cannot accept alignments, so we must convert them to an integer value.

For the Qt.TextColorRole, we return a color for the TEU column and ignore other columns. This means that the non-TEU columns will have the default text color, usually black. For the Qt.BackgroundColorRole, we provide different colored backgrounds depending on which group of countries the ship belongs to.

We can handle several other roles if we wish, including Qt.DecorationRole (the item's icon), Qt.ToolTipRole, Qt.StatusTipRole, and Qt.WhatsThisRole. And for controlling appearance, in addition to the alignment and color roles we discussed earlier, there is Qt.FontRole and Qt.CheckStateRole.

We return an invalid QVariant for all the cases we choose not to handle. This tells the model/view architecture to use a default value in these cases.

Some developers don't like mixing appearance-related information with the data, as we have done here in our data() implementation. PyQt is neutral on this issue: It gives us the flexibility to mix, but if we prefer data() to be purely concerned with data we can do that too, and leave all appearance-related issues to the delegate.

```
def headerData(self, section, orientation, role=Qt.DisplayRole):
    if role == Qt.TextAlignmentRole:
        if orientation == Qt.Horizontal:
            return QVariant(int(Qt.AlignLeft|Qt.AlignVCenter))
        return QVariant(int(Qt.AlignRight|Qt.AlignVCenter))
    if role != Qt.DisplayRole:
        return QVariant()
    if orientation == Qt.Horizontal:
        if section == NAME:
            return QVariant("Name")
        elif section == OWNER:
            return QVariant("Owner")
        elif section == COUNTRY:
            return QVariant("Country")
        elif section == DESCRIPTION:
            return QVariant("Description")
        elif section == TEU:
            return QVariant("TEU")
    return QVariant(int(section + 1))
```

Although not essential, it is a good practice to provide a headerData() implementation. The section is a row offset when the orientation is Qt.Vertical, and a column offset when the orientation is Qt.Horizontal. Here, we provide column headers, and number the rows from 1.

Like data(), this method accepts a role, and we use this to make the row numbers right-aligned and the column headers left-aligned.

The methods we have looked at so far are enough to implement read-only table models. Now we will look at the additional methods that must be implemented to make a model editable.

```
def flags(self, index):
    if not index.isValid():
        return Qt.ItemIsEnabled
    return Qt.ItemFlags(QAbstractTableModel.flags(self, index)|
                        Qt.ItemIsEditable)
```

If we have a valid model index we return a Qt.ItemFlags that combines the existing item flags with the Qt.ItemIsEditable flag. We can use this method to make items read-only by applying the Qt.ItemIsEditable flag only when the model index is for a row and column that we want to be editable.

```
        def setData(self, index, value, role=Qt.EditRole):
            if index.isValid() and 0 <= index.row() < len(self.ships):
                ship = self.ships[index.row()]
                column = index.column()
                if column == NAME:
                    ship.name = value.toString()
                elif column == OWNER:
                    ship.owner = value.toString()
                elif column == COUNTRY:
                    ship.country = value.toString()
                elif column == DESCRIPTION:
                    ship.description = value.toString()
                elif column == TEU:
                    value, ok = value.toInt()
                    if ok:
                        ship.teu = value
                self.dirty = True
                self.emit(SIGNAL("dataChanged(QModelIndex,QModelIndex)"),
                          index, index)
                return True
            return False
```

This method is called when the user completes an edit. In this case, we ignore the role, although it is possible to have separate display and edit data (for example, a spreadsheet's result and the formula behind it). If the index is valid and the row is in range we retrieve the relevant ship and update the column that has been edited. In the case of the TEU, we apply the change only if what the user typed in was converted successfully to an integer.

The dataChanged() signal *must* be emitted if a change has taken place. The model/view architecture depends on this signal to ensure that all the views are kept up-to-date. We must pass the model index of the changed item twice because the signal can be used to indicate a block of changes, with the first index being the top-left item and the second index the bottom-right item. We must return True if the change was accepted and applied, and False otherwise.

Implementing flags() and setData() (in addition to the methods necessary for a read-only model) is sufficient to make a model editable. But to make it possible for users to add or delete entire rows we need to implement two additional methods.

```
        def insertRows(self, position, rows=1, index=QModelIndex()):
            self.beginInsertRows(QModelIndex(), position,
                                 position + rows - 1)
            for row in range(rows):
                self.ships.insert(position + row,
                                  Ship(" Unknown", " Unknown", " Unknown"))
            self.endInsertRows()
```

```
        self.dirty = True
        return True
```

The call to beginInsertRows() is essential when we want to insert one or more rows into a model. The position is the row we want to insert at. The call to beginInsertRows() is taken straight from the PyQt documentation and should not need to be changed for any table model insertRows() implementation. After the insertions, we must call endInsertRows(). The model will automatically notify the views that the changes have been made, and the views will ask for new data if the relevant rows are visible to the user.

```
    def removeRows(self, position, rows=1, index=QModelIndex()):
        self.beginRemoveRows(QModelIndex(), position,
                                       position + rows - 1)
        self.ships = self.ships[:position] + \
                        self.ships[position + rows:]
        self.endRemoveRows()
        self.dirty = True
        return True
```

This method is similar to the preceding one. The call to beginRemoveRows() is taken from the documentation and is standard for table model reimplementations. After the relevant rows have been removed, we must call endRemoveRows(). The model will automatically notify the views about the changes.

We have now implemented the essential methods for an editable table model. Some models are merely interfaces to external data sources such as database tables (covered in the next chapter), or to external files or processes. In this case, we have stored the data inside the model itself and for this reason we must provide some extra methods, in particular load() and save(). We have also provided a couple of sorting methods as a convenience for the user. Sorting is expensive for large datasets, and in such cases using an ordered data structure, such as an OrderedDict, or using a list in conjunction with the bisect module's functions may prove beneficial.

Ordered-
Dict
92 ☞

```
    def sortByName(self):
        self.ships = sorted(self.ships)
        self.reset()
```

When sort() is called on a list it uses the items' __lt__() special method for comparisons, falling back to use the __cmp__() special method if __lt__() has not been implemented. We provided Ship.__cmp__() which does a locale-aware comparison of ships' names.

Sorting the data makes all model indexes invalid and means that the views are now showing the wrong data. The model must notify the views that they need to update themselves by retrieving fresh data. One way to do this is to emit a dataChanged() signal, but for big changes it is more efficient to call

Table 14.1 *Selected QAbstractItemModel Methods #1*

Syntax	Description
`m.beginInsert-Rows(p, f, l)`	Call in reimplementations of `insertRows()` before inserting data. The arguments are the parent `QModelIndex` p and the first and last row numbers the new rows will occupy; m is a `QAbstractItemModel` subclass.
`m.beginRemove-Rows(p, f, l)`	Call in reimplementations of `removeRows()` before removing data. The arguments are the parent `QModelIndex` p and the first and last row numbers to be removed; m is a `QAbstractItemModel` subclass.
`m.columnCount(p)`	Subclasses must reimplement this; the parent `QModelIndex` p matters only to tree models
`m.create-Index(r, c, p)`	Subclasses must use this to create `QModelIndexes` with row int r, column int c, and parent `QModelIndex` p
`m.data(i, rl)`	Returns the data as a `QVariant` for `QModelIndex` i and `Qt.ItemDataRole` rl; subclasses must reimplement this
`m.endInsertRows()`	Call in reimplementations of `insertRows()` after inserting new data; m is a `QAbstractItemModel` subclass
`m.endRemoveRows()`	Call in reimplementations of `removeRows()` after removing data; m is a `QAbstractItemModel` subclass
`m.flags(i)`	Returns the `Qt.ItemFlags` for `QModelIndex` i; these govern whether the item is selectable, editable, and so on. Editable model subclasses must reimplement this
`m.hasChildren(p)`	Returns `True` if parent `QModelIndex` p has children; meaningful only for tree models
`m.header-Data(s, o, rl)`	Returns a `QVariant` for "section" (row or column) int s, with `Qt.Orientation` o indicating row or column, and with `Qt.ItemDataRole` rl. Subclasses normally reimplement this; m is a `QAbstractItemModel` subclass.
`m.index(r, c, p)`	Returns the `QModelIndex` for the given row int r, column int c, and parent `QModelIndex` p; subclasses must reimplement this and must use `createIndex()`
`m.insertRow(r, p)`	Inserts one row before row int r. In tree models, the row is inserted as a child of parent `QModelIndex` p.
`m.insert-Rows(r, n, p)`	Inserts int n rows before row int r. In tree models, the rows are inserted as children of parent `QModelIndex` p. Editable subclasses often reimplement this—reimplementations must call `beginInsertRows()` and `endInsertRows()`.
`m.parent(i)`	Returns the parent `QModelIndex` of `QModelIndex` i. Tree model subclasses must reimplement this.

Table 14.2 *Selected QAbstractItemModel Methods #2*

Syntax	Description
m.removeRow(r, p)	Removes row int r. The parent QModelIndex p is relevant only to tree models; m is a QAbstractItemModel subclass.
m.removeRows(r, n, p)	Removes int n rows from row int r. The parent QModelIndex p is relevant only to tree models. Editable model subclasses often reimplement this method—reimplementations must call begin-RemoveRows() and endRemoveRows().
m.reset()	Notifies all associated views that the model's data has radically changed—this forces views to refetch all their visible data
m.rowCount(p)	Subclasses must reimplement this; the parent QModelIndex p matters only to tree models
m.setData(i, v, rl)	Sets QModelIndex i's data for Qt.ItemDataRole rl to QVariant v. Editable model subclasses must reimplement this—reimplementations must emit the dataChanged() signal if data was actually changed.
m.setHeader-Data(s, o, v, rl)	Sets the header data for section int s with Qt.Orientation o (i.e., for row or column), for Qt.ItemDataRole rl to QVariant v

QAbstractTableModel.reset(); this tells all associated views that everything is out-of-date and forces them to update themselves.

```
def sortByCountryOwner(self):
    def compare(a, b):
        if a.country != b.country:
            return QString.localeAwareCompare(a.country, b.country)
        if a.owner != b.owner:
            return QString.localeAwareCompare(a.owner, b.owner)
        return QString.localeAwareCompare(a.name, b.name)
    self.ships = sorted(self.ships, compare)
    self.reset()
```

Here we provide a custom sort method, sorting by country, by owner, and by ship's name. For a large dataset it might be more efficient to use DSU (decorate, sort, undecorate). For example:

```
def sortByCountryOwner(self):
    ships = []
    for ship in self.ships:
        ships.append((ship.country, ship.owner, ship.name, ship))
    ships.sort()
```

```
    self.ships = [ship for country, owner, name, ship in ships]
    self.reset()
```

This uses the normal `QString.compare()`, so it might be better to have used `unicode(ship.country)`, `unicode(ship.owner)`, and `unicode(ship.name)`. Of course, for very large datasets it is probably better to avoid sorting altogether and to use ordered containers instead.

Saving and Loading Binary Files

240 ☜

The `save()` and `load()` methods are very similar to ones we have seen before for handling binary data using `QDataStream`, so we will just show an extract from the heart of each, starting with the `save()` method.

```
    for ship in self.ships:
        stream << ship.name << ship.owner << ship.country \
               << ship.description
        stream.writeInt32(ship.teu)
```

Thanks to using `QDataStream` we don't have to worry about how long the strings are or about encoding issues.

The ships are loaded in correspondingly: Here is an extract from the `load()` method:

```
    self.ships = []
    while not stream.atEnd():
        name = QString()
        owner = QString()
        country = QString()
        description = QString()
        stream >> name >> owner >> country >> description
        teu = stream.readInt32()
        self.ships.append(Ship(name, owner, country, teu,
                               description))
        self.owners.add(unicode(owner))
        self.countries.add(unicode(country))
```

As noted earlier, we keep sets of owners and countries to make them available in comboboxes when we add a custom delegate.

Implementing custom models, particularly list and table models, is quite straightforward. For read-only models we need to implement only three methods, although normally we implement four. For editable models, we normally implement a total of eight methods. Once you have created a couple of models, creating others will become easy, because all list and table models follow the same pattern. Implementing tree models is more challenging; the topic is covered in the last section of Chapter 16.

Creating Custom Delegates

If we want to exercise complete control over the presentation and editing of data items, we must create a custom delegate. A delegate can be used purely to control appearance—for example, for read-only views—or to control editing by providing custom editors, or both.

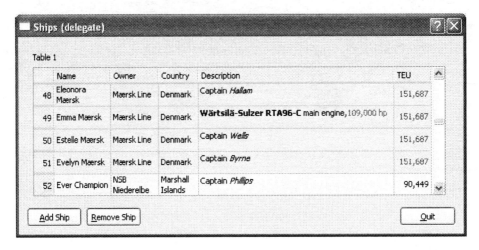

Figure 14.4 *A custom delegate in action*

Figure 14.4 looks similar to earlier screenshots, with the only noticable difference being that the description text is properly formatted rather than shown as raw HTML. However, the differences go much deeper. For example, if we edit the owner or country fields we will get comboboxes populated with the current owners and countries, and if we edit the TEU we will get a spinbox. All this control over the appearance and editing is achieved by using a delegate—and the delegate can be used with convenience views or with pure views, although in this case we have used the delegate with pure views.

For this section we are using the chap14/ships-delegate.pyw application. This is almost identical to ships-model.pyw, differing only in the window title, the fact that we resize all columns rather than skipping the description column, and the fact that we use a custom delegate. The delegate class, ShipDelegate, is in chap14/ships.py. Note that this class requires PyQt 4.1 or later.

Like model subclasses, delegates follow a fixed pattern. In the case of delegates for read-only models, the only method we must reimplement is paint(). For editable models, we must reimplement createEditor(), setEditorData(), and setModelData(). It is also common to reimplement commitAndCloseEditor() if we use QLineEdits or QTextEdits for editing. Finally, it is sometimes necessary to reimplement sizeHint(), as we will see.

It is quite common to create delegates that handle only some of the columns, particularly when it comes to painting, leaving the base class to handle columns where the default behavior is sufficient.

We will begin by looking at a small extract from the main form's constructor to see the creation of the first table:

```
class MainForm(QDialog):

    def __init__(self, parent=None):
        super(MainForm, self).__init__(parent)

        self.model = ships.ShipTableModel(QString("ships.dat"))
        tableLabel1 = QLabel("Table &1")
        self.tableView1 = QTableView()
        tableLabel1.setBuddy(self.tableView1)
        self.tableView1.setModel(self.model)
        self.tableView1.setItemDelegate(ships.ShipDelegate(self))
```

The only difference from the preceding section is that we have called setItemDelegate(), passing it a newly constructed ship.ShipDelegate. The delegate must be given the form as a parent to keep it alive while the form is in use. The code for the second table is just the same, with the same model being set, but with its own ship.ShipDelegate. This is the only change that's necessary—and now all the work of presenting and editing the data will be handled by the delegates.

```
class ShipDelegate(QItemDelegate):

    def __init__(self, parent=None):
        super(ShipDelegate, self).__init__(parent)
```

Quite often, a delegate's constructor does not need to do anything, beyond initializing the base class which is all that we do here. In fact, for cases like this we can omit the __init__() altogether.

```
    def paint(self, painter, option, index):
        if index.column() == DESCRIPTION:
            text = index.model().data(index).toString()
            palette = QApplication.palette()
            document = QTextDocument()
            document.setDefaultFont(option.font)
            if option.state & QStyle.State_Selected:
                document.setHtml(QString("<font color=%1>%2</font>") \
                        .arg(palette.highlightedText().color().name())\
                        .arg(text))
            else:
                document.setHtml(text)
            color = palette.highlight().color() \
                    if option.state & QStyle.State_Selected \
```

```
                    else QColor(index.model().data(index,
                            Qt.BackgroundColorRole))
               painter.save()
               painter.fillRect(option.rect, color)
               painter.translate(option.rect.x(), option.rect.y())
               document.drawContents(painter)
               painter.restore()
          else:
               QItemDelegate.paint(self, painter, option, index)
```

For plain text strings, numbers, dates, and so on, the base class QItemDelegate.paint() method works perfectly well, so it is very common not to reimplement it at all. However, in this example, the description column holds HTML, and this we must render ourselves.

The paint() method is called with a painter ready to draw on, a QStyleOptionViewItem which holds various pieces of information including the rectangle in which the painting should take place, and the model index of the item to be drawn.

We begin by retrieving the HTML text using the model's data() method, and relying on the Qt.DisplayRole default that we set in the model, for the second argument. Notice that a model index can give us a reference to the model it refers to with the QModelIndex.model() method.

We then retrieve the application's palette—this is based on the user's theme color preferences. If the item is selected, we apply the palette's highlighted text color to the HTML; otherwise, we use the HTML "as is". The QColor.name() method returns the color as a hexadecimal string; for example, red would be returned as the string "#FF0000", which is the same format used for HTML color specifications. Similarly, we use the palette's highlighted background color if the item is selected; otherwise, we use the background color that the model specifies by calling the data() method with the Qt.BackgroundColorRole.

The QTextDocument.drawContents() method draws relative to the painter's top-left (0, 0) coordinate. For this reason, we move (translate) the painter's top-left corner to the style option rectangle's (x, y) position, and then tell the document to paint itself on the painter.

In many cases, we don't have to bother saving and restoring the painter's state between paint events, but in this case we must. Some Qt programmers consider it a good practice to always save and restore the painter's state, whereas others prefer to do so only when necessary, that is, only when they apply a lasting change to the painter's state, such as applying a transformation, like translation, to it.

Unfortunately, this is not quite the end of the story for drawing HTML. When the view asks for the size hint of an HTML column, the default behavior will be to return a size hint based on the view's font and the number of characters.

Because HTML is rather verbose, the number of characters used in the calculation is likely to be far more than the number that are actually displayed.

There are two solutions to this problem, both of which require us to calculate the size hint for the HTML text ourselves. One solution is to change the QAbstractTableModel.data() method and to return a suitable size hint when data() is called with the Qt.SizeHintRole. The other solution is to reimplement the QItemDelegate.sizeHint() method. We prefer to reimplement sizeHint(), since that keeps the problem and its solution in the same class.

```
def sizeHint(self, option, index):
    fm = option.fontMetrics
    if index.column() == TEU:
        return QSize(fm.width("9,999,999"), fm.height())
    if index.column() == DESCRIPTION:
        text = index.model().data(index).toString()
        document = QTextDocument()
        document.setDefaultFont(option.font)
        document.setHtml(text)
        return QSize(document.idealWidth() + 5, fm.height())
    return QItemDelegate.sizeHint(self, option, index)
```

The option argument is a QStyleOptionViewItem, a QStyleOption subclass that has several useful properties. In this method, we have actually taken responsibility for two columns' size hints. For the TEU, we return a size hint wide enough for the largest TEU we expect to handle. For the description, we use a QTextDocument() to calculate the text's "ideal" width based on its fonts and font attributes, plus a small margin of 5 pixels. For the other columns, we pass the work on to the base class.

Quite often, delegates don't reimplement the paint() method at all, relying on the perfectly good default behavior for painting, and instead just providing custom methods for editing data items.

```
def createEditor(self, parent, option, index):
    if index.column() == TEU:
        spinbox = QSpinBox(parent)
        spinbox.setRange(0, 200000)
        spinbox.setSingleStep(1000)
        spinbox.setAlignment(Qt.AlignRight|Qt.AlignVCenter)
        return spinbox
    elif index.column() == OWNER:
        combobox = QComboBox(parent)
        combobox.addItems(sorted(index.model().owners))
        combobox.setEditable(True)
        return combobox
    elif index.column() == COUNTRY:
        combobox = QComboBox(parent)
```

```
                combobox.addItems(sorted(index.model().countries))
                combobox.setEditable(True)
                return combobox
            elif index.column() == NAME:
                editor = QLineEdit(parent)
                self.connect(editor, SIGNAL("returnPressed()"),
                             self.commitAndCloseEditor)
                return editor
            elif index.column() == DESCRIPTION:
                editor = richtextlineedit.RichTextLineEdit(parent)
                self.connect(editor, SIGNAL("returnPressed()"),
                             self.commitAndCloseEditor)
                return editor
            else:
                return QItemDelegate.createEditor(self, parent, option,
                                                  index)
```

When the user initiates editing on a data item, typically by pressing F2 or double-clicking, the view asks the delegate to provide an editor for the item. For any items we don't want or need to handle ourselves, we can just pass on the work to the base class, but in this delegate we prefer to deal with every column ourselves.

Rich-
Text-
LineEdit

389 ☞

For the TEU column, we create and return a spinbox. We can use any widget, whether built-in like QSpinBox, or a custom editor, such as the RichTextLineEdit that we created in the preceding chapter. In all cases, the procedure is the same: Create the editor with the given parent, and then set it up and return it.

We have populated the comboboxes with sorted lists and have made them editable so that users can add new entries. If we wanted users to be able to choose only from the list we specify, we would simply omit the setEditable(True) calls.

In the case of QLineEdit, QTextEdit, and other classes that have a returnPressed() signal to indicate that editing has been completed, we connect the signal to a reimplementation of the commitAndCloseEditor() method.

```
        def commitAndCloseEditor(self):
            editor = self.sender()
            if isinstance(editor, (QTextEdit, QLineEdit)):
                self.emit(SIGNAL("commitData(QWidget*)"), editor)
                self.emit(SIGNAL("closeEditor(QWidget*)"), editor)
```

Previously, we have always used the built-in isinstance() function to consider an object in relation to a single class, but here we have provided a tuple of two classes. This method is called when the user presses Enter and, in turn, emits signals to the editor telling it to save its data to the model and to close itself.

```
def setEditorData(self, editor, index):
    text = index.model().data(index, Qt.DisplayRole).toString()
    if index.column() == TEU:
        value = text.replace(QRegExp("[., ]"), "").toInt()[0]
        editor.setValue(value)
    elif index.column() in (OWNER, COUNTRY):
        i = editor.findText(text)
        if i == -1:
            i = 0
        editor.setCurrentIndex(i)
    elif index.column() == NAME:
        editor.setText(text)
    elif index.column() == DESCRIPTION:
        editor.setHtml(text)
    else:
        QItemDelegate.setEditorData(self, editor, index)
```

Once the editor has been created and given to the view, the view calls setEditor-Data(). This gives the delegate the opportunity to populate the editor with the current data, ready for the user to edit. In the case of TEUs, we are showing them as text, possibly containing spaces, commas, or periods. So for these we strip out the unwanted characters, convert the value to an integer, and set the spinbox's value accordingly. An alternative approach would have been to have separate Qt.DisplayRole and Qt.EditRole values for this column.

If the editor is a combobox, we set its current index to be the item that matches the data value. If there isn't a match we just make the first item the current one. For the line edit used for ships' names we use setText(), and for the rich text line edit we use setHtml() (inherited from QTextEdit). As usual, we pass on unhandled cases to the base class, although here it is a formality since we handle all the columns ourselves.

```
def setModelData(self, editor, model, index):
    if index.column() == TEU:
        model.setData(index, QVariant(editor.value()))
    elif index.column() in (OWNER, COUNTRY):
        model.setData(index, QVariant(editor.currentText()))
    elif index.column() == NAME:
        model.setData(index, QVariant(editor.text()))
    elif index.column() == DESCRIPTION:
        model.setData(index, QVariant(editor.toSimpleHtml()))
    else:
        QItemDelegate.setModelData(self, editor, model, index)
```

If the user confirms their edit, the editor's data must be written back to the model. The model will then notify the views that the item has changed, and those views that are showing the item will request fresh data to display.

In each case, we simply retrieve the value from the appropriate editor and call setData(), passing the values as QVariants.

We have now completed the delegate. Two delegates are used in the next chapter, both of which provide editors for certain fields, and both of which implement only createEditor(), setEditorData(), and setModelData(). In this chapter and the next, the custom delegates are for specific models. But in Chapter 16, we have a section devoted to "generic delegates", which can be used to create delegates for any model without having to have model-specific custom delegates—this can reduce code duplication and make maintenance easier.

Summary

PyQt's convenience item view widgets, such as QListWidget, QTableWidget, and QTreeWidget, are very useful for viewing and editing small and ad hoc datasets. They can be used in conjunction with external datasets as we did in the first section, or they can be used as data containers in their own right. Adding, editing, and removing items is straightforward, but if we use more than one view to show one dataset, we must accept the responsibility for keeping the views and dataset in sync. This problem goes away if we use the model/view approach with a custom model.

The convenience views do not provide any control over the editing of the items they handle. This deficiency is easy to rectify, both for convenience views and for pure views, by setting our own custom item delegate.

The pure views provide similar functionality to the convenience views, but do not provide sorting or direct control over the appearance of data items. These views must be used in conjunction with a model, whether a predefined one provided with PyQt, or more commonly, our own custom model.

To implement a custom table model we must reimplement rowCount(), column-Count(), and data() for both read-only and editable models; it is also usual to reimplement headerData(). In addition, we must implement flags() and set-Data() to make items editable, and insertRows() and removeRows() to allow users to insert or remove rows of data. If we want the user to be able to sort the data we can add additional sort methods, although in the case of database tables we can simply add ORDER BY clauses. Using databases with the model/view architecture is covered in the next chapter.

Creating custom delegates allows us to exercise complete control over the appearance and editing of data items. It is possible to share the responsibility for data appearance between the model and the delegate, or to give all of the responsibility to either of them. But only a custom delegate can be used to provide control over editing. For read-only delegates, and for delegates where we are concerned only with the appearance of data, we normally need to reimplement only the paint() method, although in some cases we must also reimplement sizeHint() (or handle the Qt.SizeHintRole in the model's data()

reimplementation). For most delegates, we don't need to reimplement `paint()` or `sizeHint()` at all, and only reimplement `createEditor()`, `setEditorData()`, and `setModelData()`.

In the next chapter we will see further examples of the model/view architecture, with pure views, custom delegates, and built-in SQL database models.

Exercise

Add a new method to the `ShipTableModel`, `sortByTEU()`. Use any sorting technique you like; we have used DSU. Then use this method in `MainForm.sortTable()`. In total this should take just half a dozen lines.

Extend the `ShipTableModel.data()` method to provide tooltips. The tip should simply be the text of the data item, except for TEUs, where the text should be the (localized) number followed by "twenty foot equivalents". Notice that HTML is correctly formatted in the tooltip. This is easy and takes only a dozen lines.

Modify `ShipTableDelegate.setModelData()` so that it will change the name, owner, or country, only if the new text is at least three characters long. Extend the tooltips for these columns with the text "(minimum of 3 characters)". This can be done in about half a dozen lines.

Add an Export button that, when pressed, prompts the user for a filename with the suffix `.txt`, and saves the data using the UTF-8 encoding, one ship per line, in the form:

```
name|owner|country|teu|description
```

with a bar "|" (pipe) as a separator. The data should be accessed through the model's `data()` method and output in country/owner order, with no HTML tags in the description and with TEUs output with digits only (no commas, periods, or spaces). Pop up a message box at the end, either to report an error or to report success. Use Python or PyQt for writing the file; we have used PyQt. If you write using a version of PyQt prior to 4.1, you will need to convert the TEU to a `QString` before writing it to the text stream. The `export()` method can be written in less than 50 lines.

A solution is provided in `chap14/ships_ans.py` and `chap14/ships-delegate-_ans.py`.

15

● Connecting to the Database

● Executing SQL Queries

● Using Database Form Views

● Using Database Table Views

Databases

PyQt provides a consistent cross-platform API for database access using the QtSql module and PyQt's model/view architecture.* Python also has its own completely different database API, called DB-API, but it isn't needed with PyQt and is not covered here. The commercial edition of Qt comes with many database drivers, whereas the GPL edition has fewer due to licensing restrictions. The drivers that are available include ones for IBM's DB2, Borland's Interbase, MySQL, Oracle, ODBC (for Microsoft SQL Server), PostgreSQL, SQLite, and Sybase. However, like any aspect of PyQt, it is possible to create additional database drivers if one we need is not available.

When Qt is built from source we can configure it to include SQLite, a public domain in-process database. For binary Qt packages, such as the GPL packages for Windows and Mac OS X, SQLite is built-in. The examples in this chapter use SQLite, but apart from the initial connection to the database, and a couple of aspects of raw SQL syntax that we will mention, they should work with any SQL database.

PyQt provides access to databases at two levels. The high level involves using QSqlTableModel or QSqlRelationalTableModel. These models provide abstractions for handling database tables with the same API as the other QAbstractItemModel subclasses, as well as providing some database-specific extensions. The SQL models can be used with views such as QTableView, as we will see in this chapter's last section, or with a QDataWidgetMapper for form views, the topic of this chapter's second section.

The low-level approach, also the most versatile, is based on using QSqlQuery. This class can accept any DDL (data definition language) or DML (data manipulation language) SQL statements and execute them on the database. For example, we can use QSqlQuery to create tables, and to insert, update, and delete records in tables. We will see QSqlQuery in action in this chapter's first section.

---

*This chapter assumes a knowledge of PyQt's model/view architecture, covered in the preceding chapter, as well as a basic knowledge of SQL.

Connecting to the Database

But before we can do any work with a database, we must establish a connection to it. In many database applications this is done after the creation of the QApplication object, but before the main form is created or shown. Other applications establish their connections later on—for example, only when they are needed.

To use PyQt's SQL classes we must import the QtSql module:

```
from PyQt4.QtSql import *
```

A database connection is established by calling the static QSqlDatabase.addDatabase() method, with the name of the driver we want to use. Then we must set various attributes, such as the database's name, the username, and the password. And finally, we must call open() to make the connection.

```
db = QSqlDatabase.addDatabase("QSQLITE")
db.setDatabaseName(filename)
if not db.open():
    QMessageBox.warning(None, "Phone Log",
        QString("Database Error: %1").arg(db.lastError().text()))
    sys.exit(1)
```

For SQLite we need to specify only the name of the database. This is normally a filename, but it can be the special name ":memory:" for an in-memory database. When we call QSqlDatabase.open() using the SQLite driver, if the file does not exist it will be created, in which case it will have no tables or records.

Notice that we have passed None as the message box's parent: This is because we have tried to establish the connection before creating the main window, so there is no possible parent. Since this application depends on the database, if no connection can be made it simply tells the user the error message that was received and terminates the application.

If the database connection was successfully opened, from now on all database methods will apply to this connection. If we need two or more separate connections, whether to the same database or to different databases, we must pass a second argument to addDatabase(), giving the connection a name that we can then use to distinguish between our different connections.

Executing SQL Queries

Now that we have a connection, we can execute some SQL statements.

```
query = QSqlQuery()
query.exec_("""CREATE TABLE outcomes (
        id INTEGER PRIMARY KEY AUTOINCREMENT UNIQUE NOT NULL,
        name VARCHAR(40) NOT NULL)""")
```

```
query.exec_("""CREATE TABLE calls (
            id INTEGER PRIMARY KEY AUTOINCREMENT UNIQUE NOT NULL,
            caller VARCHAR(40) NOT NULL,
            starttime DATETIME NOT NULL,
            endtime DATETIME NOT NULL,
            topic VARCHAR(80) NOT NULL,
            outcomeid INTEGER NOT NULL,
            FOREIGN KEY (outcomeid) REFERENCES outcomes)""")
```

We have not specified a particular database connection to use, so PyQt will use the default (unnamed) connection that we established earlier. The tables created by the SQL calls are shown schematically in Figure 15.1.

The AUTOINCREMENT syntax tells SQLite to populate the id field automatically with each ID being one more than the previous one, with the first being 1. Similarly, the FOREIGN KEY syntax tells SQLite about a foreign key relationship. SQLite 3 does not enforce foreign key relationships, merely allowing us to express them as a documentation aid. The syntax for achieving automatic IDs and for foreign keys may be different in other databases.

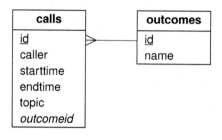

Figure 15.1 *The Phone Log database design*

Many databases have their own set of data types. For example, SQLite 3 has what it calls "storage classes", including, INTEGER, REAL, and TEXT. PyQt supports the standard SQL datatypes, including VARCHAR, NUMBER, DATE, and DATETIME, transparently converting to and from the database's native data types behind the scenes. For text, PyQt uses Unicode, except with databases that don't support Unicode, in which case PyQt converts to and from the database's native encoding.

Now that we have created the tables, we can populate them with data.

```
for name in ("Resolved", "Unresolved", "Calling back", "Escalate",
             "Wrong number"):
    query.exec_("INSERT INTO outcomes (name) VALUES ('%s')" % name)
```

We did not need to provide IDs since we have asked the database to generate them for us. Unfortunately, the preceding code is not robust: For example, it will fail if one of the names contains a single quote. One way to deal with this is to ensure that we either remove or escape unacceptable characters, but PyQt provides a better alternative: prepared queries.

There are two widely used forms of syntax for prepared queries, one based on the ODBC place holder approach, and the other based on the Oracle named variable approach. PyQt supports both, converting from one to the other behind the scenes if necessary, so that both work no matter what the underlying database is.

```
query.prepare("INSERT INTO calls (caller, starttime, endtime, "
              "topic, outcomeid) VALUES (?, ?, ?, ?, ?)")
for name, start, end, topic, outcomeid in data:
    query.addBindValue(QVariant(QString(name)))
    query.addBindValue(QVariant(start))      # QDateTime
    query.addBindValue(QVariant(end))        # QDateTime
    query.addBindValue(QVariant(QString(topic)))
    query.addBindValue(QVariant(outcomeid)) # int
    query.exec_()
```

This example uses the ODBC syntax. One benefit of using place holders is that PyQt takes care of the quoting issues, so we don't have to worry about what our data contains, as long as the types we pass are appropriate for the fields they will populate.

```
query.prepare("INSERT INTO calls (caller, starttime, endtime, "
              "topic, outcomeid) VALUES (:caller, :starttime, "
              ":endtime, :topic, :outcomeid)")
for name, start, end, topic, outcomeid in data:
    query.bindValue(":caller", QVariant(QString(name)))
    query.bindValue(":starttime", QVariant(start))
    query.bindValue(":endtime", QVariant(end))
    query.bindValue(":topic", QVariant(QString(topic)))
    query.bindValue(":outcomeid", QVariant(outcomeid))
    query.exec_()
```

This second example performs the same work as the first, but uses Oracle-style named variables. PyQt also supports a couple of other variations of prepared query syntax, but they don't add anything to what we can do with the two forms of syntax shown earlier. Prepared queries can improve performance on databases that support them, and make no difference on those that don't.

Prepared queries can also be used to call stored procedures, but we will not cover them because support for them is neither universal nor uniform. For example, not all databases support stored procedures, and the syntax for calling them and for retrieving OUT values is different from database to database. Also, stored procedures that return values are not fully supported.

We can use QSqlQuery to execute any arbitrary SQL statement. For example:

```
query.exec_("DELETE FROM calls WHERE id = 12")
```

After a query has executed we can check for errors by calling QSqlQuery.is-Active(); if this returns False an error occurred and the error message is available as a QString by calling QSqlQuery.lastError().text().

If we perform a query that may affect a number of rows, such as a DELETE or UPDATE whose WHERE clause might select more than one record, we can call QSqlQuery.numRowsAffected(); it returns -1 on error.

We can find out whether the underlying database supports various features such as transactions and BLOBs (Binary Large OBjects) by accessing the driver and calling hasFeature(). For example:

```
driver = QSqlDatabase.database().driver()
if driver.hasFeature(QSqlDriver.Transactions):
    print "Can commit and rollback"
```

When we use QSqlQuery we can initiate a transaction by calling QSqlDatabase.database().transaction(), and then either QSqlDatabase.database().commit() or QSqlDatabase.database().rollback().

We will conclude our coverage of QSqlQuery by looking at how to use it to execute SELECT statements, and how to iterate over the resultant records.

```
DATETIME_FORMAT = "yyyy-MM-dd hh:mm"
ID, CALLER, STARTTIME, ENDTIME, TOPIC, OUTCOMEID = range(6)

query.exec_("SELECT id, caller, starttime, endtime, topic, "
            "outcomeid FROM calls ORDER by starttime")
while query.next():
    id = query.value(ID).toInt()[0]
    caller = unicode(query.value(CALLER).toString())
    starttime = unicode(query.value(STARTTIME).toDateTime() \
            .toString(DATETIME_FORMAT))
    endtime = unicode(query.value(ENDTIME).toDateTime() \
            .toString(DATETIME_FORMAT))
    topic = unicode(query.value(TOPIC).toString())
    outcomeid = query.value(OUTCOMEID).toInt()[0]
    subquery = QSqlQuery("SELECT name FROM outcomes "
                         "WHERE id = %d" % outcomeid)
    outcome = "invalid foreign key"
    if subquery.next():
        outcome = unicode(subquery.value(0).toString())
    print "%02d: %s %s - %s %s [%s]" % (id, caller, starttime,
            endtime, topic, outcome)
```

When we execute a SELECT statement, we can iterate over the result set using methods such as QSqlQuery.next(), QSqlQuery.previous(), and QSqlQuery.seek(). Immediately after a successful SELECT, isActive() will return True but the inter-

Table 15.1 *Selected QSqlQuery Methods*

Syntax	Description
`q.addBindValue(v)`	Adds `QVariant` v as the next variable when using positional value binding in `QSqlQuery` q
`q.bindValue(p, v)`	Sets `QVariant` v as the value for the string p place holder when using place holder value binding in `QSqlQuery` q
`q.boundValue(p)`	Returns the `QVariant` value for the string p place holder in `QSqlQuery` q
`q.driver()`	Returns the `QSqlDriver` associated with `QSqlQuery` q. The `QSqlDriver` class provides `hasFeature()` to report which features the underlying database supports.
`q.exec_(s)`	Executes the SQL query in string s on `QSqlQuery` q
`q.first()`	Navigates to the first record in `QSqlQuery` q's result set after a `SELECT` query has been executed
`q.isActive()`	Returns `True` if the query is "active"—for example, after executing a `SELECT` query
`q.isValid()`	Returns `True` if the query is positioned on a valid record; after a `SELECT` query this will be `True` only if `isActive()` is `True` and a record has been navigated to
`q.last()`	Navigates to the last record in `QSqlQuery` q's result set after a `SELECT` query has been executed
`q.lastError()`	Returns a `QSqlError` object; this provides an errorString() method
`q.next()`	Navigates to the next record in `QSqlQuery` q's result set after a `SELECT` query has been executed. This is the only method needed to iterate forward over a result set.
`q.numRows-Affected()`	Returns the number of rows affected by the SQL query just executed, providing it was not a `SELECT`, and providing the underlying database supports this feature
`q.prepare(s)`	Prepares the query in string s ready for q to execute it
`q.previous()`	Navigates to the previous record in `QSqlQuery` q's result set after a `SELECT` query has been executed
`q.record()`	Returns a `QSqlRecord` object containing `QSqlQuery` q's current record, if any; using `QSqlQuery.value()` with a field index argument is usually more convenient
`q.size()`	Returns the number of rows in the `SELECT` result set, or -1 if a `SELECT` was not executed or if the underlying database does not support this feature
`q.value(i)`	Returns the `QVariant` value for field index int i in the current record, if there is one

nal record pointer will not be referring to a valid record. Each of the navigation methods returns True if the query's internal record pointer was successfully moved onto a valid record; this is why we call QSqlQuery.next() before accessing the first record. They return False if an error occurred or if they pass the last (or first) record.

When navigating large result sets, providing we only use next(), or only seek() forward, we can call QSqlQuery.setForwardOnly(True). This can significantly improve performance or reduce memory overhead, or both, with some databases.

The QSqlQuery.value() method takes an index position argument, based on the order of the field names given in the SELECT statement. For this reason, using SELECT * is not recommended because in that case, we don't know what the order of the fields is. Each field is returned as a QVariant and must therefore be converted to the proper type. In the case of the date/times, we first convert them from QVariant to QDateTime, then to QString, and finally to unicode, ready to be printed on the console.

We used an additional query to look up the name of the outcome from its ID, giving error text if the database does not have relational integrity. For a large dataset, it would have been more efficient to use a prepared query for the subquery.

We can use QSqlQuery to do all the database work we want, but using PyQt's SQL models is much easier for GUI programming, and it does not prevent us from using QSqlQuery when the need arises.

Using Database Form Views

One of the easiest user interfaces we can provide for database data is a form that displays the fields from a single record at a time. In this section we will develop an application that uses such a form, initially a simplified version of the phone log database introduced in the preceding section, and then the full version which includes the foreign key field.

The examples presented in this section depend on the QDataWidgetMapper class introduced with Qt 4.2. The next section's example uses SQL table models and QTableView, and can be used with Qt 4.1 or later.

The simplified application is shown in Figure 15.2, and its source code is in chap15/phonelog.pyw; the full version is in chap15/phonelog-fk.pyw. When these applications are run for the very first time they create a database of fake records which they then use on subsequent runs. Generating these records using Qt's built-in SQLite is fast on Linux but very slow on some Windows machines. (A splash screen is used to disguise the slowness.)

The simplified application has a single table, calls, and no foreign key field. The form is represented by the PhoneLogDlg class. The initializer is quite long,

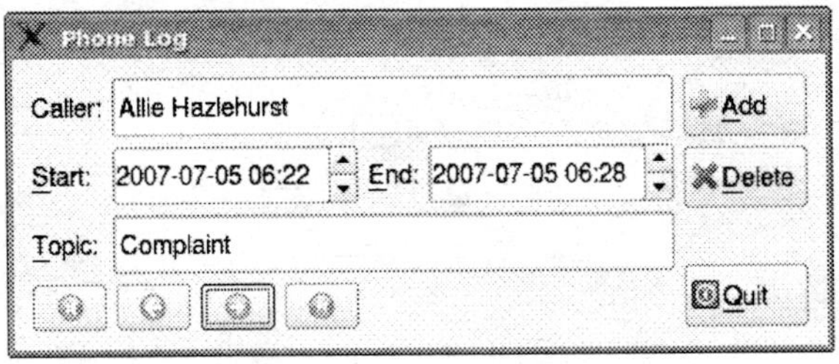

Figure 15.2 *The simplified Phone Log application*

so we will look at it in parts, skipping the layout since our focus in this chapter
is on database programming.

```
class PhoneLogDlg(QDialog):

    FIRST, PREV, NEXT, LAST = range(4)

    def __init__(self, parent=None):
        super(PhoneLogDlg, self).__init__(parent)

        callerLabel = QLabel("&Caller:")
        self.callerEdit = QLineEdit()
        callerLabel.setBuddy(self.callerEdit)
        today = QDate.currentDate()
        startLabel = QLabel("&Start:")
        self.startDateTime = QDateTimeEdit()
        startLabel.setBuddy(self.startDateTime)
        self.startDateTime.setDateRange(today, today)
        self.startDateTime.setDisplayFormat(DATETIME_FORMAT)
        endLabel = QLabel("&End:")
        self.endDateTime = QDateTimeEdit()
        endLabel.setBuddy(self.endDateTime)
        self.endDateTime.setDateRange(today, today)
        self.endDateTime.setDisplayFormat(DATETIME_FORMAT)
        topicLabel = QLabel("&Topic:")
        topicEdit = QLineEdit()
        topicLabel.setBuddy(topicEdit)
        firstButton = QPushButton()
        firstButton.setIcon(QIcon(":/first.png"))
```

We create a label and a suitable editing widget for each field. We also create
all the form's buttons, although we show the creation of only the first one. We
pass a string to the Add, Delete, and Quit buttons' constructors to give them their
captions, in addition to giving them icons.

```
        self.model = QSqlTableModel(self)
        self.model.setTable("calls")
        self.model.setSort(STARTTIME, Qt.AscendingOrder)
        self.model.select()
```

With the widgets in place, we create a `QSqlTableModel`. Since we did not specify a particular database connection, it uses the default one. We tell the model which table it is to work on and call `select()` to make it populate itself with data. We also choose to apply a sort order to the table.

Now that we have suitable widgets and a model, we must somehow link them together. This is achieved by using a `QDataWidgetMapper`.

```
self.mapper = QDataWidgetMapper(self)
self.mapper.setSubmitPolicy(QDataWidgetMapper.ManualSubmit)
self.mapper.setModel(self.model)
self.mapper.addMapping(self.callerEdit, CALLER)
self.mapper.addMapping(self.startDateTime, STARTTIME)
self.mapper.addMapping(self.endDateTime, ENDTIME)
self.mapper.addMapping(topicEdit, TOPIC)
self.mapper.toFirst()
```

To make a data widget mapper work, we must give it a model and a set of mappings between the widgets in the form and the corresponding columns in the model. (The variables, ID, CALLER, STARTTIME, and so on, are set to 0, 1, 2, and so on at the start of the file.) The mapper can be set to submit changes automatically, or only when told. We prefer the latter approach because it gives us finer control and means that when the user navigates to a different record we can make sure that any unsaved changes are saved. Once we have set up the mapping, we need to make the mapper populate the widgets with a record; we have done this by calling `toFirst()`, which means that at startup, the first record is shown.

```
self.connect(firstButton, SIGNAL("clicked()"),
            lambda: self.saveRecord(PhoneLogDlg.FIRST))
self.connect(prevButton, SIGNAL("clicked()"),
            lambda: self.saveRecord(PhoneLogDlg.PREV))
self.connect(nextButton, SIGNAL("clicked()"),
            lambda: self.saveRecord(PhoneLogDlg.NEXT))
self.connect(lastButton, SIGNAL("clicked()"),
            lambda: self.saveRecord(PhoneLogDlg.LAST))
self.connect(addButton, SIGNAL("clicked()"), self.addRecord)
self.connect(deleteButton, SIGNAL("clicked()"),
            self.deleteRecord)
self.connect(quitButton, SIGNAL("clicked()"), self.accept)

self.setWindowTitle("Phone Log")
```

The first four connections provide navigation. In each case, we call save-Record(), which saves any unsaved changes, and then navigates in accordance with the argument that has been wrapped in the `lambda` statement. This means that we need only a single method, `saveRecord()`, instead of one for each navigation button. However, the connections will work only with PyQt 4.1.1 or later. For earlier versions we must keep an instance variable (for example, a

Lambda
call-
backs
134 ☞

list) that contains references to the lambda functions to prevent them from being garbage-collected.

```
def accept(self):
    self.mapper.submit()
    QDialog.accept(self)
```

If the user clicks Quit we call QDataWidgetMapper.submit(), which writes the current record back to the underlying model, and then we close the window.

```
def saveRecord(self, where):
    row = self.mapper.currentIndex()
    self.mapper.submit()
    if where == PhoneLogDlg.FIRST:
        row = 0
    elif where == PhoneLogDlg.PREV:
        row = 0 if row <= 1 else row - 1
    elif where == PhoneLogDlg.NEXT:
        row += 1
        if row >= self.model.rowCount():
            row = self.model.rowCount() - 1
    elif where == PhoneLogDlg.LAST:
        row = self.model.rowCount() - 1
    self.mapper.setCurrentIndex(row)
```

If the user navigates, we must remember the current row, since it is forgotten after calling submit(). Then, after saving the current record, we set the row to be the one appropriate for the navigation the user requested (but kept within bounds), and then use setCurrentIndex() to move to the appropriate record.

```
def addRecord(self):
    row = self.model.rowCount()
    self.mapper.submit()
    self.model.insertRow(row)
    self.mapper.setCurrentIndex(row)
    now = QDateTime.currentDateTime()
    self.startDateTime.setDateTime(now)
    self.endDateTime.setDateTime(now)
    self.callerEdit.setFocus()
```

We have chosen to always add new records at the end. To do this we find the row after the last one, save the current record, and then insert a new record at the last row in the model. Then we set the mapper's current index to the new row, initialize a couple of fields, and give the caller field the focus, ready for the user to start typing.

```
def deleteRecord(self):
    caller = self.callerEdit.text()
```

```
starttime = self.startDateTime.dateTime().toString(
                                  DATETIME_FORMAT)
if QMessageBox.question(self,
        QString("Delete"),
        QString("Delete call made by<br>%1 on %2?") \
        .arg(caller).arg(starttime),
        QMessageBox.Yes|QMessageBox.No) == QMessageBox.No:
    return
row = self.mapper.currentIndex()
self.model.removeRow(row)
self.model.submitAll()
if row + 1 >= self.model.rowCount():
    row = self.model.rowCount() - 1
self.mapper.setCurrentIndex(row)
```

If the user clicks Delete we pick out some information from the current record and use it when we ask the user to confirm the deletion. If they confirm, we retrieve the current row, remove the row from the model, and call submitAll() to force the model to write back the change to the underlying data source (in this case the database). Then we finish up by navigating to the next record.

We have used submitAll() because we have performed the deletion on the model, not the mapper, and for databases we must confirm changes to the model by calling this method unless the view (or data widget mapper) has been set to automatically submit. The data widget mapper's API does not allow us to add or delete records, only edit existing ones, and for this reason, we must add or delete records using the underlying model.

The techniques we have used so far can be applied to any database table or editable database view to provide users with a means of navigating, adding, updating, and deleting records. However, in most cases, there are foreign keys to consider, an issue we will now address as we review the phone log application, shown in Figure 15.3.

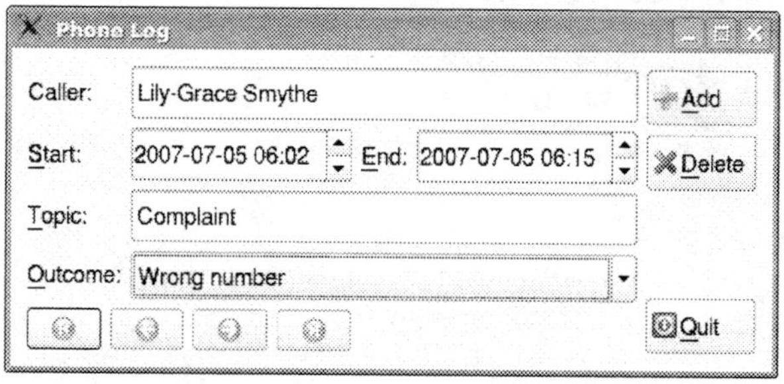

Figure 15.3 *The Phone Log application*

The calls table (shown on page 447) has a foreign key outcomeid field. We want this field to appear as a combobox in the form, showing the outcomes table's name field for each corresponding ID. To do this we create a combobox in the usual way, but we do not populate it.

Since we are now using a table that has a foreign key we must use a QSql-RelationalTableModel rather than a QSqlTableModel.

```
self.model = QSqlRelationalTableModel(self)
self.model.setTable("calls")
self.model.setRelation(OUTCOMEID,
        QSqlRelation("outcomes", "id", "name"))
self.model.setSort(STARTTIME, Qt.AscendingOrder)
self.model.select()
```

The QSqlRelationalTableModel is very similar to a QSqlTableModel, except that it provides a few extra methods for handling relations. The setRelation() method takes a field index in the model, and a QSqlRelation object. The relation object is created with the name of the foreign key's table, the field to actually store, and the field to display.

The data widget mapper code must also be changed. In particular, we must use a QSqlRelationalDelegate rather than the standard built-in delegate, and we must set up the combobox that is used for the foreign key.

```
self.mapper = QDataWidgetMapper(self)
self.mapper.setSubmitPolicy(QDataWidgetMapper.ManualSubmit)
self.mapper.setModel(self.model)
self.mapper.setItemDelegate(QSqlRelationalDelegate(self))
self.mapper.addMapping(self.callerEdit, CALLER)
self.mapper.addMapping(self.startDateTime, STARTTIME)
self.mapper.addMapping(self.endDateTime, ENDTIME)
self.mapper.addMapping(topicEdit, TOPIC)
relationModel = self.model.relationModel(OUTCOMEID)
self.outcomeComboBox.setModel(relationModel)
self.outcomeComboBox.setModelColumn(
        relationModel.fieldIndex("name"))
self.mapper.addMapping(self.outcomeComboBox, OUTCOMEID)
self.mapper.toFirst()
```

The code is similar to what we had before. Setting the relational delegate is easy, but setting up the combobox is slightly subtle. First, we must retrieve the relation model (outcomes table) used by the model (calls table) to handle the foreign key. A QComboBox is actually a convenience view widget with a built-in model, just like a QListWidget; but it is possible to substitute our own model, and that's what we have done here. However, a combobox shows a single column, and our relation model has two columns (id, name), so we must specify which one to display. We cannot be certain about the column indexes used by the relation model (since it was created for us, not by us), so we use the fieldIndex() method with a field name to specify the correct column index. Once the combobox is set up, we can add it to the mapper like any other widget.

That completes the changes for handling foreign keys. In addition, we have taken the opportunity to make a couple of other small changes to the application.

In the simplified version, we connected the Quit button to a custom accept() method and, rather unintuitively, called accept() from the reject() method. This was to ensure that the application always saved the current record's changes before terminating. In the foreign key version, we have taken a different approach, and connected the Quit button to the done() method.

```
def done(self, result=None):
    self.mapper.submit()
    QDialog.done(self, True)
```

This method is called as a result of the Quit button connection, or if the user closes the window by clicking the X close button or presses Esc. We save the current record and call the base class's done() method. The second argument is mandatory, but it doesn't matter what value it holds in this case: A True value signifies accept() and a False value signifies reject(), but either way, the window will close.

We have made one other tiny change, adding two lines to the addRecord() method:

```
self.outcomeComboBox.setCurrentIndex(
        self.outcomeComboBox.findText("Unresolved"))
```

This ensures that when the user clicks Add to add a new record, the outcome combobox will have a sensible default, in addition to the date/time defaults we already set.

Forms are very useful for tables with lots of fields, especially if a lot of validation needs to be done on the basis of interfield dependencies. But for tables with fewer fields, or where users want to see multiple records, we need to use tabular views. This is the subject of the next section.

Using Database Table Views

Probably the most natural and convenient way to present database data is to show database tables and views in GUI tables. This allows users to see many records at once, and it is particularly convenient for showing master–detail relationships.

In this section, we will examine the Asset Manager application. The code is in chap15/assetmanager.pyw. This application has four tables, created by the following SQL statements:

```
query = QSqlQuery()
query.exec_("""CREATE TABLE actions (
        id INTEGER PRIMARY KEY AUTOINCREMENT UNIQUE NOT NULL,
```

```
                    name VARCHAR(20) NOT NULL,
                    description VARCHAR(40) NOT NULL)""")
    query.exec_("""CREATE TABLE categories (
                    id INTEGER PRIMARY KEY AUTOINCREMENT UNIQUE NOT NULL,
                    name VARCHAR(20) NOT NULL,
                    description VARCHAR(40) NOT NULL)""")
    query.exec_("""CREATE TABLE assets (
                    id INTEGER PRIMARY KEY AUTOINCREMENT UNIQUE NOT NULL,
                    name VARCHAR(40) NOT NULL,
                    categoryid INTEGER NOT NULL,
                    room VARCHAR(4) NOT NULL,
                    FOREIGN KEY (categoryid) REFERENCES categories)""")
    query.exec_("""CREATE TABLE logs (
                    id INTEGER PRIMARY KEY AUTOINCREMENT UNIQUE NOT NULL,
                    assetid INTEGER NOT NULL,
                    date DATE NOT NULL,
                    actionid INTEGER NOT NULL,
                    FOREIGN KEY (assetid) REFERENCES assets,
                    FOREIGN KEY (actionid) REFERENCES actions)""")
```

The actions and categories tables are typical reference data tables, with an
ID, a short description (name), and a long description (description). The main
table is assets; this holds the name, category, and location of each asset in a
building. The logs table is used to keep track of what happens to an asset over
its lifetime. Figure 15.4 shows the tables schematically.

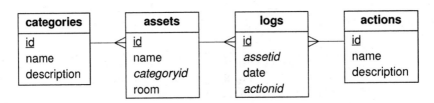

Figure 15.4 *The Asset Manager database design*

The Asset Manager application has a dialog-style main window with two
QTableViews in a master–detail relationship. It is shown in Figure 15.5. The
top table shows the assets table and the bottom one shows the records from the
logs table that correspond to the current asset record. The user can add and
delete assets and log records, and edit both tables in-place. Users can also add,
delete, and edit the categories and actions reference tables by popping up a
suitable dialog. This dialog also uses a QTableView, although it could easily have
used a QDataWidgetMapper instead.

We will begin by looking at the creation and connection to the database, then
the main form, and then we will look at the dialog that is used with the reference data. Just as with the Phone Log application, the Asset Manager generates a set of fake records the first time it is run. As noted in the preceding

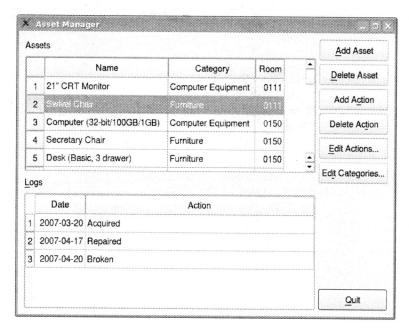

Figure 15.5 *The Asset Manager application*

section, this is fast with SQLite on Linux and very slow on some Windows machines.

```
app = QApplication(sys.argv)
db = QSqlDatabase.addDatabase("QSQLITE")
db.setDatabaseName(filename)
if not db.open():
    QMessageBox.warning(None, "Asset Manager",
        QString("Database Error: %1").arg(db.lastError().text()))
    sys.exit(1)
form = MainForm()
form.show()
app.exec_()
```

We begin as usual by creating a QApplication object. Next we create the connection; if the database file doesn't exist, SQLite will create an empty one. Then we create the main form, call show() on it to schedule a paint event, and start off the event loop.

What we haven't shown is the code that we have used to generate the fake data the first time the application is run, and to pop up the splash screen. This code is, of course, in the source file, chap15/assetmanager.pyw.

As we did in the preceding section, we will skip the form's layout and concentrate instead on the creation of the widgets and the models. We will also skip the code for creating the buttons, although we will show the first couple of signal–slot connections.

```
class MainForm(QDialog):

    def __init__(self):
        super(MainForm, self).__init__()
        self.assetModel = QSqlRelationalTableModel(self)
        self.assetModel.setTable("assets")
        self.assetModel.setRelation(CATEGORYID,
                QSqlRelation("categories", "id", "name"))
        self.assetModel.setSort(ROOM, Qt.AscendingOrder)
        self.assetModel.setHeaderData(ID, Qt.Horizontal,
                QVariant("ID"))
        self.assetModel.setHeaderData(NAME, Qt.Horizontal,
                QVariant("Name"))
        self.assetModel.setHeaderData(CATEGORYID, Qt.Horizontal,
                QVariant("Category"))
        self.assetModel.setHeaderData(ROOM, Qt.Horizontal,
                QVariant("Room"))
        self.assetModel.select()
```

The model is created in much the same way as we saw in the preceding section. The ID, NAME, and others are integer column indexes set up earlier in the assetmanager.pyw file. What's different from using a QDataWidgetMapper is that we have set the header data to give the columns titles; if we don't do this, the QTableView that presents the model will use the database field names for the column titles. Since the categoryid field is a foreign key, we have used a QSqlRelationalTableModel and called setRelation() appropriately.

```
        self.assetView = QTableView()
        self.assetView.setModel(self.assetModel)
        self.assetView.setItemDelegate(AssetDelegate(self))
        self.assetView.setSelectionMode(QTableView.SingleSelection)
        self.assetView.setSelectionBehavior(QTableView.SelectRows)
        self.assetView.setColumnHidden(ID, True)
        self.assetView.resizeColumnsToContents()
```

The view is a standard QTableView, but instead of setting a QSqlRelational-Delegate, we have set a custom delegate. We will detour to look at this in a moment. The selection mode is set so that users can navigate to individual fields; the selection behavior is that the row that has the focus is highlighted. We don't want to show the ID field since it isn't meaningful to the user, so we hide it.

We have not used a standard QSqlRelationalDelegate because we want to take control of the editing of the room numbers, since they are not straightforward to validate. We will now take a brief detour to look at the AssetDelegate class.

```
class AssetDelegate(QSqlRelationalDelegate):

    def __init__(self, parent=None):
        super(AssetDelegate, self).__init__(parent)
```

The initializer is typical of most delegate subclasses, simply calling the base class.

```
    def paint(self, painter, option, index):
        myoption = QStyleOptionViewItem(option)
        if index.column() == ROOM:
            myoption.displayAlignment |= Qt.AlignRight|Qt.AlignVCenter
        QSqlRelationalDelegate.paint(self, painter, myoption, index)
```

We have reimplemented the paint() method only to right-align the room numbers. We do this by changing the QStyleOptionViewItem, and we leave the painting itself to be done by the base class.

```
    def createEditor(self, parent, option, index):
        if index.column() == ROOM:
            editor = QLineEdit(parent)
            regex = QRegExp(r"(?:0[1-9]|1[0124-9]|2[0-7])"
                            r"(?:0[1-9]|[1-5][0-9]|6[012])")
            validator = QRegExpValidator(regex, parent)
            editor.setValidator(validator)
            editor.setInputMask("9999")
            editor.setAlignment(Qt.AlignRight|Qt.AlignVCenter)
            return editor
        else:
            return QSqlRelationalDelegate.createEditor(self, parent,
                                                       option, index)
```

The heart of the createEditor() method is the code that sets up the QLineEdit for entering room numbers. Room numbers are four digits long, made up of a floor number, in the range 01–27 (but excluding 13), and a room number on the floor in the range 01–62. For example, 0231 is floor 2, room 31, but 0364 is invalid. The regular expression is sufficient for specifying valid room numbers, but it cannot set a minimum number of digits, since one, two, or three digits may be a valid prefix for a valid four digit room number. We have solved this by using an input mask that requires exactly four digits to be entered. For the other fields, we pass the work on to the base class.

```
    def setEditorData(self, editor, index):
        if index.column() == ROOM:
            text = index.model().data(index, Qt.DisplayRole).toString()
            editor.setText(text)
        else:
            QSqlRelationalDelegate.setEditorData(self, editor, index)
```

Once the editor has been created, the view will call setEditorData() so that it can be populated with the current value. In this case, we care only about the room column, passing on the work for the other fields to the base class.

```
def setModelData(self, editor, model, index):
    if index.column() == ROOM:
        model.setData(index, QVariant(editor.text()))
    else:
        QSqlRelationalDelegate.setModelData(self, editor, model,
                                                          index)
```

We have taken a similar approach to the previous method, handling the room field and leaving the others to be handled by the base class. As a matter of fact, we could have omitted reimplementing this method, and PyQt would have been smart enough to retrieve the value from our QLineEdit. However, it is a better practice to take full responsibility for our own customizations.

We have now finished the detour and can return to the MainForm.__init__() method, beginning with the bottom table that shows the log records that are applicable to the current asset.

```
self.logModel = QSqlRelationalTableModel(self)
self.logModel.setTable("logs")
self.logModel.setRelation(ACTIONID,
        QSqlRelation("actions", "id", "name"))
self.logModel.setSort(DATE, Qt.AscendingOrder)
self.logModel.setHeaderData(DATE, Qt.Horizontal,
        QVariant("Date"))
self.logModel.setHeaderData(ACTIONID, Qt.Horizontal,
        QVariant("Action"))
self.logModel.select()
```

The code for creating the log model is almost the same as the code we used for the asset model. We use a QSqlRelationalTableModel because we have a foreign key field, and we provide our own column titles.

```
self.logView = QTableView()
self.logView.setModel(self.logModel)
self.logView.setItemDelegate(LogDelegate(self))
self.logView.setSelectionMode(QTableView.SingleSelection)
self.logView.setSelectionBehavior(QTableView.SelectRows)
self.logView.setColumnHidden(ID, True)
self.logView.setColumnHidden(ASSETID, True)
self.logView.resizeColumnsToContents()
self.logView.horizontalHeader().setStretchLastSection(True)
```

This code is also similar to what we did for the assets table, but with three differences. Here we have used a custom LogDelegate class—we won't review it because it is structurally very similar to the `AssetDelegate`. It provides custom editing of the date field. We also hide both the log record's ID field and the `assetid` foreign key—there's no need to show which asset the log records are for because we are using master–detail, so the only log records that are visible are those that apply to the current asset. (We will see how the master–detail relationship is coded shortly.) The last difference is that we have set the last column to stretch to fill all the available space. The `QTableView.horizontalHeader()` method returns a `QHeaderView`, and this is what controls some aspects of the table view's columns, including their widths.

```
self.connect(self.assetView.selectionModel(),
        SIGNAL("currentRowChanged(QModelIndex,QModelIndex)"),
        self.assetChanged)
self.connect(addAssetButton, SIGNAL("clicked()"),
        self.addAsset)
```

If the user navigates to a different row we must update the log view to show the log records for the right asset. This is achieved by the first connection in conjunction with the `assetChanged()` method that we will review in a moment.

Every view has at least one selection model that is used to keep track of which items in the view's model (if any) are selected. We connect the view's selection model's `currentRowChanged()` signal so that we can update the log view depending on the current asset.

All the other connections are button-clicked connections like the second one shown here. We will cover all the methods the buttons connect to as we progress through this section.

```
self.assetChanged(self.assetView.currentIndex())
self.setMinimumWidth(650)
self.setWindowTitle("Asset Manager")
```

The initializer ends by calling the `assetChanged()` method with the asset view's current model index—this will result in the log view showing the relevant asset's records.

```
def assetChanged(self, index):
    if index.isValid():
        record = self.assetModel.record(index.row())
        id = record.value("id").toInt()[0]
        self.logModel.setFilter(QString("assetid = %1").arg(id))
    else:
        self.logModel.setFilter("assetid = -1")
    self.logModel.reset() # workaround for Qt <= 4.3.3/SQLite bug
    self.logModel.select()
    self.logView.horizontalHeader().setVisible(
            self.logModel.rowCount() > 0)
```

This method is called once by the form's initializer and then whenever the user navigates to a different asset, that is, to a different row in the assets table view. (The call to reset() is a workaround that forces the log view to update itself.)

If the model index of the new position in the view is valid, we retrieve the row's entire record from the model and set a filter on the log model that selects only those log records which have an assetid corresponding to the asset ID of the current row. (This is the equivalent of doing SELECT * FROM logs WHERE assetid = id.) Then we call select() to refresh the log view with the selected log records. If the model index is invalid, we set the ID to be one that we know does not exist, thereby guaranteeing that no rows will be retrieved and the log view will be empty. Finally, we hide the log view's column titles if there are no log records to display.

The record() method is one of the extensions that the QSqlTableModel and QSqlRelationalTableModel classes provide in addition to the methods from their QAbstractItemModel base class, to make them easier to use with databases. Other extensions include setQuery(), which allows us to write our own SELECT statement using SQL syntax, and insertRecord(), for adding records.

The connection to the assetChanged() method, and the implementation of the method, are all we have to do to establish a master–detail relationship between two models (and therefore, between their views).

```
def done(self, result=1):
    query = QSqlQuery()
    query.exec_("DELETE FROM logs WHERE logs.assetid NOT IN"
                "(SELECT id FROM assets)")
    QDialog.done(self, 1)
```

When the application terminates we execute one final query to delete any log records that are present for nonexistent (deleted) assets. In theory, this should never be needed, and therefore should do nothing. This is because, for databases that support transactions, we use transactions to ensure that if an asset is deleted, so are its log records.

```
def addAction(self):
    index = self.assetView.currentIndex()
    if not index.isValid():
        return
    QSqlDatabase.database().transaction()
    record = self.assetModel.record(index.row())
    assetid = record.value(ID).toInt()[0]

    row = self.logModel.rowCount()
    self.logModel.insertRow(row)
    self.logModel.setData(self.logModel.index(row, ASSETID),
                          QVariant(assetid))
    self.logModel.setData(self.logModel.index(row, DATE),
```

```
                        QVariant(QDate.currentDate())))
QSqlDatabase.database().commit()
index = self.logModel.index(row, ACTIONID)
self.logView.setCurrentIndex(index)
self.logView.edit(index)
```

If the user asks to add an action (a new log record), this method is called. We retrieve the assetid for the current asset, and then insert a new log record as the last record in the logs table. We then set the record's assetid foreign key to the one we have retrieved and provide an initial default date. Finally, we retrieve a model index to the new log record's action combobox, and initiate editing ready for the user to choose a suitable action.

Before we retrieve the assetid, we begin a transaction. This is to prevent the theoretical possibility that having retrieved the assetid, the asset is deleted just before the new log record is created. If this occurred, the log record would refer to a nonexistent asset, something that might cause crashes or subtler problems later on. Once we call commit(), we know that the asset and the new log record exist. If someone now tries to delete the asset, they can do so—but the asset's log records, including this one, will correctly be deleted along with it.

For a really defensive approach we might structure our transaction code like this:

```
class DatabaseError(Exception): pass

rollback = False
try:
    if not QSqlDatabase.database().transaction():
        raise DatabaseError()
    rollback = True
    # execute commands that affect the database
    if not QSqlDatabase.database().commit():
        raise DatabaseError()
    rollback = False
finally:
    if rollback:
        if not QSqlDatabase.database().rollback():
            raise DatabaseError()
```

This tries to ensure that if some problem occurs that prevents the commit from being reached, or from being able to execute successfully if it is called, we roll back to the previous position and therefore preserve the database's relational integrity. All bets are off if the rollback fails, though. The error text can be retrieved from QSqlDatabase.database().lastError().text(), which returns a QString.

The scope of a transaction goes from when transaction() is called until the transaction is either committed or rolled back. It does not matter whether the database has been accessed through QSqlDatabase or through a model. The context of the transaction applies to all SQL statements, including those executed by independent queries and those executed by different models, as long as they apply to the same database within the same transaction's context.

If we are using Python 2.6, or use from __future__ import with_statement in Python 2.5, we could simplify the code shown earlier by creating and using a context manager.

Using a Context Manager for Unlocking sidebar
☞ 549

The transaction-oriented approach tries to arrange things so that problems cannot occur. An alternative approach is to assume that everything will work, and rely on the database to preserve foreign key relationships and other aspects of data integrity. This won't work with SQLite 3, since it does not enforce relational integrity, but it does work with some other databases. With this approach, we can often code without using transactions. Most of the time things will work fine, and for those few occasions when a problem occurs, we rely on the database to refuse to do any action that would break its rules, and to provide us with an error message that we can report to the user.

Note that transactions are set on the database, accessed through the static QSqlDatabase.database() method. The database can also be accessed by calling the database() method on a model. Each database connection can handle one transaction at a time, so if we want more than one transaction at the same time, we must establish an extra connection for each extra transaction that we want to use.

```
def deleteAction(self):
    index = self.logView.currentIndex()
    if not index.isValid():
        return
    record = self.logModel.record(index.row())
    action = record.value(ACTIONID).toString()
    if action == "Acquired":
        QMessageBox.information(self, "Delete Log",
                "The 'Acquired' log record cannot be deleted.<br>"
                "You could delete the entire asset instead.")
        return
    when = unicode(record.value(DATE).toString())
    if QMessageBox.question(self, "Delete Log",
            "Delete log<br>%s %s?" % (when, action),
            QMessageBox.Yes|QMessageBox.No) == QMessageBox.No:
        return
    self.logModel.removeRow(index.row())
    self.logModel.submitAll()
```

For deleting actions, the logic that we have implemented is that users cannot delete the "Acquired" log record, that is, the first log record. (But they can delete an asset, and with that all its log records, as we will see shortly.) If the log record is one that the user is allowed to delete and they confirm the deletion, we simply call removeRow() on the log model and then submitAll() to update the underlying database.

```
def editActions(self):
    form = ReferenceDataDlg("actions", "Action", self)
    form.exec_()

def editCategories(self):
    form = ReferenceDataDlg("categories", "Category", self)
    form.exec_()
```

Since both the actions and the categories reference tables have identical structures, we can use the same smart dialog for when we want to drill down to add, edit, and delete their records. We give the dialog the name of the table in the database, and the name of the reference data to be shown in the user interface (in the dialog's title bar, for example).

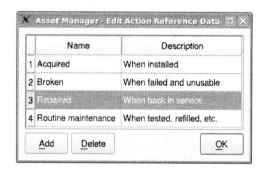

Figure 15.6 *The Asset Manager Reference Data form*

We won't review the code for the ReferenceDataDlg shown in Figure 15.6, because it does not have anything new to teach us. It uses a QTableView with a QSqlTableModel set to the table that is passed in to its constructor. Editing is in-place and handled automatically by the table view and table model. Adding a record is simply a matter of inserting a new row into the model and setting the view to it.

For reference data deletions, we execute a query to see whether the particular reference data record is being used by one of the other tables, that is, an action is used by any records in the logs table, or if a category is used by any records in the assets table. If the record is in use, we pop up an informative error message and do not permit the deletion to take place. Otherwise, we call removeRow() on the model for the relevant row and then submitAll() to commit the change to the database, just as we did when deleting an action.

Unlike reference data, adding and deleting assets is handled by the main form's methods.

```
def addAsset(self):
```

```
    row = self.assetView.currentIndex().row() \
        if self.assetView.currentIndex().isValid() else 0

    QSqlDatabase.database().transaction()
    self.assetModel.insertRow(row)
    index = self.assetModel.index(row, NAME)
    self.assetView.setCurrentIndex(index)

    assetid = 1
    query = QSqlQuery()
    query.exec_("SELECT MAX(id) FROM assets")
    if query.next():
        assetid = query.value(0).toInt()[0]
    query.prepare("INSERT INTO logs (assetid, date, actionid) "
                  "VALUES (:assetid, :date, :actionid)")
    query.bindValue(":assetid", QVariant(assetid + 1))
    query.bindValue(":date", QVariant(QDate.currentDate()))
    query.bindValue(":actionid", QVariant(ACQUIRED))
    query.exec_()
    QSqlDatabase.database().commit()
    self.assetView.edit(index)
```

When the user adds a new asset we want to create a new log record for the asset with its action set to "Acquired". Naturally, we want either both of these records created, or, if something goes wrong, neither, and to do this we must use a transaction.

We begin by initiating a transaction. Then we insert a new row and make it the current one in the asset view. If this is the very first asset, its ID will be 1, but if there are other assets, its ID will be one more than the highest asset ID. We execute a query to find the current highest asset ID and then we use a prepared query (so that we don't have to worry about quoting), to insert a new record into the logs table. Once the new record has gone into the logs table, we commit the transaction. Now we will have one log record for the new asset with an action of "Acquired", and a new blank asset record. Finally, we initiate editing on the new asset's name field.

We will finish reviewing the main form by looking at the deleteAsset() method. The method is slightly involved, so we will look at it in three parts.

```
    def deleteAsset(self):
        index = self.assetView.currentIndex()
        if not index.isValid():
            return
        QSqlDatabase.database().transaction()
        record = self.assetModel.record(index.row())
        assetid = record.value(ID).toInt()[0]
        logrecords = 1
        query = QSqlQuery(QString("SELECT COUNT(*) FROM logs "
```

```
                                "WHERE assetid = %1").arg(assetid))
        if query.next():
            logrecords = query.value(0).toInt()[0]
```

We begin by starting a transaction. This is because if an asset is to be deleted, all its log records must also be deleted, and either both of these things must happen or neither, to maintain the database's relational integrity.

We know that there must be at least one log record, the "Acquired" record, but we perform a query to see what the total number of log records is.

```
        msg = QString("<font color=red>Delete</font><br><b>%1</b>"
                      "<br>from room %2") \
                .arg(record.value(NAME).toString()) \
                .arg(record.value(ROOM).toString())
        if logrecords > 1:
            msg += QString(", along with %1 log records") \
                    .arg(logrecords)
        msg += "?"
        if QMessageBox.question(self, "Delete Asset", msg,
                QMessageBox.Yes|QMessageBox.No) == QMessageBox.No:
            QSqlDatabase.database().rollback()
            return
```

Here we give the user the opportunity to confirm their deletion or to cancel it. If they cancel, we rollback the transaction and return.

```
        query.exec_(QString("DELETE FROM logs WHERE assetid = %1") \
                    .arg(assetid))
        self.assetModel.removeRow(index.row())
        self.assetModel.submitAll()
        QSqlDatabase.database().commit()
        self.assetChanged(self.assetView.currentIndex())
```

We have deleted the log records using a SQL query, and the asset record using the model API. After the deletion we commit the transaction and call assetChanged() to make sure that the master–detail view is showing the correct log records.

We could have used the model API for both deletions. For example:

```
    self.logModel.setFilter(QString("assetid = %1").arg(assetid))
    self.logModel.select()
    if self.logModel.rowCount() > 0:
        self.logModel.removeRows(0, self.logModel.rowCount())
        self.logModel.submitAll()
```

This completes our review of the Asset Manager application. Creating master–detail relationships between tables is quite straightforward, and the same thing can be done between tables and forms using a data widget mapper. The SQL table models are very easy to use and "just work" with QTableViews. Also, we can create custom delegates to exercise complete control over the appearance and editing of fields, and where necessary we can use delegates to provide record level validation.

One issue that we have not had to concern ourselves with is that of creating unique keys for new records. We have solved the problem by using auto-incrementing ID fields in our tables. But sometimes auto-incrementing is not appropriate—for example, when a key is more complicated than a simple integer. We can handle such cases by connecting to the QSqlTableModel.beforeInsert() signal. This signal gives the method it is connected to a reference to the record that is about to be inserted (after the user has finished editing it), so we can populate or change any fields we like just before the data actually gets inserted into the database.

There are also some additional SQL-specific signals that we can connect to—for example, beforeDelete() and beforeUpdate(); these might be useful if we wanted to record deletions or changes in a separate table. Finally, there is the primeInsert() signal—this is emitted when a new record is created, but before the user has had the chance to edit it. This is where we might populate the record with helpful default values. However, in all the examples in this chapter, we have put in default values when the user clicked an Add button. Also note that since QSqlRelationalTableModel is a subclass of QSqlTableModel, it too has these signals.

Summary

PyQt provides strong support for SQL databases with a consistent API provided by the QtSql module. Database drivers are provided for all the most widely used databases, although some are available only with commercial editions of Qt due to licensing restrictions.

If we make a single database connection, all subsequent database accesses will use that connection by default. But if we need multiple connections, we can simply give each one a name, and access them by name afterward to specify which one we want to use for which particular action.

We can access the database's driver, and through that discover whether the database supports certain features such as BLOBs and transactions. And no matter what the underlying database is, PyQt allows us to use prepared queries with both ODBC and Oracle syntax, automatically handling any conversions and quoting that are necessary. PyQt supports all the standard SQL data types, and performs any necessary conversions if the database itself does not.

The QSqlQuery class allows us to execute arbitrary SQL statements using its exec_() method. This means, for example, that we can use it to create and drop tables, and to insert, update, and delete records. The QSqlQuery objects provide methods for navigating the result set produced when a SELECT statement is executed, and they can provide information on the number of rows affected by a query—for example, how many were deleted or updated.

Creating GUI forms for displaying database tables (or editable views) is straightforward using a QDataWidgetMapper. We normally use a QComboBox for each foreign key field, giving it the appropriate relation model as its internal model. Although it is possible to set a QDataWidgetMapper to submit changes automatically, this can lead to data loss when the user navigates, so if we provide a means of navigation, it is best to submit all the changes ourselves.

Displaying database tables and views is very easy using QTableView in conjunction with a QSqlTableModel or a QSqlRelationalTableModel. These classes combine to offer in-place editing of field data. Adding and deleting records can easily be achieved by inserting or deleting rows from the model, and when we need atomic actions we can use transactions.

All the functionality of PyQt's model/view architecture is available to database programmers. In addition, the SQL table models' APIs have been extended to make database programming easier. And when we need to execute raw SQL, we can easily do so using the QSqlQuery class.

We have now reached the point where you should be able to create any kind of GUI application you like, limited only by your imagination and the time available to you. In Part IV we will look at some additional topics that can be tricky to deal with, starting with more advanced material on model/view programming, then internationalization, then networking, and finishing up with multithreading.

Exercise

Create a dialog-style application for adding, editing, and deleting records in a reference table, like the one shown in Figure 15.7. The application should create the reference.db database the first time it is run, with a single, empty table:

```
CREATE TABLE reference (
    id INTEGER PRIMARY KEY AUTOINCREMENT UNIQUE NOT NULL,
    category VARCHAR(30) NOT NULL,
    shortdesc VARCHAR(20) NOT NULL,
    longdesc VARCHAR(80))
```

In addition to offering Add and Delete buttons, provide a Sort button that has a pop-up menu with three sort order options: by ID, by category, and by short description. All three could be connected to a single method using lambda or functools.partial. To make any new sort (or filter) take effect, you must call select() on the model. Use a QDialogButtonBox for all the buttons.

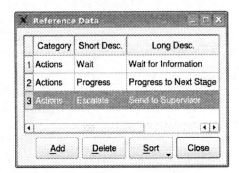

Figure 15.7 *The Reference Data dialog*

If the user clicks Delete, pop up a yes/no message box, and delete only if they click the Yes button. The application is similar to the ReferenceDataDlg from the Asset Manager application, and can be written in about 130 lines.

A solution is provided in chap15/referencedata.pyw.

Part IV

Advanced GUI Programming

16

● Custom Views

● Generic Delegates

● Representing Tabular Data in Trees

Advanced Model/View Programming

In the two preceding chapters we explored the basics of PyQt model/view programming.* We saw how to create custom models, and how to use the predefined SQL table models. We also saw how to create custom delegates to control the appearance and editing of data items. In this chapter, we will deepen our knowledge of PyQt model/view programming.

All of the topics covered in this chapter, and the ones that follow, are more advanced than the ones we have seen before, at least conceptually. However, in most cases the code is no more difficult than what we have already seen.

In the first section we will look at how to implement a custom view so that we can see how to visualize our data in any way we want. This section is useful for understanding more about how views work, and to see one straightforward approach to implementing a custom view.

The second section revisits the subject of custom delegates, showing how to minimize code duplication and how to easily create arbitrary delegates for views. This section should prove especially useful to those who need to create many delegates, especially for datasets such as SQL tables where each column is of a particular type.

In the final section we will see how to reflect tabular data into a tree view. One use of this is where we represent tables as trees when the first few columns often contain the same values—this has the effect of reducing the number of rows that the user must navigate to find the item they want. Another use is to let users pick particular values that form a "path". For example, rather than providing two, three, or more comboboxes, each with values that depend on the current values of its predecessors, we just provide a single tree for the user to navigate and choose from.

---

*This chapter assumes a knowledge of PyQt's model/view architecture, covered in Chapter 14.

Custom Views

PyQt provides several view classes that work well out of the box, including QListView, QTableView, and QTreeView. One thing that all these views have in common is that they are usually used to present data items textually—although all of them can also show icons and checkboxes if desired. An alternative to textual representations of data are visual representations, and for these we can use the graphics view classes covered in Chapter 12. Sometimes, though, we want to present data in a way that doesn't really match any of the classes that are available. In such cases we can create our own view subclass and use it to visualize our models.

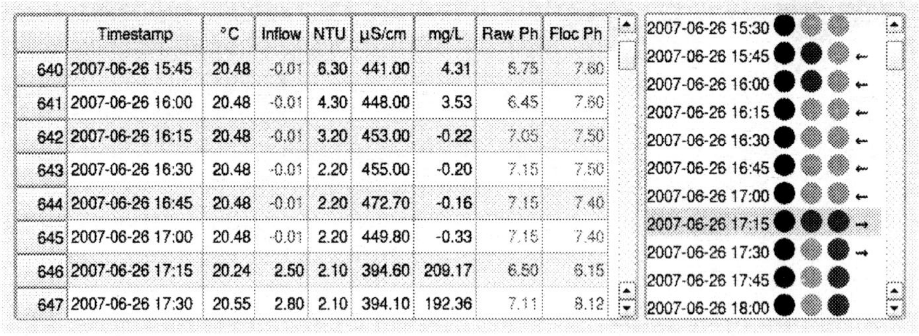

	Timestamp	°C	Inflow	NTU	μS/cm	mg/L	Raw Ph	Floc Ph
640	2007-06-26 15:45	20.48	-0.01	6.30	441.00	4.31	5.75	7.60
641	2007-06-26 16:00	20.48	-0.01	4.30	448.00	3.53	6.45	7.60
642	2007-06-26 16:15	20.48	-0.01	3.20	453.00	-0.22	7.05	7.50
643	2007-06-26 16:30	20.48	-0.01	2.20	455.00	-0.20	7.15	7.50
644	2007-06-26 16:45	20.48	-0.01	2.20	472.70	-0.16	7.15	7.40
645	2007-06-26 17:00	20.48	-0.01	2.20	449.80	-0.33	7.15	7.40
646	2007-06-26 17:15	20.24	2.50	2.10	394.60	209.17	6.50	6.15
647	2007-06-26 17:30	20.55	2.80	2.10	394.10	192.36	7.11	8.12

Figure 16.1 *Two views of water quality data*

Figure 16.1 shows the same dataset presented by two different views. The left-hand view is a standard QTableView, and the right-hand view is a custom WaterQualityView. Both show the timestamps of water quality readings textually, but the WaterQualityView shows colored circles for three key indicators, and it uses Unicode arrow symbols to signify special flow situations. Obviously, the table view presents the facts in a clear and accurate way, but the water quality view makes it easier to see what the situation is at any particular time, and it makes it easier to get an impression of any important trends, just by looking at the colors.

The water quality dataset covers a six-month period at one small water treatment plant—but with readings taken every 15 minutes, this adds up to slightly more than 17 500 readings. This implies that our view is going to need a vertical scrollbar. PyQt offers three ways to get scrollbars. One way is to create a widget that inherits QAbstractScrollArea; this approach is used by the QGraphicsView and QTextEdit widgets. Another way is to create a composite widget that includes a couple of QScrollBars. But PyQt's documentation recommends the third way—using the much simpler QScrollArea instead. The one disadvantage of using QScrollArea is that it is one of the few PyQt classes not designed to be subclassed. Instead, we must create an instance and add to it the widget for which we want scrollbars. To put this into perspective here is the Water Quality Data application's initializer:

```
class MainForm(QDialog):

    def __init__(self, parent=None):
        super(MainForm, self).__init__(parent)

        self.model = WaterQualityModel(os.path.join(
                os.path.dirname(__file__), "waterdata.csv.gz"))
        self.tableView = QTableView()
        self.tableView.setAlternatingRowColors(True)
        self.tableView.setModel(self.model)
        self.waterView = WaterQualityView()
        self.waterView.setModel(self.model)
        scrollArea = QScrollArea()
        scrollArea.setBackgroundRole(QPalette.Light)
        scrollArea.setWidget(self.waterView)
        self.waterView.scrollarea = scrollArea

        splitter = QSplitter(Qt.Horizontal)
        splitter.addWidget(self.tableView)
        splitter.addWidget(scrollArea)
        splitter.setSizes([600, 250])
        layout = QHBoxLayout()
        layout.addWidget(splitter)
        self.setLayout(layout)

        self.setWindowTitle("Water Quality Data")
        QTimer.singleShot(0, self.initialLoad)
```

The preceding code is the whole thing. The WaterQualityModel is a QAbstract-
TableModel subclass that provides read-only access to a water quality data file.
The WaterQualityView is the class we will develop in this section. One special
thing that we have done here is to create a QScrollArea widget and add the
water quality view to it—this basically means that the water quality view can
be as wide and as tall as we like and the scroll area will take care of scrolling
issues.

We will see shortly that keyboard users can navigate in the water quality
view using the up and down arrow keys, and to ensure that the selected row is
always visible we must pass the scroll area to the water quality view so that
our key press handler can interact with it. Another thing that is special is
that we have given initial sizes to the two parts of the horizontal splitter so
that at start-up, they are roughly in the right proportions for the widgets they
are holding.

We will now review the WaterQualityView, beginning with some static data and
the initializer.

```
class WaterQualityView(QWidget):

    FLOWCHARS = (unichr(0x21DC), unichr(0x21DD), unichr(0x21C9))
```

```
def __init__(self, parent=None):
    super(WaterQualityView, self).__init__(parent)
    self.scrollarea = None
    self.model = None
    self.setFocusPolicy(Qt.StrongFocus)
    self.selectedRow = -1
    self.flowfont = self.font()
    size = self.font().pointSize()
    if platform.system() == "Windows":
        fontDb = QFontDatabase()
        for face in [face.toLower() for face in fontDb.families()]:
            if face.contains("unicode"):
                self.flowfont = QFont(face, size)
                break
    else:
        self.flowfont = QFont("symbol", size)
        WaterQualityView.FLOWCHARS = (
                chr(0xAC), chr(0xAE), chr(0xDE))
```

Setting the focus policy to anything (except Qt.NoFocus) means that the widget can accept keyboard focus. We will discuss why we have done this, and the selectedRow instance variable, at the end of this section.

When water flow is going the wrong way, or too slowly, or too quickly, we want to indicate the situation with a suitable character—for example, ←, →, and ⇴. These characters are available in Unicode, but most of the default fonts supplied with Windows don't appear to include the whole Unicode character set, so all the arrows are shown as □ characters. (On Linux, if a Unicode character is not available in the current font, PyQt can usually find the character in another font, in which case it uses the found font just for that character.)

To solve this problem on Windows we iterate over the list of available fonts until we find one with "Unicode" in its name (e.g., "Lucida Sans Unicode"). If we find such a font, we store it as the flow characters' font; otherwise, we fall back to the standard (but non-Unicode) Symbol font and use the nearest equivalent characters in that font.

```
def setModel(self, model):
    self.model = model
    self.connect(self.model,
        SIGNAL("dataChanged(QModelIndex,QModelIndex)"),
        self.setNewSize)
    self.connect(self.model, SIGNAL("modelReset()"),
                self.setNewSize)
    self.setNewSize()
```

Once a model is set on the view we connect to its data-changed and reset signals so that the view can be resized to match the available data.

```
def setNewSize(self):
    self.resize(self.sizeHint())
    self.update()
    self.updateGeometry()
```

This method resizes the view to its preferred size and calls update() to schedule a repaint and updateGeometry() to tell any layout manager that is responsible for the view that its size has changed. Because we put the view in a QScrollArea, the scroll area will respond to changes in size by adjusting the scrollbars it provides.

```
def minimumSizeHint(self):
    size = self.sizeHint()
    fm = QFontMetrics(self.font())
    size.setHeight(fm.height() * 3)
    return size
```

We calculate the view's minimum size to be its preferred size's width and three characters in height. In a layout this makes sense, but since a QScrollArea is used, the minimum size will, in practice, be whatever the scroll area decides.

```
def sizeHint(self):
    fm = QFontMetrics(self.font())
    size = fm.height()
    return QSize(fm.width("9999-99-99 99:99 ") + (size * 4),
                 (size / 4) + (size * self.model.rowCount()))
```

We use the height of one character (including its interline spacing) as our unit of size for both vertical and horizontal measurements. The view's preferred size is wide enough to show a timestamp plus four units of size to allow for the colored circles and the flow character, and it's tall enough for all the rows in the model plus one-quarter of the unit of size to allow a tiny bit of margin.

The paint event isn't too difficult, but we will look at it in three parts, and show the code for only one colored circle since the code for all three is almost identical.

```
def paintEvent(self, event):
    if self.model is None:
        return
    fm = QFontMetrics(self.font())
    timestampWidth = fm.width("9999-99-99 99:99 ")
    size = fm.height()
    indicatorSize = int(size * 0.8)
    offset = int(1.5 * (size - indicatorSize))
    minY = event.rect().y()
    maxY = minY + event.rect().height() + size
    minY -= size
    painter = QPainter(self)
```

```
painter.setRenderHint(QPainter.Antialiasing)
painter.setRenderHint(QPainter.TextAntialiasing)
```

If there is no model we do nothing and return. Otherwise, we need to calculate some sizes. Just like the sizeHint(), we use the height of one character as our unit of size, setting the indicatorSize (the diameter of the colored circles) to 80% of this amount. The offset is a tiny amount of vertical spacing designed to make the circles align vertically with the timestamp text.

Given the large size of the datasets that the view might be asked to show, it seems sensible to paint only those items that are wholly or partially visible to the user. For this reason, we set the minimum y coordinate to the paint event rectangle's y coordinate (but minus one size unit), and the maximum y coordinate to be the minimum plus the paint event's height plus one size unit. This means that we will paint from the item above the topmost item that is wholly in the view (i.e., the one with the lowest y coordinate in range, since point $(0, 0)$ is the top-left corner), down to the item below the bottommost item that is wholly in the view (i.e., the one with the highest y coordinate in range).

A paint event's event parameter contains the size of the region that needs repainting. Very often we can disregard this information and simply paint the entire widget, but sometimes, as here, we use the information to make our painting more efficient.

```
y = 0
for row in range(self.model.rowCount()):
    x = 0
    if minY <= y <= maxY:
        painter.save()
        painter.setPen(self.palette().color(QPalette.Text))
        if row == self.selectedRow:
            painter.fillRect(x, y + (offset * 0.8),
                             self.width(), size,
                             self.palette().highlight())
            painter.setPen(self.palette().color(
                    QPalette.HighlightedText))
        timestamp = self.model.data(
                self.model.index(row, TIMESTAMP)).toDateTime()
        painter.drawText(x, y + size,
                timestamp.toString(TIMESTAMPFORMAT))
        x += timestampWidth
        temperature = self.model.data(
                self.model.index(row, TEMPERATURE))
        temperature = temperature.toDouble()[0]
        if temperature < 20:
            color = QColor(0, 0,
                           int(255 * (20 - temperature) / 20))
        elif temperature > 25:
```

```
            color = QColor(int(255 * temperature / 100), 0, 0)
        else:
            color = QColor(0, int(255 * temperature / 100), 0)
        painter.setPen(Qt.NoPen)
        painter.setBrush(color)
        painter.drawEllipse(x, y + offset, indicatorSize,
                                      indicatorSize)
        x += size
```

We iterate over every row in the model, but paint only those with a y coordinate that is in range. Once we have a row to paint, we set the pen (used for drawing text) to the palette's text color. If the row is selected (something we will explain after covering the paint event), we paint the background in the palette's highlight color and set the pen to the palette's highlighted text color.

Having set up the text color, and possibly painted the background, we then retrieve and draw the row's timestamp. For each row we keep an x coordinate that tells us how far across we are, and that we increment by the font metrics timestamp width we calculated earlier.

The first colored circle is used to indicate the water's temperature in °C. If the water is too cool we use a color with a blue tint; if it is too warm we use a color with a red tint; otherwise, we use a green tint. Then we switch off the pen and set the brush to the color we have set up and paint an ellipse to the right of the timestamp. The drawEllipse() method will draw a circle because the width and height of the rectangle in which the ellipse is drawn are the same.

We then increment the x coordinate. Now we repeat the process for the other two colored circle indicators, using the same tinting approach we used for temperature. We have omitted the code for these, since it is structurally identical to the code used for the temperature circle.

```
        flow = self.model.data(
                self.model.index(row, INLETFLOW))
        flow = flow.toDouble()[0]
        char = None
        if flow <= 0:
            char = WaterQualityView.FLOWCHARS[0]
        elif flow < 3:
            char = WaterQualityView.FLOWCHARS[1]
        elif flow > 5.5:
            char = WaterQualityView.FLOWCHARS[2]
        if char is not None:
            painter.setFont(self.flowfont)
            painter.drawText(x, y + size, char)
        painter.restore()
    y += size
    if y > maxY:
        break
```

If the water flow is in the wrong direction, or if it is too slow or too fast, we draw a suitable character, using the font and characters that were set in the initializer.

At the end we increment the *y* coordinate ready for the next row of data, but if we have gone past the last row that is in view, we stop.

The code we have written so far is sufficient to provide a read-only view of the dataset. But users often want to highlight an item. The easiest way to do this is to add a mouse press event handler.

```python
def mousePressEvent(self, event):
    fm = QFontMetrics(self.font())
    self.selectedRow = event.y() // fm.height()
    self.update()
    self.emit(SIGNAL("clicked(QModelIndex)"),
              self.model.index(self.selectedRow, 0))
```

The unit of size used for all our calculations is the height of a character. We divide the mouse position's *y* coordinate (which is relative to the top-left corner of the widget) by the unit of size, to find which row the user clicked. We use integer division because row numbers are whole numbers. Then we call update() to schedule a paint event. In the paintEvent() we saw that the selected row is drawn using highlighted text and background colors. We also emit a clicked() signal, with the model index of the first column of the row that was clicked. The signal is not used by this application, but providing it is a good practice when implementing custom views.

Keyboard users are catered for already by the scroll area: They can scroll using the Page Up and Page Down keys. But we ought to provide a means for keyboard users to select an item. To do this we must make sure that the widget has a suitable focus policy—we did this in the initializer—and we must provide a key press event handler.

```python
def keyPressEvent(self, event):
    if self.model is None:
        return
    row = -1
    if event.key() == Qt.Key_Up:
        row = max(0, self.selectedRow - 1)
    elif event.key() == Qt.Key_Down:
        row = min(self.selectedRow + 1, self.model.rowCount() - 1)
    if row != -1 and row != self.selectedRow:
        self.selectedRow = row
        if self.scrollarea is not None:
            fm = QFontMetrics(self.font())
            y = fm.height() * self.selectedRow
            self.scrollarea.ensureVisible(0, y)
        self.update()
```

```
            self.emit(SIGNAL("clicked(QModelIndex)"),
                    self.model.index(self.selectedRow, 0))
    else:
        QWidget.keyPressEvent(self, event)
```

We have chosen to support just two key presses: Up Arrow and Down Arrow. If the user presses either of these, we increment or decrement the selected row, make sure that the selected row is in range, and then schedule a paint event. If the user navigates to the row above the topmost visible row or below the bottommost visible row, we tell the scroll area to make sure that the row that has been scrolled to is visible—if necessary, the scroll area will scroll to achieve this. We also emit a clicked() signal with the newly selected row's model index. It is quite conventional to use a clicked() signal in this circumstance, since in effect, the user is "clicking" using the keyboard—after all, the signals and slots mechanism is concerned with what the user wants rather than how they asked for it, and here they just want to select a row.

If we do not handle the key press ourselves, that is, for all other key presses, we pass the event on to the base class.

The water quality view widget is visually very different from the table view shown beside it, yet it did not require that much code to implement and was not too difficult to program. We made the widget fairly efficient by reducing the amount of unnecessary painting. We also made the painting code as simple as possible by ensuring that the widget was always exactly the size necessary to display the entire dataset. The disadvantage of this approach is that it pushes responsibility on to the programmer using our widget to use a QScrollArea, although this saves us from having to implement scrolling ourselves.

The water quality view visualizes the data in one-to-one correspondence with the data in the model, but we are not constrained to doing this. It is also possible to create custom views that show aggregated data. In this case, for example, we could have shown one entry per day, or per hour, perhaps by averaging each day or hour's readings.

Generic Delegates

As we have seen in earlier chapters, custom delegates allow us to exercise complete control over the appearance and behavior of the data items that appear in views. Although it is obvious that if we have many models, we are likely to want a custom delegate for most if not all of them, what is not so obvious, is that the custom delegates will very likely have a lot of duplicate code.*

---

*This section is partly based on ideas from the author's whitepaper, "Qt 4's Model/View Delegates", available at http://www.ics.com/developers/papers/.

Imagine that we have just four models, each with an integer ID column, some string columns holding plain text, and a description column holding HTML text, and for some of the models, one or two floating-point columns. All the models have the ID as their first column, but the other columns don't match up, so each one requires its own custom delegate. Providing the custom delegates is not a big undertaking, but the code dealing with the integer IDs might be the same in all of them; similarly for the strings, HTML strings, and floating-point numbers.

Now imagine that we have to write custom delegates for another half dozen new models: Much of the code will again be duplicated—and this will probably make maintenance more difficult.

What would be better, particularly for models that have one data type per column, like database tables, is if instead of creating a custom delegate for each model, we could compose a delegate from a set of generic components. This would mean that the maintenance would be confined to the generic components, and a bug fix in one would automatically benefit any view that used it.

In code, the effect we are after is something like this:

```
self.table1 = QTableView()
self.table1.setModel(self.model1)
delegate1 = GenericDelegate(self)
delegate1.insertColumnDelegate(1, PlainTextColumnDelegate())
delegate1.insertColumnDelegate(2, PlainTextColumnDelegate())
delegate1.insertColumnDelegate(3, RichTextColumnDelegate())
delegate1.insertColumnDelegate(4, IntegerColumnDelegate())
self.table1.setItemDelegate(delegate1)

self.table2 = QTableView()
self.table2.setModel(self.model2)
delegate2 = GenericDelegate(self)
delegate2.insertColumnDelegate(1, PlainTextColumnDelegate())
delegate2.insertColumnDelegate(2, IntegerColumnDelegate())
delegate2.insertColumnDelegate(3, FloatColumnDelegate())
delegate2.insertColumnDelegate(4, FloatColumnDelegate())
delegate2.insertColumnDelegate(5, RichTextColumnDelegate())
self.table2.setItemDelegate(delegate2)
```

Here we have two separate models, but both use generic delegates that are composed of predefined column delegates that are data-type-specific.

With this approach, we only ever have to create a single plain text column delegate, a single rich text column delegate, and so on, for each data type we want to handle, such as integers, floating-point numbers, dates, times, and date/times. In addition, we might create some project-specific column delegates to handle custom types, but for any given data type there would be only one column delegate, drastically cutting down on code duplication and ensuring that any model can have a "custom" delegate simply by using a generic delegate with suitable column delegates added.

In this section, we will see how to create a GenericDelegate class and a couple of example column delegates. Then we will see how they are used in the context of the application shown in Figure 16.2.

	License	Customer	Hired	Mileage #1	Returned	Mileage #2	Notes	Miles	Days
37	FT56 LNC	Ms Inglis	2006-06-06	13199	2006-06-22	17055		3856	16
38	NN07 AUP	Mr Berreth	2006-06-07	18032	2006-06-26	20901	Customer **complained** about the gears	2869	19
39	YR56 JRK	Ms Boston	2006-06-09	25000	2006-06-13	25540		540	4
40	BQ07 WRM	Mr Terhune	2006-06-10	17015	2006-07-01	22769		5754	21
41	UN06 DUE	Ms Harvill	2006-06-11	14374			Sold		
42	DV58 OEJ	Ms Jolly	2006-06-11	17142	2006-06-21	19012		1870	10
43	JJ57 TDP	Ms Clemy	2006-06-12	23996	2006-06-20	26364	Returned damaged	2368	8
44	QD06 XBQ	Ms Courtice	2006-06-12	17063	2006-06-15	17600		537	3
45	SJ06 IAQ	Ms Garraway	2006-06-12	12966	2006-06-14	13508	Returned with empty fuel tank	542	2
46	JY56 RVW	Ms Verney	2006-06-14	22085	2006-06-28	26257	Returned dirty	4172	14

Figure 16.2 *A table view using generic delegates*

The GenericDelegate class is simple, because it passes almost all the work to other classes.

```
class GenericDelegate(QItemDelegate):

    def __init__(self, parent=None):
        super(GenericDelegate, self).__init__(parent)
        self.delegates = {}
```

The initializer calls super() as usual, and creates an empty dictionary. The keys will be column indexes and the values will be instances of QItemDelegate subclasses.

```
    def insertColumnDelegate(self, column, delegate):
        delegate.setParent(self)
        self.delegates[column] = delegate
```

When a new column delegate is inserted into the generic delegate, the generic delegate takes ownership of it and inserts it into the dictionary.

```
    def removeColumnDelegate(self, column):
        if column in self.delegates:
            del self.delegates[column]
```

This method is included for completeness, but it is not likely to be used. If a column delegate is removed, the generic delegate will simply use the QItemDelegate base class for that column.

```
def paint(self, painter, option, index):
    delegate = self.delegates.get(index.column())
    if delegate is not None:
        delegate.paint(painter, option, index)
    else:
        QItemDelegate.paint(self, painter, option, index)
```

The structure of this method is the key to how the GenericDelegate class works. We begin by getting the column delegate for the given column. If we get a delegate, we pass the work to it; otherwise, we pass the work to the base class.

```
def createEditor(self, parent, option, index):
    delegate = self.delegates.get(index.column())
    if delegate is not None:
        return delegate.createEditor(parent, option, index)
    else:
        return QItemDelegate.createEditor(self, parent, option,
                                                       index)
```

This method follows the same pattern as the paint() method, except that it returns a value (the editor that was created for it).

```
def setEditorData(self, editor, index):
    delegate = self.delegates.get(index.column())
    if delegate is not None:
        delegate.setEditorData(editor, index)
    else:
        QItemDelegate.setEditorData(self, editor, index)

def setModelData(self, editor, model, index):
    delegate = self.delegates.get(index.column())
    if delegate is not None:
        delegate.setModelData(editor, model, index)
    else:
        QItemDelegate.setModelData(self, editor, model, index)
```

These last two GenericDelegate methods follow the same pattern as the paint() and createEditor() methods, using the column delegate if one has been set for the given column, and using the QItemDelegate base class otherwise.

Now that we have seen the GenericDelegate's implementation, we can turn our attention to the column delegates that can be inserted into it. In chap16/genericdelegates.py we provide the IntegerColumnDelegate, DateColumnDelegate, PlainTextColumnDelegate, and RichTextColumnDelegate classes. All of them have a similar structure, so we will look at the code for only two of them, DateColumnDelegate, and RichTextColumnDelegate. Once the implementation of these is understood (and it is easy, at least for the date column delegate), creating additional column delegates, such as one for floating-point numbers, will be straightforward.

```
class DateColumnDelegate(QItemDelegate):

    def __init__(self, minimum=QDate(), maximum=QDate.currentDate(),
                 format="yyyy-MM-dd", parent=None):
        super(DateColumnDelegate, self).__init__(parent)
        self.minimum = minimum
        self.maximum = maximum
        self.format = QString(format)
```

For dates, we want to provide minimum and maximum values, as well as a display format.

```
    def createEditor(self, parent, option, index):
        dateedit = QDateEdit(parent)
        dateedit.setDateRange(self.minimum, self.maximum)
        dateedit.setAlignment(Qt.AlignRight|Qt.AlignVCenter)
        dateedit.setDisplayFormat(self.format)
        dateedit.setCalendarPopup(True)
        return dateedit
```

The code for creating the editor follows the general pattern we saw back in Chapter 14: We create the editor with the given parent, set it up, and then return it. Here we have used the minimum, maximum, and format values that were passed to the initializer.

```
    def setEditorData(self, editor, index):
        value = index.model().data(index, Qt.DisplayRole).toDate()
        editor.setDate(value)
```

We set the editor's value to be the value of the data item at the given model index. We do *not* need to check the column, since this column delegate will be called only by the GenericDelegate for the column that the user has specified.

```
    def setModelData(self, editor, model, index):
        model.setData(index, QVariant(editor.date()))
```

When writing the editor's data back to the model, again we don't have to check the column because that's taken care of by the GenericDelegate.

This is the complete DateColumnDelegate. We did not need to reimplement the paint() method because the QItemDelegate base class can draw the data perfectly well. The IntegerColumnDelegate and PlainTextColumnDelegate are both very similar to the DateColumnDelegate. The RichTextColumnDelegate is also similar, but it also reimplements the paint() and sizeHint() methods.

```
class RichTextColumnDelegate(QItemDelegate):
```

```
        def __init__(self, parent=None):
            super(RichTextColumnDelegate, self).__init__(parent)
```

The constructor is even simpler than the one used for the other column delegates. We could even omit it, but we prefer to be explicit.

```
        def createEditor(self, parent, option, index):
            lineedit = richtextlineedit.RichTextLineEdit(parent)
            return lineedit
```

We use the RichTextLineEdit that we created in Chapter 13. Structurally this method is the same as for the other column delegates, except that here we don't need to set up the editor in any particular way.

```
        def setEditorData(self, editor, index):
            value = index.model().data(index, Qt.DisplayRole).toString()
            editor.setHtml(value)
```

The RichTextLineEdit accepts HTML text if we use its setHtml() method. (It also has a setPlainText() method.)

```
        def setModelData(self, editor, model, index):
            model.setData(index, QVariant(editor.toSimpleHtml()))
```

The RichTextLineEdit has a toHtml() method, but we use the toSimpleHtml() method that we developed in Chapter 13. This ensures that we store the shortest possible HTML that validly represents the text. This is important because in the paint() method, for highlighted (i.e., selected) items, we will set the color of the text by wrapping it in a <font> tag—this will work for text that uses the simple HTML format since it is just an HTML fragment, but not for the normal HTML format which is a complete HTML document.

```
        def paint(self, painter, option, index):
            text = index.model().data(index, Qt.DisplayRole).toString()
            palette = QApplication.palette()
            document = QTextDocument()
            document.setDefaultFont(option.font)
            if option.state & QStyle.State_Selected:
                document.setHtml(QString("<font color=%1>%2</font>") \
                        .arg(palette.highlightedText().color().name()) \
                        .arg(text))
            else:
                document.setHtml(text)
            painter.save()
            color = palette.highlight().color() \
                    if option.state & QStyle.State_Selected \
                    else QColor(index.model().data(index,
                            Qt.BackgroundColorRole))
            painter.fillRect(option.rect, color)
```

```
painter.translate(option.rect.x(), option.rect.y())
document.drawContents(painter)
painter.restore()
```

Paint-
ing rich
text in a
delegate

438 ☞

The paint() method is almost the same as the one used with the ShipDelegate described in Chapter 14. The only difference is that we don't have to check for a particular column since we know that the column delegate is only ever called for the column the user has specified.

One limitation of this approach is that the highlighting works only with HTML fragments. If we want the code to work with both fragments and complete HTML documents, we could use code like this:

```
if option.state & QStyle.State_Selected:
    if text.startsWith("<html>"):
        text = QString(text).replace("<body ",
                QString("<body bgcolor=%1 ")
                .arg(palette.highlightedText().color().name()))
    else:
        text = QString("<font color=%1>%2</font>")\
                .arg(palette.highlightedText().color().name())\
                .arg(text))
document.setHtml(text)
```

Another approach would be to extract the text document's style sheet, update the background color, and set the updated style sheet back on the document.

```
def sizeHint(self, option, index):
    text = index.model().data(index).toString()
    document = QTextDocument()
    document.setDefaultFont(option.font)
    document.setHtml(text)
    return QSize(document.idealWidth() + 5,
                    option.fontMetrics.height())
```

Size
hints for
rich text
in a
delegate

439 ☞

We must calculate the size hint for a rich text column ourselves because the default calculation based on the widget's font size and the number of characters will usually give widths that are much too wide. This is because HTML text usually contains far more characters (such as tags and entities) than the number of characters that are actually displayed. This is easy to solve by using a QTextDocument. The code is almost the same as that used for the ShipDelegate's size hint method.

We can easily create other column delegates, and we could make any column delegate offer more functionality than the examples shown here provide. For example, for the IntegerColumnDelegate we have minimum and maximum values, but it would be simple to provide additional options, such as prefix and suffix text.

Now that we have seen how the `GenericDelegate` works and how to create column delegates, we can see how they are used in practice. Figure 16.2 (on page 485) shows a table view that uses a generic delegate with several column delegates to provide control over the editing and appearance of its columns. The form is in `chap16/carhirelog.pyw`; here is the beginning of its initializer:

```
class MainForm(QMainWindow):

    def __init__(self, parent=None):
        super(MainForm, self).__init__(parent)

        model = CarHireModel(self)

        self.view = QTableView()
        self.view.setModel(model)
        self.view.resizeColumnsToContents()

        delegate = genericdelegates.GenericDelegate(self)
        delegate.insertColumnDelegate(CUSTOMER,
                genericdelegates.PlainTextColumnDelegate())
        earliest = QDate.currentDate().addYears(-3)
        delegate.insertColumnDelegate(HIRED,
                HireDateColumnDelegate(earliest))
        delegate.insertColumnDelegate(MILEAGEOUT,
                MileageOutColumnDelegate(0, 1000000))
        delegate.insertColumnDelegate(RETURNED,
                ReturnDateColumnDelegate(earliest))
        delegate.insertColumnDelegate(MILEAGEBACK,
                MileageBackColumnDelegate(0, 1000000))
        delegate.insertColumnDelegate(NOTES,
                genericdelegates.RichTextColumnDelegate())

        self.view.setItemDelegate(delegate)
        self.setCentralWidget(self.view)
```

The model is a custom model similar to ones we created in Chapter 14. The view is a standard `QTableView`.

The model has nine columns: a plain text read-only license number, a plain text customer name, a hired date (a `QDate`), an integer starting mileage (mileage out), a returned date (a `QDate`), an integer returned mileage (mileage back), and a rich text notes column, as well as two columns that are generated rather than stored—a mileage column (the difference between the back and out mileages), and a days column (the difference between the returned and hired dates).

The model and the underlying data structure take care of the read-only license column and the generated columns (as we will discuss shortly), so we only need to provide column delegates for the editable columns. For the customer name we use a `PlainTextColumnDelegate`, and for the notes we use a `RichTextLineEdit`. But for the mileages and dates we have used custom column delegates that are subclasses of the `IntegerColumnDelegate` and `DateColumnDelegate`. We need these subclasses to provide cross-column validation. For example, we cannot accept a returned date that is earlier than the hired date, or a mileage back that is less than the starting mileage.

```
class HireDateColumnDelegate(genericdelegates.DateColumnDelegate):

    def createEditor(self, parent, option, index):
        i = index.sibling(index.row(), RETURNED)
        self.maximum = i.model().data(i, Qt.DisplayRole) \
                                          .toDate().addDays(-1)
        return genericdelegates.DateColumnDelegate.createEditor(
                    self, parent, option, index)
```

This is the complete `HireDateColumnDelegate` subclass. We only need to reimplement `createEditor()`. We retrieve the *returned* date and set the maximum hired date to be the day before the car was returned, since we have a minimum of one day's car hire. We actually leave the creation of the editor to the base class. We cannot set a meaningful maximum date when the column delegate is created because the user could edit the returned date at any time, so we must calculate the maximum hired date when the user starts to edit it.

Using the `sibling()` method provides us with a more convenient alternative to calling `index.model().index(index.row(), RETURNED)`.

The `ReturnDateColumnDelegate` is almost identical, except that we retrieve the hired date and set the minimum returned date to the day after the car was hired. The `MileageOutColumnDelegate` and `MileageBackColumnDelegate` are similar; they both only reimplement the `createEditor()` method, and both set the maximum (or minimum) depending on the other mileage's value.

The model's `setData()` method does not allow editing of the license number, or of the generated columns. It does this by simply returning `False` for those columns, which indicates that they were not updated. For the other columns the value passed in to the `setData()` method is set in the underlying data structure.

The model's `data()` method faithfully returns the value of the column it is asked for, as provided by the underlying data structure. The data structure returns stored values for most of the columns, but for the `MILEAGE` and `DAYS` columns it returns values calculated from the relevant values.

Creating general data-type-specific column delegates is quite easy, and subclassing them when validation must take into account the whole row (record) is not difficult either. But since it isn't hard to create a custom delegate for each model, why use the generic delegate approach at all? There are two main contexts where generic delegates don't make sense: simple applications where only a few delegates are needed, and models that have columns which contain heterogeneous data types. But for applications that need many delegates and where columns have homogeneous data types such as those used in databases, generic delegates offer three key benefits.

- It is easy to change the delegate used for a particular column, or to add additional column delegates if the model is changed to have more columns.

- Using column delegates means that we avoid the code duplication that is inevitable if we create many model-specific custom delegates—for example, we need to write only one rich text line editing delegate, one date/time editing delegate, and so on.

- Once a data-type-specific column delegate is created, it can be reused for every column that uses that data type, in any number of generic delegates used with any number of models. This means that bug fixes and enhancements need to be applied to only one column delegate for each data type.

Representing Tabular Data in Trees

Suppose we want the user to pick out a data item, but that the item they pick depends on some previous item they picked, which in turn depends on some previous item again. In concrete terms, imagine that we want the user to choose a particular airport—first they must choose the country, then the city, and then the airport. This could be done by providing three comboboxes, populating the first with country names, and populating the second with the cities in the current country, and the third with the airports in the current city. This is not difficult to program, but the user must use three separate widgets to specify their choice, and can't easily see what range of choices are available to them.

One solution to choosing dependent data items is to use a tree view. To continue the example, the roots of the tree would be the countries, and each country would have city branches, and each city branch would have airport leaves. This makes it much easier for the user to follow a path (and they can follow only valid paths), and easier for us to retrieve their complete country/city/airport choice.

Another benefit of using a tree view, compared, for example, with using a table view, is that it is more compact and easier to navigate. For example, if we had 100 countries, with an average of 4 cities each and an average of 2 airports per city, a table would require $100 \times 4 \times 2 = 800$ rows—but a tree would need only 100 rows (one per country) with each row capable of being expanded to show its cities and airports.

In this section, we will show how to represent a table of data in a tree, and how to extract the complete "path" that the user has chosen. The example application we will use is called Server Info. It reads a dataset that has six columns—country, state (meaningful only in the United States), city, provider, server, and IP address—and allows users to specify one particular 6-tuple. The sample dataset has 163 rows, but refers to only 33 unique countries, so the user

Figure 16.3 *Tabular data rendered as a tree*

need only navigate 33 top-level items rather than scrolling through almost five times that number of rows.

The heart of the application is provided by the `TreeOfTableModel` class, a `QAbstractItemModel` subclass that can represent arbitrary tabular data in a tree. We use a custom subclass of this model, along with a `QTreeView` subclass to present the data. The application itself can create the tree using different levels of nesting by running it from the console with a command-line argument of 1, 2, 3, or 4. Figure 16.3 shows the tree using the default nesting level of 3. (The nesting level does not include the leaf at the end of a series of branches.)

We will begin by reviewing the main form since it is very short. Then we will look at the table view subclass and the `TreeOfTableModel` subclass. Next, we will review the `treeoftable` module, including the `BranchNode` and `LeafNode` classes, and finally, the `TreeOfTableModel` class itself.

```
class MainForm(QMainWindow):

    def __init__(self, filename, nesting, separator, parent=None):
        super(MainForm, self).__init__(parent)
        headers = ["Country/State (US)/City/Provider", "Server", "IP"]
        self.treeWidget = TreeOfTableWidget(filename, nesting,
                                            separator)
        self.treeWidget.model().headers = headers
        self.setCentralWidget(self.treeWidget)
        self.connect(self.treeWidget, SIGNAL("activated"),
                     self.activated)

        self.setWindowTitle("Server Info")
```

The TreeOfTableWidget is similar to a convenience view, since it incorporates a model inside it. The model is a ServerModel, a small TreeOfTableModel subclass that adds the ability to show flag icons.

The filename is the name of a file that has data suitable for a TreeOfTableModel. In particular, it must have one record per line, and each column (field) must be separated by the specified separator.

The nesting value is the maximum number of branches that can spur off from a root, and does not count the leaves at the end. In this case, the nesting value passed in through the nesting parameter is 3 (unless it's changed on the command line), which means that we will have 3 levels of branches (country, state, city) and 1 level of leaves (provider). Since we have 6 fields, this means that the first 4 fields will be shown in the tree part of the tree widget, with the remaining 2 fields shown as separate columns in the rows that have leaves. The resultant tree view will have 3 columns, one containing the tree, and 2 more showing the extra fields. We set the model's headers by directly accessing the model inside the custom TreeOfTableWidget.

The activated() method is called when the user double-clicks or presses Enter on a row in the tree widget.

```
def activated(self, fields):
    self.statusBar().showMessage("*".join(fields), 60000)
```

The "path", that is, the (country, city, state, provider, server, IP address) 6-tuple that the user has chosen, is shown "*"-separated in the status bar for a minute (60 000 milliseconds), whenever a suitable row is activated. In this context, a suitable row is one containing a leaf, since these are the only ones that have all six fields.

The TreeOfTableWidget is a QTreeView subclass that contains the model it displays. It also provides a few simple convenience methods and creates some useful signal–slot connections.

```
class TreeOfTableWidget(QTreeView):

    def __init__(self, filename, nesting, separator, parent=None):
        super(TreeOfTableWidget, self).__init__(parent)
        self.setSelectionBehavior(QTreeView.SelectItems)
        self.setUniformRowHeights(True)
        model = ServerModel(self)
        self.setModel(model)
        try:
            model.load(filename, nesting, separator)
        except IOError, e:
            QMessageBox.warning(self, "Server Info - Error",
                                unicode(e))
        self.connect(self, SIGNAL("activated(QModelIndex)"),
                     self.activated)
```

```
        self.connect(self, SIGNAL("expanded(QModelIndex)"),
                     self.expanded)
        self.expanded()
```

The `ServerModel` is a `TreeOfTableModel` subclass. Its only purpose is to override the `data()` method so that it can provide suitable icons (country and state flags); we will review it shortly. After loading the model's data from the file and making the signal–slot connections, we call the `expanded()` method to give the columns suitable widths.

```
    def expanded(self):
        for column in range(self.model().columnCount(QModelIndex())):
            self.resizeColumnToContents(column)
```

Whenever the user expands a branch—for example, by clicking one of the tree's ⊞ symbols or by navigating with the arrow keys and pressing Right Arrow—this method is called. It ensures that the columns showing the expanded item's texts are wide enough for the text to be readable. In tree models, every item is either the child of another item (and therefore has a parent) or a top-level (root) item, in which case it has no parent, which is signified by an invalid model index. Therefore, when we call `columnCount()` with a `QModelIndex()` (i.e., with an invalid model index), we get the column count of top-level items.

```
    def activated(self, index):
        self.emit(SIGNAL("activated"), self.model().asRecord(index))
```

If the user activates an item by double-clicking it or by pressing Enter on it, this method is called, and in turn it emits its own `activated()` signal. Its parameter is the full path (record), as a list of field values, for the current model index.

```
    def currentFields(self):
        return self.model().asRecord(self.currentIndex())
```

This method provides the same information as the `activated()` signal, but it can be called at any time to get the current record; again, as a list of field values.

The `ServerModel` is a `TreeOfTableModel` subclass that reimplements one method, `data()`. It does so to show flags next to the names of countries and U.S. states.

```
class ServerModel(treeoftable.TreeOfTableModel):

    def __init__(self, parent=None):
        super(ServerModel, self).__init__(parent)

    def data(self, index, role):
        if role == Qt.DecorationRole:
            node = self.nodeFromIndex(index)
            if node is None:
                return QVariant()
            if isinstance(node, treeoftable.BranchNode):
```

```
            if index.column() != 0:
                return QVariant()
            filename = node.toString().replace(" ", "_")
            parent = node.parent.toString()
            if parent and parent != "USA":
                return QVariant()
            if parent == "USA":
                filename = "USA_" + filename
            filename = os.path.join(os.path.dirname(__file__),
                                    "flags", filename + ".png")
            pixmap = QPixmap(filename)
            if pixmap.isNull():
                return QVariant()
            return QVariant(pixmap)
        return treeoftable.TreeOfTableModel.data(self, index, role)
```

This data() reimplementation only handles data() requests where the role is
Qt.DecorationRole, passing on any other request to the TreeOfTableModel base
class. In list, table, and tree views, the decoration role is used to set or retrieve
icons for data items.

Tree models work in terms of parents and children. In the TreeOfTableModel
base class we have provided a method, nodeFromIndex(), that returns the node
(item) corresponding to a particular model index. We have two kinds of nodes,
branch nodes and leaf nodes. Each node can have any number of columns,
although in this case the branch nodes have only one column and leaf nodes
have at least one column. We provide icons for only the first (and only) column
of branch nodes, and then only for the branches for countries and U.S. states.

The flag icons are stored in the flags subdirectory, with country flag names
having underscores instead of spaces, and U.S. state names beginning with
"USA_". All the flag icons are .png images. Instead of using a .qrc resource
file, we retrieve the images directly from the filesystem. The os.path.dirname()
function returns the path part of a full filename, and the os.path.join() function joins two or more strings to form a single path string with the appropriate path separators. If the required image does not exist or is unreadable,
QPixmap.isNull() will return True; in this case, we return an invalid QVariant to
signify that no icon is available. Otherwise, we return the pixmap wrapped in
a QVariant.

The classes we have seen so far have been quite straightforward. This is because the real work of providing the tree model is done by the TreeOfTableModel.
This model reads in a tabular dataset and converts the row/column data into
a tree. The tree has a single branch node as its root, and then any number
of branch nodes hanging off the root, with each branch able to have its own
branches. At the end of each branch are one or more leaf nodes.

The nodes hanging off a branch are the branch's children. The children can
be branches or leaves, and they are held in a list. Each child's position in its

parent node's list of children is its row number. Column numbers refer to the items (fields) within a child (branch or leaf). A complete record (or "path") is the concatenation of all the fields in the root branch, all the intermediate branches, and the leaf at the end. The relationship between branches and leaves is shown schematically in Figure 16.4.

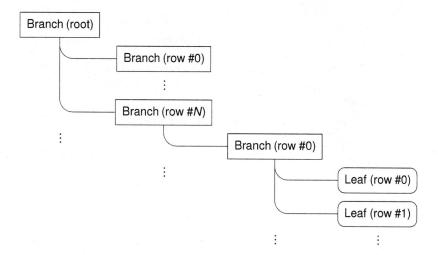

Figure 16.4 *Schematic of a tree model's branches and leaves*

In the tree of table model we have chosen to keep each branch's children in alphabetical order. To make this as fast and easy as possible, each branch's children list is actually a list of two-item lists, with the first item being the order key and the second item being the child node. We access the items in these two-item lists using the constants KEY and NODE rather than the literals 0 and 1.

We will now look at the branch node and leaf node implementations, and then at the tree of table model itself.

The branch and leaf nodes have many methods in common because in some contexts, they can be used interchangeably (thanks to duck typing).

```
class BranchNode(object):

    def __init__(self, name, parent=None):
        super(BranchNode, self).__init__(parent)
        self.name = name
        self.parent = parent
        self.children = []
```

A branch node's name is the text shown in its first (and only) column. In the Server Info example, this would be the name of a country, state, or city, depending on where the branch is in the tree's hierarchy.

```
    def orderKey(self):
        return self.name.lower()

    def toString(self):
        return self.name

    def __len__(self):
        return len(self.children)
```

The order key is a string that is used by the node's parent to position this branch correctly in the node's parent's list of children. The toString() method returns the branch's one field as a string. These methods are provided for compatibility with leaf nodes to make it easier to use either kind of node based on duck typing. The __len__() method returns how many children the branch has.

```
    def childAtRow(self, row):
        assert 0 <= row < len(self.children)
        return self.children[row][NODE]
```

assert state-ment

69 ☜

This method returns the node for the given row. We have used an assert statement here, and in many other places in the tree of table model's code. The code can be tricky to get right, but by using assertions we can at least be clear about what we expect to be true at particular points in the code.

```
    def rowOfChild(self, child):
        for i, item in enumerate(self.children):
            if item[NODE] == child:
                return i
        return -1
```

Here we return the row index of a particular child node, or -1 if the child is not one of this node's children.

```
    def childWithKey(self, key):
        if not self.children:
            return None
        i = bisect.bisect_left(self.children, (key, None))
        if i < 0 or i >= len(self.children):
            return None
        if self.children[i][KEY] == key:
            return self.children[i][NODE]
        return None
```

We sometimes want to find the first child that has a given order key. One approach would be to do what we did in the rowOfChild() method, iterating through the list of children to find the right one. Here we have taken a more efficient approach. We find the position that a node with the given key ought to occupy, and if this is in range and has the right key, we return the child.

```
    def insertChild(self, child):
        child.parent = self
        bisect.insort(self.children, (child.orderKey(), child))
```

This method inserts a new child node into a branch's list of children, and makes this branch the child's parent. By using bisect.insort() in conjunction with the child's order key, we ensure that the child is put in the correct position as quickly and efficiently as possible. The insort() function is identical to insort_right().

```
    def hasLeaves(self):
        if not self.children:
            return False
        return isinstance(self.children[0], LeafNode)
```

In the tree of table model, a branch that has children has either branches or leaves, but not a mixture of both. For this reason, if a branch has no children at all, clearly it has no leaves; and similarly, if it does have children and the first one is a leaf, all of them are leaves.

We have now seen the entire branch node class. Next, we will look at the much shorter leaf node class.

```
class LeafNode(object):

    def __init__(self, fields, parent=None):
        super(LeafNode, self).__init__(parent)
        self.parent = parent
        self.fields = fields
```

The fields in a leaf node are the node's columns.

```
    def orderKey(self):
        return u"\t".join(self.fields).lower()

    def toString(self, separator="\t"):
        return separator.join(self.fields)

    def __len__(self):
        return len(self.fields)
```

A leaf node's order key is the tab-separated concatenation of its fields. Similarly, its toString() method returns a concatenation of its fields. The __len__() method returns the number of fields; for branches it returns the number of children.

```
    def field(self, column):
        assert 0 <= column <= len(self.fields)
        return self.fields[column]
```

This method makes it easy to extract a single field's value while having the assertion that the field's column is within range.

```
def asRecord(self):
    record = []
    branch = self.parent
    while branch is not None:
        record.insert(0, branch.toString())
        branch = branch.parent
    assert record and not record[0]
    record = record[1:]
    return record + self.fields
```

The notion of a record used by the tree of table model is the concatenation of all the branches from the root to the leaf's parent, plus the leaf itself—in other words, the user's complete choice "path". In terms of the Server Info application, this is the country, state, city, provider, server, and IP address, where the country, state, and city are branches, and each leaf contains three fields: provider, server, and IP address.

To construct a record (a list of fields), we begin with the leaf node's parent branch, and walk up the tree of branches. Each branch's string is prepended to the record list. The root branch has no string, so we remove that item from the list. The list that is returned is the concatenation of all the branch strings plus the leaf's strings.

We have now completed reviewing the nodes. The tree of table model is a QAbstractItemModel subclass and it reimplements many of the methods we would expect, such as data(), headerData(), rowCount(), and columnCount(). In addition, it provides the index(), parent(), and nodeFromIndex() methods which are usually reimplemented for tree models. It also has some extra methods, namely, load() and addRecord(); these are used to load tabular data and convert it into a tree of branches and leaves. We will begin by looking at the initializer, then the methods for loading the data, and then the standard model/view methods.

```
class TreeOfTableModel(QAbstractItemModel):

    def __init__(self, parent=None):
        super(TreeOfTableModel, self).__init__(parent)
        self.columns = 0
        self.root = BranchNode("")
        self.headers = []
```

The number of columns depends on the number of columns in the data that is loaded and on the level of nesting requested. There is always one root branch node that contains no text that is used purely as the parent of all the other branches. The headers are the text used as column headers.

```
def load(self, filename, nesting, separator):
    assert nesting > 0
    self.nesting = nesting
    self.root = BranchNode("")
    exception = None
    fh = None
    try:
        for line in codecs.open(unicode(filename), "rU", "utf8"):
            if not line:
                continue
            self.addRecord(line.split(separator), False)
    except IOError, e:
        exception = e
    finally:
        if fh is not None:
            fh.close()
        self.reset()
        for i in range(self.columns):
            self.headers.append("Column #%d" % i)
        if exception is not None:
            raise exception
```

The file to be loaded must be a text file with one record per line, with each field separated by the specified separator. The file must be encoded as UTF-8 Unicode (or ASCII, since that is a subset of UTF-8). Blank lines are ignored; any other line is treated as a record and is added to the tree.

Once loading has finished (successfully or not), we call reset() to notify any views that the model has dramatically changed, and create some initial column headers. If the load failed, we then reraise the exception for the caller to handle. The columns variable is set to 0 in the initializer, and to a meaningful value in addRecord().

```
def addRecord(self, fields, callReset=True):
    assert len(fields) > self.nesting
    root = self.root
    branch = None
    for i in range(self.nesting):
        key = fields[i].lower()
        branch = root.childWithKey(key)
        if branch is not None:
            root = branch
        else:
            branch = BranchNode(fields[i])
            root.insertChild(branch)
            root = branch
    assert branch is not None
    items = fields[self.nesting:]
```

```
            self.columns = max(self.columns, len(items))
            branch.insertChild(LeafNode(items, branch))
        if callReset:
            self.reset()
```

To add a record there must be more fields than the level of nesting. The logic we use is similar to what we saw in Chapter 14 when we populated a QTree-Widget's internal model. For each field that is to be a branch we look for an existing branch with the same key. If we find one, we make it the current root branch; otherwise, we create a new branch, insert it as a child of the current root branch, and make the new branch the current root branch. As the loop progresses, we gradually walk down the tree, creating any branches that are needed, until we reach the lowest branch.

Once the loop has gone over all the branches that are necessary, creating any that did not previously exist, we can create a list of the non-nesting fields and add them as a child leaf node of the current (lowest-level) branch.

To put things in concrete terms, using the Server Info application as an example, here's what happens. When the first record is read we have a new country, new state, new city, new provider, and so on, so no suitable branches will exist. First a country branch will be created, then a state branch, and then a city branch, and finally a leaf containing the remaining provider, server, and IP address fields. If the next record read is for the same country, but for a new state, it will find the existing country node and use it as the parent node for the new state. Similarly, if a record has a country and state for which branches have already been created, these will be used. But whenever a new branch is needed the code in the loop's body will create it.

When new records are added on an ad hoc basis, we call reset() to notify any views that a significant change has taken place; but when loading from a file we pass False and call reset() in the calling code once all the records have been read.

```
        def asRecord(self, index):
            leaf = self.nodeFromIndex(index)
            if leaf is not None and isinstance(leaf, LeafNode):
                return leaf.asRecord()
            return []
```

This method provides a list of the user's chosen "path". It makes sense only for leaf nodes, since only a leaf node can represent a complete path. Returning None for nonleaf nodes would have been an equally good design choice. Notice that we use the nodeFromIndex() method to retrieve the node for a given model index: We will discuss how this works shortly.

```
        def rowCount(self, parent):
            node = self.nodeFromIndex(parent)
            if node is None or isinstance(node, LeafNode):
```

```
            return 0
        return len(node)
```

For tree models the row count is the number of children that a particular node has. Our implementation allows only branch nodes to have children, so when called on leaf nodes we always return 0. The len() function calls Branch-Node.__len__(), which returns the count of the branch's children.

```
    def columnCount(self, parent):
        return self.columns
```

The number of columns is the maximum number of non-nested fields. This may appear to be one too few, but it is correct because the first non-nested field is shown in the first (tree) column.

```
    def data(self, index, role):
        if role == Qt.TextAlignmentRole:
            return QVariant(int(Qt.AlignTop|Qt.AlignLeft))
        if role != Qt.DisplayRole:
            return QVariant()
        node = self.nodeFromIndex(index)
        assert node is not None
        if isinstance(node, BranchNode):
            return QVariant(node.toString()) \
                if index.column() == 0 else QVariant(QString(""))
        return QVariant(node.field(index.column()))
```

If the display data is requested for a branch node, we return the node's text for column 0 and an empty string for the other columns. For a leaf node, we return the field that corresponds to the requested column.

Prior to Qt 4.2, the default text alignment worked fine and did not need to be specified, but from Qt 4.2, we must explicitly return a sensible text alignment ourselves.

```
    def headerData(self, section, orientation, role):
        if orientation == Qt.Horizontal and \
           role == Qt.DisplayRole:
            assert 0 <= section <= len(self.headers)
            return QVariant(self.headers[section])
        return QVariant()
```

Tree views have only horizontal (column) headers. They don't have row headers (e.g., row numbers), because these don't really make sense since each branch has its own 0-based list of children (rows).

```
    def index(self, row, column, parent):
        assert self.root
        branch = self.nodeFromIndex(parent)
        assert branch is not None
```

```
                    return self.createIndex(row, column,
                                    branch.childAtRow(row))
```

The index() method must return the model index for the data item with the given row and column and that is a child of the given parent. In a branches and leaves tree model, this means that we must return the model index of the parent item's row-th child.

We begin by finding the branch node of the given parent model index, and return a model index with the given row and column, and with a parent that is the (branch) node's row-th child node.

```
        def parent(self, child):
            node = self.nodeFromIndex(child)
            if node is None:
                return QModelIndex()
            parent = node.parent
            if parent is None:
                return QModelIndex()
            grandparent = parent.parent
            if grandparent is None:
                return QModelIndex()
            row = grandparent.rowOfChild(parent)
            assert row != -1
            return self.createIndex(row, 0, parent)
```

The parent() method must return the model index of the given child's parent. In a branches and leaves tree model, this is the child's grandparent's row-th child.

We start by finding the child node's parent node's parent (that is, the child's grandparent). Then we return a model index that has the row the parent node occupies in the grandparent's list of children, column 0 (since all parents are branches and branches have only a zero-th column), and a parent that is the child's parent.

The reimplementations of the index() and parent() methods shown here are rather subtle. However, they are standard for tree models that take a branch and leaf approach, so their code can simply be copied "as is" in most cases.

```
        def nodeFromIndex(self, index):
            return index.internalPointer() \
                if index.isValid() else self.root
```

When we call QAbstractItemModel.createIndex(), the third argument is a reference to a node. This reference is available from a model index and is returned by the internalPointer() method. For any given model index we return a branch or leaf node, or the branch root node.

Understanding tree models is more challenging than understanding table models (or list models, which are just tables with a single column). However, in many cases the difficulties can be reduced by building upon or adapting the code presented in this section.

Summary

PyQt's built-in view widgets, and the graphics view widgets, between them provide considerable scope for visualizing datasets. But when our requirements don't really match what these classes provide, we can always create our own custom views and present our data exactly how we like.

Since a custom view could potentially be showing a portion of a very large dataset, it is usually best to optimize the paint event handler to retrieve and display only those data items that are actually visible. If scrollbars are going to be required, we could require that users of our view class use a QScrollArea, or create a composite widget with a couple of QScrollBars, or create a widget that inherits QAbstractScrollArea. The first of these approaches adds only a few lines to the user's code, and makes implementing the view much easier.

Using generic delegates with data-type-specific column delegates makes it easy to create ad hoc "custom" delegates for views. Column delegates are easy to create and can cut down on code duplication since we need only one column delegate for each data type we want to work with. The generic delegate approach is ideal for datasets where each column's data holds values of a single data type, such as database tables.

Creating tree models can be difficult because we have to think in terms of parents and children, where the children may also be parents, and so on recursively to an arbitrary level of depth. This just isn't as easy as the thinking in terms of rows and columns necessary for tree and column models. Although the tree of table model presented in this chapter is a specific example, some of the methods that provide its tree functionality, such as index(), parent(), and nodeFromIndex(), should be able to be used "as is" or with little adaptation, and other methods, such as addRecord(), should also prove to be adaptable.

Exercise

This exercise draws together many of the model/view features that have been covered in this and in earlier chapters.

Create an application that shows two widgets: a QListView and a custom BarGraphView. The data should be held in a custom BarGraphModel. The user should be able to edit the data through the QListView, using a custom BarGraphDelegate to control both the presentation and the editing of data items in the list view. The application is shown in Figure 16.5.

The model should be a `QAbstractListModel` subclass, and it should hold a list of data values (integers) and a dictionary of colors (keyed by "row"; e.g., the color with key 6 corresponds to the seventh data value and so on). The model should reimplement `rowCount()`, `insertRows()`—which should include calls to `beginInsertRows()` and `endInsertRows()` where appropriate, `flags()` to make the model editable, and `setData()` to allow the value (`Qt.DisplayRole`) and a value's color (`Qt.UserRole`) to be set and which should emit signals to indicate that data has changed—and `data()`, which should return the value, color, and for the `Qt.DecorationRole`, a 20 × 20 pixmap filled with the color. If no color has been set for a particular row, use a default of red.

The delegate is quite simple, and it is very similar to the `IntegerColumnDelegate` mentioned earlier in this chapter. The key difference is that the `paint()` method must be reimplemented, but only to set the alignment to `Qt.AlignRight`; the painting can still be done perfectly well by the base class.

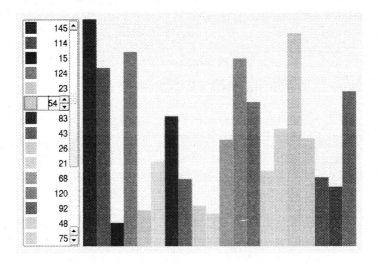

Figure 16.5 *The Bar Grapher application's widgets*

The custom view will need to reimplement `setModel()`, in which connections should be made to the base class's `update()` method so that repainting occurs when the model's data is changed, `minimumSizeHint()`, `sizeHint()`—which can simply call `minimumSizeHint()`—and `paintEvent()`. The paint event can be done in slightly more than a dozen lines—make sure that you use `QPainter.setWindow()` so that the graph always fills the available space. All the methods should work correctly even if no model has been set—for example, with no model, the paint event should paint nothing.

Here is the code for the `MainForm`, to give you a feel for how the classes are used:

```
class MainForm(QDialog):

    def __init__(self, parent=None):
```

```
        super(MainForm, self).__init__(parent)

        self.model = BarGraphModel()
        self.barGraphView = BarGraphView()
        self.barGraphView.setModel(self.model)
        self.listView = QListView()
        self.listView.setModel(self.model)
        self.listView.setItemDelegate(BarGraphDelegate(0, 1000, self))
        self.listView.setMaximumWidth(100)
        self.listView.setEditTriggers(QListView.DoubleClicked|
                                      QListView.EditKeyPressed)
        layout = QHBoxLayout()
        layout.addWidget(self.listView)
        layout.addWidget(self.barGraphView, 1)
        self.setLayout(layout)

        self.setWindowTitle("Bar Grapher")
```

In the model solution, we added some extra code to create 20 random items to create an initial bar graph. The whole thing can be done in less than 200 lines.

A solution is provided in `chap16/bargrapher.pyw`.

17

● Online Help
● Internationalization

Online Help and Internationalization

Tooltips and status tips

171 ☞

Users may be able to use a very simple application just by reading its menu options and button texts. Other applications may require a little more information, and in these cases tooltips and status tips are an easy-to-program solution. But some applications are so complex or sophisticated that users may need more extensive help to understand what facilities are available to them, and how to use the applications.

One solution to giving adequate information is to supply a printed manual; another is to provide a help system. Several possible approaches can be used to create a suitable online help system; we will mention them all, and show one of them. We will return to the Image Changer application introduced in Chapter 6, and in this chapter's first section we will show the implementation of the application's MainWindow.helpHelp() method, and how to provide an online help system.

Throughout the book, the applications shown have provided menu text, button text, labels, tips, and so on, in English. This is fine for the minority of the world's people who can read English, but not much use to those who speak the world's most widely spoken language, Mandarin Chinese, or to those who speak other major languages such as Spanish, Arabic, Hindi, Portuguese, Bengali, Russian, or Japanese.

For an application to be as widely useable as possible, it must be accessible to non-English speakers. PyQt provides a toolchain for identifying user-visible strings and for making these strings available in the easy-to-use *Qt Linguist* GUI application that human translators can use to provide suitable translations. In this chapter's second section, we will discuss the translation tools and show how to use them. We will also present a new translation-aware version of the Image Changer application suitable for use with the translation tools.

Online Help

There are three common ways to provide an online help system. One approach is to provide the help in the form of HTML files, and to launch a Web browser set to the relevant page. Another is to use the *Qt Assistant* application provided with Qt. The third approach is to provide a help form, again using HTML, but with the images and HTML files as resources.

Figure 17.1 *The Image Changer Help form*

The first approach can be achieved by launching a Web browser as a separate process, using either Python's subprocess module, or PyQt's QProcess class. Qt 4.2 introduced a new class, QDesktopServices, that makes it really easy to launch a browser in a platform-independent way with its openUrl() static convenience method.

The second approach is trickier, since it requires us to create an XML file in a special format and to distribute *Qt Assistant* with our application. The advantage of using *Qt Assistant* is that it provides automatic indexing.

The third approach, using a custom help form and with HTML files and images as resources, is the one that we will use. We saw back in Chapter 6 when we looked at resource files, that we could include arbitrary files, including HTML files, and we incorporated some demo help files in our resources.qrc file. Here is the code for the Image Changer's MainWindow.helpHelp() method:

Resource
files

172 ☜

```
def helpHelp(self):
    form = helpform.HelpForm("index.html", self)
    form.show()
```

Using our help form is easy: We just give it one of the HTML files, and `self` (over which the form will center itself). Notice that we use `show()` rather than `exec_()`; this almost always means that the form shown will have the delete on close attribute set.

The screenshot in Figure 17.1 may give the misleading impression that keyboard users are not catered to, but in fact, the class used to show the HTML files, `QTextBrowser`, provides good keyboard support. For example, users can press Tab to move the focus from hyperlink to hyperlink, and Enter to follow a hyperlink. They can go back by pressing Alt+Left Arrow, and they can go to the first page by pressing Home. And because the form is a `QDialog` subclass, they can close the window by pressing Esc.

By now we are very familiar with creating PyQt dialogs, so we will confine ourselves to showing just those extracts that are relevant to creating the online help system—specifically, a couple of extracts from the `HelpForm`'s initializer, and one of its methods. (The code is in `chap17/helpform.py`.)

```
class HelpForm(QDialog):

    def __init__(self, page, parent=None):
        super(HelpForm, self).__init__(parent)
        self.setAttribute(Qt.WA_DeleteOnClose)
        self.setAttribute(Qt.WA_GroupLeader)
```

The `Qt.WA_GroupLeader` attribute ensures that if the help form is invoked from a modal dialog, the user will be able to interact with both the modal dialog *and* the help form, something that would not be possible otherwise. If the help form is invoked from a modeless dialog or main window, the attribute has no effect, and the user can interact with both as usual.

```
        self.textBrowser.setSearchPaths([":/"])
        self.textBrowser.setSource(QUrl(page))
```

The `QTextBrowser` class is a subclass of `QTextEdit` that can be used to display a large subset of HTML tags, including images, lists, and tables. We have set its search path to the resource file's root directory, and set its initial page to be the page that was passed in. Because we have set a search path we are able to pass a page without a path (e.g., simply `index.html` or `filemenu.html`). The `QTextBrowser` understands resource paths, and is therefore able to find image resources in `<img>` tags such as `<img src=":/filenew.png">`.

```
        self.connect(backAction, SIGNAL("triggered()"),
                     self.textBrowser, SLOT("backward()"))
        self.connect(homeAction, SIGNAL("triggered()"),
                     self.textBrowser, SLOT("home()"))
        self.connect(self.textBrowser, SIGNAL("sourceChanged(QUrl)"),
                     self.updatePageTitle)
```

Navigating from page to page is handled automatically by the QTextBrowser. Nonetheless, we have provided two toolbar buttons, Back and Home, and connected them to the appropriate QTextBrowser slots to get the behavior we want. If the HTML document is changed—for example, due to the user clicking a hyperlink—we call a custom updatePageTitle() slot.

```
def updatePageTitle(self):
    self.pageLabel.setText(self.textBrowser.documentTitle())
```

This slot simply puts the HTML page's <title> text in a QLabel that is in the toolbar, to the right of the toolbar buttons.

Once we have a HelpForm class, we can implement our online help system entirely in HTML, either including the files as resources, or installing them in the filesystem and finding them using code like this:

```
helppath = os.path.join(os.path.dirname(__file__), "help")
```

This assumes that the help files are in a help directory that resides in the directory where the application's .pyw file is located.

Writing the code to provide an online help system is straightforward; but designing a system that is easy to navigate, and that is understandable, can be quite a challenge.

Internationalization

There are several issues to consider when making applications suitable for users who speak a language that is different from the one used originally. The largest and most obvious issue is that all user-visible strings must be translated into the target language—this includes not only the strings used for menu options and dialog buttons, but also tooltips, status tips, and any other online help. In addition, we must perform other localizations, such as making sure that numbers use the appropriate decimal marker and thousands symbol, that time and date formats are correct, and that paper sizes and systems of measurement are right. For example, English is spoken by most American and British people, but the two cultures have different date format conventions, different currencies, different standard paper sizes, and different systems of measurement.

Unicode strings
20 ☞

Text files
249 ☞

Thanks to the use of Unicode, any character used by just about any human language can be displayed. We saw near the beginning of the book that any unicode character can be included in unicode or QString strings using the unicode escape character and the target character's hexadecimal code point, or using the unichr() function. As for reading and writing text files containing Unicode, we can use Python's codecs.open() function, or PyQt's QTextStream as we saw in an earlier chapter.

QString
.arg()
402 ☜

When it comes to some aspects of localization we can use QString, QDate, and QDateTime. For example, assuming n is a number, QString("%L1").arg(n) will produce a QString with thousands and decimal separators suitable to the current locale. Both QDate and QDateTime have toString() methods that can accept either a custom format, or a predefined format such as Qt.SystemLocaleDate (Qt.LocalDate in older code), or Qt.ISODate, which is "universal". In addition, the QLocale class provides many methods for returning localized QStrings, and a few methods for extracting numbers from localized QStrings. It also has methods that return locale-specific characters, such as the character to use as a negative sign, a percentage symbol, and so on.

Most of the work involved with internationalizing an application is concerned with translation, so it is this topic that we will focus on for the rest of the section.

To help translate applications, PyQt provides a tool chain of three tools: pylupdate4, lrelease, and *Qt Linguist*. For these tools to be useful, every user-visible string must be specially marked. This is easily achieved by using the QObject.tr() method, which is inherited by all QWidget subclasses, including all dialogs and main windows. For example, instead of writing QString("&Save"), we write self.tr("&Save"). The text passed to tr() should be ASCII; if characters outside the ASCII range are required, use trUtf8() instead.

For each string marked for translation, the translation tools are provided with a pair of strings: a "context" string (the class name), and the marked string itself. The purpose of the context is to help human translators identify which window the string to translate is shown in, since different translations might be needed in different windows in some languages.

For strings that need translating but are not inside classes, we must use the QApplication.translate() method, and supply the context string ourselves. For example, in a main() function we might translate the application's name like this: QApplication.translate("main", "Gradgrind"). Here, the context is "main", and the string to translate is "Gradgrind".

Unfortunately, the context used by self.tr() can be different from that used by C++/Qt's tr() method, because PyQt determines the context dynamically, whereas C++ does so at compile time.[*] This may matter if translation files are being shared between C++/Qt and PyQt applications. It can also be an issue if forms are subclassed. If this is ever a problem, the solution is simply to replace each single-argument self.tr() call with a two-argument QApplication.translate() call, explicitly giving the correct context as the first argument, and the string to be translated as the second argument.

Once all of an application's user-visible strings are suitably marked, we must slightly change the way the application starts up so that it reads in the translated strings for the locale in which it is run.

---

[*]See the PyQt pyqt4ref.html documentation, under "Differences Between PyQt and Qt".

Here is how an internationalized application is created.

1. Create the application using QObject.tr() or QApplication.translate() for all user-visible strings.

2. Modify the application to read in the locale-specific .qm (Qt message) files at start-up if they are available.

3. Create a .pro file that lists the application's .ui (*Qt Designer*) files, its .py and .pyw source files, and the .ts (translation source) file that it will use.

4. Run pylupdate4 to create the .ts file.

5. Ask the translator to translate the .ts file's strings using *Qt Linguist*.

6. Run lrelease to convert the updated .ts file (that contains the translations) to a .qm file.

And here is how such an application is maintained.

1. Update the application, making sure that all user-visible strings use QObject.tr() or QApplication.translate().

2. Update the .pro file if necessary—for example, adding any new .ui or .py files that have been added to the application.

3. Run pylupdate4 to update the .ts file with any new strings.

4. Ask the translator to translate any new strings in the .ts file.

5. Run lrelease to convert the .ts file to a .qm file.

We will cover all of the preceding steps, starting with the use of QObject.tr(), using extracts from the translation-aware version of the Image Changer application in the chap17 directory.

```
fileNewAction = self.createAction(self.tr("&New..."),
        self.fileNew, QKeySequence.New, "filenew",
        self.tr("Create an image file"))
```

The first string marked for translation is the menu option string, New..., and the second is the string used for tooltips and status tips. (The "filenew" string is the name of the icon file without its .png suffix.)

```
self.fileMenu = self.menuBar().addMenu(self.tr("&File"))
```

Menu strings as well as action strings must be translated.

```
self.statusBar().showMessage(self.tr("Ready"), 5000)
```

Here we have an initial status message for the user, and again we must use tr().

It is not usually appropriate to translate the strings used as QSettings keys, especially since these strings are not normally visible to the user.

```
reply = QMessageBox.question(self,
                self.tr("Image Changer - Unsaved Changes"),
                self.tr("Save unsaved changes?"),
                QMessageBox.Yes|QMessageBox.No|
                QMessageBox.Cancel)
```

For this message box, we have marked both the window title and the message
text for translation. We don't have to worry about translating the buttons in
this case because we are using standard buttons and Qt has translations for
these.* If we had used our own text we would have had to use tr() on it, like
any other user-visible string.

```
self.tr("Saved %1 in file %2").arg(self.dataname).arg(self.filename)
```

One way to provide the preceding string is to write:

```
self.tr("Saved %s in file %s" % (self.dataname, self.filename)) # BAD
```

This is not recommended. Always use QStrings, and always use QString.arg();
this makes it easier for translators. (The tr() method returns a QString, so we
can call any QString method, such as arg(), on its return value.) For example, in
some languages the translation would be phrased "Saved in file %2 the data %1".
This is no problem using a QString with arg()s, since the translator can change
the order of the %ns in the string and the arg() methods will respect this. But
swapping one Python string's %s for another will not change anything.

We must use tr() for every user-visible string in hand-coded .pyw and .py files.
But for .py files generated from .ui files by pyuic4 we don't need to do anything,
since pyuic4 automatically uses QApplication.translate() on all strings anyway.
This works even for untranslated applications, because if there is no suitable
translation, the original language—for example, English—is used instead.

A PyQt application usually uses PyQt built-in dialogs; for example, the file
open dialog, or the file print dialog. These must also be translated, although for
several languages translations are already available in the .qm files provided
by Trolltech.

Having used tr() throughout, and having located an appropriate Qt translation, we are ready to modify the application's start-up code to load in suitable
translation files if they exist.

```
app = QApplication(sys.argv)
locale = QLocale.system().name()
qtTranslator = QTranslator()
if qtTranslator.load("qt_" + locale, ":/"):
    app.installTranslator(qtTranslator)
```

---

*Trolltech provides translations for some languages, such as French and German, and some unsup-
ported translations to various other languages. These translations are in Qt's (not PyQt's) translations directory; search your filesystem for qt_fr.qm, for example, to find the French translation.

```
appTranslator = QTranslator()
if appTranslator.load("imagechanger_" + locale, ":/"):
    app.installTranslator(appTranslator)

app.setOrganizationName("Qtrac Ltd.")
app.setOrganizationDomain("qtrac.eu")
app.setApplicationName(app.translate("main", "Image Changer"))
app.setWindowIcon(QIcon(":/icon.png"))
form = MainWindow()
form.show()
app.exec_()
```

The `QLocale.system().name()` call will return a string such as "en_US" (English, United States), or "fr_CA" (French, Canada), and so on. The `QTranslator.load()` method takes a file stem and a path. In this case, we have given the path of :/ which is the application's resource file. If the locale were "fr_CA", the file stems would be qt_fr_CA and imagechanger_fr_CA. Given these, PyQt will look for qt_fr_CA.qm, and failing that, for qt_fr.qm, and similarly for imagechanger_fr_CA.qm, and failing that, for imagechanger_fr.qm. If the locale was "en_US", no .qm files would be found, and therefore none installed—and this is fine, since the application would then fall back to using the original strings which, are in English anyway.

Notice that we had to use `QApplication.translate()` (written as app.translate()), since this code is not inside a `QObject` subclass's method. With no class name, we chose to use the text "main" for the context; some programmers might prefer to use "global". We are free to use any name we like—the purpose of contexts is purely to help human translators.

We can load only a single translation into a single `QTranslator` object, but we can add as many translators as we like to the `QApplication` object. If there are conflicts, that is, if the same string has different translations, the most recently installed translator wins.

Although we have chosen to include our translations in the resource file, there is no obligation to do so; we could just as easily have accessed them from the filesystem.

Here is an extract from the `resource.qrc` file that we have used:

```
<qresource>
<file>qt_fr.qm</file>
<file>imagechanger_fr.qm</file>
</qresource>
<qresource>
<file alias="editmenu.html">help/editmenu.html</file>
<file alias="filemenu.html">help/filemenu.html</file>
<file alias="index.html">help/index.html</file>
</qresource>
<qresource lang="fr">
```

```
<file alias="editmenu.html">help/editmenu_fr.html</file>
<file alias="filemenu.html">help/filemenu_fr.html</file>
<file alias="index.html">help/index_fr.html</file>
</qresource>
```

A resource file can have any number of <qresource> tags, although up until now we have only ever used one. If the current locale is "en_US", the main help file will be :/index.html; but if the locale is "fr_CA" or "fr" or any other "fr_*", when we seek to access file :/index.html in code, the file we will actually get is :/index_fr.html.

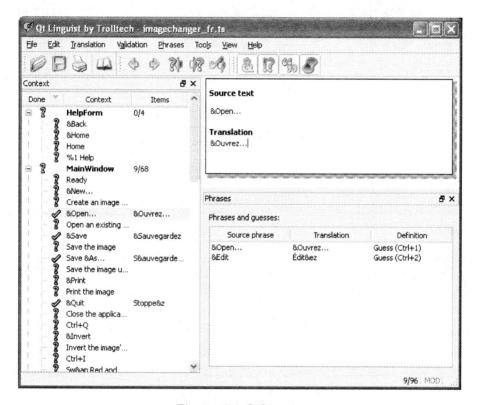

Figure 17.2 *Qt Linguist*

The tool that is used to create and update a .ts (translation source) file is pylupdate4. This program is run from the command line with the name of a .pro file as a parameter. Here is the complete imagechanger.pro file:

```
FORMS        += newimagedlg.ui
SOURCES      += helpform.py
SOURCES      += imagechanger.pyw
SOURCES      += newimagedlg.py
SOURCES      += resizedlg.py
TRANSLATIONS += imagechanger_fr.ts
```

The .pro file format is used primarily by C++/Qt programmers, but it makes using pylupdate4 and lrelease easier if we use it for PyQt projects. We care about only three kinds of entries: FORMS for .ui files, SOURCES for .py and .pyw files, and TRANSLATIONs for .ts files. Notice that we do not list .qm files (such as qt_fr.qm); this is because we do not generate the qt_fr.qm file, but simply copy it from the translations directory.

We don't have to use one line per file; instead, we can group files. For example:

```
FORMS        = newimagedlg.ui
SOURCES      = helpform.py imagechanger.pyw newimagedlg.py resizedlg.py
TRANSLATIONS = imagechanger_fr.ts
```

Once we have used tr() and translate() in our source code, and created the .pro file, we can run pylupdate4:

```
C:\>cd c:\pyqt\chap17
C:\pyqt\chap17>pylupdate4 -verbose imagechanger.pro
Updating 'imagechanger_fr.ts'...
    Found 96 source texts (96 new and 0 already existing)
```

Using the -verbose option is, of course, optional. The pylupdate4 program creates the .ts file listed in the .pro file if it doesn't exist, and puts into it all the contexts and strings for the strings marked using tr() and translate() that appear in the files listed in the FORMS and SOURCES .pro file entries. If the .ts file already exists, pylupdate4 adds any new contexts and strings that are necessary, leaving intact any translations that have been added in the meantime. Because pylupdate4 is smart, we can run it as often as we like, even if a translator has updated the .ts file by adding or changing translations, without losing any data.

When we are ready to release (or to simply test) the translated application, we can generate a .qm file for the .ts file by running lrelease:

```
C:\pyqt\chap17>lrelease -verbose imagechanger.pro
Updating 'C:/pyqt/chap17/imagechanger_fr.qm'...
    Generated 85 translations (81 finished and 4 unfinished)
    Ignored 11 untranslated source texts
```

Just like pylupdate4, we can run lrelease as often as we like. We don't need to generate the qt_fr.qm file, because we copied it.

It is possible to avoid using a .pro file entirely, and simply rely on the mkpyqt.py or Make PyQt build tools. To do this, we must run pylupdate4 once on the command line. For example:

```
C:\>cd c:\pyqt\chap17
C:\pyqt\chap17>pylupdate4 *.py *.pyw -ts imagechanger_fr.ts
```

From now on we can simply run mkpyqt.py with the -t (translate) option, or run Make PyQt and check the Translate checkbox. With translation switched on, both tools run pylupdate4 followed by lrelease.

The main piece of work left to do is the translation itself. For this, we can give the translator the *Qt Linguist* application—it is written in C++/Qt and runs on Windows, Mac OS X, and Linux—along with the .ts file, and ask them to enter translations for the strings. The *Qt Linguist* application (shown in Figure 17.2), is quite easy to use and can help minimize duplication by suggesting similar previously translated phrases. It groups translation strings by contexts (which are normally window class names). This is useful when a string might need to be translated in different ways depending on which form it appears in.

To get started with *Qt Linguist*, run it, click File→Open, and open a .ts file. Now click one of the ⊞ symbols in the Context dock window on the left to show the strings in a context, and then click one of the strings. The string will appear in the top-right panel under the "Source text" heading. Click under the "Translation" heading and type in a translation. To confirm that the translation of the string is finished, click the question mark icon in the Context dock window beside the relevant string: Clicking the icon makes it toggle between being a question mark or a tick. Translations that are ticked are "done" and will be put into the .qm file by lrelease.

Summary

Creating an HTML-based online help system using QTextBrowser or QDesktopServices.openUrl() is straightforward, whereas creating a system that uses *Qt Assistant* is trickier to set up. But no matter which approach we take to providing access to online help, the real challenge is the design and content of the online help documentation itself.

Setting up an application for translation is quite straightforward. A .pro file is normally used to list the .ts file and the .ui, .py, and .pyw files that have user-visible strings in them, and we must use pylupdate4 and lrelease to keep the .ts file up-to-date and to produce the .qm file. We can avoid using a .pro file by generating the initial .ts file and then using either mkpyqt.py or Make PyQt.

In terms of coding we must make sure that every user-visible string uses QObject.tr() or QApplication.translate(). Strings that have replaceable arguments should always use QString.arg() with its numbered %n arguments rather than the Python % operator.

For numbers we may need to use %Ln to get the correct thousands and decimal separators. One trick we can use for currency symbols is to do something like this:

```
currency = QApplication.translate("Currency", "$")
```

and translate "$" as "€", "£", "¥", or whatever else is appropriate. For dates we can use QDate.toString(Qt.SystemLocaleDate) or QDate.toString(Qt.ISODate). For units of measurement it is probably best either to provide a sensible default that the user can change through a configuration dialog, or have a "first run" dialog that asks the user to choose their units, default paper size, and so on.

Exercise

If you are multilingual, pick one of the examples or exercises, or one of your own PyQt applications, and translate it to your second language.

If you are monolingual, pick one of the examples or exercises, or one of your own PyQt applications, and add online help to it, including tooltips and status tips, as well as HTML help files.

No solutions are provided.

18

Networking

Curren-
cy
Con-
verter

121 ☞

The Python standard library has many modules that provide networking facilities. We saw one example of a standard library networking function back in Chapter 4, when we used urllib2.urlopen() to provide a "file handle" to a file on the Internet that we then read line by line using the for line in fh: idiom. It is also possible to just "grab" an entire file from the Internet:

```
source = "http://www.amk.ca/files/python/crypto/" + \
         "pycrypto-2.0.1.tar.gz"
target = source[source.rfind("/") + 1:]
name, message = urllib.urlretrieve(source, target)
```

The name holds the name that the source was saved under; it will be the same as target in this case, but if no target is specified it will be a generated name—for example, /tmp/tmpX-R8z3.tar.gz. For an HTTP download, the message is an httplib.HTTPMessage instance that contains the relevant HTTP headers.

Python's urllib and urllib2 standard library modules are very versatile. They can use the FTP and HTTP protocols, in the latter case using GET or POST, and they can use an HTTP proxy. The urllib2 module supports basic authentication and can be used to set HTTP headers. And if Python has been installed with SSL support, the urllib2 module can use the HTTPS protocol. The standard library also includes support for many other network protocols, including IMAP4, POP3, and SMTP for email, and NNTP for network news, as well as libraries for handling cookies, XML-RPC, and CGI, and for creating servers. Most of Python's networking support is based on the socket module, which can be used directly for low-level network programming.

In addition to Python's standard library, PyQt4 provides its own set of networking classes, including QFtp for client-side FTP support and QHttp for HTTP support. Low-level networking can be done using QAbstractSocket subclasses, including QTcpSocket, QTcpServer, and QUdpSocket, and from Qt 4.3, QSslSocket.

Networking support for Python can also be found in other third-party libraries, the most well known being the Twisted networking framework; see `http://twistedmatrix.com` for further details.

In this chapter we will only concern ourselves with creating a simple client/server application, and we will create both the client and the server using just two of PyQt's networking classes: `QTcpSocket` and `QTcpServer`. In the next chapter, we will look at a multithreaded version of the server that is capable of handling multiple simultaneous requests without having to block.

Client/server applications are normally implemented as two separate programs: a server that waits for and responds to requests, and one or more clients that send requests to the server and read back the server's response. For this to work, the clients must know where to connect to the server, that is, the server's IP address and port number. Also, both clients and server must send and receive data using an agreed-upon socket protocol, and using data formats that they both understand.

PyQt provides two different kinds of socket. The UDP (User Datagram Protocol) is supported by the `QUdpSocket` class. UDP is lightweight, but unreliable—there are no guarantees that data will be received. UDP is connectionless, so data is just sent or received as discrete items. The TCP (Transmission Control Protocol) is supported by the `QTcpSocket` class. TCP is a reliable connection- and stream-oriented protocol; any amount of data can be sent and received—the socket is responsible for breaking the data into chunks that are small enough to send, and for reconstructing the data at the other end.

UDP is often used to monitor instruments that give continuous readings, and where the odd missed reading is not significant. Client/server applications normally use TCP because they need reliability; this is the protocol we will use in this chapter.

Another decision that must be made is whether to send and receive data as lines of text, or as blocks of binary data. PyQt's TCP sockets can use either approach, but we have opted to work with binary data since this is the most versatile and easiest to handle.

The example we will use is the Building Services application. The server holds details of the rooms in a building and the dates they have been booked. The client is used to book and unbook particular rooms for particular dates. Any number of clients can be used, but if two clients make a request that arrives at *exactly* the same time, one will be blocked until the other's request has been handled. This problem can be mitigated by using a threaded server, as we will see in the next chapter.

For the sake of the example, we will run the server and clients on the same machine; this means that we can use "localhost" as the IP address. The server and two clients are shown in Figure 18.1. We have also chosen a port number of 9 407—this is just an arbitrary number. The port number should be greater than 1 023 and is normally between 5 001 and 32 767, although port numbers

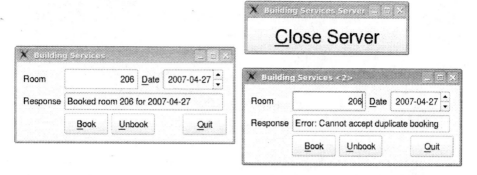

Figure 18.1 *A server with two clients*

up to 65 535 are valid. The server can accept two kinds of request, "BOOK" and "UNBOOK", and can make three kinds of response, "BOOK", "UNBOOK", and "ERROR". All the requests and responses are sent and received as binary data; we will look at their formats in the sections that follow.

In addition to the port number that is held in the PORT variable, we also create the SIZEOF_UINT16 variable and set it to 2 (meaning two bytes). In addition to the normal imports, we must also import the QtNetwork module:

```
from PyQt4.QtNetwork import *
```

The same PORT and SIZEOF_UINT16 variables, and the same QtNetwork import, are used in both the client and the server applications. In the following section, we will look at the implementation of the client, and in the second section we will review the server.

Creating a TCP Client

The Building Services client is in chap18/buildingservicesclient.pyw. It allows the user to enter a room number (with only valid room numbers being accepted) and a date, and to request that the room is booked (or unbooked) for that date. The server responds to the request and the client displays the response for the user to read in the response label.

We will begin by looking at the initializer, but omitting the creation of the widgets and layouts. We will look at it in three parts, and then go on to look at the client's methods.

```
class BuildingServicesClient(QWidget):

    def __init__(self, parent=None):
        super(BuildingServicesClient, self).__init__(parent)

        self.socket = QTcpSocket()
        self.nextBlockSize = 0
        self.request = None
```

We have subclassed QWidget rather than QDialog or QMainWindow. The only noticeable difference is that had we subclassed QDialog, pressing Esc would have terminated the application.

We have three objects to store. The first is the socket that the client will use to communicate with the server. The second is the "next block size"; this is a variable that we use to determine whether we have received sufficient response data to be able to process the response. The third is a request object; this is a QByteArray containing the request data, or None if we have no data to send.

We will skip the creation, setup, and laying out of the widgets, since all of that should all be familiar by now, although we will look at the widget connections after we have looked at the socket connections.

```
self.connect(self.socket, SIGNAL("connected()"),
             self.sendRequest)
self.connect(self.socket, SIGNAL("readyRead()"),
             self.readResponse)
self.connect(self.socket, SIGNAL("disconnected()"),
             self.serverHasStopped)
self.connect(self.socket,
             SIGNAL("error(QAbstractSocket::SocketError)"),
             self.serverHasError)
```

The first four signals are concerned with the socket. We need to know when the connection is established, since at that point we can send our request data. We also need to know whether the socket has data to read, since when it does, it will have the server's response, which we want to read. If the connection is terminated—for example, because the server has been shut down or an error has occurred—we want to know so that we can inform the user.

```
self.connect(self.roomEdit, SIGNAL("textEdited(QString)"),
             self.updateUi)
self.connect(self.dateEdit, SIGNAL("dateChanged(QDate)"),
             self.updateUi)
self.connect(self.bookButton, SIGNAL("clicked()"),
             self.book)
self.connect(self.unBookButton, SIGNAL("clicked()"),
             self.unBook)
self.connect(quitButton, SIGNAL("clicked()"), self.close)
```

The other connections are concerned with the user interface. As usual, we have an updateUi() method for doing validation and for enabling/disabling the buttons as appropriate. We also have connections to book and unbook rooms and to terminate the application.

```
def updateUi(self):
    enabled = False
    if not self.roomEdit.text().isEmpty() and \
```

```
                self.dateEdit.date() > QDate.currentDate():
                enabled = True
        if self.request is not None:
                enabled = False
        self.bookButton.setEnabled(enabled)
        self.unBookButton.setEnabled(enabled)
```

We enable the book and unbook buttons if the room edit has a room number and if the date edit has a date later than today—but we disable them if there is a pending request (i.e., if self.request is not None).

```
    def closeEvent(self, event):
        self.socket.close()
        event.accept()
```

If the application is terminated we make sure that we close the socket and we accept the close event. We don't really have to do these things, but by doing them we show that we have considered what should be done on termination.

```
    def book(self):
        self.issueRequest(QString("BOOK"), self.roomEdit.text(),
                          self.dateEdit.date())

    def unBook(self):
        self.issueRequest(QString("UNBOOK"), self.roomEdit.text(),
                          self.dateEdit.date())
```

If the user clicks Book, the book() method is called. The method simply calls issueRequest() with the request action "BOOK", the room number (as a QString), and the date. The unBook() method is almost identical, except that its request action is "UNBOOK".

```
    def issueRequest(self, action, room, date):
        self.request = QByteArray()
        stream = QDataStream(self.request, QIODevice.WriteOnly)
        stream.setVersion(QDataStream.Qt_4_2)
        stream.writeUInt16(0)
        stream << action << room << date
        stream.device().seek(0)
        stream.writeUInt16(self.request.size() - SIZEOF_UINT16)
        self.updateUi()
        if self.socket.isOpen():
            self.socket.close()
        self.responseLabel.setText("Connecting to server...")
        self.socket.connectToHost("localhost", PORT)
```

This method is used to prepare the request QByteArray and to initiate the process whereby the request is sent to the server.

Figure 18.2 shows the data that is written to the request QByteArray. A QByte-Array can be read from and written to just like any other QIODevice. The first two bytes contain an unsigned integer, initially with the value 0. This integer is used to store the number of bytes occupied by the request (excluding the size of the integer itself), that is, the number of bytes that follow it. We must start by making it 0 because we do not know how many bytes will be used.

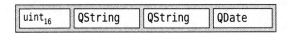

Figure 18.2 *The request format*

After the size integer, we write the data. The action string is the request action ("BOOK" or "UNBOOK"), the room string holds a room number (e.g., "213"), and the date holds a QDate. Once the data has been written to the byte array, we use seek() to move the writing position to the beginning so that what we write next will overwrite the start of the QByteArray. (We actually perform the seek on the QDataStream's underlying QIODevice, which is retrieved by the QDataStream.device() call.) We write an unsigned 16-bit integer whose value is the length of the QByteArray minus the size of the initial integer. The request byte array is now ready to be sent.

We update the user interface—this will disable the Book and Unbook buttons since the request object is not None; this is to prevent the user from making additional requests before a response has been received. We then make sure that the socket is closed, since it may have been opened to handle a previous request, and set the response label to inform the user that we are attempting to establish a connection.

Finally, we call connectToHost(). The IP address can be given as a dotted string (e.g., "82.94.237.218"), as a hostname (e.g., "www.python.org"), or as a QHost-Address object. Thanks to the signal–slot connections that we made in the initializer, we know that once the connection is established our sendRequest() method will be called, unless the connection fails, in which case either the serverHasStopped() or the serverHasError() method will be called instead.

```
def sendRequest(self):
    self.responseLabel.setText("Sending request...")
    self.nextBlockSize = 0
    self.socket.write(self.request)
    self.request = None
```

Once the connection has been established this method is called. It updates the response label to tell the user that the request it being sent, and sets the next block size to be 0. This is concerned with the *response* we hope to get back; we will see it in use in the readResponse() method. It then writes the request byte array to the socket. Once the data is written, the request is set to None, ready for a new request to be made.

If no error occurs, and providing the server has not been terminated, the server will respond, and at that point the readResponse() method will be called. (Otherwise, either the serverHasStopped() or the serverHasError() method will be called.)

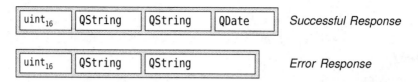

Figure 18.3 *The response formats*

The server has two different response formats, as shown in Figure 18.3. When the response is received we must begin by reading its size from the unsigned integer. Then, once we know that at least as many bytes as the size are available to read, we read the first QString. If this contains the text "ERROR", we know that we have an error response, and we can simply read the second string that contains the error message; otherwise, the text will be "BOOK" or "UNBOOK", that is, the request action, with the request's details, the room in the second QString, and the date as a QDate, to confirm that the request's action has succeeded.

```
def readResponse(self):
    stream = QDataStream(self.socket)
    stream.setVersion(QDataStream.Qt_4_2)

    while True:
        if self.nextBlockSize == 0:
            if self.socket.bytesAvailable() < SIZEOF_UINT16:
                break
            self.nextBlockSize = stream.readUInt16()
        if self.socket.bytesAvailable() < self.nextBlockSize:
            break
        action = QString()
        room = QString()
        date = QDate()
        stream >> action >> room
        if action != "ERROR":
            stream >> date
        if action == "ERROR":
            msg = QString("Error: %1").arg(room)
        elif action == "BOOK":
            msg = QString("Booked room %1 for %2").arg(room) \
                        .arg(date.toString(Qt.ISODate))
        elif action == "UNBOOK":
            msg = QString("Unbooked room %1 for %2").arg(room) \
                        .arg(date.toString(Qt.ISODate))
```

```
self.responseLabel.setText(msg)
self.updateUi()
self.nextBlockSize = 0
```

It is possible that the server's response will be returned in fragments. For this reason we use an infinite loop, first to retrieve the byte count and then to ensure that there are at least that number of bytes available to read. This leaves the responsibility for buffering with the server, and it means that when we read we know that we can read a complete response in one go.

If at least two bytes are available, we read them as an unsigned 16-bit integer: This gives us the number of bytes that are to follow. Then we test to see whether there are enough bytes to read: If there aren't, we exit the loop and wait for another readyRead() signal to result in the readResponse() method being called. If there are enough bytes, we read the action, and the string that follows—this is either the room number or an error message. If the action is not "ERROR", we also read the date. Then, depending on which action we received, we prepare a message string and display it in the response label.

Having read an entire response we reset the next block size since we have read that many bytes. Now when we loop, either another response is waiting, in which case QTcpSocket.bytesAvailable() will return a value greater than zero, and we repeat the process of reading and displaying; or there is no other response and we simply break out of the loop and finish.

```
def serverHasStopped(self):
    self.responseLabel.setText(
            "Error: Connection closed by server")
    self.socket.close()

def serverHasError(self, error):
    self.responseLabel.setText(QString("Error: %1") \
            .arg(self.socket.errorString()))
    self.socket.close()
```

If the server is terminated or if the server responds with a networking error (rather than with our own "ERROR" response), the relevant serverHas*() method is called. In both cases, we display the error message to the user in the response label and close the socket.

The BuildingServicesClient class is now complete. The user can enter their booking and unbooking requests and send them to the server by clicking the Book and Unbook buttons, and can see the results of their requests displayed in the response label. Requests are sent by writing a QByteArray to a suitably set up socket. Responses are read back from the socket through a QDataStream; this enables us to directly read QStrings, QDates, and any other data-stream-supported types, into local variables.

Now that we have seen how the client is created, we can turn our attention to the server.

Creating a TCP Server

The Building Services TCP server is in chap18/buildingservicesserver.pyw. It has three components: a GUI that holds a TCP server instance and that provides an easy means by which the user can terminate the server, a QTcpServer subclass that is instantiated to provide the server instance, and a QTcpSocket subclass that is used to handle incoming connections. We will begin by looking at the first two, since they are short, and then focus on the QTcpSocket subclass where most of the work is done.

```
class BuildingServicesDlg(QPushButton):

    def __init__(self, parent=None):
        super(BuildingServicesDlg, self).__init__(
                "&Close Server", parent)
        self.setWindowFlags(Qt.WindowStaysOnTopHint)

        self.loadBookings()
        self.tcpServer = TcpServer(self)
        if not self.tcpServer.listen(QHostAddress("0.0.0.0"), PORT):
            QMessageBox.critical(self, "Building Services Server",
                    QString("Failed to start server: %1") \
                    .arg(self.tcpServer.errorString()))
            self.close()
            return

        self.connect(self, SIGNAL("clicked()"), self.close)
```

Just for a change, and to remind us that any PyQt widget can be a top-level window, we have made the dialog a QPushButton subclass. We have also set the Qt.WindowStaysOnTopHint; most windowing systems will respect the hint and keep the widget on top of all other windows.

We won't cover the loadBookings() method; it is used to populate the in-memory data structure, the Bookings default dictionary, that holds the bookings data. The dictionary's keys are dates stored as datetime.date objects, and the values are ordered lists of room numbers stored as unicode strings. Default dictionaries were introduced with Python 2.5. They are like normal dictionaries, except that when we use a key that isn't in the dictionary, the key is inserted with a default value. What default value is used depends on how we create the dictionary. In the Building Services server we have created the dictionary like this:

```
Bookings = collections.defaultdict(list)
```

Here we have said that the default value for any new key is to be an empty list; in other cases, we might have chosen an empty set. We can always replace a default dictionary with a normal dictionary—for example, if using a Python version older than 2.5—by using the dict.setdefault() method when accessing possibly nonexistent keys, as we will show later.

We will review the TcpServer class shortly. Once we have created a server, we tell it to listen for incoming connections on the given IP address and port number. The IP address is specified as a QHostAddress, with the special address "0.0.0.0", meaning "all network interfaces"; the port number is the same arbitrary 9407 that we used for the client.

The connection ensures that if the user clicks the button, the window will close. We don't do any special cleanup for the TCP server; when it is destroyed any connected clients will be notified and their sockets' disconnected() signals will be emitted.

There is no more to the dialog, so we can now look at the tiny TcpServer class that inherits QTcpServer.

```
class TcpServer(QTcpServer):

    def __init__(self, parent=None):
        super(TcpServer, self).__init__(parent)

    def incomingConnection(self, socketId):
        socket = Socket(self)
        socket.setSocketDescriptor(socketId)
```

This is the complete code for the TCP server. Whenever an incoming connection request occurs the incomingConnection() method is called with a socket descriptor in socketId. We simply create a new Socket (a QTcpSocket subclass that we will review next), and set it to use the socket descriptor that the server has provided.

This TCP server depends on the PyQt event loop. If we wanted to create a QTcpServer-based server that did not have a GUI, there are two approaches we could take. One approach would be to use a QEventLoop, to provide an event loop without needing a GUI, and write the code in the same way as we have done here. The other approach is to not have an event loop, but in this case we would have to do things slightly differently. In particular, we would have to use the blocking QTcpServer.waitForNewConnection() method instead of reimplementing incomingConnection(). Of course, if the server does not have a GUI, it could be written purely using Python's standard libraries without needing the QtNetwork module at all. Alternatively, the server could be written using Twisted.

Once a connection is established, all the work is passed on to the Socket class, a QTcpSocket subclass that we will now review.

```
class Socket(QTcpSocket):

    def __init__(self, parent=None):
        super(Socket, self).__init__(parent)
        self.connect(self, SIGNAL("readyRead()"), self.readRequest)
        self.connect(self, SIGNAL("disconnected()"), self.deleteLater)
        self.nextBlockSize = 0
```

The socket connects its readyRead() signal to our custom readRequest() method, and its disconnected() signal to its deleteLater() slot—this ensures that the socket is cleanly deleted when the connection is terminated. The next block size variable is used for the same purpose and in the same way as in the client, to ensure that we read a request only when there are at least as many bytes available to read as are in the request.

Once the socket has been created and the connections set up, it simply waits until its readRequest() method is called. This method is a bit long, so we will review it in two parts.

```
def readRequest(self):
    stream = QDataStream(self)
    stream.setVersion(QDataStream.Qt_4_2)

    if self.nextBlockSize == 0:
        if self.bytesAvailable() < SIZEOF_UINT16:
            return
        self.nextBlockSize = stream.readUInt16()
    if self.bytesAvailable() < self.nextBlockSize:
        return

    action = QString()
    room = QString()
    date = QDate()
```

We begin by seeing whether there are at least two bytes to read: If there are, we read in the size of the next block. If there are not two bytes to read, or if there were but there are not enough bytes available to read the entire request, we return and wait for the readRequest() to be called again, when more bytes have arrived.

Once there are enough bytes, we create empty action and room strings, and a null QDate, ready to populate them from the incoming request data.

```
stream >> action
if action in ("BOOK", "UNBOOK"):
    stream >> room >> date
    bookings = Bookings.get(date.toPyDate())
    uroom = unicode(room)
if action == "BOOK":
    if bookings is None:
        bookings = Bookings[date.toPyDate()]
    if len(bookings) < MAX_BOOKINGS_PER_DAY:
        if uroom in bookings:
            self.sendError("Cannot accept duplicate booking")
        else:
            bisect.insort(bookings, uroom)
            self.sendReply(action, room, date)
```

```
            else:
                self.sendError(QString("%1 is fully booked") \
                        .arg(date.toString(Qt.ISODate)))
        elif action == "UNBOOK":
            if bookings is None or uroom not in bookings:
                self.sendError("Cannot unbook nonexistent booking")
            else:
                bookings.remove(uroom)
                self.sendReply(action, room, date)
        else:
            self.sendError("Unrecognized request")
```

The server recognizes only two request actions, "BOOK" and "UNBOOK"; if it gets one of these it reads in the room and date, and retrieves the (possibly empty) list of bookings for the given date. It also stores a unicode copy of the room number QString, since the Bookings dictionary the server uses holds all its data using Python types rather than PyQt types.

Next, the server attempts to book or unbook the given room for the given date. When booking, if there are no bookings for the given date, an empty list of bookings is created for that date. This works because we are using a default dictionary, so when we access it with a key it does not have, it automatically inserts a new item with the given key and with a default value; in this case, an empty list. The code is a little bit subtle because we begin by calling get(). We do this to avoid creating an empty list for the given date if the action is to unbook. Only when we know that the action is to book do we want to ensure that there is a list for the given date.

If we were using a normal dictionary, we would have to use dict.setdefault() to retrieve the list for the given date, creating a new item with the given date as the key and an empty list as the value, if the key is not already present. For example:

```
        bookings = Bookings.setdefault(date.toPyDate(), [])
```

The QDate.toPyDate() method was introduced in PyQt 4.1; for earlier versions we would have to perform the conversion ourselves by writing datetime.date(date.year(), date.month(), date.day()).

Once we have our (possibly empty) bookings list, and providing that there are fewer than the maximum number of bookings allowed (MAX_BOOKINGS_PER_DAY, which has a value of 5), the room number string is inserted into the list in order, and a reply is sent to the client which simply echoes the request data. If the room is already booked for the given date, or if the date has the maximum number of bookings already, an error reply is sent to the client instead.

If the action is to unbook, the room is removed from the bookings for the given date and the action echoed back to the client; or an error reply is given if the booking did not exist in the first place. Although the rooms are stored in order, we have simply used not in and list.remove(), which both do a linear search; for longer lists we would use bisect.bisect_left() to find the room using a binary chop, but that seems like overkill in this example.

If the request action is unrecognized, we simply reply with an error message.

```
def sendReply(self, action, room, date):
    reply = QByteArray()
    stream = QDataStream(reply, QIODevice.WriteOnly)
    stream.setVersion(QDataStream.Qt_4_2)
    stream.writeUInt16(0)
    stream << action << room << date
    stream.device().seek(0)
    stream.writeUInt16(reply.size() - SIZEOF_UINT16)
    self.write(reply)
```

The reply sent to the client is created in the same way as the client's requests are created. We write to a QByteArray using a QDataStream, beginning by writing an unsigned 16-bit integer and ending by overwriting the integer with the size of the reply, and then writing the reply to the socket.

```
def sendError(self, msg):
    reply = QByteArray()
    stream = QDataStream(reply, QIODevice.WriteOnly)
    stream.setVersion(QDataStream.Qt_4_2)
    stream.writeUInt16(0)
    stream << QString("ERROR") << QString(msg)
    stream.device().seek(0)
    stream.writeUInt16(reply.size() - SIZEOF_UINT16)
    self.write(reply)
```

The code for sending an error reply is almost the same as for sending a success reply, and arguably we could have used one method for both.

The server could easily be extended to handle more request types simply by adding more if statements to readRequest(). For example, the client might want to know which rooms are booked on a particular day, or which days a particular room is booked on.

Although we have used a dictionary to hold the server's data, there is no reason why the server could not hold its data in-process in a SQLite database or in an out-of-process database, or in files. Nor does the server need to have a GUI; it could have no QWidgets, and simply be run in the background as a Linux dæmon or Windows service.

Summary

The Python standard library, the Twisted networking engine, and the PyQt QtNetwork module provide considerable support for networking, from low-level sockets to various high-level protocols, including FTP and HTTP.

To write client/server applications we must ensure that the client and the server programs can communicate. This means that the server must run at a known IP address and listen at a specific port address. Both client and server must communicate using an agreed-upon protocol such as UDP, or more commonly, TCP. They must also agree on how the data is to be transmitted, whether as lines of text or as blocks of binary data—and in both cases, they must know what format each request and response must take.

The scenario shown in this chapter is a very common one: The server sits waiting for requests, and clients send requests and then read back the server's responses. Before a client can communicate at all it must establish a connection, and then, once the connection has been established, it can send its data. The server may respond with data, or some problem may have occurred. If data is received, we must make sure that we never attempt to read more bytes (or lines) than are available.

PyQt's QTcpServer and QTcpSocket classes make it very easy to implement servers. And although it is possible to read and write lines of textual data, using binary data is much more versatile, allowing us to send and receive any type of data and with no need to write a parser.

One theoretical problem with the TCP server we have implemented is that it is single threaded. This means that it may have to block to handle one request at a time if multiple requests arrive at the same moment. This can be solved by using a threaded server, as we will see in the next chapter.

Exercise

Modify the Building Services server so that it accepts a new request action, BOOKINGSONDATE. When such a request is received it should ignore the room, and instead retrieve the bookings for the given date. If there are no bookings the server should send an error reply. Otherwise, it should send as its reply not a single room string, but rather a string containing comma-space-separated room numbers as shown in Figure 18.4.

Modify the Building Services client so that it has a Bookings on Date? button, connected to a method that issues a suitable request. The client's read-Response() method will need to be modified slightly so that it can read the server's response to the new request.

The modifications necessary to provide "bookings on date" are quite straightforward. For a bit more challenge, modify the Building Services server to accept another new request action, BOOKINGSFORROOM. When one of these requests

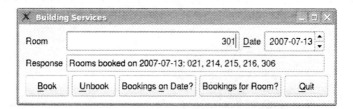

Figure 18.4 *Building Services—bookings on date*

is received it should ignore the date, and instead iterate over all the bookings, accumulating a list of the dates for which the given room is booked. If there are no bookings, it should return an error reply. Otherwise, instead of using the sendReply() method, it should send its own byte array with its length, the action, the room string, and then a 32-bit integer containing the number of dates in the list, followed by each of the dates. Since the dates are stored as datetime.date objects, they must be converted to QDates to stream them into the QByteArray.

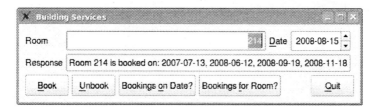

Figure 18.5 *Building Services—bookings for room*

The Building Services client must be modified to provide a Bookings for Room? button, connected to a method that issues a suitable request. The client's readResponse() method will need to be modified so that if a BOOKINGSFORROOM response is received, it reads in the dates and creates a suitable string for display in the client user interface, as shown in Figure 18.5.

The modifications to the server can be done by adding about 30 lines, and to the client by adding about 40 lines. However, the BOOKINGSFORROOM request/response does require some care.

Solutions are provided in chap18/buildingservicesserver_ans.pyw and chap18/buildingservicesclient_ans.pyw.

19

- Creating a Threaded Server
- Creating and Managing Secondary Threads
- Implementing a Secondary Thread

Multithreading

Traditionally, applications have a single thread of execution and perform one operation at a time. For GUI programs this can sometimes be a problem—for example, if the user invokes a long-running operation, the user interface might freeze up while the operation is taking place. There are a few solutions that can be tried to eliminate this problem.

One simple solution, particularly useful in long-running loops, is to call QApplication.processEvents(). This method gives the event loop the opportunity to handle any unprocessed events, such as paint events, as well as mouse and key press events. Another solution is to use zero-timeout timers. We have combined both approaches in several examples, usually when loading lots of files—for example, in Chapter 9's Text Editor's MainWindow.loadFiles() method.

A third solution is to farm the work out to another program entirely. This can be done using the Python standard library's subprocess module, or using PyQt's QProcess class. The makepyqt.pyw application supplied with the examples uses QProcess to execute PyQt's command-line tools such as pyuic4 and pyrcc4.

In some cases what we really need is a separate thread of execution within the application itself. Applications that have more than one thread of execution are said to be multithreaded.* For example, we might want to create a server that can service as many simultaneous connections as the hardware can cope with, something relatively easily done if we devote a new thread to each connection. And in some cases we might have a GUI application where we want the user to be able to start off a long-running process, and then continue interacting with the application; in such cases it may be best to pass on the processing to a separate secondary thread and leave the primary (GUI) thread free to respond to the user.

This chapter shows some common techniques used in multithreaded programming. These are enough to get started, but the coverage is not comprehensive,

---

*This chapter assumes a knowledge of the fundamentals of threading. For a thorough, but not light, introduction, see *Foundations of Multithreaded, Parallel, and Distributed Programming*.

since that would take us beyond the scope of the book and would require a book in itself.

Because several threads may access the same data concurrently, multithreaded applications are usually more difficult to write, maintain, and debug than single-threaded applications. On single-processor machines, multithreaded applications can sometimes run slower than single-threaded applications (due to the processing overhead of having the additional threads), but they are usually perceived to run faster by users because they don't freeze the user interface, and because they make it much easier for progress to be reported back to the user incrementally.

Using the right number of threads can significantly affect performance. For example, in the Page Indexer example covered later in the chapter, we have a primary (GUI) thread and a secondary thread. The exercise involves changing this example to use multiple secondary threads. If too many are used, the application runs slower than the version with one secondary thread, but with the right number, we can start up the one secondary thread version, and then start up the multiple secondary thread version, and see the multiple secondary thread version catch up, overtake, and finish, before the one secondary thread version has finished. How many secondary threads should we use? The answer depends on what processing must be done and on the particular machine and operating system that the application is run on. We could experiment with realistic datasets to fix a number, or we could make our code use more or fewer secondary threads depending on circumstances.

Python's standard library provides the low-level thread module and the higher-level threading module, but for PyQt programming, we recommend using the PyQt threading classes. PyQt's threading classes offer a high-level API, but under the hood some of their basic operations are implemented in assembly language to make them as fast and fine-grained as possible, something not done in Python's threading modules.

PyQt applications always have at least one thread of execution, the primary (initial) thread. In addition, they may create as many secondary threads as they need. However, if the application has a GUI, the GUI operations, such as executing the event loop, may only take place in the primary thread. New threads are created by instantiating QThread subclasses that reimplement the QThread.run() method.

It is possible to create PyQt applications that do not have a GUI, using QCoreApplication instead of QApplication. Just like GUI PyQt applications, they have one primary thread and may have any number of secondary threads.

Communication between secondary threads and the primary thread is often desirable—for example, to keep the user informed of progress, to allow the user to intervene during processing, and to let the primary thread know when processing is complete. Traditionally, such communication has taken place by using shared variables in conjunction with a resource protection mechanism.

PyQt has classes to support this approach, including `QMutex`, `QReadWriteLock`, and `QSemaphore`. In addition, PyQt applications can use the signal–slot mechanism to communicate between threads; this is very convenient and useful.

In this chapter's first section we will look at a threaded TCP server; it does the same job as the server described in the preceding chapter's last section, but it can serve several clients simultaneously because it is threaded. In the second and third sections we will look at a GUI application that has some potentially very time-consuming processing to do, and that passes on the processing to a secondary thread. This application uses signals and slots to keep the user interface up-to-date regarding progress, and to provide the user with some control over the secondary thread. This example also uses some of the resource protection classes so that the user interface can access work in progress.

Creating a Threaded Server

Unlike some other GUI libraries, PyQt's network socket classes are integrated with the event loop. This means that the user interface remains responsive during network processing, even in single-threaded PyQt applications. But if we want to be able to handle multiple simultaneous incoming connections, we might prefer to use a multithreaded server.

Making a multithreaded server is no more complicated than making a single-threaded server—the difference between the two being that instead of creating a separate socket to handle incoming connections, a multithreaded server creates a new thread for each new connection, and creates a new socket inside each new thread. For example, here is a complete threaded server:

```
class TcpServer(QTcpServer):

    def __init__(self, parent=None):
        super(TcpServer, self).__init__(parent)

    def incomingConnection(self, socketId):
        thread = Thread(socketId, self)
        self.connect(thread, SIGNAL("finished()"),
                     thread, SLOT("deleteLater()"))
        thread.start()
```

The `incomingConnection()` method is reimplemented from the `QTcpServer` base class. It is called whenever a new network connection is made to the server.

The signal–slot connection is necessary to ensure that the thread is deleted when it is no longer needed, thereby keeping the server's memory footprint as small as possible. Although we must reimplement `QThread.run()` in a `QThread` subclass, the thread is always started by calling `QThread.start()` (and *never* by calling `run()` directly).

The Thread subclass has one static variable and four methods. The sendReply() and sendError() methods are identical to those shown in the preceding chapter, so we will omit them.

```
class Thread(QThread):

    lock = QReadWriteLock()

    def __init__(self, socketId, parent):
        super(Thread, self).__init__(parent)
        self.socketId = socketId
```

The Thread.lock variable is static, so all the Thread instances share it. The initializer simply takes note of the socket descriptor ready for when the thread is started. The run() method is quite long, so we will review it in parts.

```
    def run(self):
        socket = QTcpSocket()
        if not socket.setSocketDescriptor(self.socketId):
            self.emit(SIGNAL("error(int)"), socket.error())
            return
        while socket.state() == QAbstractSocket.ConnectedState:
            nextBlockSize = 0
            stream = QDataStream(socket)
            stream.setVersion(QDataStream.Qt_4_2)
            while True:
                socket.waitForReadyRead(-1)
                if socket.bytesAvailable() >= SIZEOF_UINT16:
                    nextBlockSize = stream.readUInt16()
                    break
            if socket.bytesAvailable() < nextBlockSize:
                while True:
                    socket.waitForReadyRead(-1)
                    if socket.bytesAvailable() >= nextBlockSize:
                        break
```

We begin by creating a new socket and setting its socket descriptor to the one we were given. We take a slightly more robust approach than before, checking the return value of the QTcpSocket.setSocketDescriptor() call, and giving an error message on failure. Once the run() method finishes, the finished() signal is emitted and, thanks to our earlier signal–slot connection, the thread will be deleted.

As long as the socket is connected, we can use it to receive requests and send responses. Unlike the TCP server we created in the preceding chapter, rather than running asynchronously and waiting for things to happen, such as data being available, through signal–slot connections, here we block using wait-ReadyRead() until there is data. (The -1 argument means "wait forever".) It does not matter that we block, because we are in a separate thread of execution, so the rest of the application, its primary thread, and any other connection-handling secondary threads can continue unhindered.

Once there are two bytes available, we read the unsigned 16-bit byte count, and once at least that number of bytes is available to read, we can continue.

```
action = QString()
room = QString()
date = QDate()
stream >> action
if action in ("BOOK", "UNBOOK"):
    stream >> room >> date
    try:
        Thread.lock.lockForRead()
        bookings = Bookings.get(date.toPyDate())
    finally:
        Thread.lock.unlock()
    uroom = unicode(room)
```

We read in the request action, which should be "BOOK" or "UNBOOK", and if it is one of these, we then read in the room number string and the date. The Bookings default dictionary holds all the bookings data, and any number of threads could be accessing it simultaneously. For this reason we must protect each access. Here, we only want to read, so we call lockForRead(), extract the data we want, and then unlock the lock. We use a try ... finally block to guarantee that the lock will be unlocked when we have finished accessing the shared data.

Default dictionaries
529 ☜

Python 2.6 (and 2.5 with a suitable from __future__ statement) offers a nicer and more compact syntax that can replace the try ... finally, as the Using a Context Manager for Unlocking sidebar on page 549 shows.

One well-known locking mechanism is a mutex (also called a binary semaphore), provided by PyQt's QMutex class. A mutex allows only the thread that locks it to have access to the protected resource. PyQt also offers a more fine-grained mechanism, the read/write lock, provided by the QReadWriteLock class that we have used here. Whenever a lock is in force in one thread, other threads may be blocked, waiting for access. We can minimize this problem in two ways. First we can use read locks whenever possible—if the only locks in force are read locks, none of the threads is blocked since it is safe for all threads to read if no thread is writing. And second, we can minimize the amount of processing we do when a lock is in force. We have used both of these techniques in the run() reimplementation; the downside is that the code is much longer than might be expected.

QMutex, QReadWriteLock, and the other protection mechanisms work because they are all "thread-safe". Any number of threads can simultaneously call the methods of a thread-safe object, and can rely on the underlying system, that is, PyQt, to automatically serialize any accesses to shared data that might

occur. This means, for example, that if two or more threads attempt to lock
a `QReadWriteLock` for writing, only one will succeed, and all the others will be
blocked. This allows the thread that gained the lock to perform its updates on
the shared data, and when it releases the lock one of the other threads that
wants to write will be given access, and so on until no more threads require
write access.

The PyQt documentation indicates which classes, or which methods within
classes, are thread-safe. It also indicates which methods are reentrant. Reentrant methods are more constrained than thread-safe methods. This is because
it is safe to call reentrant methods simultaneously from multiple threads only
if each invocation results only in unique data being accessed, such as local
variables. A reentrant method can be made thread-safe by using locks for all
accesses to instance variables, and to any variables that refer to shared data.

```
if action == "BOOK":
    newlist = False
    try:
        Thread.lock.lockForRead()
        if bookings is None:
            newlist = True
    finally:
        Thread.lock.unlock()
    if newlist:
        try:
            Thread.lock.lockForWrite()
            bookings = Bookings[date.toPyDate()]
        finally:
            Thread.lock.unlock()
```

If the request is to book a room we begin by examining the `bookings` variable.
This is either `None` or a reference to a list held by the shared `Bookings` default
dictionary, so we must use a read lock when accessing it. If `bookings` is `None`, we
insert a new empty list into the dictionary with the given date as its key; this
time we must use a write lock.

```
error = None
insert = False
try:
    Thread.lock.lockForRead()
    if len(bookings) < MAX_BOOKINGS_PER_DAY:
        if uroom in bookings:
            error = "Cannot accept duplicate booking"
        else:
            insert = True
    else:
        error = QString("%1 is fully booked").arg(
                date.toString(Qt.ISODate))
```

```
            finally:
                Thread.lock.unlock()
        if insert:
            try:
                Thread.lock.lockForWrite()
                bisect.insort(bookings, uroom)
            finally:
                Thread.lock.unlock()
            self.sendReply(socket, action, room, date)
        else:
            self.sendError(socket, error)
```

If the room is already booked for the given date, we do not duplicate the booking, but instead send an error response to the client. In the nonthreaded server, we simply called sendError() in this case, but here we just assign an error text. We do this to keep the processing that is done within the context of the lock to a minimum.

If the booking can be made, we take a write lock, insert the room into the bookings list, and send a response indicating success. Otherwise, we send an error response. Neither response is sent within the context of a lock, again to minimize the time that locks are in force.

```
        elif action == "UNBOOK":
            error = None
            remove = False
            try:
                Thread.lock.lockForRead()
                if bookings is None or uroom not in bookings:
                    error = "Cannot unbook nonexistent booking"
                else:
                    remove = True
            finally:
                Thread.lock.unlock()
            if remove:
                try:
                    Thread.lock.lockForWrite()
                    bookings.remove(uroom)
                finally:
                    Thread.lock.unlock()
                self.sendReply(socket, action, room, date)
            else:
                self.sendError(socket, error)
```

The unbooking if branch follows the same pattern as the booking branch. We begin by checking whether the booking can be made, using a read lock, and if necessary, storing an error message rather than doing a time-consuming send while the lock is in force. Then we either unbook the room by removing it from the Bookings dictionary's list for the given date and send a success response, or we send an error response. Again, the responses are sent when no lock is in force.

```
else:
    self.sendError(socket, "Unrecognized request")
socket.waitForDisconnected()
```

If the server received a request that it does not recognize, it simply sends an error response. At the end, we call QTcpSocket.waitForDisconnected(); this blocks until the connection is closed, that is, until after the response has been sent. We don't need or want to keep the connection open, since our client/server application operates in terms of pairs of independent request–response transactions. Once the connection has been closed, the run() method finishes, and thanks to the deleteLater() signal–slot connection, the thread will be deleted.

Creating and Managing Secondary Threads

One common use case for threads in GUI applications is to pass processing on to a secondary thread so that the user interface can remain responsive and can show the secondary thread's progress. In this section, we will look at the Page Indexer application, shown in Figure 19.1, which indexes HTML files in a specified directory and all its subdirectories. The indexing work is passed off to a secondary thread that communicates with the primary thread to notify it of the progress that has been made as well as when the indexing is complete.

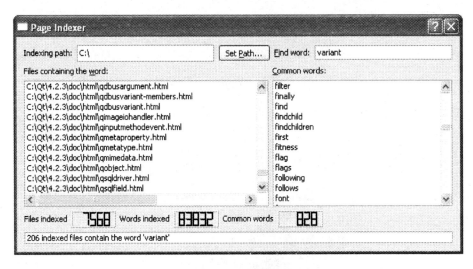

Figure 19.1 *The Page Indexer application*

The algorithm we will use for indexing is this: For each HTML file that is encountered, its text is read, entities are converted to the equivalent Unicode character, and the HTML tags are stripped out. Then the text is split into

Default dictio- naries

529 ☞

words and each word of 3–25 characters in length inclusive that isn't in the set of common words is added to the `filenamesForWords` default dictionary. Each of the dictionary's keys is a unique word, and each associated value is a set of the filenames where the word occurs. If any word occurs in more than 250 files, it is deleted from the dictionary and added to the set of common words. This ensures that the dictionary is kept to a reasonable size and means that searches for words like "and" and "the" won't work—which is a good thing, since such words are likely to match in thousands of files, far too many to be useful.

We will begin by looking at two extracts from the application's main form, which is in file `chap19/pageindexer.pyw`.

```
class Form(QDialog):

    def __init__(self, parent=None):
        super(Form, self).__init__(parent)

        self.fileCount = 0
        self.filenamesForWords = collections.defaultdict(set)
        self.commonWords = set()
        self.lock = QReadWriteLock()
        self.path = QDir.homePath()
```

The `fileCount` variable is used to keep track of how many files have been indexed so far. The `filenamesForWords` default dictionary's keys are words and its values are sets of filenames. The `commonWords` set holds words that have occurred in at least 250 files. The read/write lock is used to ensure that access to the `filenamesForWords` dictionary and to the `commonWords` set are protected since they will be read in the primary thread and read and written in the secondary thread. The `QDir.homePath()` method returns the user's home directory; we use it to set an initial search path.

```
        self.walker = walker.Walker(self.lock, self)
        self.connect(self.walker, SIGNAL("indexed(QString)"),
                     self.indexed)
        self.connect(self.walker, SIGNAL("finished(bool)"),
                     self.finished)
        self.connect(self.pathButton, SIGNAL("clicked()"),
                     self.setPath)
        self.connect(self.findEdit, SIGNAL("returnPressed()"),
                     self.find)
```

The secondary thread is in the `walker` module (so named because it walks the filesystem), and the `QThread` subclass is called `Walker`. Whenever the thread indexes a new file it emits a signal with the filename. It also emits a `finished()` signal when it has indexed all the files in the path it was given when it was started.

Signals emitted in one thread that are intended for another work asynchronously, that is, they don't block. But they work only if there is an event

loop at the receiving end. This means that secondary threads can pass information to the primary thread using signals, but not the other way around—unless
we run a separate event loop in a secondary thread (which is possible). Behind
the scenes, when cross-thread signals are emitted, instead of calling the relevant method directly as is done for signals emitted and received in the same
thread, PyQt puts an event onto the receiving thread's event queue with any
data that was passed. When the receiver's event loop gets around to reading
the event, it responds to it by calling the relevant method with any data that
was passed.

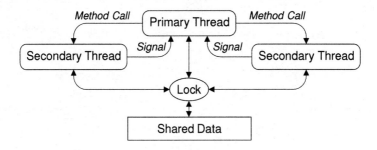

Figure 19.2 *A schematic of typical PyQt inter-thread communication*

As Figure 19.2 shows, the primary thread normally passes information to
secondary threads using method calls, and secondary threads pass information
to the primary thread using signals. Another communication mechanism,
used by both primary and secondary threads, is to use shared data. Such data
must have accesses protected—for example, by mutexes or read/write locks.

If the user clicks the Set Path button, the setPath() method is called, and if the
user presses Enter in the find line edit, the find() method is called.

The Form class is a QDialog, but we have designed it so that if the user presses
Esc while the indexing is ongoing, the indexing will stop, and if the user
presses Esc when the indexing has finished (or been stopped), the application
will terminate. We will see how this is done when we look at the accept() and
reject() reimplementations.

```
def setPath(self):
    self.pathButton.setEnabled(False)
    if self.walker.isRunning():
        self.walker.stop()
        self.walker.wait()
    path = QFileDialog.getExistingDirectory(self,
                "Choose a Path to Index", self.path)
    if path.isEmpty():
        self.statusLabel.setText("Click the 'Set Path' "
                                 "button to start indexing")
        self.pathButton.setEnabled(True)
```

```
            return
        self.path = QDir.toNativeSeparators(path)
        self.findEdit.setFocus()
        self.pathLabel.setText(self.path)
        self.statusLabel.clear()
        self.filesListWidget.clear()
        self.fileCount = 0
        self.filenamesForWords = collections.defaultdict(set)
        self.commonWords = set()
        self.walker.initialize(unicode(self.path),
                self.filenamesForWords, self.commonWords)
        self.walker.start()
```

When the user clicks Set Path, we begin by disabling the button and then stopping the thread if it is running. The stop() method is a custom one of our own. The wait() method is one inherited from QThread; it blocks until the thread has finished running, that is, until the run() method returns. In the stop() method, we indirectly ensure that the run() method finishes as soon as possible after stop() has been called, as we will see in the next section.

Next we get the path the user chose (or return, if they canceled). We have used QDir.toNativeSeparators() since internally PyQt always uses "/" to separate paths, but on Windows we want to show "\"s instead. The toNativeSeparators() method was introduced with Qt 4.2; for earlier versions use QDir.convertSeparators() instead. By default, getExistingDirectory() shows only directories because there is an optional fourth argument with a default value of QFileDialog.ShowDirsOnly; if we want filenames to be visible, we can clear this flag by passing QFileDialog.Options().

The user interface is set up by moving the keyboard focus to the find line edit, setting the path label to the chosen path, and clearing the status label that is used to keep the user informed about progress. The files list widget lists those files that contain the word in the find line edit. We don't need to protect access to the filenamesForWords default dictionary or to the commonWords set since the only thread running at this point is the primary thread.

We finish off by initializing the walker thread with the path and references to the data structures we want it to populate, and then we call start() to start it executing.

```
        def indexed(self, fname):
            self.statusLabel.setText(fname)
            self.fileCount += 1
            if self.fileCount % 25 == 0:
                self.filesIndexedLCD.display(self.fileCount)
                try:
                    self.lock.lockForRead()
                    indexedWordCount = len(self.filenamesForWords)
                    commonWordCount = len(self.commonWords)
```

```
            finally:
                self.lock.unlock()
            self.wordsIndexedLCD.display(indexedWordCount)
            self.commonWordsLCD.display(commonWordCount)
        elif self.fileCount % 101 == 0:
            self.commonWordsListWidget.clear()
            try:
                self.lock.lockForRead()
                words = self.commonWords.copy()
            finally:
                self.lock.unlock()
            self.commonWordsListWidget.addItems(sorted(words))
```

Whenever the walker thread finishes indexing a file, it emits an indexed() signal with the filename; this signal is connected to the Form.indexed() method shown earlier. We update the status label to show the name of the file that has just been indexed, and every 25 files we also update the file count, words indexed, and common words LCD widgets. We use a read lock to ensure that the shared data structures are safe to read from, and we do the minimum amount of work inside the context of the lock, updating the LCD widgets only after the lock has been released.

For every 101st file processed we update the common words list widget. Again we use a read lock, and we use set.copy() to ensure that we do not refer to the shared data once the lock has been released.

```
    def finished(self, completed):
        self.statusLabel.setText("Indexing complete" \
            if completed else "Stopped")
        self.finishedIndexing()
```

When the thread has been stopped or has finished, it emits a finished() signal, connected to this method and passing a Boolean to indicate whether it completed. We update the status label and call our finishedIndexing() method to update the user interface.

```
    def finishedIndexing(self):
        self.walker.wait()
        self.filesIndexedLCD.display(self.fileCount)
        self.wordsIndexedLCD.display(len(self.filenamesForWords))
        self.commonWordsLCD.display(len(self.commonWords))
        self.pathButton.setEnabled(True)
```

When the indexing has finished we call QThread.wait() to make sure that the thread's run() method has finished. Then we update the user interface based on the current values of the shared data structures. We don't need to protect access to the dictionary or the set because the walker thread is not running.

Using a Context Manager for Unlocking

In this chapter, we use `try ... finally` blocks to ensure that locks are unlocked after use. Python 2.6 offers an alternative approach using the new `with` keyword, in conjunction with a context manager. Context managers are explained in `http://www.python.org/dev/peps/pep-0343`; suffice it to say that we can make a context manager by creating a class that has two special methods: `__enter__()` and `__exit__()`. Then, instead of writing code like this:

```
try:
    self.lock.lockForRead()
    found = word in self.commonWords
finally:
    self.lock.unlock()
```

we can write something much simpler and shorter:

```
with ReadLocker(self.lock):
    found = word in self.commonWords
```

This works because the semantics of the object given to the `with` statement (at its simplest) are:

```
ContextManager.__enter__()
try:
    # statements, e.g., found = word in self.commonWords
finally:
    ContextManager.__exit__()
```

The `ReadLocker` context manager class itself is also easy to implement, assuming it is passed a `QReadWriteLock` object:

```
class ReadLocker:
    def __init__(self, lock):
        self.lock = lock
    def __enter__(self):
        self.lock.lockForRead()
    def __exit__(self, type, value, tb):
        self.lock.unlock()
```

If fact, since PyQt 4.1, `QReadLocker` and `QWriteLocker` can be used as context managers, so with Python 2.6 (or Python 2.5 with a `from __future__ import with_statement`), we don't need to use `try ... finally` to guarantee unlocking, and can instead write code like this:

```
with QReadLocker(self.lock):
    found = word in self.commonWords
```

The files `pageindexer_26.pyw` and `walker_26.py` in `chap19` use this approach.

At any time during the indexing, the user can interact with the user interface with no freezing or performance degradation. In particular, they can enter text in the find line edit and press Enter to populate the files list widget with those files that contain the word they typed. If they press Enter more than once with a bit of time between presses, the list of files may change, because in the interval more files may have been indexed. The find() method is slightly long, so we will review it in two parts.

```python
def find(self):
    word = unicode(self.findEdit.text())
    if not word:
        self.statusLabel.setText("Enter a word to find in files")
        return
    self.statusLabel.clear()
    self.filesListWidget.clear()
    word = word.lower()
    if " " in word:
        word = word.split()[0]
    try:
        self.lock.lockForRead()
        found = word in self.commonWords
    finally:
        self.lock.unlock()
    if found:
        self.statusLabel.setText(
                "Common words like '%s' are not indexed" % word)
        return
```

If the user enters a word to find, we clear the status label and the file list widget and look for the word in the set of common words. If the word was found, it is too common to be indexed, so we just give an informative message and return.

```python
    try:
        self.lock.lockForRead()
        files = self.filenamesForWords.get(word, set()).copy()
    finally:
        self.lock.unlock()
    if not files:
        self.statusLabel.setText(
                "No indexed file contains the word '%s'" % word)
        return
    files = [QDir.toNativeSeparators(name) for name in \
            sorted(files, key=unicode.lower)]
    self.filesListWidget.addItems(files)
    self.statusLabel.setText(
            "%d indexed files contain the word '%s'" % (
            len(files), word))
```

If the user's word is not in the set of common words, it might be in the index. We access the `filenamesForWords` default dictionary using a read lock, and copy the set of files that match the word. The set will be empty if no files have the word, but in either case, the set we have is a copy, so there is no risk of accessing shared data outside the context of a lock. If there are matching files we add them to the files list widget, sorted and using platform-native path separators.

The `sorted()` function returns its first argument (e.g., a list or set), in sorted order. It can be given a comparison function as the second argument, but here we have specified a "key". This has the effect of doing a DSU (decorate, sort, undecorate) sort that is the equivalent of:

```
templist = [(fname.lower(), fname) for fname in files]
templist.sort()
files = [fname for key, fname in templist]
```

This is more efficient than using a comparison function because each item is lowercased just once rather than every time it is used in a comparison.

```
def reject(self):
    if self.walker.isRunning():
        self.walker.stop()
        self.finishedIndexing()
    else:
        self.accept()
```

If the user presses Esc, the `reject()` method is called. If indexing is in progress, we call `stop()` on the thread and then call `finishedIndexing()`; the `finishedIndexing()` method calls `wait()`. Otherwise, indexing has either been stopped by a previous Esc key press or has finished; either way, we call `accept()` to terminate the application.

```
def closeEvent(self, event=None):
    self.walker.stop()
    self.walker.wait()
```

When the application is terminated, either by the `accept()` call that occurs in the `reject()` method, or by other means, such as the user clicking the close X button, the close event is called. Here we make sure that indexing has been stopped and that the thread has finished so that a clean termination takes place.

All the indexing work has been done by the walker secondary thread. This thread has been controlled by the primary thread calling its methods (e.g., `start()` and `stop()`), and has notified the primary thread of its status (file indexed, indexing finished) through PyQt's signals and slots mechanism. The the shared data has been accessed—for example, when the user has asked which files contain a particular word, or when the data has been updated by the walker thread, using the protection of a read/write lock. In the following section we will see how the Walker thread is implemented, how it emits its signals, and how it populates the data structures it is given.

Implementing a Secondary Thread

The Page Indexer's secondary thread is implemented in the Walker class in the file chap19/walker.py. The class is a QThread subclass that uses a QMutex to protect accesses that it makes to its own private data, and that uses the QReadWriteLock passed to it to protect accesses to data it shares with the primary thread.

```
class Walker(QThread):

    COMMON_WORDS_THRESHOLD = 250
    MIN_WORD_LEN = 3
    MAX_WORD_LEN = 25
    INVALID_FIRST_OR_LAST = frozenset("0123456789_")
    STRIPHTML_RE = re.compile(r"<[^>]*?>", re.IGNORECASE|re.MULTILINE)
    ENTITY_RE = re.compile(r"&(\w+?);|&#(\d+?);")
    SPLIT_RE = re.compile(r"\W+", re.IGNORECASE|re.MULTILINE)
```

The class begins with some static variables that govern how many files a word can occur in before it is considered to be a common word, the minimum and maximum lengths of a word, and what characters a word may not begin or end with. The "strip HTML" regular expression is used to strip out HTML tags, the entity regular expression is used to pick out entities to be converted to Unicode characters, and the split regular expression is used to split a file's text into its constituent words. A more realistic application might use an HTML parser rather than regular expressions.

```
    def __init__(self, lock, parent=None):
        super(Walker, self).__init__(parent)
        self.lock = lock
        self.stopped = False
        self.mutex = QMutex()
        self.path = None
        self.completed = False
```

The application creates one walker thread object but does not start it off straight away. The lock is the same QReadWriteLock used by the primary thread—the walker thread uses it to protect all accesses to the shared filenamesForWords default dictionary and to the commonWords set. The stopped variable is used inside the class to determine whether the thread has been asked to stop (by a call to the stop() method). The mutex is used to protect access to the stopped variable by the walker thread itself. This is necessary because while the run() method is executing it is possible that another of the thread's methods, such as stop(), is called. The completed variable is used to indicate whether the indexing was completed when the thread stopped.

```
def initialize(self, path, filenamesForWords, commonWords):
    self.stopped = False
    self.path = path
    self.filenamesForWords = filenamesForWords
    self.commonWords = commonWords
    self.completed = False
```

This method is designed to be called just before QThread.start() is called, to set up the thread for doing the indexing. It should not be called while the thread is running. (If we were paranoid we could put an if not self.isStopped(): return at the beginning.)

Although it would be harmless to use the mutex and the lock, neither is necessary. When this method is called the walker thread is not running, so assigning to stopped is no problem, and in the case of the dictionary and set passed in, we are just taking references to them, not altering them in any way.

```
def run(self):
    self.processFiles(self.path)
    self.stop()
    self.emit(SIGNAL("finished(bool)"), self.completed)
```

When the caller calls start(), the thread in turn calls the run() method—something we must never do ourselves. The method has only three statements, but processFiles() can take a long time to execute since it involves recursively reading and indexing all the HTML files in the path. This isn't a problem, though, because the processing is taking place in the walker thread's own thread of execution, so the user interface remains responsive, and the primary thread can call the walker thread's methods, and respond to the walker thread's signals, as we saw in the preceding section. At the end, the run() method emits a finished() signal, with a Boolean flag that indicates whether the indexing was finished; if it wasn't, the user must have stopped it through the user interface.

```
def stop(self):
    try:
        self.mutex.lock()
        self.stopped = True
    finally:
        self.mutex.unlock()
```

Using a Context Manager for Unlocking sidebar

This blocks until the lock is obtained and, thanks to the try ... finally block, guarantees that the mutex is unlocked at the end.

If we were using Python 2.6, or Python 2.5 with a suitable from __future__ statement, we could rewrite this method as:

```
                def stop(self):
                    with QMutexLocker(self.mutex):
                        self.stopped = True
```

Since PyQt 4.1, the QMutexLocker class can be used as a context manager. It locks the QMutex it is given as an argument (blocking until it can obtain the lock), and unlocks the mutex when the flow of control leaves the with scope (even if the scope is exited as the result of an exception).

```
                def isStopped(self):
                    try:
                        self.mutex.lock()
                        return self.stopped
                    finally:
                        self.mutex.unlock()
```

Notice that the return statement is inside the try ... finally block. When the return is reached the method will attempt to return the value, but it will be forced to enter the finally block, after which the method will return with the return statement's value.

If we were using Python 2.6 (or 2.5 with a suitable from __future__ statement), we might omit this method entirely, and in some of the other methods, instead of writing:

```
            if self.isStopped():
                return
```

we might write this:

```
            with QMutexLocker(self.mutex):
                if self.stopped:
                    return
```

There should not be any significant difference in the overhead of any of these approaches, although using with with a QMutexLocker seems to be the cleanest and clearest approach.

The processFiles() method is rather long, so we will review it in three parts.

```
                def processFiles(self, path):
                    def unichrFromEntity(match):
                        text = match.group(match.lastindex)
                        if text.isdigit():
                            return unichr(int(text))
                        u = htmlentitydefs.name2codepoint.get(text)
                        return unichr(u) if u is not None else ""
```

We begin with a nested function definition. It is used in conjunction with the entity regular expression (shown on page 552). This expression has two match groups, only one of which can match at any one time. Given a match object matched by the regular expression, the function takes the last, that is, the only, match group, and if it is all digits, it returns the Unicode character for the corresponding code point. Otherwise, the function returns the Unicode character matching the entity name, or an empty string if the name is not in the htmlentitydefs.name2codepoint dictionary.

```
for root, dirs, files in os.walk(path):
    if self.isStopped():
        return
    for name in [name for name in files \
                if name.endswith((".htm", ".html"))]:
        fname = os.path.join(root, name)
        if self.isStopped():
            return
        words = set()
        fh = None
        try:
            fh = codecs.open(fname, "r", "UTF8", "ignore")
            text = fh.read()
        except (IOError, OSError), e:
            sys.stderr.write("Error: %s\n" % e)
            continue
        finally:
            if fh is not None:
                fh.close()
        if self.isStopped():
            return
        text = self.STRIPHTML_RE.sub("", text)
        text = self.ENTITY_RE.sub(unichrFromEntity, text)
        text = text.lower()
```

The os.walk() method recursively walks a directory tree starting from the given path. For each directory it finds, it returns a three-tuple of the root path, a list of subdirectories, and a list of files in the directory.

We iterate over each of the directory's files that has a .htm or .html suffix. The unicode.endswith() and str.endswith() methods accept either a single string or a tuple of strings to match against. For each matching file we create a filename with the full path and create a local empty set that will contain the unique words found in the file.

We should really check the encoding used by the HTML files, but instead we have just assumed that they are either UTF-8 Unicode, or ASCII (which is a strict subset of UTF-8). We have also passed an additional parameter to indicate how decoding errors should be dealt with (i.e., they should be ignored).

Once we have the file's text, read in as a single large string, we strip out its HTML tags, convert any entities to their Unicode equivalents, and lowercase the text that remains. The re.sub() ("substitute") method takes the text to work on as its second argument; its first argument is either a literal string to replace each match, or a function to call. In the case of a function, for each match a match object is passed to the function, and the function's return value (which should be a string) is used as the replacement string.

At several points we check to see whether the stopped variable is True, which will be the case if the stop() method has been called. If this has occurred, we do no further indexing, and simply return. If we have too few checks, the user may experience a delay between requesting that the indexing stop and the thread actually stopping. But on the other hand, the more checks we put in, the slower the thread will run. So how often we check, and where we place the checks, may require a bit of trial and error before we get it right.

```
for word in self.SPLIT_RE.split(text):
    if self.MIN_WORD_LEN <= len(word) <= \
        self.MAX_WORD_LEN and \
        word[0] not in self.INVALID_FIRST_OR_LAST and \
        word[-1] not in self.INVALID_FIRST_OR_LAST:
        try:
            self.lock.lockForRead()
            new = word not in self.commonWords
        finally:
            self.lock.unlock()
        if new:
            words.add(word)
    if self.isStopped():
        return
    for word in words:
        try:
            self.lock.lockForWrite()
            files = self.filenamesForWords[word]
            if len(files) > self.COMMON_WORDS_THRESHOLD:
                del self.filenamesForWords[word]
                self.commonWords.add(word)
            else:
                files.add(unicode(fname))
        finally:
            self.lock.unlock()
    self.emit(SIGNAL("indexed(QString)"), fname)
self.completed = True
```

For each word in the file's text that is not too long or too short and which does not start with an unacceptable character, we first look to see whether it is in the set of common words, and if it is not, we add it to the local set of words.

Once we have gathered all the file's uncommon words in the words set, we iterate over this set. New words are added to the filenamesForWords default dictionary. If the dictionary's set of filenames for the word is too large, we delete the dictionary entry and add the word to the set of common words; otherwise, we add the filename to the dictionary's set for the current word. We must, of course, use a write lock to ensure that no other thread (e.g., the primary thread) can access the dictionary or the common words set while they are being updated.

After the file has been indexed, the indexed() signal is emitted with the file's name as a parameter. The primary thread has a connection to this signal and shows the filename in a label so that the user can see which file has just been indexed.

Once the os.walk() loop finishes, the completed variable is set to True, the method ends, and control returns to the caller, run(). It is possible that the last statement is never executed, because if the user stops the indexing (by pressing Esc, which causes stop() to be called, which sets stopped to True and means that isStopped() will return True), one of the if isStopped(): statements will cause the processFiles() method to return immediately. In this case the completed variable will (correctly) be False.

This completes our review of the walker thread. Using with statements and context managers instead of try … finally blocks can make the code much shorter and easier to understand, as can be seen by comparing pageindexer.pyw with pageindexer_26.pyw, and walker.py with walker_26.py. Having a stop() method and a stopped variable is quite common for secondary threads that serve a primary thread, so the Walker class, though specific in its processing, is quite general in its structure.

Summary

Writing threaded servers using PyQt's threading and networking classes is relatively straightforward. For non-GUI servers, it is possible to use QCore-Application rather than QApplication, or to avoid using PyQt classes at all, relying instead on the Python standard library threading and networking classes, or using Twisted.

Farming out processing to secondary threads is not difficult in theory, but in practice we must be very careful to ensure that any data that is accessible by more than one thread uses a protection mechanism such as QMutex, QReadWrite-Lock, or QSemaphore. Inside the context of a protection mechanism we must make sure that we do the least amount of work possible to minimize the time that other threads might be blocked. And in the case of reading data, especially if the data is not too large, it is often best to copy it to avoid the risk of accessing it outside the scope of the protection.

It is quite common for the primary thread to communicate with secondary threads by calling the secondary threads' methods—for example, start() to start them and stop() to stop them. Secondary threads can communicate with the primary thread by emitting signals that the primary thread connects to. Both primary and secondary threads can also use shared data structures protected by QMutexes, QReadWriteLocks, or QSemaphores—with one common scenario being that the primary reads and the secondary threads read and write shared data. Threads may need to protect accesses to their own data—for example to a secondary thread's stopped variable—since more than one of their methods may be active at the same time (e.g., both run() and stop() in a secondary thread).

Multithreaded programs are more difficult to write and maintain than single-threaded programs, so it is often worthwhile to see whether simpler alternatives, such as calling QApplication.processEvents() or calling external processes using QProcess, can be used instead.

Exercise

Modify the Page Indexer application so that it uses multiple secondary threads instead of just one. By getting the number of secondary threads right, the application could be made to run faster than the single secondary thread version. Although this exercise involves writing or modifying only about 100 lines of code, it is quite subtle and challenging.

The approach taken in the solution is to move os.walk() to the primary thread, and create a list of filenames. Whenever the list has 1 000 files, a secondary thread is created to process those files. At the end, another secondary thread is created to process whatever files remain. The Walker.initialize() method is not required since we can pass all the parameters to the constructor. And changes to Walker.run() and Walker.processFiles() are quite small. Most of the changes must be made in the pageindexer.pyw file.

The setPath() method is where the filenames can be gathered and secondary threads created to process them. In the solution we used a separate method to create the secondary threads. Since there could be many secondary threads we also added a stopWalkers() method and modified the finished(), accept(), reject(), and finishedIndexing() methods. Since some of the widgets in the user interface could potentially be accessed in response to signals from more than one thread, we protect accesses to them with a mutex.

Make sure that the threads are deleted when they are no longer needed to avoid creating more and more threads each time setPath() is called.

The new version of the walker module should be a bit shorter than the original, but the new page indexer will be about 90 lines longer than the original. A solution is provided in chap19/pageindexer_ans.pyw and chap19/walker_ans.py.

This Is Not Quite the End

We have reached the end of the book, but by no means have we reached the end of what Python or PyQt has to offer. Python's standard library is very large, and because of our focus on PyQt we have hardly used a fraction of what is available in it. Many other libraries are also available as add-ons for Python and PyQt, so in many cases, we can program by composing existing components rather than having to build everything ourselves from scratch. A good place to begin looking for add-ons is the Python Package Index at `http://pypi.python.org/pypi`. And a good place to look for tricks, tips, and ideas is the *Python Cookbook* at `http://aspn.activestate.com/ASPN/Python/Cookbook`.

Our coverage of PyQt has been extensive, and all the major features have been shown and described. But PyQt has hundreds of classes, so we have not been able to cover, or even mention, all of them. For example, PyQt includes more widgets than we have used, including `QCalendarWidget`, `QGroupBox`, `QProgressBar`, and `QToolBox`. There are also lots of useful nonwidget classes, such as `QCompleter` (text completion), `QFileSystemWatcher` (to observe changes to files or directories in the filesystem), and `QSystemTrayIcon` (to put an icon with a popup menu in the system tray). It also has support for accessibility and an undo/redo framework. In addition, PyQt has some platform-specific features, including ActiveX support on Windows, session management on the X Window System, and sheets and drawers on Mac OS X. All of these are described in the extensive online documentation. PyQt is also provided with its own set of examples—those that cover areas similar to the ones you are interested in will be well worth looking at.

This book has laid a solid foundation in GUI programming with Python and PyQt. The principles and practices it shows should make it straightforward to learn new PyQt classes from the documentation and examples supplied with PyQt, and to be able to successfully create your own classes. Programming with PyQt is both productive and enjoyable, and it leaves us free to ignore irrelevant details. This means that we can concentrate on building great applications that look good and that work well.

● Installing on Windows

● Installing on Mac OS X

● Installing on Linux and Unix

Installing

All the tools described in this book are freely available for downloading online. Note, however, that some of the packages are quite large (~50MB for Qt, ~12MB for Python, ~6MB for PyQt, and ~0.5MB for SIP★), so they are only really suitable for downloading with broadband connections. In this appendix we cover both downloading and installing, on Windows, Mac OS X, and most X11-based forms of Unix and Unix clones, including Linux and BSD.

All of the packages come with their own installation instructions, which will probably be more up-to-date and comprehensive than those given here, so ideally they are the instructions that you should follow. However, in many cases, this appendix contains sufficient information to get the tools installed and working. One approach would be to use this appendix to identify the packages that need to be obtained (and the order in which they should be downloaded, which matters for Windows users), as well as the order they should be installed (which matters for all platforms). Then, once the tools are downloaded, use the official instructions to install each one, and skim this appendix's instructions to help clarify what needs to be done, as well as to learn a couple of tips, one for Windows users and one for Mac OS X users, that may prove helpful.

Installing on Windows

For Windows, there are four tools to install: a C++ compiler, the Qt C++ application development framework, the Python interpreter and its accompanying libraries, and PyQt4 (which includes SIP in the Windows binary package). We assume that the GPL editions are being used, in which case the *only* C++ compiler that will work with Qt is MinGW. (Visual C++ can be used only with the commercial editions of Qt and PyQt and the instructions for installing them are provided when you buy them.)

★SIP is a tool used to create "bindings" that allow C++ classes to be accessible from Python.

At the time of this writing, an all-in-one package was under development. This package is an executable setup file that is expected to contain all the PyQt modules (except the QtDesigner module), QScintilla, the translation and *Qt Designer* support tools, the documentation and examples, the SQLite database, and support for .png, .svg, .gif, and .jpeg image formats. This package is complete and self-contained and requires no other software to be installed apart from Python itself. However, the package is not extensible. If you are learning or evaluating PyQt for the first time, using this package is probably the easiest way to begin. You can always uninstall it and install the precise set of components you need later on when you have gained experience. When the package is available it will be on the Web site http://riverbankcomputing.com. After intalling Python, simply download and execute the all-in-one package to install everything else.

In the instructions that follow, we are using Windows XP Home edition and are installing each component separately. There may be differences for other Windows versions, but they should not be so different that they can't be worked out from what's written here.

The files required for installation are MinGW-3.4.2.exe, qt-win-opensource-4.2.3-mingw.exe, python-2.5.1.msi, and PyQt-gpl-4.2-Py2.5-Qt4.2.3.exe. The book's examples are in the file pyqtbook.zip.

The first item to get is PyQt itself. This is because the versions of Python and Qt you will need depend on the version of PyQt you get. Go to http://www.riverbankcomputing.co.uk/pyqt/download.php and download the binary package PyQt-gpl-4.2-Py2.5-Qt4.2.3.exe. The filename has version numbers embedded in it and these may differ from the ones shown here: The first number is the PyQt version which must be at least 4.2 to get the most out of this book; the second number is the Python version that you must get; and the third number is the Qt version—you must download this precise version.

Now get Qt. Go to http://www.trolltech.com/developer/downloads/qt/index and click the Qt/Windows Open Source Edition link; at the bottom of the page, download qt-win-opensource-4.2.3-mingw.exe. The version number should exactly match the one in the PyQt package name, so if, for example, you downloaded PyQt-gpl-4.3-Py2.5-Qt4.3.1.exe, you will need to get qt-win-opensource-4.3.1-mingw.exe.

The MinGW C++ compiler is also available from Trolltech's Web site, but from a completely different URL. Go to ftp://ftp.trolltech.com/misc/ and download MingGW-3.4.2.exe. (You can skip this step and let the Qt installer download the compiler for you, but by downloading it yourself you have the package in hand, which is more convenient for installing on other machines, or for restoring if your Windows installation goes bad.)

Now it is time to get Python. Go to http://www.python.org/download and download one of the Windows installers. (The ones at the top of the page do not include the source code; this is fine, as you need the source only if you want to modify Python itself.) There may be more than one Windows installer; click a hardware-specific one such as the AMD64 or Itanium one if that matches your machine's processor; otherwise click the first one—for example, "Python 2.5.1 Windows installer". Save the installer to disk; this will give you a Microsoft Installer file—for example, python-2.5.1.msi. Note that the first two parts of the version number *must* match the equivalent part of the PyQt version number; so for PyQt-gpl-4.2-Py2.5-Qt4.2.3.exe, *any* Python 2.5 version is acceptable, such as Python 2.5, or Python 2.5.1, for example.

If you want to run the examples that are shown in the book or you want to see the model answers to the exercises, you can unzip the pyqtbook.zip file available from http://www.qtrac.eu/pyqtbook.html.

Now that all the pieces are at hand, you can perform the installation. The order of installation is important, and is different from the downloading order. (You needed to download PyQt first, to make sure you got the right versions of Python and Qt; but for installing you must start with the C++ compiler, and finish by installing PyQt.) We will assume that the versions are those mentioned earlier, but obviously use whichever versions you downloaded and adjust accordingly.

Figure A.1 *The MinGW and Qt installers on Windows*

If you did not download the MinGW installer, either because you have the compiler already installed or because you want the Qt installer to fetch and install it for you, skip to the next paragraph. Otherwise, start up the MinGW installer (e.g., double-click MinGW-3.4.2.exe), and follow the installer's instructions. The installer's first screen is shown on the left in Figure A.1. The only decision that you must make is where to install MinGW. We have assumed that you accepted the default of C:\MinGW; but you can put it anywhere. If you do not use the standard location, though, make a note of its path since you will need it when you install Qt.

To install Qt, start up its installer by double-clicking qt-win-opensource-4.2.3-mingw.exe (or whichever version you downloaded). The installer's first screen is shown on the right in Figure A.1. The instructions are easy to follow, and again, we have assumed that you have accepted the default directory (e.g., C:\Qt\4.2.3). When you get to the "MinGW Installation" screen, if you put MinGW in the standard location, the "Previously installed MinGW" path should be correct. If it is not, or if you installed MinGW in a nonstandard location, you must type in its path or use the browse button (...) to locate it. If you did not install MinGW, check the "Download and install minimal MinGW" checkbox so that the Qt installer can fetch and install it for you.

Unfortunately, the GPL Qt installer does not add Qt to the path; this means that applications that depend on the Qt DLLs, such as `QtCore4.dll`, `QtGui4.dll`, `QtXml4.dll`, and so on, or that depend on the MinGW DLL, `mingwm10.dll`, will not find them. Since PyQt applications depend on these libraries, you must manually add the path to them so that double-clicking a PyQt `.pyw` application will work. Without this path, any PyQt program you attempt to run will not work, and instead an error message box will pop up, such as, "pythonw.exe - Unable To Locate Component", that says it can't find `mingwm10.dll`.

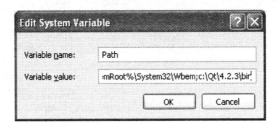

Figure A.2 *Setting the Windows path*

Click Start→Control Panel, then click System, to pop up the System Properties dialog. Click the Advanced tab, then the Environment Variables button (near the bottom of the dialog). Click the Path variable in the "System variables" section (in the bottom half of the dialog), and then click Edit.

The Edit System Variable dialog, as shown in Figure A.2, has the Windows path. Be very careful not to delete the existing path! If you delete it by mistake, click Cancel, and then try editing the path again. Press End to deselect the path and to put the text cursor at the far right of the line edit, then add the text ";C:\Qt\4.2.3\bin". The leading semicolon is essential; obviously, use the version number of the Qt you actually installed, if it's different from the one shown here. This path works for all the Qt DLLs and for the MinGW DLL (since the Qt installer copies it into the Qt `bin` directory).

You are now ready to install Python. Start up the Python installer by double-clicking `python-2.5.1.msi` or whichever other `.msi` file you downloaded. The installer's first screen is shown on the left in Figure A.3. The installer is straightforward to use; the only information you need to type in is Python's path if you don't want to use the default of `C:\Python25`. If you use a nonstandard path, keep a note of it since you will have to type it into the PyQt installer. If you are desperate for disk space you don't have to install the test suite or the utility scripts, but we assume that you keep all the other components complete, including Tcl/Tk. Once Python has been installed, the installer may ask you to reboot—you should do so before going on to install PyQt.

Figure A.3 *The Python and PyQt installers on Windows*

Now you can install PyQt4 itself. Start up the PyQt installer by double-clicking PyQt-gpl-4.2-Py2.5-Qt4.2.3.exe, or whichever version of PyQt you downloaded. The installer's first screen is shown on the right in Figure A.3. If you installed Python in a nonstandard location you must enter the correct location in the Choose Install Location screen—PyQt is installed as a Python extension, so its libraries are placed inside the Python directories. (For this reason, if you ever want to uninstall Python, you should uninstall PyQt first, then Python.)

PyQt is the last tool that must be installed to have everything set up and working. To test things, click Start→All Programs→PyQt GPL v4.2→Examples and Demos. This launches a PyQt version of the standard Qt demo application. From inside this application you can run many of the demo applications that are supplied with PyQt. The source code to the demos, and to many other PyQt examples, are normally installed in C:\Program Files\PyQt4\examples.

If you downloaded the book's examples, you might like to unzip pyqtbook.zip in C: to get a C:\pyqt directory with all the book's examples, along with model answers to the exercises, categorized by chapter. In the C:\pyqt directory itself you will find mkpyqt.py and makepyqt.pyw; these utilities are explained on page 207. If you want to try out any of the examples before reading the book, make sure that you run makepyqt.pyw first. (When you run makepyqt.pyw, set its path to C:\pyqt, check its Recurse checkbox, and then click the Build button. Now all the examples will be ready to run.)

That completes the installation for Windows, and is sufficient for PyQt GUI programming. But if you also want to write some console applications, or to sometimes run PyQt applications in a console (which can be useful for debugging), a few more steps will make this much more convenient.

Click Start→All Programs→Accessories→Windows Explorer. Once Windows Explorer is running, navigate to My Computer\Local Disk (C:)\Documents and Settings, and then to the directory that has your username, and inside that, navigate to Start Menu\Programs\Accessories. Copy and paste the Console (or MS-DOS Prompt) shortcut, and rename the copy "Console (PyQt)". Right-click the new Console (PyQt) shortcut to edit its properties. On the General page, change the Target to cmd.exe /k C:\pyqt\pyqt.bat. Now when you want a PyQt-friendly console you can click Start→All Programs→Accessories→Console (PyQt) and the console that appears will automatically run C:\pyqt\pyqt.bat. This batch file contains only two lines:

```
set QMAKESPEC=win32-g++
path=C:\pyqt;C:\MinGW\bin;c:\Python25;c:\Python25\lib\idlelib;%path%
```

You might like to edit this file (using a plain text editor) to add a third line containing a cd command—for example, cd C:\pyqt—so that the console starts up in a convenient directory. If you installed MinGW or Python in nonstandard locations you will need to edit this file anyway, to put in their correct paths.

You are now ready to write and run PyQt applications on your Windows machine—and they will run unchanged on Mac OS X and Linux too!

Installing on Mac OS X

To install PyQt on Mac OS X, you must already have the Xcode tools installed. This is because a compiler and build tool are required to install PyQt. Xcode is a very large package, normally supplied on a separate developer's CD provided with the machine; it is also available online from http://developer.apple.com/tools/xcode. The following instructions assume that Xcode is already installed.

Although Macs are normally supplied with a version of Python preinstalled, it may be an old version, in which case we recommend installing an up-to-date version for PyQt development. To check the Python version, start up a Terminal, and type in python -V; if this prints "Python 2.5", or a higher version number, there is no need to install a new version of Python.

The files required for installing PyQt are qt-mac-opensource-4.2.3.dmg, python-2.5.1-macosx.dmg (unless you already have Python 2.5 or later installed), sip-4.6.tar.gz, and, PyQt-mac-gpl-4.2.tar.gz. The book's examples are in the file pyqtbook.tar.gz.

Start by getting Qt. Go to http://www.trolltech.com/developer/downloads/qt/index and click the Qt/Mac Open Source Edition link, and near the bottom of the page, download qt-mac-opensource-4.2.3.dmg. A later version number, say, 4.3.1, should also be fine.

If you need to install an up-to-date version of Python, go to http://www.python.org/download and download the Python 2.5.1 for Macintosh OS X version—for example, python-2.5.1-macosx.dmg. A later $2x$ series version, such as 2.5.2 or

2.6.0, should also be okay, providing they are production releases (not alphas, betas, or release candidates).

The last two tools that must be obtained are SIP and PyQt. Go to `http://www.` `riverbankcomputing.co.uk/sip/download.php` and download the source package `sip-4.6.tar.gz`, then go to, `http://www.riverbankcomputing.co.uk/pyqt/download` `.php` and download the source package `PyQt-mac-gpl-4.2.tar.gz`. Again, the version numbers may be higher—for example, 4.3—for PyQt.

If you want to run the examples that are shown in the book or to see the model answers to the exercises, you can unpack the `pyqtbook.tar.gz` file available from `http://www.qtrac.eu/pyqtbook.html`.

Now that all the pieces are at hand, and assuming that Xcode is already installed, you can perform the PyQt installation. Both Qt and Python must be installed first, then SIP, and finally PyQt itself. We will assume that the versions are those mentioned earlier, but obviously, use whichever versions you downloaded and adjust accordingly. We assume that all the downloaded files are on the Desktop, and that you know the administration password (which is normally your own password).

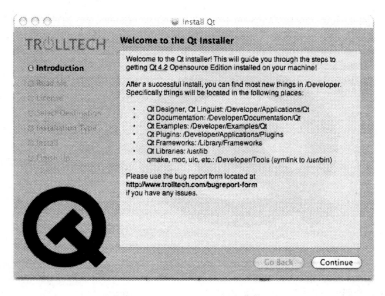

Figure A.4 *Installing Qt on Mac OS X*

First set up Qt by double-clicking `qt-mac-opensource-4.2.3.dmg`, or whichever Qt package you downloaded, and following the instructions. The installer's first screen is shown in Figure A.4. We assume that you accept all the defaults and install in the standard locations. Older Qt versions have an unoptimized build tool, and this means that the setup can take a surprisingly long time. More up-to-date versions have an optimized build tool which works much faster.

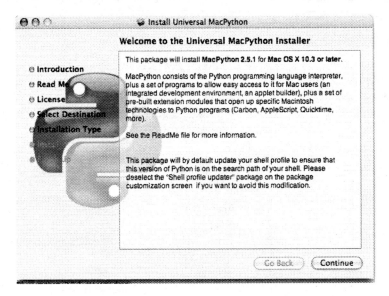

Figure A.5 *Installing Python on Mac OS X*

Once Qt is installed, it is time to install Python, if you need to. Double-click `python-2.5.1-macosx.dmg` or the package you downloaded. The installer's first screen is shown in Figure A.5. This may pop up a new window with a `MacPython.mpkg` file—just double-click this to start up the installer, and follow the instructions. Just as for Qt, we assume that you accept the defaults and install in the standard locations. If you already have one or more older Python versions you will find that these remain intact, with two new Python executables added to `/usr/local/bin` along with their names, including the version numbers—for example, `python2.5` and `pythonw2.5`. The first executable is used in Terminal windows, and the second is used for running GUI applications and avoids a Terminal from being needlessly popped up in the background.

The installation should make the Python version just installed the default version. To check, close any existing Terminal windows, and then start up a fresh Terminal window, and type `python -V`. If the version is not the one installed, the settings will need to be changed manually. Close the Terminal, and then in Finder, go to Applications→MacPython 2.5, and start up the Python Launcher. Open the Preferences dialog (shown in Figure A.6), and for each item in the Settings for file type combobox—for Python Scripts, Python GUI Scripts, and Python Bytecode Documents—change the version of Python. For the Python Scripts and Python Bytecode Documents entries, change to `/usr/local/bin/python2.5`, and for the Python GUI Scripts entry, change to `/usr/local/bin/pythonw2.5` (note the "w" in the executable's name). These values may not be available in the drop-down lists, in which case they must be typed in manually. For each entry, also be sure to uncheck the Run in a Terminal window checkbox.

Both SIP and PyQt must be built in a Terminal. Close all open Terminals, and then start a fresh one. Type `python -V` to make sure that the correct Python is be-

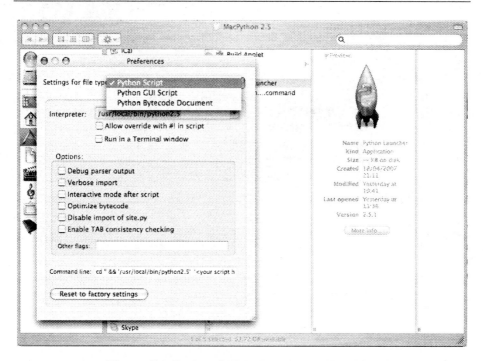

Figure A.6 *Setting which Python to use on Mac OS X*

ing used. If it is not, see the preceding paragraph; alternatively, enter the full name of the version of Python you want to use—for example, python2.5 configure.py.

SIP must be built first, by typing the following into the Terminal:

```
cd $HOME/Desktop
tar xvfz sip-4.6.tar.gz
cd sip-4.6
python configure.py
make
sudo make install
```

You will be asked for the administration password (normally your own password) when you execute the sudo command at the end. Now, PyQt can be installed.

```
cd $HOME/Desktop
tar xvfz PyQt-mac-gpl-4.2.tar.gz
cd PyQt-mac-gpl-4.2
python configure.py
make
sudo make install
```

Again, you will be prompted for a password when you execute the sudo command. Building PyQt can take quite a long time, so you will need to be patient.

The Qt documentation is available through *Qt Assistant*, which can be run from Finder. PyQt's documentation is supplied in HTML format in the $HOME/Desktop/PyQt-mac-gpl-4.2/doc directory. It is worthwhile moving this somewhere permanent and adding a suitable bookmark to your browser. It also comes with numerous examples; at the very least it is worth looking at the PyQt examples and running the demo. (For example, change the directory to $HOME/Desktop/PyQt-mac-gpl-4.2/examples/tools/qtdemo and run ./qtdemo.py.)

If you downloaded the book's examples, you might like to unpack pyqtbook. tar.gz in $HOME to get a $HOME/pyqt directory with all the book's examples, and model answers to the exercises, categorized by chapter. In the $HOME/pyqt directory itself you will find mkpyqt.py and makepyqt.pyw; you might like to move (or soft-link) these to a directory on your $PATH—for example, $HOME/bin—to make them more convenient to use. Some of the examples depend on *Qt Designer* .ui files or on .qrc resource files. How to turn these into Python modules is covered on page 207, but for now it might be convenient to simply perform the conversions:

```
cd $HOME/pyqt
./mkpyqt.py -r
```

This will convert any .ui and .qrc files that are found in the pyqt directory and in its subdirectories.* If you prefer to use the GUI makepyqt.pyw tool, you may have to click its More→Tool paths option and set the path to pyuic4. It may also be necessary to set the paths to the other tools too.

This completes the installation for Mac OS X. If you unpacked the examples, you could go to the Desktop and click the pyqt directory, then the chap12 directory, and then click multipedes.pyw to see a graphics application. If an unwanted Terminal window pops up, right-click multipedes.pyw, and click the Info dialog; change the Open with setting to the Python Launcher for the correct version of Python, and apply the change to all files with the .pyw suffix.

You are now ready to write and run PyQt applications on your Mac OS X machine—and they will run unchanged on Windows and Linux too!

Installing on Linux and Unix

If you are running Kubuntu (7.04 Fiesty Fawn and later), you already have PyQt4 installed! So, you only need to install the book's examples (see page 573), and the documentation packages python-doc and python-qt4-doc.

---

*If mkpyqt.py does not work, you will have to edit the mkpyqt.py file and at least hard-code the path to pyuic4.

For Linux and most other Unixes that don't have PyQt4 preinstalled, there are four tools to install: the Qt C++ application development framework, the Python interpreter and its accompanying libraries, the SIP bindings tool, and PyQt4 itself. The most convenient way to get everything up and running is to install the tools using standard packages for the Linux or Unix distribution being used.

For ArchLinux, Debian, Fedora, Gentoo, Kubuntu, Pardus, Ubuntu, and many others, the necessary components are available as packages. These can be installed using Adept, Pirut, apt-get, yum, or whatever other package manager the system uses. For PyQt4, the package is usually called pyqt4 or PyQt4 or pyqt4-dev-tools. PyQt4's documentation package is usually called pyqt4-doc or python-qt4-doc or PyQt4-examples. Python's documentation is usually in a package called python-doc or python-docs. IDLE is often available separately in a package called idle or python-tools. If you want a more powerful IDE, Eric4, itself written in PyQt, is available in a package for many popular distributions. The package manager should be able to figure out the dependencies, but if it cannot, you may have to also request that it install Python itself, and maybe even Qt and the g++ compiler. The *Qt Designer* visual design tool and the translation support tools are often packaged separately—for example, in packages called qt4-designer and qt4-dev-tools.

If you are fortunate enough to be able to install using standard packages, once you have done so, you are all set for writing PyQt programs, and can skip to installing the book's examples, described on page 573.

For users of older distributions, for those who don't have suitable packages available or who have only some of the components available in packages, and for those who want to build manually to get the most up-to-date versions, building and installing by hand is quite straightforward. However, we make two assumptions if you are building from source—First, that a C++ compiler and tool chain, such as make, are already installed and operational, and second, that you install as *root* (using su or sudo), or know how to use configure's --prefix option to install locally.

The files required for installation are qt-x11-opensource-src-4.2.3.tar.gz, Python-2.5.1.tgz, sip-4.6.tar.gz, and PyQt-x11-gpl-4.2.tar.gz. The book's examples are in the file pyqtbook.tar.gz.

Start by getting Qt. Go to http://www.trolltech.com/developer/downloads/qt/index and click the Qt/X11 Open Source Edition link, and near the bottom of the page, download qt-x11-opensource-src-4.2.3.tar.gz. A later version number, say, 4.3.1, should also be fine.

Now it is time to get Python. Go to http://www.python.org/download and then click the current production version link, and download one of the other platforms source versions—for example, Python-2.5.1.tgz or Python-2.5.1.tar.bz2. We will assume you got the .tgz version—later 2*x* series versions such as 2.5.2

or 2.6.0 should be okay, providing they are production releases (not alphas, betas, or release candidates).

The last two tools that must be obtained are SIP and PyQt. Go to http://www.riverbankcomputing.co.uk/sip/download.php and download the source package sip-4.6.tar.gz, then go to, http://www.riverbankcomputing.co.uk/pyqt/download.php and download the source package PyQt-x11-gpl-4.2.tar.gz. Again, the version numbers may be higher—for example, 4.3—for PyQt.

If you want to run the examples that are shown in the book or to see the model answers to the exercises, you can unpack the pyqtbook.tar.gz file available from http://www.qtrac.eu/pyqtbook.html.

Now that all the pieces are at hand, you can perform the installation. Both Qt and Python must be installed first, then SIP, and finally PyQt itself. We will assume that the versions are those mentioned earlier, but obviously, use whichever versions you downloaded and adjust accordingly. We assume that the downloaded tarballs are in the $HOME/packages directory, and that either you do everything as superuser having done su, or that you do every make install as superuser using sudo.

First you need to build Qt. The last line should be sudo make install if you are using sudo.

```
cd $HOME/packages
tar xvfz qt-x11-opensource-src-4.2.3.tar.gz
cd qt-x11-opensource-src-4.2.3
./configure -fast -qt-sql-sqlite -no-qt3support
make
make install
```

The -qt-sql-sqlite option will build the SQLite in-process database; this is used in Chapter 15 but can be omitted if desired. The -fast and -no-qt3support options should reduce the build time slightly, but both can be safely omitted. If you want to see what other options are available, including the database drivers that can be installed, run ./configure -help. Building Qt can take quite a while (from half an hour to more than three hours depending on the processor), since it is more than 600 000 lines of C++ code.

Python and SIP don't take anywhere near as long. You should build Python next, again using sudo make install if you are using sudo (We'll take this for granted from now on.).

```
cd $HOME/packages
tar xvfz Python-2.5.1.tgz
cd Python-2.5.1
./configure
make
make install
```

This should be a lot faster than the Qt build. Once it is complete, you can perform the last two phases, building SIP and then PyQt, doing so in a slightly different way than you built Qt and Python.

```
cd $HOME/packages
tar xvfz sip-4.6.tar.gz
cd sip-4.6
python configure.py
make
make install
```

This assumes that (the correct version of) Python is in your $PATH. If that is not the case (i.e., because you have two or more versions of Python installed), give the full path to the appropriate Python executable—for example, $HOME/opt/python25/bin/python configure.py. Once SIP is installed, you can install PyQt.

```
cd $HOME/packages
tar xvfz PyQt-x11-gpl-4.2.tar.gz
cd PyQt-x11-gpl-4.2
python configure.py
make
make install
```

Just like the SIP installation, this assumes that the correct version of Python is in your $PATH. Again, if this is not the case, give the full path to the appropriate Python executable when running configure.py. The make phase can take a long time (but not as long as building Qt).

Qt, Python, and PyQt are supplied with documentation in HTML format. It is worthwhile moving this somewhere permanent and adding suitable bookmarks to your browser. All three also come with numerous examples; at the very least it is worth looking at the PyQt examples and running the demo. (For example, change the directory to $HOME/PyQt-x11-gpl-4.2/examples/tools/qtdemo and run ./qtdemo.py.)

If you downloaded the book's examples, you might like to unpack pyqtbook.tar.gz in $HOME to get a $HOME/pyqt directory with all the book's examples, and model answers to the exercises, categorized by chapter. In the $HOME/pyqt directory itself, you will find mkpyqt.py and makepyqt.pyw; you might like to move (or soft-link) these to a directory on your $PATH—for example, $HOME/bin to make them more convenient to use. Some of the examples depend on *Qt Designer* .ui files or on .qrc resource files. How to turn these into Python modules is covered on page 207, but for now it might be convenient to simply perform the conversions:*

---

*If mkpyqt.py does not work, you will have to edit the mkpyqt.py file and at least hard-code the path to pyuic4.

```
cd $HOME/pyqt
./mkpyqt.py -r
```

This completes the installation for X11-based forms of Unix and Unix clones, including Linux and BSD. You are now ready to write and run PyQt applications on your Unix or Unix-like platform—and they will run unchanged on Mac OS X and Windows too!

Selected PyQt Widgets

The screenshots shown here were taken on Linux using KDE to provide an eye-pleasing consistency. In the body of the book, screenshots are shown for Windows, Linux, and Mac OS X, generally varying from chapter to chapter.

QCalendarWidget

This widget can be used as a display widget, although it was designed primarily as an input widget through which the user can choose a particular date. The widget's display is highly configurable; for example, week numbers can be displayed or not, day names can be represented by a single letter, or in short or full forms, the colors and fonts used can be set, and so can which day is treated as the first day of the week. Minimum and maximum allowable dates can also be set. Calling setCalendarPopup(True) on a QDateEdit or a QDateTimeEdit will cause their spin buttons to be replaced by an arrow button. If the user clicks the arrow button, a QCalendarWidget will pop up.

☒ Ignore Case

QCheckBox

A checkbox can be used to present users with a simple yes/no choice. If QCheckBox.setTristate(True) is called, the checkbox will have three states: The user checked it, the user unchecked it, or the user did not change it from whatever it was before. The tri-state approach may be useful for representing Boolean database fields where IS NULL is allowed.

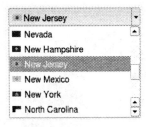

QComboBox

The screenshot shows a QComboBox with its list popped down. A combobox is used to present the user with a list of items where too little vertical space is available for a QListView to be used. Calling QCombo-Box.setEditable(True) allows the user to either choose one of the items in the list, or to type in their own text instead. Each combobox item has text, an optional icon, and optional data. We can populate a combobox using QComboBox.addItem() or QComboBox.addItems(), or we can use a custom or built-in QAbstractItemModel subclass with QComboBox.setModel().

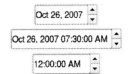

QDateEdit,
QDateTimeEdit, and
QTimeEdit

The QDateEdit is used for displaying and entering dates, the QDateTimeEdit is used for dates and times, and the QTimeEdit is used for times. By default, the widgets use locale-specific date and time formats—they are shown here using a U.S. locale. The formats can be changed, and minimum and maximum allowable dates and times can be set.

QDialogButtonBox

This widget can be used to create a row or column of buttons. The buttons can be standard buttons with predefined roles and text, or can be added with the roles and text of our choice. This widget automatically arranges the buttons according to their roles and the underlying windowing system's user interface guidelines.

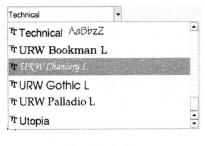

QFontComboBox

PyQt provides a pop-up font dialog, using the native font dialog where available. If we want to provide font choices ourselves—for example, in a toolbar—we can use the QFontComboBox, shown here popped down. For Qt 4.0 and Qt 4.1, the nearest equivalent (but without font previewing) is to use an ordinary QComboBox, populating it with the list returned by QFontDatabase.families().

QGroupBox and
QRadioButton

A group box can be used purely as a visual grouping device, or it can be made checkable, as shown here. If checkable, the widgets contained in the group box can be interacted with only when the group box is checked. If a frame is required without a title, a QFrame can be used instead. When QRadioButtons are put in a group box they automatically behave correctly, that is, the user can choose only one of them. QComboBoxes and QListViews are often more convenient than QRadioButtons.

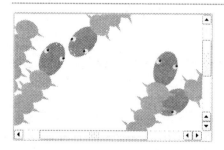

QGraphicsView

This widget is used to view the QGraphics-Items in a QGraphicsScene. Any number of QGraphicsViews can view the same scene, each with its own transformations (e.g., scaling and rotation), in effect. The scrollbars appear automatically if they are needed. Each QGraphicsView can provide its own background and foreground, overriding those provided by the scene.

A multi-line **QLabel**,
showing <u>HTML</u> text
with *font effects.*

QLabel

The QLabel widget is a display widget that can be used to show an image, a plain text string, a QTextDocument, or HTML. A label with an accelerator (a single underlined character) can be associated with a "buddy" widget, passing the keyboard focus to the buddy when the accelerator is pressed.

84.5

QLCDNumber

This is a display widget for showing numbers in the style of a seven-segment LCD.

Elephantine

QLineEdit

This widget can accept one line of text from the user. The text can be constrained by using a validator (e.g., a QIntValidator or a QRegExpValidator), or by setting an input mask, or both. The echo mode can be set to show "*"s (or nothing) instead of the text entered.

QListView and QListWidget

Through these widgets users can choose an item, or with a suitable selection mode, multiple items. The widgets can be in list mode (as shown), or icon mode, where the icons appear larger and the text is displayed under the icons. A QList-View must be used in conjunction with a custom or built-in QAbstractItemModel subclass using QListView.setModel(). A QListWidget has a built-in model, so items can be added to it directly using QListWidget.addItem() and QListWidget.addItems(). Where vertical space is at a premium, a QComboBox can be used instead.

QProgressBar

This widget can be used to show users the progress of long-running operations. It is often put in a QMainWindow's status bar using QStatusBar.addWidget() or addPermanentWidget(). An alternative is to pop up a QProgressDialog.

QPushButton

Buttons are used to invoke actions. If a button click will lead to a dialog being popped up, we normally add an ellipsis (...) to the end of the button's text. Buttons can also be set to have pop-up menus (in which case, PyQt will add a little triangle indicator), or they can be set as toggle buttons, staying down when clicked an odd number of times and coming back up when clicked an even number of times. Since Qt 4.2, most applications use QDialogButtonBoxes rather than individual QPushButtons.

QSlider

A slider is often used to show proportionality, and is commonly used in conjunction with a QLabel or QLCDNumber that shows an actual amount. Sliders can be aligned vertically or horizontally. A QScrollBar could be used for a similar purpose.

QDoubleSpinBox and
QSpinBox

These widgets are used to accept and display numbers. The number can be shown with a prefix or suffix and with a particular alignment. (The QDoubleSpinBox shown here has a "$" prefix.) They can have minimum and maximum values set, and for the QDoubleSpinBox, the number of digits shown after the decimal point can be set. An alternative is to use a QLineEdit in conjunction with a QInt-Validator or a QDoubleValidator.

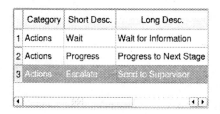

QTableView and QTableWidget

These widgets are used to present data in tabular form. A QTableView must be used in conjunction with a custom or built-in QAbstractItemModel subclass, such as QSqlTableModel, using QTableView.setModel(). A QTableWidget has a built-in model, so items can be added to it directly—for example, using QTableWidget.setItem(). Both widgets can show icons as well as text in every cell, including in the header cells.

QTabWidget

This widget is used when space is at a premium, or simply as a means of logically grouping widgets. The tabs have two shape settings and can appear at the top, left, right, or bottom, with the text rotated when shown left or right.

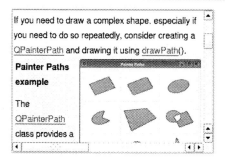

QTextEdit and QTextBrowser

These widgets can display HTML, including lists, tables, and images. The QTextEdit can also be used as an editing widget, either for plain text or for PyQt "rich text" (essentially HTML, although a custom subclass would be needed to provide table and image editing). The QTextBrowser supports clickable links, so it can be used as a simple Web browser. Both widgets have support for CSS (Cascading Style Sheets).

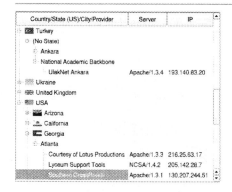

QTreeView and QTreeWidget

These widgets are used to present hierarchical data. A QTreeView must be used with a custom or built-in QAbstractItemModel subclass using QTreeView.setModel(). Like all widgets that use a model, only the data that is visible to the user is retrieved, so even large datasets are very fast. A QTreeWidget has a built-in model, so items can be added to it directly using QTreeWidget.insertTopLevelItem() and insertTopLevelItems(), or by creating QTreeWidgetItems as children of other items.

Selected PyQt Class Hierarchies

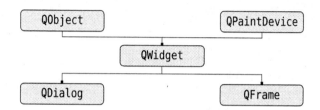

Figure C.1 *Selected base classes*

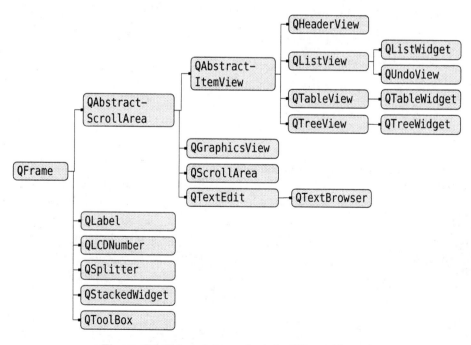

Figure C.2 *Selected classes from the QFrame hierarchy*

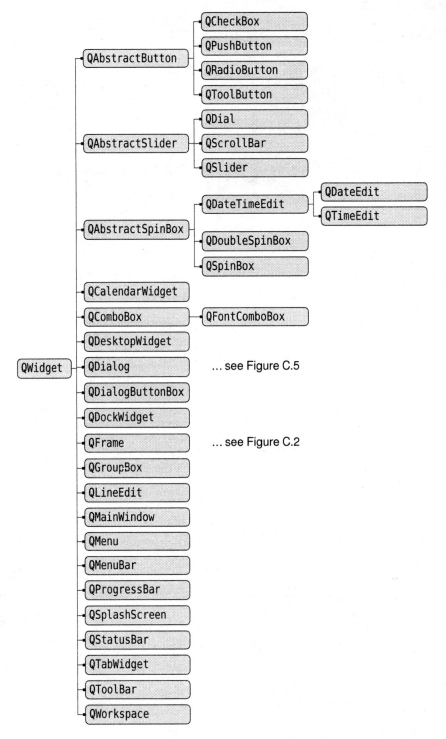

Figure C.3 *Selected classes from the QWidget hierarchy*

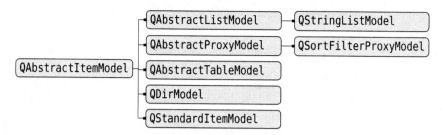

Figure C.4 *Selected classes from the QAbstractItemModel hierarchy*

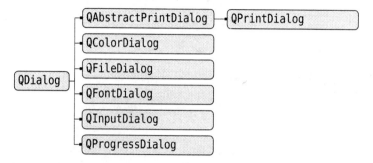

Figure C.5 *Selected classes from the QDialog hierarchy*

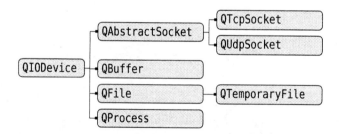

Figure C.6 *Selected classes from the QIODevice hierarchy*

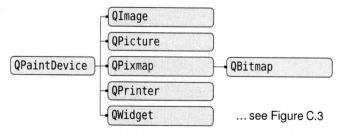

Figure C.7 *Selected classes from the QPaintDevice hierarchy*

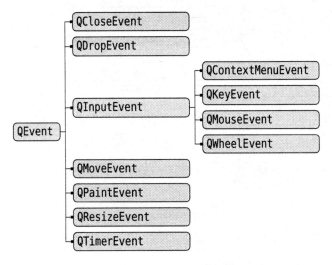

Figure C.8 *Selected classes from the QEvent hierarchy*

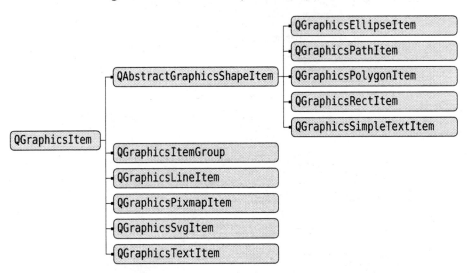

Figure C.9 *Selected classes from the QGraphicsItem hierarchy*

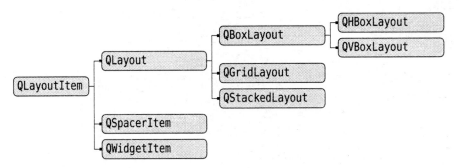

Figure C.10 *Selected classes from the QLayoutItem hierarchy*

Index

When looking up methods for PyQt widgets, also consider looking under their base classes, such as QFrame, QWidget, *and* QObject. *Functions and methods are listed in their own right, and in most cases under their module or class. Where a method or function name is close enough to a concept, the concept is not listed. For example, there is no entry for "splitting strings", but there is an entry for the* split() *methods.*

Symbols

!= (not equal operator), 47, 81, 82

" (double quote), 21

% (modulus/remainder operator, string formatting operator), 24, 26, 53, 84, 98

%= (modulus augmented assignment operator), 84

& (bitwise and operator, accelerator indicator), 38, 47, 143

' (single quote), 21

() (tuple creation operator, function and method call operator, expression operator), 30, 51, 54, 55, 81

* (multiplication operator, replication operator, positional argument list indicator, from ... import operator), 19, 25, 84, 91

** (power/exponentiation operator, keyword argument list indicator), 40

*= (multiplication augmented assignment operator), 84, 91

+ (addition operator, concatenation operator), 25, 33, 84, 90, 500

+= (addition augmented assignment operator, append operator), 84, 90, 234

- (subtraction operator, negation operator), 84

-= (subtraction augmented assignment operator), 84

. (dot operator), 78

/ (division operator), 84, 91

/= (division augmented assignment operator), 84, 91

// ("true" division operator), 84, 86, 91

//= ("true" division augmented assignment operator), 84, 91

: (suite follows indicator, slice index separator), 46

:/ (resource path, root of), 173

< (less than operator), 47, 81, 82

<< (QDataStream and QTextStream write operator, int and long shift left operator), 242, 245, 250, 254, 359, 435, 525, 533

<= (less than or equal to operator), 38, 47, 81, 82

<> (not equal operator—deprecated), 47

= (name binding operator, object reference creation and assignment operator), 81, 82, 83

== (equal operator), 13, 47, 81, 82

> (greater than operator), 47, 81, 82

>= (greater than or equal to operator), 38, 47, 81, 82

>> (QDataStream and QTextStream read operator, int and long shift right operator), 245, 360, 435, 528, 532, 541

@ (decorator operator), 85
[] (indexing operator, slicing operator), 22, 54, 93
\ (escape character), 21, 51, 220
\n (newline character), 51
^ (bitwise xor operator), 47
_ (underscore character), 76, 80
__ (double underscore), 77, 80, 82, 88
`` (repr() operator), 83
{} (braces), 46
| (bitwise or operator), 38, 47
~ (bitwise not operator), 47
€ (euro symbol), 21

A

about() (QMessageBox), 200
aboutToShow() signal (QMenu), 178, 187, 285, 292
abs(), 40, 84, 403
__abs__() (abs()), 84
absolute positions and sizes, 119
abstract base class, 102
accelerator; *see* keyboard accelerator
"accept" button, 141, 188
accept()
    QDialog, 151, 154, 425
    QEvent, 314, 333, 391
accepted() signal (QDialogButtonBox), 145, 150
access, private and public, 76, 88
accessor methods, 79–80
action; *see* QAction
action group; *see* QActionGroup
activateWindow() (QWidget), 160, 289
activeWindow() (QWorkspace), 296
add() (set), 37, 38, 372, 556
__add__() (+), 84, 90
addAction() (QWidget), 172, 178, 180, 307, 330, 365, 392, 393
addActions() (QWidget), 178
addBindValue() (QSqlQuery), 448, 450
addButton() (QDialogButtonBox), 150

addDatabase() (QSqlDatabase), 446, 459
addDays() (QDate), 491
addDockWidget() (QMainWindow), 169, 186
addEllipse()
    QGraphicsScene, 354
    QPainterPath, 374, 376
addItem()
    QComboBox, 276
    QGraphicsScene, 354, 356, 362, 364, 371
    QListWidget, 418
addItems() (QComboBox), 440
addLayout()
    QBoxLayout, 146
    QGridLayout, 146, 151
addLine() (QGraphicsScene), 354
addMapping() (QDataWidgetMapper), 453, 456
addMenu() (QMenu and QMenuBar), 177, 178
addPath() (QGraphicsScene), 354
addPixmap() (QGraphicsScene), 354
addPolygon()
    QGraphicsScene, 354
    QPainterPath, 376
addRect() (QGraphicsScene), 354, 355
addSeparator(), 178, 180, 307
    QMenu, 178, 180
    QToolBar, 178, 180
addSpacing() (QBoxLayout), 146
addStretch() (QBoxLayout), 146
addText() (QGraphicsScene), 354
addToolBar() (QMainWindow), 179, 186
addWidget()
    QLayout, 146, 151, 273
    QToolBar, 180
addYears() (QDate), 490
adjusted() (QRect/QRectF), 355, 367
aggregation, 93
Alert application, 112–116
alignment, 168, 338, 429
aliveness, of PyQt objects, 287–288, 289
all(), 38

and operator, 47
anonymous functions; *see* lambda statement
antialiasing, 337, 342, 361, 369
any(), 38
append()
    list, 33
    QTextEdit, 120
application modal dialogs, 140
application termination, 115, 185
applicationDirPath() (QCoreApplication), 173
applicationName() (QCoreApplication), 194
applications
    lrelease, 207, 513, 518
    Make PyQt (makepyqt.pyw), 174, 206, 207, 216, 519
    mkpyqt.py, 174, 206, 207, 216, 519
    pylupdate4, 207, 513, 517, 518
    pyrcc4, 173, 174, 207
    pyuic4, 206, 207, 216, 221, 515
    Qt Assistant, 510
    Qt Linguist, 513
arg() (QString), 402, 418, 419, 423, 427, 428, 455, 513, 515
arguments; *see* parameters
argv variable (sys), 114
array module, 29
as keyword, 104
ASCII, 20, 22, 250, 501, 513, 555
    see also codecs, QString, and Unicode encodings
aspect ratio, 329, 400
assert statement, 69, 498, 500, 501, 502, 503, 504
AssertionError exception, 69
Asset Manager application, 457–470
assignment operators, 15, 83
associative array; *see* dict, defaultdict, and OrderedDict
atEnd() (QDataStream and QTextStream), 245, 252, 253, 254
attribute() (QDomElement), 261
AttributeError exception, 89, 101
attributes, 75, 78, 103, 106, 125

augmented assignment operators, 15, 16, 84, 90, 91
automatic disconnection, 130
automatic garbage collection; *see* garbage collection
automatic reparenting, 119
automatic signal–slot connections, 217
automatically deleting windows, 156, 284, 286

B

backslash escapes, 21, 22, 51
base class, 75, 76, 102
basename() (os.path), 189
beforeInsert() (QSqlTableModel), 470
beginInsertRows() (QAbstractItemModel), 432, 433
beginRemoveRows() (QAbstractItemModel), 433
bibliography; *see* books
binary chop algorithm, 93, 95, 238
binary data, 20
binary files, 240–248
binding names, 14–16
    see also assignment operators
bindValue() (QSqlQuery), 448, 450, 468
bisect module, 93, 238
bisect_left() (bisect), 95, 239, 498
bitwise operators, 47
BLOBs (Binary Large OBjects), 449
block of code; *see* suite of code
block structure, 46
blockSignals() (QObject), 135
.bmp (image file), 193
books
    Core PYTHON Programming, 27
    Dive into Python, 327
    Mastering Regular Expressions, 220
    Python and XML, 256
    Python Cookbook, 27
    Python in a Nutshell, 27

books *(cont.)*
 XML Processing in Python, 256
bool(), 83
bool type, 16–17, 46
Boolean context, 83
Booleans, 45, 46
bounding rectangle, 338, 367, 373,
 377
boundingRect()
 QGraphicsItem, 365, 366, 367, 373,
 377
 QPainterPath, 377
boundValue() (QSqlQuery), 450
braces, no need for, 46
break statement, 49, 50, 53
buddies, 143, 206, 215, 217
 see also QLabel.setBuddy()
built-ins
 != operator, 47, 81, 82
 % operator, 24, 26, 53, 84
 & operator, 38, 47
 * operator, 19, 25, 84, 91
 ** operator, 40
 *= operator, 84, 91
 + operator, 25, 33, 84, 90
 += operator, 84, 90
 - operator, 38, 84
 -= operator, 84
 . operator, 78
 / operator, 84, 91
 /= operator, 84, 91
 // operator, 84, 86, 91
 //= operator, 84, 91
 < operator, 47, 81, 82
 <= operator, 38, 47, 81, 82
 = operator, 81, 82, 83
 == operator, 13, 47, 81, 82
 > operator, 47, 81, 82
 >= operator, 38, 47, 81, 82
 @ operator, 85
 [] operator, 22, 54
 ^ operator, 47
 | operator, 38, 47
 ~ operator, 47
 abs(), 40, 84, 403
 all(), 38

built-ins *(cont.)*
 and operator, 47
 any(), 38
 as keyword, 104
 assert statement, 69, 498, 500,
 501, 502, 503, 504
 bool(), 83
 bool type, 16–17, 46
 break statement, 49, 50, 53
 callable(), 102
 chr(), 21, 39
 class statement, 69, 75, 76, 77, 85,
 86, 103, 115
 cmp(), 82, 89
 complex type, 17–20
 continue statement, 53
 def statement, 55, 62–63, 77
 del statement, 32, 355, 359, 361,
 372, 556
 dict type, 35–36, 51, 93
 dir(), 39, 40
 divmod(), 40
 enumerate(), 87, 419, 498
 eval(), 39, 81, 83, 89, 120, 247
 except statement, 66–67
 exceptions; *see* exceptions
 False constant, 45
 finally statement, 66, 70–71, 78,
 541, 542, 543, 548, 550, 551, 553,
 554, 556
 float(), 40, 84, 91
 float type, 17–20, 241
 for loop, 50–51, 54, 59
 frozenset type, 37, 552
 hasattr(), 39, 102, 218, 336
 help(), 37, 39
 hex(), 40
 id(), 13, 39, 231, 237, 418
 if statement, 46–49
 import statement, 18, 19
 in operator, 25, 33, 36, 38, 45, 96
 int(), 40, 84, 91, 256
 int type, 16–17, 241
 is statement, 13, 47, 57

built-ins *(cont.)*
  isinstance(), 39, 94, 102, 135, 289, 296, 359, 372, 375, 393, 395, 440, 496, 499, 502, 503
  iter(), 97, 237
  lambda statement, 61–62, 134, 453
  len(), 20, 25, 33, 36, 38, 96, 237, 503
  list type, 31–35, 93
  long(), 40
  long type, 16–17, 231, 241
  max(), 38
  min(), 38
  None constant, 13, 57
  not operator, 47
  object type, 76, 77, 78
  oct(), 40
  open(), 39, 70
  or operator, 47
  ord(), 21, 39, 50
  pass statement, 47
  pow(), 40
  print statement, 10, 26
  property(), 80
  range(), 39, 50–51, 54
  repr(), 81, 83, 89, 90, 98
  return statement, 58, 97, 554
  round(), 40, 91, 333
  set type, 37, 93
  sorted(), 52, 53, 63, 432, 434, 551
  special methods; *see* special methods
  staticmethod(), 85, 239, 288
  str type; *see* str type
  sum(), 38
  super(), 100, 153, 217
  True constant, 45
  try statement, 66, 70, 78, 541, 542, 543, 548, 550, 551, 553, 554, 556
  tuple type, 29–31, 30, 50, 87
  type(), 18, 39, 102
  unichr(), 21, 39, 236, 554
  unicode type; *see* unicode type
  while loop, 49–50

built-ins *(cont.)*
  with statement, 549
  xrange(), 51, 54
  yield statement, 58, 97, 237
button()
  QDialogButtonBox, 150, 158
  QMouseEvent, 333
buttons; *see* QAbstractButton, QDialogButtonBox, and QPushButton
byte array; *see* QByteArray
bytecode, 11, 111
bytesAvailable() (QIODevice), 528, 531, 540

C

Calculate application, 116–121
__call__(), 81
callable(), 102
callables, 63, 97, 102, 115, 128, 131
callbacks; *see* object references to, under functions
calling context, 64
canPaste() (QTextEdit), 385
case statement; *see* if statement
center() (QRect/QRectF), 392, 393
centering, 168, 338
central widget, 168
character escapes, 21, 22
character formatting, 397
characters() (QXmlContentHandler), 263
checkable actions, 176, 177
chr(), 21, 39
class statement, 69, 75, 76, 77, 85, 86, 103, 115
clear(), 98
  dict, 36
  QListWidget, 418
  QTableWidget, 418
  QTextDocument, 383
  QTreeWidget, 420
  set, 38
clearMessage() (QStatusBar), 170, 232

clearSelection() (QGraphicsScene), 356, 361, 362, 364

click; *see* mousePressEvent() and mouseReleaseEvent()

clicked() signal (QPushButton), 219

client/server applications, 522

clipboard; *see* QClipboard

clipboard() (QApplication), 297, 311

close button, 118, 121

close()
    file, 70, 555
    QIODevice, 243, 259, 525, 528
    QWidget, 175, 285, 289, 330

closeAllWindows() (QMainWindow), 289, 293

closeEvent() (QWidget), 175, 185, 187, 282, 285, 289, 293, 309, 551

closeSubPath() (QPainterPath), 376

closing dialogs, 118, 121

closures; *see* partial function application

cmp(), 82, 89

__cmp__() (cmp()), 81, 82, 89, 416, 432

code suite, 46

codecs; *see* encodings

codecs module, 255–256
    open(), 255, 260, 501, 555
    readline(), 255

collections, 29–37, 92–98

collections module, 29
    defaultdict type, 529, 532, 545

collidesWithPath() (QGraphicsItem), 366

collidingItems()
    QGraphicsItem, 366
    QGraphicsScene, 354, 375

collision detection, 349, 374, 375

color palette; *see* QPalette

column() (QModelIndex), 428, 431, 439, 461, 462, 486, 496, 503

columnCount() (QAbstractItemModel), 427, 428, 433, 503

combining comparison expressions, 47

combobox; *see* QComboBox

command-line arguments, 113, 114

commercial licensing, 3

commit() (QSqlDatabase), 449, 465, 468, 469

communication mechanisms; *see* events and signals and slots

compare() (QString), 435

comparisons, 13, 38, 47, 57, 63, 82
    cmp(), 89
    __cmp__(), 89, 416, 432
    creating operators for, 82
    disallowing, 83
    expressions, 47
    operators, 47
    see also == operator, != operator, id(), and is statement

compile() (re), 220

complex type, 17–20

composite widgets, 168, 280, 325–326

composition, 93

conditional expression, 49, 390

connect() (QObject), 124, 130, 133, 145, 146, 151, 158, 453

connecting to databases, 446

connections; *see* signals and slots

Connections application, 132–135

connectSlotsByName() (QMetaObject), 217

connectToHost() (QAbstractSocket), 525

constructors; *see* initializers, __init__(), and __new__()

containers; *see* collections, and dict type, list type, and tuple type

contains()
    QGraphicsItem, 366
    QRect/QRectF, 357
    QString, 234
    QStringList, 189

__contains__() (in), 93, 96

context managers, 549, 554

context menus, 168, 180–181, 307, 365, 390

contextMenuEvent()
    QGraphicsItem, 365

contextMenuEvent() *(cont.)*
    QWidget, 307, 309, 390
continue statement, 53
control structures; *see* if, for, while,
    and try statements
controls; *see* QWidget
convenience widgets; *see* QList-
    Widget, QTableWidget, and QTree-
    Widget
conventional entry point, 62
conversions
    bool() conversion, 83
    float() conversion, 40, 84, 91
    generator to list, 58
    int() conversion, 40, 84, 91
    int to float, 14, 20
    int to long, 17
    long() conversion, 40
    str() conversion, 81, 83, 90, 98
    str to unicode, 20
    unicode() conversion, 81, 83
    unicode to QString, 28
coordinates, 309, 328–331, 339, 342,
    350, 357, 374
copy constructor, unnecessary, 83
copy(), 98
    copy module, 83, 88, 89
    dict, 36
    set, 38, 548, 551
copy module
    copy(), 83, 88, 89
    deepcopy(), 34, 83
copy_reg module, 247
copying, 34, 51, 88, 89, 98
cos() (math), 371, 375
count()
    list, 33
    str/unicode, 25
cPickle module, 235, 246–248
    see also pickle module
createActions() helper, 174–175
createEditor() (QAbstractItem-
    Delegate), 436, 440, 461, 486,
    487, 488, 491
createIndex() (QAbstractItemModel),
    433, 504

critical() (QMessageBox), 188
cStringIO module, 23
    see also StringIO module
Currency Converter application,
    121–127
current mouse position, 318
currentCharFormat() (QTextEdit), 393,
    395
currentColumn() (QTableWidget), 422
currentDate() (QDate), 46, 236, 401,
    490
currentDateTime() (QDateTime), 454
currentFrame() (QTextCursor), 404
currentIndex()
    QAbstractItemView, 427, 463, 465,
    466, 468, 469
    QDataWidgetMapper, 454, 455
currentIndexChanged() signal
    (QComboBox), 124, 275
currentItem() (QTableWidget), 422
currentRowChanged() signal (QList-
    Widget), 275
currentText() (QComboBox), 441
currying; *see* partial function appli-
    cation
cursor, text; *see* insertion point
cursorRect() (QTextEdit), 392, 393
custom data containers, 235
custom delegates, 436–442
custom models, 423–435
customized message boxes, 188
cut() (QTextEdit), 385
cycles, avoiding in signal–slot con-
    nections, 135

D

dangling else trap, not possible, 48
data containers, 235
data dictionary; *see* dict type
data()
    QAbstractItemModel, 414, 427, 428,
    429, 430, 433, 438, 441, 462, 481,
    487, 488, 489, 491, 496, 503
    QAction, 172, 393, 395
    QMimeData, 315, 316

data() *(cont.)*
    QTableWidgetItem, 422
data stream; *see* QDataStream
data structures; *see* dict type, list
    type, and tuple type
database forms; *see* QDataWidgetMap-
    per and QSqlTableModel
database() (QSqlDatabase), 465, 468,
    469
database queries; *see* QSqlQuery and
    SQL statements
databases
    connecting to, 446
    data types, 447
    drill-down, 467
    drivers, 445
    foreign keys, 455–457
    in-memory, 446
    master-detail forms, 458, 464,
        469
    prepared queries, 447
    SELECT statements, 449–451
    stored procedures, 448
    transactions, 465–466, 468
    see also SQL statements
dataChanged() signal (QAbstractItem-
    Model), 431, 432, 478
date formats, 250, 258
date() (QDateTimeEdit), 487
dates; *see* QDate and QDateTime
dateTime() (QDateTime), 455
DB2 database, 445
Decimal class (decimal), 17–20
decorations, window, 112
decorators, 85–86, 218, 219
deepcopy() (copy), 34, 83
deeply nested loops, 69
def statement, 55, 62–63, 77
default arguments, 56
defaultdict type (collections), 529,
    532, 545
    base class, dict
del statement, 32, 355, 359, 361, 372,
    556
__del__() (del statement), 78

delegates; *see* custom delegates and
    QItemDelegate
deleteLater() (QObject), 287, 531,
    539, 544
deleting; *see* del statement, delete-
    Later(), garbage-collection, and
    remove()
deleting windows, automatically,
    156, 284, 286
__delitem__() (del statement), 93,
    95
destroyed() signal (QObject), 286,
    288
destructors, 78
device coordinates; *see* viewport co-
    ordinates
device() (QDataStream), 525, 533
dial; *see* QDial
dialog buttons; *see* QDialogButtonBox
    and QPushButton
dialogs, 145
    closing, 118, 121
    hiding, 118, 121, 160
    modal, 140, 142, 511
    modeless, 140, 155
    showing, 160
    see also QDialog
dict type, 35–36, 51–53, 93
    clear(), 36, 98
    __contains__() (in), 96
    copy(), 36, 98
    get(), 36, 95, 420, 532, 541, 551
    has_key(), 96
    items(), 36, 52, 97
    __iter__(), 97
    iterating, by keys, 50
    iteritems(), 53, 97, 98
    iterkeys(), 53, 97
    itervalues(), 53, 97
    keys(), 36, 51, 52
    pop(), 36, 96
    popitem(), 96
    remove(), 95, 532, 543
    __repr__(), 98
    setdefault(), 36, 95, 532
    values(), 36, 52, 96

dict type *(cont.)*
  see also defaultdict type and
    OrderedDict example class
difference() (set), 38
dir(), 39, 40
dirname() (os.path), 173, 477, 496,
  512
dirty flag, 168, 187, 192, 232, 356,
  361, 362, 364, 365, 422, 425, 431
disabling widgets and actions, 219,
  274, 385
discard() (set), 38
disconnect() (QObject), 130
division (/ and //), 17, 84, 86, 91
divmod(), 40
dock window; *see* QDockWidget
dock windows, 169–170
docstrings, 57, 77, 105
doctest module, 105–107
document() (QTextEdit), 286, 287, 383,
  384, 385, 396
documentation, 27, 111
documentElement() (QDomDocument),
  260
DOM parser, 259–262
done() (QDialog), 154, 457, 464
double-click; *see* mouseDoubleClick-
  Event()
double-quoted strings, 21
drag and drop, 312–317
drag icon, 316
dragEnterEvent() (QWidget), 309, 314,
  316
dragMoveEvent() (QWidget), 309, 314,
  315, 316
drawArc() (QPainter), 344
drawChord() (QPainter), 344
drawContents() (QTextDocument), 438,
  489
drawConvexPolygon() (QPainter), 344
drawEllipse() (QPainter), 344, 374,
  377, 481
drawImage() (QPainter), 344, 363, 400
drawLine() (QPainter), 338, 344
drawPath() (QPainter), 344, 377
drawPicture() (QPainter), 363

drawPie() (QPainter), 344
drawPixmap() (QPainter), 344, 363,
  408
drawPoint() (QPainter), 344
drawPolygon() (QPainter), 338, 343,
  344, 345
drawPolyline() (QPainter), 344, 345
drawRect() (QPainter), 337, 344, 368,
  410
drawRoundRect() (QPainter), 344
drawText() (QPainter), 306, 338, 344,
  408, 410, 481
drill-down, 467
driver()
  QSqlDatabase, 449
  QSqlQuery, 450
drivers, for databases, 445
dropEvent() (QWidget), 309, 315, 316
DSU (decorate, sort, undecorate),
  551
duck typing, 101, 222, 497
dump() (pickle/cPickle), 248
duplicated data, avoiding, 413
dynamic attributes, 78
dynamic function definitions, 62–63
dynamic menus; *see* menus and
  QMenu
dynamic typing, 12, 13–15, 101

E

edit() (QAbstractItemView), 426, 465,
  468
editing, in-place, 414, 458
editing, initiating, 417, 426, 440, 465,
  468
editItem() (QTableWidget), 422
editor, IDLE, 10, 105, 382
editors; *see* IDEs
elif statement; *see* if statement
else statement; *see* if statement
emit() (QObject), 130, 131, 219, 333,
  340, 391, 431, 440, 556
enabling widgets and actions, 219,
  274, 385
encodings, 20, 250, 258, 501

encodings *(cont.)*
    ASCII, 20, 236, 250, 501, 555
    Latin1, 20
    UTF-8, 236, 250, 258, 501, 555
    see also codecs module, QString,
        and Unicode
endElement() (QXmlContentHandler),
    263
endInsertRows() (QAbstractItem-
    Model), 432, 433
endRemoveRows() (QAbstractItem-
    Model), 432, 433
endswith() (str/unicode), 25, 31, 555
endsWith() (QString), 240
ensureCursorVisible() (QTextEdit),
    392, 393
Enter keypress, 120, 145, 188, 391,
    421, 422, 440, 511
entities; *see* HTML
entry point, no fixed, 62
enumerate(), 87, 419, 498
__eq__() (==), 81
Eric4, IDE, 2, 10, 105, 382
error handling, for files, 244
errorString() (QIODevice), 241, 243,
    250, 252, 258, 259, 528
Esc keypress, 121, 161, 188, 421, 422
escape()
    Qt namespace, 258, 397, 401
    re, 220
escaped characters, 21, 22, 401
    newlines, 51
euro symbol (€), 21
eval(), 39, 81, 83, 89, 120, 247
event handlers; *see* events
event loop, 115–116, 184, 221, 537,
    539
event() (QObject), 304, 309, 310, 384
events, 115, 303–310
    see also closeEvent(), keyPress-
        Event(), keyReleaseEvent(),
        paintEvent(), resizeEvent(),
        timerEvent(), and wheelEvent()
examples
    Alert application, 112–116
    Asset Manager application,
        457–470

examples *(cont.)*
    Calculate application, 116–121
    Connections application,
        132–135
    Currency Converter application,
        121–127
    FractionSlider class, 331–338
    frange(), 55–57
    Image Changer application,
        165–200
    Length class, 86–91
    Multipedes application, 368–377
    My Movies application, 227–265
    OrderedDict class, 92–98
    Page Designer application,
        351–368
    partial(), 64–65, 133
    RichTextLineEdit class, 389–398
    RomanSpinBox class, 326–328
    Signals and Slots application,
        128–131
    simplified(), 61
    simplify(), 59, 61
    YPipe class, 339–345
except statement, 66–67
    see also finally statement and
        try statement
exceptions, 52, 66–71
    AssertionError, 69
    AttributeError, 89, 101
    Exception, 68, 69
    handling, 66–71
    hierarchy, 67
    IOError, 243, 244
    KeyError, 94
    NotImplementedError, 83, 102
    OSError, 243, 244
    RuntimeError, 288
    StopIteration, 52, 58, 59
    TypeError, 56
    ValueError, 68, 114
    vs. testing for errors, 68
exec_()
    QCoreApplication, 115, 184
    QDialog, 142, 154, 511
    QDrag, 316

exec_() *(cont.)*
    QMenu, 307, 365, 392, 393
    QSqlQuery, 447, 448, 449, 450, 464, 468, 469
exists() (QFile), 294
exiting applications; *see* terminating applications
expandItem() (QTreeWidget), 421
exporting files, 229
extend() (list), 33
extension; *see* file extensions
extension dialogs, 276–280

F

F2 keypress, 417, 422, 440
False constant, 45
fatalError() (QXmlErrorHandler), 263
field-level validation, 140
fieldIndex() (QSqlTableModel), 456
file; *see* file type, open(), and QFile
file dialog; *see* QFileDialog
file error handling, 244
file extensions
    .bmp, .jpg, .jpeg, and .png (image files), 193
    .pro (C++/Qt project file), 518
    .py and .pyw (Python file), 11, 111, 207
    .pyc and .pyo (Python bytecode file), 11, 207
    .qm (Qt message file), 516, 518
    .qrc (PyQt resource file), 173, 207, 517
    .ts (translation source file), 517, 518, 519
    .ui (user interface file), 206, 207, 515
file formats, 241
file handle, generator, 70
file type
    close(), 70, 555
    __file__ variable, 173
fileName() (QFileInfo), 189
files, 70, 229
fill() (QPixmap), 392

fillPath() (QPainter), 344
fillRect() (QPainter), 344, 438, 481, 489
finally statement, 66, 70–71, 78, 541, 542, 543, 548, 550, 551, 553, 554, 556
    see also except statement and try statement
financial calculations, 18
find() (str/unicode), 24, 25, 68
findText() (QComboBox), 142, 441, 457
first() (QSqlQuery), 450
firstChild() (QDomNode), 260
fixed size, of widget, 277
flags() (QAbstractItemModel), 427, 430, 433
flags, window, 115
float(), 40, 84, 91
float type, 17–20, 241
    %f format specifier, 26
__float__() (float()), 84, 91
floating-point division; *see* "true" division
__floordiv__() (//), 84
focus; *see* keyboard focus
font; *see* QFont
font()
    QGraphicsTextItem, 359
    QWidget, 336, 342
for loop, 50–51, 54, 59
    break statement, 53
    continue statement, 53
    else statement, 50, 53, 254
    vs. list comprehensions, 96–97
foreign keys, 455–457
form design; *see* user interface design
form-level validation, 140, 158, 491
format specifiers, for %, 26
formats, of images, 193
formatting, of characters, 397
forms, previewing, 215
FractionSlider example class, 331–338
frame; *see* QFrame
frange() example, 55–57

from __future__ import division, 86
from __future__ import
    with_statement, 549
from ... import statement; *see* import
    statement
fromImage() (QPixmap), 199
frozenset type, 37, 552
function definitions, nested, 261
functions; *see under the functions'*
    names, and built-ins
    as closures, 64
    dynamic definitions, 62–63
    nested, 65, 261
    object references to, 63, 64
    signatures, 56
    wrapping; *see* partial function
        application
functools module
    partial(), 64–65, 133, 365

G

garbage collection, 15, 78, 168, 169,
    170
__ge__() (>=), 81
generating lists, 54
generators, 54–55, 58–59, 70, 92, 97
geometry() (QWidget), 357
get() (dict), 36, 95, 420, 532, 541,
    551
getcwd() (os), 173
getDouble() (QInputDialog), 199
getExistingDirectory() (QFile-
    Dialog), 547
getInteger() (QInputDialog), 199
getItem() (QInputDialog), 199
__getitem__() ([]), 93, 94
getOpenFileName() (QFileDialog), 193,
    194, 233, 234, 287, 295, 356
getSaveFileName() (QFileDialog), 196
getText() (QInputDialog), 199
global functions; *see under the func-*
    tions' names, and built-ins
global scope, 55
globalPos() (QEvent), 307, 309
gradient fills; *see* QLinearGradient

graphics items; *see* QGraphicsItem
graphics scenes; *see* QGraphicsScene
graphic transformations; *see* trans-
    formations
graphics item coordinates, 350
graphics, rotating, 349
graphics, scaling, 349, 370, 374
grid layout; *see* QGridLayout
group() (re), 554
__gt__() (>), 81
gzip module, 248

H

handling errors, reading and writ-
    ing files, 244
has_key() (dict), 96
hasattr(), 39, 102, 218, 336
hasChildren() (QAbstractItemModel),
    433
hasFeature() (QSqlDriver), 449
hasFocus() (QWidget), 330, 426
hasFormat() (QMimeData), 314, 316
hash, Perl; *see* dict type
hasHtml() (QClipboard), 312
hasMouseTracking() (QWidget), 308
hasSelection() (QTextCursor), 385
headerData() (QAbstractItemModel),
    427, 430, 433, 503
height() (QWidget), 330
help(), 37, 39
hex(), 40
hide() (QWidget), 280, 330
hiding dialogs, 118, 121, 160
hiding widgets, 277, 280
high-level communication mecha-
    nisms; *see* signals and slots
homePath() (QDir), 545
horizontal layout; *see* QHBoxLayout
horizontal lines; *see* QFrame
horizontalHeader() (QTableView), 463,
    464
hotspot, icon, 316
HTML (Hyper-Text Markup Lan-
    guage), 114, 117, 168, 188, 311,

349, 381, 396, 397, 401, 488, 511, 552
html() (QMimeData), 312

I

__iadd__() (+=), 84, 90
icon; *see* QIcon
icon, for dragging, 316
icon, hotspot, 316
id(), 13, 39, 231, 237, 418
idealWidth() (QTextDocument), 390, 439, 489
identifiers, 36
identity
    comparison of, 13, 57
    operators, 47
    see also id(), and is statement
IDEs (integrated development environments)
    Eric4, 2, 10, 382
    IDLE, 9, 10, 60, 105, 382
if statement, 46–49
    conditional expression, 49
__ifloordiv__() (//=), 84
ignore() (QEvent), 186, 314
image; *see* QImage
image formats, 193
Image Changer application, 165–200
images, 168, 193, 195, 196
images, printing, 363
immutable objects, 15, 16, 20, 23, 29, 34, 35, 37, 57
__imod__() (%=), 84
import statement, 18, 19
    from __future__, 86, 549
    paths, 60
importing files, 229
__imul__() (*=), 84, 91
in-memory databases, 446
in operator, 25, 33, 36, 38, 45, 96
in-place editing, 414, 458
incomingConnection() (QTcpServer), 530, 539
indentation, 46

index()
    list, 33
    QAbstractItemModel, 433, 465, 468, 504
    QModelIndex, 427
    str/unicode, 24, 25, 68
indexing, 22, 30, 32
indexOf() (QString), 306, 387, 388
infinite recursion, risk of, 100
information() (QMessageBox), 188
inheritance, 76, 99–103, 103
__init__.py module, 104
__init__(), 77, 78, 437
initial processing, 184
initializers, 77
inputMask property (QLineEdit), 157
insert() (list), 33, 500
insertBlock() (QTextCursor), 404
insertImage() (QTextCursor), 404
insertion point, 386, 392, 393, 404
insertPlainText() (QTextEdit), 297
insertRecord() (QSqlTableModel), 464
insertRow() (QAbstractItemModel), 433, 465, 468
insertRows() (QAbstractItemModel), 426, 427, 432, 433
insertTable() (QTextCursor), 404
insertText() (QTextCursor), 384, 404
insort() (bisect), 499, 532, 543
insort_left() (bisect), 95, 238
insort_right() (bisect), 499
installEventFilter() (QObject), 304
installTranslator() (QCoreApplication), 516
instances
    callable, 97, 102
    copying, 88, 89
    see also objects
int(), 40, 84, 91, 256
int type, 16–17, 241
    %i and %d format specifiers, 26
    promotion to float, 14, 20
    promotion to long, 17
    see also long type
__int__() (int()), 84, 91
integer literals, 17

integrated development environ-
    ments; *see* IDEs
interactive, use of Python, 60
Interbase database, 445
interdependent actions; *see also* QAc-
    tion, 176
interdependent values; *see*
    form-level validation
interfaces, 102
internalPointer() (QModelIndex), 504
interpreter, Python, 60
intersection() (set), 38
introspection, 102, 105
invertPixels() (QImage), 197
IOError exception, 243, 244
is statement, 13, 47, 57
isActive() (QSqlQuery), 449, 450
isAlive() helper, 287–288, 289
isalpha() (str/unicode), 25
isChecked() (QAction), 172, 176
isdigit() (str/unicode), 25, 238, 554
isEmpty()
    QString, 233
    QTextDocument, 385
isEnabled() (QAction), 172
isFile() (QFileInfo), 294
isinstance(), 39, 94, 102, 135, 289,
    296, 359, 372, 375, 393, 395, 440,
    496, 499, 502, 503
isModified() (QTextDocument), 287,
    385
isNull()
    QDate, 45
    QDateTime, 45
    QDomNode, 260
    QImage, 400
    QPixmap, 496
    QString, 45
    QStringList, 45
    QTime, 45
ISO date format, 250, 258
isObscured() (QGraphicsItem), 366
isOpen() (QDataStream), 525
isRunning() (QThread), 547, 551
isSelected() (QGraphicsItem), 366
issubset() (set), 38

issuperset() (set), 38
__isub__() (-=), 84
isValid()
    QModelIndex, 427, 428, 504
    QSqlQuery, 450
item() (QTableWidget), 422
itemChange() (QGraphicsItem), 362,
    366
itemChanged() signal (QTableWidget),
    417
items(), 97
    dict, 36, 97
    QGraphicsScene, 354, 372
iter(), 97, 237
__iter__() (iter()), 93, 97, 237
iterable, 50
iteration; *see* for loop, while loop,
    and generators
iterator protocol, 52
iterators, 52, 54, 87, 92, 97
iteritems() (dict), 97, 98
iterkeys() (dict), 97
itervalues() (dict), 97
__itruediv__() (/=), 84, 91

J

join()
    os.path module, 496, 512, 555
    str/unicode, 23, 25, 61, 193, 477
.jpg and .jpeg (image file), 193

K

key() (QKeyEvent), 307, 334, 365, 384,
    391, 483
key sequences, 171–172, 175, 176
    see also QKeySequence
keyboard accelerator, 143, 144, 189,
    299
keyboard focus, 206, 218, 304, 351,
    364, 478
keyboard shortcut, 144, 394
keyboard users, support for, 149,
    218, 390, 417, 482, 511

KeyError exception, 94
keypresses, 483
  Enter, 120, 145, 188, 391, 421, 422,
    440, 511
  Esc, 121, 161, 188, 421, 422
  F2, 417, 422, 440
  Shift, 365
  Tab, 206, 218, 310, 421, 422, 511
keyPressEvent()
  QGraphicsItem, 365
  QWidget, 307, 309, 334, 391, 483
keyReleaseEvent() (QWidget), 307
keys() (dict), 36
keyword arguments, 55, 59–61
keywords, table of, 16

L

label; *see* QLabel
lambda statement, 61–62, 134, 453
last() (QSqlQuery), 450
lastError()
  QSqlDatabase, 446, 450, 459, 465
  QSqlQuery, 449
lastIndexOf() (QString), 234
Latin1 encoding, 20
layout managers, 118–120, 123,
    144–146, 145, 150, 209–210,
    212, 213–215, 270–271, 332
layout() (QWidget), 277
layout policies, 270–271
__le__() (<=), 81
left() (QString), 234, 306
len(), 20, 25, 33, 36, 38, 96, 237, 503
__len__() (len()), 93, 96, 237, 503
Length example class (length),
    86–91
length() (QString), 388
level of detail, 374
licensing, 3
lifetime, of PyQt objects, 287
line editor; *see* QLineEdit
line width; *see* pen width
lineEdit() (QAbstractSpinBox), 327
list comprehensions, 53–54, 96–97
list type, 31–35, 33, 38, 93

list type *(cont.)*
  + concatenation operator, 33
  append(), 33, 53
  count(), 25, 33
  extend(), 33
  generating, 54
  index(), 24, 33
  indexing, 32
  insert(), 33, 500
  iterating, 50
  pop(), 33, 355, 361
  remove(), 32, 33
  reverse(), 33
  slicing, 32
  sort(), 33, 53, 63, 95, 239
  title(), 24
list widget; *see* QListWidget
listen() (QTcpServer), 529
literals
  integer, 17
  string, 20
live dialogs, 159–162
loading files, 184, 229, 240–248,
    249–256, 256–265
local scope, 55
local variables, 87
locale; *see* QLocale and
    QString.arg()
localeAwareCompare() (QString), 416,
    434
lock() (QMutex), 553, 554
lockForRead() (QReadWriteLock), 541,
    542, 543, 548, 550, 551, 556
lockForWrite() (QReadWriteLock), 542,
    543, 556
logical coordinates; *see* window coor-
    dinates
logical operators, 47
long(), 40
long type, 16–17, 231, 241
  %i and %d format specifiers, 26
  see also int type
loops; *see* for statement and while
    statement
  deeply nested, 69

low-level communication mechanisms; *see* events
lower() (str/unicode), 25, 238
lrelease application, 207, 513, 518
__lt__() (<), 81, 82, 432

M

Mac OS X detection, 218
magic number, 241
mailing lists, 5
main(), conventional entry point, 62
main window; *see* QMainWindow
__main__ module attribute value, 106
Make PyQt application (makepyqt.pyw), 174, 206, 207, 216, 519
mangling names, 77, 88, 89
mapFromGlobal() (QWidget), 357
mapToGlobal() (QWidget), 309, 392, 393
mapToScene() (QGraphicsView), 357
master-detail forms, 458, 464, 469
math module, 40, 117, 371, 375
matrix()
    QGraphicsItem, 359, 377
    QGraphicsView, 370
max(), 38
maximum size, of layouts and widgets, 271
maximumHeight() (QWidget), 390
MDI (Multiple Document Interface), 290–300
membership operators, 47
menu separators, 178, 180
menuBar() (QMainWindow), 186
menus, 168, 177–178
    see also QMenu and QMenuBar
mergeCurrentCharFormat() (QTextEdit), 395
message box; *see* QMessageBox
meta-characters
    regular expression, 220
    XML, 257, 258
methods, 81

methods *(cont.)*
    static, 78
    virtual, 75, 99
mid() (QString), 252
MIME (Multipurpose Internet Mail Extensions) format, 310, 313
mimeData()
    QClipboard, 312
    QDropEvent, 314
min(), 38
minimizing windows, 297
minimum size, of layouts and widgets, 270, 271, 335
minimumHeight() (QWidget), 390
minimumSizeHint() (QWidget), 271, 335, 340, 341, 479
mirrored() (QImage), 198
mkpyqt.py application, 174, 206, 207, 216, 519
__mod__() (%), 84
modality, 140, 142, 511
model() (QModelIndex), 438, 441, 462, 489
modeless dialogs, 140, 155, 159, 286
models; *see* custom models and QAbstractItemModel
modifiers() (QInputEvent), 307, 365, 391
modules, 104
modulus (%), 53
mouse position, 318
mouse tracking; *see* hasMouseTracking() and setMouseTracking()
mouseDoubleClickEvent()
    QGraphicsItem, 362
    QWidget, 308, 309, 417, 422, 440
mouseMoveEvent() (QWidget), 309, 317
mousePressEvent() (QWidget), 309, 333, 482
mouseReleaseEvent() (QWidget), 308, 309
move() (QWidget), 183, 330, 341
moveBy() (QGraphicsItem), 366
__mul__() (*), 84, 91
multifile applications, 104
Multipedes application, 368–377

multiple document interface; *see* MDI

multiple inheritance, 76, 103, 216, 217, 373

multiway branching; *see* if statement

mutable objects, 16, 23, 28, 29, 31, 32, 34, 35, 37, 51, 57

mutually exclusive actions, 176
  see also QAction

My Movies application, 227–265

MySQL database, 445

N

name mangling, 77, 88, 89

__name__ module attribute, 106

names, of variables, 76, 80, 88

namespaces, 19

__ne__() (!=), 81

__neg__() (–), 84

negative lookahead, in regular expressions, 387

nested functions, 65, 261, 554

network protocols, 521

new-style vs. old-style classes, 76

__new__(), 77, 78, 81

newlines, escaping, 51

newlines, universal, 256

newPage() (QPrinter), 410

next()
  iterator method, 52, 59, 97
  QSqlQuery, 449, 450, 451, 468, 469

nextSibling() (QDomNode), 260

nodeType() (QDomNode), 261

None constant, 13, 45, 57

__nonzero__() (bool()), 81, 83

not operator, 47

notify() (QCoreApplication), 305

NotImplementedError exception, 83, 102

number() (QString), 338

numRowsAffected() (QSqlQuery), 449, 450

O

object names; *see* QObject.setObject-Name()

object references, 12, 55, 57, 58, 63, 64

object type, 76, 77, 78

objects
  callable, 97, 102
  comparing, 13
  copying, 88, 89
  function references, 63, 64
  immutable, 15, 16, 20, 23, 29, 34, 35, 37, 57
  mutable, 16, 23, 28, 29, 31, 32, 34, 35, 37, 51, 57
  ownership of, 119, 168, 170, 172, 180, 355, 357, 359, 372, 376
  references, 12, 15, 55, 57, 58, 63, 64

oct(), 40

ODBC database, 445, 448

okToContinue() helper, 187

old-style vs. new-style classes, 76

open()
  built-in, 39, 70
  codecs, 255, 260, 501, 555
  gzip, 248
  QIODevice, 241, 243, 250, 252, 258, 259
  QSqlDatabase, 446, 459

Open Source licensing, 3

or operator, 47

Oracle database, 445, 448

ord(), 21, 39, 50

OrderedDict example class, 92–98

orientation, 430

os module
  walk(), 555

os.path module
  basename(), 189
  dirname(), 173, 477, 496, 512
  join(), 496, 512, 555

OSError exception, 243, 244

overloading, 75

ownership, of objects, 119, 168, 170, 172, 180, 355, 357, 359, 372, 376

P

page size, printer, 400
Page Designer application, 351–368
pageRect() (QPrinter), 408
paint devices; *see* QImage, QPainter,
    QPicture, QPixmap, QPrinter,
    QSvgGenerator, and QWidget
paint()
    QAbstractItemDelegate, 436, 438,
      461, 486, 489
    QGraphicsItem, 366, 368, 374, 377
paintEvent() (QWidget), 306, 309, 336,
    342, 480
palette; *see* QPalette
palette()
    QApplication, 438, 489
    QWidget, 337
parameters, 55, 56
    default, 56
    keyword, 55, 59–61
    passing by value, 57
    positional, 55
parent() (QObject), 433, 504
parent, of widget, 118, 119, 172, 340,
    372
parenting, automatic, 119
parse() (QXmlReader), 262
parsing XML, 259–262, 262–265
partial() example, 64–65
partial() (functools), 64–65, 133,
    365
partial function application, 63–65,
    133, 365
pass-by-value, 57
pass statement, 47
pasteboard; *see* QClipboard
patents, disadvantages of, for soft-
    ware, 222
path() (QFileInfo), 233, 356
path variable (sys), 60, 104
PDF (Portable Document Format),
    398, 401
pen width, 144
physical coordinates; *see* viewport
    coordinates

pickle() (copy_reg), 247
pickle module, 235, 246–248
    see also cPickle module
pixmap; *see* QPixmap
pixmap()
    QClipboard, 311
    QGraphicsPixmapItem, 359
platform module
    python_version(), 200
    system(), 200, 217, 336, 390
.png (image file), 193
pointers; *see* object references
policies for
    file error handling, 244
    size and layout, 270–271, 335
    strings, 28, 228
polymorphism, 99–103
pop(), 96
    dict, 36, 96
    list, 33, 355, 361
    set, 372
popitem() (dict), 96
populating list widgets, 418
populating table widgets, 418
populating trees, 420, 502
portable document format; *see* PDF
pos()
    QCursor, 318, 357
    QGraphicsItem, 359, 366
    QMouseEvent, 309
positional arguments, 55
post-mortem validation, 140, 150,
    151
PostgreSQL database, 445
PostScript, 401
pow(), 40
preferred size, of layouts and wid-
    gets, 271, 335
prepare() (QSqlQuery), 448, 450, 468
prepared queries, 447
prepend() (QStringList), 189
preserving aspect ratio, 329
preventative validation, 140, 157,
    159, 162, 327
previewing forms, 215
previous() (QSqlQuery), 449, 450

print statement, 10, 26
  trailing comma, 49
print_() (QTextDocument), 403, 407
printer; *see* QPrinter
printImage() helper, 363
printing, 170, 363, 398–410
printing images, 363
private names, 76, 80, 88
.pro (C++/Qt project file), 518
processEvents() (QCoreApplication),
  294, 537
processing, at start-up, 184
propagating hide and show calls,
  280
properties, 80, 211, 322
properties, of QObjects, 157, 211
property()
  built-in, 80
  QObject, 322, 324
.py and .pyw (Python file), 11, 111,
  207
.pyc and .pyo (Python bytecode file),
  11, 207
pylupdate4 application, 207, 513,
  517, 518
PyQt4 modules; *see the individual
  modules*, QtCore, QtGui, etc.
pyqtProperty() (QtCore), 322
@pyqtSignature decorator (QtCore),
  218, 219
PYQT_VERSION_STR variable, 200
pyrcc4 application, 173, 174, 207
python_version() (platform), 200
pyuic4 application, 206, 207, 216,
  221, 515

Q

QAbstractButton (QtGui)
  base class, QWidget
  setCheckable(), 276, 278
  setText(), 370
  toggled() signal, 277, 280
QAbstractItemDelegate (QtGui)
  base class, QObject

QAbstractItemDelegate (QtGui) *(cont.)*
  createEditor(), 436, 440, 461,
    486, 487, 488, 491
  paint(), 436, 438, 461, 486, 489
  setEditorData(), 436, 441, 462,
    486, 487, 488
  setModelData(), 436, 441, 462,
    486, 487, 488
  sizeHint(), 436, 439, 489
QAbstractItemModel (QtCore), 425,
    433, 434, 445, 500
  base class, QObject
  beginInsertRows(), 432, 433
  beginRemoveRows(), 433
  columnCount(), 427, 428, 433, 503
  createIndex(), 433, 504
  data(), 414, 427, 428, 429, 430,
    433, 438, 441, 462, 481, 487, 488,
    489, 491, 496, 503
  dataChanged() signal, 431, 432,
    478
  endInsertRows(), 432, 433
  endRemoveRows(), 432, 433
  flags(), 427, 430, 433
  hasChildren(), 433
  headerData(), 427, 430, 433, 503
  index(), 433. 465, 468, 504
  insertRow(), 433, 465, 468
  insertRows(), 426, 427, 432, 433
  removeRow(), 434, 466, 469
  removeRows(), 427, 432, 434, 470
  reset(), 432, 434, 501, 502
  rowCount(), 426, 427, 428, 434,
    454, 455, 479, 481, 503
  setData(), 414, 427, 431, 434, 441,
    462, 465, 487, 488
  setHeaderData(), 434, 460, 462
QAbstractItemView (QtGui)
  base class, QAbstractScrollArea
  currentIndex(), 427, 463, 465,
    466, 468, 469
  edit(), 426, 465, 468
  selectionModel(), 463
  setAlternatingRowColors(), 231,
    477
  setCurrentIndex(), 426, 465, 468

QAbstractItemView (QtGui) *(cont.)*
  setDragEnabled(), 312, 313, 315
  setEditTriggers(), 231
  setItemDelegate(), 437, 460, 463, 490
  setModel(), 425, 437, 460, 463, 477, 490
  setSelectionBehavior(), 231, 460, 463, 495
  setSelectionMode(), 231, 460, 463
  startDrag(), 316
QAbstractScrollArea (QtGui)
  base class, QFrame
  viewport(), 392, 393
QAbstractSlider (QtGui)
  base class, QWidget
  setRange(), 369
  setValue(), 128, 369
QAbstractSocket (QtNetwork), 521
  base class, QIODevice
  connectToHost(), 525
  state(), 540
  waitForDisconnected(), 544
QAbstractSpinBox (QtGui)
  base class, QWidget
  lineEdit(), 327
  setAlignment(), 340, 487
  validate(), 327, 328
QAbstractTableModel (QtCore), 425, 427
  base class, QAbstractItemModel
QAction (QtGui), 171–172, 175, 194, 385
  base class, QObject
  data(), 172, 393, 395
  editor, visual, 206
  isChecked(), 172, 176
  isEnabled(), 172
  setCheckable(), 393
  setChecked(), 172, 177, 393
  setData(), 172, 189, 392, 393
  setEnabled(), 172
  setSeparator(), 172
  setShortcut(), 171, 172
  setStatusTip(), 172
  setText(), 172

QAction (QtGui) *(cont.)*
  setToolTip(), 172
  setwhatsThis(), 172
  toggled() signal, 172, 176, 177
  triggered() signal, 172, 176
QActionGroup (QtGui), 176
QApplication (QtGui), 113, 115, 304
  base class, QCoreApplication
  clipboard(), 297, 311
  palette(), 438, 489
  setQuitOnLastWindowClosed(), 121
QBoxLayout (QtGui), 146, 326
  base class, QLayout
  addLayout(), 146
  addSpacing(), 146
  addStretch(), 146
  setStretchFactor(), 146
QBrush (QtGui), 374, 377
QByteArray (QtCore), 313, 316, 358, 359, 525, 526, 533
QCalendarWidget (QtGui), 575
QCheckBox (QtGui), 575
QClipboard (QtGui), 297, 310–312
  base class, QObject
  hasHtml(), 312
  mimeData(), 312
  pixmap(), 311
  setImage(), 311
  setMimeData(), 311
  setPixmap(), 311
  setText(), 297, 311
  text(), 297, 311
QCloseEvent (QtGui), 186
QColor (QtGui), 337, 345, 371, 392, 393, 438, 481, 489
QComboBox (QtGui), 440, 576
  base class, QWidget
  addItem(), 276
  addItems(), 440
  currentIndexChanged() signal, 124, 275
  currentText(), 441
  findText(), 142, 441, 457
  setCurrentIndex(), 441, 457
  setEditable(), 440
  setModel(), 456

QComboBox (QtGui) *(cont.)*
  setModelColumn(), 456
QContextMenuEvent (QtGui), 307
  base class, QInputEvent
QCoreApplication (QtCore), 538
  base class, QObject
  applicationDirPath(), 173
  applicationName(), 194
  exec_(), 115, 184
  installTranslator(), 516
  notify(), 305
  processEvents(), 294, 537
  quit(), 115
  translate(), 513, 515
QCursor (QtGui), 318
  pos(), 318, 357
QDataStream (QtCore), 240–246, 242,
    245, 315, 316, 358, 359, 435, 525,
    528, 531, 533, 540
  atEnd(), 245
  device(), 525, 533
  isOpen(), 525
  readBool(), 245
  readDouble(), 241, 245
  readInt*n*(), 243, 245, 360, 435
  readUInt*n*(), 245, 528, 540
  setVersion(), 241, 243, 245, 525,
    528, 531, 533, 540
  write(), 526, 533
  writeBool(), 245
  writeDouble(), 241, 245
  writeInt*n*(), 241, 242, 245, 359,
    435
  writeUInt*n*(), 245, 525, 533
QDataWidgetMapper (QtGui), 453, 456
  base class, QObject
  addMapping(), 453, 456
  currentIndex(), 454, 455
  setCurrentIndex(), 454, 455
  setItemDelegate(), 456
  setModel(), 453, 456
  setSubmitPolicy(), 453, 456
  submit(), 454
  toFirst(), 453, 456
QDate (QtCore), 19, 45, 253, 513
  addDays(), 491

QDate (QtCore) *(cont.)*
  addYears(), 490
  currentDate(), 46, 236, 401, 490
  isNull(), 45
  toPyDate(), 532, 541
  toString(), 258, 401
QDateEdit (QtGui), 487, 576
  base class, QDateTimeEdit
QDateTime (QtCore), 45, 454, 513
  currentDateTime(), 454
  dateTime(), 455
  isNull(), 45
  setDateTime(), 454
  toString(), 455
QDateTimeEdit (QtGui), 452, 576
  base class, QAbstractSpinBox
  date(), 487
  setCalendarPopup(), 487
  setDate(), 487
  setDateRange(), 452, 487
  setDisplayFormat(), 452, 487
QDesktopServices (QtGui), 510
QDial (QtGui), 128
QDialog (QtGui), 118, 154, 217
  base class, QWidget
  accept(), 151, 154, 425
  done(), 154, 457, 464
  exec_(), 142, 154, 511
  reject(), 215
  setSizeGripEnabled(), 154
QDialogButtonBox (QtGui), 145, 150,
    576
  base class, QWidget
  accepted(), 145, 150
  addButton(), 150
  button(), 150, 158
  default button, 145, 188
  rejected(), 145, 150
QDir (QtCore)
  homePath(), 545
  toNativeSeparators(), 547, 551
QDockWidget (QtGui), 169
  base class, QWidget
  setAllowedAreas(), 169, 170
  setFeatures(), 170
QDomDocument (QtXml), 257, 259–262
  base class, QDomNode

QDomDocument (QtXml) *(cont.)*
  documentElement(), 260
  setContent(), 259
  toString(), 257, 260
QDomElement (QtXml)
  base class, QDomNode
  attribute(), 261
  tagName(), 260
QDomNode (QtXml)
  firstChild(), 260
  isNull(), 260
  nextSibling(), 260
  nodeType(), 261
  toElement(), 260
  toText(), 261
QDoubleSpinBox (QtGui), 123, 578
  base class, QAbstractSpinBox
QDrag (QtGui), 316
  base class, QObject
  exec_(), 316
  setHotSpot(), 316
  setMimeData(), 316
  setPixmap(), 316
  start(), 316
QDropEvent (QtGui)
  base class, QEvent
  mimeData() (QDropEvent), 314
  setDropAction(), 314, 315, 316
QEvent (QtCore)
  accept(), 314, 333, 391
  globalPos(), 307, 309
  ignore(), 314
  type(), 384
QFile (QtCore), 241, 243, 250, 252,
    258, 259, 262
  base class, QIODevice
  exists(), 294
QFileDialog (QtGui)
  getExistingDirectory(), 547
  getOpenFileName(), 193, 194, 233,
    234, 287, 295, 356
  getSaveFileName(), 196
QFileInfo (QtCore), 189
  fileName(), 189
  isFile(), 294
  path(), 233, 356

QFont (QtGui), 335, 336, 408, 478
  setPointSize(), 335, 336
QFontComboBox (QtGui), 576
  base class, QComboBox
QFontMetrics/QFontMetricsF (QtGui),
    335, 336, 340, 341, 342, 390, 408,
    439
QFrame (QtGui), 277
  base class, QWidget
  setFrameStyle(), 170, 278
QGraphicsItem (QtGui), 349, 364, 365,
    366, 367, 373, 376
  boundingRect(), 365, 366, 367,
    373, 377
  collidesWithPath(), 366
  collidingItems(), 366
  contains(), 366
  contextMenuEvent(), 365
  isObscured(), 366
  isSelected(), 366
  itemChange(), 362, 366
  keyPressEvent(), 365
  matrix(), 359, 377
  mouseDoubleClickEvent(), 362
  moveBy(), 366
  paint(), 366, 368, 374, 377
  pos(), 359, 366
  resetMatrix(), 366
  rotate(), 360, 366, 371, 375, 377
  scale(), 366
  scene(), 366, 375
  sceneBoundingRect(), 366, 379
  setCursor(), 366
  setEnabled(), 366
  setFlag(), 366
  setFlags(), 351, 356, 362, 364
  setFocus(), 364, 366
  setFont(), 362
  setMatrix(), 362, 364, 367, 377
  setPos(), 356, 362, 364, 367, 373,
    375
  setSelected(), 356, 362, 364, 367
  setZValue(), 367
  shape(), 365, 367, 374, 377
  shear(), 367
  translate(), 367

QGraphicsItem (QtGui) *(cont.)*
  update(), 365, 367
  zValue(), 367
QGraphicsLineItem (QtGui), 349
  base class, QGraphicsItem
QGraphicsPixmapItem (QtGui), 349,
  356
  base class, QGraphicsItem
  pixmap(), 359
QGraphicsRectItem (QtGui), 355
  base class, QAbstractGraphics-
  ShapeItem
QGraphicsScene (QtGui), 349, 354, 369
  base class, QObject
  addEllipse(), 354
  addItem(), 354, 356, 362, 364, 371
  addLine(), 354
  addPath(), 354
  addPixmap(), 354
  addPolygon(), 354
  addRect(), 354, 355
  addText(), 354
  clearSelection(), 356, 361, 362,
  364
  collidingItems(), 354, 375
  items(), 354, 372
  removeItem(), 354, 355, 359, 361,
  372
  render(), 354, 361
  selectedItems(), 358, 360, 361
  setBackgroundBrush(), 354
  setSceneRect(), 354, 369
  update(), 354
  views(), 354, 362
QGraphicsSceneContextMenuEvent (Qt-
  Gui), 365
  base class, QEvent
  screenPos(), 365
QGraphicsSimpleTextItem (QtGui), 349
  base class, QAbstractGraphics-
  ShapeItem
QGraphicsTextItem (QtGui), 349, 362
  base class, QGraphicsItem
  font(), 359
  toPlainText(), 359

QGraphicsView (QtGui), 349, 351–352,
  369, 577
  base class, QAbstractScrollArea
  mapToScene(), 357
  matrix(), 370
  render(), 361
  scale(), 352
  setDragMode(), 352
  setMatrix(), 370
  setRenderHint(), 352, 369
  setScene(), 354, 369
QGridLayout (QtGui), 123, 144, 146,
  150, 270, 273
  base class, QLayout
  addLayout(), 146, 151
  setColumnStretch(), 146
  setRowStretch(), 146
QGroupBox (QtGui), 577
QHBoxLayout (QtGui), 144, 146, 270
  base class, QBoxLayout
QIcon (QtGui), 173, 313, 392
QImage (QtGui), 168, 195, 197, 198,
  199, 329, 400
  base class, QPaintDevice
  invertPixels(), 197
  isNull(), 400
  mirrored(), 198
  rgbSwapped(), 197
  save(), 196
  scaled(), 199
  size(), 363, 400
QImageReader, 193
QImageWriter, 196
QInputDialog (QtGui), 199
QInputEvent (QtGui)
  base class, QEvent
  modifiers(), 307, 365, 391
QIODevice (QtCore), 526
  base class, QObject
  bytesAvailable(), 528, 531, 540
  close(), 243, 259, 525, 528
  errorString(), 241, 243, 250, 252,
  258, 259, 528
  open(), 241, 243, 250, 252, 258,
  259
  readAll(), 254

QIODevice (QtCore) *(cont.)*
  waitForReadyRead(), 540
QItemDelegate (QtGui), 436, 437,
    485–489
  base class, QAbstractItemDelegate
QKeyEvent (QtGui), 307
  base class, QInputEvent
  key(), 307, 334, 365, 384, 391,
    483
QKeySequence (QtGui), 171, 175, 285,
    292, 393
QLabel (QtGui), 114, 168, 340, 577
  base class, QFrame
  setAlignment(), 168, 340
  setBuddy(), 143, 425
  setPixmap(), 199
QLayout (QtGui), 146
  base class, QLayoutItem
  addWidget(), 146, 151, 273
  setSizeConstraint(), 277, 279
QLCDNumber (QtGui), 577
QLinearGradient (QtGui), 343
QLineEdit (QtGui), 117, 310, 314, 440,
    461, 577
  base class, QWidget
  inputMask property, 157
  returnPressed() signal, 440
  setAlignment(), 461
  setInputMask(), 461
  setText(), 441, 462
  setValidator(), 461
  text(), 441
  textEdited() signal, 161, 217,
    218
QListView (QtGui), 415, 578
  base class, QAbstractItemView
QListWidget (QtGui), 275, 312, 315,
    414, 418, 578
  base class, QListView
  addItem(), 418
  clear(), 418
  currentRowChanged() signal, 275
  populating, 418
  setCurrentItem(), 418
QListWidgetItem (QtGui), 316, 418
  setIcon(), 316

QListWidgetItem (QtGui) *(cont.)*
  takeItem(), 316
QLocale (QtCore), 513, 516
.qm (Qt message file), 516, 518
QMainWindow (QtGui), 168, 186, 284,
    290
  base class, QWidget
  addDockWidget(), 169, 186
  addToolBar(), 179, 186
  closeAllWindows(), 289, 293
  menuBar(), 177, 186
  restoreState(), 183, 186
  saveState(), 183, 186
  setCentralWidget(), 168, 186, 285
  statusBar(), 170, 186
QMatrix and QTransform (QtGui), 356
  reset(), 370, 377
  scale(), 370
QMdiArea (QtGui), 290
QMenu (QtGui), 307, 365, 392, 393
  base class, QWidget
  aboutToShow() signal, 178, 187,
    285, 292
  addMenu(), 178
  addSeparator(), 178, 180, 307
  exec_(), 307, 365, 392, 393
QMenuBar (QtGui), 177, 178
QMessageBox (QtGui), 153, 187, 188,
    200, 361, 423, 455
QMetaObject (QtCore), 217
  connectSlotsByName(), 217
QMimeData (QtCore), 311, 313, 316
  base class, QObject
  data(), 315, 316
  hasFormat(), 314, 316
  html(), 312
  setData(), 316
  setHtml(), 311
QModelIndex (QtCore), 414, 432, 504
  column(), 428, 431, 439, 461, 462,
    486, 496, 503
  index(), 427
  internalPointer(), 504
  isValid(), 427, 428, 504
  model(), 438, 441, 462, 489
  row(), 427, 491

QModelIndex (QtCore) *(cont.)*
  sibling(), 491
QMouseEvent (QtGui), 309
  base class, QInputEvent
  button(), 333
  pos(), 309
QMutex (QtCore), 541, 552, 553, 554
QMutexLocker (QtCore), 554
QObject (QtCore), 119, 127, 304, 322,
    370
  blockSignals(), 135
  connect(), 124, 130, 133, 145, 146,
    151, 158, 453
  deleteLater(), 287, 531, 539, 544
  destroyed() signal, 286, 288
  disconnect(), 130
  emit(), 130, 131, 219, 333, 340,
    391, 431, 440, 556
  event(), 304, 309, 310, 384
  installEventFilter(), 304
  parent(), 433, 504
  properties, 157, 211
  property(), 322, 324
  sender(), 135, 289, 393, 395, 440
  setObjectName(), 169, 183, 324
  setProperty(), 322, 324
  startTimer(), 370
  timerEvent(), 372
  tr(), 513, 514, 515
  trUtf8(), 513
QPainter (QtGui), 306, 328, 337, 342,
    343, 344, 361, 363, 400, 407–410,
    408, 480
  drawArc(), 344
  drawChord(), 344
  drawConvexPolygon(), 344
  drawEllipse(), 344, 374, 377, 481
  drawImage(), 344, 363, 400
  drawLine(), 338, 344
  drawPath(), 344, 377
  drawPicture(), 363
  drawPie(), 344
  drawPixmap(), 344, 363, 408
  drawPoint(), 344
  drawPolygon(), 338, 343, 344, 345
  drawPolyline(), 344, 345

QPainter (QtGui) *(cont.)*
  drawRect(), 337, 344, 368, 410
  drawRoundRect(), 344
  drawText(), 306, 338, 344, 408,
    410, 481
  fillPath(), 344
  fillRect(), 344, 438, 481, 489
  restore(), 343, 346, 410, 438, 482,
    489
  rotate(), 343
  save(), 343, 346, 438, 481, 489
  scale(), 343
  setBrush(), 337, 344, 345, 374,
    377, 481
  setFont(), 344, 408, 482
  setMatrix(), 343
  setPen(), 337, 338, 343, 344, 345,
    374, 377, 409, 410, 481
  setRenderHint(), 306, 337, 342,
    343, 363
  setViewport(), 329, 342, 343, 363
  setWindow(), 329, 342, 343, 363
  shear(), 343
  translate(), 343, 438, 489
  viewport(), 363, 400
QPainterPath (QtGui), 374, 376
  addEllipse(), 374, 376
  addPolygon(), 376
  boundingRect(), 377
  closeSubPath(), 376
QPaintEvent (QtGui), 480
  base class, QEvent
  rect(), 480
QPalette (QtGui), 337, 481
QPen (QtGui), 368
  setColor(), 368
  setWidth(), 368
QPicture (QtGui), 329
  base class, QPaintDevice
QPixmap (QtGui), 199, 329, 392, 404,
    408, 496
  base class, QPaintDevice
  fill(), 392
  fromImage(), 199
  isNull(), 496

QPoint/QPointF (QtCore), 309, 338, 343, 371

QPolygon/QPolygonF (QtGui), 343, 345, 376

QPrintDialog (QtGui), 361, 363, 400, 403, 404, 408

QPrinter (QtGui), 170, 329, 353, 361, 363, 398, 400, 401
    base class, QPaintDevice
    newPage(), 410
    pageRect(), 408
    setPageSize(), 353, 398, 400

QProcess (QtCore), 537

QProgressBar (QtGui), 578

QPushButton (QtGui), 276, 278, 369, 578
    base class, QAbstractButton
    clicked() signal, 219
    default button, 145, 188
    see also QDialogButtonBox

QRadioButton (QtGui), 577

.qrc (PyQt resource file), 173, 207, 517

QReadWriteLock (QtCore), 540, 541, 545, 552
    lockForRead(), 541, 542, 543, 548, 550, 551, 556
    lockForWrite(), 542, 543, 556
    unlock(), 541, 542, 543, 548, 550, 551, 556

QRect/QRectF (QtCore), 355, 357, 364, 376, 410
    adjusted(), 355, 367
    center(), 392, 393
    contains(), 357
    setBottom(), 365
    setRight(), 365
    size(), 400

QRegExp (QtCore), 327, 386, 387, 461

QRegExpValidator (QtGui), 157, 327, 461

QScintilla add-on, 381, 382

QScrollArea (QtGui), 476, 477, 479

QSettings (QtCore), 182–183, 228, 282, 293, 514
    base class, QObject

QSettings (QtCore) *(cont.)*
    IniFormat constant, 228
    value(), 183

QSignalMapper (QtCore), 292, 297–300

QSize (QtCore), 183, 335, 341, 390, 400, 439, 489
    scale(), 363, 400

QSlider (QtGui), 369, 578
    base class, QAbstractSlider

QSpacerItem (QtGui), 212
    base class, QLayoutItem

QSpinBox (QtGui), 180, 326, 340, 440, 578
    base class, QAbstractSpinBox
    setRange(), 180, 340, 440
    setSingleStep(), 440
    setSuffix(), 180, 340
    setValue(), 128, 180, 340, 441
    textFromValue(), 327, 328
    value(), 441
    valueChanged(), 124, 128, 199
    valueFromText(), 327, 328

QSplitter (QtGui), 280–283, 477
    base class, QFrame
    restoreState(), 282
    saveState(), 282
    setStretchFactor(), 283

QSqlDatabase (QtSql), 446
    addDatabase(), 446, 459
    commit(), 449, 465, 468, 469
    database(), 465, 468, 469
    driver(), 449
    lastError(), 446, 450, 459, 465
    open(), 446, 459
    rollback(), 449, 465, 469
    setDatabaseName(), 446, 459
    transaction(), 449, 465, 468, 469

QSqlDriver (QtSql), 449
    base class, QObject
    hasFeature(), 449

QSqlQuery (QtSql), 445, 446–451, 450, 464, 468, 469
    addBindValue(), 448, 450
    bindValue(), 448, 450, 468
    boundValue(), 450
    driver(), 450

QSqlQuery (QtSql) *(cont.)*
  exec_(), 447, 448, 449, 450, 464,
    468, 469
  first(), 450
  isActive(), 449, 450
  isValid(), 450
  last(), 450
  lastError(), 449
  next(), 449, 450, 451, 468, 469
  numRowsAffected(), 449, 450
  prepare(), 448, 450, 468
  previous(), 449, 450
  record(), 450
  seek(), 449, 451
  setForwardOnly(), 451
  size(), 450
  value(), 449, 450, 451
QSqlQueryModel (QtSql)
  base class, QAbstractTableModel
  record(), 464, 465, 466, 469
  setQuery(), 464
QSqlRecord (QtSql)
  value(), 464, 465, 466, 469
QSqlRelation (QtSql), 456, 460, 462
QSqlRelationalDelegate (QtSql), 456,
    460, 461
QSqlRelationalTableModel (QtSql),
    445, 456, 462
  base class, QSqlTableModel
  relationModel(), 456
  setRelation(), 456, 460, 462
QSqlTableModel (QtSql), 445, 453
  base class, QSqlQueryModel
  beforeInsert(), 470
  fieldIndex(), 456
  insertRecord(), 464
  select(), 453, 456, 460, 462, 464,
    470
  setFilter(), 464, 470
  setSort(), 453, 456, 460, 462
  setTable(), 453, 456, 460, 462
  submitAll(), 455, 466, 469, 470
QSslSocket (QtNetwork), 521
QStackedWidget (QtGui), 274–276
  base class, QFrame
  setCurrentIndex(), 275
QStatusBar (QtGui)

QStatusBar (QtGui) *(cont.)*
  base class, QWidget
  clearMessage(), 170, 232
  setSizeGripEnabled(), 170
  showMessage(), 170, 233
QString (QtCore), 19, 23, 28, 233, 234,
    256, 313, 402
  arg(), 402, 418, 419, 423, 427, 428,
    455, 513, 515
  compare(), 435
  contains(), 234
  endsWith(), 240
  indexOf(), 306, 387, 388
  isEmpty(), 233
  isNull(), 45
  lastIndexOf(), 234
  left(), 234, 306
  length(), 388
  localeAwareCompare(), 416, 434
  mid(), 252
  number(), 338
  simplified(), 61, 422
  split(), 253
  startsWith(), 252
  toInt(), 251, 422
  toUpper(), 327
  trimmed(), 252, 422
  see also str type and unicode
    type
QStringList (QtCore), 45, 189
  contains(), 189
  isNull(), 45
  prepend(), 189
  takeLast(), 189
QStyleOptionGraphicsItem (QtGui),
    374
QStyleOptionViewItem (QtGui), 438,
    439, 461
QSvgGenerator (QtGui), 329, 363
  base class, QPaintDevice
QSvgRenderer (QtSvg), 363
QSyntaxHighlighter (QtGui), 386–389
Qt namespace, 258
  escape(), 258, 397, 401
  WindowStaysOnTopHint, 529
Qt Assistant application, 510

Qt Designer application, 205–216,
        272, 274, 275, 276, 277, 280, 324,
        326, 333
Qt.ItemDataRole (QtGui), 231
Qt Linguist application, 513
Qt.WidgetAttribute (QtGui)
    WA_DeleteOnClose, 156, 158, 284,
        286
    WA_GroupLeader, 511
QTableView (QtGui), 415, 425, 437, 458,
        460, 463, 477, 490, 579
    base class, QAbstractItemView
    horizontalHeader(), 463, 464
    resizeColumnsToContents(), 232,
        419, 460, 463, 490
    setColumnHidden(), 460, 463
    setSortingEnabled(), 418, 419
QTableWidget (QtGui), 230–232, 310,
        313, 414, 418, 579
    base class, QTableView
    clear(), 418
    currentColumn(), 422
    currentItem(), 422
    editItem(), 422
    item(), 422
    itemChanged() signal, 417
    populating, 418
    scrollToItem(), 232
    setColumnCount(), 231, 418
    setCurrentItem(), 232, 419
    setHorizontalHeaderLabels(),
        231, 418
    setItem(), 231, 419
    setRowCount(), 231, 418
QTableWidgetItem (QtGui), 231–232,
        418, 419
    data(), 422
    setData(), 419
    setSelected(), 232, 419
    setTextAlignment(), 231, 419
    text(), 422
QTabWidget (QtGui), 272–274, 579
    base class, QWidget
QtCore module (PyQt4), 19
    pyqtProperty(), 322
    @pyqtSignature(), 218, 219

QtCore module (PyQt4) *(cont.)*
    PYQT_VERSION_STR variable, 200
    QT_VERSION_STR variable, 200
    SIGNAL(), 131
    SLOT(), 131
    see also under class names
QTcpServer (QtNetwork), 529, 530, 539
    incomingConnection(), 530, 539
    listen(), 529
QTcpSocket (QtNetwork), 522, 524, 531,
        540
    base class, QAbstractSocket
QTextBlock (QtGui), 396
QTextBlockFormat (QtGui), 404
QTextBrowser (QtGui), 117, 381, 511,
        579
    base class, QTextEdit
QTextCharFormat (QtGui), 386, 387,
        404
QTextCursor (QtGui), 297, 384,
        403–407
    currentFrame(), 404
    hasSelection(), 385
    insertBlock(), 404
    insertImage(), 404
    insertTable(), 404
    insertText(), 384, 404
    removeSelectedText(), 297
    selectedText(), 297
    setPosition(), 406
QTextDocument (QtGui), 381, 383, 396,
        398, 401–407, 403, 438, 439,
        489
    base class, QObject
    clear(), 383
    drawContents(), 438, 489
    idealWidth(), 390, 439, 489
    isEmpty(), 385
    isModified(), 287, 385
    print_(), 403, 407
    setDefaultFont(), 438, 439, 489
    setHtml(), 403, 438, 439, 489
    setModified(), 286, 383, 384
    toHtml(), 407
QTextEdit (QtGui), 285, 310, 381, 383,
        390, 392, 579

QTextEdit (QtGui) *(cont.)*
  base class, QAbstractScrollArea
  append(), 120
  canPaste(), 385
  currentCharFormat(), 393, 395
  cursorRect(), 392, 393
  cut(), 385
  document(), 286, 287, 383, 384,
    385, 396
  ensureCursorVisible(), 392, 393
  insertPlainText(), 297
  mergeCurrentCharFormat(), 395
  setHtml(), 488
  setLineWrapMode(), 390
  setPlainText(), 384
  setTabChangesFocus(), 390
  setTextColor(), 393
  textCursor(), 297, 384, 385
  toHtml(), 395
  toPlainText(), 384, 395
QTextOption (QtGui), 409
QTextStream (QtCore), 250–255, 254,
  258, 384
  atEnd(), 252, 253, 254
  readAll(), 384
  readLine(), 252, 253, 254
  setCodec(), 250, 252, 254, 258,
    384
QTextTableFormat (QtGui), 404
QtGui module (PyQt4), 19
  see also under class names
QThread (QtCore), 538, 540
  isRunning(), 547, 551
  run(), 538, 540, 548, 553
  start(), 539, 547, 553
  wait(), 547, 548, 551
QTime (QtCore), 45
  isNull(), 45
  see also time module
QTimeEdit (QtGui), 576
  base class, QDateTimeEdit
QTimer (QtCore), 373, 376
  base class, QObject
  singleShot(), 115, 306
  start(), 373, 376
  timeout() signal, 373, 376

QtNetwork module (PyQt4), 521, 523
  see also under class names
QToolBar (QtGui), 179–180, 180
  base class, QWidget
  addSeparator(), 178, 180
QToolTip (QtGui), 171, 200, 514
QTransform (QtGui), 356
QTranslator (QtCore), 516
QTreeView (QtGui), 415, 495, 579
  base class, QAbstractItemView
  populating, 502
  setItemsExpandable(), 420
  setUniformRowHeights(), 495
QTreeWidget (QtGui), 414, 579
  base class, QTreeView
  clear(), 420
  expandItem(), 421
  populating, 420
  setColumnCount(), 420
  setCurrentItem(), 421
  setHeaderLabels(), 420
QTreeWidgetItem (QtGui), 420, 421
QtSql module (PyQt4), 445, 446
  see also under class names
QtSvg module (PyQt4), 363
  see also under class names
QT_VERSION_STR variable, 200
QtXml module (PyQt4), 235
  see also under class names
QUdpSocket (QtNetwork), 522
  base class, QAbstractSocket
queries, database; *see* QSqlQuery and
  SQL statements
question() (QMessageBox), 187, 188,
  361, 423, 455
quit() (QCoreApplication), 115
quitting applications; *see* terminating applications
quoted strings; *see* string literals
QVariant (QtCore), 183, 185, 231, 323,
  392, 414, 427, 428, 429, 430, 441,
  448, 451, 488, 496
  toBool(), 324
  toDate(), 487, 491
  toDateTime(), 449
  toDouble(), 481

QVariant (QtCore) *(cont.)*
    toInt(), 395, 431, 449
    toLongLong(), 422
    toString(), 427, 431, 441, 449,
      488
QVBoxLayout (QtGui), 146, 270
    base class, QBoxLayout
QWidget (QtGui), 118, 119, 127, 168,
      273, 305, 306, 309, 322–324, 324,
      325–326, 328, 329, 330, 331, 370,
      421
    base classes, QObject and QPaint-
      Device
    activateWindow(), 160, 289
    addAction(), 172, 178, 180, 307,
      330, 365, 392, 393
    addActions(), 178
    close(), 175, 285, 289, 330
    closeEvent(), 175, 185, 187, 282,
      285, 289, 293, 309, 551
    contextMenuEvent(), 307, 309, 390
    dragEnterEvent(), 309, 314, 316
    dragMoveEvent(), 309, 314, 315,
      316
    dropEvent(), 309, 315, 316
    font(), 336, 342
    geometry(), 357
    hasFocus(), 330, 426
    hasMouseTracking(), 308
    height(), 330
    hide(), 279, 330
    keyPressEvent(), 307, 309, 334,
      391, 483
    keyReleaseEvent(), 307
    layout(), 277
    mapFromGlobal(), 357
    mapToGlobal(), 309, 392, 393
    maximumHeight(), 390
    minimumHeight(), 390
    minimumSizeHint(), 271, 335, 340,
      341, 479
    mouseDoubleClickEvent(), 308,
      309, 417, 422, 440
    mouseMoveEvent(), 309, 317
    mousePressEvent(), 309, 333
    mouseReleaseEvent(), 308, 309

QWidget (QtGui) *(cont.)*
    move(), 183, 330, 341
    paintEvent(), 306, 309, 336, 342,
      480
    palette(), 337
    raise_(), 160, 289, 330
    rect(), 306, 330
    resize(), 183
    resizeEvent(), 306, 309, 341
    restoreGeometry(), 183, 186, 330
    saveGeometry(), 183, 186, 330
    setAcceptDrops(), 312, 313, 314,
      315, 316, 330
    setAttribute(), 156, 284, 330,
      511
    setContextMenuPolicy(), 168, 330,
      365
    setCursor(), 330
    setEnabled(), 219, 330
    setFocus(), 120, 310, 330, 422
    setFocusPolicy(), 180, 217, 331,
      369, 478
    setFont(), 330
    setLayout(), 273, 279, 330
    setMaximumHeight(), 390
    setMinimumHeight(), 390
    setMinimumSize(), 168, 340
    setMinimumWidth(), 340
    setMouseTracking(), 308, 334
    setSizePolicy(), 330, 331, 340
    setStatusTip(), 171, 180
    setStyleSheet(), 323, 330
    setTabOrder(), 206
    setToolTip(), 171, 180, 390
    setVisible(), 277, 280
    setWindowFlags(), 529
    setWindowIcon(), 186, 330
    setWindowModified(), 192
    setWindowTitle(), 146, 151, 186,
      330, 370
    show(), 115, 155, 280, 286, 330,
      511
    showMinimized(), 297
    showNormal(), 297
    sizeHint(), 335, 390, 479
    update(), 306, 330, 332, 479, 482

QWidget (QtGui) *(cont.)*
  updateGeometry(), 330, 332, 479
  wheelEvent(), 352
  width(), 330
QWorkspace (QtGui), 290, 297
  base class, QWidget
  activeWindow(), 296
  setActiveWindow(), 292, 295
  windowList(), 295
QXmlContentHandler (QtXml)
  characters(), 263
  endElement(), 263
  startElement(), 263
QXmlDefaultHandler (QtXml), 263
  base class, QXmlContentHandler
QXmlErrorHandler (QtXml)
  fatalError(), 263
QXmlInputSource (QtXml), 262
QXmlReader (QtXml)
  parse(), 262
  setContentHandler(), 262
  setErrorHandler(), 262
QXmlSimpleReader (QtXml), 262–265
  base class, QXmlReader

R

__radd__() (+), 84
radians() (math), 371, 375
raise_() (QWidget), 160, 289, 330
raising windows, 160
randint() (random), 19, 357, 371, 375
range(), 39, 50–51, 54
  see also xrange()
"raw" strings, 157, 220
re module, 219, 220, 554, 556
read-only models, 427
read-only widgets, 421
readAll()
  QIODevice, 254
  QTextStream, 384
readBool() (QDataStream), 245
readDouble() (QDataStream), 241, 245
readI*n*() (QDataStream), 243, 245, 360, 435
readline() (codecs), 255

readLine() (QTextStream), 252, 253, 254
readUInt*n*() (QDataStream), 245, 528, 540
rebinding names; *see* binding names
recently used files, 187–190
record-level validation, 140, 491
record()
  QSqlQuery, 450
  QSqlQueryModel, 464, 465, 466, 469
rect()
  QPaintEvent, 480
  QWidget, 306, 330
recursion, risk of infinite, 100
reentrant methods, 542
references; *see* object references
regression testing, 105
regular expressions, 157, 220, 327, 386, 387, 461, 552
"reject" button, 141, 188
reject() (QDialog), 215
rejected() signal (QDialogButtonBox), 145, 150
relationModel() (QSqlRelational-TableModel), 456
remainder (%), 53
remove()
  dict, 95, 532, 543
  list, 32, 33
  set, 38
removeItem() (QGraphicsScene), 354, 355, 359, 361, 372
removeRow() (QAbstractItemModel), 434, 466, 469
removeRows() (QAbstractItemModel), 427, 432, 434, 470
removeSelectedText() (QTextCursor), 297
render()
  QGraphicsScene, 354, 361
  QGraphicsView, 361
  QSvgRenderer, 363
replace() (str/unicode), 25, 238
repr(), 81, 83, 89, 90, 98

__repr__() (repr()), 81, 83, 90, 98
reset()
    QAbstractItemModel, 432, 434, 501,
        502
    QMatrix, 370, 377
resize() (QWidget), 183
resizeColumnsToContents() (QTable-
    View), 232, 419, 460, 463, 490
resizeEvent() (QWidget), 306, 309,
    341
resource path, root of (:/), 173
resource files, 173–174, 206, 401,
    517
restore() (QPainter), 343, 346, 410,
    438, 482, 489
restoreGeometry() (QWidget), 183,
    186, 330
restoreState()
    QMainWindow, 183, 186
    QSplitter, 282
restoring windows, 297
Return keypress; *see* Enter keypress
return statement, 58, 97, 554
returnPressed() signal (QLineEdit),
    440
reverse() (list), 33
rfind() (str/unicode), 25
__rfloordiv__() (//), 84
rgbSwapped() (QImage), 197
rich text; *see* HTML
RichTextLineEdit example class,
    389–398
rindex() (str/unicode), 25
__rmod__() (%), 84
__rmul__() (*), 84, 91
rollback() (QSqlDatabase), 449, 465,
    469
RomanSpinBox example class,
    326–328
rotate()
    QGraphicsItem, 360, 366, 371, 375,
        377
    QPainter, 343
rotating, graphics, 349
round(), 40, 91, 333
row() (QModelIndex), 427, 491

rowCount() (QAbstractItemModel), 426,
    427, 428, 434, 454, 455, 479, 481,
    503
__rsub__() (-), 84
__rtruediv__() (/), 84
rubber band, 352
run() (QThread), 538, 540, 548, 553
RuntimeError exception, 288

S

save()
    QImage, 196
    QPainter, 343, 346, 438, 481, 489
saveGeometry() (QWidget), 183, 186,
    330
saveState()
    QMainWindow, 183, 186
    QSplitter, 282
saving files, 229, 240–248, 249–256,
    256–265
SAX parser, 262–265
scale()
    QGraphicsItem, 366
    QGraphicsView, 352
    QMatrix, 370
    QPainter, 343
    QSize, 363, 400
scaled() (QImage), 199
scaling, graphics, 349, 370, 374, 400
scaling, widgets, 329, 331
scene coordinates; *see* window coor-
    dinates
scene() (QGraphicsItem), 366, 375
sceneBoundingRect() (QGraphicsItem),
    366, 379
scenes, graphic; *see* QGraphicsScene
Scintilla; *see* QScintilla add-on
scope, 55
screen coordinates, 309, 357
screenPos() (QGraphicsSceneContext-
    MenuEvent), 365
scrollbars and scrolling, 393, 476,
    479
scrollToItem() (QTableWidget), 232

SDI (Single Document Interface), 283–290
search() (re), 219
seek() (QSqlQuery), 449, 451
select() (QSqlTableModel), 453, 456, 460, 462, 464, 470
SELECT statements, 449–451
selected text, 392
selectedItems() (QGraphicsScene), 358, 360, 361
selectedText() (QTextCursor), 297
selecting graphics items, 352
selectionModel() (QAbstractItem-View), 463
self, 77, 78
sender() (QObject), 135, 289, 393, 395, 440
separators, menu, 178, 180
sequences, 22
set type, 37, 38, 93, 551
    add(), 37, 38, 372, 556
    clear(), 38
    copy(), 38, 548, 551
    discard(), 38
    pop(), 372
    remove(), 38
setAcceptDrops() (QWidget), 312, 313, 314, 315, 316, 330
setActiveWindow() (QWorkspace), 292, 295
setAlignment()
    QAbstractSpinBox, 340, 487
    QLabel, 168, 340
    QLineEdit, 461
setAllowedAreas() (QDockWidget), 169, 170
setAlternatingRowColors() (QAbstractItemView) (QAbstractItem-View), 231, 477
setAttribute() (QWidget), 156, 284, 330, 511
setBackgroundBrush() (QGraphics-Scene), 354
setBottom() (QRect/QRectF), 365
setBrush() (QPainter), 337, 344, 345, 374, 377, 481

setBuddy() (QLabel), 143, 425
setCalendarPopup() (QDateTimeEdit), 487
setCentralWidget() (QMainWindow), 168, 186, 285
setCheckable()
    QAbstractButton, 276, 278
    QAction, 393
setChecked() (QAction), 172, 177, 393
setCodec() (QTextStream), 250, 252, 254, 258, 384
setColor() (QPen), 368
setColumnCount()
    QTableWidget, 231, 418
    QTreeWidget, 420
setColumnHidden() (QTableView), 460, 463
setColumnStretch() (QGridLayout), 146
setContent() (QDomDocument), 259
setContentHandler() (QXmlReader), 262
setContextMenuPolicy() (QWidget), 168, 330, 365
setCurrentIndex()
    QAbstractItemView, 426, 465, 468
    QComboBox, 441, 457
    QDataWidgetMapper, 454, 455
    QStackedWidget, 275
setCurrentItem()
    QListWidget, 418
    QTableWidget, 232, 419
    QTreeWidget, 421
setCursor()
    QGraphicsItem, 366
    QWidget, 330
setData(), 189, 231
    QAbstractItemModel, 414, 427, 431, 434, 441, 462, 465, 487, 488
    QAction, 172, 189, 392, 393
    QMimeData, 316
    QTableWidgetItem, 231
    QTableWidgetItem, 419
setDatabaseName() (QSqlDatabase), 446, 459
setDate() (QDateTimeEdit), 487

setDateRange() (QDateTimeEdit), 452, 487

setDateTime() (QDateTime), 454

setdefault() (dict), 36, 95, 532
see also defaultdict type

setDefaultFont() (QTextDocument), 438, 439, 489

setDisplayFormat() (QDateTimeEdit), 452, 487

setDragEnabled() (QAbstractItemView, 312, 313, 315, 316

setDragMode() (QGraphicsView), 352

setDropAction() (QDropEvent), 314, 315, 316

setEditable() (QComboBox), 440

setEditorData() (QAbstractItem-Delegate), 436, 441, 462, 486, 487, 488

setEditTriggers() (QAbstrac-tItemView), 231

setEnabled()
    QAction, 172
    QGraphicsItem, 366
    QWidget, 219, 330

setErrorHandler() (QXmlReader), 262

setFeatures() (QDockWidget), 170

setFilter() (QSqlTableModel), 464, 470

setFlag() (QGraphicsItem), 366

setFlags() (QGraphicsItem), 351, 356, 362, 364

setFocus()
    QGraphicsItem, 364, 366
    QWidget, 120, 310, 330, 422

setFocusPolicy() (QWidget), 180, 217, 331, 369, 478

setFont()
    QGraphicsItem, 362
    QPainter, 344, 408, 482
    QWidget, 330

setForwardOnly() (QSqlQuery), 451

setFrameStyle() (QFrame), 170, 278

setHeaderData() (QAbstractItem-Model), 434, 460, 462

setHeaderLabels() (QTreeWidget), 420

setHorizontalHeaderLabels() (QTableWidget), 231, 418

setHotSpot() (QDrag), 316

setHtml()
    QMimeData, 311
    QTextDocument, 403, 438, 439, 489
    QTextEdit, 488

setIcon() (QListWidgetItem), 316

setImage() (QClipboard), 311

setInputMask() (QLineEdit), 461

setItem() (QTableWidget), 231, 419

__setitem__() ([]), 93, 95

setItemDelegate()
    QAbstractItemView, 437, 460, 463, 490
    QDataWidgetMapper, 456

setItemsExpandable() (QTreeView), 420

setLayout() (QWidget), 273, 279, 330

setLineWrapMode() (QTextEdit), 390

setMatrix()
    QGraphicsItem, 362, 364, 367, 377
    QGraphicsView, 370
    QPainter, 343

setMaximumHeight() (QWidget), 390

setMimeData()
    QClipboard, 311
    QDrag, 316

setMinimumHeight() (QWidget), 390

setMinimumSize() (QWidget), 168, 340

setMinimumWidth() (QWidget), 340

setModel()
    QAbstractItemView, 425, 437, 460, 463, 477, 490
    QComboBox, 456
    QDataWidgetMapper, 453, 456

setModelColumn() (QComboBox), 456

setModelData() (QAbstractItem-Delegate), 436, 441, 462, 486, 487, 488

setModified() (QTextDocument), 286, 383, 384

setMouseTracking() (QWidget), 308, 334

setObjectName() (QObject), 169, 183, 324

setPageSize() (QPrinter), 353, 398, 400

setPen() (QPainter), 337, 338, 343, 344, 345, 374, 377, 409, 410, 481

setPixmap()
QClipboard, 311
QDrag, 316
QLabel, 199

setPlainText() (QTextEdit), 384

setPointSize() (QFont), 335, 336

setPos() (QGraphicsItem), 356, 362, 364, 367, 373, 375

setPosition() (QTextCursor), 406

setProperty() (QObject), 322, 324

setQuery() (QSqlQueryModel), 464

setQuitOnLastWindowClosed() (QApplication), 121

setRange()
QAbstractSlider, 369
QSpinBox, 180, 340, 440

setRelation() (QSqlRelationalTableModel), 456, 460, 462

setRenderHint()
QGraphicsView, 352, 369
QPainter, 306, 337, 342, 343, 361, 363

setRight() (QRect/QRectF), 365

setRowCount() (QTableWidget), 231, 418

setRowStretch() (QGridLayout), 146

setScene() (QGraphicsView), 354, 369

setSceneRect() (QGraphicsScene), 354, 369

setSelected()
QGraphicsItem, 356, 362, 364, 367
QTableWidgetItem, 232, 419

setSelectionBehavior() (QAbstractItemView), 231, 460, 463, 495

setSelectionMode() (QAbstractItemView), 231, 460, 463

setSeparator() (QAction), 172

setShortcut() (QAction), 171, 172

setSingleStep() (QSpinBox), 440

setSizeConstraint (QLayout), 277, 279

setSizeGripEnabled()
QDialog, 154
QStatusBar, 170

setSizePolicy() (QWidget), 330, 331, 340

setSort() (QSqlTableModel), 453, 456, 460, 462

setSortingEnabled() (QTableView), 418, 419

setStatusTip()
QAction, 172
QWidget, 171, 180

setStretchFactor()
QBoxLayout, 146
QSplitter, 283

setStyleSheet() (QWidget), 323, 330

setSubmitPolicy() (QDataWidgetMapper), 453, 456

setSuffix() (QSpinBox), 180, 340

setTabChangesFocus() (QTextEdit), 390

setTable() (QSqlTableModel), 453, 456, 460, 462

setTabOrder() (QWidget), 206

setText()
QAbstractButton, 370
QAction, 172
QClipboard, 297, 311
QLineEdit, 441, 462

setTextAlignment()
QTableWidgetItem, 231, 419
QTreeWidgetItem, 421

setTextColor() (QTextEdit), 393

setToolTip()
QAction, 172
QWidget, 171, 180, 390

setUniformRowHeights() (QTreeView), 495

setupUi() (generated by pyuic4), 217, 218

setValidator() (QLineEdit), 461

setValue()
QAbstractSlider, 128, 369
QSpinBox, 128, 180, 340, 441

setVersion() (QDataStream), 241, 243, 245, 525, 528, 531, 533, 540

setViewport() (QPainter), 329, 342, 343, 363
setVisible() (QWidget), 277, 280
setWhatsThis() (QAction), 172
setWidth() (QPen), 368
setWindow() (QPainter), 329, 342, 343, 363
setWindowFlags() (QWidget), 529
setWindowIcon() (QWidget), 186, 330
setWindowModified() (QWidget), 192
setWindowTitle() (QWidget), 146, 151, 186, 330, 370
setZValue() (QGraphicsItem), 367
shallow copying, 34, 51, 98
shape() (QGraphicsItem), 365, 367, 374, 377
shear()
    QGraphicsItem, 367
    QPainter, 343
Shift keypress, 365
short-circuit logic, 47
short-circuit signals, 130–131
    see also signals and slots
shortcut; *see* keyboard shortcut and QKeySequence
show() (QWidget), 115, 155, 280, 286, 330, 511
showing dialogs, 160
showing images, 168
showing widgets, 277, 280
showMessage() (QStatusBar), 170, 233
showMinimized() (QWidget), 297
showNormal() (QWidget), 297
sibling() (QModelIndex), 491
SIGNAL() (QtCore), 131
signals and slots, 115, 120, 124, 127–136, 206, 215, 217, 292, 307, 333, 385, 440, 482, 539, 544
    see also short-circuit signals
Signals and Slots application, 128–131
signature of, function, method, signal or slot, 56, 129
simplified() (QString), 61, 422
sin() (math), 371, 375
single click; *see* mousePressEvent() and mouseReleaseEvent()

single document interface; *see* SDI
single-quoted strings, 21
singleShot() (QTimer), 115, 306
sip module, 288
size; *see* QSize
size grip, 170
size hint, 271
size()
    QImage, 363, 400
    QRect/QRectF, 400
    QSqlQuery, 450
size of layout or widget
    fixed, 277
    maximum, 271
    minimum, 270, 271, 335
    preferred, 271
size policies, 270–271, 335
sizeHint()
    QAbstractItemDelegate, 436, 439, 489
    QWidget, 335, 390, 479
sleep() (time), 114, 115
slicing, 22, 30, 32
slot; *see* signals and slots
SLOT() (QtCore), 131
__slots__ class attribute, 103, 115
software patents, disadvantages of, 222
sort() (list), 33, 53, 63, 95, 239
sorted(), 52, 53, 63, 432, 434, 551
sorting, 52, 418, 425, 432–435
spacer; *see* QSpacerItem
spacers, in layouts, 212, 214
special methods, 81
    __abs__() (abs()), 84
    __add__() (+), 84, 90
    __call__(), 81
    __cmp__() (cmp()), 81, 82, 89, 416, 432
    __contains__() (in), 93
    __del__() (del statement), 78
    __delitem__() (del statement), 93, 95
    __eq__() (==), 81
    __float__() (float()), 84, 91
    __floordiv__() (//), 84

special methods *(cont.)*
    __ge__() (>=), 81
    __getitem__() ([]), 93, 94
    __gt__() (>), 81
    __iadd__() (+=), 84, 90
    __ifloordiv__() (//=), 84
    __imod__() (%=), 84
    __imul__() (*=), 84, 91
    __init__(), 77, 78, 437
    __int__() (int()), 84, 91
    __isub__() (-=), 84
    __iter__() (iter()), 93, 97
    __itruediv__() (/=), 84, 91
    __le__() (<=), 81
    __len__() (len()), 93, 96
    __lt__() (<), 81, 82, 432
    __mod__() (%), 84
    __mul__() (*), 84, 91
    __ne__() (!=), 81
    __neg__() (-), 84
    __new__(), 77, 78, 81
    __nonzero__() (bool()), 81, 83
    __radd__() (+), 84
    __repr__() (repr()), 81, 83, 90
    __rfloordiv__() (//), 84
    __rmod__() (%), 84
    __rmul__() (*), 84, 91
    __rsub__() (-), 84
    __rtruediv__() (/), 84
    __setitem__() ([]), 93, 95
    __str__() (str()), 81, 83, 90, 98, 100
    __sub__() (-), 84
    __truediv__() (/), 84, 91
    __unicode__() (unicode()), 81, 83
spinbox; *see* QDoubleSpinBox and QSpinBox
split()
    QString, 253
    str/unicode, 25, 114, 238, 501
splitter; *see* QSplitter
SQL queries; *see* QSqlQuery and SQL statements
SQL Server database, 445
SQL statements, 445, 446, 447, 448, 449, 449–451, 458, 464, 468, 469

SQLite database, 445, 446, 447
stacked widgets; *see* QStackedWidget
standard key sequence; *see* keyboard shortcut and QKeySequence
start()
    QDrag, 316
    QThread, 539, 547, 553
    QTimer, 373, 376
start-up processing, 184
startDrag() (QAbstractItemView), 316
startElement() (QXmlContentHandler), 263
startswith() (str/unicode), 25, 238, 255
startsWith() (QString), 252
startTimer() (QObject), 370
state, changes; *see* signals and slots
state() (QAbstractSocket), 540
state, preserving using generators, 58, 97
statement separators, 51
static data, 85–86
static methods, 78, 85–86
static typing, 12
staticmethod(), 85, 239, 288
status bar; *see* QStatusBar
statusBar() (QMainWindow), 170, 186
StopIteration exception, 52, 58, 59
stored procedures, in databases, 448
str type, 20–28, 25
    % formatting, 24, 98
    %s format specifier, 26
    * replication operator, 25
    + concatenation operator, 25
    count(), 25
    endswith(), 25, 31, 555
    find(), 24, 25, 68
    index(), 24, 25, 68
    indexing, 22
    isalpha(), 25
    isdigit(), 25, 238, 554
    iterating, 50
    join(), 23, 25, 61, 193, 477
    literals, 21

str type *(cont.)*
  lower(), 25, 238
  promotion to unicode, 20
  replace(), 25, 238
  rfind(), 25
  rindex(), 25
  slicing, 22
  split(), 25, 114, 238, 501
  startswith(), 25, 238, 255
  strip(), 25, 59, 255
  title(), 24
  upper(), 25
  see also QString and unicode type
__str__() (str()), 81, 83, 90, 98, 100
stream reading and writing, 242,
    245, 250, 252, 258
streams; *see* QDataStream and
    QTextStream
stretch factors, 144, 212, 271, 283
string literals, 20
string module, 26
  Template class, 26
StringIO module, 23
    see also cStringIO module
strings; *see* QString, str type, and
    unicode type
strip() (str/unicode), 25, 59, 255
style sheets, 322–324
sub() (re), 220, 556
__sub__() (-), 84
subcontrols, in widgets, 324
submit() (QDataWidgetMapper), 454
submitAll() (QSqlTableModel), 455,
    466, 469, 470
suite of code, 46, 47
sum(), 38
super(), 100, 153, 217
support for keyboard users; *see* key-
    board users, support for
supportedImageFormats()
  QImageReader, 193
  QImageWriter, 196
SVG (Scalable Vector Graphics) for-
    mat, 363
switch statement; *see* if statement
Sybase database, 445

sys module, 60, 63, 114
  argv variable, 114
  path variable, 60, 104
  version_info tuple, 63
system() (platform), 200, 217, 336,
    390

T

Tab keypress, 206, 218, 310, 386, 390,
    421, 422, 511
tab order, 206, 215, 217, 310
tab widget; *see* QTabWidget
table widget; *see* QTableWidget
tagName() (QDomElement), 260
takeItem() (QListWidgetItem), 316
takeLast() (QStringList), 189
taskbar entries, 142
TCP (Transmission Control Proto-
    col), 522
Template class (string), 26
terminating applications, 115, 121,
    185
terminology, 13, 75
ternary operator; *see* conditional ex-
    pression
testing for errors vs. exception han-
    dling, 68
testing, user interface, 221–222
testmod() (doctest), 106
text cursor; *see* insertion point
text editor; *see* QTextEdit
text files, 249–256
text()
  QClipboard, 297, 311
  QLineEdit, 441
  QTableWidgetItem, 422
text stream; *see* QTextStream
text stream reading and writing,
    250, 252, 258
textCursor() (QTextEdit), 297, 384,
    385
textEdited() signal (QLineEdit), 161,
    217, 218
textFromValue() (QSpinBox), 327, 328
this pointer; *see* self

thread safety, 541–542
time module
    sleep(), 114, 115
    see also QTime
timeout() signal (QTimer), 373, 376
timer; *see* QTimer
timerEvent() (QObject), 372
times; *see* QDateTime, QTime, and time
    module
title bar, 115
title() (str/unicode), 24
toBool() (QVariant), 324
toDate() (QVariant), 487, 491
toDateTime() (QVariant), 449
toDouble() (QVariant), 481
toElement() (QDomNode), 260
toFirst() (QDataWidgetMapper), 453,
    456
toggle actions, 176
    see also QAction
toggle button, 276, 278
    see also QPushButton
toggled() signal
    QAbstractButton, 277, 280
    QAction, 172, 176, 177
toHtml()
    QTextDocument, 407
    QTextEdit, 395
toInt()
    QString, 251, 422
    QVariant, 395, 431, 449
toLongLong() (QVariant), 422
toNativeSeparators() (QDir), 547,
    551
toolbar; *see* QToolBar
toolbar buttons, 169
tools; *see* applications
tooltip; *see* QToolTip
top-level windows, 115, 118, 221
toPlainText()
    QGraphicsTextItem, 359
    QTextEdit, 384, 395
toPyDate() (QDate), 532, 541
toString()
    QDate, 258, 401
    QDateTime, 455

toString() *(cont.)*
    QDomDocument, 257, 260
    QVariant, 427, 431, 441, 449, 488
toText() (QDomNode), 261
toUpper() (QString), 327
tr() (QObject), 513, 514, 515
transaction() (QSqlDatabase), 449,
    465, 468, 469
transactions, database, 465–466,
    468
transformations, graphics, 349, 350,
    356, 360, 370, 374, 376, 438
translate()
    QCoreApplication, 513, 515
    QGraphicsItem, 367
    QPainter, 343, 438, 489
triggered() signal (QAction), 172,
    176
trimmed() (QString), 252, 422
triple quoted strings, 21, 57
True constant, 45
"true" division, 17, 84, 86
__truediv__() (/), 84, 91
truncating division, 17, 84, 86, 91
trUtf8() (QObject), 513
try statement, 66, 78, 541, 542, 543,
    548, 550, 551, 553, 554, 556
    else statement, 70, 295
    see also except statement and fi-
        nally statement
.ts (translation source file), 517,
    518, 519
tuple type, 29–31, 30, 50, 87
Twisted networking framework,
    522
type conversions; *see* conversions
type(), 18, 39, 102
    see also isinstance()
type() (QEvent), 384
type promotion; *see* conversions
type testing, 94
TypeError exception, 56
typing; *see* duck typing, dynamic
        typing, and static typing

U

UDP (User Datagram Protocol),
    522
.ui (user interface file), 206, 207,
    515
ultimate base class; *see* object type
underscores, leading, 77, 80, 82
unichr(), 21, 39, 236, 554
Unicode, 20, 117, 236, 250, 258, 447,
    478, 512, 552, 555
    characters, 22
    encodings, 20, 21, 250, 258, 501
    see also ASCII, codecs, and
        QString
unicode type, 20–28, 25, 256, 401
    % formatting, 24
    %s format specifier, 26
    * replication operator, 25
    + concatenation operator, 25
    count(), 25
    endswith(), 25, 31, 555
    find(), 24, 25, 68
    index(), 24, 25, 68
    indexing, 22
    isalpha(), 25
    isdigit(), 25, 238, 554
    iterating, 50
    join(), 23, 25, 61, 193, 477
    literals, 20, 21
    lower(), 25, 238
    promotion to QString, 28
    replace(), 25, 238
    rfind(), 25
    rindex(), 25
    slicing, 22
    split(), 25, 114, 238, 501
    startswith(), 25, 238, 255
    strip(), 25, 59, 255
    title(), 24
    upper(), 25
    see also str type and QString
__unicode__() (unicode()), 81, 83
union() (set), 38
unit testing, 105–107
universal newlines, 256
unlock()

unlock() *(cont.)*
    QMutex, 553, 554
    QReadWriteLock, 541, 542, 543,
        548, 550, 551, 556
unpacking tuples, 87
unsaved changes, 168, 187, 192, 232,
    293, 356, 361, 362, 364, 365, 425,
    453
update()
    QGraphicsItem, 365, 367
    QGraphicsScene, 354
    QWidget, 306, 330, 332, 479, 482
updateGeometry() (QWidget), 330, 332,
    479
upper() (str/unicode), 25
urlopen() (urllib2), 126
urlretrieve() (urllib), 521
user actions; *see* QAction
user interface design, 205–216
user preferences; *see* QSettings
UTF-8 encoding, 236, 250, 258, 501,
    555

V

validate() (QAbstractSpinBox), 327,
    328
validation, 140, 151, 157, 327, 328,
    491
value comparison, 13, 57
value()
    QSettings, 183
    QSpinBox, 441
    QSqlQuery, 449, 450, 451
    QSqlRecord, 464, 465, 466, 469
valueChanged()
    QDial, 128
    QSpinBox, 124, 128, 199
ValueError exception, 68, 114
valueFromText() (QSpinBox), 327, 328
values() (dict), 36, 96
variable names, 15, 76, 80, 88
version_info tuple (sys), 63
version string, application, 167
__version__, application variable,
    167

vertical layout; *see* QVBoxLayout
vertical lines; *see* QFrame
view widgets; *see* QGraphicsView,
    QListView, QTableView, and
    QTreeView
viewport coordinates, 328–331, 339,
    342, 350, 400
viewport()
    QAbstractScrollArea, 392, 393
    QPainter, 363, 400
views() (QGraphicsScene), 354, 362
virtual methods, 75, 99
visual design tool; *see Qt Designer*

W

wait() (QThread), 547, 548, 551
waitForDisconnected() (QAbstract-
    Socket), 544
waitForReadyRead() (QIODevice), 540
walk() (os), 555
warning() (QMessageBox), 153, 188,
    293
Web browser, launching, 510
wheelEvent() (QWidget), 352
while loop, 49–50
    break statement, 53
    continue statement, 53
    else statement, 49–50, 254
widget attributes; *see*
    Qt.WidgetAttribute
widget coordinates, 309
widget-level validation, 140, 144
widget stack; *see* QStackedWidget
widgets; *see* QWidget
width() (QWidget), 330
window coordinates, 328–331, 339,
    342, 350, 354, 357
window decorations, 112
window flags, 115
window menu, MDI, 292–293,
    297–300
window menu, SDI, 285, 288–289
window modal dialogs, 140, 511
window system detection, 218, 336,
    389, 390

windowList() (QWorkspace), 295
windows, 115, 118, 160
    see also widgets, QWidget, QDialog,
    and QMainWindow
Windows detection, 389, 390
windows, previewing, 215
WindowStaysOnTopHint (Qt name-
    space), 529
with statement, 549
wrapping functions; *see* partial func-
    tion application
write() (QDataStream), 526, 533
writeBool() (QDataStream), 245
writeDouble() (QDataStream), 241,
    245
writeInt*n*() (QDataStream), 241, 242,
    245, 359, 435
writeUInt*n*() (QDataStream), 245, 525,
    533
writing files; *see* saving files

X

X Window System detection, 336
XML files, 256–265
XML meta-characters, 257, 258
XML parser, DOM, 259–262
XML parser, SAX, 262–265
xrange(), 51, 54
    see also range()

Y

yield statement, 58, 97, 237
YPipe example class, 339–345

Z

z value, 349
zoom; *see* scaling, graphics
zValue() (QGraphicsItem), 367

About the Author

Mark Summerfield

Mark graduated in computer science with first class honors from the University of Wales Swansea. He followed this with a year's postgraduate research before going into industry. He spent many years working as a software engineer for a variety of firms before joining Trolltech. He spent almost three years as Trolltech's documentation manager, during which he founded and edited Trolltech's technical journal, *Qt Quarterly*, and co-wrote *C++ GUI Programming with Qt 3*, and later *C++ GUI Programming with Qt 4*. Mark owns Qtrac Ltd., www.qtrac.eu, where he works as an independent author, editor, trainer, and consultant, specializing in C++, Qt, Python, and PyQt.

Production

The text was written using gvim and marked up with the Lout typesetting language. The index was compiled by the author, with the assistance of a PyQt program developed for the purpose. All the diagrams were produced using Lout. Almost all of the code snippets were extracted directly from the example programs using Lout in conjunction with a Python script. The icons used in the example programs are mostly from KDE (The "K" Desktop Environment), with a few created by the author. The images used in the book's margins are from the Open Clip Art Library, with some other images coming from Project Gutenberg. SVG images were converted to EPS using Inkscape. The Linux screenshots were taken with KSnapshot, and the Windows screenshots were captured and saved using a tiny PyQt application; in both cases, the .png images were converted to .eps using ImageMagick. The monospaced font used for code is derived from a condensed version of DejaVu Mono and was modified using FontForge. Wikipedia proved itself to be useful in all kinds of ways, including being the source of the flag images, and was frequently referred to for ideas, information, and sample data. The marked-up text was previewed using gv and evince, and converted to PostScript by Lout, then to PDF by Ghostscript.

All the editing and processing were done on Fedora and Kubuntu systems. The cover was provided by the publisher, with the picture suggested by the author in view of the fact that Python is used to calibrate and analyze data from the Hubble Space Telescope. The screenshots were taken on Windows XP, Mac OS X, and Linux/KDE. All the example programs have been tested on Windows, Linux, and Mac OS X, using Python 2.5, Qt 4.2, and PyQt 4.2, and additionally on Windows and Linux using Qt 4.3 and PyQt 4.3, and also with Python 2.6 using Qt 4.4 and PyQt 4.4.